Tanavala

SECOND EDITION

INDUSTRIAL MARKETING
Analysis, Planning, and Control

ROBERT R. REEDER
*Southwestern Oklahoma
State University*

EDWARD G. BRIERTY
*Southern Oregon
State College*

BETTY H. REEDER
*Betty Reeder
Enterprises*

Prentice Hall, Englewood Cliffs, New Jersey 07632

Library of Congress Cataloging-in-Publication Data

Reeder, Robert R.
    Industrial marketing : analysis, planning, and control / Robert R.
    Reeder, Edward G. Brierty, Betty H. Reeder.—2nd ed.
        p.   cm.
    Includes index.
    ISBN 0-13-457110-X
    1. Industrial marketing.   I. Brierty, Edward G.   II. Reeder, Betty H.
    III. Title.
    HF5415.R355   1991
    658.8—dc20   90-41004
                                                                     CIP

Editorial/production supervision and
    interior design: Joanne Palmer
Cover design: Franklyn Graphics
Prepress buyer: Trudy Pisciotti
Manufacturing buyer: Robert Anderson

 © 1991 by Prentice-Hall, Inc.
A Paramount Communications Company
Englewood Cliffs, New Jersey 07632

Printed in the United States of America

10 9 8 7 6 5 4 3 2

ISBN 0-13-457110-X

Prentice-Hall International (UK) Limited, *London*
Prentice-Hall of Australia Pty. Limited, *Sydney*
Prentice-Hall Canada Inc., *Toronto*
Prentice-Hall Hispanoamericana, S.A., *Mexico*
Prentice-Hall of India Private Limited, *New Delhi*
Prentice-Hall of Japan, Inc., *Tokyo*
Simon & Schuster Asia Pte. Ltd., *Singapore*
Editora Prentice-Hall do Brasil, Ltda., *Rio de Janeiro*

We dedicate this book to our friends in the Philippines.

Contents

PART VIII   INTERNATIONAL INDUSTRIAL MARKETING

*The Case for International Marketing/The International Marketing Environment/
Forms of International Market Entry/International Adaptation of Conventional
Marketing Strategies/Looking Back/Questions for Discussion/Suggested Additional Readings*

CASES

Chapters

1. The Nature of Industrial Marketing
2. Understanding Industrial Markets
3. The Industrial Marketing Environment
4. The Nature of Industrial Buying
5. The Interpersonal Dynamics of Industrial Buying Behavior
6. The Strategic Planning Process in Industrial Marketing
7. Assessing Market Opportunities
8. Industrial Market Segmentation, Target Marketing, and Positioning
9. Developing Product Strategy
10. New Product Development Strategy
11. Marketing Channel Participants
12. Physical Distribution Strategy
13. Developing the Industrial Sales Force
14. Planning, Organizing, and Controlling the Selling Function
15. Managing Advertising, Sales Promotion, and Publicity Strategy
16. Price Determinants: Customers, Competition, and Costs
17. Pricing Decision Analysis
18. Industrial Marketing in the International Environment

Case \ Chapter	1	2	3	4	5	6	7	8	9	10	11	12	13	14	15	16	17	18
1. C N Information Services	S				S			S					S					
2. Crofton–Wagley, Inc.		S														S	P	
3. Edward F. Crow Company		S	P			S			S		P							
4. Cumberland Gasket Company, Inc.	S			P	S	S			S									
5. Double L Company		S		P														
6. Grey Electronics, Inc.					S												P	
7. Huntington Electronics			S	P	S					P								
8. Kruger–Montini Manufacturing Co.						P	S	P	S				P	P				
9. Lewiston–Copeland Company			S	S		P	S	P	S	S			S	S				
10. Modern Medical Prouducts Co.			S	S				P	S	S	P							
11. Parker Instruments Ltd.										P								P
12. Power Tools, Inc.	S		S			P			P									S
13. Precision Parts, Inc.							P											
14. Prentice Machine Tools						P		S						S		P		P
15. Starnes–Brenner Machine Co.											S	S						
16. Frank Sud Furniture						P		S										P
17. Titan Controls Corporation					S	P	P	P			S			S				
18. The Top Plastics Company			P	S	S	S	P	S	P									
19. Trans–Europa Business Credit			P										P					
20. Universal Motor Parts Division				S								P						

P = primary area
S = secondary area

Preface

As I reviewed the preface to our first edition, I was caught up in the excitement Betty, Ed and I felt at that time. We had wanted so strongly to contribute, to have a part in focusing the educational emphasis on the industrial marketing field, an emphasis which was then in the count-down stage. I recall the day Whitney Blake from Prentice Hall phoned to tell me that the book was "a go." Though I live in the heart of the Bible Belt, I bought a bottle of champagne and two plastic glasses. As I reached our small home atop a hill surrounded by endless miles of wheat fields, I stopped in the carport and laid on the horn. When Betty came out and saw me pouring the champagne—she knew!

Today, as I write this preface to our second edition, I'm not caught up in that champagne excitement of years ago, but somehow I am filled with a more relaxed, though very real feeling, a sort of tempered exhilaration. However, I know it is a feeling that is just as compelling as the champagne scene of yesteryear. Perhaps it is a deeper and more meaningful empathically inspired commitment, because it is infused by (1) the determination of so many, as evidenced by so much research, thought, and writing, (2) the great improvements that American businesses have accomplished in these last few years, and (3) the gratification of knowing that, once again, we are being allowed to summarize, comment, and even contribute a small suggestion here and there to this dynamic and most important area.

I just can't help but think of what Lee Iacocca said in the closing of his autobiography: "People say to me: 'You're a roaring success. How did you do it?' I go back to what my parents taught me. Apply yourself. Get all the education you can, but then, by God, do something! Don't just stand there, make something happen." So many vigorous researchers, writers, students, and, especially, young people entering the work force are no longer "just standing there." And Betty, Ed, and I, who consider that "hope for tomorrow," are very thankful to again be a part of it, and proud to say of industrial marketing, "We have liftoff; we have achieved liftoff!"

OVERALL

Once again, in our wake we see no unturned stones that would disavow our considerable and earnest efforts to ferret out the archetypical research, writings, and examples that illustrate the greatest accomplishments in the field of industrial marketing, but without question we have surely erred here and there, since so very much has been written and done. But at least we can say that one perplexing problem that dogged us in our first edition no longer remains. In those early years, we were frequently concerned with presenting industrial marketing materials rather than with rehashing time-worn consumer marketing concepts. Given today's abundance of industrial information, that concern has gone by the boards.

With a great deal of pride I can tell you—and in reviewing the text you will quickly realize—that we do not present research findings and then drop them, leaving you in silent orbit, to wonder, "Just what is the significance of this for me?" We spell out the significance, the implications for real marketers in real businesses in this very real world. Our commitment to do so is absolute.

FEATURES OF THIS EDITION

We have made major additions to reflect new and growing practices, as well as new ways of doing old things. These changes and additions involve such topics as marketing services; competitive intelligence; selling to the government; determining the composition of organizational buying centers; JIT systems; improving conflict-resolution strategies; small business decision making, including "humble decision making"; computerized secondary data sources, including those in the international environment; forecasting sources that are actually used; how to survey groups; executive information systems; segmentation, including benefit segmentation; channel and physical distribution strategies; auditioning; accelerated learning; current methods of motivation; tailoring compensation to achieve goals and objectives; sales force automation; the intrapreneurial philosophy; changes in sales force structure for the 1990s; telemarketing; setting advertising budgets; the learning curve controversy and its solution; and sharpening pricing decisions.

We have updated many examples and vignettes and added new ones. Just a few of the topics include the Exxon Valdez, Toxic Chemicals in California, Japanese

Workers Come to America, UNISYS, and Training Isn't Micro at IBM. Of course, we have carefully preserved the "classic" vignettes of our first edition, such as Part Seven's General Dynamics introductory story.

Finally, to prepare this edition we updated a seemingly endless number of items. We had to use government documents to make many of these changes in the chapter on the international marketing environment. That may not sound particularly difficult, and it isn't. If one is clairvoyant.

THIS TEXT'S CONTINUING COMPARATIVE ADVANTAGES

This text continues to be organized so as to enhance learning. For example, the discussion of strategy begins with Chapter Six. This provides an early framework for mentally organizing the balance of the text, as well as enabling case analysis during the beginning weeks of the course. Concepts brought up in earlier chapters are carried thoughout the text rather than being dropped when different topics are discussed. Materials within each chapter are also organized in a more logical manner to assist student learning.

This remains the only industrial marketing text with an international chapter. This might be justified by the fact that seventy percent of United States businesses face international competition, though such a justification isn't likely to be necessary; polls show that most of us are quite worried about international competition, having seen foreign companies buy up everything but the Washington Monument.

Additionally, this text devotes two chapters to the sales force, since it is far and away the main method of selling in the industrial area. The text devotes an entire chapter to the industrial environment, since our industrial experiences indicated its importance, and studies have shown that industrial marketing managers are held much more accountable for knowledge in that area than are consumer marketing managers. Finally, we continue to be very pleased with the two pricing chapters. The discussion of the learning curve was excellent in the first edition, but has been made even better in this edition. The Chapter Seventeen pricing discussion is excellent in the way that it weaves several pricing concepts together using a single set of data.

CASES

We have placed twenty cases at the end of the book. We have also included a cross-reference page that relates cases to chapters. The cases range from two to eighteen pages in length and vary considerably in levels of difficulty, facilitating professors' discretionary judgments as to just which cases might be right for class discussions, debates, and written papers. We have placed these cases in the text only after giving them classroom testing.

ACKNOWLEDGMENTS

Of course, we shall always remember those fine people who, as reviewers, suffered through our original manuscript. They were Sue E. Neeley (University of Houston, Clear Lake), Alvin J. Williams (University of Southern Mississippi), William C. Rodgers (St. Cloud State University), David Lambert (Suffolk University), Jon M. Hawes (University of Akron), Gary Young (University of Massachusetts), Ernest Cooke (Memphis State University), and Roger Bennet (McGill University). As we laid the foundation, they were the ones who did the leveling, troweling, and chucking aside of many a questionable brick that might otherwise have caused the entire structure to crumble.

For this edition, we would like to acknowledge librarians. How quickly we writers forget them! Yet they are the ones who greet us with a smile as we trudge in, among the "no smoking—eating—chewing—drinking—talking" signs, for some very long hours and days of searching. They are there to lend a hand when our searches are fruitless; they are there when we can't cajole the microfiche machine into lighting up; they are there to advise us that we ought to use the hardbound indexes and not just the computer with its quick CD-ROMs; they are there to tell us that the back door will be open during vacation; and they do indeed send us through intra-university mail an endless stream of documents, the likes of which no one ever dreamed existed. Perhaps too often, they send us things that make a chapter; things that clarify a point we've never been able to clarify; things that give our writings a spark, a flare, a dynamic quality; things that enable us to achieve paragraphs and chapters that we would never ever otherwise have achieved. And, too, they can almost always break the government documents' cryptographic code!

We salute them for this text and for all the texts which they have done so much to help create through the years, but for which they have received so little acknowledgment: Sheila Hoke (who doesn't know what a frown is); Matt Berry (an eternal kidder); Jo Hagerman (who loves the world); Jim Wilkerson, Vicki Buettner and Mary Robertson, who are always there to lend a hand. Most of all, we would like to thank Carol Torrence, the most dynamic lady who has done so much from day one of this text, who can not only break the secret code to the government documents, but who actually comprendos the on-line data bases. She is a marvel.

Bob Reeder
Binger, Oklahoma

About the Authors

BETTY REEDER was the inspiration for this text. Thus, when Ed and I grow weary of analyzing and writing, we frequently proclaim her to be the cause of our innumerable problems. However, she has also been the inspirational fire that has kept all of our work alive and moving. She has provided the needed word of encouragement, the gifted thought, the right idea, and the intuitive interpretation, just when each of these things have been most needed.

After fifteen years of teaching, Betty has moved into her third career change. She has opted to return to the life of an entrepreneur, a vocation for which she is unquestionably suited. Her leaving is a considerable loss to higher education, but an equal or greater profit for private enterprise.

ED BRIERTY is a methodically prodigious perfectionist. The fruits of one week of his efforts can surpass a month's worth of efforts of most writers. He has long been an outstanding researcher and writer. Additionally, he is the most experienced industrial marketer on this team.

Ed continues to teach at Southern Oregon State College, and continues, rightfully, to devote much time to his exceptionally large and fine family. His colleagues have twice elected him to preside over the college's faculty senate.

BOB REEDER, author of this introduction, has taught at Southwestern Oklahoma State University for 7.5 years, a tenure record for his career. He has usually left jobs in businesses and universities long before 7.5 years, before they discovered his errors!

He basically loves to live in isolation from the world. This allows him to write, paint, and play his guitar where others cannot interfere.

PART ONE

Dimensions of Industrial Marketing

THE CAT FIGHTS BACK

Caterpillar Inc., long number one, is driving especially hard to beat off its Japanese competitors. In just four years, it has doubled its product offerings by producing new varieties of Cats it never would have considered in bygone times.

In those glorious olden days, a fifteen foot, seventy-three ton Cat tractor could push, crush, and role over the best that competition could offer. And Cat users were happily willing to pay premiums for that excellence. But in the 1980s things began to head for a sudden downturn. Construction markets collapsed, a long long-term recession insidiously set in, and the U.S. dollar took flight; suddenly the number one feline found both her flanks exposed to attack by Japanese competitors. Profits fell. She saw a 1981 $579 million profit figure sink into the depths of a $953 million loss in just three quick years. A mandate for change was dramatically painted across her balance sheet.

She began cutting her marginally productive facilities, pruning excessive pay-rolls, and reorganizing her 60,000 Cat-people. She cut prices in world markets, introduced new, smaller Cats, which ranged from backhoes to farm tractors, and built a six-year modernization program for the updating of 36 million square feet of factory space, with an estimated cost of $1.2 billion.

> By late 1988, Cat sales had jumped up twenty-two percent, and losses had turned to profits. By the end of the year, profits totalled $616 million, excelling all previous years.
>
> *Source:* Reprinted by permission of Fortune magazine, "This Cat is Acting Like a Tiger," by Ronald Henkoff, *Fortune,* © 1988 Time Inc. All rights reserved.

Caterpillar is but one of many firms that are feeling the impact of both domestic and international competition. It is also quickly coming to understand the totality of company commitment required in those organizations labeled "industrial." Their responses must, without question, be more complex, more organizationally appropriate, more holistic.

This text is written with such important thoughts in mind, written to aid and inspire those whose careers will be spent within the crucial industrial marketing sphere. It is an addition to the limited number of texts written to facilitate the education of those who will be involved in the complexities of industrial marketing: those who will struggle with the worldwide business changes—changes that impact our nation's economy, our standard of living, and our very way of life in America.

Assuming that you have a good grasp of the basic principles of marketing, the purpose of Chapters One through Three is to lay a foundation for an understanding of industrial marketing and the role of industrial marketing management.

CHAPTER 1

The Nature of Industrial Marketing

While the basic tenets of consumer marketing are equally applicable to industrial marketing, the composition of the industrial market is uniquely different, as are the forces that affect industrial demand. Industrial marketing managers must react differently to changing markets, develop products to meet those changes, and market them in uniquely specialized ways to sophisticated customers while maintaining corporate objectives and profits. Thus, industrial marketers face many unique marketing situations not normally encountered in the consumer market. The intent of this chapter, then, is to introduce you to

1. The difference between consumer and industrial marketing management.
2. The basic composition of the industrial market.
3. The economic factors that influence the demand for industrial goods and services.
4. How the reseller's market parallels the industrial market.
5. The importance of the industrial marketing concept in developing marketing strategy.

Since the Industrial Revolution, the industrial market has been the backbone of the high standard of living enjoyed by consumers in the United States. It is dynamic and challenging, accounting for well over half of our economic activity.[1] In-

---

[1]Frederick E. Webster, Jr., "Management Science in Industrial Marketing," *Journal of Marketing* (January 1978), pp. 21–27.

terestingly though, while more than half of our business school graduates are employed in this arena, less than 2 percent have been exposed to industrial marketing courses during their college educations.[2]

While the principles, knowledge, and practice of marketing cut across all industries, to market effectively in the industrial market we must understand industrial marketing problems.[3] The industrial market, while similar in many respects to the consumer market, functions differently and, therefore, merits separate study.

WHY STUDY INDUSTRIAL MARKETING?

Unquestionably, employment opportunities for college graduates are quite broad. So why study industrial marketing? The heart of that question lies in the observation that, while many industrial executives saw increased marketing competency as the key priority for the 1980s, they recognize that the "historical weakness in their firms" has been the lack of marketing orientation, which has resulted in

> A failure to provide proper guidance and stimulation for research and development of new products.
> A failure to exploit and develop markets for new products.
> An inability to define new methods for promoting products to customers in the face of major increases in the cost of media advertising and personal selling.
> A failure to innovate in distribution and other areas to keep up with changing requirements of industrial customers doing business on a multinational basis.
> An attempt to meet significant new competition through traditional ways of doing business.
> An inability to refine and modify product positioning.
> A tendency for product managers and higher levels of management to approach problems in the same old way.[4]

The marketing competency needed to correct such situations will only come through painful experience in the marketplace. However, to overcome our industrial marketing weaknesses, the foundation for achieving that competency must be laid here, in the academic setting.

The skills needed for success in industrial marketing have been defined by industrial practitioners. Since they are the ones who dictate hiring practices, you should find Table 1-1 to be of special interest, particularly if you are planning a career in industrial marketing. As Table 1-1 shows, marketing research, planning, and forecasting are viewed as the most important areas to study.[5]

[2]James D. Hlavacek, "Business Schools Need More Industrial Marketing," *Marketing News* 13 (April 4, 1980), p. 1.

[3]Webster, "Management Science in Industrial Marketing."

[4]Frederick E. Webster, Jr., "Top Management's Concern About Marketing: Issues for the 1980's," *Journal of Marketing* 45 (Summer 1981), pp. 9–16.

[5]Richard E. Plank, "Industrial Marketing Education: Practitioner's Views," *Industrial Marketing Management* 11 (1982), pp. 311–315.

TABLE 1-1 Practitioners' Ranking of Marketing Skills

Topic	Ranking	Topic	Ranking
Market Planning	1	Proposal Writing	20
Market Analysis	2	Distribution Service	21
Sales Forecasting	3	List Pricing	22
Market Research	4	R&D Management	23
Product Planning	5	Value Analysis	24
New Product Development	6	Trade Shows	25
Product Management	7	Manufacturers' Representatives	26
Pricing Strategies	8	Regulation	27
Price Theory	9	Purchasing	28
Sales Management	10	Vendor Analysis	29
Field Sales Management	11	Logistics	30
Advertising	12	Environmental Factors	31
Sales Promotion	13	Channel Management	32
Buyer Behavior	14	Personal Inducements	33
Buyer-Seller Relations	15	Women in Sales	34
Financial Interface	16	Leasing	35
Price and the Law	17	Government Markets	36
Marketing Control	18	Wholesaling	37
Technical Sales	19		

Source: Reprinted by permission of the publisher from "Industrial Marketing Education: Practitioners' Views," Richard E. Plank, *Industrial Marketing Management,* 11 (1982), pp. 311–315. Copyright © 1982 by Elsevier Science Publishing Co., Inc.

INDUSTRIAL VERSUS CONSUMER MARKETING MANAGEMENT

While the basic tasks of marketing management apply in both the consumer and industrial markets, unique forces combine to pose special challenges for the industrial marketing manager. In the industrial market, markets are relatively concentrated and channels of distribution are shorter; buyers are well informed, highly organized, and sophisticated in purchasing techniques; and multiple influencers contribute different points of view to purchasing decisions. Thus, industrial marketing creates its own set of conditions for marketing decisions.

As in the consumer market, industrial marketers must define their target markets, determine the needs of those markets, design products and services to fill those needs, and develop programs to reach and satisfy those markets. However, in comparison to consumer marketing, industrial marketing is more a responsibility of general management. In fact, many industrial executives have difficulty in separating marketing from corporate strategy and policy.[6]

In consumer marketing, changes in marketing strategy are often carried out completely within the marketing department through changes in advertising, promotion, and packaging. However, as Figure 1-1 indicates, changes in industrial market-

[6]Webster, "Top Management's Concern About Marketing: Issues for the 1980's."

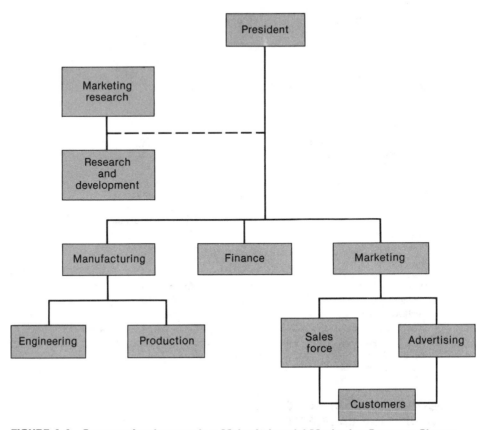

FIGURE 1-1   Company Involvement in a Major Industrial Marketing Strategy Change

ing strategy tend to have companywide implications. Such implications may involve departures from traditional engineering and manufacturing techniques or major shifts in developmental emphasis. As in the case of Caterpillar, this may require capital commitments for new plants and equipment. (To revamp one 40-year old facility will take Caterpillar five years and $200 million).[7] Although the need for such departures from tradition may be identified by marketing, decisions on such departures are often the responsibility of general management, which must provide the follow-through in all functional areas.[8]

INDUSTRIAL MARKETING DEFINED

Industrial marketing consists of all activities involved in the marketing of products and services to organizations (i.e., commercial enterprises, profit and not-for-profit

[7]"This Cat is Acting Like a Tiger," *Fortune,* December 18, 1988, pp. 71–76.

[8]B. Charles Ames, "Trappings vs Substance in Industrial Marketing," *Harvard Business Review,* 48 (July-August 1970), pp. 93–102.

institutions, government agencies, and resellers) that use products and services in the production of consumer or industrial goods and services, and to facilitate the operation of their enterprises.[9] Viewed from the perspective of "marketing," industrial marketing is, then, human activity directed toward satisfying wants and needs of organizations through the exchange process.[10]

Figure 1-2 shows that exchange transactions in the industrial market consist of (1) product or service exchange, (2) information exchange, (3) financial exchange, and (4) social exchange.[11]

Product Exchange. The characteristics of the product or service involved have a significant effect on the industrial exchange process. The ease of exchange depends upon the ability of the seller to identify the buyer's needs and the product's potential to satisfy those needs.

Information Exchange. Information exchange often consists of answering technical, economic, and organizational questions regarding pre- and postsale maintenance and servicing. Products must be planned and designed to serve customers. To

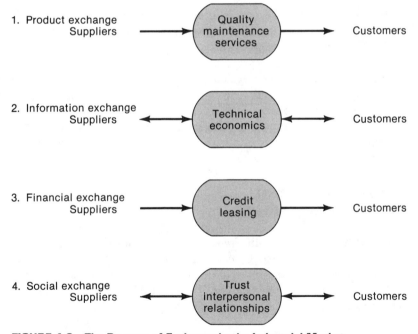

FIGURE 1-2   The Process of Exchange in the Industrial Market

[9]Industrial Marketing Committee Review Board, "Fundamental Differences Between Industrial and Consumer Marketing," *Journal of Marketing* 19 (October 1954), p. 153.

[10]Philip Kotler, *Marketing Management: Analysis, Planning, and Control,* 5th ed. (Englewood Cliffs, N.J.: Prentice-Hall, Inc., 1984), p. 4.

[11]IMP Project Group, Hakan Hakanson ed., *International Marketing and Purchasing of Industrial Goods* (New York: John Wiley & Sons, Inc., 1982), pp. 16–17.

DON'T CONFUSE MOTIVES WITH ACTIONS

An often heard theme is that industrial purchasing is almost wholly rational economic behavior. In fact, as any experienced industrial marketing person will tell you, it is nearly as often a personality sales situation as is any consumer transaction. Were this not so, no company would find it necessary to allocate as much of its marketing budget to direct sales as it does. The fact of the matter is that the demand or need for industrial products is usually economically motivated and rational, but this should not be confused with the actions taken to satisfy that need or the behavioral aspects of the industrial purchase.

Source: Reprinted by permission of the publisher from ''Industrial Marketing Myths,'' by W. S. Penn, Jr., and Mark Mougel, *Industrial Marketing Management,* 7 (1978), pp. 133–138. Copyright © 1978 by Elsevier Science Publishing Co., Inc.

---

accomplish this, buyers and sellers tend to work together, exchanging product-specific information over long periods of time.

Financial Exchange. Financial exchanges may involve such considerations as the granting of credit or the need to exchange money from one currency into another when dealing with foreign buyers.

Social Exchange. Social exchange is important in such areas as reducing uncertainty between buyer and seller, avoiding short-term difficulties, and maintaining the exchange relationship over a lengthy transaction period. Many aspects of an agreement between buyers and sellers in the industrial market are not fully formalized or based on legal criteria until the end of the transaction period. Rather, much of the process of exchange is based on mutual trust.

CONTRASTING INDUSTRIAL AND CONSUMER MARKETING

An appreciation of the differences between industrial and consumer marketing is probably best facilitated by comparing the two markets. As Table 1-2 indicates, considerable differences exist in (1) the structure of the market, (2) product usage, (3) the nature of buying behavior involved, (4) the channels of distribution, (5) promotional variables, and (6) pricing strategies.

Market Characteristics

Significant differences exist between industrial and consumer market characteristics that affect the nature of industrial marketing. These differences exist in (1) the size, (2) the geographic concentration, and (3) the competitive nature of the markets.[12]

[12]Webster, ''Management Science in Industrial Marketing.''

TABLE 1-2 Industrial versus Consumer Marketing Areas of Differences

	Industrial Markets	*Consumer Markets*
Market structure	Geographically concentrated Relatively fewer buyers Oligopolistic competition	Geographically dispersed Mass markets Monopolistic competition

Products	Technical complexity
	Customized
	Service, delivery and availability very
	   important
		Standardized
		Service, delivery, and availability
		   somewhat important

Buyer behavior	Functional involvement Rational/task motives predominate Technical expertise Stable relations Interpersonal relationships Reciprocity	Family involvement Social/psychological motives pre- dominate Less technical expertise Nonpersonal relationships
Decision making	Distinct, observable stages	Unobservable, mental stages
Channels	Shorter, more direct, fewer link- ages	Indirect, multiple linkages
Promotion	Emphasis on personal selling	Emphasis on advertising
Price	Competitive bidding, negotiating on complex purchases List prices on standard items	List prices

Size of the Market.   Compared to the great number of households that constitute the mass market for consumer goods and services, it is not 1   ᵐmon to find fewer than 20 companies representing the entire market for an '   ᵣoduct or ser- vice. In fact, only three or four customers may compr'   ᵗᶦon of a total market. For example, in the small town of Weathe   ᶫier of industrial packaging, Raven Company, has less tha' 1 is a major customer, 3-M. It is not difficult to imᵣ are for aircraft carriers, huge trucks that haul coppᵣ

While there are relatively few industrial custᵣ chase larger quantities, and engage in this volᵣ Ford Motor Company, for instance, spends ovᵣ than 100,000 different items to support its pᵣ

Geographical Concentration.   Industrial ᶜ specific areas of the United States such aᵣ

[13]Gordon T. Brand, *The Industrial Buying* *trial Marketing* (New York: John Wiley & Sonᵣ

Pacific Coast.[14] Such concentration occurs mainly because of natural resources and manufacturing processes.[15] For instance, the geographic location of natural resources explains the concentration patterns of most energy-producing firms. Only a handful of counties in California, Oklahoma, Texas, and Louisiana produce the bulk of our gas and oil. Manufacturers whose production processes add weight to their products tend to locate near customers, while those whose processes subtract weight tend to locate near sources of input.

Manufacturers of computers and other advanced electronic products present an interesting case of plant location. They tend to concentrate in areas that have advanced teaching and research facilities and desirable living locales such as the Silicon Valley near San Francisco and Route 128 surrounding Boston. Such locations are chosen to facilitate the attraction of intelligent, educated employees, who seek both intellectual challenges and physical pleasures.

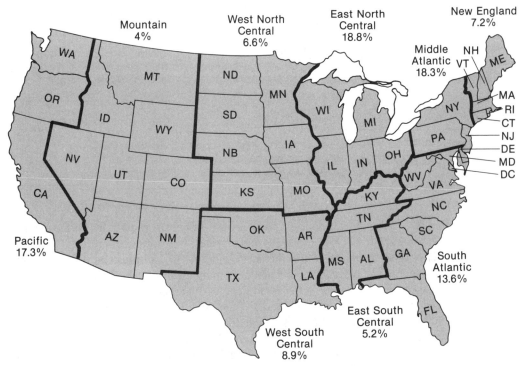

FIGURE 1-3 Geographical Distribution of U.S. Manufacturing Plants

Source: Reprinted by permission from Cahners Advertising Research Report No. 711.1 [Boston: Cahners Publishing ....ny, 1977; updated July 9, 1985).

[14]Cahners Advertising Research Report No. 7102, "19% of All the U.S. Manufacturing Plants ... All the Business" (Boston: Cahners Publishing Company, 1977; updated).

... of Industrial and Commercial Buying Power," *Sales and Marketing Management* (April

   The geographical distribution of manufacturing plants in the United States is illustrated in Figure 1-3. As you can see, approximately 37 percent of all manufacturing plants are located in the East North Central and Middle Atlantic states, with 17.3 percent on the Pacific Coast and 13.6 percent in the South Atlantic states.

Competitive Nature. A further difference between the two markets is the nature of oligopsonistic buying. In the industrial arena, oligopsonistic buying organizations, organizations that are very large firms, tend to dominate many markets. For instance, the small number of large automobile producers in the United States purchase 60 percent of all synthetic rubber, 60 percent of all lead, and 72 percent of all plate glass produced in the United States.[16] These oligopsonists' reactions to changes in one another's buying practices affect industrial marketing strategy decisions.

   Due to the fact that technological or cost-effective advantages override geographical considerations, industrial organizations are more directly involved in international purchasing. Thus, the major finished goods exports of industrialized nations tend to be industrial rather than consumer goods manufacturers. Industrial demand as well as industrial supply, therefore, is more apt to cross international boundaries than are demand and supply in the consumer market. (Table 1-3 indicates that, with the exception of three motor vehicle companies and Phillip Morris, the remaining top twenty exporters are industrial corporations. Additionally, Fortune magazine explains that much of both GM's and Ford's exports are component parts shipped for assembly to Canadian plants, and that most of the completed cars are returned to the United States. Therefore, industrial exports are an even more significant proportion of total exports than one might realize in first glancing at Table 1-3.) However, because of increasing improvements in foreign technology and marketing skills, subsidized by government policies, worldwide competition makes it more difficult for U.S. suppliers of industrial goods to compete not only in foreign markets, but domestically as well. Industrial marketers, then, are more subject to world political, economic, and competitive changes than are their consumer counterparts.

Product Characteristics

In the industrial market, products are not purchased for personal use. Rather, they are purchased as component parts of the products and services to be produced or to serve the operation of the firm in some way. Thus, there is greater concern with the technical aspects of products, and purchases are often controlled by the use of customer-generated specifications. While a product in both the industrial and consumer market should be thought of as a bundle of problem-solving attributes, service and support variables in addition to the physical product itself assume greater importance in the marketing of industrial goods. For instance, timeliness

[16]Brand, *The Industrial Buying Decision,* p. 82.

TABLE 1-3 The Top 20 U.S. Exporters

	Export Sales [Millions of $]	Percent of Total Sales
1. General Motors	$9,392	7.8%
2. Ford Motor	8,822	9.5
3. Boeing	7,849	46.3
4. General Electric	5,744	11.6
5. Int'l Business Machines	4,951	8.3
6. Chrysler	4,344	12.2
7. E. I. Du Pont De Nemours	4,196	12.9
8. McDonnell Douglas	3,471	23.0
9. Caterpillar	2,930	28.1
10. United Technologies	2,848	15.8
11. Eastman Kodak	2,301	13.5
12. Digital Equipment	2,083	18.2
13. Hewlett-Packard	2,064	21.0
14. Unisys	2,013	20.3
15. Philip Morris	1,863	7.2
16. Motorola	1,742	21.1
17. Occidental Petroleum	1,684	8.7
18. General Dynamics	1,597	16.7
19. Allied-Signal	1,464	12.3
20. Weyerhaeuser	1,398	14.0

and certainty of delivery are usually critical due to the significant costs of production delays and are, thus, considered important aspects of the total product package.

Buyer Characteristics

While the typical consumer buyer has little technical knowledge regarding most products purchased, buyers in the industrial market are professionally trained and technically qualified. Purchasing decisions are generally made on the basis of compliance with specifications, cost-effectiveness, and dependability of supply, rather than on social or psychological needs. Due to the technical complexity of many of these decisions, the large amounts of money involved, and the corresponding risks and uncertainties, purchasing decisions may take up many months and involve several individuals. Reciprocity is also a unique characteristic of the industrial market. That is, when an opportunity is present, buyers tend to buy from their own customers. Thus, both buyer and seller become customers of one another.

Stable Relationships.   While most consumers frequently change their purchasing strategies and habits, this is not so in industrial buying. Empirical studies of industrial markets indicate that the relationships between sellers and buyers develop over time and are usually highly stable. Changes are few and occur relatively slowly.[17] Buyers face problems in searching out and qualifying suppliers. The cost of selecting a supplier who cannot meet delivery requirements or who delivers an unsatisfactory product can be high. Thus, the purchasing firm must be certain of a potential supplier's technical, administrative, and financial capabilities.[18]

Buyer-Seller Interfaces. Agreements, orders, and contracts require offers and counteroffers; thus, considerable negotiating and information exchange takes place between individual specialists and representatives from the various functional areas within both the customer and supplier firms. Individuals from both firms bring to the relationship special knowledge and interests. Thus, a network of interorganizational contacts emerges, and interpersonal relationships develop. These relationships are highly valued and are an integral part of the buyer-seller interface, as well as the foundation of successful overall organizational interrelationships.[19]

Channel Characteristics

Because of production line inventory requirements and other unique needs of industrial buyers, physical distribution is extremely important. Thus, as Figure 1-4 shows, fewer channel alternatives are feasible in the industrial market than in the consumer market.

In the industrial market, channels tend to be more direct. With the exception of small manufacturers, or in situations where geographical markets are considerably dispersed, manufacturers tend to utilize their own sales forces to sell directly to customers. Since there are relatively fewer buyers and they tend to be concentrated, fewer layers of intermediaries exist. Where intermediaries are used, manufacturers' representatives and industrial distributors or dealers facilitate the flow of goods.

Promotional Characteristics

Generally, in the industrial market, there is a much greater emphasis on personal selling. Advertising is used to lay a foundation for the sales call rather than serve as the primary communication tool. Sales people act more as consultants and technical problem solvers, utilizing in-depth product knowledge and technical understanding of the buyers' needs, whereas industrial advertising normally stresses more factual

---

[17]For example, see S. Levin and P. White, "Exchange as a Conceptual Framework for the Study of Interorganizational Relationships," *Administrative Science Quarterly* 5 (1961), pp. 583–601; R. Warren, "The Interorganizational Field as a Focus for Investigation," *Administrative Science Quarterly* 12 (1967), pp. 396–419; C. B. Marett, "On the Specification of Interorganization Dimensions," *Sociology and Social Research* 61 (1971), pp. 83–99; and H. E. Aldrich, *Organizations and Environments* (Englewood Cliffs, N.J.: Prentice-Hall, Inc. 1979).

[18]Hakanson, ed., *International Marketing and Purchasing of Industrial Goods,* pp. 3–4.

[19]Ibid., p. 4.

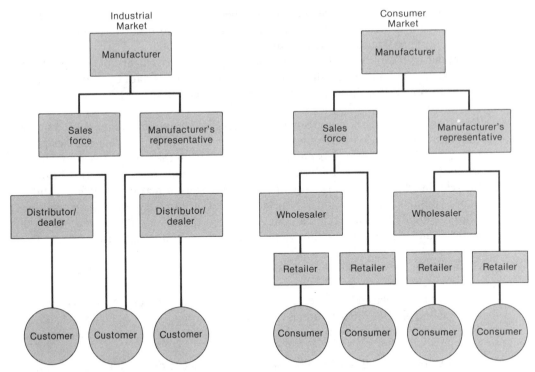

FIGURE 1-4 Channel Distribution in the Industrial versus the Consumer Market

and technical data. While some industrial advertisers, such as IBM, Xerox, and Union Carbide, use television to reach potential customers, the primary means of reaching the market is through business magazines, traditional trade journals, and direct mail. Sales promotion activities tend to center on trade shows and catalogs.

Price Characteristics

Although still important, price is less critical in industrial buying decisions. In one recent study of industrial buying in high-tech markets, researchers found that price ranked low in the purchasing criteria. In fact, purchasers were willing to pay a "premium price for equipment from a supplier who could provide superior technical and after sales service." It is not surprising, then, that quality and consistency of products, certainty of delivery, service, and technical support are often the most important criteria.[20] Competitive bidding and negotiated prices are very common, and financing arrangements are often considered part of the pricing package. In the case of capital goods, leasing is often included as a price alternative. Trade and quantity discounts off published price lists are widely used.

[20]Russell Abratt, "Industrial Buying in High-Tech Markets," *Industrial Marketing Management* 15 (1986), pp. 293–298.

NEVER TALK PRICE

Inexperienced salespeople invariably start by thinking and talking price when money is the last thing they should discuss. They probably reason: "If a buyer bases decisions on quality, service, and price, how can I prove good quality and service when I'm not shipping anything? The only thing left is price."

. . . never talk price with anyone before you've sold him on your company and yourself. The purchaser will generally guide the salesperson he or she wants to do business with to the lower price. This leads to my first rule of selling: people buy from whom they want to buy and make price and all other decision factors fit.

Source: Reprinted by permission of the *Harvard Business Review.* An excerpt from "Industrial Selling: Beyond Price and Persistence," by Clifton J. Reichard [March—April 1985]. Copyright © 1985 by the President and Fellows of Harvard College; all rights reserved.

Price stabilization is quite common and results in nonprice competition. In oligopolistic industries, firms readily respond to competitors' moves, particularly price changes. Large steel producers have long tended to change their prices within only a few days of one another. Therefore, price receives much less attention as a promotional tool.

From the following discussion, it should be evident that many fundamental differences exist between consumer and industrial marketing. Consumer marketing managers, when crossing over to the industrial market, cannot easily transfer their cultivated knowledge. They must understand the differences between the two markets. Yet even these differences in characteristics do not provide a complete picture. To understand more fully the differences between the markets, it is necessary to understand some underlying economic peculiarities of the industrial market.

ECONOMICS OF INDUSTRIAL DEMAND

Economic demand in the industrial market involves dimensions not prevalent in consumer demand. Demand for industrial goods and services is *derived* from the ultimate demand for consumer goods and services. That is, demand is derived from expectations of the actions of ultimate consumers. Demand for industrial products is also often joint. *Joint demand* occurs when the demand for a product depends upon its use in conjunction with another product or products. While *cross-elasticity of demand* exists in both markets, it is more important in industrial marketing since it can have a major effect on a firm's entire corporate strategy.

Derived Demand

Derived demand is the single most important force in the marketing of industrial goods and services. Industrial customers purchase goods and services for use in producing other goods and services. Eventually, whatever is finally produced will be sold to the consuming public or kept forever in inventory. The demand for wool does not exist in and of itself. Wool is demanded to spin yarn because yarn is demanded to weave cloth because cloth is demanded to make coats, and all these demands are derived from forecasts of ultimate consumer demand for coats. Thus, real inventory problems can develop when final demand is over or under that which has been estimated. Consequently, forecasts of ultimate consumer demand determine the levels of demand throughout the entire industrial pipeline.

Dramatic Shifts in the Demand Curve. Demand for needed materials is normally determined by actual (historical) as well as expected (future) sales. As you can see in Figure 1-5, when consumers demand increases and expectations are bright, purchasing managers increase their inventory objectives. However, when projected demand in the consumer market becomes shaky during recessionary periods, inventory objectives may be abruptly reduced due to the uncertainties of future demand for end products. Such actions magnify fluctuations in demand, dramatically shifting the demand curve in the short run throughout the entire industrial pipeline, often with a domino-like effect—much like a car hitting its brakes as it moves along a congested freeway.

Capital goods—machinery and equipment used to produce other goods—are also purchased in anticipation of future needs but require major expenditures, and are subject to closer scrutiny than are industrial goods in general. Consequently, a variation in the level of expected business will usually have a more pronounced impact on the sale of capital goods. A vivid example of this occurred during the 1929–1932 depression when production of consumer goods dropped 20 points from an index of 100 to 80, while spending for capital equipment dropped 65 points from an index of 100 to 35.[21] In periods of recovery—real or anticipated—and in times of prosperity, sales of capital goods are notably stimulated.

During periods of reduced or uncertain demand, industrial firms usually employ a dual strategy regarding capital equipment: the life of older equipment is stretched out through increased maintenance and repair, while demand peaks are handled with labor force fluctuations (e.g., temporary help, overtime, and additional shifts) rather than capital expenditures.

Stimulating Industrial Demand. Because of this derived nature of industrial demand, the influence of final consumers is well recognized. Obviously, then, one way in which industrial marketers attempt to increase sales is by stimulating increases in the demand of ultimate consumers. By directing advertising to ultimate consumers, industrialists can often increase consumer demand for final products, which, in turn, increases their industrial sales. This is precisely the philosophy behind much industry advertising directed toward consumers. Industrial advertising to ultimate

[21]Robert W. Haas, *Industrial Marketing Management,* 2nd ed. (Boston: Kent Publishing Co., 1982), p. 40.

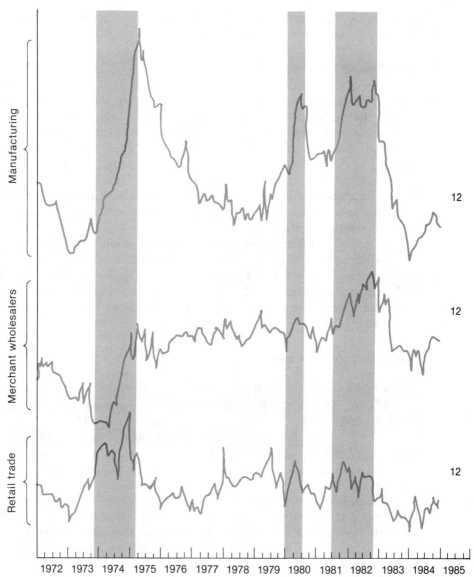

FIGURE 1-5   Ratios of Manufacturing, Wholesale, and Retail Inventories to Sales, 1972–1985 (in 1972 dollars)

Source: 1985 U.S. Industrial Outlook, U.S. Department of Commerce, U.S. Government Documents Depository Library No. 496, January 1985, p. 34–16.

consumers is also a method of increasing goodwill and achieving a favorable position with an industrialist's immediate customers.

Joint Demand

Joint demand is commonplace in the industrial market. It occurs when one product requires the existence of others to be useful. While exceptions may be found (as in the manufacturing of nails), most products require several component parts or ingredients. Food processors, for instance, require flour, yeast, eggs, salt, and preservatives in the production of bread. If, for some reason, any one of these ingredients cannot be obtained, other purchases will be curtailed or discontinued. Joint demand situations can also be affected by changes in product specifications. For example, should the food processor switch to self-rising flour, the demand for yeast should diminish and disappear.

Industrial customers often prefer to buy joint product items or complete product lines from one supplier rather than purchase individual products from different suppliers. Thus, a firm may not purchase any of a supplier's products if a gap exists in the supplier's product line. The individual products required, then, do not have individual demand, but are demanded only if the "other" products are available in the supplier's line.

Cross-Elasticity of Demand

Cross-elasticity of demand, that is, the responsiveness of the sales of one product to a price change in another, can have a dramatic impact on the marketing strategy of an industrial firm. The demand for many industrial goods is influenced by the price of other goods. For example, the quantity of steel demanded is related to the price of a close substitute, aluminum. This direct relationship between the price of one good and the quantity demanded of a second good holds true for all substitute products.

The degree to which resources are substitutable for one another is an important issue in the industrial market. The larger the number of substitute resources available, the greater the cross-elasticity of demand for a particular resource. Should a housing contractor, for instance, find that different types of wood are about equally satisfactory for home construction, such as cedar and redwood, a rise in the price of redwood may cause a sharp rise in the demand for cedar and a corresponding decrease in the demand for redwood.

Other goods, such as printers and word processors, illustrate a completely different relationship. As the price of word processors falls, the demand for printers increases. Goods that are inversely related in this manner are complementary goods—they are used together rather than in place of one another. This is a situation of joint demand as previously discussed.

Cross-elasticity for substitutes is always positive; that is, the price of one good and the quantity demanded of the other always move in the same direction. The more positive this ratio, the higher the cross-elasticity and the more definite it is that the products compete in the same market. Cross-elasticity for complements (joint demand) is negative—price and quantity move in opposite directions. The more negative this relationship, the more closely the demand for the products is related.

The concept of cross-elasticity of demand can be very useful to industrial marketers. First, it is important that a firm know how the demand for its products is likely to be affected by changes in the prices of other goods. Second, it is useful in measuring the interrelationships among industries. Therefore, it is used by industrial organizations to identify areas of competition between industrial goods and between industries.[22]

THE RESELLER'S MARKET

So far our discussion has centered on organizations that purchase industrial goods and services to produce other goods and services (e.g., commercial enterprises). Purchasing considerations of resellers in the consumer market, however, parallel those of the industrial market—particularly when they are large organizations. Because of their many marketing similarities to industrial organizations, it is important to give this market its proper attention in the study of industrial marketing. Resellers, like industrial firms, do not purchase goods and services for personal consumption, but do so to facilitate the operations of their businesses. That is, everything that is purchased is purchased to make a profit.

In the conventional study of consumer marketing, the emphasis is primarily upon the behavior of ultimate consumers; wholesalers and retailers are treated as an element of the marketing mix (place or distribution) rather than as a served market. But these firms also represent a sizable and important buying group whose behavior is similar to that of industrial buyers. Consideration must be given to both the similarities and differences in this market so that a suitable and effective marketing strategy can be devised.

Market Characteristics

Many merchandising firms are very large and have few competitors in their particular market arenas. There are, for instance, approximately 50,000 fast-food outlets of which over 70 percent are chains. McDonald's alone operates nearly 6,000 outlets.[23] While these outlets are scattered throughout the United States, most of the buying is conducted through central headquarters; thus, the market tends to be small and concentrated. This is true also for large retailers, such as J. C. Penney, Montgomery Ward, Sears, and Homeland.

---

[22]Eugene F. Brigham and James L. Pappas, *Managerial Economics* (Hindsdale, Ill.: The Dryden Press, 1972), pp. 102–104.

[23]"Industrial Surveys," *Standard & Poors* (1979), p. 172.

These retailers have strong bargaining power when they purchase from suppliers. For instance, Atari originally entered through the market through Sears, so its single major competitor at the time, Mirco, had to find an equally effective channel if it hoped to compete with Atari. Mirco chose Montgomery Ward and was then faced with negotiating a contract that also had to compete with the Atari-Sears agreement. For example, to enable Wards to sell the Mirco home video machines successfully, Mirco's retail price had to be competitive with Atari's retail price. Thus, Mirco's marketing strategy was impacted significantly by the concentrated buying power of these resellers.

Product Characteristics

Many large sellers are technically oriented in their purchasing procedures and set detailed specifications that govern the production of goods that are purchased under the buyer's private brand. Buyers often require alterations to enhance the quality of materials, workmanship, and styling. They may specify the elimination of factors that add to the cost without providing additional retail value to the product. To differentiate their product versions from other merchants, they often specify changes in product components, such as switches, motors, and batteries.[24] Sears, with 90 percent of its offerings privately branded, normally functions in this manner.[25]

For some products, attributes such as delivery, availability of spare parts, and maintenance can play a heavy role in determining a product's success or failure in the reseller's market. Service availability for major durable goods such as television sets and appliances, and high-tech equipment such as home computers, is often a major criterion in the purchasing decision. When such factors as maintenance and delivery are considered critical, resellers also look for stability in their relationships with suppliers.

Buyer Characteristics

Although resellers do not always have the technical background of purchasers in the industrial market, they do tend to compare technical features of products when making purchasing decisions. For instance, K-Mart would not sell Coleco's Adam computer because all the peripheral equipment was built in. Instead, K-Mart carried Atari's 600XL and 800XL models so that customers could add desired peripheral equipment in stages.[26]

---

[24]John W. Wingate and Joseph S. Friedlander, *The Management of Retail Buying,* 2nd ed. (New York: John Wiley & Sons, Inc., 1978), pp. 274–275.

[25]Ibid., p. 274.

[26]"Warner's Atari Is Trying to Regain Top Spot in Consumer Electronics," *The Wall Street Journal* (July 6, 1983), p. 25.

As in industrial buying, purchasing decisions in this market are approached primarily on the basis of rational rather than social or psychological criteria. Often, multiple buying influencers and decision makers are involved in a single major purchase.

Channel Characteristics

The length of channels of distribution in the reseller's market depends on the type of product being marketed. Manufacturers of durable goods and textile products sell directly to retailers and seldom use intermediaries (e.g., wholesalers). Basic commodities, such as hardware, however, tend to flow through a variety of intermediaries.

Because these wholesalers and retailers, as well as industrial producers, depend upon the profits obtained from the resale of goods to the ultimate consumer, physical distribution is also extremely important. When the flow of goods to this market bogs down and the consumer is unable to find a desired brand, that sale may be lost forever. Not only will the consumer buy elsewhere, cutting into the reseller's profit, he or she may purchase another manufacturer's product.

Promotional Characteristics

As in the industrial market, there is a much greater emphasis on personal selling to reach buyers in the reseller's market. While advertising is directed to ultimate consumers to "pull" products through the channel, it is the manufacturer's sales force, or the manufacturer's representatives, who call on wholesalers and retailers. So important is direct selling in the textile industry that clothing retailers no longer have to travel to New York to see the new seasonal lines; New York comes to them. And manufacturers of consumer durable goods, such as General Electric, have their own sales forces dispersed throughout the United States to serve their retailers more efficiently.

Price Characteristics

Resellers are more concerned with the price of goods than are industrial buyers. This is true because of the emphasis that their customers, the ultimate consumers, place on price. Moreover, a reseller's eventual profits are primarily determined by gross product margin: the difference between "buy price" (trade discount) and the manufacturer's suggested resale price. Thus, a manufacturer's product will be attractive to resellers only if it can be retailed competitively and still provide a reasonable profit margin. Contrasted to the industrial market, price in this market is used by manufacturers as a promotional tool. It is common practice to allow special discounts for extra shelf-facings and in-store promotions.

Economics of Demand

Wholesale and retail inventory levels are part of the chain reaction linking consumer demand and derived industrial demand. When wholesale and retail stocks of consumer goods are relatively high in the face of declining consumer demand as they were during the 1981–82 recession (see Figure 1-5), resellers naturally reduce their purchases from manufacturers. However, due to their particular marketing function, resellers can be of special assistance to the industrial marketer. First, retailers have the ability to affect consumer demand directly through increased promotion, value-enhancing services, or reduced price. Vendors who maintain strong relationships with resellers may achieve some degree of preferential treatment, such as special promotions or increased shelf-facings for their products and, thus, obtain a greater share of consumer demand.

Second, resellers are positioned closest to ultimate consumers so that they have the opportunity to obtain and furnish feedback regarding consumers' desires and preferences. Hence, they can act as an informational catalyst for industrial firms that want to implement the marketing concept.

Joint demand is also an economic reality for most resellers. For example, a meat market wants its supplier to carry all the varieties of meats, poultry, and fish that the meat market will sell. Such desires are equivalent to demanding a full line of products. Many small, independent retailers depend on their suppliers to provide full lines of needed items.

Overall, the reseller's market confronts the industrial marketer with both similarities and differences in market characteristics, buyer behavior, channels of distribution, promotion, price, and demand. Those factors are sufficiently important to warrant specific thought as to what tactical variations in industrial marketing strategy are necessary to serve this market successfully.

THE INDUSTRIAL MARKETING CONCEPT

The marketing concept holds that the key task of the organization is to define the needs of a target market and adapt the organization's product or service to satisfy those needs more effectively than its competitors.[27] While the nature of the markets differs, the marketing concept is applicable and important in both the industrial and consumer markets. However, evidence indicates that consumer marketers have embraced the marketing concept more fully than their industrial counterparts.[28]

Industrial customers are organizations—businesses, institutions, and government agencies—with unique needs. The industrial marketing concept involves more than facilitating exchange with these customers; it is a philosophical point of view

[27]Kotler, *Marketing Management,* p. 76.

[28]Frederick E. Webster, Jr., ''Management Science in Industrial Marketing,'' *Journal of Marketing* 42 (January 1978), p. 23; see also, Grandhi Balakrishma, ''Better Use of the Industrial Marketing Concept,'' *Industrial Marketing Management* 7 (January 1978), pp. 71–76.

that has as its basis the formation of a partnership between buyer and seller for the purpose of achieving the organizational goals of both.

Often a major barrier to a true industrial marketing orientation lies in a frequently found excessive preoccupation with products. Effective marketing planning is not so much concerned with what management thinks the company is producing but, rather, with what customers think they are buying. Given the nature and purpose of industrial products, to be part of the customer's product or organizational process, a seller literally becomes part of the buyer's technology, productivity, end-market satisfaction, and profit plan—in short, total corporate strategy.[29]

Too often, industrial organizations tend to be technically oriented—much more interested in a particular product and its technical development. Many managers in such firms are promoted out of engineering and research and development departments. It is not unusual therefore, that technical values tend to dominate their decision making. When this occurs, there is a risk of "becoming so enamored with a technical accomplishment or particular product parameters that the necessary flexibility for responding to customer needs in a competitive market place disappears."[30] This is more serious in industrial marketing due to the complexity of the problems customers are attempting to solve. For marketing effectiveness, the product should always be regarded as a variable and should be viewed from the perspective of the customer. Customer benefits and need satisfaction, rather than the physical product, should be the center of attention.

It should be noted, however, that a marketing-oriented firm is not run by the marketing department. Customer satisfaction should be paramount in all corporate decision making; therefore, it cannot be the exclusive domain of the marketing department. Providing customer satisfaction must involve all decision makers and will affect product design, demand analysis, manufacturing techniques, resource utilization, and long-range profits.

LOOKING BACK

It should be obvious from reading this chapter that industrial marketing is more complex than is consumer marketing and that marketing success depends on understanding the complexities involved. Industrial marketing strategy has companywide implications and is, therefore, more of a general management function, affecting various departments within the marketing firm.

Compared to consumer markets, the majority of industrial markets are oligopsonistic, with relatively few large buyers that tend to be geographically concentrated. Industrial buyers are also more rational in their purchasing strategy, and purchasing tends to be influenced by many members of the buying organization. Differences

---

[29]Frederick E. Webster, Jr., *Industrial Marketing Strategy* (New York: John Wiley & Sons, Inc., 1979), pp. 15–16.

[30]Ibid., pp. 15–16.

also exist in the nature of the products sold, the channels of distribution, and the criteria used in the purchase decision.

While price is an extremely important consideration in the purchase of consumer goods, this is not as true in the industrial market. Price importance is tempered by product quality, dependability of supply, and technical innovation.

Because of the unique characteristics of derived demand, industrial marketers are faced with the necessity of anticipating demand increases or decreases at several market levels, including the ultimate consumer. They must be on the lookout for any factors that may affect demand for their products, including joint demand. They must monitor the cross-elasticity of demand for their products to recognize all competition, both direct and indirect.

Manufacturers selling in the reseller's market must also be aware of how this market parallels the industrial market.

QUESTIONS FOR DISCUSSION

1. "Marketing is marketing—no matter what the product. . . . A good marketing person can move products in any part of the marketplace." Do you agree with this statement?
2. In the marketing of goods and services, information, financial, and social exchanges take place in both the consumer and industrial market. Do you see any significant differences in these exchanges between the two markets? Explain your answer.
3. Some people maintain that the distinctions between consumer and industrial marketing are unjustified and that the similarities between the two markets are more useful in developing marketing knowledge. Do you agree?
4. Of the several basic differences between industrial and consumer marketing covered in this chapter, which, from your point of view, would have the most significant impact on the development of marketing strategy? Why?
5. How would the desire for stable relationships in the industrial market affect a firm's ability to sell its products to a manufacturer currently buying from another source?
6. Would a price decrease be an effective marketing strategy if the demand for an industrial product was falling because of decreased consumer demand? Justify your response.
7. Using a product with which you are familiar, illustrate the concept of joint demand.
8. How does the concept of joint demand impact the firm selling to resellers?

SUGGESTED ADDITIONAL READINGS

AMES, B. CHARLES, "Trappings vs Substance in Industrial Marketing," *Harvard Business Review,* 48 (July-August 1970):93–102.

HLAVACEK, JAMES D., "Business Schools Need More Industrial Marketing," *Marketing News,* 13 (April 4, 1980):1.

LEVIN, S., AND P. WHITE, "Exchange as a Conceptual Framework for the Study of Interorganizational Relationships," *Administrative Science Quarterly,* 5 (1961):583–601.

PLANK, RICHARD E., "Industrial Marketing Education: Practitioner's Views," *Industrial Marketing Management,* 11 (1982):311–315.

WEBSTER, FREDERICK E., JR., "Top Management's Concern About Marketing: Issues for the 1980's," *Journal of Marketing,* 45 (Summer 1981):9–16.

WEBSTER, FREDERICK E., JR., "Management Science in Industrial Marketing," *Journal of Marketing* (January 1978):21–27.

CHAPTER 2

Understanding Industrial Markets

The industrial market is composed of commercial enterprises, governmental organizations, and institutions whose purchasing decisions vary with the type of industrial good or service under consideration. Effective marketing programs thus depend upon a thorough understanding of how marketing strategy should differ with the type of organization being targeted and the products being sold. The objective of this chapter, then, is to expose you to

1. The diversity of industrial customers and the types of products and services they purchase.
2. How marketing strategy is influenced by the type of customer being served and the product or service being marketed.
3. The unique characteristics of organizational purchasing.

The industrial market is characterized by tremendous diversity both in customers served and products sold. General Motors, for instance, purchases $500 worth of electronic fuel injectors, microelectronic sensors, and electronic noses for each subcompact car it produces; the federal government purchases $2,900 Allen wrenches to keep its spare parts inventory up to date; universities purchase $100 surge suppressors to protect their investment in IBM computers; while Computer

Land, the largest U.S. computer chain, sells maintenance agreements to its corporate customers to keep their computers operating.[1]

Component parts, spare parts, accessory equipment, and services are only a small example of the types of products purchased by the variety of customers in the industrial market. As indicated in Figure 2-1, industrial distributors or dealers who in turn sell to other industrial customers, commercial businesses, government, and institutions buy a variety of products that, in one way or another, are important to the functioning of their business endeavors. Knowing how this vast array of industrial customers purchase and use products and what criteria are important in their purchasing decision is an important aspect of industrial marketing strategy.

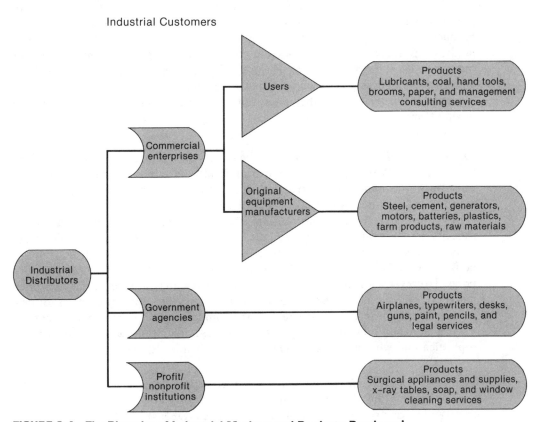

FIGURE 2-1 The Diversity of Industrial Markets and Products Purchased

[1]See Louis S. Richman, "Bosch: The King of Black Boxes," and "Defense Contractors Under Fire," *Fortune* (April 29, 1985), pp. 228–232, 237.

ORGANIZATIONAL CUSTOMERS

One way to understand the diversity of industrial customers and the products they purchase is to begin by examining the various types of customers. Industrial customers are normally classified into three groups: (1) commercial enterprises, (2) governmental agencies, and (3) institutions.

Commercial Enterprises

Commercial enterprises, such as IBM, General Motors, Computer Land, and Raven Company, purchase industrial goods and/or services for purposes other than selling directly to ultimate consumers. However, since they purchase products for different uses, it is more useful from a marketing point of view to define them in such a way as to understand their purchasing needs and, when we have examined the variety of products they purchase, how marketing strategy can be developed to meet their needs. Thus, it is more logical to look at commercial enterprises as consisting of (1) industrial distributors or dealers, (2) original equipment manufacturers (OEMs), and (3) users. These categories, which at times tend to overlap, are useful to the industrial marketer because they point out how products and services are used by buying firms.

Industrial Distributors and Dealers.   When a commercial enterprise, such as Computer Land, or VWR, purchases industrial goods and resells them in basically the same form to commercial, government, and institutional markets, we classify them as industrial distributors or dealers. Industrial distributors and dealers take title to goods; thus, they are the industrial marketer's intermediaries—acting in a similar capacity to wholesalers or even retailers. For instance, while living in California, your authors often patronized industrial plumbing, lumber, and electronic supply houses to purchase, at wholesale prices, products needed for home remodeling purposes. However, as Figure 2-1 indicates, while a few may also serve the consumer market, they generally serve other business enterprises, government agencies, or private and public institutions. Because of their importance in the industrial channel to both large and small manufacturers and because they are growing in number and sophistication, we shall discuss them further in Chapter Eleven.

Original Equipment Manufacturers.   When enterprises such as Hyster, Xerox, or Ford purchase industrial goods to incorporate into products that they produce, we classify them as original equipment manufacturers (OEMs). That is, the electronic engine controls producer who sells parts to Ford would view Ford as an OEM. The important point, however, is that with this type of customer (Ford), the product of the industrial marketer (in this case, Motorola) becomes a part of the customer's product.

LOW-TECH DISTRIBUTORS ARE NOT SMALL OPERATORS

VWR Scientific is no tiny operation. Bringing in $330 million in sales, VWR distributes labware and equipment, microscopes, specialty chemicals, and graphic arts supplies to electronics manufacturers, research labs, hospitals, and schools, supplying both commercial enterprises and institutions. Some 75,000 items, representing 2,000 suppliers, are listed in its catalog, and 32 national sales offices serve its large market base.

Over the past several years, VWR has been actively consolidating its inventory, moving away from local distribution. To maintain one-day delivery service to sales centers, warehouses are located in Bridgeport, Connecticut; Chicago; San Francisco; and, soon, Dallas.

The backbone of these regional warehouses is what VWR calls its "VWR Interactive Purchasing System," or "VIPS." VIPS enables customers to communicate directly with VWR's mainframe computer system to check inventory, prices, and place orders. Customers can also check on open or back orders, and request written replies.

Source: See *Purchasing* magazine, John F. Russell, "Why Not Walk to Your Distributor's Office . . . Just Down the Hall," March 14, 1985, pp. 30–34. Copyright © by Cahners Publishing Company, 1985.

User. On the other hand, when a commercial enterprise, be it Hyster, Montgomery Ward, or VWR, purchases industrial products or services to support its manufacturing process or facilitate the operation of its business, we classify it as a user. Products used to produce output consist of items such as lathes, drilling machines, and grinding wheels, whereas products that facilitate the operation of a business might consist of computers, typewriters, and adding machines. In contrast to the products purchased by OEMs, products purchased by users are not incorporated into the final product.

Overlap of Categories. It should be obvious that the preceding classifications center on how products and services serve the customer. A manufacturer of forklifts can be a *user,* purchasing metal-cutting machine tools to support the manufacturing process, or an *OEM,* purchasing gear drives and transmissions to incorporate into the forklifts being manufactured. The important point is that OEM purchasers will be concerned with the impact that products have on the quality and dependability of the end products they produce. Since users buy products for use in the production process or to facilitate the operations of their businesses, their concerns will center on prompt, predictable delivery and maintenance service. And industrial distributors or dealers will be more concerned with how products match the needs of their customers. On one point, however, all commercial customers agree: their purchases are expected to enhance the profit-making capability of the firm.

GOVERNMENTAL AGENCIES

The largest purchasers of industrial goods in the United States are the various federal, state, and local governments—spending nearly a trillion dollars annually for products and services. These government units purchase virtually every kind of good—from $2900 Allen wrenches to multimillion-dollar ICBM missiles—and represent a huge market, accounting for approximately thirty-seven percent of our total gross national product. The result of this volume purchasing is that procurement administration and practices are highly specialized and very often confusing. When a particular product or service is needed, government buyers may negotiate directly with vendors or carefully develop detailed specifications and invite qualified suppliers (through the media) to submit a price bid in writing, usually awarding the bid to the lowest, qualified supplier. In the case of the $2900 Allen wrench, in accordance with customary contract specifications at the time, overhead and direct engineering man-hours were allocated across all items in the "kit." Thus, for the limited production run of the single Allen wrench, direct engineering costs came to $1,034.64; engineering overhead came to $503; $507 was necessary for fringe benefits, $149 for general and administrative costs and $388.79 was billed for profits, plus some other costs. The total price—though thoroughly documented and necessary in view of cost allocations, various actions necessary to comply with contract specifications and many visits, discussions, and inspections by government officials—appeared to be an unrealistic $2,917.45 per wrench.[2] Since effective marketing strategy for reaching government customers lies in the marketer's understanding of these complex purchasing procedures, we will discuss government purchasing in more detail when we introduce the unique characteristics of organizational procurement later in this chapter.

INSTITUTIONS

Public and private institutions such as churches, hospitals, colleges, sanitariums, and prisons are another important classification of industrial customers. Some of these institutions follow rigid rules and purchasing procedures while others follow far more casual procedures. The important difference with this type of industrial customer is that effective marketing rests on the industrial marketer's ability to recognize the way in which each institution purchases its goods or services.

CLASSIFYING INDUSTRIAL PRODUCTS

As further indicated by Figure 2-1, wide arrays of goods and services are required by industrial organizations. Although solutions to industrial customers' problems

---

[2]William H. Gregory, "A $2,000 Misunderstanding," *Aviation Week & Space Technology,* 122 (May 13, 1985), p. 9.

go far beyond a preliminary identification of which products belong under which classification, classifying industrial goods gives the industrial marketer a better indication of the scope of the market, who is involved in the purchasing process, and what marketing factors affect the buying decision.[3]

Whereas there are various methods for classifying industrial goods, the most useful method analyzes how products or services enter the production process or affect the cost structure of the firm.[4] This enables marketers to view their offerings from the customer's perspective and adapt or adjust marketing strategy to maximize potential customer benefits based on the product's intended use.

Given this perspective, the following three broad classifications are useful: (1) materials and parts, goods that enter the product directly; (2) capital items, goods that affect the cost structure of the firm; and (3) supplies and services, goods that facilitate the firm's operation. Figure 2-2 highlights this classification method.

Materials and Parts

Goods that enter the product directly consist of raw materials, manufactured materials, and component parts. The costs of these items are treated by the purchasing firm as expenses that are assigned to the manufacturing process.

Raw Materials. Raw materials such as agricultural products or natural gas normally enter the production process with little or no alteration. They may be marketed as either OEM or user products. For instance, when Sara Lee purchases gas to fire the massive ovens used to produce all those delicious cakes in the freezer sections of the grocery stores, it is a "user" customer. When it purchases fruits for further processing to fill those delicious delicacies, it is an OEM.

Manufactured Materials and Component Parts. Manufactured materials include all types of raw materials that are subjected to some amount of processing before

FIGURE 2-2   Classification of Industrial Products

Source: Philip Kotler, *Marketing Essentials* [Englewood Cliffs, N.J.: Prentice-Hall, Inc., 1984], p. 190. Reprinted with permission.

[3]George Risley, *Modern Industrial Marketing* (New York: McGraw-Hill Book Company, 1972), pp. 22–24.

[4]Phillip Kotler, *Marketing Management: Analysis, Planning, and Control,* 3rd ed. (Englewood Cliffs, N.J.: Prentice-Hall, Inc., 1980), pp. 100–101.

entering the manufacturing process. For example, latex can be processed into giant tires as the Foxboro advertisement features (see Figure 2-3), copper formed into wire, aluminum into extruded shapes, or plastic powder into molded parts. Materials such as leather or chemicals, however, require considerably more processing

FIGURE 2-3   An Example of How Raw Material Is Processed into Component Parts

Source: Courtesy of PALM·DEBONIS·RUSSO·INC. Advertising and Public Relations, Bloomfield, CT.

before reaching the shoe or drug manufacturer, but will undergo a series of further changes before becoming part of the finished product.

Component parts such as switches, motors, and customized gears (see Figure 2-4), however, can be installed directly into products with little or no additional changes. When these products are sold to customers who use them in their production processes, they are marketed as OEM goods. Component parts, however, are also sold to distributors who resell them into the replacement or "after" market. Champion, for instance, will sell spark plugs directly to Ford or General Motors and, through distributors, to the many automotive parts dealers throughout the country.

Marketing Implications. Marketing strategy for materials and parts depends on additional factors related to the goods' subclassification. Most component parts and materials are standardized and are normally purchased in large quantities on a contractual basis by OEMs. However, some components are custom made to the buyer's specifications. When component parts are custom made, considerable interaction is necessary between the engineering departments of both the buyer and seller. Such interaction normally dictates that marketers sell directly rather than through industrial distributors. Direct selling is also prompted when large-volume orders are involved. However, when selling standard parts to the smaller OEM or user, it is usually more cost effective to market through industrial distributors.

With the exception of custom-made parts, these goods are normally sold through the purchasing department of buying firms. However, engineers and production people in buying firms usually develop the product specifications used in the purchase and, occasionally, will even limit the choice of suppliers. Therefore, marketers must communicate their product information to those influencers. This is usually done through trade advertising and personal contact; and because of standardization, the basic appeals used center on product quality and performance, delivery dependability, price, and supportive service.

Where component parts such as tires and batteries are sold in the consumer replacement market, sellers must strive to create product differentiation or be willing to sell primarily on a price basis. Consumer advertising becomes an important part of the marketing strategy. Manufacturers who succeed in building consumer preference for their products usually find it much easier to attract industrial customers selling to these same consumers. A consumer, presold on Michelin tires, will be favorably disposed toward a car that includes Michelins as standard equipment.

Capital Items

Capital items are used in the production process and wear out over time; thus, they are treated as a depreciation expense by the buying firm. This category consists of installations and accessory equipment.

Installations. Installations are major, long-term investment items such as factories and office buildings and fixed equipment such as generators, lathes, furnaces, com-

FIGURE 2-4   An Example of Customized Component Parts

Source: Courtesy of Winzeler, Chicago, IL.

DETROIT REDISCOVERS HIGH-PERFORMANCE TIRES

The burgeoning fleet of sporty cars in the United States and Detroit's concern for enhancing car handling and traction are creating a hot market for high-performance tires. Once the hot-rod mania of youth, the high-performance market is luring so many buyers that major tire makers are beefing up promotion on present lines and introducing new ones. These new tires have a high speed capability of at least 130 mph and a low profile. This low profile gives the tires a shorter and wider road-surface contact. It is this special contact, called a footprint, that improves traction and handling, enabling cars to take corners at increased speeds. Stiffer sidewalls, revised tread patterns, and different internal belt configurations also add to this cornering and handling ability.

With some industry sources speculating that thirty percent of the OEM market will soon be equipped with high-performance tires, many tire makers are challenging industry leader Goodyear and its Eagle VR S. The hottest challengers are Bridgestone's Potenza RE71, Pirelli's P7, and Goodrich's Comp T/A. Yet tire manufacturers aren't overlooking the replacement market; Goodyear's VR S and Goodrich's Comp T/A are both primarily aimed at the aftermarket segment.

Source: See "Hot New Tires—Racetrack Performance for Your Car," by Herbert Shuldiner, *Popular Science* 228, February 1986, pp. 76–114.

---

puters, and the custom-made equipment used by Raven Company to manufacture custom-made parts for 3-M. (See Figure 2-5.)

Accessories. Light equipment and tools (portable power drills, typewriters, etc.), which are generally less expensive and not considered part of the fixed plant, are classified as accessory equipment. Accessories are more apt to have wide usage throughout the buying organization as compared with capital equipment. For example, a firm may have only one mainframe computer, within and controlled by the data processing department, but hundreds of computer terminals bought specifically for accounting, engineering, production, personnel, and marketing.

Purchasers of installations and accessory equipment are normally user customers. Installations and accessories can be purchased outright or leased by industrial users. When capital equipment is leased, the cost is treated for tax purposes as an expense by the purchaser rather than as a depreciable item. Leasing versus selling is a growing trend in the capital goods market and often paves the way for a company to penetrate markets that might not otherwise exist if its products had to be sold outright.

Marketing Implications. Marketing strategy for capital items hinges on whether the product is classified as an installation or an accessory. Direct manufacturer-to-user distribution is normally utilized when marketing major installations because of the extensive interaction involved. The impact of these purchases on the buyer's

FIGURE 2-5 **An Example of Customized Capital Equipment. An employee at Raven Company, Weatherford, Oklahoma, operating the computer-controlled Film Disk Core machine. The machine, custom built for Raven, produces 1.5 million disk cores each month that are supplied to 3-M—Raven Company's major OEM.**

Source: Photo courtesy of Brian Merritt, student, Southwestern Oklahoma State University, Weatherford—phtographed by permission of Raven Company.

scale of operations requires that sellers work closely with prospective buyers. Negotiations often take many months and may involve top executives in both the buying and selling firms. This is particularly true for buildings or custom-made equipment. While buying executives may apply different criteria to the purchase decision, buying motives center on factors such as impact on costs, return on investment, or a desire for industry leadership. Personal selling is the primary promotional effort.

In the marketing of less costly, more standardized installations and accessories, it is not uncommon to use industrial intermediaries. However, advertising in trade journals to reach final users, and the deployment of missionary salespersons who provide selling support to intermediaries, are often necessary in the marketing program. Missionary salespersons are the manufacturers' sales people who make "buddy calls" with intermediaries to provide additional information, usually technical, to customers.

Supplies and Services

Supplies and services support the operation of the purchasing firm. Since these goods do not become part of the finished product or support the production process, they are treated as operating expense items for the periods in which they are consumed.

Supplies. Supplies, such as soap, cleaning compounds, typing paper, and paper clips are required by all organizations to maintain their day-to-day operations. These items are generally standardized, marketed to a broad cross section of industrial users, and are not very different from the types of supplies that consumers purchase.

Services. Organizations require a rapidly increasing range of services. These have been categorized as operating, maintenance, and repair services. Operating services facilitate the functioning of a firm. These operating services might be further differentiated by whether they are primary or secondary. An accounting firm facilitating the functioning of an organization by doing individualized work for that firm would illustrate a primary operating service. An online database which enables the day-to-day functioning of many firms, but is not prepared for a specific firm's original use, would exemplify a secondary operating service. Maintenance and repair services would be exemplified by a farmer returning his combine to the John Deere retailer for preventive maintenance or repair. Other authorities have pointed out that services ought to be further differentiated by a classification specifically used for those services employed in the production process.[5] The federal government provides inspection and grading in meat-processing plants; such production facilitation could be classified as "production services." As the number of service jobs and industries continues to grow, we will doubtless see many new service classification systems.

Marketing Implications. In the case of supplies, marketing strategy differs because most supplies are marketed to many organizations in almost all industries. While direct marketing is used to reach large users, normally a wide variety of intermediaries is required to reach this broad and diverse market.

In the purchase of supplies, purchasing agents dominate. They choose and evaluate alternative suppliers based on criteria such as dependability of delivery, convenience, price, and breadth of assortment. Because these purchasing agents normally lack sufficient time to evaluate carefully all alternatives each time repeat purchases are required, the key to successful marketing lies in the supplier's reputa-

[5]Ralph W. Jackson and Philip D. Cooper, "Unique Aspects of Marketing Industrial Services," *Industrial Marketing Management* pp. 111–118.

HELPING CUSTOMERS TO SELL

With the aftermarket contributing eighty percent of its corporate profits these days, Federal Mogul Corp. will pin its marketing efforts on new ways to reach and help those customers. . . . The heavier emphasis on the aftermarket often includes going beyond just having sales staffs make calls and talk products. It means providing a lot of technical information and marketing variables—looking at our strengths and trying to help customers as much as we can to market their products. . . .

Among recent new programs is a hot line for technical services, generating about 150 customer calls a day. The company promoted it through direct mail, customer announcements and hot-line stickers with an 800 number. . . . A technical services manager and his staff field calls from end-users, mostly automotive and heavy-duty vehicle customers, who might check on whether F-M produces particular parts for particular engines, or from people looking for technical installations information.

Source: Joseph Bohn, "Federal Mogul Tries Service Marketing Strategy," *Business Marketing*, April 1983, pp. 22, 26. Reprinted with permission.

---

tion for dependability. Personal selling is not as cost effective for supplies as it is for other classifications of products; thus, firms often limit their direct selling efforts to major resellers and large users. Advertising, including the use of catalogs and trade journals, is the primary vehicle employed to reach most users and resellers.

Marketing strategy for professional services is more subtle. Buying firms usually contact professionals on the basis of their word-of-mouth reputations. In turn, the selling firm's efforts are more consultative in nature, aimed at helping the customer develop an objective, relevant definition of the need or problem so that the implemented solution will be effective and beneficial.

UNIQUE CHARACTERISTICS
OF ORGANIZATIONAL PROCUREMENT

Selling in the industrial market is complicated by a broad spectrum of customers. Commercial enterprises (including resellers), governmental organizations, and institutions give buying responsibility to individuals who are quite knowledgeable in their particular markets. These individuals are often more realistic in assessing the competitive value of a vendor's product than is the vendor. Thus, they normally identify, evaluate, and select suppliers, domestic or foreign, who provide the greatest value. The foundation for formulating successful industrial marketing strategy, then, lies in knowing how the buying function is administered in a diversity of markets and situations.

Purchasing in Commercial Enterprises

How goods and services are purchased by commercial enterprises depends on the nature of the business, the size of the firm, and the volume, variety, and technical complexity of the products purchased.

Multiple Influencers.   With the exception of very small organizations, the purchasing decision is usually shared by several people. Multiple influencers in commercial purchasing can include production people, engineers, cost accountants, middle and upper management, and purchasing agents.

Technical Sophistication.   Techniques such as materials requirement planning, supplier rating systems (both discussed in Chapter Five), economic order quantity (discussed in Chapter Twelve), and value analysis (discussed shortly), are commonly used in the industrial market. Purchasing managers now make greater use of the firm's internal engineering capability to evaluate competitive products. They are more knowledgeable of price trends, and quite expert in the art of negotiation, and tend to be specialists capable of developing detailed knowledge with respect to manufacturing processing and design specifications of those products and materials for which they are responsible.

Knowledge of the buyer's needs, the products that can fulfill those needs, and the capabilities of existing and potential competition is essential. Industrial marketers can develop a more realistic perception of customer needs by understanding a process called *value analysis*. While value analysis is used more frequently by buyers, suppliers who can predict or anticipate a customer's value judgments are in a better position to react in accordance with these judgments.

VALUE ANALYSIS SAVES ELECTRIC BRAKE MANUFACTURER BIG BUCKS

According to *Purchasing World*, disc drives must be stopped within three seconds after shutoff or a computer memory wipeout could result. In order to stop disc drives so quickly, power-off electric brakes are generally used.

These electric brakes must employ considerable stopping force, and the resultant stresses cause vibrations that tend to dislodge disc drive screws. Because of this, Inertia Dynamics Inc., of Collinsville, CT, began using specially designed socket screws from HoloKrome when assembling its brakes. These screws proved to be especially vibration-resistant. They stayed locked in place.

"We decided to utilize Corlex-Taptite screws," said Dennis Geyer of Inertia Dynamics. "We were attracted to this company because of its reputation for furnishing quality merchandise and for meeting long-term customer needs." The result was a savings of $120,000 annually for Inertia Dynamics.

Source: Edward J. Walter, "Value Analysis—It's Not Just Parts," *Purchasing World*, February 1988, pp. 28–38.

**TABLE 2-1 End-Product Improvements
from Value Analysis**

A. Maintenance and handling
   1. Fewer parts
   2. Easier maintenance
   3. Less frequent maintenance
   4. Easier transport
B. Operations
   1. Faster operation
   2. Easier operation
   3. More accuracy
   4. Reduced fuel/energy
   5. Less pollutants

Source: Reprinted from *Purchasing*, "Selling Value Analysis: When Your Customer Is the Supplier," and "Selling Value Analysis: When Your Customer is Operating Personnel," March 28, 1985, pp. 111, 119. Copyright © by Cahners Publishing Company, 1985.

Value Analysis. Value analysis involves systematized techniques for reducing costs and improving the performance value of materials, components, and manufacturing processes. (See Table 2-1.) The first industrial application of value analysis, attributed to Larry Miles of the General Electric Purchasing Department, occurred in 1947. The Department of Defense, which has done much to promote value analysis (sometimes referred to as value engineering), defines value analysis as

> an intensive appraisal of all the elements of the design, manufacture, or construction, procurement, inspection, installation, and maintenance of an item and its components, including the applicable specifications and operational requirements in order to achieve the necessary performance, maintainability, and reliability of the item at minimum cost.[6]

Value analysis, as developed by General Electric, involves a step-by-step procedure:

1. **Selection.** A product that is ripe for improvement is selected for value analysis.
2. **Information gathering.** Drawings, costs, scrap rates, usage forecasts, and operations sheets are collected by the team coordinator before the team first meets. Team members are asked to send in whatever information they have.
3. **Function definition.** The team meets and defines each function of the product. A function is defined in two words, a verb and a noun (e.g., a flower pot *contains soil*). Only essential functions are included. Next the team determines the present cost of each function. This reveals which functions represent major expenditures.

[6]In Richard B. Chase and Nicholas J. Aquilano, *Production and Operations Management,* Armed Services Procurement Regulations, Section 3–406.3 (Homewood, Ill.: Richard D. Irwin, Inc., 1973), p. 567

4. **Generation of alternatives.** Team members suggest ideas for new and different ways to accomplish the functions. This is known as brainstorming. All ideas are recorded and later culled to a list of manageable size.
5. **Evaluation of alternatives.** Alternatives are evaluated on various factors, including feasibility and cost. This further reduces the list to one or two good ideas.
6. **Presentation.** The final alternatives are refined and presented to a management committee as value analysis change proposals.
7. **Implementation.** The approved value analysis change proposal is translated into an analysis change order and implemented.[7]

The two-word function definitions, step 3, stimulate thinking by requiring individuals to search for the primary and secondary functions of items. For example, possible definitions of a soft drink container could include "contains cola," "contains beverage," "contains liquid." By moving away from specifics (cola and beverage) toward a generality (contains liquid), mental restrictions regarding the product are removed. Thus, containers that customarily contain liquids other than soft drinks can be considered. Secondary function definitions are also listed, such as "maintains fizz," "provides access," "enables dispensing," "promotes selling," and "allows stacking." Secondary functions usually account for at least 80 percent of the cost of all items.[8]

The values of the basic and secondary functions are analyzed in terms of four definitions of value: use, esteem, cost, and exchange. The "use value" of an item refers to its ability to perform a specific function; "esteem value" deals with its ability to inspire people to want the item; "cost value" quantifies the money or labor cost of the product; and "exchange value" refers to the trade-in value of the product. Esteem, cost, and exchange values of the Rolls-Royce account for its high price.

Brainstorming, step 4, involves asking questions such as:

To what other uses can the product be put?
What other products or substitutes might be used?
How might this item be modified?
How might this item be magnified or "minified"?
How might the item be rearranged?
How might the item be reversed?
How might the item be combined with other items?[9]

Once alternatives are evaluated, costs are considered from several perspectives: the costs of elements (labor, material, etc.), the cost of increments (how costs build up through various assembly stages), cost change over time, cost per unit of dimension (length, area, weight, etc.), and cost per function.

[7]Richard J. Schonberger, *Operations Management* (Plano, Tex.: Business Publications, Inc., 1981), pp. 614–615.
[8]Marsolais, *Handouts for Naval Reserve Officers School,* p. H1–5.
[9]Ibid., pp. H4–2 to H4–4.

Value analysis teams often include purchasing specialists, design and production engineers, marketing and finance managers, as well as technical sales people from supplying firms. The important point is that when sales people are knowledgeable in value analysis, the marketing firm can play an active role in the process, predict or anticipate customer needs, or even initiate a value analysis study.

Value analysis continues to serve our current life-styles and make our latest technological achievements even better. Edward Walter depicts the role value analysis played in cutting the size of Jacuzzi Motor inventories by fifty percent, he tells of how Xerox used it to develop an electronic voice recognition system and successfully inventory over two million parts, and he explains how value analysis was used by a disc drive manufacturer to save $120,000 through the use of better fitting screws to overcome the severe braking forces needed in disc drives.[10]

Purchasing in Government Units

As stated earlier, the largest purchaser of goods and services in the United States is government. To compete in this market, industrial marketers must develop a thorough understanding of the complexities involved in selling to the government. While the scope of this text does not allow a detailed coverage of government purchasing practices, perhaps a few comments will provide an idea of just how specialized and complex governmental purchasing really is.

Widely Dispersed Markets. There are many functional areas within both federal and state government organizations. In addition to the various agencies of the federal government (e.g., defense, space, interior, transportation, and the postal service), there is a broader range of government units at the state, county, and municipal levels. Thus, the industrial marketer is faced with a widely dispersed market. There are more than 70,000 buying centers at the federal, state, and local levels. Compounding this fact is the large number of influencers in the purchasing process. Government buyers are responsible to and/or influenced by numerous interest groups who specify, legislate, evaluate, and use the goods and services purchased.[11]

Complicated Procurement Laws. Government purchasing, regardless of the level, is also based on legal requirements that establish the guidelines for contractual arrangements.[12] Government contracts often contain provisions that have little to do with the product or service under consideration. Rather, they are more concerned with broader, social goals. They may require the contractor to give preference to small subcontractors, to employ a certain proportion of minorities, or pay the mini-

---

[10]Edward Walter, "Value Analysis—It's Not Just Parts," *Purchasing World* (February 1988), pp. 28–39.

[11]Cecil Hynes and Noel Zabriskie, *Marketing to Governments* (Columbus, Ohio: Grid, Inc., 1974), p. 1.

[12]Hynes and Zabriskie, *Marketing to Governments,* p. 67.

mum wage. Where the federal government is concerned, all contractors must meet general contract provisions that are set forth by law and are published as part of the federal procurement regulations. These provisions include product inspection requirements, payment methods, actions to be taken as a result of default and disputes, and many other provisions relative to the supplier's performance.

Understanding Government Contracts. Besides the need to understand procurement laws, marketing to the government also requires an understanding of the types of contracts that might be employed. Basically, there are two types: fixed-price contracts and cost-reimbursement contracts. In the fixed-price contract, a firm price is agreed upon before the contract is awarded, and full payment is made when the good or service is delivered in the condition agreed upon in the contract. Under cost-reimbursement contracts, the supplier is reimbursed for allowable costs incurred in performing the contract. A provision is made for profit, either a specified dollar amount above cost (cost plus fixed fee) or a predetermined percentage of total contract price. In most cases, the fixed-price contract permits the greatest profit potential; however, greater risks are involved if unforeseen expenses are incurred. But if the supplier can effect unforeseen cost reductions during the contract period, profits may be earned beyond those originally estimated. Because of the low incentives for contractor efficiency contained in cost-reimbursement contracts, they are carefully administered by the government. They are usually employed for developmental work where is is difficult to forecast efforts and expenses.

When nonstandardized products are involved, or when there are very few suppliers capable of providing a product, negotiated contract buying is employed. This type of purchasing strategy is much more flexible, since the government purchasing office has a wide range of personal judgment it can exercise. However, in its attempts to provide some uniformity to the negotiation process, the military has set up a uniform negotiation procedure that specifies the manner in which purchase needs are to be established, potential suppliers identified, proposals evaluated, and contracts negotiated and awarded.

In summary, selling to the government is very involved, complex, and time consuming. Within this market can be found some of the most sophisticated buyer-seller environments. To assist suppliers in selling to the government, numerous manuals and publications are provided that explain the process, such as "Selling to the Military" and "Selling to the U.S. Air Force," which are available through the Department of Defense.

Institutional Purchasing

Purchasing in the institutional market, as previously discussed, involves practices lying somewhere between commercial enterprises and government. For instance, a multicampus state university with centralized buying for all its campuses may purchase products much like a government customer, while another multicampus university with decentralized purchasing authority may purchase products in the same manner as commercial customers. Institutional buyers are a mixture of government and private organizations, and the industrial marketer must consider them on an individual basis to respond successfully to their unique needs and characteristics. On one hand, public institutional buyers are quite similar to government buyers due to the constraints of political considerations and dictates of law; on the other hand, private institutions are managed very much like commercial enterprises. Thus, institutional marketers may have to develop separate strategies to meet the needs of a purchasing agent who buys for an entire school system through formal bidding as opposed to a purchasing agent for a private health care institution.

Purchasing in the Reseller's Market

Buyers in the reseller's market select vendors by evaluating them primarily on their expected contribution toward increased sales volume and profits. Thus, buyers in the reseller's market are not only interested in the products of potential suppliers, but in their marketing policies as well (e.g., their choice among intensive, selective, or exclusive distribution, and their attitude toward cooperative advertising and the provision of point-of-purchase displays).[13]

Both products and policies affect resellers' ability to match, beat, or avoid competition. Suppliers who can assist resellers in their selling effort, counsel them on inventory management and procurement, and provide prices, terms, and financing policies that enable the reseller to function competitively and with reasonable risk, are virtually assured a share of the business. However, some manufacturers of well-known consumer brands have chosen to depend upon consumer acceptance rather than supportive policies to maintain reseller allegiance. But resellers say, "I buy from XYZ Corp. because I have to, not because I want to. When the day comes that I no longer have to buy from them, watch how fast I change suppliers!"

LOOKING BACK

Customers in the industrial market are a diverse group of organizations that were defined as commercial enterprises, governmental agencies, and institutions. Commercial enterprises were categorized as original equipment manufacturers (OEMs) that purchase goods to incorporate into products that they produce; users, organizations that purchase goods and services to either support their manufacturing process or to facilitate the operation of their businesses; and industrial distributors that are the intermediaries in the industrial market. How these enterprises are classified depends on how they use products. Thus, these categories tend to overlap and are not mutually exclusive.

Because of the diversity of products sold in the industrial market, a classifica-

[13]Michael E. Leenders, Harold E. Fearson, and Wilbur B. England, *Purchasing and Materials Management* (Homewood, Ill.: Richard D. Irwin, Inc., 1980), p. 490.

tion system was introduced: (1) materials and parts, (2) capital items, and (3) supplies and services. By looking at the way products enter the production process or cost structure of the buying organization, marketers are better able to develop differentiated marketing strategies. This is necessary because the focus and direction of marketing programs change from one product category to another.

Purchasing practices in the industrial market are highly specialized and technical, employing analytical tools such as material requirements planning, economic order quantity, value analysis, and supplier rating systems.

QUESTIONS FOR DISCUSSION

1. Why are government agencies and institutions classified as industrial organizations?
2. What differences must be considered in developing a marketing strategy for an OEM firm versus a user firm?
3. If you were selling in both the commercial market and the government market, could you employ a single marketing strategy? Explain your answer.
4. How would you direct your marketing program for an entering good versus a facilitating good?
5. "Marketing to industrial firms is enhanced through the understanding of value analysis." Do you agree or disagree? Explain why.
6. How does government purchasing differ from purchasing by commercial organizations?

SUGGESTED ADDITIONAL READINGS

DEVLIN, JOAN C., "Uncle Sam Needs You," *Entrepreneur* (April 1988):32–36.

RICHMAN, LOUIS S., "Bosch: The King of Black Boxes," and "Defense Contractors Under Fire," *Fortune* (April 29, 1985).

VYAS, NIREN, AND ARCH G., WOODSIDE, "An Inductive Model of Industrial Supplier Choice Processes," *Journal of Marketing,* 48 (Winter 1984):30–45.

WALTER, EDWARD J., "Value Analysis—It's Not Just Parts," *Purchasing World* (February 1988): 28–38; and Edward J. Walter, "Bar Codes, Buyers, and Value Analysis," *Purchasing World* (February 1988):6.

CHAPTER 3

The Industrial Marketing Environment

Industrial buyers and sellers operate in a dynamic environment, one constantly posing new opportunities and threats. Chipmakers overestimate demand, build productive capacity, and then, as sales fall short of expectations, begin an all-out drive to reduce unsold inventories. And the boom in telecommunications spurs the demand in a new technology of fiber-optic cables, while falling demand in an older technology forces U.S. Steel to close its largest iron-ore facility indefinitely.[1] To survive the turbulent industrial environment, marketers must keep abreast of significant changes and be prepared to adapt to or influence them. In reading this chapter, you should become aware of

1. How major participants and forces in the industrial marketing environment affect marketing decisions of both buyers and sellers.
2. The various steps buyers and sellers take in reacting to or attempting to influence and control those components.
3. Strategies available to the industrial marketer for managing the industrial marketing environment.

[1]See John W. Wilson, Scott Ticer, and Otis Port, "Chipmakers Are Choking on a Sudden Inventory Glut," *Business Week* (October 10, 1984), p. 91; "Boon in Electronic Messages Spurs Demand for Systems Using Fiber-Optic Cable," *The Wall Street Journal* (November 9, 1984), p. 3; and "Steel Corp. to Close Plant, Lay Off 1,600," *The Wall Street Journal* (November 21, 1984), pp. 3, 4.

How well buyers and sellers understand the environment within which they operate, and how well they communicate with one another, foretells their capabilities of profiting from or being damaged by the environment's many surprises and shocks. The effectiveness of the buyer-seller interface hinges on monitoring and adapting to or developing strategies to affect environmental changes that directly impact either or both organizations.

The traditional view of marketing has been one of achieving organizational goals through satisfying the needs of identified markets by adapting the organization to deliver the desired satisfaction "more effectively and efficiently than competitors."[2] Thus, marketing strategies have been "viewed as a set of adaptive responses",[3] that is, marketing strategies appear to begin with a system of environmental constraints. Marketers gather and analyze information on forces in the environment (e.g., competitors, politics, and economics) and implement strategies to adapt to environmental demands.

Adaptation strategies, however, are not sufficient in today's turbulent environment. Marketers must adopt a proactive orientation so that marketing strategy can be developed not only to adapt to but to change or affect, when possible, the environment in which the firm operates. Thus, in this chapter we discuss the environment within which buyers and sellers operate, how it impacts their marketing operations, and strategies they can adopt to adapt to or counteract environmental forces.

THE INDUSTRIAL MARKETING ENVIRONMENT

The environment within which industrial firms operate is depicted in Figure 3-1. Due to the several interfaces that exist between firms that interact directly with one another, we refer to the first level as the *interface level.* The next two levels we refer to as the *publics* and the *macroenvironment.* All three discernible levels of a firm's environment exist within the purview of a final environmental entity, government.

The Interface Level

The interface level involves those key participants who immediately interface with an industrial firm (buyer or seller) in facilitating production, distribution, and purchase of a firm's goods and services. Supply inputs are transformed by a company and its competitors into outputs with added value that move on to end markets, the move being made through the firm's interface with industrial distributors and dealers, manufacturers' representatives, and the company's own sales force. That

---

[2]Philip Kotler, *Marketing Management: Analysis, Planning, and Control,* 5th ed. (Englewood Cliffs, N.J.: Prentice-Hall, Inc., 1984), p. 22.

[3]Carl P. Zeithaml and Valarie A. Zeithaml, "Environmental Management: Revising the Marketing Perspective," *Journal of Marketing* (Spring 1984), pp. 46–53.

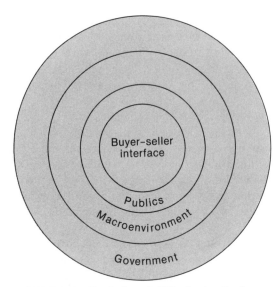

FIGURE 3-1 The Industrial Marketing Environment

move is made possible by a firm's interface with facilitating institutions such as banking, transportation, research, and advertising firms.

As Figure 3-2 shows, the distinctive nature of the industrial market allows a firm to view its operations from several perspectives. The industrial firm may view itself as an "industrial marketer," a "competitor," an "input supplier," a "distributor," or an "industrial buyer." A moment's reflection on the nature of industrial firms should indicate that an OEM, user, distributor, or buyer can and does occupy all these positions.

Input Suppliers. Input goods (e.g., raw materials and component parts), labor, and capital are supplied by organizations to industrial firms for use in producing output goods and services. Industrial OEMs and distributors purchase from supplier firms but are themselves suppliers to other firms. The survival and success of a firm, whether buyer or seller, depends on its knowledge of and relationships with its input

FIGURE 3-2 Participants in the Interface Level

PROMISES OF SUPPLY SHORTAGES POSE MANY PROBLEMS

Faced with continuing shortages of electronic components, steel, coated paper products, and corrugated packaging in 1985, many U.S. manufacturers considered foreign sourcing or product rejection as quality dropped, prices rose, and lead times extended.

Supply shortages occurred for many reasons. As the U.S. recovered from the 1981–82 recession and government increased its defense spending, the resurgence in economic activity swallowed up supply. Shutdowns and layoffs in the steel mills created long lead times and a drop in product quality—while prices fluctuated wildly.

Source: Reprinted from *Purchasing* magazine, "Buyers Say 1985 Will Bring Many Old Supply Headaches," *Purchasing,* January 31, 1985, p. 23. Copyright © by Cahners Publishing Company, 1985.

---

suppliers. In the fall of 1984 United Auto Workers closed 13 General Motors' facilities by striking for better wages, pensions, job security, and a curb on "outsourcing" (the purchasing of cars and parts from nonunion domestic or foreign sources). Every day the walkout continued GM lost production of approximately 8,000 cars, 40 percent of its normal U.S. output, and 1,700 trucks, 31 percent of its normal U.S. output.[4]

Such interruptions in the flow of inputs (in this case, labor) cause repercussions throughout the entire industrial pipeline, affecting not only the buyer's production and marketing plans (in this case, GM), but also the production and marketing plans of suppliers. The demand for aluminum, steel, plastic, batteries, and tires comes to a standstill. Clearly, both industrial sellers and buyers must, and do, monitor activities of suppliers and anticipate possible effects on customers' objectives as well as their own. In a recent study, for instance, one buyer reported that when potential suppliers are in the midst of negotiating labor contracts, the firm hesitates to give them a major share of its business.[5]

Distributors. The importance of distributors to buyers as well as to sellers has been evidenced in one study that found that most organizational buyers purchase from five or more industrial distributors.[6] In addition to contacting potential buyers and negotiating orders, they provide buffer inventories, credit, and technical advice to potential buyers. They are also particularly important when joint demand is present because they bring together the heterogeneous inputs needed for the production of

---

[4]Dale D. Buss, "GM Labor Talks Set to Resume to End Walkout," *The Wall Street Journal* (September 18, 1984), p. 3.

[5]Niren Vyas and Arch G. Woodside, "An Inductive Model of Industrial Supplier Choice Processes," *Journal of Marketing* 48 (Winter 1984), pp. 30–45.

[6]"Distributor Image: '79—How the Buyer See It," *Industrial Distribution* 69 (February 1979), p. 54.

COMPETITIVE INTELLIGENCE: A VALUABLE STRATEGIC TOOL

As corporate America enters the twentieth century, it faces highly competitive markets. Economic growth has slowed down, competition from overseas has heightened, and many end-use industries have matured. The result is that few opportunities exist for improving performance through market growth. According to Dominick Attanasio, vice president of Planning and Business Development for Pfizer, Inc., expansion will occur mainly through market share gains. Such an environment, however, significantly intensifies competition. Thus, competitive intelligence becomes a more valuable tool for strategic planning.

The objectives of competitive intelligence are 1, to identify competitors' weaknesses, thereby providing the firm with possible new market share opportunities; 2, to anticipate competitors' market thrusts; and 3, to allow the firm to react more quickly and effectively to changes in the market.

Competitive intelligence as practiced today, however, functions as a formal information system that monitors the external world of the organization—the industry, the markets, the industry suppliers of technology and materials, the competition, and the global economy. In the same manner that management information systems formalized information for internal operations, competitive intelligence formalizes information for tactical and strategic management.

Source: Dominick B. Attanasio, "The Multiple Benefits of Competitor Intelligence," The Journal of Business Strategy (May/June 1988), pp. 16–19.

---

end products. The supplier of valves for PVC (plastic) pipe uses distributors who also provide users with complementary products, such as the PVC pipe itself, the pipe cleaner, and the glue necessary for attaching valves to the pipe.

Facilitators. Advertising agencies and public relations firms provide the necessary communication flow between sellers and buyers through the formulation of meaningful information and media strategies. The use of advertising in reaching potential buyers and the multitude of buying influencers is vital in the overall communication plan of industrial marketers. Rarely can sales people personally contact all potential buying influencers. Public relations firms are particularly adept in the development and dissemination of commercially significant news used by organizations to enhance their public image. Trade journal advertising and publicity releases are an important source of supplier location and selection to buyers.

Transportation and warehouse companies facilitate the physical flow of goods that must be delivered in usable condition to industrial customers and distributors when and where they are required. When goods are not delivered on time and in usable condition, buyers can be forced to shut down production lines. Thus, physical distribution is critical in the industrial market. And resources, as they move from supply inputs to end users, must be financed and insured.

Competitors.   Competitors' actions, whether domestic or foreign, ultimately influence the company's choice of target markets, distributors, product mix, and, in fact, its entire marketing strategy. For several years now, as productivity declines and labor costs rise, as economic growth slows down, end-use markets mature, and American businesses lose market share to foreign rivals both at home and abroad, gathering information on competitors will become increasingly important in the development of business strategy.[7] To survive the ever-growing "global" perspective of competition, both buyers and sellers will also be giving their marketing people (purchasing as well as selling) more responsibility in their respective areas.

Implications.   Industrial firms are part of a chain of organizations. Each firm is both buyer and supplier. As buyers, firms form less populated markets than in the consumer area. Their buying decisions are more technical, logical, and expert. And they recognize that what they buy and how they buy can affect the cost and efficiency of their manufacturing process or alter the quality and performance of the output products that are sold to firms farther along the industrial chain.

To deal with such interdependencies, industrial firms form long-term buyer-seller interfaces. Individuals in various functional areas, such as research, engineering, and production, meet with their counterparts in other firms to exchange information on technological developments and processing innovations. And they will be expecting more assistance in the areas of technical innovation, manufacturing, and other cost-cutting areas from their suppliers.

GAINING COST EFFICIENCY THROUGH COOPERATION

Some years ago, automobile manufacturers who wanted steel made to precise specifications were often told they would have to accept the standards and tolerances of the American Iron and Steel Institute. Neither buyers nor suppliers paid much attention to quality, an oversight that led to thousands of tons of rejected steel piled up at many automobile plants. But when consumers were no longer willing to absorb the price increases caused by the industry's wastefulness, business as usual could not continue. As a result, General Motors reduced its list of steel mill suppliers from 341 to 272, began giving advanced notice of its production plans to help suppliers with their planning, and demanded adherence to product-quality specifications. GM gained in cost-effectiveness through lower rejection rates, lower inventories, and manufacturing efficiencies due to the greater reliability of suppliers' materials.

Source: See Steven Glax, "How Detroit Is Reforming the Steelmakers," *Fortune,* May 16, 1983.

---

[7]Dominick B. Attanasio, "The Multiple Benefits of Competitor Intelligence," *The Journal of Business Strategy* (May/June 1988), pp. 16–19.

Industrial marketing is no longer domestically oriented; it is global in nature. For both buyers and sellers to survive and compete, they must work together to fend off foreign competition. At the same time, industrial marketers must constantly monitor their competitive situation, both at home and abroad, and take the necessary steps to defend their position in the marketplace by exploiting their distinctive competencies or improving the internal efficiencies of their resources, as well as helping customers to accomplish these same goals. When all goes well in the interface environment, when the several interfaces work cooperatively and beneficially, with individual firms making necessary contributions, a synergistic effect results.

Publics

The sphere of activity of the various participants in the interface level of the industrial marketing environment is greatly influenced by the multiple publics shown in Figure 3-3. Publics are distinct groups that have an actual or potential interest or impact on each firm's ability to achieve its respective goals.[8] Publics have the ability to help or hinder a firm's effort to serve its markets. Financial institutions influence the ability to obtain funds, favorable or unfavorable press affects marketing activities, interest groups demand social responsibility, and the attitudes of employees and the general public toward a firm's activities and products affect a firm's ability to do business.

Financial Publics. Financial institutions, such as investment houses, stock brokerage firms, and individual stockholders, invest in an organization on the basis of its ability to return profits. This type of investment is different from that of financial organizations serving as facilitators in the interface environment where those organizations finance the flow of goods and services and, therefore, tend to be less involved in overall organizational considerations.

Institutional investors, such as public employee pension funds, tend to concern themselves with the total operation of a firm, even to the point of operating by the "rules of Wall Street." In buying stock, these investors often become involved with voting for the management of a company. When they become unhappy with management or dissatisfied with a company's social policies, they sell their shares. Some have become angry in recent years with what they consider self-serving actions by some corporate managers and have begun to act aggressively, exerting their influence to make sure that management acts in the best interests of its shareholders.

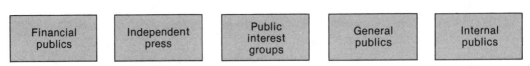

FIGURE 3-3 Publics that Influence the Industrial Market

[8]Philip Kotler, *Marketing Essentials* (Englewood Cliffs, N.J.: Prentice Hall, Inc., 1984), pp. 82–83.

When organizations are not totally honest with shareholder publics, they can also run into serious difficulties with the Securities and Exchange Commission, which regulates the stock market. General Dynamics, for instance, found itself under investigation by the SEC when it was revealed that top management wasn't as forthcoming as it should have been in fully and promptly disclosing to its shareholders cost overruns and other problems.[9] To achieve support of the financial community, a firm must evaluate its actions in light of that public's interpretations and attempt to cultivate its goodwill.

Independent Press. Industrial organizations must be acutely sensitive to the role that the mass media (including trade media) play and how they can affect the achievement of marketing objectives. The independent press is capable of publishing news that can either boost or destroy the reputation of a firm as well as the sales potential of a product. Unfavorable publicity, as in the General Dynamic's case, can also severely hamper a company's ability to float stock or issue bonds.

Many industrial firms have experienced the effects of negative publicity. Tenneco Shipbuilders has been cited as "overcharging the Navy" for a nuclear aircraft carrier. Caterpillar Tractor received free, but undesired, publicity when Moody's Investors Service reviewed its debt and commercial paper ratings for possible downgrading. And Texas Instruments found a spotlight in the press when it came under scrutiny by the Pentagon for possible failure to provide adequate testing for integrated circuits used in military weapons systems.[10]

Public Interest Groups. Industrial marketing decisions are being increasingly affected by public interest groups. And hundreds of these groups have developed and expanded over the last two decades. Organizations like the Sierra Club and Greenpeace seek to protect the environment. Other organizations such as NOW, the NAACP, and the Gray Panthers seek to protect and expand the rights of women, blacks, and senior citizens.

Clearly, these various public interest groups limit the freedom of suppliers and buyers in the industrial market. While some organizations respond by fighting, others accept these groups as another variable to be considered in developing strategic planning, working through public affairs departments to determine their interests and to express favorably the company's goals and activities in the press. The impact of these groups, however, is felt by all participants in the interface level.

General Public. Although the general public does not react in an organized way toward a firm or industry, as interest groups do, when a sizable portion of a popu-

[9]"A Move to Make Insitutions Start Using Their Stockholder Clout," *Business Week,* August 6, 1984, pp. 70–71.

[10]See *The Wall Street Journal,* Robert S. Greenberger, "Texas Instruments Is Under Inquiry by Pentagon Office," (September 27, 1984), p. 7; "Moody's Is Reviewing Ratings on Caterpillar Debt, Commercial Paper," (October 29, 1984), p. 18; and Tim Carrington, "Tenneco Shipbuilding Unit Overcharged Navy for Carrier, Senate Investigators Say," (December 6, 1984), p. 10.

CAN EXXON ASSUAGE THE PUBLIC?

When Joseph Hazelwood's ship ran aground, spilling eleven million gallons of crude oil on the Alaskan shores of Prince William Sound, Exxon found itself locked in a public relations offensive which many say was poorly handled. While Exxon recited statistics on what it had accomplished—60,000 barrels of oil recovered and 1,087 miles of beach rendered "environmentally stable"—the State of Alaska filed a multibillion-dollar lawsuit, claiming that the company had "cut and run with the work unfinished." T-shirts sold in Valdez, Alaska, summed up the problems that pervaded Exxon's $1 billion effort:

"Cleanup '89. It's not just a job,

It's a —— waste of time."

While many say that Prince William Sound is no longer an ecological disaster, Exxon's failure to respond openly and immediately to the spill, which it called an "act of God," has cast a shadow over the oil industry. Instead of showing its concern and commitment to the public by flying to Valdez immediately after the spill, Exxon's Chairman Lawrence Rawl remained in New York, silent and unavailable to the press. To avoid the barrage of unanswered questions, other executives went underground. And Otto Harrison, Exxon's cleanup engineer, waiting for heavy cleanup equipment, set hundreds of people to wiping off the oil-laden rocks by hand, "a spectacle that fixed in the public's mind images of a bumbling and ludicrous Exxon effort."

Since the accident, environmentalists have continued to battle the oil industry and its allies, preaching energy conservation. Congress also postponed new offshore drilling in Alaska's Bristol Bay, along the California coast, and on several sections of the East Coast from Massachusetts to Florida.

Source: See "A Disaster That Wasn't," *U.S. News & World Report* (September 18, 1989), pp. 60–69.

---

lace approaching a quarter of a billion people shifts its attitudes toward a firm or industry, there is a definite impact. Exxon is still wondering if it will survive the public outcry over the Alaskan oil spill. In its attempt to win the hearts and minds of the public, environmentalists, and Congress, Exxon mobilized an army of workers to repair the damage and launched and multi-million-dollar public-relations campaign.[11]

Internal Publics. The board of directors and managers, as well as blue- and white-collar workers, are important emissaries between an organization and other participants in the interface and publics levels. Corporate policy must give consideration to employees and others who are held responsible for the overall operation of the firm. Employee morale is an important factor in all business decisions. And, when morale is low, organizational efforts suffer.

---

[11]"A Disaster That Wasn't," *U.S. News & World Report* (September 18, 1989), pp. 60–69.

PROTECTING WORKERS' REPRODUCTIVE HEALTH

As more and more women enter the work force, many organizations find that they are faced with the dilemma of protecting them from potential hazards that may affect their ability to reproduce. In 1983, expectant mothers working at a Digital Equipment Corporation plant were experiencing an unusually high number of miscarriages. In an effort to determine what was causing the phenomenon, Digital commissioned the University of Massachusetts to study the problem. While the study did not uncover the specific cause, it did find that the miscarriage rate among a group of sixty-seven women who worked in the plant's so-called clean room was thirty-nine percent, nearly twice the national average.

Responses to the study, however, were mixed. Digital urged pregnant women to leave their positions, American Telephone & Telegraph Company removed them from their computer chip production jobs, and National Semiconductor Corporation and others left the decision to the employees themselves.

According to a recent study, only fifteen of the largest American companies have policies dealing with reproductive hazards, even though evidence suggests that a variety of chemicals and even video display terminals may pose reproductive health risks.

Solutions to protecting workers' reproductive health, however, remain difficult. When policies are established to ban pregnant women from certain jobs, they often touch off controversy or lawsuits alleging discrimination. Another problem that makes it difficult to establish policies is that few industrial compounds have been tested for their potential reproductive hazards. Some courts have even ruled that reproductive protection policies are discriminatory without a strong scientific showing that workplace hazards pose a particular risk to unborn children.

Source: See Barry Meier, "Companies Wrestle With Threats To Workers' Reproductive Health." Reprinted by permission of *The Wall Street Journal.* Copyright © Dow Jones & Company, Inc., February 5, 1987, p. 21. All rights reserved.

A firm's employees spend more than two-thirds of their time off the job, interacting with their families and the community, so employees' attitudes do influence the public. Many television viewers were reassured by the positive attitudes expressed by people who lived near Union Carbide's West Virginia plant as those individuals were interviewed on television shortly after the debacle in Bhopal, India. On the other hand, General Dynamics' investigation by the SEC was brought about by tapes of telephone conversations secretly made by one company executive while he was still general manager of the company's troubled Electric Boat Division.[12]

Implications. Since the ultimate function of business is to serve society, publics are a composition of tangible interest groups that (1) indicate how well that service

---

[12]Bruce Ingersoll, "SEC Begins Inquiry of General Dynamics' Disclosure of Cost Overruns to Submarines," *The Wall Street Journal* (October 3, 1984), p. 16.

is being performed, (2) actively work to assure that society is in fact being served, and (3) act as a societal sounding board upon which business can make its case heard.

When one of this nation's major railroads was performing poorly in serving customers, who were primarily industrial, financial institutions were reluctant to underwrite further operations. Its own employees became demoralized, and their negative perceptions further impaired the company's reputation and operations, so that the stocks and bonds of the firm dropped considerably in value. Stories of the railroad's problems appeared in newspapers across the nation. Government agencies and legislators began to respond, stimulated by public interest groups concerned with averting the demise of one of the nation's primary railroads. The company itself appealed for support, making its case through the print media and television, in the courts, and before government agencies. Today, Penn Central is again serving a viable function along America's Eastern seaboard.

A firm's management must always bear in mind the ultimate mission of business—service to society—and be sensitive to the publics that monitor and evaluate performance against that mission. At the same time, a firm must not hesitate to initiate pronouncements through corporate advertising and public relations campaigns of its service accomplishments to its various publics.

The Macroenvironment

The dynamic forces of the macroenvironment, shown in Figure 3-4, have a major impact on both the publics and interface levels of the industrial environment.[13] Shifts in U.S. and world economics, demographics, ecology and culture, changing technology, and the physical plant location of suppliers and buyers impact both levels. While any participant in the interface level can adjust its marketing or operating strategy to counteract the actions, or meet the needs of others and attempt to influence or adjust to the actions of publics, forces in the macroenvironment are usually beyond an individual firm's ability to influence or control.

The primary problem with the macroenvironment is that it keeps changing, and it does so at an accelerating rate. Over the last decade, dramatic changes have occurred not only in technologies, but in economics, politics, demographics, and cultural ideologies, and they have occurred not only in the United States, but worldwide. Thus, industrial organizations are constantly in precarious balance with forces

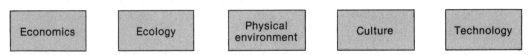

FIGURE 3-4   Forces in the Macroenvironment

[13]Philip Kotler, *Marketing Management: Analysis, Planning, and Control,* 5th ed. (Englewood Cliffs, N.J.: Prentice-Hall, Inc., 1984), p. 87.

in the macroenvironment, forces that, ironically, are often brought about by activities within the industrial arena.

Technology arises through its adoption by industry and, in turn, causes changes in demographics, ecology, cultural ideologies, and economics. A moment's reflection will bear this point out. One of the newest technologies, gene splicing (a form of biotechnology), is just beginning to come of age. Born in Monterey, California, where the world's scientists gathered in 1975 to decide its fate, the potential benefits of recombinant DNA are already beginning to bear their fruit through the combined effort of many industrial firms.[14]

Biotechnology has not only brought about a fundamental shift in drug research and development, it also promises to increase milk production significantly and give civilization the capability of producing drought-resistant crops as well as crops that can thrive in high-salinity soil. Improved food production will eventually reduce world hunger (bringing about a change in world demographics), enable many of the Third World nations to become self-supporting (leading to changes in world economics), allow these nations to move from subsistence economies to industrial economies (ultimately changing cultural ideologies), and, due to the production of stronger, hardier food varieties, permit a lower use of herbicides (improving world ecology).

Economic Influences. General American and worldwide economic conditions greatly influence an organization's ability and willingness to buy and sell. Thus, emerging changes in the economic environment, both at home and abroad, must be closely monitored.

Because of the derived nature of industrial demand, changes in economic variables that affect consumers' discretionary purchasing power have an impact on the industrial producer. As consumers' discretionary incomes change, pronounced shifts in the demand for different categories of durable goods occur. When consumers tighten their belts and wait for better economic times, demand for raw materials, component parts, and associated services also tightens.

When American interest rates are high, the dollar tends to gain value in comparison to major foreign currencies, enhancing the price competitiveness of foreign imports and cramping U.S. exports, further reducing the demand for industrial goods. For instance, during the early 1980s, the U.S. dollar was persistently overvalued with respect to foreign currencies, and many U.S. firms were forced to change their manufacturing and marketing strategies as well as their relations with key suppliers and labor unions. Beckman Instruments, for instance, was forced to move the manufacturing of two of its European-sold product lines overseas. Foreign suppliers were supplying component parts at thirty-three percent less than what U.S. suppliers were charging.[15]

---

[14]Biotech Comes of Age: More than 100 Gene-Splicing Companies Launch a Barrage of Products," *Business Week* (January 23, 1984), pp. 84–94.

[15]"For Multinationals, It Will Never Be the Same," *Business Week* (December 24, 1984), p. 57.

GETTING TOUGH ON TOXICS IN CALIFORNIA

Proposition 65, passed by California voters in November 1986, may change the way products are sold, packaged, and labeled. Once called the Safe Drinking Water and Toxic Enforcement Act, Prop 65 (as it is popularly called) goes far beyond existing state or federal toxic control laws by forcing the hand of government and industry.

Not only does Prop 65 order the governor to create a list of chemicals "known to the state to cause cancer or reproductive toxicity," it puts the burden on business to provide "clear and reasonable" warnings to those who may be exposed to designated chemicals—whether in the workplace, in consumer products, or in the environment at large. It also set in motion an inflexible timetable for implementation, and provisions for enforcement by civil suits from those who are dissatisfied.

According to David Roe, a lawyer for the Environmental Defense Fund who was a principal draftsman of the new law, this is a powerful approach that has potential repercussions in virtually every area of risk; the assessment, regulation, and management of toxic substances.

Source: Christine Russell, "California Gets Tough on Toxics," *Business and Society Review* (August 1989), pp. 47–53.

Shifts in economic conditions, however, do not affect all sectors of the market equally. While the demand for aluminum, copper, and component parts to produce autos may experience dramatic effects when interest rates are rising and credit is tight, other industries such as textiles and chemicals may be minimally affected. Therefore, firms that market to more than one industry must carefully monitor the impact of selective economic shifts on potential buyers. It should be noted, however, that profit versus nonprofit purchasing decisions differ. While commercial enterprises may cut back on capital goods spending during periods of high interest, nonprofit organizations tend to justify purchasing on the rationale that funds allocated for a particular item must be spent during that fiscal year or the budget will be cut the next year.[16]

Ecological Influences. Within the United States and around the globe, industrial organizations face public reaction and government intervention when industrial activities pose potential danger to the earth's resources. Government officials are becoming increasingly concerned with environmental damage to the earth's water, land, air, and people. Industrial organizations involved in the manufacture of such products as chemicals and pesticides constantly pose severe threats to the environment. The disposal of waste materials from these products has already created dan-

---

[16]Thomas V. Bonoma and Gerald Zaltman, "Introduction," in Bonoma and Zaltman, eds., *Organizational Buyer Behavior* (Chicago: American Marketing Association, 1978), p. 23.

gerously high levels of mercury in our oceans, DDT in our soil and food supplies, and numerous toxic-waste dump sites.

Industrial accidents, such as occurred in Bhopal, India, and Chernobyl in the Soviet Union, generate stern consequences as governments tighten safety and environmental regulations. During the Bhopal incident, Brazil, the world's fourth largest user of agricultural chemicals, immediately banned the use of deadly methyl isocyanate. Large multinational companies also faced a move by the Organization for Economic Cooperation and Development—a coalition of twenty-four nations—to pass a long-delayed code of conduct for chemical companies, a code that the United States and several other European countries had been opposing. Many American cities and states have passed "right-to-know" laws that force companies to give detailed information about the hazards of chemicals made and used in factories.[17]

Physical Environmental Influences. The ability to produce and market goods and services at a profit necessitates a favorable combination of the inputs needed. Certain advantages stem from the natural endowments of an environment, such as raw materials, water, and power, or the favorable combination of production inputs, such as adequately skilled management, low-cost labor, and transportation facilities. Industrial suppliers who are able to work out low-cost combinations of these factors of production often have a differential advantage over their competitors.

Nations with histories of political stability also offer greater assurances to both buyers and sellers than those that are constantly in upheaval. Tariff barriers and trade restrictions have traditionally been used by governments to close off outside competition and enhance the production advantage of domestic producers.

Location and transportation considerations, particularly when procurement requirements necessitate a close buyer–seller relationship, are often of paramount consideration in the supplier-sourcing decision.[18] As transportation costs increase, buyers are beginning to prefer suppliers whose mining, manufacturing, or storage facilities are nearby.[19]

Cultural Influences. Cultural mores, customs, habits, norms, and traditions greatly influence the structure and function of an organization as well as the interpersonal relationships of organizational members. While cultural differences have little effect on the product specifications of industrial products, there is a growing trend in the United States toward joint venturing with foreign partners to take advantage of production techniques that are the products of other cultures.

While the growing links between U.S. and foreign companies have taken place to improve competitive positions in the United States and abroad, they all run the

---

[17]Maria Recio and Vicky Cahan, "Bhopal Has Americans Demanding the 'Right to Know,'" *Business Week,* (February 18), 1985, pp. 36–37.

[18]Raleigh Barlowe, *Land Resource Economics,* 2nd ed. (Englewood Cliffs, N.J.: Prentice-Hall, Inc., 1972), Chap. 9.

[19]Vyas, "An Inductive Model of Industrial Supplier Choice Process," pp. 30–45.

COMING TO AMERICA

More and more managers from Japanese companies are coming to America. They are joining existing staffs of subsidiaries and branches to work with teams of their American counterparts. Integrating these newcomers into the American culture and value system is a big job, according to Sy Corenson of Hewlett-Packard's International Operations. But when United States managers understand the cultural differences, they can help these newcomers "get up to speed."

The first step is to recognize that differences in cultural attitudes toward work exist. For example, Americans generally are more interested in the rewards that are earned through working, such as money, status, or promotion. Japanese people, on the other hand, see work as a "consecrated" task. Work enables the Japanese manager to build a legacy that can be passed on to his sons and grandsons. In contrast to the American manager, then, the Japanese manager is more willing to take work home, to study each assignment carefully, and to work long hours.

Americans also tend to be individualistic, looking to individual performance and appraisals as the major determinants of their salaries and bonuses. The Japanese, however, emphasize group cohesiveness and consensus. Thus, while American managers expect to be held individually accountable and receive the lion's share of the bonus, Japanese managers expect to share recognition and responsibility—and any bonuses—with the group.

To avoid a collision of cultural values and work styles, Hewlett-Packard provides intensive training and orientation for Japanese managers to assist them in adjusting to the differences they find in working in the American culture.

Source: From "Working Better with Japanese Managers" by Louis A. Allen, from *Management Review.* Reprinted, by permission of publisher, from *Management Review,* November 1988 © 1988. American Management Association, New York. All rights reserved.

---

risk of cultural incompatibility. For example, Japanese methods of consensual decision making, long-term employment, and the use of quality control circles have all experienced difficulties when attempted in the United States. Despite the risks, and even though some ventures have already failed when corporate objectives diverged, more and more U.S. companies are looking for ways to team up in joint ventures with foreign partners.[20]

Technological Influences. Technological developments and changes in the industrial market strongly affect both buyers and sellers. Buyers wonder whether their profitability and market acceptance will be favorably impacted by changes in suppliers' product design or manufacturing process. Suppliers are equally concerned whether their customers will perform well enough in the downstream markets to

---

[20]Are Foreign Partners Good for U.S. Companies?" *Business Week* (May 28, 1984), pp. 58–59.

maintain or increase their share of derived demand. Rapidly changing technology can also restructure an entire industry, dramatically altering both purchasing and marketing plans.

According to a recent "technology forecast,"[21] marketing in the future will require an understanding and close working relationship with computer-based manufacturing systems. CAD and CAM (computer-aided design and manufacturing) and robotics will affect the future of marketing. While the range of marketing options is limited by factory capabilities today, with the advent of such technologies, continuous assembly-line flows of dissimilar items will be possible through simple programming changes that will lead to greater production of customized products.

Given the rate of technological change in industries such as telecommunications, computers, and semiconductors, large buying firms are developing forecasting techniques to enable them to estimate time periods in which major technology developments might occur. Marketers must also monitor technological change if they hope to adapt marketing strategy with sufficient speed and accuracy to make the most of scientific breakthroughs. Industrial strategy will increasingly require that marketing work more closely with other functional areas, such as research, engineering, and manufacturing.

Demographic Influences.   Industrial firms cannot ignore the demographic environment because of the derived nature of industrial demand. World population explosion and the changing population structure of the world and the United States provide both opportunities and threats. The world's population has reached 4.5 billion, and every 30 seconds 115 babies are born but only 45 people die.[22] As world population increases, it becomes more and more difficult to ration the earth's resources. Not only is the rate of population increasing geometrically, placing tremendous demands upon the earth's exhaustible resources, but that population is also growing unevenly. Those nations that can least afford to support increased populations are experiencing the greatest growth rates.

It has been estimated that Sweden's population will double in 1,386 years and England's in 1,155, but India's will double in only thirty-six years and Mexico's in just twenty-five.[23] Such imbalance bodes continuing economic woes for the entire world and immediate problems for many Third World countries. At the same time, many of the problems that accompany such increases can be mitigated by advanced technology. For example, industrial firms have been evaluating the possibilities of farming the oceans to lessen world hunger problems.

No industrial firm should be caught unprepared by changing demographic conditions. Trends develop slowly and are easy to monitor, and reliable data are available for short- and intermediate-range planning.

---

[21]E. Warren McFarlan, "Information Technology Changes the Way You Compete," *Harvard Business Review* (May-June 1984), pp. 98–103.

[22]American Association for the Advancement of Science, *Science 80* (November 1980), p. 11.

[23]Ibid.

GOVERNMENT'S INFLUENCE
ON THE INDUSTRIAL MARKETING ENVIRONMENT

Government, charged with administering and controlling nations and their subdivisions, transcends the industrial marketing environment. As world competition increases, the industrial manager gives greater attention to the actions of governments around the world, as well as within the United States. In performing its multifaceted functions, government enables and facilitates, but also hampers and disallows, industrial actions.

In the interface environment, government laws, regulations, and activities affect all participants. Some of government's diversified actions, shown in Table 3-1, include providing input monies by funding various programs, effecting changes in interest rates and taxes, specifying product safety standards, sponsoring research and development (Figure 3-5), issuing regulations that protect the environment, and perhaps most important, facilitating actions that are believed to be in accordance with the desires of the society that it regulates.

In contemplating government's performance of these various activities, one can easily see that government transcends the industrial environment. For example, government may become attentive to public opinion aroused by the independent press. That opinion may involve some ecological problem that can only be overcome by banning a particular pesticide—a pesticide that must eventually be replaced by another that will ultimately be developed through new and different technology.

Anticipating Governmental Actions. Industrial leaders have long realized that it is often to their benefit to beat government to the punch. Government, in its omnipo-

TABLE 3-1 Government Activities Influencing the Industrial Marketing Environment

Primary Functions of Government Are to

1. Protect companies from each other.
2. Protect consumers from unfair business practices.
3. Protect the larger interests of society against unrestrained business behavior.
4. Ameliorate income inequality in society.
5. Provide economic stabilization through control of unemployment and inflation.

These Functions Involve

1. Regulating agencies.
2. Laws/politics.
3. Program funding.
4. Research funding.
5. Import/export regulation.
6. Levying taxes.
7. Providing social programs.
8. Controlling interest rates.

Who's footing the bill   Who's doing the work

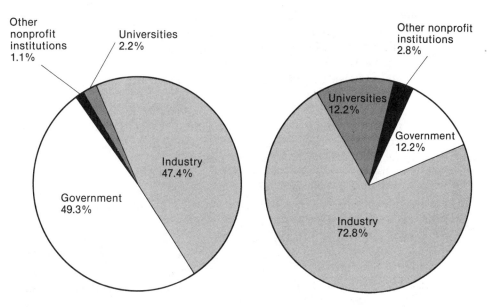

Source: Battelle's Columbus Division

FIGURE 3-5   Research & Development—Who's Footing the Bill Who's Doing the Work

Source: Battelle's Columbus Division, found in Purchasing World, February 1988, p. 18.

tence, does sometimes yield to advocacy in the face of logic, to public opinion despite heavy investment, and to the free press regardless of a firm's best intentions. Governmental regulations and laws often favor whichever environmental entity has the most influence in Washington, the state capital, or city hall.

An industrial firm's own best interests are particularly furthered if and when that firm anticipates government regulation by changing before being mandated to do so. The lone industrial firm's vote is biggest only when it votes first. At the same time industrial managers must remember that government is an enabler and facilitator as well as a regulator.

Industrial marketers have frequently reaped considerable benefit by anticipating, planning, and assisting government with some new research project or product development. For example, new metal alloys and fabrics developed for NASA space projects has spawned entire product lines aimed at industrial and consumer applications with similar temperature, weight, or volume requirements. As discussed next, the influence of government on the industrial environment is brought to bear through political and legal systems as well as through its many agencies and legislators.

Influencing Governmental Action.   Since government transcends all levels of the industrial environment, it is capable of influencing and being influenced by environmental elements at all levels. Each element of the public and macroenvironment level influences government, whether it does so intentionally or unintentionally. Public interest groups fight intentionally to save a wilderness area, while the demographic consideration of a growing segment of older citizens influences governmental actions unintentionally when planned social security increases are sidetracked.

As international competition heats up, industrial firms, which have long intentionally influenced government, must attempt to exert even more influence. The Japanese government, through the broadly powerful Ministry of International Trade and Industry (MITI), provides considerable guidance and assistance to Japan's industrial firms such as direct financial assistance; recommendations regarding product lines, type of technology, and most profitable world areas for export; and the establishment of import barriers.[24]

The United States government's last major attempt to bring financial, governmental, and industrial entities together by enabling the establishment of export trading companies accomplished little because of economic conditions in the macroenvironment during the 1980s.[25] Such failure not only impedes U.S. competitiveness abroad, it also does little toward alleviating the growing U.S. trade deficit—a deficit that amounted to $152 billion in 1987 and has been predicted to reach $200 billion.[26] And "Our ability to compete in world markets," according to the President's Commission on Industrial Competitiveness, "is eroding. . . . Even our lead in high technology is slipping."[27] U.S. industry may well need to increase its share of governmental influence. (See Figure 3-6.)

Political and Legal Influences

The political environment includes international trade restrictions, government attitudes toward business and social activities, and government funding of selected programs. United States businesses, for instance, currently import foreign goods at the rate of $335 billion a year. In fact, twenty cents out of every dollar Americans now spend goes for imported goods.[28] While consumer goods, including autos, make up the largest segment of foreign imports, the fastest-growing area is in capital goods.

Protection against foreign imports is brought about through government pressure on foreign nations to restrict exports "voluntarily," through quota restrictions,

[24]Naoto Sasaki, *Management & Industrial Structure in Japan* (New York: Pergamon Press Ltd., 1981), p. 95.

[25]Jennifer Stoffel, "Why the Export Trading Act Failed," *Business Marketing* (January 1985), pp. 54–58.

[26]See Edward Mervosh and Karen Pennar, "Yes, the Dollar Is Down. No, It Won't Do Much Good," *Business Week* (August 19, 1985), pp. 52–53; "The Trade Deficit in 1983," in *Financial Letter,* Federal Reserve Bank of Kansas, Vol. 10, No. 3 (Kansas City, Missouri, March 1984), p. 1; and "The Trade Deficit's Ominous Outlook," in "Readers Report," *Business Week* (December 31, 1984), p. 5.

[27]See The Report of the President's Commission on Industrial Competitiveness, "Global Competition: The New Reality," Volume II, Superintendent of Documents, U.S. Government Printing Office, Washington, D.C. 1984.

[28]See "The Import Invasion: No Industry Has Been Left Untouched," *Business Week* (October 8, 1984), pp. 172–174.

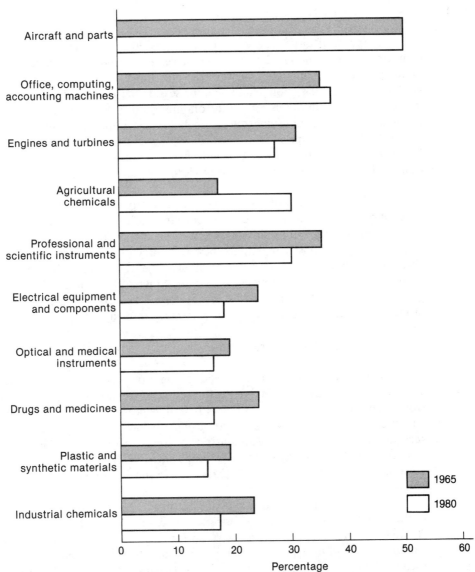

FIGURE 3-6 U.S. Share of World High-Technology Exports, 1965 and 1980
The declining U.S. share of world technology markets is particularly trou-
bling. First, the demand for these products has been growing very rapidly,
and they represent a major growth opportunity. Second, technology's value
is far greater than the dollars it represents in our trade ledger. Innovation
leads to productivity gains that allow us to earn more than our counterparts
abroad, and technologically unique products have been able to command premium prices in world markets. Finally, technology changes fast, with one
round of advances building on those that precede it. Loss in one round of
innovation makes it much harder to enter the competition later on.

Source: Report of the President's Commission on Industrial Competitiveness, Volume II, "Global Competition:
The New Reality," Superintendent of Documents, U.S. Government Printing Office, Washington, D.C., 1984.

through the use of tariffs, or through the imposition of artificial barriers, such as cumbersome rules and regulations. How successful an industry is in gaining United States government support of such restrictions, however, is a matter of politics. In an "around-the-clock" political bargaining session before Congress in 1984, several proposed tariffs and other restrictions on imports of specific products were struck down. Instead of establishing quotas to hold steel imports to fifteen percent of United States consumption, for instance, legislators called on the Reagan administration to reduce imports by seventeen to twenty percent through voluntary restrictions and urged the steel industry to modernize and improve its competitive position.[29]

Political decisions with regard to tariffs and import quotas can have worldwide implications. China, for example, threatened to retaliate against a number of United States exports, "including politically sensitive farm products," when the Reagan administration proposed to impose new "country-of-origin" regulations on imports. The new regulations would have changed the way a country's quota on textile products is charged when it enters the United States. The country of origin, whose quota is charged, is determined by the degree of "substantial transformation" a product undergoes in that country prior to entry into the United States.[30]

Government Agencies and Legislators

Buyers and sellers in the industrial market are firmly regulated by governmental agencies, agencies that are charged with the responsibility of protecting businesses from each other, protecting consumers from businesses, and protecting the larger interests of society from unrestrained business behavior. The dictates of agencies, such as the Food and Drug Administration, the Federal Trade Commission, the Environmental Protection Agency, and the Federal Communications Commission, must be adhered to by both buyers and sellers in the development of their products and overall marketing strategies.

Manufacturers must carefully consider product safety and ecological impact in the design of products and the location of plants or face the same situation as Aerojet General. Aerojet General has, so far, spent more than $20 million in attempting to clean up its environmental pollution. TCE, a cancer-causing chemical used by Aerojet in the manufacture of rockets, was discovered in the groundwater under its California plant—a plant that is being called California's worst toxic-waste site.[31]

Over the last several years, there has been a major trend toward more government regulation and intervention in marketing decisions. Thus, both buyers and

---

[29]See Thomas F. O'Boule, "U.S. Steelmakers Buoyed by Reagan Plan to Seek Voluntary Restraints on Imports," *The Wall Street Journal* (September 20, 1984), p. 2; and "Trade Talks: Congress Hands Reagan a Carrot and a Stick," *Business Week* (October 12, 1984), p. 38.

[30]"U.S. Textile Quotas: Mending Loopholes Has Frayed Nerves," *Business Week* (September 15, 1984), p. 39.

[31]Ingersoll, "SEC Begins Inquiry of General Dynamics."

sellers must keep careful watch on pending regulation to ensure that their respective business plans will meet with government approval. Industrial organizations respond to government agencies and legislators by seeking legal advice from internal or external legal staffs as to what they can and cannot do. They also monitor and attempt to effect regulation by working with key legislators at local, state, and national levels when unfavorable situations develop. This can be done individually or jointly with other firms in the industry—commonly known as lobbying.

Implications. Implications relating to our discussion of the macroenvironment and the influence of government can best be made with regard to all influences within the environment of industrial marketing. The importance of environmental elements will vary with the decision being made and the impact of associated environmental considerations. Support from the financial community, for instance, will be important to a firm constructing office buildings, but the amount of concern will vary with the overall strength of the economy and the current phase of the business cycle.

As the pace of worldwide competition accelerates, the cultures and demographics of different nations are of primary concern to the international marketer attempting to perform comparative marketing, a type of segmentation that divides nations on the basis of similarities and dissimilarities. And as the pace of technological change increases geometrically, firms have begun to monitor actively the environment for technological changes and to predict the technological life cycles of their industrial processes. In fact, some authorities advocate that more effort be spent to develop new technologies rather than to attempt to compete using a dying technology.

Since government is the single entity that transcends all environmental levels, exerts influence on all other environmental entities, and is itself capable of being influenced, it can be of considerable benefit to industry. If governments of other industrial nations act more effectively to shape the industrial environment for the benefit of their own industries, U.S. industries could continue to suffer and the trade deficit could continue to worsen.

STRATEGIES FOR MANAGING
THE INDUSTRIAL MARKETING ENVIRONMENT

This overview of the industrial environment clearly dictates the need for industrial marketers to develop and implement strategies to influence, modify, or respond to actions within the environment that may hinder or aid the achievement of organizational objectives. Manipulation of the marketing mix variables is not enough to ensure success and survival in such a dynamic environment.[32]

---

[32]See Carl P. Zeithaml and Valarie A. Zeithaml, "Environmental Management: Revising the Marketing Perspective," *Journal of Marketing* (Spring 1984), pp. 46–53; and Zeithaml and Zeithaml, "Kotler: Rethink the Marketing Concept," *Marketing News* 18 (September 14, 1984), p. 1.

Marketers must adopt a proactive, creative stance with respect to the external environment. Through ongoing research and forecasting, a firm can anticipate change, predict its impact on organizational goals and performance, and develop strategies to protect its market position. Market intelligence gathering, market research, and economic forecasting are essential factors in monitoring competitive actions, identifying technological innovations, assessing political and regulatory developments, evaluating social change, and identifying changing market demand trends.

As indicated in Table 3-2, marketers have various strategies available to use in influencing their respective environments. Once threats or opportunities are identified through environmental monitoring, three types of environmental management strategies are open to the firm: independent strategies, cooperative strategies, and strategic maneuvering of the environment.

Independent Strategies. Independent environmental management strategies are efforts by the company to reduce environmental uncertainty through the use of its

TABLE 3-2 Environmental Management Strategies

Independent strategies	Competitive aggression	Product differentiation
		Aggressive pricing
		Comparative advertising
	Competitive pacification	Improved competitive relationships
		Industry promotion
		Price umbrellas
	Publics	Corporate image advertising
		Voluntary environmental control
		Commitment to interest groups
	Political/legal	Direct lobbying
		Issue advertising
		Education of regulators
	Resource supplies	Resolution of irregular demand
		Demarketing
	Implicit cooperation	Price leadership
		Technological leadership
Cooperative strategies	Contracting	Vertical/horizontal market systems
	Cooptation	Absorption of publics on board of directors
	Coaltion	Industry associations
		U.S. Chamber of Commerce associations
Strategic maneuvering	Domain selection	Discovery of markets with limited competition and regulation
		Entry into high-growth markets
	Diversification	Vertical integration
		Geographic expansion

Source: Adapted from Carl P. Zeithaml and Valerie A. Zeithaml, "Environmental Management: Revising the Marketing Perspective," *Journal of Marketing*, 48 [Spring 1984], pp. 46–53. Reprinted with permission.

own resources and ingenuity, such as the use of more aggressive pricing strategies in retaliation against competitors or a corporate advertising campaign to enhance or correct a public image.

Cooperative Strategies. Cooperative environmental management strategies involve cooperation, implicit or explicit, with other groups, firms, or industries in the environment, such as joint venturing with foreign or domestic competitors, or including ecologists, women, or bankers on the board of directors. Myriad computer manufacturers, the self-designated IBM compatibles, use an interesting combination of these strategies. Cooperatively, they want potential customers to view them as a technological equivalent to IBM, thus eliminating any trade-off decision by engineers or user groups. But, independently, many of these manufacturers try to establish price levels sufficiently below IBM's to attract the attention of price-conscious purchasing agents.

Strategic Maneuvering. Strategic maneuvering of the environment involves strategies that are designed to alter or change the firm's relationship with respect to its interface environment, such as Eastman Kodak's entry into the telecommunication market or AT&T's venture into computers.

The type of strategy a firm implements depends on the environmental situation it faces as well as its resources. The strategic choice also requires an analysis of costs versus the benefits to be gained immediately and over the long run.

In subsequent chapters, strategies will be proposed in areas such as pricing, promotion, and distribution with the explicit purpose of affording the firm greater control, or at least advantageous influence over a volatile environment. For now, it is sufficient to recognize the beneficial importance of environmental management as well as the interesting paradox associated with this strategic concept. The paradox lies in the fact that firms that could benefit most by skillful management of their environment are usually the least able to do so effectively.

Those firms lacking product advantages or service enhancements are most in need of a favorable price differential. Their limited market share, and subsequent production level, does not yield the cost savings necessary for price leadership. Similarly, firms sorely in need of a technological edge will often lack the money required to support an extensive development program, or the creative people to spend the money profitably, or both. Finally, there are those firms whose risk-averse, reactive managements simply refuse to consider the possibility that anything outside the corporate walls can be proactively changed or influenced.

LOOKING BACK

In this chapter, we set out to increase your awareness of the industrial marketing environment, to expose you to the major elements within that environment, and to increase your understanding of how buyers and sellers influence and control, and sometimes simply respond to, their environments. We have viewed the environment as being composed of three distinct levels—the interface, the publics, and the macro-environment—that exist within the purview of government.

The interface level is composed of key participants (e.g., suppliers, distributors, facilitators, and buyers) who interface with one another in producing goods and moving them through the channel. Influencing the various actions of participants within the interface level are the many and varied publics. Impacting both levels are the uncontrollable forces in the macroenvironment. And transcending the entire industrial marketing environment are those governmental entities charged with assuring that industrial firms serve the nation-state and its subdivisions.

The various strategies available to industrial marketers to better manage their environments include independent and cooperative strategies and strategic maneuvering.

QUESTIONS FOR DISCUSSION

1. Is it most appropriate to view a typical industrial firm as a supplier of inputs to the productive process, as a user of these inputs, or as a marketer of output products? Explain your response.

2. Given the current business and social environments, do you see the mass media as a valuable ally to industry or as a troublesome adversary? Should the media play any role other than that of an unbiased informer?

3. Producers of industrial goods do not deal directly with the general public. Why, then, should they be concerned with this level of the industrial environment?

4. While U.S. manufacturers of semiconductor equipment still hold the upper hand, they have been losing market share to the Japanese. To hold its share of the U.S. market, would it be good strategy for a producer of semiconductors to seek a joint venture with a Japanese manufacturer?

5. "Industrial firms can exert influence over their target markets and even competitors, but they can only sit and watch what happens in the macroenvironment." What is your reaction to this statement?

6. Give examples of the U.S. government's positive and helpful influence upon industry. On the other hand, what actions appear detrimental to industrial progress?

7. What, in your opinion, are the most important conclusions to draw from the environment of industrial marketing?

SUGGESTED ADDITIONAL READINGS

"A Disaster that Wasn't," *U.S. News & World Report,* (September 18, 1989): 60–69.

"Are Foregin Partners Good for U.S. Companies?" *Business Week* (May 28, 1984): 58–59.

ATTANASIO, DOMINICK B., "The Multiple Benefits of Competitor Intelligence," *The Journal of Business Strategy* (May/June 1988): 16–19.

BAKER, M. J., *Marketing New Industrial Products* (New York: Holmes & Meier Publishing Co., 1975).

"For Multinationals, It Will Never Be the Same," *Business Week* (December 24, 1984): 57.

"A Move to Make Institutions Start Using Their Stockholder Clout," *Business Week* (August 6, 1984): 70–71.

RUSSELL, CHRISTINE, "California Gets Tough on Toxics," *Business and Society Review* (August, 1989): 47–53.

ZEITHAML, CARL P., and VALARIE A. ZEITHAML, "Environmental Management: Revising the Marketing Perspective." *Journal of Marketing* (Spring 1984): 46–53.

PART TWO

Organizational Buying and Buyer Behavior

FORD KILLS THE BIG ORDER

In June 1983, after months and months of negotiating with suppliers, Ford Motor Company killed a plan to have its North American truck and van transmissions built in Mexico. During those many months a half-dozen suppliers had negotiated for the work, work that would bring in several hundred million dollars. Two Japanese firms, Toyo Kogyo and Mitsubishi Motors, competed against such U.S. companies as Dana, Borg-Warner, and Eaton. The competition was keen. Not only were these companies competing with each other, but they were also competing with Ford. If none of those suppliers could undercut Ford's manufacturing costs, Ford had the option of producing the transmissions itself.

Purchasing at Ford is serious business. Suppliers must be located who can deliver needed parts, in required quantities, at the right times, in accordance with specifications, and at competitive prices.

Designing new cars and trucks starts years before they are finally produced; consumer demand must be estimated four or more years in advance of sales. Throughout the entire process, from idea inception to production, purchasing plays a big part in establishing cost controls for parts and materials, advising design engineers on anticipated costs, and, once designs are finalized, studying blueprints and specifications to begin the long, involved process of searching for suppliers.

The ability to produce a needed part is so crucial that Ford people often visit potential suppliers' plants to determine their capabilities. They may evaluate suppliers' managerial abilities, business reputations, and even their financial responsibility. Ford's considerations are numerous; its requirements are many and detailed. So important is production flow at Ford that should suppliers fail to meet quality and delivery requirements, experience financial difficulties, or become unable to maintain the smooth flow of supplies needed by Ford, they will be dropped as supply sources.

In the case of the manual transmissions, several years of work, involving numerous individuals in various Ford departments, culminated in the decision that the company itself would produce the parts. Although Ford spends over $5 billion a year purchasing thousands of items from more than 25,000 independent suppliers, it is precise in its attention to detail. Perhaps Ford's purchasing department does not "know all and see all," but it comes very close.

Source: Joseph Bohn, "Ford Mexican Plants Key to U.S. Suppliers," *Industrial Marketing*, January 1983, p. 10; telephone conversation with Don Edwards of Ford Motor Company, June 1983; and Gordon T. Brand, *The Industrial Buying Decision* (New York: John Wiley & Sons, Inc., 1972], pp. 114–124.

In contrast to consumer purchasing, organizational purchasing is much more complex. Multiple forces both internal and external to the firm exert various pressures on the ultimate decision as buyers move from problem or need recognition to their final purchase decision. Thus, the effectiveness of industrial marketing strategy hinges on how well the industrial marketer understands the different types of buying situations that organizational buyers face, how they proceed through the purchasing decision process, and how that process is influenced by the various needs and expectations of those who are involved in the purchasing decision. In the next two chapters, then, we discuss how marketing strategy is affected by the type of purchasing situation industrial buyers face, where they are in their decision-making process, and how organizational buyer behavior influences buying decisions.

CHAPTER 4

The Nature of Industrial Buying

Industrial buying adds extensions and entirely new dimensions to the traditionally studied consumer buying process. In making decisions, purchasing managers must coordinate with numerous people with diverse organizational responsibilities who apply different criteria to purchasing decisions. Developing effective marketing strategy to reach organizational buyers rests on the industrial marketer's understanding of the nature of industrial buying. Thus, this chapter discusses

1. The purchasing decision process that organizational buyers apply when confronted with different buying situations and how marketing strategy is affected.
2. The various roles of buying influencers in the purchasing decision process and why it is important to identify those influencers.
3. The criteria that organizational buyers apply in making purchasing decisions.

Just as Ford's purchasing managers must understand the needs of Ford Motor Company, so must the industrial marketer who is interested in selling to Ford or any other industrial organization. This point cannot be overstressed. Effective industrial marketing strategy *must* begin with an understanding of industrial buying behavior. This entails knowledge of the different types of buying situations that organizations encounter, the process that organizational buyers go through in reaching purchasing decisions, how those decisions are affected by different members of the firm and the criteria they apply in making purchasing decisions.[1]

[1]Earl Naumann, Douglas J. Lincoln, and Robert D. McWilliams, "The Purchase of Components: Functional Areas of Influence," *Industrial Marketing Management* 13 (1984), pp. 113-122.

ORGANIZATIONAL BUYING ACTIVITIES

Organizational buying activities center on the level of experience and information that firms have in purchasing certain products and services. In making a routine purchase, buyers have little need for information because of their past experience with the purchasing situation. When a purchasing situation is entirely new, information needs may be extensive due to the firm's lack of experience with the product, service, or suppliers. In the purchase of a new computer system, for example, buyers will be very concerned with identifying computer characteristics (e.g., programs and peripheral equipment) that will satisfy their needs, services provided to maintain the system, and the supplier's capability to provide those services.

Buying activity also consists of various phases of decision making. Depending on the type of buying situation, whether it is routine or new, these phases will vary in their degree of importance. Effective industrial marketing strategy, then, requires that marketers focus their attention on the type of buying situation a firm is facing, where it is in its decision-making process (which phase), and what criteria various influencers will emphasize in the purchasing decision.

THE BUYGRID MODEL

Understanding organizational buying behavior is easier if it is divided into the various phases and these phases are analyzed under different buying situations. This enables the marketer to identify critical decision phases, the information needs of purchasing organizations, and the various criteria buyers consider when making purchase decisions.[2] A conceptual model, referred to as the *Buygrid*, is quite useful in analyzing the purchasing decision process over various buying situations.

As shown in Table 4-1, the Buygrid incorporates three types of buying situations—(1) the "new task," (2) the "straight rebuy," and (3) the "modified rebuy"—as well as eight phases in the buying decision process. Thus, it provides a frame of reference for dividing the overall decision-making process into distinct segments that are useful for recognizing critical decisions and specific information requirements.

Buying Situations

As mentioned, buyers have various levels of experience and information to use in purchasing products and services.[3] The same purchase in two different organizations may elicit markedly different purchasing strategies if the buying situation is different (e.g., a straight rebuy in one and a new task in the other). Therefore, marketing

---

[2]Joseph A. Bellizzi and Philip McVey, "How Valid Is the Buy-Grid Model?" *Industrial Marketing Management* 12 (1983), pp. 57–62.

[3]The following discussion is based on Patrick J. Robinson, Charles W. Faris, and Yoram Wind, *Industrial Buying and Creative Marketing* (Boston: Allyn & Bacon, Inc., 1967), Chaps. 3, 4, and 5.

TABLE 4-1 A Buygrid Analytic Framework for Industrial Buying Situations

	Buyclasses		
	New Task	*Modified Rebuy*	*Straight Rebuy*
B u y P h a s e s	1. Anticipation or recognition of problem (need) and a general solution		
	2. Determination of characteristics and quantity of needed item		
	3. Description of characteristics and quantity of needed item		
	4. Search for and qualification of potential sources		
	5. Acquisition and analysis of proposals		
	6. Evaluation of proposals and selection of suppliers		
	7. Selection of an order routine		
	8. Performance feedback and evaluation		

Notes

1. The most complex buying situations occur in the upper left portion of the Buygrid matrix, when the largest number of decision makers and buying influences are involved. Thus, a new task in its initial phase of problem recognition generally represents the greatest difficulty for management.

2. Clearly, a new task may entail policy questions and special studies, whereas a modified rebuy may be more routine and a straight rebuy essentially automatic.

3. As Buyphases are completed, moving from phase 1 through phase 8, the process of "creeping commitment" occurs, and there is diminishing likelihood of new vendors gaining access to the buying situation.

Source: From Marketing Science Institute Series, *Industrial Buying and Creative Marketing* by Patrick J. Robinson, Charles W. Faris, and Yoram Wind. Copyright © 1967 by Allyn & Bacon, Inc. Reprinted by permission.

strategy must begin with identifying the type of buying situation the purchasing firm is facing.[4]

New Task.   In the new task buying situation, the problem or need is considerably different from past experiences. Problem recognition may be triggered by internal or external factors. For instance, the firm's decision to add a new product line may necessitate the purchase of new equipment, parts, or materials. Or a change in customer requirements may necessitate the purchase of new machinery to meet the changed need. Since both situations are new, decision makers lack the experience and product knowledge to make comparisons of alternative products and suppliers. In the new task purchasing situation, decision makers and influencers enter into extensive problem-solving activity. They must obtain a variety of information to explore alternative solutions adequately before a purchase can be made.

Modified Rebuy.   Organizational decision makers enter into a modified rebuy situation when they feel that significant benefits such as quality improvements or cost

[4]Naumann, Lincoln, and McWilliams, "The Purchase of Components: Functional Areas of Influence," pp. 113–122.

reductions may be derived from reevaluating alternatives. Although well-defined criteria may be employed in the purchase decision, there may be uncertainty about which supplier can best fill specific needs. In such instances, buyers will seek additional information. Re-evaluation of supply alternatives may be triggered by internal and/or external forces. The modified rebuy situation, however, occurs most often when the firm is displeased with the performance of present suppliers.

Straight Rebuy. The most common buying situation in industrial purchasing is the straight rebuy. When purchases are continuing or recurring, little or no information is required; routine response is the normal buying pattern. Organizational buyers usually have well-developed choice criteria that have been used and refined over time. One purchasing agent, for example, states that so long as delivery is prompt, quality is consistent, and price is reasonably competitive, he will not switch suppliers. As long as choice criteria are met, alternative solutions are seldom evaluated.[5]

Phases in the Purchasing Decision Process

As Figure 4-1 shows, by tracing the sequence of activities that occur in the organizational buying process, it is not difficult to uncover the critical decision phases and evolving information requirements of buying situations.[6]

The consumer purchasing decision process is usually described as a series of mental stages that include problem recognition, information search, information evaluation, purchase decision making, and postpurchase behavior.[7] The industrial purchasing decision process, on the other hand, accents physical, observable stages, as opposed to mental stages, because several people are usually involved in various ways in each phase. Phase 3, for example, is the description of the characteristics and quantity of the needed item; the original developers of the Buygrid model wrote: "Since this description becomes the basis for action by people inside and outside of the buying organization, it must be detailed and precise to facilitate later phases in the buying process.[8]

Phase 1. Anticipation or Recognition of a Problem (Need). The purchasing decision process is triggered by the recognition of a problem, need, or potential opportunity. Such recognition may originate within the buying organization, especially when products become outmoded, equipment breaks down, or existing materials are unsatisfactory in quality or availability. It may also originate outside the buying orga-

[5]Peter Doyle, Arch G. Woodside, and Paul Mitchell, "Organizations Buying in New Task and Rebuy Situations," *Industrial Marketing Management* 8 (1979), pp. 7–11.

[6]The following discussion is based on Gordon T. Brand, *The Industrial Buying Decision* (New York: John Wiley & Sons, Inc., 1972), Chap. 9; J. M. Stevens and J. P. Grand, *The Purchasing/ Marketing Interface* (New York: John Wiley & Sons, Inc., 1975); and Robinson, Faris, and Wind, *Industrial Buying and Creative Marketing*, pp. 11–18, 185–193.

[7]Philip Kotler, *Principles of Marketing* (Englewood Cliffs, N.J.: Prentice-Hall, Inc., 1980), pp. 252–260.

[8]Robinson, Faris, and Wind, *Industrial Buying and Creative Marketing*, p 3.

DO-IT-YOURSELF PROBLEM SOLVING CAN BE COSTLY

For 11 years, Polakoff Bros., a tax accounting firm, mailed its general ledger work to a local data processing time-share company, ADP. When annual costs exceeded $30,000, ADP talked Polakoff into using a terminal and telephone connection from its office. ADP's system, however, had no display—what went in could not be reviewed, errors and all were transmitted. Consequently, costs increased and Polakoff returned to the tried, but true, mail-them-in method.

Two years later, as business was being lost to competitors who were using computerized reports, Polakoff tried Commerce Clearing House, Inc., which promised everything: general ledgers, tax processing, work processing, you name it. But when the new trainees attempted to use the system, disaster struck. The software was not capable of handling a multiuser system. Polakoff crated up the gear and shipped it back. Total loss, $3,000 and two months' time.

Desperate, Polakoff finally responded to an ad. Computer Advisory Services, Inc., suppliers of "turnkey" tailored accounting systems, responded, analyzed Polakoff's needs, and recommended a $12,000 system based on IBM's PCXT. After five years of wasting time and money, for $5,000 worth of problem-solving consultation Polakoff finally got it right.

Source: See "A Do-It-Yourself Approach That Proved Disastrous." *Business Week*, October 8, 1984, p. 134.

---

nization with a marketer who recognizes and reveals opportunities for potential performance improvement. The marketer who initiates or becomes involved in the buying process at this phase, particularly in a new task situation, will have a distinct advantage in influencing the final decision and, thus, a greater probability of being selected as a supplier. Since research has shown that new product ideas frequently originate with customers, early involvement in the new task/problem recognition phase also offers the marketer a differential advantage over competitive suppliers.[9]

Phase 2. Determination of the Characteristics and Quantity of Needed Item. Once a problem has surfaced, organizational members must determine specifically how the situation may be resolved; that is, the problem and solution alternatives must be narrowed and precisely analyzed. Thus, the firm will seek answers to such questions as: "What performance specifications need to be met?" "What are the application requirements?" "What types of goods and services should be considered?" and "What quantities will be needed?"

In the case of technical products, either the user department or engineering will usually prepare performance specifications. For nontechnical items, the user department might determine that products currently on the market could solve the

[9]Eric Von Hippel, "Successful Industrial Products from Customer Ideas," *Journal of Industrial Marketing* 42 (January 1978), pp. 39–49.

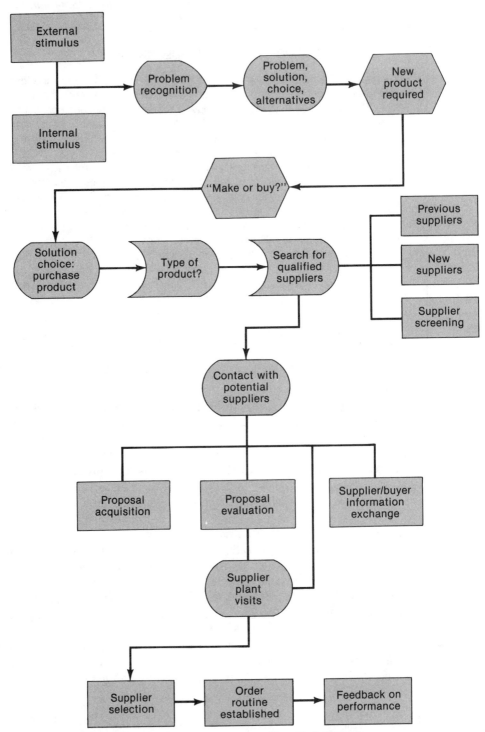

FIGURE 4-1 Purchasing Decision Process in a New Task Situation

problem. The narrowing of the problem and alternatives is, thus, a task internal to the user department. While influencers from outside the department may be used as additional sources of information, critical decisions and information needs at this phase lie chiefly within the user department.

Phase 3. Description of the Characteristics and Quantity of the Needed Item. This is often a critical phase for the marketer. It is during this phase that those influencers who prepare or affect specifications enter the purchasing process. During this phase, buying influencers may change from department heads to engineers and manufacturing personnel. It is at this phase, too, that buying influencers begin to look outside the firm for supplier and product information and for assistance in developing product specifications.

Many suppliers do not become aware that a buying situation is in progress until the firm begins its outside search for information. Because of the opportunity to develop a close working relationship with organizational influencers prior to other competitors coming on the scene, a definite advantage accrues to the marketer who triggered the need, or who is aware of the need at this point in time.

ATTRACTING GOOD SUPPLIERS ENTAILS A LOT OF PLANNING

At first blush, DMA isn't that much different from thousands of other firms struggling to take a new idea or product into the marketplace. In DMA's case the product is a new type of Winchester computer disk drive . . . named after the famous Winchester rifle.

. . . What sets DMA apart from the average small company trying to hit the market with a running start is its sophisticated approach to integrating vendor~ directly into its production operation.

. . . The big question, of course, is how does a purchasing department in an emerging company attract good and competent suppliers, get them to produce great parts, and provide these parts at prices that the emerging company can afford: The answer comes in two parts: [1] finding the vendors you want, [2] making them want to work for you. . . . The purchasing department has to have a good understanding of the product and the suppliers who will be asked to bid on a piece of the action. This entails talking informally with suppliers, following up with a letter introducing DMA to the prospective vendor describing the company, the product, and giving some general information about production and market goals.

. . . Before DMA sets down to negotiate on a contract, it knows the vendor's quality history, and what his tooling, production, delivery performance, leadtimes, and costs are like. To get suppliers to want a close relationship with DMA, DMA builds a "believable management team and a plan of operation" which results in real numbers and a long-term contract offer "based on a five-year production plan."

Source: Reprinted from *Purchasing* magazine, "Putting Success in Your Vendors' Hands," *Purchasing,* April 29, 1982, pp. 81–84. Copyright © by Cahners Publishing Company, 1982.

Phase 4. Search for and Qualification of Potential Sources. Once solutions have been identified and precisely described, a buying organization begins to search for alternative sources of supply. This leads to the qualification of suppliers. However, qualifications sought will vary with the type of buying organization, the specific buying situation, and the buying influencers involved. For example, a firm may have made its new task decision based primarily on price, with the accounting department acting as the major decision influencer. The important end result of phase 4 is that decision makers have determined which suppliers will be considered as potential vendors.

Phase 5. Acquisition and Analysis of Proposals. When qualified suppliers have been identified, requests for specific proposals will be made. Phases 4 and 5 may occur simultaneously in a straight rebuy—buyers may merely check a catalog or contact suppliers to obtain up-to-date information about prices and deliveries. However, in more complex situations, phases 4 and 5 are separate and distinct. Many months may be spent in exchanging proposals and counterproposals. In such purchase situations, the need for information is extensive, and a great deal of time is given to analyzing proposals and comparing products, services, and costs. Thus, phase 5 emerges as a distinct component of the purchasing process.

Phase 6. Evaluation of Proposals and Selection of Suppliers. Various proposals of competing suppliers are weighed and analyzed. If a firm is facing a make-or-buy decision, proposals are compared to the cost of producing the needed item within the buying firm. If the buying firm decides it can produce the needed item more economically, the buying process terminates.[10] If the firm is not facing a make-or-buy decision, one or more offers from competing suppliers are accepted. Further negotiations may continue with selected suppliers on terms, prices, deliveries, or other aspects of suppliers' proposals.

Phase 7. Selection of an Order Routine. Order routines are established by forwarding purchase orders to the vendors and status reports to the using department and by determining the levels of inventory that will be needed over various time periods. While this phase begins with the placement of an order, the purchase process is not actually completed until the ordered item is delivered and accepted for use. The user department, where the need originated, does not view its problems solved until the specified product has been received and is available for use. The effectiveness of suppliers in handling this phase is, therefore, critical.

Phase 8. Performance Feedback and Evaluation. The final phase in the purchasing process consists of a formal or informal review and feedback regarding product

---

[10]Robert W. Haas, *Industrial Marketing Management*, 2nd ed. (Boston: Kent Publishing Co., 1982), p. 85.

performance, as well as vendor performance.[11,12] This phase involved a determination by the user department as to whether the purchased item solved the original problem. If it did not, suppliers that were screened earlier may be given further consideration. Feedback that is critical of the chosen vendor or product can cause the various members of the decision-making unit to reexamine their positions. Research indicates that when this occurs, views regarding previously rejected alternatives become more favorable.[13] How buyers evaluate competing suppliers is discussed in Chapter 5.

Overview of the Buygrid

In the foregoing discussion of the Buygrid, it is important to note that it is the decision-making process that is the subject of analysis.

Creeping Commitment. Decision making, according to the concept of "creeping commitment," involves a sequence of choices, each of which eliminates certain alternatives from further consideration.[14] As decisions are made over the various phases of the purchasing process, the range of alternatives is narrowed. At some point, the number of alternatives will have been narrowed so that only a few alternative solutions remain feasible. The problem-solving process will continue until a final decision is made. For example, by the time purchasing personnel at Ford begin their search for qualified suppliers, design engineers have already completed phase 3; that is, they have specified the parts and materials to be used and the opportunity for sellers to influence their specifications has passed—Ford is now committed to the parts and materials to be used in producing the new model, and the bulk of alternative choices has been eliminated. In other words, commitment to the final solution is becoming firmer and more specific ("creeping") with each phase.

Center of Gravity. The concept of the "center of gravity" holds that various phases or combinations of phases become more critical to final outcomes of purchase decisions (depending on the purchasing situation) and that individuals involved in these critical phases have greater power than do individuals in other phases.[15] For instance, a critical decision phase occurs at Ford when final design decisions are being implemented and Purchasing is asked to assist design engineers in estimating costs. It is this critical decision phase or center of gravity on which all

[11]Doyle, Woodside, and Michell, "Organizations Buying in New Task and Rebuy Situations," pp. 7–11.

[12]Lambert, Dornoff, and Kernan, "The Industrial Buyer and the Postchoice Evaluation Process," *Journal of Marketing Research* 14 (May 1977), pp. 246–251.

[13]Doyle, Woodside, and Michell, "Organizations Buying in New Task and Rebuy Situations," p. 19.

[14]Robinson, Faris, and Wind, *Industrial Buying and Creative Marketing*, p. 19.

[15]Ibid., p. 20.

other phases tend to focus. It should also be noted that the relative importance of each phase will vary from purchase to purchase.

Marketing Implications

The direction of marketing strategy is greatly affected by both the purchasing situation and decision phase of customer firms. Progressively greater amounts of information will be needed by organizational buyers as the purchase situation changes from a straight rebuy to a modified rebuy to a new task situation. Information needs, as well as individual involvement in the purchase decision, will also be affected by the phase of the purchasing process.[16] Anderson, Chu, and Weitz, for example, have found that when organizational buyers are facing a new task, they will be (1) uncertain about their needs and the appropriateness of the possible solutions; (2) more concerned about finding a good solution than getting a low price or assured supply; (3) more willing to entertain proposals from "out" suppliers and less willing to favor "in" suppliers; (4) more influenced by technical personnel; and (5) less influenced by purchasing agents.[17] Thus, marketing strategy depends on both the purchasing situation and the decision-making process.

The most important phases affecting marketing strategy, particularly for a new task or modified rebuy situation, are phases 1 through 5. While Table 4-2 summarizes how the following discussion of marketing strategy differs over these phases and buying situations, the astute marketer should be aware that not all organizational members may view the buying situation from the same perspective. That is, a purchasing agent might view a given buying situation as a new buy and an engineer might view it as a straight rebuy. Such a situation could easily occur where an engineer, for instance, had been routinely involved with a product (or supplier) while employed with a different organization within the same industry.[18]

Phase 1. Problem Recognition. In the new task situation, marketing opportunities depend upon anticipating, recognizing, and understanding customer problems to provide the right information and assistance at the right time. This is difficult because problem recognition is largely internal to the buying firm. Thus, marketers need to use appropriate advertising media, as well as creative sales people, to alert prospective customers to potential problems and to convince them of their problem-solving capabilities.

Because a straight rebuy situation is rather routine, the "in" supplier (a current supplier to the organization) should maintain a close relationship with users and purchasing personnel. To prevent or minimize shifts to a modified rebuy, consistent quality and service standards must be provided. Research has shown that customers,

---

[16]Naumann, Lincoln, and McWilliams, "The Purchase of Components: Functional Areas of Influence," pp. 113–122.

[17]Eric Anderson, Wujin Chu, and Barton Weitz, "Industrial Purchasing: An Empirical Exploration of the Buyclass Framework," *Journal of Marketing* 51 (July 1987), pp. 71–85.

[18]Ibid.

TABLE 4-2 Appropriate Marketing Strategies over Various Buying Situations and Phases

Phases	New Task	Modified Rebuy	Straight Rebuy
1. Problem recognition	Anticipate problem; use advertising and creative sales people to convince buyers of problem-solving capabilities.	In supplier: maintain quality/service standards; out supplier: watch for developing trends.	In supplier: maintain close relationship with users and buyers; out supplier: convince firm to reexamine alternatives.
2. Solution determination	Provide technical assistance and information.	In supplier and out supplier: stress capability, reliability, and problem-solving capabilities.	Same as phase 1.
3. Determining needed item	Provide detailed product/service information to decision makers.	Same as phase 2.	Same as phase 1.
4. Searching for and qualifying supplier	In supplier: maintain dependability; out supplier: demonstrate ability to perform task.	In supplier: watch for problems; out supplier: demonstrate ability to perform task.	Same as phase 1.
5. Analyzing proposals	Understand details of customer problem/needs; make timely proposals.	Understand details of customer problem/needs; make timely proposals.	Make timely proposal.

Source: Marketing Science Institute Series, *Industrial Buying and Creative Marketing,* by Patrick J. Robinson, Charles W. Faris, and Yoram Wind. Copyright ©1967 by Allyn & Bacon, Inc. Used with permission.

dissatisfied with present suppliers, often react by changing suppliers without first attempting to correct the situation with the existing source.[19]

"Out" suppliers (not a current supplier to the organization) need to develop systematic sources of information to detect and respond quickly to any developing trends that might lead to a modified rebuy. When out suppliers attempt to modify a straight rebuy, they face a major task. Buying influencers must be convinced that a reexamination of alternative solutions is appropriate. This requires the customer to expend time, personnel, and money. The out supplier's ability to bring about a modified rebuy will depend greatly upon that firm's reputation for being creative, objective, and dependable.

[19]Doyle, Woodside, and Michell, "Organizations Buying in New Task and Rebuy Situations," p. 9.

Phase 2. Determining Solution Characteristics. Marketing opportunities at this phase consist of providing information, technical assistance, and suggested direction while the customer is in the process of narrowing solutions. In the new task or modified rebuy situation, the major marketing task for both the in and the out supplier is that of gaining acceptance for participation in the problem-solving process. Being able to do this depends, to a significant degree, on the marketer's reputation. "In" suppliers should have previously established their reputations for providing capable technical assistance to the purchasing firm through prior marketing efforts or actual performance. "Out" suppliers need to stress their general capability, reliability, and problem-solving skills and address any special information requirements.

The marketing task in a straight rebuy situation requires that in suppliers maintain information flow to discourage departure from established routines that might lead to a modified rebuy.

Phase 3. Characteristics/Quantity of Needed Item. In the new task or modified rebuy situation, decision makers are primarily interested in the total offerings that competing suppliers can provide, particularly those related to products and support services. Marketing opportunities at this phase, therefore, depend primarily upon providing detailed product, production, and service information. It is at this phase that a marketer has the best opportunity to influence the preparation of specifications that favor his or her organization's products or services. For the straight rebuy situation, marketing strategy is essentially the same as in phase 2.

During the first three phases, it is particularly important for the marketer to "find the decision maker." The normal buyer-seller interaction point is in the purchasing department. This is where sellers should concentrate their efforts to develop strong personal relationships. Unfortunately, the purchasing department usually has minimum involvement in these early stages with a new task situation. In fact, the buyer is often "the last to know" that major changes are being considered. Middle and upper management, engineering (especially in high-tech firms), manufacturing and research and development are the likely spots to find the decider and major influencers in the problem recognition and solution-choice phases.[20] To complicate matters further, the cast of actors will not be the same from firm to firm, or even from situation to situation within any given firm.

Phase 4. Searching for and Qualifying Suppliers. In the new task or modified rebuy situation, out suppliers must demonstrate ability to perform the job. As in the case of Ford, technical experts may visit plant facilities, examine equipment, and talk with technical personnel. Buyers may evaluate the suppliers' managerial capabilities, general business reputation, and financial responsibility. The marketing task for the out supplier in a modified rebuy situation is to convince the potential cus-

---

[20]Naumann, Lincoln, and McWiliams, "The Purchase of Components: Functional Areas of Influence," pp. 113–122.

tomer firm that superior value, such as better quality control, faster deliveries, or significant cost savings, are possible. The primary task in a straight rebuy situation for the in supplier is to maintain performance and communication flow so that the customer will not consider alternative suppliers.

Phase 5. Acquiring and Analyzing Proposals.   Marketing strategy in the new task or modified rebuy situation should be directed at understanding the specific details of the customer's problems and providing technical assistance. This may include cooperative involvement in cost studies, product testing, and evaluation. During this phase it is also critical for the supplier (particularly in new task situations) to determine the relative importance of the various specification details to the customer. These details will fall into three basic categories:

1.   What is essential to solve the problem (e.g., electric motor with 1-horsepower output).
2.   What is desirable, but not essential (e.g., weight less than 25 pounds).
3.   What is added for clarification only (e.g., painted black with white letters).

With this understanding, the supplier is in a much better position to emphasize those factors of greatest importance to the customer and avoid designing product characteristics that increase cost without increasing the customer's value perception. This understanding also allows the supplier to know which specifications are open to value-enhancing revisions (e.g., our standard 30-pound, 1-horsepower motor will cost fifteen percent less than a 25-pound version requiring special metal alloys).

In the straight rebuy, in suppliers should make timely proposals and quotations upon request. The goal, as in the previous phases, is to maintain quality service to prevent or forestall a shift to a modified rebuy.

BUYING CENTERS
AND MULTIPLE BUYING INFLUENCERS

To be successful, marketing communication strategy must address the significant variation in information needs of those individuals involved in the purchasing decision as it progresses through its many phases. A major task, then, facing the industrial marketer is identifying those individuals who are in any way involved in the purchasing decision process, that is, the *decision-making unit.*

A decision-making unit may consist of only one person, but it is normally a group of individuals "who share a common goal or goals which the decision will hopefully help them to achieve, and who share the risks arising from the decision."[21] It is not unusual to encounter groups consisting of fifteen to twenty individuals,[22]

[21]R. D. Buzzell and others, *Marketing: A Contemporary Analysis*, 2nd ed. (New York: McGraw-Hill Book Company, 1972), p. 62.

[22]G. Van Der Most, "Purchasing Process: Researching Influencers Is Basic to Marketing Planning," *Industrial Marketing* (October 1976), p. 120.

and some have been known to involve more than 50 people. In industrial marketing, these decision makers are referred to as the *buying center.*[23]

Identifying Buying Center Members

The buying center gives a good framework for answering the question: "Who is really involved?" The buying center is an "informal, cross-departmental decision unit in which the primary objective is the acquisition, impartation, and processing of relevant purchasing-related information."[24] Generally, people within an organization become involved in the buying center for one of two reasons—they have formal responsibility, though this is not always discernible, or they have importance as a source of information.[25] The emphasis of this discussion regarding buying centers is, then, upon functional areas, that is, various organizational groups that exert influence on the purchasing decision.[26] Table 4-3, however, also indicates how these various functional areas are involved in the purchasing decision process over different buying situations.

Marketing. When a purchasing decision has an effect on the marketability of a firm's product, such as altering the product's materials, packaging, or price, marketing people become active influencers in the purchase decision process. The perspective of marketing in the purchasing process is: "Will it enhance salability?" The purchase of parts and materials tends to influence the salability of final products.

Manufacturing. When new products or models are being developed, manufacturing plays a significant role. Manufacturing is responsible for determining the feasibility and economic considerations of producing end products. Thus, engineering decisions on specifications, parts, and materials are confirmed in this department, and equipment needs, costs, and impacts on current production are given careful consideration. Continuous feedback to the purchasing department on the performance of suppliers also makes manufacturing a key influencer in the selection and retention of suppliers and the allocation of quantities among suppliers.

It should be noted that manufacturing will not always welcome technical changes, even obvious improvements, with complete enthusiasm. Top management holds manufacturing primarily responsible for product cost reductions, and changes have a tendency to increase costs, at least temporarily, due to an interruption of the learning curve process (see Chapter Seventeen).

[23]Frederick E. Webster, Jr., and Yoram Wind, *Organizational Buying Behavior* (Englewood Cliffs: N.J.: Prentice-Hall, Inc., 1972), p. 6.

[24]Robert E. Speckman and Louis W. Stern, "Environmental Uncertainty and Buying Group Structure: An Empirical Investigation," *Journal of Marketing* 43 (Spring 1979), p. 56.

[25]Brand, *The Industrial Buying Decision*, p. 30.

[26]See Robinson, Faris, and Wind, *Industrial Buying and Creative Marketing*, Chap. 9; E. Raymond Corey, *Industrial Marketing: Cases and Concepts* (Englewood Cliffs, N.J.: Prentice-Hall, Inc., 1983), pp. 59–63; and Brand, *The Industrial Buying Decision*, Chap. 4.

TABLE 4-3 Buying Center Influence Matrix

Phase	New Buy	Modified Rebuy	Straight Rebuy
Need identification	Engineering Purchasing Research and Development Production	Purchasing Production Engineering	Production Purchasing

Establishment of
  specification
	Engineering
	Purchasing
	Production
	Research and
	  Development
		Engineering
		Purchasing
		Production
		Research and
		  Development
		Quality Control
			Purchasing
			Engineering
			Production

Modification and
  evaluation of buy-
  ing alternatives
	Engineering
	Purchasing
	Research and
	  Development
		Purchasing
		Engineering
		Production
			Purchasing
			Engineering
			Production

Supplier selection	Purchasing Engineering Research and Development Quality Control	Purchasing Engineering Production	Purchasing Engineering Production

Source: Reprinted by permission of the publisher from "The Purchase of Components: Functional Areas of Influence," by Earl Naumann, Douglas J. Lincoln, and Robert D. McWilliams, *Industrial Marketing Management*, Vol. 13 (1984), pp. 113–122. Copyright © 1984 by Elsevier Science Publishing Co., Inc.

ARE CORPORATE JETS A WASTE OF COMPANY RESOURCES?

Shareholders as well as employees are beginning to believe that corporate planes (ninety percent of the aircraft industry's market) represent a waste of company profits. But it is doubtful that corporate jets, a status symbol, will disappear. Since 1980, the industry has invested $750 million in research to develop lighter, advanced electronic planes with more efficient engines targeted for the corporate market. Their strategy may work. While companies are reluctant to expand their fleets, they are consolidating them and buying from the top of the line. The industry may be selling fewer planes, but it is selling more at the high end of the market.

Source: See "New Corporate Planes: Fewer but Fancier," *Business Week*, February 18, 1985, p. 102.

Research and Development. Research and development departments are involved in the initial development of products and processes and set broad specifications for component and materials criteria, minimum end-product performance standards, and occasionally, manufacturing techniques. Because these departments have a number of projects in various stages, they are important to marketers for two major reasons. First, the earlier the marketer becomes involved in the development process, the greater the chance of incorporating a product into the final design. Second, by understanding the direction in which customers or prospective customers are moving, marketers are better able to plan the direction of their own business.

General Management. Top management becomes involved in purchasing decisions when the firm is faced with unfamiliar situations not related to day-to-day activities, or when purchasing decisions are likely to have major consequences on the firm's operations. For instance, the purchase of an executive airplane is most likely to be strongly influenced by top management. Such major acquisitions are also likely to be decided at the top with little information requested from lower levels. When top management is directly involved in a purchase, it is also likely to be actively involved in establishing guidelines and criteria for future purchases of similar products.

Purchasing. As you can see in Table 4-4, contrary to widely held beliefs, purchasing is not the most central figure in the purchasing process.[27] In fact, research consistently indicates that purchasing's dominant sphere of influence falls within phases 4, 5, and 6 of the purchasing decision process—when specifications of products to be purchased have been established and suppliers qualified.[28,29]

Because purchasing agents are specialists who have negotiation expertise, knowledge of buying products, and close working relationships with individual suppliers, they are the dominant decision makers and influencers in repetitive buying situations. They also exercise a high level of influence over selected types of purchases when uncertain environmental conditions are present, as when the probability of interrupted supply or shortages is high.[30] How purchasing influences buying decisions is discussed in Chapter Five.

Influence Patterns Vary

It is important to note, however, that functional responsibility and job titles are often not true indicators of the relative influence of buying center members in a purchase decision task. Any one person can assume several or all the roles shown in Table 4-5. Since buyers have differing levels of experience and use different

---

[27]Joseph A. Bellizzi and C. K. Walter, "Purchasing Agent's Influence in the Buying Process," *Industrial Marketing Management* 9 (1980), pp. 143–156.

[28]Ibid.

[29]Corey, *Industrial Marketing*, p. 34.

[30]Speckman and Stern, "Environmental Uncertainty and Buying Group Structure," pp. 54–61.

TABLE 4-4 The Most Central Individual(s) in Each Buying Center for the Purchase of Capital Equipment

Type of Company	Equipment Purchase	Central Figure(s)
Chemical manufacturer	Heat exchanger	Purchasing manager
Industrial safety products manufacturer	Automatic drilling machine	Engineer and vice president of manufacturing
Steel mill furnace manufacturer	Standby oil heating system	Purchasing manager
Steel manufacturer	Coke oven	Purchasing manager
	River tow barge, galvanized steel processor	Vice president of production
Water transportation and construction companies	Locomotive crane	Purchasing manager
Heating equipment manufacturer	Large industrial press	Engineer
Specialty steel manufacturer	Hot piercer mill	Purchasing manager
	Steel plate leveler	Manufacturing engineer
Industrial products distributor	Plasma cutting equipment	Vice president of operations
	Storage shelving	Director of materials
Metal and wire manufacturer	Wrapping machine	Division manager
Aerospace and automotive products manufacturer	Metal working	Divisional purchasing
	Machine tool	Manager
Paper products manufacturer	Banding system	General manager
		Project manager
Steel mill builder	Processing pump	Project manager
Refractory	Forklift trucks	Plant purchasing manager
Pipe fabricator	Presses	Safety engineer, maintenance supervisor
Petroleum products manufacturer	Gasoline storage tank	Buyer
Power plant builder	Nuclear load cell	Job-shop order department manager
Mining equipment manufacturer	Executive office desk	Purchasing agent
Chemicals & scientific instrument distributor	Medical instruments	District vice president of sales
Electrical parts distributor	Recessed lighting	Company vice president
Electrical parts manufacturer	Resistor	General manager and Purchasing manager
Building materials manufacturer	Pump	Engineer
Cement manufacturer	Forklift truck	General manager and vice president

Source: Adapted from Wesley J. Johnston and Thomas Bonoma, "The Buying Center: Structure and Interaction Patterns," *Journal of Marketing*, Summer 1981, p. 143–56. Reprinted by permission of the American Marketing Association.

TABLE 4-5 Buying Center Roles

Primary roles

Deciders. Those organizational members who have formal or informal authority who actually make the buying decision. Identifying deciders, or decision makers, is often the most difficult task. In routine purchases of standard items, the buyer is usually the decider. However, in complex purchasing decisions, the officers of the company are often the deciders. An engineer who designs specifications such that only one vendor can meet them becomes, in effect, an informal decision maker.

Influencers. Those individuals inside or outside the organization who influence the decision process (directly or indirectly) by providing information on criteria for evaluating buying alternatives or by establishing product specifications. Technical people, such as design engineers and quality control inspectors, typically have significant influence in the purchase decision. Individuals outside the buying firm, such as architects who draw up building specifications, may also assume this role.

Secondary roles

Users. Those organizational members who use the products and services. Users may exert from a minor to a very significant degree of influence on the purchasing decision. They may even initiate the purchasing process and play an important role in defining purchase specifications.

Buyers. Buyers are organizational members who have formal authority in the selection of suppliers and in the implementation of procedures involved with purchasing. In complex purchasing, buyers might include high-level officers of the company who may well be the decision makers. Buyers may be involved in developing specifications, but their major role is in selecting suppliers and negotiating purchases within buying constraints.

Gatekeepers. Those organizational members who control the flow of information into the buying center. This can be done by controlling printed information and advertisements, as well as by controlling which salespersons are allowed to speak to individuals within the buying center.

Source: Adapted from Frederick E. Webster, Jr., and Yoram Wind, Organizational Buyer Behavior (Englewood Cliffs, N.J.: Prentice-Hall, Inc., 1972], pp 77–80.

problem-solving approaches in various situations, role influence will vary over the different phases of the purchasing process depending on the purchasing situation, the number of individuals involved, the complexity of the purchase, and functional lines involved.[31]

Identifying the various roles of buying center members across functional lines is important to both marketing managers and sales people in developing the most effective marketing communication strategy. However, it has been estimated that the industrial salesperson typically contacts only one or two persons in a buying organization. One study of industrial buying practices concluded that

> Suppliers have significant misconceptions about who in their customers' companies initiates purchases, selects a supplier "pool" and actually approves the final supplier. The role of middle management in these three functions is underestimated, particularly in regard to initiation and conclusion of a purchase, while the importance of top management and the purchasing department is correspondingly inflated.[32]

[31]Murray Harding, "Who Really Makes the Purchasing Decision?" *Industrial Marketing* 51 (September 1966), p. 76.

[32]Mary R. O'Rourke, James M. Shea, and William M. Solley, "Survey Shows Need for Increased Sales Calls, Advertising and Updated Mailing Lists to Reach Buying Influences," *Industrial Marketing* 58 (April 1973), p. 38.

Gatekeeper's Influence

Understanding the role of the gatekeeper is critical in the development of industrial marketing strategy. Information that flows between a source and its destination is filtered by gatekeepers who, in effect, become decision makers by allowing only information favorable to their opinion to flow to decision makers. By being closest to the action, purchasing managers, or those persons involved in a buying center, may act as gatekeepers and filter information reaching decision makers.[33]

The basic functions of the purchasing department are to negotiate prices and place orders on the best terms in accordance with requisitions and to expedite orders to assure a smooth flow of supplies. Purchasing agents often wish to expand beyond these functions and feel that they have important contributions to make by keeping management informed of developments in materials, sources, and price trends. Therefore, they want to be consulted before requisitions are drawn up, and this tends to enhance and protect their position as gatekeepers.[34]

Because of this, industrial salespersons often take on expanded roles to bypass purchasing agents to ensure that the information gets to those who should receive it.[35] Such expanded roles take the form of gourmet diner, theatergoer, golfer, waterskier, and so on. Sales people find it beneficial to have hobbies that mesh well with those of key decision makers in customer organizations.

Identifying Key Buying Influencers

Because members of buying centers change as an organization moves through the purchasing process, the task of identifying key buying influencers becomes quite complex. Further, research indicates that key influencers are most often located outside the purchasing department. For example, in buying centers for highly technical products, purchasing agents, engineers, scientists, production, and quality control personnel are usually included in the buying center; the engineers and scientists, however, have the greatest level of influence.[36]

Key buying influencers are those persons who are capable of swaying other influencers, either knowingly or unknowingly.[37] For instance, a buying center involved in the purchase of capital equipment may consist of fifteen buying influencers, yet three or four of these influencers are able to influence the others because of their authority, knowledge, information, or gatekeeper status. The ability to identify

---

[33]Thomas V. Bonoma and Gerald Zaltman, "Introduction," in Bonoma and Zaltman, eds., *Organizational Buying Behavior* (Chicago: American Marketing Association, 1978), p. 14.

[34]Mary Ellen Mogee and Alden S. Bean, "The Role of the Purchasing Agent in Industrial Innovation," in Bonoma and Zaltman, eds., *Organizational Buying Behavior*, p. 126.

[35]George Strauss, "Workflow Frictions, Interfunctional Rivalry, and Professionalism: A Case Study of Purchasing Agents," in A. H. Rubenstein and C. Haberstroh, eds., *Some Theories of Organizations* (Homewood, Ill.: Richard D. Irwin, Inc., 1966).

[36]James R. McMillan, "Role Differentiation in Industrial Buying Decisions," *Proceedings of the American Marketing Association* (Chicago: American Marketing Association, 1973), pp. 207–211.

[37]Corey, *Industrial Marketing*, p. 97.

key buying influencers and sell them on product attributes (defined in terms of customer benefits) is vital to good marketing strategy.

A MODEL FOR DETERMINING THE COMPOSITION OF THE ORGANIZATIONAL BUYING CENTER

As we have discussed, the composition and varying influences within a buying center will change, depending on the buying situation and the phase in the purchasing decision process.[38] Mattson has developed a model, shown in Figure 4-2, which assists marketers in analyzing and predicting buying center membership and influence. The variables shown in Figure 4-2 relate to the buying firm's environments, mission, purchase needs, and organizational structure.

Environment and Mission

Environment and mission variables may place constraints on how organizational authority is delegated, or change the level of managerial interest in a particular purchase decision. In industries with strong channel leaders, for instance, a firm may not be allowed flexibility in its choice of transportation carriers. Where no channel leaders exist, transportation decisions may be totally routinized or be made by habit rather than by rational choice of the firm.

Different organizations have different missions that affect the importance of the purchasing decision. For example, automobiles will have a different function in the ability of Hertz to serve its mission than they would to the mission of Bethlehem Steel. The determination of a firm's mission, according to Mattson, is the first step in determining who in the buying organization will be interested in the purchasing decision.

Purchase Needs

Identifying influences and buying center composition depends on the marketer's understanding of the product's potential uses and priorities within the firm. For example, when products are developed to department specifications, that department may also specify the supplier.

Buy Class/Buy Phase

As previously discussed, in the new task buying situation buying center membership tends to be larger than in the modified or straight rebuy situation. Departmental influence also tends to vary with the type of product and the buy phase and, while

---

[38]Melvin R. Mattson, "How to Determine the Composition and Influence of a Buying Center," *Industrial Marketing Management* 17 (1988), pp. 205–214.

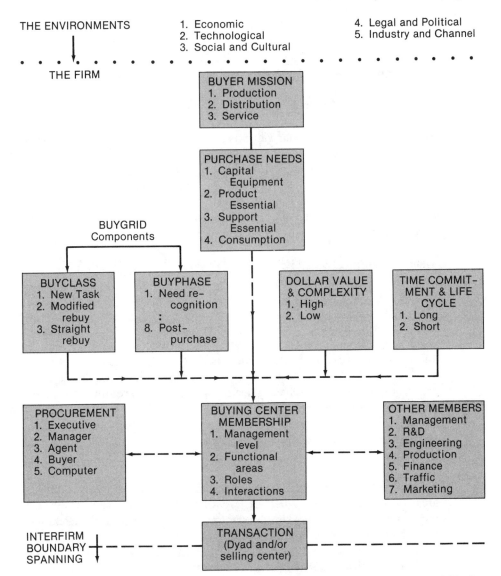

THE ENVIRONMENTS

1. Economic
2. Technological
3. Social and Cultural

4. Legal and Political
5. Industry and Channel

THE FIRM

BUYER MISSION
1. Production
2. Distribution
3. Service

PURCHASE NEEDS
1. Capital
   Equipment
2. Product
   Essential
3. Support
   Essential
4. Consumption

BUYGRID
Components

BUYCLASS
1. New Task
2. Modified
   rebuy
3. Straight
   rebuy

BUYPHASE
1. Need re-
   cognition
   :
8. Post-
   purchase

DOLLAR VALUE
& COMPLEXITY
1. High
2. Low

TIME COMMIT-
MENT & LIFE
CYCLE
1. Long
2. Short

PROCUREMENT
1. Executive
2. Manager
3. Agent
4. Buyer
5. Computer

BUYING CENTER
MEMBERSHIP
1. Management
   level
2. Functional
   areas
3. Roles
4. Interactions

OTHER MEMBERS
1. Management
2. R&D
3. Engineering
4. Production
5. Finance
6. Traffic
7. Marketing

INTERFIRM
BOUNDARY
SPANNING

TRANSACTION
(Dyad and/or
selling center)

FIGURE 4-2 A Model for Determining the Composition of the Organizational Buying Center

Source: Reprinted by permission of the publisher from "How to Determine the Composition and Influence of a Buying Center," by Melvin R. Mattson, *Industrial Marketing Management* 17, (1988), pp. 200–214. Copyright 1988 by Elsevier Science Publishing Co., Inc.

each buy phase may have different buying center members, purchasing is generally represented in each phase. However, it should be remembered that purchasing's influence in the purchasing decision increases as the products and method of purchase become more routine.

Dollar Value and Complexity

Purchasing agents use dollar value as an indication of management involvement in the purchasing decision process and level of criteria to be employed. In very small firms, when the dollar amount is relatively large, purchasing managers generally have little influence. In medium sized firms, purchasing agents have more authority as the relative size of each purchase gets smaller. In large firms, the authority of purchasing managers decreases as purchasing decisions become more compartmentalized and purchasing managers become specialists.

Time Commitment and Life Cycle

Purchasing activities tend to vary with the buying firm's product life cycle. While the buy class suggests that the amount of management involvement decreases as the firm moves from a new task to a straight rebuy, Fox and Rink have found that purchasings' involvement is high during the product decision (introduction stage) and maturity stages of the buying firm's product life cycle.[39]

As time horizons increase, buyers and sellers tend to develop mutually beneficial relationships and purchasing decisions can be made routine; thus, they are delegated to managers lower in the hierarchy.

Buying Center Membership, Procurement, and Other Members

As discussed, buying center involvement can be determined by examining functional areas of influence. The higher the level of managerial interest, however, the lower the influence of purchase. This does not mean that industrial marketers should overlook their importance. Due to their special knowledge, their involvement in asset-management teams, and their negotiating skills, they are highly influential during the interorganizational steps of the purchasing process.

Industrial buying must be viewed as a multidimensional, complex process which is affected by organizational, individual, social, and environmental variables. Therefore, purchasing decisions are frequently team decisions which often overlap among several departments and top management.

---

[39]Harold W. Fox and David R. Rink, "Purchasing's Role Across Life Cycle," *Industrial Marketing Management* 7 (June 1978), pp. 186–192.

OBJECTIVES IN ORGANIZATIONAL BUYING

Before vendors can respond effectively to customer information needs, they must understand the various criteria that customers use in evaluating potential suppliers. Different groups of individuals will view the supplier's offering from their unique perspectives. While industrial buying tends to reflect organizational goals, organization members are influenced by both task and nontask objectives.

Task-oriented objectives involve pragmatic considerations such as price, quality, service, and return on investment. Nontask objectives center on personal factors such as the desire for job security, recognition, promotion, and salary increases. When suppliers' offerings are similar in such factors as product attributes, price, and delivery, buyers have little basis for task-oriented choices. Since they can effectively satisfy organizational goals through several suppliers, buyers often tend to be more influenced by personal factors, or nontask objectives. However, when pronounced differences exist in product/service factors, industrial buyers are more accountable for their choices and tend to place more emphasis on economic factors.[40]

The problem facing the industrial marketer is to define the buying goals of organizational buyers. This task is difficult. Generalizations of organizational buying objectives across industrial buying decisions cannot be made. In fact, research indicates that buying center members often employ different criteria in evaluating suppliers.[41] Purchasing agents, for example, may value price and delivery factors; engineers, product quality; and comptrollers, return on investment. Additionally, the importance placed on such criteria varies with the type of purchase being considered. The challenge, then, is to examine the purchasing decision from the buying firm's point of view, determine the roles of buying center members, and ascertain the task and nontask objectives that motivate key buying influencers. Table 4-6 shows how buying influencers rank the factors that affect their supplier choice decision.

Task-Oriented Objectives

Organizations that are in business to make a profit are predominantly oriented to purchase at the lowest possible price while avoiding compromises on such factors as technical service, product quality, and certainty of delivery. Nonprofit organizations, however, are concerned with budgetary constraints, and buying at the lowest possible price may be necessary to operate within predetermined budgets. Therefore,

[40]Philip Kotler, *Marketing Management: Analysis, Planning and Control*, 5th ed. (Englewood Cliffs, N.J.: Prentice-Hall, 1984), p. 168.

[41]J. Patrick Kelly and James W. Coaker, "Can We Generalize About Choice Criteria for Industrial Purchasing Decisions?" in Kenneth L. Bernhardt, ed., *Marketing: 1976 and Beyond* (Chicago: American Marketing Association, 1976), pp. 33–43.

TABLE 4-6 Ranking of Factors Motivating Buying Influences in Various Departments in Selecting Suppliers of a Standard Industrial Product

Accounting Department
1. Offers volume discounts.
2. Regularly meets quality specifications.
3. Is honest in dealings.
3. Answers all communications promptly.
5. Has competitive prices.
5. Handles product rejections fairly.
5. Provides needed information when requested (such as bids).

Production Control Department
1. Can deliver quickly in an emergency.
2. Ships products when wanted (for example, when move-up and/or push-back deliveries are necessary).
3. Regularly meets quality specifications.
4. Is willing to cooperate in the face of unforeseen difficulties.
4. Is helpful in emergency situations.

Purchasing Department
1. Regularly meets quality specifications.
2. Advises of potential trouble.
2. Is honest in dealings.
2. Provides products during times of shortages.
5. Is willing to cooperate in the face of unforeseen difficulties.
5. Deliveries when promised.
5. Provides needed information when requested (such as bids).
5. Is helpful in emergency situations.

Manufacturing
Engineering Department
1. Delivers when promised.
2. Is honest in dealings.
2. Provides products during times of shortages.
4. Regularly meets quality specifications.
5. Can deliver quickly in an emergency.

Quality Control Department
1. Regularly meets quality specifications.
2. Is honest in dealings.
3. Allows credit for scrap or rework.
3. Provides products during times of shortages.
5. Has a low percentage of rejects.

Special Machinery
Engineering Department
1. Provides products during times of shortages.
2. Regularly meets quality specifications.
3. Has a low percentage of rejects.
4. Delivers when promised.
5. Is honest in dealings.

Tool Design Department
1. Is honest in dealings.
2. Has technical ability and knowledge.
2. Handles product rejections fairly.
2. Allows credit for scrap or rework.
2. Invoices correctly.
2. Provides products during times of shortages.
2. Answers all communications promptly.

*Duplicate numbers indicate ties in rankings. A standard product was defined as having three or more of the following characteristics: (1) low unit cost, (2) little additional information required, (3) few people involved in the purchase, (4) short commitment (one year or less) to the product, and (5) little or no supplier modification of the product needed before use.

Source: Stanley D. Sibley, "How Interfacing Departments Rate Vendors," *National Purchasing Review,* 5 (August–October 1980), p. 11. Reprinted with permission.

economic task objectives that achieve the organizational goals are of significant consideration to the marketer.[42]

Price. Buyers are concerned with the "evaluated price" of a product. Customers do not buy products; they buy value (satisfaction). Therefore, in evaluating price, buyers consider a variety of factors that generate or minimize costs, such as: "What amount of scrap or waste will result from the use of the material?" "What will the cost of processing the material be?" and "How much power will the machine consume?" Quantifiable economic measures of return on investment are also used when purchasing capital equipment. The proposed purchase of a new machine, for example, may be supported by expected increases in productivity or reduced labor costs.

Price, however, cannot be considered in isolation. A supplier who has a reputation for high-quality products and dependable delivery may be awarded a contract even though his prices are higher. The costs of shutting down manufacturing due to faulty equipment or missed deliveries may far outweigh the greater price. Industrial marketers, then, should not overestimate the importance of price; they should also know that low bidders often fail to meet other important criteria of buyers.[43]

Services. Multiple services are required by industrial buyers to achieve organizational goals. Such services include technical assistance, availability of spare parts, repair capability, and training information.

Technical contributions of suppliers are highly valued wherever equipment, materials, or parts are in use. Many firms tend to favor suppliers with reputations for being technical leaders in their fields. The availability of replacement parts is often vital to manufacturers who prefer to make their own repairs. Complex manufacturing and office equipment requires user training to ensure maximum productivity. The marketer who can offer sound technical advice, adequate training, and a ready supply of replacement parts very often has a differential advantage over less capable competitors.

Quality. Organizational customers search for quality levels that are consistent with specifications and the intended use of the product. They are reluctant to pay for extra quality and are unwilling to compromise specifications for a reduced price. The crucial factor is uniformity or consistency in product quality that will guarantee uniformity in end products, reduce costly inspections and testing of incoming shipments, and ensure a smooth blending with the production process. When consistency or uniformity requirements are not met, costly problems are created for the buying firm. Marketers can determine the degree of consistency and uniformity

---

[42]The following discussion is based on Richard M. Hill, Ralph S. Alexander, and James S. Cross, *Industrial Marketing* (Homewood, Ill.: Richard D. Irwin, Inc., 1975), pp. 54–58; and Corey, *Industrial Marketing*, pp. 36–37.

[43]Kelly and Coaker, "Can We Generalize About Choice Criteria," pp. 330–333.

needed by, and the tolerance levels acceptable to, a customer firm only through close communications and coordination with that firm.

Assurance of Supply.   Interruptions in the flow of parts and materials can cause a shutdown of the production process, resulting in costly delays and lost sales. Physical distribution services rank second to product quality in influencing the purchasing decision.[44] To guard against interruptions in supply, which can be caused by a number of factors (e.g., strikes, accidents, fires, or natural catastrophes), purchasing agents are reluctant to rely on a single source of supply. Instead, they often choose to spread their buying over two or more suppliers whenever possible. When buyers split their purchases between suppliers, one of them, the preferred supplier, often gets the lion's share of the order quantities. The marketer should understand the policies that customers follow in seeking continuity of supply and develop marketing strategy around them.

Reciprocity.   Giving consideration to selecting suppliers because of their value as customers is known as "reciprocity." "The objective of reciprocity is, in theory at least, for the buyer and seller to reach an agreement on an exchange of business that is mutually beneficial" and has become an important part of the trade relations responsibility of purchasing and materials management.[45] Large-volume purchasing and the need for specialty suppliers (brought about by intensified national and foreign competition and increased product differentiation) leads to close relationships at the executive level that foster awareness of mutual dependence for achieving increased profits.[46] Reciprocity is legal if it is not enforced through coercive power or if a reciprocal agreement does not substantially lessen competition. Because of the increasing shortages in raw materials and the soaring costs of production inputs, purchasing managers may initiate reciprocal arrangements to "meet their firms' basic purchasing needs."[47]

Nontask Objectives

People join organizations to accomplish personal objectives such as greater status, promotions, salary increases, increased job security,[48] and social interaction.[49] In the

---

[44]William D. Perreault, Jr., and Frederick A. Russ, "Physical Distribution Services in Industrial Purchasing Decisions," *Journal of Marketing* 40 (April 1976), pp. 3–10.

[45]Lamar Lee, Jr., and Donald W. Dobler, *Purchasing and Materials Management* (New York: McGraw-Hill Book Company, 1971), pp. 90–91.

[46]Ibid.

[47]Gregory D. Upah and Monroe M. Bird, "Changes in Industrial Buying: Implications for Industrial Marketers," *Industrial Marketing Management* 9 (1980), pp. 117–121.

[48]See Delbert J. Duncan, "Purchasing Agents: Seekers of Status, Personal and Professional," *Journal of Purchasing.* 2 (August 1966), pp. 17–26; and George Strauss, "Tactics of Lateral Relationships: The Purchasing Agent," *Administrative Science Quarterly* 7 (September 1962), pp. 161–186.

[49]Thomas V. Bonoma and Wesley J. Johnston, "The Social Psychology of Industrial Buying and Selling," *Industrial Marketing Management* 17 (1978), pp. 213–234.

sphere of industrial marketing, it has been found that major factors that influence the purchasing decision are social considerations, such as friendship, reputation, and mutually beneficial interactions.[50]

Organizations work best when people accomplish personal and organizational objectives simultaneously. A buyer can take pride, a personal objective, in making a correct buying decision that also accomplishes an organizational objective. In this instance, a single action accomplishes two different objectives. To avoid an incomplete picture of organizational buying, vendors need to keep both sets of objectives in mind. Marketers can open doors to future business by simply remembering to send a letter of appreciation and praise to a buyer or even a buyer's supervisor. At the same time, caution must be exercised to avoid overemphasizing the buyer's personal goals at the expense of the organization's objectives.

PRODUCT ANALYSIS FOR IDENTIFYING INFORMATION NEEDS OF KEY INFLUENCERS

A product is a bundle of promises to perform, and any one promise may be highly significant to certain individuals and only incidental to others. Product characteristics are viewed by influencers in accordance with how well those characteristics assist in meeting task objectives and the impacts they have on different functional areas. Equally important is the translation of product characteristics into need satisfactions, or customer benefits. As stated in the classic example, "customers don't want quarter-inch drill bits, they want quarter-inch holes." Marketers must understand what need satisfactions are important to those who influence buying. When information needs vary, no single sales presentation can be targeted simultaneously to the purchasing agent, the engineer, and the vice president of manufacturing.

Product analysis consists of developing a list of criteria considered relevant to the needs of the target market, assigning weights to each of those criteria, and developing a rating scale to determine whether the product under consideration has a high or low probability of success in the marketplace. Lists of product criteria that specifically relate to functional areas of customer firms can also be developed. By questioning purchasing agents and other influencers within customer firms, and by exercising judgment based on past experience, weights can be assigned to the importance of criteria for various functional areas.

Where weights are comparatively high, effective communication strategy must be developed to reach key influencers involved with those functional areas. For instance, in Table 4-7, the product analysis matrix for a new computer installation pinpoints the relevant information needs of key functional influencers. Information most important to management involves knowledge of the supplier's technical competency (.4) and personnel training ability (.5). Purchasing, on the other hand, is

---

[50]Ibid.

TABLE 4-7 Product Analysis for a New Computer Installation

Product Information Needs	Functional Influencers				
	Marketing	Engineering	Management	Comptroller	Purchasing
Technical competency	.2	.2	.4		
Expansion capability	.1	.2	.1	.1	.4
Installation		.1			.1
Credit terms				.2	
Personnel training	.3	.3	.5		.1
Programs	.4	.2			
Investment payback period				.7	
Maintenance service					.4
	1.0	1.0	1.0	1.0	1.0

more concerned with expansion capabilities (.4) and maintenance service (.4) than with installation (.1) and training (.1). Comptrollers are vitally interested in the investment payback period (.7). Marketing communication strategy must be developed to address these concerns of the various functional people and emphasis should correlate with the levels of importance the different people assign to their information needs.

LOOKING BACK

Insight into how industrial organizations purchase goods and services enables the industrial marketer to reach the right influencers with information that satisfies their various needs. Industrial purchasing is a problem-solving process that evolves in sequential steps. The level of a firm's experience with purchasing problems is the key to how the marketer should define the buying situation. Discussion in this chapter has pointed out that each purchasing situation—new task, modified, or straight rebuy—requires a different type of response from the industrial marketer.

In developing marketing strategy, industrial marketers must be aware of the concept of "creeping commitment" and recognize that some phases in the purchasing process are more critical than others. Influencers involved in these phases tend to have more power in affecting the final choice. Marketing efforts must, therefore, be concentrated at these critical phases, and marketers must be continually on the search for *who* is making *what decisions* based on *which criteria*.

Marketing strategy is influenced by the number and background of influencers in the buying center who may cut across functional lines and assume several different roles during the purchasing decision process. Task as well as nontask objectives of buying influencers should also be considered. As buying influencers move through the purchasing decision process, they have information needs that must be met if they are to evaluate alternatives and make the best supplier selection. Such information needs are product and service related and should be viewed with regard to the firm's task objectives and the product's impact upon functional areas. Since various influencers will evaluate product characteristics from their individual perspectives, product analysis can and should be used to identify the major interests of key influencers and their respective information needs.

QUESTIONS FOR DISCUSSION

1. In which phases of the purchasing process will upper management most likely be involved? At what stage should the marketer attempt to become involved? What types of action should be taken?

2. As an "out" supplier, would it be possible to penetrate a firm by offering (a) very attractive prices or (b) substantial improvements in production efficiencies?

3. Industrial marketers rarely call upon their counterparts in the buying firm. What advantages might accrue to the seller if a relationship were to be established in this area?

4. Consider the scenario wherein a young, insecure buyer is clearly acting as an information gatekeeper. The order cannot be won unless important information reaches the decision makers, but unfortunately, the buyer will not pass along the information and cannot be bypassed without his knowledge and subsequent wrath. How can a creative salesperson turn this potentially disastrous situation into a clear-cut advantage?

5. Functional areas are generally perceived to have varying amounts of influence across both the purchase situation and purchase phases. In a new task purchasing situation, some authorities believe that engineering will have the most influence, and in modified or straight rebuy situations, purchasing. Discuss how this could be so.

6. Analyze the medium-sized (several hundred employees) manufacturing firm in the process of purchasing, for the first time, an expensive, multipurpose computer system to be used by various functional departments. List the individuals and name the one or more roles they will play in this buying situation.

7. What would your reaction be if advised that social and psychological persuasion played no part in the industrial buying process? How would you prefer to differentiate consumer and industrial buying motives?

8. One authority has concluded that the type of buying situation a firm is facing is not as important in the buying decision process as are other factors such as the product under consideration and the market/economic environment. Do you agree?

SUGGESTED ADDITIONAL READINGS

ANDERSON, ERIC, WUJIN CHU, and BARTON WEITZ, "Industrial Purchasing: An Empirical Exploration of the Buyclass Framework," *Journal of Marketing* 51 (July 1987):71–85.

BELLIZZI, JOSEPH A., and PHILLIP MCVEY, "How Valid Is the Buy-Grid Model?" *Industrial Marketing Management*, 12 (1983):57–62.

BELLIZZI, JOSEPH A., and C. K. WALTER, "Purchasing Agent's Influence in the Buying Process," *Industrial Marketing Management*, 9 (1980):143–156.

DOYLE, PETER, ARCH G. GOODSIDE, and PAUL MICHELL, "Organizations Buying in the New Task and Rebuy Situations," *Industrial Marketing Management*, 8 (1979):7–11.

LAMBERT, DORNOFF, and KERNAN, "The Industrial Buyer and the Postchoice Evaluation Process," *Journal of Marketing Research*, 19 (May 1977):246–251.

MATTSON, MELVIN R., "How to Determine the Composition and Influence of a Buying Center," *Industrial Marketing Management* 17 (1988):205–214.

SHETH, JAGDISH N., WILLIAMS, and HILL, "Government and Business Purchasing: How Similar Are They?" *Journal of Purchasing and Materials Management* (Winter 1983):7–13.

VAN DER MOST, G., "Purchasing Process: Researching Influencers Is Basic to Marketing Planning," *Industrial Marketing* (October 1976):120.

VON HIPPEL, ERIC, "Successful Industrial Products from Customer Ideas," *Journal of Industrial Marketing*, 42 (January 1978):39–49.

CHAPTER 5

The Interpersonal Dynamics of Industrial Buying Behavior

Organizational buying behavior is ultimately influenced by forces within the organization as well as environmental forces. The status and operating procedures of purchasing, the degree of involvement and interaction of various groups and group members, and their different perceptions, have a significant impact on purchasing decisions. Knowledge of these forces is an essential ingredient in the development of effective industrial marketing strategy. The purpose of this chapter, then, is to discuss

1. How purchasing activities within the organizational structure influence buying behavior.
2. The factors influencing the size and interaction of buying centers.
3. How groups and individuals differ in their approach to buying.
4. How organizational buyers choose and evaluate suppliers.

Effective and responsive industrial marketing strategy rests on the industrial marketer's knowledge of how organizational buying behavior is affected by forces within the organization. Seldom does an organizational buyer make a decision in isolation. Purchasing decisions are influenced by organizational, group, and individual forces, as well as forces within the external environment.[1] The position of purchasing and its status within the organization has a significant influence on industrial buying behavior. Purchases are also affected by a complex set of decisions made by the several individuals in buying centers—individuals with different levels of information and expertise and different backgrounds, who interact at different stages of the purchasing decision process. For marketing strategy to be successful, the industrial marketer must have a clear understanding of how organizational groups interact, the amount of influence the various group members may possess, and how this influence varies throughout the purchasing decision process.[2]

Environmental forces that influence buyers as well as sellers were discussed in Chapter Three. In Chapter Four we discussed how purchasing activities depend on the type of buying situation a firm is facing and where it is in the decision-making process. We also discussed the role of purchasing and other buying influencers and the criteria they apply in making purchasing decisions. The purpose of this chapter is to examine the influence of purchasing activities on organizational buyer behavior and how groups and individuals differ in their approach to buying decisions.

PURCHASING'S INFLUENCE ON BUYER BEHAVIOR

International material shortages, skyrocketing costs of materials and energy, fluctuating nationalistic moods, conflicting social goals, profit squeezes, and greater government regulation of business during the mid–1970s brought about a recognition of the importance of the purchasing function. Contributing to this recognition and the growing status of purchasing is the realization that efficient and effective purchasing, through the use of material requirements planning and just-in-time inventory control systems, is a key factor in maintaining profits and alleviating cash flow problems. The average industrial firm spends approximately 60% of its sales dollars on materials, services, and capital equipment.[3] Purchasing is now being viewed as "asset-management through asset-utilization and inventory control."[4] Today, purchasing managers regularly attend meetings with other major functional depart-

---

[1]Frederick E. Webster, Jr., and Yoram Wind, *Organizational Buying Behavior* (Englewood Cliffs, N.J.: Prentice-Hall, Inc., 1972), pp. 26–37.

[2]Earl Naumann, Douglas J. Lincoln, and Robert D. McWilliams, "The Purchase of Components: Functional Areas of Influence," *Industrial Marketing Management* 13 (1984), pp. 113–122.

[3]Robert F. Reck and Brian G. Long, "Purchasing: A Competitive Weapon," *Journal of Purchasing and Materials Management* (Fall 1988), pp. 2–8.

[4]See Gregory D. Upah and Monroe M. Bird, "Changes in Industrial Buying: Implications for Industrial Marketers," *Industrial Marketing Management* 9 (1980), pp. 117–121; Gary J. Zenz, *Purchasing and the Management of Materials*, 5th ed. (New York: John Wiley & Sons, Inc., 1981), pp. 6–7; and Wolfgang U. Mayer, "Situational Variables and Industrial Buying," *Journal of Purchasing and Materials Management* (Winter 1983), pp. 21–26.

ments of the firm. A typical asset management team includes procurement specialists, cost/price analysts, and engineers.[5]

Material Requirements Planning

One major change in the purchasing function is the use of *material requirements planning (MRP)*. Under MRP a firm estimates its future sales, schedules production accordingly, and then orders parts and materials to coordinate with production schedules so that inventories will not become too large or too small. MRP is conceptually simple, but in practice it can require diverse considerations. An input part, for example, may be used at more than one stage in a production process that takes place over a period of time. Thus, multiple deliveries may be necessary to minimize inventory costs and existing inventories continuously monitored to accommodate for inaccuracies in sales forecasts and subsequent production.

To utilize MRP, a growing number of firms are combining the functions of purchasing, transportation, inventory control, receiving, and, in some instances, production control under one functional area referred to as *materials management*. For example, to improve its accuracy of inventory records and achieve its objective of a 15 percent annual growth, Tennant Company reorganized the functions of purchasing, production planning, and material planning into one 33-member unit. One of the advantages of Tennant's reorganization, shown in Figure 5-1, is that procurement specialists have more time to negotiate with vendors, to work on cost-reduction plans, and to consult with engineers on prototype products.[6]

To keep track of orders and the various supply sources available, many organizations have also begun using computers, some of which are directly linked to suppliers. Since irregular deliveries and defective parts furnished by suppliers can require numerous adjustments in a producer's MRP scheduling, these computerized systems are used to find and eliminate weak suppliers.[7]

In general, the effectiveness of MRP depends on the buyer notifying the supplier of material needs in advance of production schedules. Since irregular deliveries and defective parts furnished by suppliers can require numerous adjustments in a producer's MRP scheduling, suppliers who sell to organizations using MRP must work closely with customer firms to ensure that MRP systems are effective. The resultant benefits of MRP to both the supplier and customer, however, are con-

---

[5]Naumann, Lincoln, and McWilliams, "The Purchase of Components: Functional Areas of Design," pp. 113–122.

[6]Margaret Nelson, "MRP War-Gaming via Market Simulation," *Business Marketing* (September 1984), pp 20–22.

[7]See John C. Fisk, "MRP: A Tool for Product and Sales Management," *Industrial Marketing Management* 7 (1978), pp. 32–36; and Joseph R. Biggs, Donald C. Bopp, Jr., and William M. Campion, "Material Requirements Planning and Purchasing: A Case Study," *Journal of Purchasing and Materials Management*, Spring 1984, pp. 15–22.

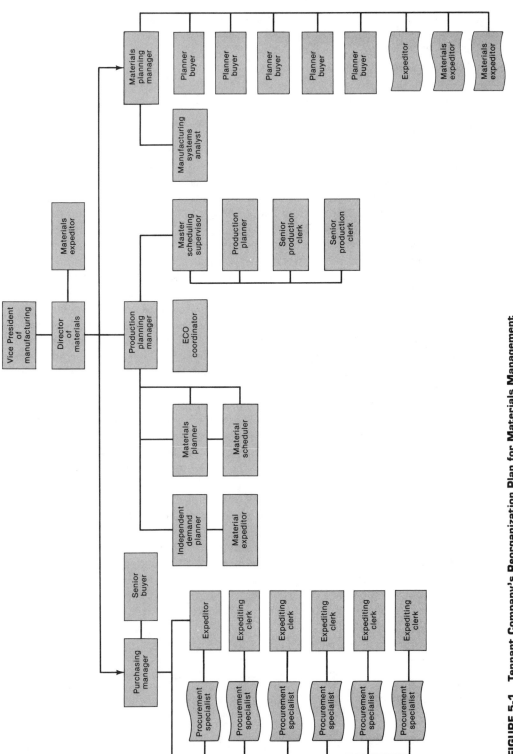

FIGURE 5-1 Tennant Company's Reorganization Plan for Materials Management

Source: "MRP War Gaming via Market Simulation," Business Marketing, (September 1984), pp. 20–22. Reprinted with permission.

trolled inventory levels, better management of production costs, timely deliveries, and an overall increase in efficiency and effectiveness of operations.[8]

Just-in-Time Purchasing

During the last decade, a new form of exchange has developed between suppliers of component parts and materials and OEMs. Rather than using multiple sourcing, many OEMs are using just-in-time (JIT). Just-in-time is an inventory control system which enables a manufacturer to maintain minimum inventory levels by relying on only one supplier to deliver frequent shipments (sometimes daily) just in time for assembly into final products.

One objective of JIT is to develop long-term, one-supplier relationships to reduce the risk of interrupted material flows. An advantage of such a relationship is the resultant improved quality of items supplied, referred to as "zero-defect quality levels." For instance, AMP, a manufacturer of connectors, has embarked on a program to upgrade the quality of incoming parts and materials. Through its Vendor Quality Awareness Program, AMP suppliers receive monthly reports on product quality and delivery performance.[9]

The use of JIT necessitates that the supplier deliver the ordered product at the precise time in the precise quality. It also requires the integration of the buyer-seller's materials management, engineering, purchasing, production, and marketing systems to promote the efficient flow of parts and materials.[10] Under JIT, then, cost factors are less dominant and material specifications are more flexible. This does not imply a lack of concern for costs or quality. Rather, it creates an atmosphere

---

JUST-IN-TIME PURCHASING CHANGES THE BUYER'S ROLE

Buyers have always done a certain amount of "missionary" work before placing their orders to get suppliers to adjust to their quality, delivery, and service needs. But JIT requires more than just getting suppliers to adjust. Now buyers have to explain the advantages of JIT, long-term contracts, stable relationships, and the potential to shave peak plant capacity. Buyers aren't just adjusting anymore, they're selling too.

Source: See Richard J. Schonberger and James P. Gilbert, "Just-in-Time Purchasing: A Challenge for U.S. Industry," *California Management Review* 26 (Fall 1983), pp. 54–68.

---

[8]See Zenz, *Purchasing and the Management of Materials*, pp. 4–5; Upah and Bird, "Changes in Industrial Buying: Implications for Industrial Marketers," pp. 117–21.

[9]"AMP Buyers Aim for Defect-Free Material," *Purchasing* (March 14, 1985), pp. 68A3, 68A5.

[10]Gary L. Fraizer, Robert E. Spekman, and Charles R. O'Neal, "Just-In-Time Exchange Relationships in Industrial Markets," *Journal of Marketing* 52 (October 1988), pp. 52–67.

which both buyer and seller contribute toward optimal cost/benefit trade-offs, with cost and performance each receiving full consideration.[11]

Centralized Purchasing

In addition to MRP and JIT, there is a growing tendency toward centralization of purchasing. Important differences in buying behavior occur between centralized and decentralized purchasing functions.[12] When purchasing is centralized, purchasing specialists concentrate their attention on selected items, developing extensive knowledge of supply and demand conditions. Thus, they are more familiar with cost factors that affect the supplying industry and understand well how vendors within the industry operate. This specialized knowledge, when combined with the volume buying that centralized purchasing controls, increases the firm's buying strength and its supplier options.

Centralized purchasers also tend to place different priorities on selected buying criteria. In comparison to local units where the emphasis is more on short-term cost efficiency and profit considerations, centralized units place more emphasis on long-term supply availability and supplier relationships. Further, influencers outside the purchasing unit appear to have more influence on purchasing decisions at the local level. Engineers and other technical personnel are inclined to be overly specific in their preferences regarding materials, component parts, and sources of supply. Less

---

HOW GENERAL FOODS BARGAINS FOR BETTER BUYS

Negotiation often hinges on the search for alternatives. Here are three examples of how GF buying pros go about it:

- In today's world of declining oil prices, says vice president Korn, material manager Ed Plucenik uses that decline to negotiate favorable natural gas prices.
- When purchasing director Ted Schultz saw a price increase coming on a chemical where GF didn't have much buying clout, he got the technical people to OK a switch to another chemical where purchasing had more leverage.
- Although meat by-products are not traded on an exchange and can't be bought as futures, Bruce Burnham occasionally covers his meat by-product position by buying soybean meal futures. "They're both high-protein supplements," Burnham explains, "so the price of meat and bone meal tends to follow the price of soybean meal even though it doesn't parallel it exactly."

Source: Reprinted from *Purchasing* magazine, "Fast-Track Purchasing at General Foods," by Somerby Dowst, *Purchasing* [July 22, 1982], pp. 44–50. Copyright © at Cahners Publishing Company, 1982.

---

[11]Joseph Bohn, "Suppliers Must Change," *Business Marketing* (August 1983), pp. 10–30.

[12]See Raymond Corey, *The Organizational Context of Industrial Buying Behavior* (Cambridge, Mass.: Marketing Science Institute, 1978), pp. 6–12.

specialized, nontechnical local purchasing agents often lack the expertise and self-perceived status to challenge these preferences.[13]

Buyer Technology

The advent of computers has significantly improved the function of purchasing. Typical computer applications in purchasing include calculating economic order quantities, determining optimal lead times, tracking critical delivery schedules, and monitoring supplier performance indices. In fact, computers have been the primary factor in the implementation of MRP. (See Table 5-1.)[14]

While many significant advancements in computer applications of purchasing decisions remain for the future, computer systems are already employed in highly repetitive buying due to their ability to handle such tasks faster, cheaper, and more accurately than buyers. Although totally computerized handling of new task buying situations is unlikely in the near future, computerized data analysis allows purchasing managers more time to evaluate and negotiate with potential suppliers.[15]

Marketing Implications

MRP, JIT, and centralized purchasing have a definite impact on industrial marketing programs. To remain compatible with the growing professionalism of purchasing managers who are more technical and financially oriented in their approach to buying, marketers must keep up to date with industrial purchasing practices. Buyers are not only becoming more professional, but, in many cases, the scope of their responsibility has broadened considerably. Sales people must possess the tools necessary to respond properly to their needs and be able to provide information on a broad range of functions and buying criteria.

Marketing to these firms will be even more difficult for out suppliers because

**TABLE 5-1 How Purchasing Uses Its Computers
[% of computerized departments]**

We have an on-line decision support system.	37.2%
We do on-line purchase order processing.	56.5
We do batch processing of purchase orders.	56.5
We use computers for preparing status reports.	65.6
We use computers for special off-line problem-solving applications.	31.5

Source: Reprinted from *Purchasing* magazine, "Computers Begin to Take off in Purchasing Departments," [April 25, 1985]. Copyright © Cahners Publishing Company, 1985.

[13]Ibid., p. 13.

[14]Zenz, *Purchasing and the Management of Materials*, p. 372.

[15]David T. Wilson and H. Lee Mathews, "Impact of Management Information Systems Upon Purchasing," *Journal of Purchasing* 7 (February 1971), pp. 48–56.

MEETING THE MRP CHALLENGE WITH MRP II

With the advent of new software tools, marketers' detachment and their occasional hostility to manufacturing is changing fast. That's because the new technologies— once marketers learn the ropes—can be used to make companies become marketing-driven, rather than manufacturing-oriented.

In recent years, with the increasing computerization of production scheduling and inventory control, the information networks of manufacturing databases have begun to extend into marketing offices. These systems are described as 'Integrated' manufacturing systems and include formerly independent departmental databases. It's no easy task, but the ultimate goal of the integrated database is to get the entire business enterprise operating as a team.

Now this is happening, thanks to a relatively new, yet controversial, system catching on fast in companies across the country called Manufacturing Resource Planning [MRP II].

Source: John Couretas, "The Challenge to Marketing of Integrated Manufacturing Databases," *Business Marketing* [March 1985], pp. 10, 51. Reprinted with permission.

---

of the close buyer-seller relationships that develop through MRP and JIT. In suppliers, to serve their customers better, will eventually find it necessary to link (by computer) directly with the customer. The utilization of computer systems for MRP and JIT will also necessitate that suppliers constantly monitor product quality and delivery capability.

BUYING CENTER INVOLVEMENT AND INTERACTION PATTERNS

The industrial purchase decision is an outcome of the interactions that take place between the various members of the buying center. Except for very small firms and most routine purchases, rarely will one person be responsible for the purchasing decision. Multiple buying influencers and group forces play critical roles in organizational buying. Industrial marketers must not only address the question of who participates in the decision process, they must also "understand the involvement and interaction of organizational members, . . . the leadership pattern, and the formal and informal network of communications among the center's members."[16]

Many models have been developed in attempting to explain organizational buying behavior.[17] The use of buyer-behavior models gives those who wish to under-

---

[16]Wesley J. Johnston and Thomas V. Bonoma, "The Buying Center: Structure and Interaction Patterns," *Journal of Marketing* 45 (Summer 1981), pp. 143–156.

[17]See Jagdish N. Sheth, "Research in Industrial Buying Behavior—Today's Needs, Tomorrow's Seeds," *Marketing News* 13 (April 4, 1980), p. 14; and Robert W. Haas, *Industrial Marketing Magazine*, 2nd ed. (Boston: Kent Publishing Co., 1982), pp. 77–84.

stand and affect industrial buying behavior a common and useful starting point. One of the most intuitively appealing of these models is the Sheth model of industrial buyer behavior. Although not all of its many considerations have yet been empirically substantiated, it offers us insight into the factors that appear to influence organizational buying behavior within the organization.

The Sheth model, shown in Figure 5-2, focuses on the complex relationships involved with joint decision making. While the model appears complicated, it is quite useful for examining organizational buying behavior from the perspective of [18] (1) the conditions that precipitate joint decision making, (2) the psychological world of the individuals involved, and (3) the inevitable conflict among those involved in the decision process and resolution of this conflict.

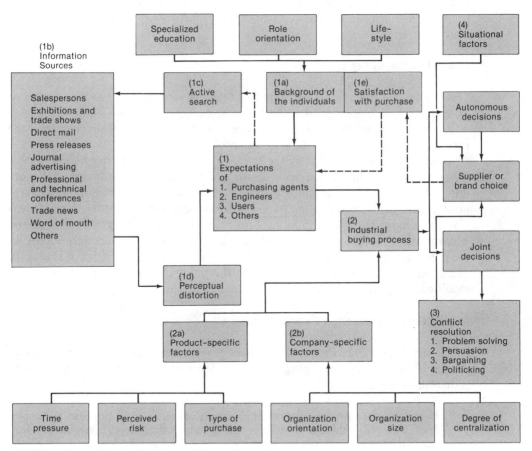

FIGURE 5-2 A Model of Industrial Buyer Behavior

Source: Jadish N. Sheth, "A Model of Industrial Buyer Behavior," *Journal of Marketing* 37 [October 1973], pp. 50–56. Reprinted with permission of the American Marketing Association.

[18]The following discussion is based mostly on Jagdish N. Sheth, "A Model of Industrial Buyer Behavior," *Journal of Marketing* 37 (October 1973), pp. 50–56.

JOINT DECISION MAKING

While methods of reaching buying decisions differ widely, even within the same firm, there appear to be underlying patterns of organizational structure and behavior that establish similarities for analyzing organizational decision making. Whereas recent evidence indicates that when supplier loyalty is high, modified or straight rebuy purchasing decisions are frequently made by individuals within the firm. Studies have shown that the number of organizational members involved in a buying decision depends on (1) the characteristics of the firm (e.g., organization orientation and size), (2) the type of purchasing situation (e.g., routine versus new task), (3) the perceived importance of the product (e.g., risk involved), and (4) the available resources for handling the purchase (e.g., degree of centralization).[19] Sheth refers to these areas in his model as company-specific factors (1, 4) and product-specific factors (2, 3).

Characteristics of the Firm

Findings from a recent study indicate that two characteristics of the firm appear to have a strong influence on the number of influencers involved in the purchasing decision: the size of the firm as determined by the number of employees and the firm's orientation (e.g., profit versus nonprofit).[20]

Table 5-2 indicates that as the size of the firm increases, the number of influencers involved in the purchase decision increases. It also indicates that more influencers are involved when the organization is a nonprofit institution or governmental agency. Two variables may account for these findings. First, functional areas tend to be more specialized in larger firms. Second, nonprofit, governmental, and educational organizations, because of their high visibility, are more accountable to the public sector. Thus, more individuals may be involved as a matter of safeguard and cross-check. It also indicates that as the purchasing situation moves from a modified rebuy to a new task, more influencers are involved.

Buying Center Interaction Patterns

One in-depth study into the social dynamics of the buying center has concluded that the size of the buying center and the amount of interaction between those involved is dependent upon

1. **Vertical involvement**—the number of organizational levels in the hierarchy (from production people up through the board of directors) exerting influence and communicating within the buying center.

---

[19]W. E. Patton III, Christopher P. Puto, and Ronald H. King, "Which Buying Decisions Are Made By Individuals and Not By Groups?" *Industrial Marketing Management* 15 (1986), pp. 129–138.

[20]Lowell F. Crow and Jay D. Lindquist, "Impact of Organizational and Buyer Characteristics on the Buying Center," *Industrial Marketing Management* 14 (1985), pp. 49–58.

TABLE 5-2 The Average Number of Persons Influencing the Decision in a Modified Rebuy and New Task Purchasing Decision versus the Firm's Characteristics

Characteristics	Average Number of Persons Influencing Decisions	
	Modified Rebuy	*New Task*
Number of Employees		
Less than 100	1.82	1.96
100–250	1.97	2.10
251–500	1.58	2.00
501–1000	1.85	2.63
1001–1500	3.16	2.75
Over 1500	2.60	2.81
Significance level	.0001	.165
Function of the Firm		
Manufacturing	1.90	2.20
Service for profit	1.86	2.40
Nonprofit, government, education	2.58	2.70
Significance level	.005	165

Source: Lowell E. Crow and Jay D. Lindquist, "Impact of Organizational and Buyer Characteristics in the Buying Center," *Industrial Marketing Management* 14 [1985], pp. 49–58. Used with permission.

2. **Lateral involvement**—the number of departments, divisions, or functional areas that become involved in the purchase decision.
3. **Extensivity**—the total number of individuals involved in the communication network of the buying center.
4. **Connectedness**—the degree to which buying center members directly communicate with one another regarding the purchase.[21]

Purchase Situation Influence.   As Table 5-3 shows, the greater the importance and complexity of the purchase situation, the greater the vertical involvement, the lateral involvement, and the extensivity. Thus, greater numbers of people are involved in the buying center, and they come from other divisions and departments as well as from other levels in the hierarchy.

Organizational Influence.   The more complex the organization, as evidenced by more written communications, the greater the lateral involvement and extensivity

[21]Johnston and Bonoma, "The Buying Center: Structure and Interaction Patterns," pp. 143–156.

TABLE 5-3 Positive Relationships Between Situational/Organizational and Buying Center/Interaction Variables

	Organizational Structural Variables		Purchase Situation Attributes			
	Formalization [increased written communication]	Centralization [control of purchasing]	Importance	Complexity [long time frame]	Novelty [from rebuy to modified rebuy]	Capital Good versus Service
Vertical involvement			+	+		+
Lateral involvement	+		+	+	+	
Extensivity	+		+	+		+
Connectedness		+				

Source: Adapted from Wesley J. Johnston and Thomas V. Bonoma, "The Buying Center: Structure and Interaction Patterns," *Journal of Marketing* 45 [Summer 1981], pp. 143–56. Reprinted with permission of the American Marketing Association.

and the lesser the connectedness. As more written communications are required by a buying organization, more people are called on to help in the buying decision. However, since many of the communications take on a written form (such as purchase orders), there is less face-to-face communication. On the other hand, when sign-off power for purchasing decisions is concentrated at corporate headquarters, as is often the case in formal organizational structures, the degree of connectedness between buying center members tends to be high. This is due to the amount of interaction that must take place to see that everything is in order before the decision can be moved upward.

Marketing Implications

The foregoing studies give the marketer important insights for determining the size and interaction of buying center members. Two variables that impact upon buying center size are the firm's characteristics and the type of purchasing situation the firm is in, neither of which is difficult to determine. Secondary data are available for determining organizational size and orientation, and sales people are quite adept at discovering the type of purchasing task customer firms are facing.

Insight into the degree of vertical and lateral involvement, extensivity, and connectedness and how they are affected by both the purchasing situation and organizational structure is quite useful for developing a proactive communication strategy. Marketers who anticipate that various hierarchical levels will be involved in complex purchasing decisions can structure a sales force that embodies individuals who can relate to various hierarchical levels.

The greater the degree of lateral involvement, the greater the potential for diversity of viewpoints in the buying organization. Thus, the potential to influence the buying organization lies in communicating with different functional areas within the firm. As lateral involvement increases, the more important it is to have a broadly trained sales force with access to the expertise of the different functional specialists within their firm.

Extensivity and connectedness affect the buyer's ability to process information. When the various people involved in a purchasing decision communicate directly, information is processed quickly and relatively accurately. However, in those purchasing situations that are important and complex, it should be recognized that the buying center will be larger and less connected.

When there are several divisions in the buying firm and the purchasing department is centralized, it should be recognized that face-to-face communications in the buying center will tend to decrease. When a high degree of centralization exists, it may only be necessary to persuade the purchasing manager of the vendor's capabilities. When the purchasing manager's control is low, marketers will find it necessary to influence other members of the buying center, each with a unique perspective of the purchasing problem.

PSYCHOLOGICAL FACTORS INFLUENCING INDIVIDUAL DECISION MAKING

Knowledge of the similarities and differences in the psychological worlds of individuals involved in the buying center and how their behavior can affect the purchase decision is critical in directing the firm's communication strategy. It is not unusual to find purchasing, engineering, manufacturing, and marketing personnel involved both individually and jointly at various phases in the purchasing decision process, particularly in a modified or new task purchasing situation. Due to the differences in their psychological makeups, expectations regarding the potential of alternative suppliers to satisfy a number of different purchasing criteria will substantially differ in any given purchasing task. Two significant factors, as indicated in Sheth's model, appear to account for these differences: role orientation and information exposure.[22]

Differences in Role Orientation

Because of their different areas of functional responsibility, each individual has a different perception of his or her role in the decision process. Thus, they tend to view the importance of the various buying criteria differently. Purchasing agents, for instance, look for price advantage and economy in shipping; engineers look for quality and pretesting.

Due to the fact that organizations typically reward individuals for achieving their respective departmental goals, they will also have experienced different levels of satisfaction with past suppliers. Purchasing agents, for example, are rewarded for economic achievement and engineers for product performance. The result is that the respective objectives and reward criteria of individuals may conflict when applied to a supplier choice decision.

Differences in Information Exposure

Expectations and, thus, objectives are further influenced by the type and source of information exposure. Purchasing agents, because of their position within the organization, are not only exposed to greater amounts of commercial sources of information, but are normally delegated the task of actively searching for information. Personnel in engineering and production, however, typically have a disproportionately smaller amount of information. What information is obtained is often gathered primarily through trade reports, professional meetings, and word of mouth.

Due, perhaps, to individual educational pursuits and life-styles, information is also subject to the individual's cognitive process of selective distortion and retention: the tendency to sytematically select, change, and retain information so that it

---

[22]Sheth, "A Model of Industrial Buyer Behavior," pp. 50–56.

conforms to prior knowledge, expectations, or needs. Therefore, given the different goals and values of these individuals, the same information will be interpreted differently, leading to further differences in expectations and objectives.

Perceived Risk in the Vendor Selection Process

Industrial purchasing decisions often involve an element of functional risk, such as uncertainty with respect to product or supplier performance, or psychological risk, such as negative reactions from other organizational members. The greater the uncertainty in a buying situation and the greater the adverse consequences associated with making the wrong choice, the greater the perceived risk in the purchasing decision.[23] The different types of perceived personal risk associated with making buying decisions, and how purchasing agents rank them are shown in Table 5-4.[24]

TABLE 5-4 Magnitude of Various Components of Perceived Personal Risk

Component	Average Risk[1]	Rank
You will feel personal dissatisfaction	6.32	1
Your relations with the users of the purchased product will be strained	5.13	2
The status of the purchasing department will decrease	3.59	3
Your next performance review will be less favorable	3.41	4
You will have less chance for promotion	2.92	5
Your next raise will be smaller	2.71	6
You will lose status among your peers	2.68	7
You will lose your job	2.25	8
Your personal popularity will diminish	1.78	9

[1] Where risk is computed as the product of seriousness [1 = annoying but not serious, 2 = somewhat serious, 3 = very serious] and probability [1 = not probable, 2 = somewhat probable, 3 = very probable].

Source: Reprinted by permission of the publisher. From "How Purchasing Agents Handle Personal Risk," by Jon M. Hawes and Scott H. Barnhouse, *Industrial Marketing Management* 16 (1987) pp. 287–292. Copyright © 1987 by Elsevier Science Publishing Co., Inc.

[23]Raymond A. Bauer, "Consumer Behavior as Risk Taking," in R. L. Hancock, ed., *Dynamic Marketing for a Changing World*, (Chicago: American Marketing Association, 1960), pp. 389–400.

[24]Jon M. Hawes and Scott H. Barnhouse, "How Purchasing Agents Handle Personal Risk," *Industrial Marketing Management* 16 (1987), pp. 287–293.

When uncertainty exists in any given purchasing decision, research indicates that decision makers tend to reduce the level of risk by remaining loyal to existing suppliers who represent a known entity. They also tend to adopt one or more of the following strategies in an attempt to minimize or avoid the perceived risk:

1. *Reduce uncertainty*—uncertainty may be reduced by gathering additional information, such as consulting with other influencers or visiting potential suppliers' plants.
2. *Play the odds*—through sophisticated, quantitative methods of vendor analysis and selection, often involving expected value analysis, which considers both the probability of and magnitude of the consequence, the industrial buyer can "play the odds" by selecting the supplier with the most favorable expected value.
3. *Spread the risk*—the consequences of choosing the wrong supplier can also be reduced through multiple sourcing, thus, enabling buyers to choose the proportion of risk to be assumed by allocating it among different suppliers.[25]

A recent study, however, indicates that strategies for handling risk may be related to the way in which decision makers approach the situation.[26] In attempting to reduce uncertainty, buyers may adopt decision-making strategies such as (1) use performance measures (i.e., examining past historical data of current suppliers, looking for guaranteed performance levels, or utilizing break-even criteria), (2) use expected value analysis, and (3) choose between certainty and risk.

According to the findings, when past historical data alone are utilized, or buyers prefer certainty to risk, buyers tend to split their orders between suppliers, thus avoiding or minimizing the uncertainties involved in the purchasing decision. However, when suppliers are willing to guarantee performance, reducing the element of risk considerably, this does not appear to be the case.

When break-even criteria or expected value analysis is employed, buyers are more willing to accept the elements of uncertainty. The assumption for this phenomenon under the use of break-even criteria is that decision makers may be expected value maximizers. However, in the case of expected value analysis, buyers appear to be willing to accept the best course of action, given the possible consequences—choosing those suppliers that have the most favorable expected value.

Marketing Implications

The significance of these findings relate more to out suppliers than to in suppliers. In view of the fact that supplier loyalty represents a formidable obstacle for out suppliers, the most effective strategy approach for out suppliers is to offer perform-

[25]See T. W. Sweeney, H. L. Mathews, and D. T. Wilson, "An Analysis of Industrial Buyers' Risk Reducing Behavior: Some Personality Correlates," *Proceedings of the American Marketing Association* (Chicago: American Marketing Association, 1973), pp. 217–221; and D. T. Wilson, "Industrial Buyers' Decision Making Styles," *Journal of Marketing Research* 8 (November 1971), pp. 433–436.

[26]Christopher P. Puto, Wesley E. Patton III, and Ronald H. King, "Risk Handling Strategies in Industrial Vendor Selection Decisions," *Journal of Marketing* 39 (Winter 1985), pp. 89–98; and Christopher P. Puto, Wesley E. Patton III, and Ronald H. King, "Risk Handling Strategies in Industrial Vendor Selection Decisions," *Journal of Marketing* 50 (Winter 1985), pp. 89–98.

ance guarantees as part of their proposals. Out suppliers might also want to consider encouraging split procurement, offering their services as a backup or secondary supplier, and, whenever an opportunity exists to service a portion of a new account, be willing to accept it when submitting a proposal.

In developing marketing strategy, however, both in and out suppliers should be aware of buyers' decision strategies in reducing uncertainty and how they affect supplier choice. Industrial sales people should, for instance, emphasize guarantees when applicable or the expected value considerations of their offer.

CONFLICT AND RESOLUTION IN JOINT DECISION MAKING

Whenever two or more individuals have to reach an agreement over issues such as product specifications, information credibility, vendor capabilities, multiple sourcing, contract terms, or order routines, the potential for conflict exists.[27] The potential for conflict emanates from differences in expectations regarding suppliers, differences in the evaluative criteria employed, differences in buying objectives, and differences in decision-making styles of the individuals involved.[28] Whether conflict is good or bad depends upon the type of conflict that emerges and how it is resolved. Conflict that supports the goals of the organization and improves the firm's performance rather than hinders it is good. What is important from the marketer's perspective is how conflict is resolved.

When conflict is resolved through cooperation and the search for a mutually beneficial solution, joint decision making tends to be rational. However, when conflict is resolved through bargaining or politicking, joint decision making tends to be based on irrational criteria.

Conflict-Resolution Strategies

As Figure 5-3 shows, when conflict arises, individuals may resort to several different types of conflict-resolving strategies.[29]

1. Competing—"Let's do it my way!": The desire to win one's own concerns at the other party's expense—the desire to dominate, to yield no quarter, to envision the interaction as a win–lose power struggle; assertive, uncooperative behaviors.
2. Accommodating—"I see your point of view.": The desire to satisfy the other's concerns without attending to one's own concerns—peaceful coexistence, perhaps entertaining long-run motives; unassertive, cooperative behaviors.

---

[27]Michael H. Morris and Stanley M. Freedman, "Coalitions in Organizational Buying," *Industrial Marketing Management* 13 (1984), pp. 123–132.

[28]Sheth, "A Model of Industrial Buyer Behavior," pp. 50–56.

[29]Ralph L. Day, Ronald E. Michaels, and Barbara C. Purdue, "How Buyers Handle Conflicts," *Industrial Marketing Management*, 17 (1988), pp. 153–169. Copyright by Elsevier Science Publishing Co. Inc. Reprinted by permission.

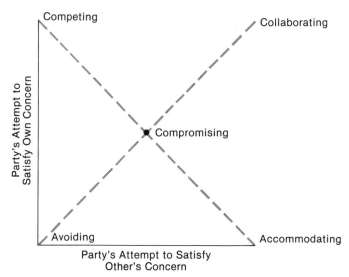

FIGURE 5-3   Resolution Strategies

Source: Reprinted by permission of the publisher. Adapted from "How Buyers Handle Conflicts," by Ralph L. Day, Ronald E. Michaels, and Barbara C. Purdue, *Industrial Marketing Management* 17 (1988), pp. 153–169. Copyright by Elsevier Science Publishing Co., Inc.

3. Collaborating—"Maybe we can work this one out.": The desire to fully satisfy the concerns of both parties—sharing responsibility, problem-solving, in-depth exploration of issues, reaching a mutually beneficial agreement; assertive, cooperative behaviors.

4. Avoiding—"Better let the situation cool down before we act.": Exerting an attitude of indifference to the concerns of either party, not immediately addressing the conflict— diplomatically sidestepping an issue, postponing an issue until a more opportune time, or withdrawal from a threatening situation; unassertive, uncooperative behaviors.

5. Compromising—"Let's split the difference!": The desire to reach an expedient, mutually acceptable agreement which is somewhere short of total satisfaction for either party—exchanging concessions or seeking a middle-ground solution; intermediate in both assertive and cooperative behaviors.

Coalition.   Perhaps the most prevalent and yet ignored form of conflict resolution found among buying center members is coalition formation.[30] When coalition is used to resolve conflict, individuals within the formation attempt to cooperate with specific other group members to enhance their competitive position with respect to the entire group. Since it tends to enhance the individuals' influence and represents a positive channel for airing and resolving conflict, it may be the most rational approach to conflict resolution.

The type of conflict-resolution strategy that individuals use, however, depends

[30]See Robert J. Thomas, "Bases of Power in Organizational Buying Decisions," *Industrial Marketing Management*, 13 (1984), pp. 209–217; and Morris and Freedman, "Coalitions in Organizational Buying," pp. 123–132.

on several mediating variables, such as the characteristics of the purchase situation, the size of the buying center, the network of communication links, and their base of power in the organizational buying decision.[31]

For example, two important reasons for utilizing coalition behavior are (1) the rewards available through various coalitional alternatives and (2) the resource/power positions of group members.[32] It is not unusual for individual objectives and reward criteria to be in conflict when applied to group decision making due to the differences in expectations of the individuals involved. Coalition formation is one way of neutralizing conflict (i.e., joining with other individuals who have the same objectives and reward systems to strengthen one's position in the conflict situation). Coalition formation is also a means of compensating for resource of power inequalities and enhancing one's influence on the decision. When alliances form between weaker group members, more strength results to bargain for control of the group decision.

Power in Conflict Resolution

It is becoming increasingly important for marketers to understand and identify the source of power held or sought by key decision makers in customer firms.[33] The use of power in resolving conflict is common in industrial buying.[34] Unfortunately, power does not always correlate with organizational rank or the functional area of an individual. Buying centers do, however, tend to display one dominant power base. It may be a combined power base (e.g., purchasing and marketing, or engineering and production)[35] or an individual with little formal power who is able to stop or hinder a purchase by virtue of his or her attributed power.[36] As Table 5-5 indicates, common bases of power include reward, coercive, legitimate, referent, and expertise power.[37]

Reward Versus Coercive Power. The ability to influence a purchasing decision by granting monetary, social, political, or psychological benefits refers to reward power. The opposite of reward power is coercive power. Coercive power depends on fear of the ramifications that could result from noncompliance and the coercer's

[31]Morris and Freedman, "Coalitions in Organizational Buying," pp. 123–132.

[32]Ibid.

[33]Thomas V. Bonoma, "Major Sales: Who Really Does the Buying?" *Harvard Business Review* 60 (May–June 1982), pp. 111–119.

[34]George Strauss, "Tactics of Lateral Relationships: The Purchasing Agent," *Administrative Science Quarterly* 7 (September 1962), pp. 161–186.

[35]Morris and Freedman, "Coalitions in Organizational Buying," pp. 123–132.

[36]Bonoma, "Major Sales: Who Really Does the Buying?" pp. 111–119.

[37]See J. R. P. French and B. H. Raven, "The Bases of Social Power," in D. Cartright, ed., *Studies of Social Power* (Ann Arbor: University of Michigan Press, 1959); Samuel B. Bachrach and Edward J. Lawler, *Power and Politics in Organizations* (San Francisco: Jossey-Bass, Inc., Publishers, 1980); and Bonoma, "Major Sales: Who Really Does the Buying?" pp. 111–119.

TABLE 5-5 Sources of Power in Conflict Resolution

Reward power	The ability to influence a decision by granting monetary, social, political, or psychological benefits.
Coercive power	The ability to impose monetary or psychological punishment.
Legitimate power	Formal authority or position within the organizational structure.
Personality power	The ability to inspire and convince others because of one's own physical appearance or attitude, wit, charm, or status.
Expertise power	The possession, access to, or even the withholding of information.

Source: See J. R. French and B. H. Raven, "The Bases of Social Power," in D. Cartright ed., *Studies of Social Power* [Ann Arbor: University of Michigan Press, 1959], pp. 150–167.

ability and discretion to impose the penalty. Threats are not the same as having the power to impose them.

Legitimate Power.   The power to reward or coerce is closely related to an individual's formal position within the organizational structure. Legitimate power grants one the right to reward or punish (coerce) to carry out organizational tasks or functions. When authority is granted to prescribe behavior, both reward and punishment are used to bring about the desired behavior. Such power is exercised in the superior-subordinate relationship and in the control of resources laterally between departments and divisions; for example, the computer department manager may make additional computer time available to the marketing department if certain concessions are agreed upon.

Expert Power.   In the area of organizational buying behavior, expert power has been found to be a more important source of influence over other buying center members than legitimate power.[38] Purchasing behavior, particularly in a new task situation, has a relatively high element of risk. Uncertainty may exist in the need itself, the technical aspects of the product, in market availability, whether funds are available, or with respect to delivery dates or terms of the sale.[39] An important source of credible information for reducing the uncertainty is the expertise of another buying center member. Further, when the purchasing decision cuts across functional areas, as in the case of a computer purchase, hierarchical lines of authority over the purchase tend to become diffused.

Identifying Power Bases

In a small firm, it is not unusual to find a combination of several power bases, such as organizational authority and personality power, being enjoyed by a single member of a buying center. On the other hand, in a large diverse firm, purchasing deci-

[38]Thomas, "Bases of Power in Organizational Buying Decisions," pp. 209–217.

[39]Richard N. Cardoza, "Situational Segmentation of Industrial Markets," *European Journal of Marketing* 14 (1980), pp. 264–276.

EXPERT POWER CAN MEAN VETO POWER TOO

The chief pilot, as an equipment expert, often has veto power over purchase decisions and may be able to stop the purchase of one or another brand of jet by simply expressing a negative opinion about, say, the plane's bad weather capabilities. In this sense, the pilot not only influences the decision but also serves as an information "gatekeeper" by advising management on the equipment to select.

Source: Reprinted by permission of the *Harvard Business Review.* An excerpt from "Major Sales: Who *Really* Does the Buying?" by Thomas V. Bonoma [May–June 1982]. Copyright © 1982 by the President and Fellows of Harvard College; all rights reserved.

---

sions may be subject to influence by a number of individuals relying on various sources of power. Effective marketing strategy rests on the ability to determine which individuals hold and utilize power to influence various decisions, or if coalitions of power exist.[40]

The power obtained through one's organizational position and through the ability to reward and punish is frequently discernible in a simple organization chart. There are of course other rewards and punishments that are given by peers and subordinates that are not so easily discernible, such as a secretary who bars a salesperson's visit to a purchasing manager because of a real or imagined discourteous treatment.

A marketing person contacting a new organization might begin with the assumption that the organizational hierarchy appropriately depicts power bases, but that person should be aware of other buying center members who seem to have unexplained influence. Those buying center members with expertise are often easily discernible because of their questions, apparent comprehension, or job function. Those possessing referent power, however, are often the most difficult to determine.

It may be possible to determine the existence of coalitions by examining the network of communication links between and among group members, that is, the interaction patterns of the buying firm as discussed earlier. It has been found that when two-way versus one-way communication is possible, coalition formations are more likely.

Marketing Implications

The more detailed the salesperson's understanding of how power is distributed within the buying center and the resulting interactions (how conflict is resolved), the better his or her ability to communicate effectively with buying center members. For example, when individuals within the buying center are politicking, it is possible for a salesperson to find herself in the middle of opposing interests. An awareness of

---

[40]Morris and Freedman, "Coalitions in Organizational Buying," pp. 123–132.

the situation may enable the salesperson to decide which political camp will best serve the company's interest and, thus, develop a strategy that may bridge the gap between the opposing parties.

It is wise to acknowledge those who hold power bases and give them the attention and respect consistent with their power. In this regard the amount of time spent with various buying center members should be related to their ability to influence decisions. Spending an undue amount of time and effort to persuade an ineffective buying center member who is consistently overruled can work to the disadvantage of a vendor.

THE BUYING COMMITTEE

So far, much of our discussion has focused on the buying center. A more formalized buying center, the buying committee, is used extensively in the resellers' market and by many industrial organizations, particularly when purchasing is centralized. In the resellers' market, organizations such as food chain retailers form buying committees that meet on a regular basis to decide on new product purchases. In the industrial market, institutions such as universities and hospitals often appoint temporary buying committees to make joint decisions regarding which products can best satisfy organizational needs. And, in the commercial market, representatives from engineering, production, and accounting often establish formal buying committees to review and approve major purchases. Committee buying is also prevalent in the government market.

In the typical buying committee, one or two individuals set the direction while "rubber stamp" decision makers go along. Determining who these direction setters are and understanding their motives is the key in selling to buying committees.[41]

Committee buying generally involves a lengthy selling process during which the vendor meets much more frequently with individuals on the buying committee than with the entire committee. While the salesperson must provide product-related information to all accessible committee members, the real selling effort needs to be targeted to those one or two individuals who are most influential on the committee. Identifying those individuals and determining the structure of the decision-making unit depends on an analysis of the seller's past experience with the buying firm with respect to product purchases, technical expertise of committee members, individual personalities and objectives, and organizational structure.[42]

SUPPLIER CHOICE AND EVALUATION

Regardless of the diversity of expectations and objectives, buyers seek to find the best possible source of supply for their respective needs. In repetitive purchasing situations, such as a straight or modified rebuy, where buyers are familiar with cur-

---

[41]John W. Wingate and Joseph S. Friedlander, *The Management of Retail Buying* (Englewood Cliffs, N.J.: Prentice-Hall, Inc., 1978), pp. 235–237.
[42]Ibid., see footnote, p.225.

rent suppliers and the purchase involves a standardized product, it may be a simple matter of choosing a supplier from the list of sources already identified and evaluated.[43] A supplier may even be recommended for selection on the basis of reciprocity considerations. For example, in one study it was noted that buyers sometimes want to favor a specific vendor in return for a favor.[44]

In a new task situation, or when the purchase involves a substantial expenditure or the quality of the needed product is critical, the selection may involve an extensive search to find the one qualified supplier. When no current source of supply exists, it may even require that the firm work with many suppliers to develop the needed product.

The development of a new source can take months, even years. In some cases, the buying organization may have to help a supplier develop the necessary level of needed performance by providing financing for equipment, by assisting in developing job scheduling and quality control techniques, or by participating in the development of bid preparations and cost accounting procedures.[45]

Supplier Choice and Qualifying Process

How buyers choose and qualify suppliers depends upon the type of buying situation and the importance of the purchase in terms of complexity and dollar value. When the procurement need is complex or involves a substantial expenditure, it is common practice for personnel from purchasing, quality control, engineering, and production to evaluate the supplier's facilities and production capacity to ensure, for instance, an uninterrupted flow of product, to evaluate product quality via product samples, to approve technical competency and manufacturing efficiency via plant visits, and to verify the supplier's financial stability through sources such as Moody's Industrials, Dun & Bradstreet reports, or annual corporate reports. They may even evaluate the supplying firm's position in the industry, its progressiveness, its interest in the firm's order, and its cooperative attitude.[46] Factors important to buyers in the supplier selection process are shown in Table 5-6.

Qualifying factors, however, may limit buyers' choice of suppliers. For instance, with the increasing cost of transportation, buyers may limit their choice to local suppliers, or in the case of dependency on uninterrupted shipments, the suppliers' capacity and capability may become a deciding factor in supplier choice.[47] The point is that the buying organization's objective in carefully evaluating and qualifying potential vendors is to locate those suppliers that have the capacity to produce the needed item in the required quality and quantity, are capable of fulfill-

---

[43]Stuart F. Heinritz and Paul V. Farrell, *Purchasing Principles and Applications*, 5th ed. (Englewood Cliffs, N.J.: Prentice-Hall, Inc., 1971), p. 222.

[44]Niren Vyas and Arch G. Woodside, "An Inductive Model of Industrial Supplier Choice Processes," *Journal of Marketing* 48 (Winter 1984), pp. 30–45.

[45]B. Charles Ames and James D. Hlavacek, *Managerial Marketing for Industrial Firms* (New York: Random House, Inc., 1984), p. 57.

[46]Heinritz and Farrell, *Purchasing Principles and Applications*, p. 222.

[47]Vyas and Woodside, "An Inductive Model of Industrial Supplier Choice Processes," pp 30–45.

**TABLE 5-6   Ten Criteria Viewed as Most Appropriate
in Measuring Buyer's Performance**

 1. Making purchases that arrive on time
 2. Making purchases that pass incoming Quality Assurance inspection
 3. Meeting target costs
 4. Knowledge of commodities in the buyer's area of responsibility
 5. Ability to control purchase order cycle time
 6. Ability to cultivate qualified suppliers
 7. Ability to perform work with a minimum of errors
 8. Ability to determine the bottom price a supplier will take
 9. Amount of complexity of commodities in buyer's responsibility
10. Providing timely responses to inquiries from suppliers and internal customers

Source: Thomas E. Hendrick and William A. Ruch, "Determining Performance Appraisal Criteria for Buyers," *Journal of Purchasing and Materials Management,* (Summer 1988), pp. 18-24.

ing delivery and other service needs, are price competitive and can be relied upon as a continuous source of supply.

Evaluating Supplier Performance

Qualification of suppliers does not end with the purchase. The real test of a supplier is the ability to perform effectively and consistently over time. This is the deciding factor as to whether the supplier will continue as the "in" supplier or be replaced. Buyers use both objective and subjective evaluations to rate suppliers' performance. Supplier evaluation, however, generally involves four basic considerations: quality, service, delivery, and price. The most common methods used to evaluate suppliers are (1) the categorical method, (2) the weighted-point method, and (3) the cost-ratio method.[48]

The Categorical Method.   The least precise of the three methods is the categorical method because supplier evaluation is based on the experience and opinions of the user departments. Thus it is subjective rather than objective. A list of significant performance factors is drawn up by purchasing, and users merely assign a grade of plus, minus, or neutral to each factor. At regularly scheduled meetings (usually monthly), the ratings are discussed, and those suppliers with overall high, low, or neutral ratings are notified.

While the categorical method is nonquantitative, it is an inexpensive way for the buyer to keep records of supplier performance. The main disadvantage to the vendor, however, is that it relies heavily on the memory and opinion of the different evaluators and is subject to their perceptual biases.

[48]The following discussion is based on Zenz, *Purchasing and the Management of Materials*, pp. 140–146.

The Weighted-Point Method.   Under the weighted-point method, the organization assigns weights to the different evaluation criteria. While any number of evaluative factors may be included, the assigning of weights to each factor enables the buyer to develop a composite performance index that can be quantitatively used to compare suppliers.

For example, if quality and delivery are the first and second most important performance factors, with frequency of cost-reducing suggestions and price being third and fourth in importance, then quality might be given a weight of 40, delivery 30, cost-reducing suggestions 20, and price 10. A performance score can then be developed for each factor, and the factor scores of each supplier can be totaled for comparative analysis of supplier performance. Buyers can also assign acceptable and unacceptable ranges to apply to the composite ratings of competing suppliers such as excellent = 85 or above, acceptable = 84 to 75, unacceptable = 74 and below. An example of a composite rating for one supplier is shown in Table 5-7.

The advantage of the weighted-point method of supplier evaluation to the buyer is that a number of evaluative criteria can be proportioned to correspond with the values of the firm. It also forces the buyer to define the key attributes of a supplier and objectively evaluate them, thus minimizing much of the subjective evaluation that occurs under the categorical method.

The regular notification of suppliers concerning their respective performance assists in isolating supplier problems, stimulates improved supplier performance, and, most important, strengthens the buyer–seller relationship.

The Cost-Ratio Method.   The cost-ratio method is based on the use of cost analysis in evaluating suppliers and has become increasingly important in the way purchasing managers evaluate suppliers.[49] Under this method, all identifiable purchasing costs are related to the value of products received. When the ratio of costs to products is

TABLE 5-7 Weighted-Point Method of Supplier Evaluation

Factor	Weight	Actual Performance	Performance Score
Quality	40	90% acceptable	$40 \times .9 = 36$
Delivery	30	90% on schedule	$30 \times .9 = 27$
Cost-reducing suggestions	20	% of total received = 60	$20 \times .6 = 12$
Price	10	125% of lowest price $100/125 = .8$	$10 \times .8 = 8$
			Total composite peformance score = 83

[49]Robert M. Manzka and Steven J. Trevcha, "Cost-Based Supplier Performance Evaluation," *Journal of Purchasing and Materials Management* (Spring 1988), pp. 2–7.

high, the supplier's rating is low; when the ratio is low, the supplier's rating is high. While the choice of costs depends on the products involved, quality, delivery, service, and price are the most commonly used categories.

From the buyer's perspective, costs associated with quality include such factors as visits to the vendor's plant, evaluation of samples, inspection of incoming shipments, and the costs associated with defective products (for example, unusual inspection procedures, rejected parts, and manufacturing time lost due to defective parts). Thus, when cost-ratio methods of supplier evaluation are used, not only can purchasing managers rationalize lowest total cost suppliers, they can also measure nonperformance costs.[50]

To arrive at a cost/quality ratio, the vendor's quality cost is totaled and equated to the value of goods received. For instance, if the buyer's quality costs were $8,000, and the value of the purchase $800,000, the cost/quality ratio would be .01 or 1 percent.

Cost ratios are also computed for costs associated with delivery, such as the cost of paperwork involved in expediting the order, telephone follow-ups, factory downtime and rescheduling due to delayed shipments, and emergency transportation. However, the intangible costs of supplier service capability, such as financial stability, geographical location, innovativeness, and flexibility in providing short lead time, are difficult to measure and evaluate but often considered necessary to the evaluation. Intangible costs are measured by assigning relative weights to each factor considered important by the firm. Once costs have been computed, they are combined with the supplier's quoted prices to determine the "net adjusted price."

A summary of cost comparisons for four suppliers is shown in Table 5-8. As you can see, under this method of supplier evaluation, the buying organization assigns a minus (−) weight for favorable service and a (+) for unfavorable service. In this example, supplier B had a bid price of $95.00, but a total cost penalty of +7 percent (2 + 3 + 2 = 7). Thus, the adjusted net cost to the buyer was $101.65. The firm will select the supplier with the most economical total offer that fulfills

TABLE 5-8 Summary of Suppliers' Cost Comparisons

Supplier	Quality/ Cost Ratio	Delivery/ Cost Ratio	Service/ Cost Ratio	Total Cost Penalty	Quoted Price per Unit	Net Adjusted Price per Unit
A	2%	1%	−4%	−1%	$95.50	$ 94.55
B	2	3	+2	+7	95.00	101.65
C	2	1	+1	+4	94.75	98.54
D	1	1	−1	+1	95.25	96.20

Source: Adapted from Gary J. Zenz, *Purchasing and the Management of Materials* [New York: John Wiley & Sons, Inc., copyright © 1981], p. 144. Reprinted with permission.

[50]Ibid.

other salient criteria considered important to the firm, such as company image and supplier reputation and attitude, rather than the supplier with the lowest bid, supplier A in this example.

Marketers Too Can Develop Supplier Rating Systems

Industrial marketers must be aware of the criteria that buyers employ in evaluating their offerings. Since buying organizations have varying objectives, requirements, and structures, the evaluation criteria used will differ from firm to firm. Each buying organization will have product and service needs that are unique to its operation. The systematic evaluation of suppliers by buyers, however, offers the marketer unique opportunities. By developing a rating system based on customer criteria, a similar system can be used by the selling firm to[51]

1. Promote and enhance the value of the company's product and services.
2. Provide special control over items that customers consider critical to their operation.
3. Substantiate performance in response to customer requests.
4. Improve efficiency of internal planning and control.
5. Supply "hard data" in support of contract negotiations.

Benefits to the marketer include more effective buyer-seller communications, better customer services, and, thus, enhanced buyer-supplier relationships. As buyers increase their use of the computer, and purchasing becomes more expert and centralized, the performance of suppliers will be subject to greater quantitative scrutiny. Therefore, industrial marketers must view their product offering from the perspective of the buying organization. The use of a self-evaluation, based on customer needs, is one way of ensuring this view.

LOOKING BACK

Industrial marketers must thoroughly understand the influence of industrial purchasing practices on organizational buying behavior. The power and status of purchasing has been enhanced by such factors as material requirements planning, just-in-time purchasing, centralization, and advanced quantitative techniques brought about by increased computer technology. Where the purchasing function is centralized, buyers tend to become specialists in repetitive buying situations, are long-term rather than short-term oriented, and have more influence on the purchasing decision than those at decentralized locations.

Industrial purchase decisions are often the outcome of interactions that take place between various members of the buying center. Thus, it is important for mar-

---

[51]David Wieters and Lonnie L. Ostrom, "Supplier Evaluation as a New Marketing Tool," *Industrial Marketing Management* 8 (1979), pp.161–166.

keters to understand the interaction, the leadership patterns, and the formal and informal network of communication among buying center members. The number of organizational members involved in the buying center depends on the characteristics of the firm, the type of purchasing situation, the perceived importance of the product, and the resources available for handling the purchase.

Group decision making is affected by the different personalities, experiences, organizational functions, and perceptions of the individuals involved. In joint decision making, the potential for conflict is always present due to the different goals and expectations of organizational members. When conflict occurs, individuals resort to one of several means for resolving it, depending on their respective sources of power.

After applying a wide range of criteria, both subjective and objective, to the choice of a supplier, firms usually evaluate and monitor supplier performance through the use of formal rating systems. These systems center on supplier attributes that are important to the firm, such as quality, service, delivery, and price. Vendor rating systems can range from the easily administered categorical plan to the more complex cost-ratio method.

QUESTIONS FOR DISCUSSION

1. Is the combination of purchasing, material flow, and production control into one functional department a logical, evolutionary change or simply "empire building" by or for the purchasing manager? Justify your opinion.

2. The advantages of a just-in-time purchasing system to a large-scale, continuous-flow manufacturing operation are fairly obvious. However, would this system have any advantages for a smaller-scale, discontinuous job-order type of operation?

3. From a marketer's perspective, what are the advantages and disadvantages of dealing with a modern, centralized purchasing function compared to a decentralized department of the 1960s?

4. Suppose that you were asked to compare the impact of social classes and reference groups upon consumer buying with vertical and lateral involvement in the industrial buying process. Is there any logical comparison? If so, describe it.

5. The buying committee is made up of a chief engineer who wants technical innovation regardless of price, a purchasing agent committed to driving component costs down, and a manufacturing manager who insists on the status quo so manufacturing costs can be stabilized. How can a seller develop a strategy to handle these contradictory objectives?

6. "In selling to a committee, it is definitely more effective to make an initial presentation to the group as a whole and then handle objections and problems in separate, individual sessions." Agree or disagree with this statement and explain why.

7. Consider a situation in which three different members of a chemical firm are involved in a purchasing decision for a computer. The scientist wants a service that generates a particular output form, the manager wants a service emphasizing low cost and speed of information recovery, and the librarian wants a service in which his department plays a role. Discuss how sources and bases of power might impact the situation. Considering the risk involved in such a purchase, what types of strategies might these decision makers employ?

8. If a selling firm wants to encourage an evaluation visit by a potential customer, what steps can it take beforehand to increase the probability that the visit will be made, and what actions during the visit will increase the likelihood of a fair and objective evaluation?

9. Given a choice, which evaluation method would you prefer your customers employ: categorical, weighted-point, or cost-ratio? Why?

SUGGESTED ADDITIONAL READINGS

BIGGS, JOSEPH, DONALD C. BOPP, JR., and WILLIAM M. CAMPION, "Material Requirements Planning and Purchasing: A Case Study," *Journal of Purchasing and Materials Management* (Spring 1984): 15–22.

BONOMA, THOMAS V., "Major Sales: Who Really Does the Buying?" *Harvard Business Review* 60 (May–June 1982): 111–119.

CROW, LOWELL F., and JAY D. LINDQUIST, "Impact of Organizational and Buyer Characteristics on the Buying Center," *Industrial Marketing Management* 14 (1985): 49–58.

DAY, RALPH L., RONALD E. MICHAELS, and BARBARA C. PERDUE, "How Buyers Handle Conflicts," *Industrial Marketing Management* 17 (1988): 153–169.

FRAIZER, GARY L., ROBERT E. SPEKMAN, and CHARLES R. O'NEAL, "Just-In-Time Exchange Relationships in Industrial Markets," *Journal of Marketing* (October 1988): 52–67.

JOHNSTON, WESLEY J., and THOMAS V. BONOMA, "The Buying Center: Structure and Interaction Patterns," *Journal of Marketing* 45 (Summer 1981): 143–156.

KOHLI, AJAY, "Determinants of Influence in Organizational Buying: A Contingency Approach," *Journal of Marketing* 53 (July 1989): 50–65.

MANZKA, ROBERT M., and STEVEN J. TREVCHA, "Cost-Based Supplier Performance Evaluation," *Journal of Purchasing and Materials Management* (Spring 1988): 2–7.

MORRIS, MICHAEL H., and STANLEY M. FREEDMAN, "Coalitions in Organizational Buying," *Industrial Marketing Management* 13 (1984): 123–132.

PUTO, CHRISTOPHER P., WESLEY E. PATTON III, and RONALD H. KING, "Risk Handling Strategies in Industrial Vendor Selection Decisions," *Journal of Marketing* 39 (Winter 1985): 89–98.

RECK, ROBERT F., and BRIAN G. LONG, "Purchasing: A Competitive Weapon," *Journal of Purchasing and Materials Management* (Fall 1988): 2–8.

THOMAS, ROBERT J., "Bases of Power in Organizational Buying Decisions," *Industrial Marketing Management* 13 (1984): 202–17.

UPAH, GREGORY D., and MONROE M. BIRD, "Changes in Industrial Buying: Implications for Industrial Marketers," *Industrial Marketing Management* 9 (1980): 117–121.

PART THREE

Strategy Formulation in the Industrial Market

MILITARY SPECIFICATIONS DETOUR MILITARY SALES

Outdated military specifications and inspection procedures have caused considerable hardships, leading to drastic strategic changes in companies supplying military products. Within five years after 1982, only 38,000 of 118,000 firms supplying goods to the Pentagon continued to do so. The other 80,000 had either gone bankrupt or changed their missions to supplying organizations other than the United States armed services.

Military specifications for something as simple as a fruitcake had grown to eighteen pages in length. Inspection procedures often required numerous and costly additions to equipment. Because of such Pentagon demands, one company found that it could produce only 25 percent as many shotgun shells on its military production line as it produced on its civilian line, that is, sixty versus 240 rounds per minute.

Additionally, because of constraining military bureaucracy, the customary side benefit of creativity, once a major effect of spending military research & development dollars, has all but vanished, as more and more R&D money has been committed to development of proposed products rather than creative new products. The president of Hunter Manufacturing, a former producer of heaters for military planes and vehicles, said "We had to go commercial to stay on the cutting edge. It was becoming more and more apparent that the designs the government used were archaic."

Source: Bruce B. Auster, "A Healthy Military–Industrial Complex," *U.S. News & World Report* (February 12, 1990), pp. 42–48. Reprinted by permission.

Industrial marketing success depends on identifying promising market segments to serve, understanding their needs, and then developing marketing strategy and plans to satisfy those needs better than competitors in such a way as to achieve organizational objectives. This is not easy to accomplish in today's rapidly changing environment. In the next three chapters, then, we will discuss how industrial marketing firms develop their strategy to meet those changes, the resources available for analyzing marketing opportunities and developing strategic decisions, and how industrial marketers can discover attractive markets to serve.

CHAPTER 6

The Strategic Planning Process in Industrial Marketing

If industrial marketers are to meet the challenges of today's rapidly changing markets and increasing global competition, marketing decisions must be based on well-conceived strategies. Clearly defined strategies and resulting plans are vital if the firm is to achieve its objectives while optimizing the use of its limited resources. How well strategy is conceived, and the success of its implementation, however, is greatly dependent on careful coordination between marketing and other functional areas of the firm. The objective of this chapter, then, is to discuss

1. Some of the problems involved in developing strategic plans in the industrial market and how they may be solved.
2. Strategic planning at the corporate level and the areas that must be assessed if resulting decisions are to be successful.
3. The role of marketing in the strategic planning process.

Success in the industrial market, as in the consumer market, depends on recognizing the importance of strategic planning. To deal with all the factors that can affect a firm's ability to grow profitably, however, management must design and follow a viable strategic planning process, a process that consists of developing a system of objectives and plans as well as the allocation of resources to achieve objectives. Strategic planning, then, involves an organization in recognizing, anticipating, and responding to changes in the marketplace to ensure that resources are directed toward achieving those opportunities that are consistent with the firm's capabilities.

Strategic planning, for most businesses, however, takes place at three levels: the corporate, the business, and the functional level.[1]

Strategic planning at the corporate level involves the firm in deciding on which markets to compete in, establishing corporate objectives, acquiring needed resources, and allocating those resources among the different markets to achieve corporate objectives. Strategic planning at the business level addresses how and on what basis the firm will compete in a market and provides guidance as to how the various functional areas (e.g., production, marketing, R&D, finance, and personnel) will be coordinated to achieve corporate objectives. And strategic planning at the functional level involves the development of short-term strategies to implement or execute the strategic plans made at both the corporate and business level.

While businesses vary in the approach they use in developing their strategies, *strategies* consists of the long-term objectives and plans with which the organization will relate its particular characteristics and capabilities to customers, competitors, and regulators.[2] *Plans*, on the other hand, consist of the various actions that must take place if resources are to be utilized effectively in implementing strategies. Thus, plans are more specific and detailed, answering such questions as: "What will be done?" "Who will do it?" "When will it be done?" and "How much will it cost?" Tactics are the on-the-spot decisions taken during the planning execution stage to ensure that plans are modified with events that materialize during the planning period. In this chapter, we are concerned with how the industrial firm identifies and selects strategies at the corporate level and the role of marketing in the strategic planning process.

STRATEGIC PLANNING IN THE INDUSTRIAL MARKET

While the basic principles of planning apply in both markets, many organizations have found that what works well in the consumer market fails to do so in the industrial market. Two significant differences between these markets appear to account for this phenomenon.[3]

First, unlike the consumer market where products are normally marketed through one or two channels, most industrial marketers face diverse markets that must be reached through a multiplicity of channels—each requiring a different marketing approach. A producer of communication equipment, for instance, may market to such diverse segments as the commercial, institutional, and governmental market, each of which will require a unique marketing plan.

Second, in contrast to consumer marketing, successful industrial marketing

---

[1]See, for instance, John A. Pearce II and Richard B. Robinson, Jr., *Strategic Management* (Homewood, Ill.: Richard D. Irwin, Inc., 1982), pp. 6–7; and Donald L. Bates and David L. Elderedge, *Strategy and Policy*, 2nd ed. (Dubuque, Iowa: William C. Brown Co., Publishers, 1984), p. 12.

[2]Henry L. Tosi and Stephen J. Carroll, *Management*, 2nd ed. (New York: John Wiley & Sons, Inc., 1982), p. 196.

[3]This section is based on B. Charles Ames, "Marketing Planning for Industrial Products," *Harvard Business Review* (September–October 1968), pp. 100–111.

strategy depends more on other functional areas. Where the elements of planning in consumer marketing can often be contained within specific areas of marketing, such as advertising, selling, and product management, planning in the industrial market is largely dependent on, or constrained by, the activities of other functional areas—for example, engineering, manufacturing, and technical services. When marketing emphasizes tailor-made products and fast deliveries, for instance, manufacturing must be prepared to follow through with product output. Planning, then, in the industrial marketing arena requires a higher degree of integrated effort across functional areas and a closer relationship with overall corporate strategy than in the consumer market.

Functional Isolation

While planning in the industrial market is as sophisticated as it is in the consumer arena, too often industrial firms concentrate planning efforts in the marketing department, failing to recognize the interdependency between marketing and other functional areas. Perhaps this is due to what may be referred to as "functional isolation."[4] That is, not only does marketing tend to ignore its interface with other areas such as finance, manufacturing, and R&D, but "marketing concepts, methods and inputs are frequently ignored in the decision perspectives of other business functions."[5] While marketing should take the lead in defining market segments, needs, and opportunities and in determining what it will take to satisfy the various markets and segments, planning in the industrial arena must be a collaborative effort between all key functional areas. Unfortunately, as Wind and Robertson point out, the isolation between marketing and other functional areas may continue until we:

> Find solutions to the inherent conflict between marketing and other functional areas.
> Develop organizational structures that explicitly incorporate marketing and nonmarketing considerations.
> Begin using marketing decision models that are based on relevant input from other functional areas besides marketing.[6]

Functional Conflict

While successful planning depends on cooperation between the different functional areas, whenever tasks and objectives are different or unclear between two or more departments a strong tendency for disharmony exists.[7] As Table 6-1 highlights, po-

[4]Yoram Wind and Thomas S. Robertson, "Marketing Strategy: New Directions for Theory and Research," *Journal of Marketing* 47 (Spring 1983), pp. 13–25.

[5]B. Charles Ames, "Trappings vs. Substance in Industrial Marketing," *Harvard Business Review* (July–August 1970), pp. 93–103.

[6]Wind and Robertson, "Marketing Strategy: New Directions for Theory and Research," pp. 13–25.

[7]J. Donald Weinrauch and Richard Anderson, "Conflicts Between Engineering and Marketing Units," *Industrial Marketing Management* 11 (1982), pp. 291–301.

TABLE 6-1 A Catalog of Potential Conflicting Areas Between Marketing/Engineering

Areas	Marketing Responses	Engineering Responses
New product design	They don't give us products we can sell. By the time we get them to design the product it will be obsolete.	We're limited in what we can design because we have to keep it simple for marketing.
Breadth of the product line	We need more variety.	We have too much variety now.
Product appearance	Our line looks so inferior.	Our line does not need a lot of fancy window dressing.
Product problems	Why can't engineering make workable products?	Neither the customer nor our marketing department understand the product and how it is supposed to work.
Product promotion	The information we get from engineering is so dull and technical that no one would read it.	The information that marketing includes is so exaggerated. We could get sued for false advertising.
Packaging	It looks so cheap and functions so poorly that it makes our products hard to sell.	Trying to package so many products and hold costs down is extremely difficult.
Quality	Why can't we have reasonable quality at reasonable costs.	We must design so many products with numerous options that it is hard to maintain quality and keep costs down.
Technical	We need a technical expert to soothe customers even though they really do not have a problem.	We don't have enough manpower to hold the hand of some pet customers of marketing.
Warranty	Engineering always goes by the book, they don't understand that you have to bend a little.	Marketing wants us to pay the full amount of every claim, even an invalid one.

Source: Reprinted by permission of the publisher from "Conflicts Between Engineering and Marketing Units," by J. Donald Weinrauch and Richard Anderson, *Industrial Marketing Management* 11 (1982), pp. 291–301. Copyright © 1982 by Elsevier Science Publishing Co., Inc.

tential areas of conflict between marketing and engineering exist in such basic matters as new product development, product quality, and technical services. Potential conflict also exists between marketing and manufacturing in such areas as sales forecasting and production planning, and between marketing and R&D in the area of new product development.

Alleviating Conflict.   Alleviating conflict begins with developing an understanding of the basic causes of interdepartmental conflict. As discussed in Chapter Five, conflict arises due to the fact that each area is evaluated and rewarded on the bases of different criteria, the inherent complexities of the different functional areas, and the different perceptions of the individuals involved. Conflict can also arise through differences in how departmental individuals perceive their prestige, power, and knowledge. Budget constraints, rapid company growth, and the rapid pace of technological change can also yield potential areas of conflict.

JAPANESE MARKETERS IDENTIFY WITH THEIR COMPANIES

Whereas American marketers such as marketing researchers, advertising, or sales managers tend to identify with their professions, Japanese marketers identify with their companies. While American companies hiring marketing personnel pay particular attention to such factors as educational background, industry experience, accomplishments and technical capabilities, Japanese companies place more emphasis on human factors. They see the main marketing management duties as being involved with developing people, getting them to agree, cooperate, work harmoniously, and contribute as much as they can to the company.

. . . In American companies, marketing is considered to be an area of business specialization delegated to a group of experts and professionals, the marketing staff, who are well versed in marketing approaches, models, and techniques, and are aware of the profit levels to be achieved. The marketing department's espoused marketing philosophy may or may not be accepted by other functional areas in the company. In Japanese companies, by contrast, responsibilities for marketing are in the hands of a broader but less sophisticated and technically trained group of managers. The marketing turf is not solely the responsibility of the marketing department, for other departments accepting the company's philosophy and the logic of the marketing concept and its approach to business become directly involved in applying it throughout the organization. It is a group responsibility, with a group approach for the performance of marketing activities resulting.

Source: William Lazar, Shoji Murata, and Hiroshi Kosaka, "Japanese Marketing: Towards a Better Understanding," *Journal of Marketing* 49 [Spring 1985], pp. 69–81. Reprinted with permission.

Some degree of conflict is necessary and can be very constructive in that it promotes more efficient and effective use of the company's resources. However, when conflict begins to diminish the ability of the organization to coordinate the efforts of its various functional areas, it becomes counterproductive and impedes the organization's effectiveness in achieving its primary goals. Alleviating conflict, however, is top management's responsibility. Conflict can only be alleviated when an atmosphere of cooperation is created through (1) promotion of clear and straightforward corporate policies, (2) evaluation and reward systems that stress interfunctional cooperation and responsiveness, and (3) formal and informal interfunctional contacts (e.g., including manufacturing people in sales meetings and marketing people in product design decision meetings or establishing squash courts for noon-hour use by all company members).

Marketing executives, however, can assist in alleviating conflict by building their marketing plans around each functional area's ability to service the firm's markets and customers and by analyzing the strengths, weaknesses, and competitiveness of each respective area, similar to analyzing customers and competitors.[8]

[8]Benson P. Shapiro, "Can Marketing and Manufacturing Coexist?" *Harvard Business Review* 46 (September–October 1968), pp. 100–111.

Organizational Design for Interfunctional Cooperation

While many types of organizational structures exist, organizations are typically designed around what Galbraith and Nathanson have defined as the "segmentation of work into roles such as production, finance, and marketing and recombining roles into departments or divisions around functions, products, regions, or markets and the distribution of power across this role structure."[9] To resolve conflict and disputes between areas of specialty and to assure that broad organizational goals will be obtained, coordination of the various functional activities is normally achieved vertically through the hierarchy of authority or through committee work and liaison roles. Due to upper management concentrating on the internal efficiency and effectiveness of individual departments, methods of organizing that would achieve cooperation among departments or functional areas are often overlooked.

Designing for Competitive Advantage. MacMillan and Jones have suggested that an organization can better serve its purpose if it is designed to be competitive rather than efficient.[10] That is, typical organizational designs can be expanded so that they relate better to competitors in a firm's environment. In so doing, the organization must ask itself several key questions that will, ironically, lead to an optimal alignment of functional interdependency. For instance, in pursuing a competitive organizational structure, an organization must address such important issues as (1) "What major task groupings are feasible design alternatives?" (2) "What linkages are necessary between groupings?" and (3) "What support systems are needed?"

In asking itself "What major task groupings are feasible design alternatives?" to maintain its desired competitive advantage in the area of product development and cost leadership, one industrial foods producer established two developmental functions under research and development to serve, individually, its commercial and institutional markets. Further, to ensure that the research function was in line with organizational needs and environmental demands, product managers became the formal linkage, interacting with developmental people in the area of new product development. They were also given the explicit responsibility of coordinating and interacting with manufacturing to manage conflicting needs between marketing and manufacturing. Thus, when an organization also asks, "What linkages are necessary between groupings?" it may find it necessary to develop linking mechanisms, such as those shown in Table 6-2, to coordinate and control critical interfaces.

"What support systems are needed?" ultimately leads the organization to ask whether planning, control, and reward systems are designed so as to focus on achieving organizational objectives. Additionally, it forces the organization to address the question of the skills necessary to achieve those objectives. For example, IBM's success is, to a great degree, built on its recognition that it was vital to spend

---

[9] J. R. Galbraith and D. A. Nathanson, *Strategic Implementation: The Role of Structure and Process* (St. Paul, Minn.: West Publishing Co., 1978), pp. 12–16.

[10] This section is based on Ian C. MacMillan and Patricia E. Jones, "Designing Organizations to Compete," *The Journal of Business Strategy* 5 (Spring 1984), pp. 11–26.

TABLE 6-2 Key Linking Mechanisms

Task force	A group is selected from various activities to tackle a specific intergroup problem. It is automatically disbanded after the problem is solved.
Team	A group is selected from various activities in the organization to respond to recurring problems that cross over group boundaries. It is a permanent coordinative arrangement that is only disbanded by a higher level in the hierarchy.
Integrating role	An individual is charged with formal responsibilities for coordinating between two groupings. A common example is the product manager whose task it is to see that specific products get adequate attention from the marketing, production, and service functions.
Integrating department	A department with independent resources and staff whose task is to ensure coordination between different functions. A typical example is an expediting department in a manufacturing firm whose task is to coordinate between specific projects and the various technical departments supplying skills to execute the projects.
Matrix	A person simultaneously reports to and has responsibility for a number of managers, each in charge of different activities or resources which must be coordinated. Below this matrix manager is a structure in which competing tasks must be executed. The classic example is the project manager in a construction company who is required to report both to operations and to the technical manager while managing a specific project under his/her control.

Source: Ian C. MacMillan and Patricia E. Jones, "Designing Organizations to Compete." Reprinted by permission from *The Journal of Business Strategy*, Spring 1984. Published by Warren, Gorham & Lamont, Inc., 210 South St., Boston, Mass. Copyright © 1984. All rights reserved.

millions of dollars educating and training its personnel in programming areas so that they could, in turn, pass their knowledge and skills on to what were unknowledgeable users in IBM's customer companies.

The important point is, that in designing to compete more effectively in the marketplace, an organization is forced to reconsider and develop synergy between its various functional areas—the focus is on serving external rather than internal forces.

Decision Support Systems

A relatively new tool, *decision support systems (DSS)*, contributes much toward integrating personnel in different departments, enabling a firm to use its competitive advantages better and to overcome interdepartmental conflict. Decision support systems are computer systems developed to aid managerial decision making by employing state-of-the-art quantitative models that analyze proposed actions by evaluating how those actions would affect all primary areas of an organization. For example, if a DSS were to analyze the effects of a product's price reduction, it would be able to include in its analysis such considerations as effects on (1) amount sold, (2) inventory levels, (3) manufacturing scheduling, (4) input availabilities, (5) capital expenditures, (6) additional revenues, and (7) anticipated competitor reactions.

Such integrated models help firms pinpoint competitive advantages and recognize their opportunities and threats, as well as their strengths and weaknesses. Interdepartmental teams are employed to supply the data necessary for the models, thus causing managers to become more company oriented in their thinking. Management's use of these systems also increases its perception of company, as well as departmental, implications of particular actions. Such increased perceptions of decision effects serve to alleviate conflict brought about by more customary, limited departmental views of consequences of actions. Decision support systems are discussed in more detail in Chapter 7.

MANAGING THE DEVELOPMENT
OF STRATEGIC PLANNING

Strategic planning, however, is not the total answer to marketing success. A firm must be managed effectively. And many companies are coming to recognize that effective management does not just lie solely in the area of strategic decision making, it also depends on other factors. According to one of the world's leading consulting firms, McKinsey & Company, strategy is only one of seven factors that the best managed organizations exhibit.[11]

As a result of studying a large sample of excellently managed companies, such as IBM, Boeing, and 3-M, and discovering that their strengths included more than strategy, structure, and systems, consultants at McKinsey added four other factors. Figure 6-1 shows the seven factors that McKinsey considers necessary for a company to perform successfully over time.

The first three factors—strategy, structure, and systems—are what McKinsey sees as the hardware of success. The next four—style, staff, skills, and shared values—are seen as the software of success.

Style refers to the fact that employees share a common style in behaving and thinking, sometimes referred to as "culture." *Skill* refers to the fact that the necessary skills needed to carry out the strategies, such as marketing planning and financial analysis, have been mastered by the firm's employees. *Staffing* means that the company has hired capable people and placed them in the right positions to take full advantage of their respective talents. The last factor, *shared values*, means that employees share the same guiding values and mission, that is, an excellently managed company has a driving purpose and philosophy that is known and practiced by everyone.

---

[11]See Thomas J. Peters and Robert H. Waterman, Jr., *In Search of Excellence: Lessons from America's Best-Run Companies* (New York: Harper & Row, Publishers, Inc., 1982), pp. 9–12. This framework, however, has been developed by and is used in Richard Tanner Pascale and Anthony G. Athos, *The Art of Japanese Management: Applications for American Executives* (New York: Simon & Schuster, Inc., 1981).

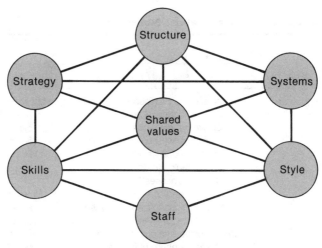

FIGURE 6-1   McKinsey's 7-S Framework

Source: Thomas J. Peters and Robert H. Waterman, Jr., *In Search of Excellence: Lessons from America's Best Run Companies.* Copyright © 1982 by Thomas J. Peters and Robert H. Waterman, Jr. Reprinted by permission of Harper & Row, Publishers, Inc.

Strategy: An Intellectual and Social Process

In his study of large international companies, Horovitz has discovered that management is becoming more and more concerned with three areas, areas that are believed to be the key to quality in strategic decision making: (1) the organization structure, (2) the planning process, and (3) the activating modes used to produce strategic changes (people and style).[12]

To overcome the problems and challenges faced in today's market, all companies studied were looking for "cleaner, simpler structures . . . and a better balance between line and top management." Thus, many companies are moving away from the matrix structure of the 1970s toward smaller, more manageable units. Further, to create an entrepreneurial spirit, the capacity for innovation, and a sense of responsibility, many companies are undergoing a complete realignment of their organization structure so that each manager will have the necessary resources, responsibility, and scope of decision making (including financing, asset management, and legal problems) for his or her business unit.

Most companies, however, felt that the greatest need for improvement was in the area of developing people—people who are able to present alternatives, make judgments, and think strategically. When a firm fails to choose the right people, to train, educate, and motivate them, it can affect the firm's ability to adapt to its environment.

---

[12]Jacques Horovitz, "New Perspectives on Strategic Management," *The Journal of Business Strategy* 4:3 (Winter 1984), pp. 19–33.

TABLE 6-3 Concerns in Strategic Management

Steps	Process	
	Intellectual Process	Social Process
Strategy formulation	What are the prospects in a particular industrial sector? Can we handle a changing environment with our current resources and capabilities? What should we do in our current businesses? How can profits be restored? What businesses should we be in? What portfolio should a business have, given its objectives? What firms can be bought? What units/activities should be sold?	How should the responsibilities to prepare, present, defend, and carry out plans (SBUs) be defined? How much more should be spent on planning processes and systems in the organization? How can staff be involved and a balance of viewpoints be maintained? How can innovative ideas be fostered and the right issues be addressed? How can checks be made to ensure that plans presented make sense? How can priorities be selected? How should no/yes be said? How can corporatewide spirit and concerns be instilled?
Strategy implementation	How well does the structure fit the purpose? How can our efforts be organized to generate new businesses, innovation, and new strategic alternatives? What delegation is required for fast adaptation to changes in the marketplace? How detailed should we plan the different aspects of the business? What information is needed and at what level to respond to the requirements of markets, to anticipate problem areas, and to trigger in advance strategic responses? What training and reward systems best fit our strategy?	How can we get our managers to think strategically? How can we get people committed to make it happen? How can new ideas be made standard practice? How can individual motivation be kept high? How can we ensure that broad objectives are carried out effectively through the chain of command? How can efforts be mobilized around a few values and objectives? How can withholding of information, deformation of purpose, resistance to change, and defiance toward innovation be prevented?

Source: Jacques Horovitz, "New Perspectives on Strategic Management." Reprinted by permission from *The Journal of Business Strategy* 4 (Winter 1984). Published by Warren, Gorham & Lamont, Inc., 210 South St., Boston, Mass. Copyright © 1984. All rights reserved.

According to Horovitz, the concerns of management in the development of strategy, shown in Table 6-3, are best understood when viewed from two dimensions: (1) the steps necessary to formulate and implement strategy and (2) the processes that are used (see Table 6-3). Steps involve:

1. **Strategy formulation**—deciding in which direction to go
2. **Strategy implementation**—deciding how the organization is going to get there internally

The processes by which strategies are formulated and implemented involve:

1. **An intellectual process.** A decision maker, through certain methodologies and tools, thinks through the best way to formulate a strategy and the organizational arrangements that best suit the orientation chosen or helps managers define better their long-term orientations.
2. **A social process.** Through the planning process, the members of an organization participate one way or the other in the formulation of strategy. The people's profile and ability, as well as the CEO's activating mode, will determine whether and how well the strategies actually "happen." These factors also ensure that the actual behavior within the organization supports the accomplishment of the purpose.

THE STRATEGIC PLANNING PROCESS

As previously mentioned, the strategic planning process, shown in Figure 6-2, involves the organization in recognizing, anticipating, and responding to changes in the marketplace to ensure that resources are directed toward achieving opportunities that are consistent with the firm's capabilities. Strategic planning is a formal, long-range planning process that focuses on an organization's basic mission, objectives, and the long-range strategies needed to carry them out.

The Corporate Mission as a Directing Force in the Development of Strategy

All successful companies exhibit a distinct and widely shared culture that directs corporate strategy.[13] A corporation's culture, like a society's culture, "is reflected in the attitudes and values, the management style, and the problem-solving behavior of its people."[14] The foundation for the development of that culture lies in a systematically and comprehensively developed *mission statement*.[15] It is the company mission, or purpose, that provides the basis for the culture that guides executive action and directs the formulation and implementation of strategy. When manage-

---

[13]"Corporate Culture," *Business Week* (October 27, 1980), pp. 148–160.

[14]George A. Steiner, John B. Miner, and Edmund B. Gray, *Management Policy and Strategy*, 2nd ed. (New York: Macmillan Publishing Company, 1982), p. 477.

[15]John A. Pearce II, "The Company Mission as a Strategic Tool," *Sloan Management Review* (Spring 1982), pp. 15–24.

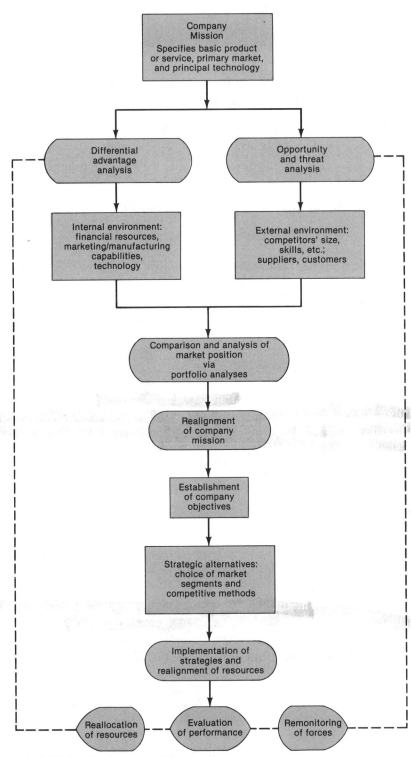

FIGURE 6-2 The Strategic Planning Process

148

ment addresses such fundamental questions as "What business are we in?" "Who are the customers we serve?" and "Why does this organization exist?" the organization achieves a heightened sense of purpose.

A carefully conceived mission statement is necessary if individuals within the various functional areas of the company are to work independently and at the same time cooperatively toward realizing organizational goals. It is the company mission that embodies the business philosophy of those who direct the company, reveals the image the firm seeks to project, reflects the firm's self-concept, and specifies the business domain within which the firm will operate. A company's business domain consists of the customer groups that will be served, the customer needs that will be met, and the technology that will satisfy those needs.[16] For example, IBM has been guided over the years by recognizing that it was not in business to "manufacture and sell computers" but "to solve data storage, retrieval, and processing problems of large organizations."

A well-conceived mission statement should provide a view of what an organization seeks to accomplish and the markets and customers it seeks to pursue now and in the future. It should be broadly outlined or implied, rather than specified, to enable the organization to expand or contract its business domain as it attempts to adjust to environmental change. As a business grows, or is forced by environmental pressures to alter its product/market/technology position, the need will arise to redefine the company mission. Thus, a firm's mission should be conceived in such a way as to provide for the enterprise's growth and development as it is forced to adapt to changing business and economic conditions.

Opportunity and Threat Analysis

The question, "What business are we in?" can only be answered through the accurate evaluation of present and future marketing opportunities and threats. Opportunity and threat assessment shapes organizational efforts, determines how resources should be deployed, and guides the organization's future. It answers questions relative to such critical issues as the markets to serve, which products to add or drop, how the sales force should be deployed, and what support services should be offered. In effect, it guides the organization in the development and revisions of its mission statement. And it is essential to the development of profitable marketing strategies and plans.

Threat Analysis. Environmental threats must be identified and evaluated with respect to their seriousness and probability of occurrence to enable management to adopt strategies to counteract them. An environmental threat is a threat that is likely to affect significantly the strategic planning process over the planning horizon. Kotler has identified such a threat as

---

[16]Derek Abell, *Defining the Business: The Starting Point of Strategic Planning* (Englewood Cliffs, N.J.: Prentice-Hall, Inc., 1980), Chap. 3.

a challenge posed by an unfavorable trend or development in the environment that would lead, in the absence of purposeful marketing action, to the erosion of the company's position.[17]

Opportunity Analysis. Opportunity analysis, the opposite of threat analysis, is undertaken to anticipate favorable situations within the scope of the firm's present or future domain capabilities. A marketing opportunity depends not only on environmental factors, but on the organization's actual and potential resources as well. Kotler defines a company marketing opportunity as

> an attractive arena for company marketing action in which the particular company would enjoy a competitive advantage.[18]

The purpose of assessing opportunities and threats is to enable an organization to capitalize on its ability to develop, maintain, and defend a specific position in the market. This involves

1. Monitoring the external environment for forces that are likely to affect markets and the demand for current and future products.
2. An internal analysis of the firm to identify its strengths and weaknesses with respect to its management, its organizational structure, and its current position in the market to identify its future capabilities.
3. The determination of which market opportunities the organization should pursue and which threats should be assessed as to their implications for company planning and marketing decision making.

Monitoring the External Environment

Environmental monitoring or scanning is becoming an increasingly important function of the firm. Managers must cope with changing forces in the external environment that may affect the organization, its markets, or the demand for its current and future products. A firm's external environment consists of those forces within the interface, public, and macro levels that can affect its strategic alternatives. Of course, forces in a firm's environment have positive or negative impacts. Zenith, for instance, whose major business domain was in the consumer market, is now the nation's largest supplier of computer terminal monitors in the institutional and government market—selling mainly to colleges and the military. Zenith's move into the industrial market arena was prompted by a decade of competitive price cutting that led to a loss of market share in all three of its consumer product areas.[19]

Environmental monitoring requires the analyses of past developments and cur-

---

[17]Philip Kotler, *Marketing Management: Analysis, Planning, and Control,* 5th ed. (Englewood Cliffs, N.J.: Prentice-Hall, Inc., 1984), p. 41.

[18]Kotler, *Marketing Management: Analysis, Planning, and Control*, 5th ed. (Englewood Cliffs, N.J.: Prentice-Hall, Inc., 1984), p. 42.

[19]"Zenith Wants to Give the Boob Tube a Brain," *Business Week* (May 6, 1985), pp. 69–72.

MAXIMUM RETURN FOR MAXIMUM RISK? STICK TO YOUR AREA OF
DISTINCTIVE COMPETENCY

Many companies that aggressively diversified in the late 1960s and 1970s have
been actively divesting a good percentage of the businesses they acquired. Such
conglomerates as Ashland Oil, R. J. Reynolds, Atlantic Richfield, and Armco have
taken millions of dollars worth of losses in their attempts to shed business areas,
purchased for a multitude of reasons (most of them invalid), that failed to match
their areas of distinctive competency. Armco, for one, who moved aggressively over
a fifteen-year period into such diversifications as titanium and insurance to shelter
itself from earning swings in the steel industry ran into real problems when it moved
into financial services. While the market was healthy, Armco had very few people in
its management group who were capable of asking the right questions and trouble
shooting in that part of its operations.

Although these newly trimmed companies say they haven't entirely given up
on diversification, "Many managers have come to feel in their gut that the way you
create maximum return for minimum risk is by sticking within your area of distinctive
competence." They are beginning to ask if potential businesses can be managed
properly and, if they can, will it make economic sense.

rent situations, as well as future projections to discover trends and identify likely
opportunities and threats. It relies on quantitative analysis such as time-series analysis and other extrapolation methods that are useful in projecting economic and
demographic data, as well as management judgment. To monitor political developments, foreign competition, or other issues that may affect their future, many organizations also gather information from government sources such as the Bureau of
the Census, the Bureau of Economic Analysis, and the Bureau of Labor Statistics,
as well as from banks and universities, or from services such as the Yankelovich
Monitor.

Differential Advantage Analysis

At the heart of successful marketing strategy is differentiation. Effective differentiation brings with it recognition and reward in such forms as customer awareness,
brand switching, improved sales, better market shares, and heftier cash flows. "The
survival of a firm requires that for some group of buyers it should enjoy a differential advantage over all other suppliers."[20] The assumption is that every firm occupies

[20]Wroe Alderson, "The Analytical Framework for Marketing," in Ben M. Enis and Keith K. Cox,
eds., *Marketing Classics: A Selection of Influential Articles*, 4th ed. (Boston: Allyn & Bacon, Inc., 1981),
pp. 24–34.

a unique position in the market, somehow differentiating itself from others on the basis of product or service characteristics, management or engineering expertise, geographical location, or some other area that gives it a specific distinctive competency.[21]

A firm's differential advantage, however, is subject to change as elements within its external environment neutralize its existing position. The marketing environment is never static. Marketing success, then, also necessitates an ongoing evaluation of the firm's distinctive competencies and its position of differential advantage within the marketplace. A threat in one market may lead to an opportunity in another, but only when a firm is able to transfer its distinctive competencies in such a manner as to develop a new differential advantage. Zenith, for instance, was able to successfully enter the personal computer market by building on its distinctive competency in electronics. In fact, according to one industry analyst, Zenith's successful entry into other electronic fields (e.g., microcomputers, monitors, and power plants for computer terminals) would not have been achieved if Jerry Pearlman, the company's chief executive, had not been at the helm—a second facet of Zenith's distinctive competency.[22]

Internal Company Analysis

Three ingredients are essential for successful strategic planning: (1) it must be consistent with conditions in the external environment, (2) it must be realistic in terms of the requirements it places on the firm, and (3) it must be carefully executed.[23] The purpose of an internal company analysis, then, is to identify the specific strengths and weaknesses upon which strategic planning should be based. In seeking to take advantage of opportunities yet minimize the impact of threats, an organization must develop its strategies around its key strengths, or distinctive competencies, and its weaknesses. This is accomplished by reviewing the company's past and present performance with respect to its products and markets as well as industry trends and characteristics. Specifically, the organization should analyze sales trends by product lines, customer groups, geographic regions, channels of distribution, the cost and profitability of the respective areas, and its industry position.

When internal factors are isolated for analysis, the firm is in a better position to determine which factors (e.g., products, markets, channels, or pricing) to place emphasis on when developing future strategy. In actuality, an internal company analysis involves analyzing all aspects of the firm, including finance and accounting, production operations, and the organization's structure and personnel as well as marketing.

[21]Laurence D. Ackerman, "Identity Strategies That Make a Difference," *The Journal of Business Strategy* (May/June 1988), pp. 28–32.

[22]"Zenith Wants to Give the Boob Tube a Brain."

[23]John A. Pearce II and Richard B. Robinson, Jr., *Strategic Management* (Homewood, Ill.: Richard D. Irwin, Inc., 1982), p. 155.

CAPITALIZE ON INHERENT CAPABILITIES

To sustain differentiation over the long term, a company must distinguish itself from competitors in ways that are so basic they are almost impossible to duplicate. And these distinctions must be inherent rather than fabricated. This means going beyond quantitatively based economic and marketing considerations such as production cost advantages, technology improvements, pricing schemes, special product features, and product warranties. . . . Differentiation . . . {means} capitalizing on inherent capabilities that define the organization in terms of its basic identity—who it is and, by extension, who it is not—and making sure that these capabilities are fully manifested and recognized in the marketplace.

Identity is the unique capabilities of a company—the cross-functional mix of experience, skills, knowledge, and talents—which distinguish the corporation and determine its ability to create value in proprietary ways.

Alcoa provides an illustration of how identity affects value creation. Although the company's business and its image have focused on aluminum for a century, the identity of Alcoa is characterized by a genius for transformation. The company has a marked ability to constantly convert materials into new products, products into new markets (where the company is always the leader), and markets into societal change based on scientific precedents.

For example, aluminum was converted into can sheet, which revolutionized the packaging industry, which in turn fundamentally changed food preservation techniques.

In effect, Alcoa's ability to create proprietary value has been driven not just by its aluminum know-how, but by its ability to manage the process of transformation as a discrete, human technology over and over again.

Source: Laurence D. Ackerman, "Identity Strategies That Make a Difference," Reprinted with permission from *The Journal of Business Strategy* 1988 May/June. Copyright © Warren, Gorham & Lamont, Inc., 210 South Street Boston, MA 02111. All rights reserved.

Portfolio Analysis

The increased complexity of the industrial environment, coupled with the multi-product, multimarket, and multinational nature of industrial marketing, has led many organizations to develop their strategies around portfolio analysis. Portfolio analysis enables organizations to make better decisions with respect to which market or product should be maintained, which expanded, which phased out, and which new ventures pursued. Several organizations have developed analytical models to assist them in selecting the appropriate marketing strategy. One of the most widely used approaches for analyzing current market situations is the General Electric business screen.

Identifying Strategic Business Units. The first step, however, in portfolio analysis is to carefully identify *strategic business units (SBUs)* within the company. An SBU can consist of a collection of businesses or divisions, a single business or division, a product line, or on occasion, a single product. Ideally, an SBU, which is a single business, would have a distinct mission, a responsible manager, and its own competition; be independent of other business units; benefit from strategic planning; and be planned independently of other business units.[24] For instance, General Electric has identified forty-nine separate business areas.

Business Screening. General Electric's business screen is used to combine a number of factors into a composite value to determine each SBU's strengths and weaknesses and to assess environmental factors that represent risks and opportunities. Thus, the method uses multiple factors to assess each unit's business strengths and market attractiveness.

The business screen matrix, presented in Figure 6-3, is divided into nine cells to represent high, medium, and low market attractiveness and strong, average, and weak business strengths. Each cell is placed into zones to represent high, medium,

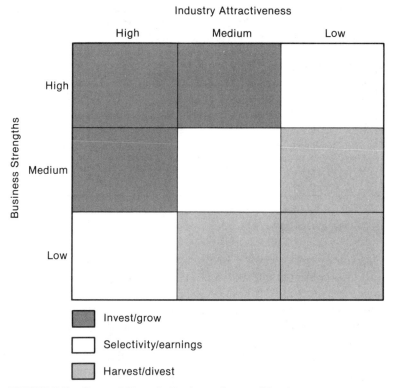

FIGURE 6-3   **General Electric Business Screen Matrix**

---

[24]Kotler, *Marketing Management*, 5th ed., p. 51.

or low overall attractiveness. The horizontal axis is traditionally labeled "Industry Attractiveness"; the vertical axis, "Organizational Strengths."

Industry attractiveness is defined as a *composite projection* of the size and growth potential of the market, competitive structure, industry profitability, and environmental impact (e.g., economic, social and legal considerations). Organizational strength is viewed as a function of market size and growth rate, technological position, image, price competitiveness, product quality, sales force effectiveness, market location, profitability, environmental impact, and caliber of management.[25] The strategies that a business screen might suggest, depending on where an SBU is located, are illustrated in Table 6-4.

The advantages of using business screening are twofold. First, it allows SBUs to be ranked intermediately between high and low and strong and weak. Second, it forces management to consider a wide range of strategically relevant variables. Once businesses have been evaluated and positioned, the appropriate marketing strategies can be determined. For example, business units falling in the "high overall attractiveness" zone should be given heavy marketing support; those in the "low overall attractiveness" should be considered for either harvesting or divesting.

Profit Impact of Marketing Strategies.[26] Portfolio models, such as the business screen model, imply the need for measuring return on investment for a given business unit, under given industry and market conditions, following a given marketing strategy. Some methods of doing this have emerged from a unique research project called *Profit Impact of Marketing Strategies (PIMS)*.

The PIMS program is administered by the Strategic Planning Institute, which gathers data from a number of corporations to establish a relationship between a variety of business factors and two measures of organizational performance—return on investment (ROI) and cash flow. By examining PIMS data, an organization can determine the effects of various marketing strategies on performance.

According to PIMS's findings, those factors having the greatest impact on ROI are market share relative to the company's three largest competitors, the value added to a product by the company, industry growth, product quality, level of innovation/differentiation, and vertical integration (ownership of other channel members). With respect to cash flow, PIMS's data suggest that growing markets and high levels of investment drain cash, while high relative market share improves cash flow. PIMS information is conveyed to participating firms through the following reports:

[25]See, for instance, Charles W. Hofer and Dan Schendel, *Strategy Formulation: Analytical Concepts* (St. Paul, Minn.: West Publishing Co., 1978), pp. 32–34; and William K. Hall, "SBU's: Hot, New Topic in the Management of Diversification," *Business Horizons* 21 (February 1978), p. 20.

[26]See Paula Smith, "Unique Tool for Marketers: PIMS," *Dun's Review* 108 (October 1976), pp. 95–106; Sidney Schoeffer, Robert D. Buzzell, and Donald F. Heany, "Impact of Strategic Planning on Profit Performance," *Harvard Business Review* 52 (March–April 1974), pp. 137–145; and D. F. Abell and J. S. Hammond, *Strategic Marketing Planning* (Englewood Cliffs, N.J.: Prentice-Hall, Inc., 1979), pp. 272–278.

TABLE 6-4 Strategies Suggested for the Placement of SBUs in the Business Screen Matrix

Organizational Strength	Industry Attractiveness		
	High	Medium	Low
High	Premium: Invest for growth. Provide maximum investment. Diversify worldwide. Consolidate position. Accept moderate near-term profits.	Selective: Invest for growth. Invest heavily in selected segments. Share ceiling. Seek attractive new segments to apply strength.	Protect/Refocus: Selectively invest for earnings. Defend strengths. Refocus to attractive segments. Evaluate industry revitalization. Monitor for harvest or divestment timing.
Medium	Challenge: Invest for growth. Build selectively on strengths. Define implications of leadership challenge. Avoid vulnerability—fill weaknesses.	Prime: Selectively invest for earnings. Segment market. Make contingency plans for vulnerability.	Restructure: Harvest or divest. Provide no unessential commitment. Position for divestment. Shift to more attractive segment.
Low	Opportunistic: Selectively invest for earnings. Ride market. Seek niches, specialization. Seek opportunity to increase strength [e.g., acquisition].	Opportunistic: Preserve for harvest. Act to preserve or boost cash flow out. Seek opportunistic sale. Seek opportunistic rationalization to increase strengths.	Harvest or divest: Exit from market or prune product line. Determine timing so as to maximize present value.

Source: D. D. Monieson, ''An Overview of Marketing Planning.'' In Executive Bulletin No. 8, [Ottawa: The Conference Board of Canada, 1978], p. 5.

Par reports—showing average return on investment and cash flow on the basis of market, competition, technology, and cost structure that enable managers to consider what would be reasonable expectations for their business and to set control standards.

Strategy sensitivity reports—predicting effects of strategy changes on short-run and long-run ROI and cash flow.

Optimum strategy reports—suggesting combinations of strategies that will maximize results in income or cash flows.

Look-alike reports—examining tactics of similar competitors, both successful and un-successful.

Integrated Portfolio Models. In an empirical study of 15 SBUs, using PIMS data, Wind, Mahajan, and Swire have found that where an SBU is placed in a matrix depends on the type of portfolio model being used as well as the factors used to determine high/low industry growth and share, or industry attractiveness and organizational strengths. Specifically, they have discovered that a minor change in the definition of the dimensions used, the rules used to divide those dimensions into low or high categories, how those dimensions are weighted, and the cutoff points used can result in a different classification of the SBU involved (i.e., a business may appear to be located in a high-high position in one model but a high-low position in another model). Thus, they advise that rather than use a single portfolio model, integrated models should be used to take advantage of various methods of classification as well as to test the sensitivity of portfolio classifications of particular models. Such an integration would eliminate the risk "involved in employing a single standardized portfolio model as a basis for portfolio analysis and strategy." They further suggest that the classification of an SBU with respect to the dimensions used, cutoff rules, and weights be carefully examined.[27]

Evaluating the Portfolio Matrix. It may make little difference, however, which type or combinations of portfolio matrices are used. Their main purpose is to identify the character and market position of a firm's business portfolio. Thus, once the matrices are constructed, their classifications should be supplemented by additional analysis that adds to what the matrices indicate and that further indicates which strategies should be pursued. As Hofer and Schendel point out, those additional analyses should include

1. An assessment of each SBU's industry to identify key trends and market changes, strengths and weaknesses of competitors, technological changes, and supply conditions.
2. An examination of the firm's competitive position within each industry and how it ranks on factors important to successful performance in those industries.
3. An identification of opportunities and threats that might arise in each area.
4. An assessment of corporate resources and skills needed to improve the competitive strength of each SBU.
5. A comparison of the relative short- and long-run attractiveness of each SBU.
6. An evaluation of the overall portfolio to determine whether the mix of SBUs is adequately balanced, for example, whether there are sufficient cash-producing SBUs in relation to the number of those that are heavy cash consuming, so that internal control is maximized with respect to resource deployment.[28]

[27]Yoram Wind, Vijay Mahajan, and Donald J. Swire, "An Empirical Comparison of Standardized Portfolio Models," *Journal of Marketing* 47 (Spring 1983), pp. 89–99.
[28]Hofer and Schendel, *Strategy Formulation*, pp. 32–34.

Establishing Company Objectives

In effect, opportunity and threat analysis is the intermediate step between defining the firm's mission and the setting of corporate objectives. Analysis may reveal that to take advantage of an environmental opportunity, or avoid a threat, the organization may have to redefine its business domain, adopt a more effective strategy, or both.

While mission statements identify the underlying design, aim, or thrust of a company, objectives are the specific results desired. For example, the mission statement of Nicor, Inc., reads

> The basic purpose of Nicor, Inc., to perpetuate an investor-owned company, engaging in various phases of the energy business, striving for balance among those phases so as to render needed satisfactory products and services and earn optimum, long-range profits.[29]

To achieve its underlying thrust, Nicor must develop specific objectives in such areas as profitability, return on investment, and technological leadership. Thus, a specific corporate objective to optimize profits might read

> Double earnings per share within five years with increases in each interim year.

Objectives are important in the strategic planning process because they provide people with a specific sense of their role in the organization, lead to consistency in decision making among the various functional managers, stimulate exertion and accomplishment, and most important, provide the bases for specific planning, corrective actions, and control.[30] Most organizations, however, pursue a number of objectives. Thus, when possible, they should be ranked in order of importance. They should also be stated in specific quantitative terms with respect to what is to be achieved and when it is to be achieved if they are to be useful for developing plans and implementing controls. Other criteria for establishing useful objectives are outlined in Table 6-5.

MARKETING'S ROLE IN THE STRATEGIC PLANNING PROCESS

"Marketing plays an important, indeed critical, role in company strategic planning."[31] Successful planning at both the corporate level and the business level depends on the ability of marketing to generate ideas for new product development, to spot and evaluate new market opportunities, to develop detailed marketing plans,

[29]Bates and Eleredge, *Strategy and Policy*, p. 97.

[30]Kotler, *Marketing Management*, 3rd ed., p. 53.

[31]Kotler, *Marketing Management*, 5th ed., p. 35.

TABLE 6-5 Criteria for Establishing Useful Objectives

Acceptable	When objectives are consistent with managers' perceptions and preferences, they are more likely to be pursued. If objectives are inappropriate, unfair, or offensive, management may ignore or even obstruct their achievement.
Flexible	In the event of unforeseen or extraordinary changes in the firm's environment, objectives must be capable of modification.
Motivating	If objectives are to stimulate exertion and accomplishment, they must be set high enough to provide a challenge and yet not so high as to cause frustration or so low as to be easily attained.
Consistent	Objectives must be consistent and suited to the overall mission of the firm as well. Objectives that are inconsistent or unsupportive of company goals can be counterproductive.
Understandable	If objectives are to be achievable, they must be stated in clear, meaningful, and unambiguous terms. Managers at all levels must have a clear understanding of what is to be achieved and the criteria by which they will be evaluated.
Achievable	To be achievable, objectives must be realistic and feasible. Thus, they should come from the company's external and internal analysis, not out of wishful thinking.

to implement and evaluate ongoing results, to take corrective action where necessary, and to determine when a business venture is no longer viable. However, since the success of marketing planning in the industrial arena is greatly dependent on the activities of other functional areas, marketing's role in the strategic planning process involves analyzing and interpreting market requirements to enable corporate management to decide how best to respond.[32]

The relationship between marketing and the various business units during the strategic planning process is shown in Figure 6-4. Marketing supplies each unit with information and opinion inputs (step 1), which are analyzed and evaluated by each unit (step 2), which then establishes its mission and formulates its objectives (step 3). Once each business unit has established its mission and objectives, marketing managers can formulate marketing plans (step 4), implement them (step 5), and evaluate the results (step 6), which triggers the next cycle in the strategic planning process.[33]

Situational Analysis

As Figure 6-5 shows, marketing plays a major role in the development of strategic plans, particularly at the business level. Each business unit within a firm relies on marketing "as the main system for monitoring opportunities and developing mar-

[32]Ames, "Marketing Planning for Industrial Products," p. 100–111.
[33]Kotler, *Marketing Management*, 5th ed., p. 61.

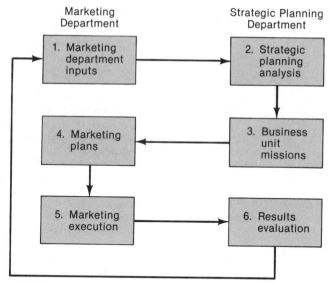

FIGURE 6-4   Relationship Between Marketing and Strategic Planning

Source: Philip Kotler, *Marketing Management: Analysis, Planning, and Control,* 5th ed. [Englewood Cliffs, N.J.: Prentice-Hall, Inc. © 1984], p. 61. Reprinted by permission of Prentice-Hall.

keting objectives and plans for achieving that business's objectives.''[34] To carry out their role in the strategic planning process then, marketing managers (1) assess the current market situation and (2) determine forces that will affect the market situation during the future planning period. Situational analysis, then, is the information gathering stage in which marketing managers assimilate and assess external or market-related information and internal or company-related information to assist each business unit in identifying opportunities and threats to make the best of its differential advantages. Current and potential market opportunities, marketing objectives, and marketing plans cannot be determined without knowing where the company presently stands in its total marketing environment.[35]

A necessary part of marketing's role in analyzing and interpreting market requirements, then, is to assess realistically the present and future market situation and identify the company's strengths and weaknesses with respect to its present and future capability of competing in the marketplace. The types of information that marketing managers most often seek during the situation analysis stage are outlined in Table 6-6.

Establishing Marketing Objectives

Marketing objectives are derived directly from the objectives set forth by each business unit during the strategic planning process and the situational analysis. Given

[34]Ibid.

[35]See Robert W. Haas and Thomas R. Wotruba, *Marketing Management: Concepts, Practice and Cases* (Plano, Tex.: Business Publications, Inc., 1983), pp. 285–289.

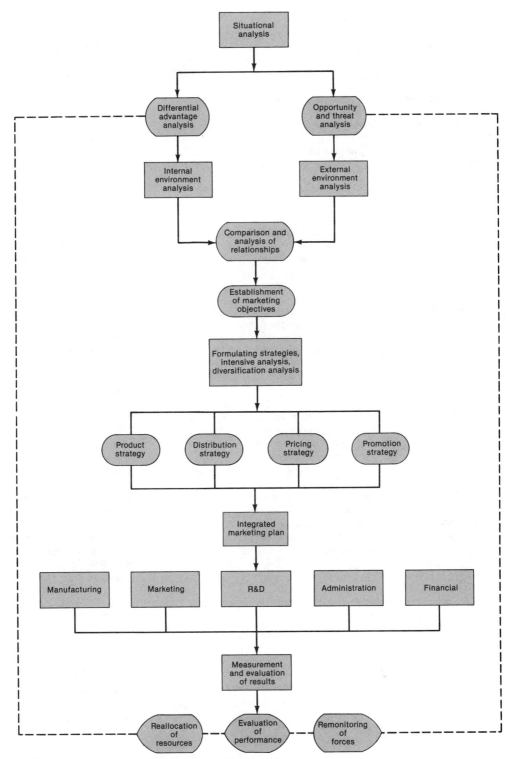

FIGURE 6-5   The Industrial Marketing Planning Process

TABLE 6-6 Internal and External Information Gathering in the Situational Analysis

Internal Information		External Information	
Categories	Types of Information	Categories	Types of Information
Organization	Company mission, objectives; company growth strategies; portfolio plans, organizational problems, power center/struggles, company strengths/weaknesses	Environmental factors	Cost and availability of needed resources: economic conditions [e.g., recession, inflation and interest rates]; technological/social changes; environmental policies/regulations; industry/business regulations
Financial resources	Profitability by product/market geographic areas; cost data by product/market geographic areas; budgets; financial ratios; credit position	Market conditions	Market size/growth; geographic concentration; market share/sales penetration
Forecasts and projections	Sales and market share forecasts and projections by products/markets; production and manpower forecasts	Market segments	Rate of product usage, product applications and benefits; decision makers' and influencers' receptivity to sales force, advertising and promotion, prices, price changes, and channel arrangements
Operating capabilities	Manufacturing/production/ purchasing capacity; quality of engineering and R&D; service facilities/expertiese; inventory levels	Channels	Present channel relations; motivation of channel members; costs of alternative arrangements; inventory levels, f.o.b. points; effect of pricing strategies
Competitive strengths and weaknesses	Current status of company products, sales force, distribution advertising and promotion, compared to competitors	Competitors	Number, location, and market share; strengths and weaknesses with respect to products, prices, advertising and promotion, channels, R&D, engineering; possible competitive reactions

the assessment of current and future market situations, specific marketing objectives are normally established in terms of some desired sales volume, market share, gross margin, profits, and return on investment. Since performance is usually measured in relation to desired objectives, marketing objectives should have those attributes discussed in Table 6-5, "Criteria for Establishing Useful Objectives."

Formulating Marketing Strategies

Once marketing objectives have been determined, alternative marketing strategies must be analyzed. Two levels of analysis are available for determining strategic marketing alternatives:[36] (1) intensive analysis, which identifies possible strategic alternatives within the company's current business areas, and (2) diversification analysis, which identifies strategic alternatives outside the firm's current business areas.

Intensive Analysis.   Intensive analysis consists of reviewing existing business units (i.e., portfolio analysis) to determine whether opportunities exist for improving their performance.[37] When the current product/market position has not been fully exploited, the potential for market share growth exists. Through more aggressive marketing efforts such as offering quantity discounts and increasing advertising and selling efforts, current customers can be encouraged to buy more, and, where competitors are weak, their customers can be attracted.

Strategic alternatives may also be generated by developing new markets through regional, national, or international expansion or by developing differentiated product versions that appeal to new market segments. Or they may exist in the development of improved products for present markets (e.g., improving product features, creating different quality versions, or developing additional models and sizes).

Diversification Analysis.   By looking outside its present product/market area for opportunities that are both highly attractive and are related to its business strengths and distinctive competencies, the firm may also discover strategic alternatives via diversification. Three types of diversification are worth considering: (1) concentric diversification, which consists of searching for new products that have technological and/or marketing synergies with the firm's existing product lines and that will appeal to new customers; (2) horizontal diversification, which consists of adding new, technologically unrelated products that appeal to the firm's present customer base; and (3) conglomerate diversification, which consists of seeking new businesses that are totally unrelated to the company's present technology, products, or markets.

Mobility Barriers.   Factors that may inhibit a firm's entry into new businesses or industry segments have been generalized as mobility barriers. Mobility barriers consist of factors that may be deterrents to a shift in the strategic position of one firm and advantages to another.[38] These barriers can be described as

[36]Kotler, *Marketing Management*, 5th ed., pp. 57–60.

[37]H. Igor Ansoff, "Strategies for Diversification," *Harvard Business Review* (September–October 1957), pp 113–24.

[38]John H. Grant and William R. King, *The Logic of Strategic Planning* (Boston: Little, Brown and Company, 1982), pp. 48–49.

1. **Economies of scale**—can force an organization to enter on a large scale or accept the cost disadvantages inherent in low production volume. Economies of scale may exist in research, marketing, distribution, and finance as well as manufacturing.
2. **Product differentiation**—can create customer loyalty, which would force an organization to spend heavily to overcome the loyalty. Where products are clearly differentiated, it can be a strong entry barrier.
3. **Capital requirements**—where substantial capital is needed for physical facilities, R&D, advertising, credit, inventories, or other areas can be a clear barrier to entry.
4. **Cost disadvantages**—due to the considerable expenditures necessary to overcome a lack of experience in proprietary technology, existing supplier relationships, location, or existing assets an organization may be impeded from entry.
5. **Access to distribution channels**—may make entry difficult if channels are limited or an organization is required to develop entirely new channels.
6. **Government policy**—such as license requirements and environmental and safety regulations, can serve to give entrenched firms significant advantages over potential entrants.

Since the ease of entry into new businesses or industry segments depends on the strategic position that firm may choose to adopt, mobility barriers to intensive or diversification strategies must be carefully analyzed before deciding which strategic alternative will achieve marketing objectives.

DEVELOPING MARKETING STRATEGY

Once strategic alternatives have been decided upon, the development of marketing strategy, rests on (1) market segmentation analysis, (2) target market(s) selection, and (3) the development of the marketing mix strategies.

Market Segmentation and Target Marketing

Market segmentation analysis is fairly well recognized by most marketing managers and can be thought of as a process of dividing a larger market into submarkets, each having different demand patterns, needs, buying styles, and responses to various suppliers' marketing strategies. Market segments must be assessed, however, in terms of their market potential, competition, customer profiles, and the company's capability in serving them. How industrial markets are segmented is covered in Chapter Eight. The important point is that marketing planning cannot be undertaken until the firm has carefully chosen those markets it is capable of serving. Assessment of potential target markets must be based on

1. **Their current size**—which must be sufficient if marketing objectives in terms of sales volume, market share, profitability, or return on investment are to be achieved.
2. **Their potential for future growth**—if the firm is to realize a sufficient return for its efforts to serve a particular market.

3. **Whether they are owned or overoccupied by existing competition**—if the firm is to assess realistically its capability of penetrating a particular market.
4. **Whether there exists a relatively unsatisfied need that the firm can satisfy better than its competitors.**[39]

Formulating Marketing Mix Strategy

Once a target market has been identified, marketing strategy can address the components of product, place, price, and promotion. Table 6-7 briefly outlines the decision areas covered by these four components.

Decisions with respect to how product lines, features, quality levels, services, and new product development will be used to satisfy customer needs must be clearly formulated and integrated with manufacturing, R&D, and technical services.

Since products or services must be delivered to customers when and where they are wanted, distribution strategy is primarily concerned with developing the right combination of factors (e.g., inventory levels, storage facilities, and transportation modes) to ensure consistency with the total marketing strategy.

Promotion strategy defines the manner in which the firm will communicate with its target market and provides the bases for formulating personal selling, advertising, sales promotion, and media selection plans. Not only must promotion strategy be consistent with other strategic components, it must be closely integrated with financial strategy due to cost requirements.

Pricing strategy, because of its influence on demand and supply, profitability, customer perception, and regulatory response must be carefully developed in conjunction with internal factors (e.g., cost, return on investment, and profitability). When strategies in the four areas of the marketing mix are properly developed, they should produce a synergistic marketing effect.

Developing Marketing Plans

Marketing planning involves considerations with respect to developing specific marketing activities to implement strategies such as test marketing a new product, training sales personnel, and developing advertising programs. It also involves developing budgets, based on realistic sales projections for each of the company's divisions and products, and allocating those budgets across the various components of the marketing mix.

Successful marketing planning, however, also requires careful timing and implementation. Hofer and Abel have suggested that in many industries there are "strategic windows"—limited periods of time during which a firm may successfully adopt and implement a completely new strategy.[40] Thus, timing is particularly critical when a firm is developing, or radically changing, its strategy. Scheduling is a

---

[39]Kotler, *Marketing Management*, 3rd ed., p. 58.
[40]Derek F. Abell, "Strategic Windows," *Journal of Marketing* (July 1978), pp. 21–29.

TABLE 6-7 Industrial Marketing Strategy Components

Product Planning and Development
1. Distinguish product from that of competitors as viewed by customers.
2. Offer only one product and try to attract all buyers [i.e., use an "undifferentiated" strategy].
3. Develop separate products and marketing programs for each market segment [i.e., use a "differentiated" strategy].
4. Create new uses for existing products [through improved performances and/or exclusive features].
5. Diversify into new markets with new products, either through acquisition of companies or through internal development of new products.
6. Establish product leadership through development of quality products.
7. Develop new products for commercialization consideration each year, beating competition to marketplace and establishing a reputation for innovation.

Distribution
1. Warehouse products at locations that enable quick delivery to each distributor and customer.
2. Provide additional outlets to reduce distribution cost per sale.
3. Use only one warehouse to minimize inventory control problems.

Sales/Service
1. Expand geographic area of operations to penetrate high-potential regions not currently approached.
2. Reshape distribution channels [i.e., dealers, distributors, agents, and company sales force] to satisfy market buying preferences more closely.
3. Develop more competent sales force and/or dealer/distributor organization.
4. Require sales force to improve its knowledge of customers and their products.
5. Employ target marketing to identify and reach high-potential customers and prospects.
6. Maximize reciprocal purchases with suppliers where prudent.
7. Increase sales effort on most profitable products and customers.

Advertising/Promotion
1. Employ "push" strategy to encourage dealers, distributors, and company sales force to move your product lines [good margins, bonuses, services, advertising, and promotional subsidies].
2. Employ "pull" strategy to stimulate customer demand through increased brand, concept, and product acceptance.
3. Maximize advertising and promotion coverage to increase volume, which will permit mass production and distribution.
4. Address advertising and promotion to key customers and "best" prospects to maximize the benefits of these expenditures in a limited market segment.

Pricing
1. Set low price for new products to discourage competitive entry into market.
2. Set low price for products to encourage high sales volume, which permits mass production and low unit cost.
3. Provide minimum "extra" services to permit lower prices.
4. Price parts, service, and repairs at cost or with slight markup to gain maximum goodwill.
5. Price products to obtain principal profit on original sale rather than on follow-up service and parts.
6. Offer quantity discounts to encourage larger unit purchases.

Source: Adapted from Cochrane Chase and Kenneth L. Barasch, *Marketing Problem Solver* [Radnor, PA.: Chilton Book Company, 1977], pp. 79–80. Reprinted with permission.

useful means of controlling the timing of activities, as well as the deployment of resources, in implementing plans.

Scheduling can be accomplished through the use of such techniques as the *critical path method (CPM)* and *program evaluation and review technique (PERT)*. Both CPM and PERT are especially useful when major changes in purchasing or production schedules are called for in the implementation of marketing plans.

Implementing and Controlling Marketing Plans

Once marketing strategies and plans have been determined, they must be implemented and carried out. To evaluate and control their performance, standards for control must also be established. Since marketing strategies and plans are formulated to achieve objectives, these same objectives can be used to establish standards against which performance can be measured, such as objectives regarding profit, market share, and sales penetration. The company's historical trends can also be used to establish objective targets in these areas. Industry trends, such as sales per salesperson or percentage return on sales, can also be used.

Evaluation and control methods "make it possible not only to determine better the impact of current marketing activities on costs, revenues, and profits but also to respond more quickly to opportunities and threats.[41] A number of different performance measures are available for purposes of control:

1. *Sales analysis*—provides valuable data and serves as an early warning system for identifying declining or rapidly growing sales.
2. *Sales performance analysis*—compares sales volume to predetermined objectives or quotas and provides a benchmark against which to evaluate sales. Sales can also be compared to last year's sales, competitors' sales, forecasted sales, or industry sales.
3. *Marketing cost analysis*—measures marketing expenses against their magnitude and gives insight into the costs of doing business and the patterns of these costs.
4. *Contribution margin analysis*—subtracts direct costs from sales to determine contribution to overhead and profits.
5. *Net profit analysis*—subtracts both direct and indirect costs from sales to determine profitability.
6. *Return on investment analysis*—compares profits to the assets involved in generating profits to measure marketing productivity.[42]

Common performance measures and the extent of their use in the industrial market are shown in Table 6-8.

Schedules and Control Charts.   Schedules and charts are two common and logical types of control tools. As mentioned, CPM and PERT are used to plan and monitor schedules of activities. Gantt charts can also be used. Control charts are used more

---

[41]Donald W. Jackson, Jr., Lonnie L. Ostrom, and Kenneth R. Evans, "Measures Used to Evaluate Industrial Marketing Activities," *Industrial Marketing Management* 11 (October 1982), pp. 269–274.
[42]Ibid.

TABLE 6-8 Common Performance Measures Used in the Industrial Market

Measure	Percentage of Responding Firms
Customer performance measures [n = 116]	
Sales volume by customer (units or dollars)	90.5%
Sales volume as compared to a predetermined objective set for the customer	48.3
Contribution of customer profit	41.4
Net profit of customer (sales less direct costs less indirect costs allocated)	24.1
Return on assets committed to the customer	9.5
Product performance measures [n = 142]	
Sales volume by product (units or dollars)	91.5
Sales volume as compared to a predetermined quota by product	54.2
Market share by product	59.9
Expenses incurred by product	40.0
Contributions of product to profit (sales less direct cost)	75.4
Net profit of product (sales less direct costs less indirect costs allocated)	57.0
Return on assets committed to the product	28.9
Order size performance measures [n = 37]	
Sales volume by order size (units or dollars)	81.1
Sales volume as compared to a predetermined quota set for order sizes	18.9
Expenses incurred in relation to size of order	43.2
Contribution of a particular order size to profit (sales less direct costs)	45.9
Net profits of each order size (sales less direct costs less indirect costs allocated)	35.1
Geographic area performance measures [n = 110]	
Sales volume by area (units or dollars)	91.8
Sales volume as compared to a predetermined quota set for the area	70.0
Expenses incurred for sales to a particular area	38.2
Contribution of a particular area to profit (sales less direct costs)	25.5
Net profit of each area (sales less direct costs less indirect costs allocated)	11.8
Return on assets (committed to a particular area)	7.3

Source: Adapted by permission of the publisher from "Measures Used to Evaluate Industrial Marketing Activities," by Donald W. Jackson, Jr., Lonnie L. Ostrom, and Kenneth R. Evans, *Industrial Marketing Management* 11 (October 1982), pp. 269–274. Copyright © 1982 by Elsevier Science Publishing Co., Inc.

for repetitive-type activities to detect when an activity deviates significantly enough to warrant investigation.

Reports. To assist those persons responsible for implementing, evaluating, and controlling marketing strategy, companies' information systems produce periodic reports. These reports are helpful if they are prepared so as to report on how well objectives are being accomplished. Too frequently, though, once an information system begins producing reports relative to particular objectives, it will continue to do so, long after the objectives have changed.

Budgets. Budgets are an excellent control and evaluation tool, usually established for a one-year period and projecting costs for each budgeted category, such as sales and advertising. Since each budgeted item can be isolated for departments and individuals, deviations can be traced to the responsible activities or persons.

Sales and Cost Analyses. Sales and cost analyses are an effective means of discovering unexpected problems. Since sales analyses are subdivided by product, product line, customer type, and geographic area, components that need attention can be easily pinpointed. Where possible, when costs are separated and matched to specific products, product lines, customers, and geographic areas, profit measures can also be obtained.

Marketing Audits. A marketing audit consists of a systematic, periodic assessment of the entire marketing program with respect to its objectives, strategies, activities, organization structure, and individual personnel. It also includes an assessment of the firm's environment with respect to company image, customer characteristics, competitive activities, regulatory constraints, and economic trends. To ensure that an audit is carried out objectively and in an unbiased manner, however, it should be performed by persons who have no vested interests in the findings.

LOOKING BACK

Successful planning in the industrial market as compared to the consumer market requires a higher degree of functional coordination. Thus, regardless of the difficulties involved, the interfaces between marketing and manufacturing, R&D, and finance must not be ignored. Both top management and marketing management must search for ways to overcome the traditional isolation of functional areas—isolation that is brought about by (1) the inherent conflict between marketing and other functional areas, (2) organizational structures that are typically internally oriented rather than externally oriented, and (3) the failure to incorporate input from other functional areas into marketing decisions.

Strategic planning is not only an intellectual process, it is a social process that involves the firm in recognizing, anticipating, and responding to changes in the marketplace. To direct resources effectively so that objectives are achieved, management must begin the strategic planning process with a careful evaluation of its mission, which embodies the organization's business philosophy and defines its business domain; analyze opportunities and threats by examining both internal and external forces; evaluate the firm's distinctive competencies and differential advantages; and when necessary, realign its mission to adapt better to changing business and economic conditions.

Marketing's role in strategic planning should be one of analyzing and interpreting market requirements to assist management in deciding how to respond best. This involves gathering, analyzing, and interpreting external, or market-related, information as well as internal, or company-related, information to spot opportunities and assess the company's strengths and weaknesses with respect to competing in the marketplace.

The development of marketing strategy consists of identifying strategic alternatives within the company's current business domain—intensive analysis—or businesses not related to the firm's current businesses—diversification analysis.

Implementing and controlling marketing strategy involves the development of specific plans with respect to how the marketing mix will be implemented to deliver the desired satisfaction of target markets and monitored for corrective action. How the specific elements of each variable within the marketing mix (product, distribution, promotion, and price) are developed and controlled is addressed in Parts IV through VII.

QUESTIONS FOR DISCUSSION

1. A large component manufacturer was recently revising one of its leading product lines for the automotive industry. Engineers wanted a simple, cost-effective, technically consistent product line. Marketing wanted the technical aspects varied for product differentiation. After months of customer dissatisfaction and inefficient engineering designs and tests, the issue was still unresolved. What are the real issues involved and how would you solve them?

2. "Japanese companies place less reliance on the formal and conceptual aspects of formulating marketing goals and strategies and more emphasis on the implementation and human relations aspects than do American companies." Would this work in American organizations?

3. "People's behavior, judgment, and past experience and the CEO's style very much influence the quality and type of strategic decisions made." Do you agree?

4. The objective behind portfolio analysis is to "emphasize the balance of cash flows, by ensuring that there are products that use cash to sustain growth and others that supply cash. . . . The problem with concentrating on cash flow to maximize income and growth is that strategies to balance risks are not explicitly considered." If this is true, what other factors would you consider in developing your strategy besides organizational strengths and industry attractiveness?

5. "The success of any marketing strategy depends on the strength of the competitive analysis on which it is based." Thus, before marketing strategy can be developed, specific competitors must be identified and their strengths and weaknesses evaluated. "Yet present concepts of competitive analysis in marketing are almost useless." If that is true, can you improve on them?

6. "A marketing strategy is the manner in which company resources are put at risk in the search for differential advantage." Do you agree? If so, what are the firm's sources of differential advantages? How can management calculate the strength of its differential advantages?

SUGGESTED ADDITIONAL READINGS

ACKERMAN, LAURENCE D., "Identity Strategies That Make a Difference," *The Journal of Business Strategy* (May/June 1988):28–32.

COOK, VICTOR J., "Understanding Marketing Strategy and Differential Advantage," *Journal of Marketing* 49 (Spring 1985): 137–142.

DAY, GEORGE S., "Diagnosing the Product Portfolio," *Journal of Marketing* (April 1977):29–38.

GUPTA, ANIL K., and V. GOVINDARAJAN, "Build, Hold, Harvest: Converting Strategic Intentions into Reality," *The Journal of Business Strategy* 4 (Winter 1984):34–47.

HELMEKE, TODD M., "Strategic Business Unit Market Planning: An Industrial Case History," *Business Marketing* (November 1984):42–55.

HOROVITZ, JACQUES, "New Perspectives on Strategic Management," *The Journal of Business Strategy* 4 (Winter 1984):19–32.

HUTT, MICHAEL D., and THOMAS W. SPEH, "The Marketing Strategy Center: Diagnosing the Industrial Marketer's and Interdiscipinary Role," *Journal of Marketing* 48 (Fall 1984):53–61.

JACKSON, DONALD W., JR., Lonnie L. Ostrom, and Kenneth R. Evans, "Measures Used to Evaluate Industrial Marketing Activities," *Industrial Marketing Management* 11 (1982):269–274.

LAZER, WILLIAM, SHOJI MURATA, and HIROSHI KOSAKA, "Japanese Marketing: Towards a Better Understanding," *Journal of Marketing* 49 (Spring 1985):69–81.

MACMILLAN, IAN C., and PATRICIA E. JONES, "Designing Organizations to Compete," *The Journal of Business Strategy* 5 (Spring 1984):11–26.

PEARCE, JOHN A., "The Company Mission as a Strategic Tool," *Sloan Mangement Review* (Spring 1982):15–24.

WEINRACH, J. DONALD, and RICHARD ANDERSON, "Conflicts Between Engineering and Marketing Units," *Industrial Marketing Management* 11 (1982):291–301.

WIND, YORAM, VIJAN MAHAJAN, and DONALD J. SWIRE, "An Empirical Comparison of Standardized Portfolio Models," *Journal of Marketing* 47 (Spring 1983):89–98.

CHAPTER 7

Assessing Market Opportunities

Assessing market opportunities is basic to strategic planning. In our increasingly competitive and changing world, effective market performance depends on the continuous gathering and analysis of information on customers, competitors, and internal and external forces to support strategic decision making. This chapter, then, discusses the various methods that industrial organizations use to gather and analyze relevant marketing information to identify marketing opportunities and mitigate problems. When you have completed this chapter, you should

1. Understand the role of marketing research in strategic decision making.
2. Understand how secondary and primary data are collected and used.
3. Become aware of the vast changes taking place in the area of secondary research.
4. Appreciate the industrial applications of decision support systems and the software for them.

Strategic decision making must be based on knowledge about market potential, customer segments, and requirements and other forces in the firm's internal and external environment. Thus, to analyze, plan, implement, and control marketing strategy effectively, information must be gathered, organized, and analyzed. The assessment of environmental opportunities and threats, and the company's capacity to respond, however, must be performed with systematic care. According to a study of more than four hundred industrial firms, seventy percent of today's industrial organizations use marketing research in the strategic decision-making process to analyze market potential, market share, sales, business trends, and competition. They also use market research to establish sales forecasts and quotas for customers and territories, to study new product acceptance and potential, and to determine market characteristics.[1] In this chapter, then, we are concerned with how organizations systematically assess the marketing environment through marketing research.

As we move into the era of computer-designed support systems, the perspective and use of research in strategic decision making has changed considerably. Computerized systems now store, calculate, and retrieve data and enable managerial interaction to facilitate decision making at conveniently located terminals. Thus, today's decision makers use both primary and secondary research via a dynamic manager/machine interface in which a synergistic effect is achieved in analyzing the marketing environment and mitigating problems.[2]

THE ROLE OF MARKETING RESEARCH IN STRATEGIC DECISION MAKING

Marketing research consists of "the systematic design, collection, analysis, and reporting of data and findings relevant to a specific marketing situation facing the company."[3] As discussed, it is frequently used in areas such as analyzing and forecasting market and sales potential. It is also used to conduct market surveys, experiments, and other studies, such as those involving buying attitudes and practices, and to create an information base for making individual decisions in areas such as new product development. Thus, marketing research provides the data that are used in planning and controlling marketing efforts.

Differences Between Industrial and Consumer Marketing Research

While the basic objectives of marketing research apply in both the industrial and consumer market arena, due to the industrial marketing environment and the nature of organizational buying and behavior, significant differences exist between industrial and consumer marketing research.[4]

---

[1]William Cox, *Industrial Marketing Research* (New York: John Wiley & Sons, Inc., 1979), p. 10.

[2]Robert Thierauf, *Decision Support Systems for Effective Planning and Control* (Englewood Cliffs, N.J.: Prentice-Hall, Inc., 1982), pp. 26–27.

[3]Philip Kotler, *Principles of Marketing* (Englewood Cliffs, N.J.: Prentice-Hall, Inc., 1980), p. 139.

[4]William Cox and Luis Dominguez, "The Key Issues and Procedures of Industrial Marketing Research," *Industrial Marketing Management* 8 (1979), pp. 81–93.

Technical Orientation. As compared to consumer marketing researchers, industrial marketing researchers are considerably more technically oriented due to their interaction with engineers, production, and purchasing personnel during the collection of data and the development of technical reports.

Concentrated Access to Information. Due to the smaller concentration of industrial buyers, information sources tend to be concentrated. Thus, there is a greater reliance on secondary data sources, exploratory studies, and expert judgment.

Survey Techniques. Because it is normally easier to identify specific respondents within a much smaller sample base, personal interviewing rather than telephone or mail is the predominant survey tool.

Respondent Cooperation. For a variety of reasons, such as the hesitancy to give information and time constraints, data from industrial respondents are often more difficult to obtain than they are from consumers.

Competitive Intelligence

Competitive intelligence is receiving increased attention from businesses because of the long-term growth of competition and a persistently stagnant United States economy. Competitive intelligence, as the name implies, involves learning about a firm's competitors. It emphasizes increased learning about competitor's opportunities, threats, strengths, weaknesses, and strategic actions. Its intention is to enhance responses to competitors' planned and existent actions.

Upon arriving at his office one morning, the president of a large Eastern firm was informed of an unpleasant rumor. A competitor was said to be readying for a major attack on the company's primary products. Initially, management contemplated major price cuts; however, instead it called a consulting firm specializing in gathering competitive intelligence.

The consulting firm used computer-accessible databases to learn that the competitor (1) had done no borrowing to finance such an expansion; (2) had not hired an ad agency to handle the rumored attack; (3) had been put up for sale, unsuccessfully, by its parent company; (4) was the subsidiary of a parent company whose debentures were being downgraded; (5) lost a senior executive who had retired without being replaced; and (6) also lost two other executives who, hinting of company turmoil, had left the firm. This new intelligence allowed the president of the large Eastern firm to maintain existing prices and, thus, to preserve profits.[5]

Decision Making

Tremendous and constantly increasing amounts of easily accessible information have inspired much recent thought in the area of decision making. One direction of

[5]Tim Miller, "Staying Alive in the Jungle," *Online Access* (March–April 1987), pp. 44–57.

thought holds that, despite the ominous amount of information and the "high-tech" methods used to obtain much of it, smaller organizations should gain access to and take advantage of the information. One researcher points out that many newly created information sources are inexpensive, easy to access, easy to interpret, and relevant even to small, day-to-day business decisions.[6]

Two engineers established themselves as a consulting firm and, in an effort to obtain clients, ran trade journal ads that cost $15,000. However, the ads resulted in only one project, which yielded no more than the cost of the ads. Based on this disappointment, the engineers called on a marketing firm for help. That firm used several online data bases to analyze and segment the market. It billed the engineers only $3,000 and provided names of fifty potential clients. The engineers then conducted a direct mail and phone campaign, offering half-day seminars on quality assessment and production enhancement. Thirty of the companies requested the seminar. After the seminars, the engineers obtained contracts totaling over $300,000.[7]

Amitai Etzioni describes another direction of thought, which he calls "humble decision making." Among other avenues of decision making, he compares it to rationalism and incrementalism. Rationalism involves evaluating all possible courses of action, while incrementalism employs many very small decisions. Etzioni holds that rationalism is no longer feasible in view of the great amounts of information available. He says that decision making no longer resembles evaluating an "open book" but more of "an entire library of encyclopedias under perpetual revision." Incrementalism involves "trying this or that small maneuver without any grand plan or sense of ultimate purpose."[8]

On the other hand, humble decision making incorporates a "generalized consideration of a broad range of facts and choices followed by detailed examination of a focused subset of facts and choices."[9] As a method lying somewhere between rationalism and incrementalism, humble decision making can be viewed as necessitating a number of facilitating concepts.

Focused trial and error, the first facilitating concept, involves searching based on logic or intuition, as well as periodic checking to assure that one is still on course, according to Etzioni. Another concept is tentativeness, which involves "a willingness to change directions" when the results are not satisfactory—thus the term "humble" decision making. Procrastination, another useful concept, relates to a willingness to delay a decision so that a better decision might be made at a later date. The concept of decision staggering involves effecting the decision in increments over time rather than all at once. This enables the marketer to evaluate whether incre-

[6]Alan R. Andreasen, "Simple, Low-Cost Marketing Research: A Manager's Guide," *Marketing News* (May 25, 1984), Section 2, pp. 6–9.

[7]Ken Landis, "Focus: Information Goldmines," *Online Access* (September–October 1987), pp. 46–55.

[8]Amitai Etzioni, "Humble Decision Marking," *Harvard Business Review* (July–August 1989), pp. 122–126.

[9]Ibid.

ments are having the expected results. Fractionalizing is a concept similar to procrastination. Etzioni says that it "treats important judgments as a series of subdecisions and may or may not also stagger them in time." For example, buying a truck may involve several subdecisions and some of those decisions might be delayed in order to await the publication on consumer satisfaction surveys. Hedging bets, yet another facilitating concept, involves implementing the decision in more than one area, or, in other words, not putting all the eggs in one basket. Maintaining strategic reserves another facilitating concept, would lead to maintaining reserves in case of adversity. Etzioni's final implementing concept is that of reversible decisions. It is a way of avoiding "overcommitment" and involves making decisions which can be easily reversed—for example, before buying a truck, one might lease it with an option to buy, thus allowing for a chance to better evaluate the vehicle before assuming a hefty obligation.[10]

THE MARKETING RESEARCH PROCESS

Marketing research is undertaken to gather reliable marketing information to facilitate planning and control. Therefore, the value of the results will depend on the design and implementation of research methods. Marketing research, then, as shown in Figure 7-1, should be viewed as a process, moving from problem definition to presentation of the findings.[11]

Industrial research is intended to provide benefits to the firm by indicating environmental opportunities and threats, and how the firm can best pursue or react to them. Research can also indicate lesser contingencies (e.g., unforeseen chances) and constraints (e.g., restrictions) as well as how to operate in regard to them. The first step in the research process involves defining the problem (e.g., the basis of concern), which, in turn, establishes what is to be researched—the nature of the opportunity to be sought or the threat to be overcome. Research problems are sometimes but not always causes. A gifted inventor may be a cause of market success, but the firm may want to investigate the question, "Is there a profitable market for an item invented by the gifted individual?" In some cases, when not enough is known to allow adequately for problem definition, "exploratory research" (covered later in this chapter) is performed to learn more about the problem.

Defining the Problem

Too often decision makers define a problem in such general terms in their own minds as well as those of others who are to perform research that considerable misdirected work takes place. Weeks and months can be spent looking into areas that are related to but are not the problem or that are only effects of the problem.

[10]Ibid.
[11]Philip Kotler, *Marketing Essentials* (Englewood Cliffs, N.J.: Prentice-Hall, Inc., 1984), p. 60.

FIGURE 7-1 **The Marketing Research Process**

Source: Philip Kotler, *Marketing Essentials* [Englewood Cliffs, N.J.: Prentice-Hall, Inc., 1984], p. 60. Reprinted by permission.

The real problem is often unknown by even the decision maker and, like an iceberg, only a small portion of the problem or its effects may be visible.[12]

Thus, both those who ask for research and those who perform it must take time to describe the problem clearly and precisely. One industrial decision maker, for instance, who only needed information regarding what his firm's computerized information system could provide regarding specific services, formulated the problem to indicate that printouts of all current marketing information were needed. Had he provided the more specific problem of concern, such as, "to determine service shortcomings in areas A and B," his desk would not have, as it did, become completely covered with large boxes of computer printouts.

When attempting to determine problems and reduce the possibilities of wasteful research, considerable thought-provoking probing is called for. One expert researcher repeatedly asks variations of the question, "And what do you mean by that?" There are numerous examples of such strategies among researchers. Another individual charges over $1,000 an hour for constantly asking, "Why would that be a problem?" For such probing to be effective, the researcher must be sure that he or she is asking questions of the individual who will be the decision maker (the one who will actually be using the information), not someone delegated by the decision maker to get the research accomplished.

Research Objectives

Another method of pinpointing the problem involves joint consideration of research objectives. Research objectives are statements of the various specific aims of the research and are derived from the problem definition. They describe and limit the extent of the research. A problem definition such as, "Is there a sufficient demand for product X?" would lead to several research objectives. These objectives might include (1) determining the number of firms in three different industries that should desire the product, (2) for large firms in those industries, estimating the present consumption of products similar to X, (3) estimating the competitive product market shares in each of those industries, and (4) estimating the potential gross sales possible in each industry.

[12]William G. Zikmund, *Business Research Methods* (Hinsdale, Ill.: The Dryden Press, 1984), p. 54.

Whether the objectives are prepared by the decision maker or the researcher, they should be jointly reviewed by those individuals. Such a review has considerable value. Primarily, it forces those involved to question further whether or not the true problem has been properly defined. It frequently reveals differences in perception relating to the problem and often leads to a redefinition of the problem. Its importance in this regard should not be underestimated; that is, the joint review of objectives is a necessary requirement for effective research. Additionally, since the review deals more with specifics, it properly focuses attention on necessary details before research is conducted. For example, a research objective that states that "three industries will be evaluated" causes those involved to question such areas as whether a fourth should be added or which would be the best three to examine. Because of the importance of this step, research objectives should be prepared in written form.[13]

Research Methodologies.   Research objectives call for exploratory, descriptive, or experimental research. When problems are not clearly defined, the objectives would require performing an exploratory study, that is, one involved more with gathering preliminary data from secondary information sources, or knowledgeable people within the company or industry to shed more light on the problem. Exploratory research not only assists in defining a problem and the variable of interest; when thoroughly performed, it can often indicate a problem solution.

When the problem involves measuring awareness, knowledge, attitudes, opinions, or developing market and sales potential forecasts, research objectives would necessitate a descriptive study (i.e., describing the way things are).

While industrial marketing research is normally more involved with surveys than experiments or observations; when the problem centers on a cause-and-effect relationship (e.g., will sales increase if we lower price or make more frequent sales calls) to test the hypothesis, the research objective would call for an experiment (e.g., increase sales call frequency in one territory while holding it constant in another) to determine if a causal relationship exists.

DEVELOPING INFORMATION SOURCES

The second step in the marketing research process is to specify the type of information needed. Information is developed from secondary or primary data sources. *Secondary data* are data that already exist, not having been prepared for the specific problem at hand. Data specially prepared for a problem, to aid decision making relating to that problem, are called *primary data.*

Secondary Data Sources

Many secondary data sources used in industrial marketing research, such as *Predicasts,* the *Census of Manufacturers,* and *Sales and Marketing Management's* "Sur-

---

[13]Ibid., p. 57.

vey of Industrial Purchasing Power," have their data arranged in accordance with codes established by the Office of Management and Budget of the federal government, as described in the *Standard Industrial Classification Manual*. These codes, commonly referred to as SIC codes, categorize business establishments in the United States according to the industries in which they are engaged.

As shown in Table 7-1, the U.S. economy is divided into 11 divisions, A through K. Within each division, major industry groups are classified by two-digit numbers. For example, all manufacturing firms are in division D, with the two-digit numbers (ranging from 20 to 39) indicating major manufacturing industries within that division. Industry subgroups are further delineated by a third digit; detailed industries by a fourth digit—the longer the number, the more detailed the industry being defined. For example, SIC 2491213 includes manufacturers of lumber and wood products of more than 15 feet in length. Thus, a producer of forklifts that

TABLE 7-1 The Standard Industrial Classification System

The *SIC Manual* provides codes for 11 industries, A through K:

Division	Industry Classification	First Two-Digit SIC	Major Groups Within Industries
A	Agriculture, forestry, and fishing	01–09	20 Food and kindred products
B	Mining	10–14	21 Tobacco manufactures
C	Construction	15–17	22 Textile mill products
D	Manufacturing	20–39	23 Apparel . . .
.			24 Lumber and wood products . . .
.			.
K	.		.

And 2 additional digits for industry series within major groups:
    2441   Nailed wood boxes and shook
    2448   Wood pallets and skids
    2449   Wood containers . . .
    2491   Wood preserving
          .
          .
          .

The *Census of Manufactures* provides additional codes up to 7 digits:
    24912   Wood poles, piles, and posts . . .
    2491211   15 ft or less in length
    2491213   More than 15 ft in length
          .
          .

Source: Adapted from Office of Management and Budget, *Standard Industrial Classification Manual* [Washington, D.C.: U.S. Bureau of the Census, 1982], and *Census of Manufactures: Wooden Containers and Miscellaneous Wood Products* [Washington, D.C.: U.S. Government Printing Office, 1985].

are capable of carrying lengthy wood poles can consult the *SIC Manual* and determine that code 2491213 designates industrial firms that produce wood poles, piles, and posts that are more than 15 feet long.

Generally, however, the most common aggregate level is the four-digit code, as little published data are available for five- and seven-digit codes. Using code 2491, for instance, other secondary data sources can be searched to determine where those firms are located, their names, the number of their employees, and other pertinent information. Because SIC codes establish a means of locating data about firms within particular industries, they can be a valuable tool to industrial researchers.

SIC Code Limitations. Effective use of SIC data requires an understanding of their major limitations. First, SIC codes are not completely up-to-date; for example, in recent years they have been updated on an average of about every four years. Second, SIC codes are based on the major product produced or operation performed by the establishment. Thus, the classification assigned to an individual establishment will depend on the "principal product or operation." Where two or more products are produced, the principal product is determined by the one with the largest amount of activity associated with it—either by the amount of value added, sales, or shipments. Third, several different types of firms are often aggregated under one SIC code. Thus, for many marketers, the four-digit codes are not as "clean" as they should be. In fact, according to one industry source, as many as one hundred different industries are lumped into a single four-digit code.[14] Jerry Reisberg tells of one telemarketer attempting to promote personal computer boards to microcomputer dealers who used SIC code 5081—Commercial Machines and Equipment Wholesalers. The telemarketer became very frustrated because firms listed under that code include dealers of such products as coffee machines, neon signs, copiers, and restaurant equipment. Reisberg says that because of such frustrations, a number of people in private businesses are presently working on developing an expanded SIC Code system, one which will have eight rather than seven digits.[15] Overall, the advantages of SIC codes outweigh the disadvantages, as evidenced by the large number of secondary information sources that use them.

In using SIC codes, however, care must be exercised. As discussed, the basic reporting unit in the SIC system is the *individual establishment,* a single physical location where business is conducted, or where services or industrial operations are performed. Thus, establishments should not be confused with entire companies that may consist of more than one establishment. Further, to obtain a more up-to-date picture of potential market segments, governmental SIC sources should be supplemented with nongovernmental data sources, such as *Predicasts* or *Sales and Marketing Management's* "Survey of Industrial Purchasing Power."

---

[14]John Couretas, "What's Wrong with the SIC Code . . . And Why," *Business Marketing* (December 1984), pp. 108–116.

[15]Jerry Reisberg, "An Expanded SIC Code: Let's Do It Ourselves," *Direct Marketing* (October 1987), pp. 148–151.

HOW MEGATREND'S NAISBITT SEES IT

We now mass-produce information the way we used to mass-produce cars.

In the information society, we have systematized the production of knowledge and amplified our brainpower. To use an industrial metaphor, we now mass-produce knowledge and this knowledge is the driving force of our economy.

Source: Reprinted with permission of John Naisbitt, *Megatrends* (New York: Warner Books, © 1982), p. 7.

To overcome the fact that data are gathered by "establishments" and are assigned a SIC by the "primary" product produced or operation conducted, the marketer can also turn to the *Census of Manufacturers,* which uses two ratios to indicate the degree of error involved: the primary product *specialization ratio* and the *coverage ratio.* Specialization ratios are used to indicate the percentage of total shipments for a given four-digit industry that is accounted for by its primary product or operation. The higher the ratio, the higher the production activity associated with the primary product, that is, the more homogeneous the industry. Thus, where ratios exceed ninety percent, the date is more reliable.

Coverage ratios indicate the extent to which the primary product is produced by other industries. Where coverage ratios are low, the marketer would want to investigate other industries than those in the SIC under consideration. When they are high, 90 percent or more, this would not be the case.

Computerized Secondary Data Sources. When information was gathered in 1985 for our first edition, there were 2,000 on line databases, but by 1989 there were more than 3,500. And back in 1985 people were just beginning to discuss the possibilities of the CD-ROM (compact disk/read-only memory) technology. One 4 3/4 inch CD-ROM can hold the contents of 1,600 flexible diskettes or eighteen complete normal-size textbooks.[16] Additionally, the *Encyclopedia of Information Systems and Services* now not only speaks of the availability of so many on line databases, but also of CD-ROM data, and data available on "diskette, and magnetic tape."[17] Recent studies have indicated that not only are organizations satisfied with more accessible information but, in one instance, engineers chose to use a more accessible, though lower quality, source.[18] These data sources not only make a great amount of information readily available, but they usually do so at relatively low cost, ranging from fifty to a few hundred dollars per hour. One study, receiving responses

---

[16]*Encyclopedia of Information Systems and Services,* Ninth Edition, Gale Research Inc., (Detroit: 1989, Book Tower, preface).

[17]Ibid.

[18]Mary Culnan, "Environmental Scanning: The Effects of Task Complexity and Source Assessability on Information Gathering Behavior." *Decision Sciences* 14:2 (April 1983), pp. 194–206.

TABLE 7-2 Average Yearly Usage of Forecasting Sources

Name of Source	Average Times Used Per Year
Census of Manufacturers	3.0
Annual Survey of Manufacturers	1.9
County Business Patterns	2.8
Input-Output Analysis	1.9
Business Conditions Digest	3.2
Survey of Industrial Purchasing Power	3.0
SIC codes	37.2
Computerized Data Sources	61.2
Trade Association Publications	36.9
State and Local Industrial Directories	21.9

from thirty-four large firms, each with over 5,000 employees and over $100 million in sales (in random SIC codes), indicated that computerized data sources are used an average of 61.2 times per year by each firm, an average far exceeding that of any other secondary data source.[19] (See Table 7-2.) Time and money can also be expended collecting a good deal of redundant or even irrelevant data. A person with experience can usually bypass irrelevant data and quickly locate valuable information. Examples of some data bases are included in Table 7-3. Because of their training and experience with computerized data sources, librarians are well qualified to do computer searches; in fact, many of them are being lured from their jobs in public or academic institutions by higher-paying business organizations.

Noncomputerized Secondary Data Sources. Numerous noncomputerized sources of free data are available for providing needed information, such as business periodicals, trade magazines, newspapers, business reference services, federal banks, and annual operating reports that are listed in such sources as Dunn & Bradstreet, Moody's, and Standard and Poor's Industrial Surveys. One marketing researcher claims that for less than $400 a firm can purchase a core of reference books that will provide the essential noncomputerized secondary data sources for market research and planning. He states that "for every significant economic activity, there is (1) an association that represents it, (2) a government agency that monitors it, and (3) a magazine that covers it.[20]

Government Sources. Government, at all levels, gathers and publishes a great deal of economic data on a national, state, and county basis (four-digit codes), and a

---

[19]Robert Reeder, Richard Sewell, and Betty Reeder, "A Survey of Empirical Industrial Marketing Research." (Southwestern Oklahoma State University 1988), p. 3. Typescript.

[20]Stephen M. Baker, "Find Marketing Data Fast!" *Sales and Marketing Management* (December 6, 1982), pp. 32–36.

TABLE 7-3 Some On-Line Data Bases

Data Base	Description	Producer
PTS Annual Reports Abstracts	Provides national and international data from more than 175,000 abstracts pertaining to 4,000 companies. Covers industries, companies, products, and services. Firms are classified by SIC code, name, and several other methods. Data is updated monthly.	Predicasts, Inc.
Disclosure Database	Provides extracts on more than 12,000 companies based on their Securities and Exchange Commission reports. Data is updated weekly. Also available on CD-ROM.	Disclosure, Inc.
The WEFA Group	Formed by a merger of the Chase and Wharton Econometric groups. Provide multiple data bases and econometric models that cover all major sectors of the U.S. economy as well as much international data.	The WEFA Group
Commerce Business Daily (CBD)	Provides daily data on U.S. government purchasing and selling.	U.S. Department of Commerce
Dow Jones News/Retrieval	Makes up-to-the-minute business and financial information available. It contains 40 online data bases containing both national and international information.	Dow Jones & Company, Inc.

For a thorough listing of indices, see the *Encyclopedia of Information Systems and Services* (1989) and its periodic updates, produced by Gale Research Company of Detroit, Michigan.

product-by-product basis (seven-digit codes). Since these data are classified by SIC codes, they allow for analyzing data on an industry-by-industry basis. The challenge, however, is to develop familiarity with these sources to understand how they can be used in the area of industrial marketing research.

Some of the government publications that are most useful to industrial marketers are presented in Table 7-4. Due to the considerable data these reports contain, only the *Business Conditions Digest* can be maintained on a current, up-to-date basis. For example, though the Census of Manufacturers is scheduled to be released every five years, in practice it takes a number of additional years to release it, so that the data it contains upon release is already dated. There is, however, a positive side to using these dated sources. The information they provide is available from few other sources; they provide excellent starting points (or "benchmarks") for additional research; they can be quite useful in indicating what market share was; and, in industries that change slowly and where SIC codes sufficiently differentiate, they

TABLE 7-4 Reference Sources for Marketing Research and Planning

Name	Producer	Description
Census of Manufacturers	U.S. Department of Commerce	Provides data for industries, states, and SMSAs. Data involve materials consumed, employment, payroll, value added, and capital goods expenditures, among others. *Problems:* Differing firms lumped under same SIC code. Census lacks currency.
Annual Survey of Manufacturers	Bureau of the Census	Provides same industry data (employment, payroll, value of shipments, etc.) as the *Census of Manufacturers.* Also provides data on assets, rents, supplemental labor cost, fuels, etc. Intended to cover the four interim years between issues of the Census. *Problems:* Although the Survey is intended to be issued during each year the Census is not issued, this rarely occurs.
County Business Patterns	Bureau of the Census	Provides information on numbers of employees and payrolls by state counties for various SIC codes. *Problems:* A sampling of the reports indicates they are issued two years after the data are obtained.
Survey of Business (Input-Output Analysis)	Office of Business Economics (U.S. Department of Commerce)	Provides data showing value of outputs of 370 industries and what portions of the outputs various industries purchase. Also shows percentages of outputs (e.g., industry A sells 10% of its output to industry B, 30% to industry C, etc.). If, then, industry B is expected to increase production 50%, sales to B can be estimated. *Problems:* A firm in industry A wishing to forecast sales to industry B must first have a forecast of B's production/sales. A firm must then determine how similar firms are within industry B and determine how similar it (A) is to firms within industry A. Data are for industries, not products. In reality firms within industries can widely differ in what they produce and consume.
Business Conditions Digest	Bureau of Economic Analysis (U.S. Department of Commerce)	Provides economic time series data on a monthly (and timely) basis. Includes about 150 time series classified by their relationship to fluctuations in economic activity. These include leading, roughly coincident, and lagging indicators relative to business cycle peaks and troughs. Monthly historical data are included (as far back as 1950). This publication is produced and distributed in a timely fashion. Its numerous indices offer the researcher the opportunity to find existing data which can indicate future changes in sales, business trends, etc.

CORDIS CORPORATION LOOKS AT COMPETITORS

Cordis Corporation, a manufacturer of heart pacemakers, made a major advancement in pacemaker technology in 1980. The new technology was superior to that of any pacemaker on the market. However, sales did not increase and in fact dropped in some sales territories. Cordis sales representatives were asked to investigate. The sales reps learned that physicians were being enticed by gifts of cars, boats, and the like to buy competitors' products. Cordis responded by putting more money into physician education, putting more sales reps into the field, and establishing its own gift program—though its gifts were of equipment that was related to pacemakers. And Cordis' sales soared.

Source: See Steven Flax, "How to Snoop on Your Competitors," *Fortune,* May 14, 1984, pp. 28–33.

---

can be of considerable use in researching such areas as markets that need more attention, sales force routing, designing distribution channels, and market share analysis. For instance, the director of Faxfinder depends on the *Census of Manufacturers* as a benchmark of industrial production, for determining which companies dominate a given market, and in designing distribution channels.[21]

A more timely annual source of similar information is *Sales and Marketing Management's* "Annual Survey of Industrial Purchasing Power." Table 7-5 depicts a portion of the contents of the survey. The survey lists all counties that have at least one manufacturing firm with twenty or more employees. Data, however, are reported only for those counties with more than 1,000 employees working in firms classified within the same SIC code. "Large Establishments" refers to those firms with over one hundred employees. "Shipments/Receipts" refers to goods produced. The "% of U.S. Shipments/Receipts" refers to the percentage of goods produced with the SIC (or "All Manufacturing" category) in the United States. The final column, which presents the percentage produced in large establishments, can, as the survey points out, be worthwhile in determining the necessary level of sales coverage (greater percentages indicate the need for fewer sales people.)[22]

The survey can be used alone or in conjunction with those sources listed in Table 7-4. Since it does use four-digit SIC codes and does not give SIC codes for firms with less than 100 employees, using it in conjunction with government sources can prove beneficial. It is also an excellent source for determining if some of the data presented in those government sources are still current.

[21]Couretas, "Counting Smokestacks," pp. 86–88.

[22]*Sales and Marketing Management,* "Guide to Using S&MM's Survey of Industrial & Commercial Buying Power," April 22, 1985, p. 58.

TABLE 7-5 A Portion of the Contents of the Annual Survey of Industrial Purchasing Power

County SIC	Industry	Establishments Total	Establishments Large	Shipments/ Receipts ($ millions)	% of U.S. Shipments/ Receipts	% in Large Establishments
California						
San Joaquin	All manufacturing	143	56	$2,432.6	.1121	81%
2033	Canned fruits and vegetables	13	11	611.3	6.1997	98
3231	Products of purchased glass	1	1	104.0	3.5062	100
8062	General medical and surgical hospitals	9	7	183.5	.1278	96
San Luis Obispo	All manufacturing	20	4	277.9	.0128	16
8062	General medical and surgical hospitals	7	5	94.2	.0656	92
San Mateo	All manufacturing	285	64	2,553.8	.1180	67
2711	Newspapers	11	3	107.7	.4462	69
2851	Paints and allied products	6	3	168.6	1.7732	91
3662	Radio and TV communications equipment	8	5	238.6	.6400	95
8062	General medical and surgical hospitals	9	7	223.6	.1557	97

Source: Sales and Marketing Management (April 22, 1985), p. 66. Reprinted by permission from Sales and Marketing Management news magazine, copyright © 1985.

Primary Data Sources

While industrial marketers rely heavily on secondary data sources, when research objectives cannot be met by secondary data sources, primary data must be collected. Primary data collection, however, should never be undertaken before a search of secondary data sources have been completed, or the problem and variables of interest have been clearly defined, if necessary through exploratory research. Although primary data can be collected through surveys, observation, and experimentation, as previously mentioned, the most common method of obtaining primary data in the industrial market is through surveys.

Surveys involve questioning subjects and collecting their responses through person-to-person interviews, telephone interviews, or mailed questionnaires. Depending on the method employed and the vehicle used to collect the data, responses can be recorded directly by the respondents themselves, or by researchers who may complete the questionnaires, take notes, or record the data.[23] While individuals, as well as groups, may be surveyed, the use of groups is generally restricted to surveys of knowledgeable people within the industrial marketer's firm.

Unstructured Surveys. In general, surveys in the industrial market are unstructured as well as nondisguised. Unstructured surveys consist of asking respondents open-ended questions (questions that require more than a yes or no answer) to encourage in-depth responses so that motivations, priorities, problems, perceptions, and attitudes can be better understood and evaluated by the researcher. Nondisguised refers to the use of straightforward open questions that do not attempt to hide the purpose of the survey as is often done in the consumer area.[24]

Depending on the form of data collection, unstructured surveys can involve minimal costs and effort or consume a relatively high amount of time and money. Information types of unstructured surveys (e.g., using the sales force to collect data from distributors, customers, or various other outsiders) can be very effective and relatively inexpensive. Such surveys also fit well with the industrial peculiarities of relatively limited research budgets and concentrated customers who possess considerable expertise and are readily accessible to sales people.

Formal unstructured, nondisguised surveys, while flexible and effective, are more difficult to undertake and require the use of skilled interviewers and sophisticated analysts. Thus, they are relatively more costly and time consuming.[25]

Structured Surveys. Structured surveys—questionnaires that seek specific, quantifiable answers—are used in the industrial market, though not to the extent of unstructured surveys. For instance, the primary planning instrument of one multinational corporation is a questionnaire that is mailed to its own sales people for

---

[23]C. William Emory, *Business Research Methods* (Homewood, Ill.: Richard D. Irwin, Inc., 1980), p. 87.

[24]Cox, *Industrial Marketing Research,* pp. 244–245.

[25]Ibid.

completion rather than directly to customers or distributors. Where sales people can complete the questionnaire for a single customer without contacting the customer for additional information, the questionnaire may take up to 4.5 hours to complete. However, when sales people must contact customers or other sources, it can consume up to 15 hours to complete.[26]

While structured surveys are more easily quantified and lead to more standardized information, they are normally used only when the sample population is relatively large, the market is not concentrated, and the information of interest consists of measuring awareness and knowledge, attitudes and opinions, or prior and present buyer behavior.[27]

Surveying Individuals. Surveying individuals in the industrial market is not as difficult, or as costly, as in the consumer market because customers are more geographically concentrated and thus easier to contact. Further, since unstructured surveys are the preferred means of gathering information, surveys tend to be more qualitative than quantitative in nature.

Surveying Customers. The major problem with surveying individuals within current and potential customer firms is that these individuals are often hesitant to cooperate, or unwilling to share information with their suppliers because they are afraid that (1) the information may be used against them during negotiations, (2) it may cause the seller to develop unreasonable expectations or make premature commitments, and (3) the information may inadvertently or knowingly be disclosed to the buyer's competitors.[28] Not only are they hesitant about disclosing information, they may color data—particularly if they are requested by a trade association—so that competitors will be misinformed or misled. Thus, secondary data in trade magazines that have been made available by industrial buyers are not of the same quality as are secondary data in the consumer market.[29]

At the same time a good case can be made for going directly to individuals within customer firms for information, particularly current customers. The longtime buyer-seller interface results in very close intercompany personal relationships that generate trust and cooperation. Also, since selling in the industrial market often requires major adjustments to develop unique products for particular customers, buyers often want to allow sellers sufficient lead time to prepare for changes in buyer requirements.

Surveying Experts. The more limited nature of industrial research budgets, the concentration of industrial information within limited number of people, and the

[26]David Grace and Tom Pointon, "Marketing Research Through the Salesforce," *Industrial Marketing Management* 9 (1980), pp. 53–58.

[27]Cox, *Industrial Marketing Research,* p. 84.

[28]Frederick Webster, Jr., "Management Science in Industrial Marketing," *Journal of Marketing* (January 1978), pp. 21–27.

[29]Ibid.

limited numbers of customers all encourage obtaining data from a relatively few experts—internal or external to the firm. Within the firm, for instance, technical information can be obtained from research and development, engineering, manufacturing, and service personnel, as well as sales people who may be quite knowledgeable with respect to customers' needs. External experts may consist of people within customer and prospect firms, industry consultants, trade journal editors or association executives, government officials, and university professors. External experts are often located by asking internal experts to identify them.[30]

There are problems, however, with regard to the biases that can be present with individuals who are experts in their field. As humans, we tend to become overconfident in our opinions and predictions and do not always relay information that might conflict with our position on a particular situation. Thus, opinions and predictions that are obtained from a few individual experts may not be representative of the opinions and predictions of many.[31] Therefore, information should be pooled from several experts, with careful attention given to the selection of those experts.

Surveying Groups.   Focus group interviewing is often beneficial in industrial marketing. It is conducted much the same way as a group discussion: the trained moderator ensures that (1) a thorough discussion of all items about which a client wants to learn is conducted; (2) everyone becomes involved; (3) monopolists are held in check; and (4) the moderator gives frequent and brief summaries, asks open-ended questions, and never expresses a personal opinion. Robert Inglis, a consultant and frequent moderator, often uses rooms with one-way mirrors, so that people from the client company can listen, observe, and learn from the comments made by the participants, usually seven or eight current or potential customers who have been invited to participate. He claims that most information is obtained from the discussants' tone of voice and nonverbal actions. Thus, more than quantitative information, opinions and pertinent issues are revealed.[32]

Inglis points out that focus groups have the advantages of examining issues in greater depth than structured questionnaires; they are faster and less expensive than most other types of research, and they are flexible in that they can include examination of unplanned areas.[33]

Inglis also indicates a number of differences between consumer and industrial focus groups. Group members are usually chosen from a list provided by the industrial client, and these members are generally more articulate and capable of discussing product concepts based on drawings or brief verbal descriptions than are participants in consumer groups. However, due to the make or buy abilities of many firms, discussants can sometimes be the clients' potential or actual competitors and thus

---

[30]Cox, *Industrial Marketing Research,* pp. 22–23.

[31]Robin Hogarth and Spyros Makridakis, "Forecasting and Planning: An Evaluation," *Management Science* 27:2 (February 1981), pp. 115–138.

[32]Robert C. Inglis, "Focus Groups are a Powerful Technique for Researching Business Buyers," *Business Marketing* (November 1987), pp. 79–82.

[33]Ibid.

may be a bit reluctant to be completely open and frank. Moderators also have difficulty in the more technical industrial market and often require more lengthy brief-
ings and preparations.[34]

Group discussions not involving expert moderators have also proven to be an
effective means of obtaining primary data with regard to customers' needs or current satisfaction, market characteristics, and competitors' actions, particularly when
sales people are involved in the discussions. Sales people, because of their day-to-
day interaction with customers, tend to be knowledgeable with respect to market,
industry, and customer trends. When estimates are needed from experts, data collection may be approached by

1. Group discussion—where experts are gathered and asked to discuss an issue collectively
   and produce a group estimate.
2. Pooling individual estimates—where experts are asked to discuss an issue collectively
   and produce individual estimates that can be pooled into a single estimate.
3. Delphi method—where a group of experts are asked separately to provide individual
   estimates and assumptions that are reviewed, averaged, and returned with comments.
   Requests for a new round of estimates are then made, and the process continues until
   the estimates converge.[35]

The use of simple averages of individual estimates have been shown to be
considerably more accurate than the more sophisticated Delphi technique in predicting future events.[36] Though industrial companies continue to use the Delphi technique, current reviews indicate that it is "unreliable and scientifically unvalidated."
It appears that the feedback of results at each round of estimating causes certain
estimators to yield to group opinion, which biases the final results.[37]

Improving Group Surveys.   A number of suggestions have been made for improving formal group methods of obtaining data such as (1) using larger groups, (2)
using more than one group, (3) avoiding the hasty acceptance of forecasts, (4) attempting to find disconfirming information, and (5) institutionalizing "devil's advocates."[38]

Benefits of Group Surveys.   There is, however, a positive side to formal, future-
oriented, group research. First, it has beneficial side effects, such as creating improved communications and coordination, causing people to be more motivated and

---

[34]Ibid.

[35]Philip Kotler, "A Guide to Gathering Expert Estimates," *Business Horizons* (October 1970),
pp. 78–87.

[36]Robert M. Hogarth, "Methods for Aggregating Opinions," in H. Jungermann and G. de Zeeuw,
eds., *Decision Making and Change in Human Affairs* (Dordrecht, Holland: D. Reidel Publishing Co.,
1977), pp. 231–235.

[37]H. Sackman, *Delphi Assessment: Expert Opinion, Forecasting, and Group Process* (Santa Mon-
ica, Calif.: Rand Corporation, April 1974), p. vi.

[38]Hogarth and Makridakas, "Forecasting and Planning," pp. 115–138.

future oriented in their thinking.[39] Additionally, experts sometimes know of key future events that would not be reflected through statistical techniques based upon historical data. Also, sometimes there are no extant historical data available. For instance, when a major food producer, Conoisseur Foods, establishes a new brand for which it has no existing data, it uses a "model specialist" to obtain subjective estimates from knowledgeable people within the organization to update its computer information system. Though the manager of marketing services sees the role of the model specialist as "crucial, . . . wherever possible, the analysis of historical data is used to validate subjective opinions."[40]

Competitive Intelligence Surveys.　Because of dramatically increasing competition and a stagnant economy, gathering competitive intelligence has recently received a great deal of attention. The developments resulting from that attention, coupled with the rather clandestine nature of gathering such intelligence, make this area of research intriguing and thought-provoking. It is a research area that makes use of a number of previous types of survey methods as well as additional methods. Table 7-6 lists some possible competitor information-gathering strategies suggested by one research organization.

ANALYZING THE DATA

The increased use of computers and the considerable number of software programs available have led to greater usage of quantitative methods of analyzing data.[41] Software programs make available simple but highly useful techniques for analysis. (See Table 7-7.) For example, computerized cross-tabulations can summarize data quickly and provide researchers with useful comparisons of portions of data that are arranged into easily readable matrices. Table 7-8, for instance, reflects a simplified cross-tabulation matrix for analyzing customer attitudes on salesperson visits.

Analysis of Table 7-8 indicates that twice as many customers in the territory of Illinois feel that salesperson visits are excessive as compared to customers in the territory of Texas. Had Table 7-8 been an actual computer printout, it would have also contained percentages that would have shown that forty-two percent of the customers in Texas feel that salesperson visits are excessive compared to twelve percent in Illinois. Such comparisons, provided by cross-tabulation software, considerably enhance the understanding and usefulness of secondary and primary data.

In addition to software programs such as chi-square, graphics and frequency distribution, which are excellent techniques for summarizing, displaying, and evaluating *descriptive data* (data that enable comparisons of existing factors), simple

---

[39]Ibid.

[40]Steven Alter, *Decision Support Systems: Current Practice and Continuing Challenges* (Reading, Mass.: Addison-Wesley Publishing Co., 1980), p. 15.

[41]Neil Seitz, *Business Forecasting on Your Personal Computer* (Reston, Va.: Reston Publishing Company, Inc., 1984).

TABLE 7-6 Competitive Intelligence Strategies

TAKING A LOCAL APPROACH
Search publications from the hometown of the competitor; newspapers and city business publications, as well as regional publications. Phone calls to authors of articles will often yield much additional worthwhile information.

INTIMATE CONTACTS
Try contacting your competitor's suppliers, distributors and customers, since they may know and share "intimate details."

EDUCATED GUESSING
In the case of private companies, try researching some similar public companies—this can allow some educated guessing.

CALLING IN THE REPS
As both your reps and your competitors are close to your customers, your reps' opportunities to learn about the competition are very close at hand.

TAPPING INTO UNIVERSITIES
Companies are generally open to students and written accounts of competitors are thus often easily accessible through dissertations, company cases, and various written student projects.

COMBING THROUGH CASES
Your attorneys can often access court cases and records that will yield valuable insights regarding competitors.

FEDERAL, STATE, AND MUNICIPAL FILINGS
Government agencies can frequently provide records regarding competitors' future actions; construction permits regarding new facilities, for example, or applications relating to new products or services.

SOMEONE HAS THE ANSWERS
Remember that if you devote enough thought to the question "Who would know about this?" there will, with few exceptions, be someone, somewhere, who knows.

Source: Tim Miller, "Focus: Competitive Intelligence," *Online Access* [March-April 1987], pp. 43–57.

techniques such as trend analysis, moving averages, and exponential smoothing are used to analyze *predictive data* (data that enable forecasting future events, e.g., sales forecasting, competitive reactions, and general business trends).

Exponential Smoothing

The simplest form of exponential smoothing can be expressed by the equation,

$$F_{t+1} = F_t + \alpha(X_t - F_t)$$

TABLE 7-7 Use of Computers for Measurement

Computer Capability	Market Potentials	Market Characteristics	Market Shares	Business Trends	New Products/Line Extensions	Competitive Activities	Sales [Analysis]	Distribution Channels	Acquisitions	Imports/Exports	Marketing Planning Inputs
Provided by external vendors											
Data bases											
Time series	X	X	X	X	X	X	X	X	X	X	X
Secondary literature	X	X	X	X	X	X		X	X	X	X
Input/output services	X	X	X		X		X	X	X		X
Time-series software		X		X	X			X			X
Multivariate software		X	X		X	X	X	X	X		X
Computerized planning systems		X			X	X			X		X
Created internally											
Data bases											
Time series	X	X	X	X	X	X	X	X	X	X	X
Other intelligence	X	X	X	X	X	X		X	X		X
Input/output tables	X	X	X		X		X	X	X		X
Sales reporting systems		X	X		X	X	X	X		X	X
Marketing intelligence systems	X	X	X	X	X	X	X	x	X	X	X

Source: Applications for computers in industrial marketing research progress during the 1970s. Reprinted by permission from Craig M. Collins, "Major Industrial Marketing Research Computer System Developments Will Be in Graphics and Planning in '80s," *Marketing News* 13 [April 4, 1980], p. 5.

TABLE 7-8 Sample Cross-tabulation Matrix

No. of Salesperson Visits	Target Markets			
	Illinois	California	Texas	Total
Excessive	10	0	5	15
Satisfactory	60	10	7	77
Too few	12	5	0	17
Total	82	15	12	109

where F_{t+1} is the forecast for the present time period and α is the weight given to the difference between the actual value of the variable in the present time period (X_t) and the forecasted value.

The use of simple predictive techniques, however, can lead to incorrect predictions and costly errors because, in most situations, they do not include a sufficient number of variables for accurate forecasting, as the exponential smoothing formula reflects. This problem in predicting arises in the industrial market because derived demand is considerably affected by such factors as world political and economic conditions, the cost of money, the level of disposable income, the stage of the business cycle, seasonable considerations, the availability of resources, and many other factors that, in many cases, must be taken into consideration.

Although some of these factors can be analyzed by simple predictive techniques, generally the methods do not consider a sufficient number for purposes of accurately predicting. Thus, many firms use more sophisticated programs, such as linear regression and time-series models, to analyze predictive data. The previously cited study regarding thirty-four large firms in random SIC code areas indicated that time series and linear regression techniques ranked one and two in business-world forecasting techniques, with sales force composites a close third.[42] However, all other statistical techniques ranked comparatively much lower (see Table 7-9).

Linear Regression

Simple linear regression involves predicting the level of one variable, Y (the dependent variable), on the basis of another variable, X (the independent variable). That is, the level of Y is dependent on—brought about or reflected by—changes in the X variable. Multiple linear regression, on the other hand, involves predicting the level of a Y variable with the use of more than one X variable. For example, the level of sales (Y) might be predicted on the basis of gross national product (X_1), the prime interest rate (X_2), and the cost of foreign imports (X_3). The equation for this relationship would appear as

$$Y = a + b_1X_1 + b_2X_2 + b_3X_3 + e$$

where Y is the dependent variable, a is the Y intercept (the expected level of Y given zero levels for all independent variables), X_1 through X_3 are the independent variables, b_1 through b_3 are the linear regression coefficients (see Table 7-10 for an explanation), and e is the error term (the difference between the actual Y level and Y predicted using the independent variables and their regression coefficients).

The theory behind the use of more than one X variable to predict the level of Y is that the Y variable is usually affected by more than one factor. For example, the level of U.S. automobile sales is dependent on the rate of interest, tariff restrictions, and the level of consumers' disposable income. Thus, any change in one or

---

[42]Reeder, Sewell, and Reeder, "A Survey of Empirical Industrial Marketing Research," p. 5.

TABLE 7-9 Average Yearly Usage of Statistical Tools

Name of Tool	Average
Delphi Technique	1.8
Exponential Smoothing	2.4
Linear Regression	8.7
Time Series	10.6
ARIMA/Box-Jenkins	1.0
Decision Support Systems	2.8
Venture Analysis	2.0
Executive Panels	3.2
Sales force Composites	6.0

more of these variables can have a negative or positive affect on U.S. auto producers' sales, eventually affecting the industrial marketer's sales.

Choosing X Variables.   Care must be taken in choosing X variables that will accurately predict the level of Y. Some industrial companies use numerous, very broad X variables, such as gross national product, and prepare what are called econometric models. Most researchers, however, try to limit the number of predictor variables to as few as possible. This saves time and money in collecting and processing data and is particularly important when several linear regression models are run fre-

TABLE 7-10 Commonly Used Linear Regression Terms

X variable	The variable used to predict, also called the independent or predictor variable.
Y variable	The variable being predicted, also called the dependent, criterion, or predicted variable.
b coefficient	The amount of an X variable necessary to estimate a change of one unit in the Y variable.
Beta coefficient	The b coefficient determined after the X and Y data have been normalized; that is, the data for each variable are entered into the regression only after they have been changed from their raw b form into the number of standard deviations they are above or below the average.
Syx (standard error)	The standard deviation running along each side of the regression line. After computing the regression, for any particular value of X, there is a 68% chance that the predicted Y will fall between one standard error above and one standard error below the regression line.
t test	A test used to determine if a particular b coefficient is large enough to be meaningful (other than zero) or if that particular predictor variable should be omitted. Sometimes called Student's t test.
F test	A test to determine if an entire set of different X variables (GNP, disposable income, etc.) is meaningful enough to be used as a set or if one, some, or all of them should be replaced.

quently. Also, there is increasing evidence that simpler regression and time-series models perform as well as and often better than those that are more complicated.[43]

Using Lag Variables. It is worthwhile for researchers to spend extra time locating X variables for which data become available before the period the company is attempting to forecast. For example, one roofing shingle manufacturer predicts future sales using, among other variables, present building permits. The data for this building permit X variable are available before the period Y is to be predicted. This X variable is called a lag variable. The use of lag variables allows researchers to predict on the basis of data from events that have already occurred rather than basing predictions on data that are projected to occur at the same time as their forecasts.

To locate lag variables, researchers obtain data from several, preferably easily accessible, indices and compare plots of that data against plots of the variable to be predicted. To do this, past data for the Y variable are plotted alongside past data for various indices of X variables, but one, two, or three time periods behind the X variable data. Researchers then visually observe the plotted data to determine if they are related positively or negatively; that is, both the X and Y data move up and down together or both move in opposite directions. If the two variables appear to be related (move in a positive or negative relationship), as shown in Figure 7-2 (for a positive relationship), researchers can use the X indices to predict or study the relationship further. Further study of the relationship can involve using the X indices to predict values of Y for different past time periods, or it can involve determining how well the variables X and Y are correlated.

Correlation Analysis. Linear regression computer programs usually produce two coefficients, the coefficient of correlation and the coefficient of determination, which estimate how well X and Y are correlated (whether X is related to Y). The coefficient of correlation, which ranges between positive and negative one, indicates whether X and Y are positively or negatively related. The nearer the coefficient is to negative or positive one, the greater the relationship between the two variables. The coefficient of determination (the square of the coefficient of correlation) ranges between zero and one and indicates what percentage of the variation in Y is explained by X. The closer the coefficient of determination is to one, the more likely it is that X is a good predictor of Y.

Computer Programs. There are several excellent software programs that perform linear regression. Dynacomp's Regression I, which is inexpensive and "available for all computers," has several worthwhile features; among other things, it provides automatic data sorting, plots both data and curves, and produces the coefficient of correlation.[44] A frequently used program for macro computers is the SPSS (Statistical Package for the Social Sciences).

[43]Hogarth, "Forecasting and Planning," pp. 115–138.
[44]*Dynacomp Catalog No. 28,* (Rochester, N.Y.: DYNACOMP, Inc.), p. 54.

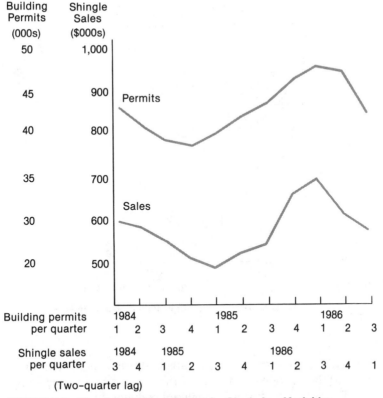

Building Permits (000s)	Shingle Sales ($000s)
50	1,000
45	900
40	800
35	700
30	600
20	500

Building permits per quarter: 1984 (1 2 3 4) 1985 (1 2 3 4) 1986 (1 2 3)

Shingle sales per quarter: 1984 (3 4) 1985 (1 2 3 4) 1986 (1 2 3 4 1)

(Two-quarter lag)

FIGURE 7-2 Graphic Determination of a Single Lag Variable

Understanding Linear Regression

To guide research efforts and evaluate and adjust the findings, marketing managers must understand the strong and weak points of linear regression. Some commonly used linear regression terms that appear on computer printouts and aid in interpreting regression results have been shown in Table 7-8.

Standard Error.   Although linear regression is normally more effective than simpler predictive models, it does have its own inherent problems. One such problem involves the standard error (see Table 7-8 for a definition). As Figure 7-3 indicates, the standard error allows the forecaster to establish confidence intervals for estimates. When the researcher is forecasting Y based on an X value near the center of the X's (300 in Figure 7-3), the standard error will be smaller than when the researcher is forecasting Y based on an X value more distant from the center X value. Thus when an unusually high or low X value occurs, indicating a forecast that would

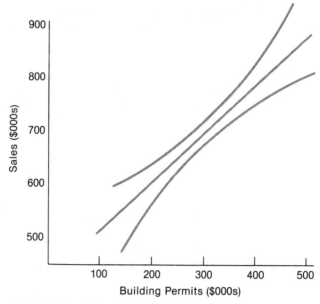

FIGURE 7-3 Sales Regressed on Building Permits

require the organization to make larger adjustments than usual, the standard error and thus the confidence interval of the forecast becomes less accurate.

Four other problems, though not common to all regression models, that present difficulties in preparing or interpreting linear regression models are the following.

Multicollinearity. Multicollinearity refers to using predictor variables that are very much the same (more correlated among themselves than with the variable they are predicting). Either of two such variables may alone predict well, but when both variables are used, very little additional information is added. Although this does not adversely affect forecasting, researchers attempt to avoid multicollinear variables, since much time and money can be spent gathering data that add little predictive ability. Researchers normally determine the presence of multicollinearity when it is noted that a new variable seems to lack additional predictive impact. The problem is corrected by eliminating or replacing one of the correlated variables with a different, more predictive variable.

Autocorrelation. Autocorrelation can be seen on a plot of actual data points around a regression line. (See Figure 7-4.) Sometimes the actual data points seem to be related to one another rather than to the line, as, for example, when several adjacent points are above the line and then when several adjacent points go below the line. The points are correlated among themselves, or autocorrelated, and seem

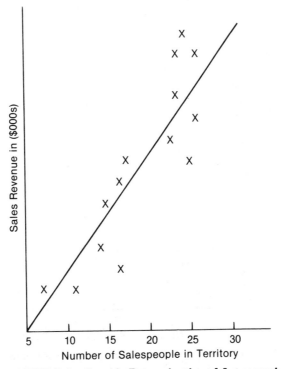

FIGURE 7-4 Graphic Determination of Autocorrelation

to be marching to a different drummer than to the line. When autocorrelation is present, an overestimate in one period will likely be followed by an overestimate in the next, while an underestimate will likely be followed by another underestimate.

Computer plots that indicate autocorrelation visually are usually verified by the Durbin-Watson statistic present on many computer printouts. If the Durbin-Watson statistic is less than 1.5 or greater than 2.5, autocorrelation is indicated. To remove autocorrelation, the forecaster should search for more predictive variables.[45]

Heteroscedasticity.   Heteroscedasticity occurs when the variance of a Y variable is not constant for different X values. This condition reduces the accuracy of the standard error and thus the accuracy of the confidence interval of estimates. To determine if heteroscedasticity exists, some computer programs will present a plot of the "error data"; that is, they will plot the actual input data around a line that represents the mean of Y for different X levels. (See Figure 7-5.) Heteroscedasticity can be corrected by transforming the Y values in various ways before placing them into

[45]Dick Berry, "Inside the Art of Regression-Based Sales Forecasting," *Business Marketing* (June 1984), pp. 100–111.

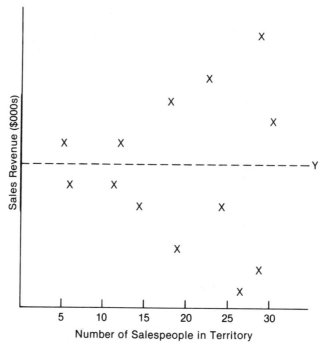

FIGURE 7-5   Graphic Determination of Heteroscedasticity

the computer. For example, one can simply take the square root of each Y value and use them in place of the original Y values.[46]

Nonlinearity.   Nonlinearity refers to situations in which Y variables do not have straight-line relationships with X variables. This is true of learning curves, where X represents quantity produced and Y represents total production costs. If researchers do not recognize the nonlinearity and assume a straight-line relationship, forecast estimates and confidence intervals will be incorrect. The presence of nonlinearity can best be determined by having the computer plot a regression graph for the data entered and examining the plotted points. It can also be indicated by the F test. Nonlinearity can be overcome by transforming both the X and Y data elements before performing computations. The square roots of the data elements can be used or, as is done in the case of learning curves, the logs of the data elements can be used.

Time Series

A second method of analyzing data to predict is called time series. Time series is used to analyze changes in a variable on the basis of events and their periods of

---

[46]John Neter and William Wasserman, *Applied Linear Statistical Models* (Homewood, Ill.: Richard D. Irwin, Inc., 1974), p. 507.

occurrence, which tend to be repetitive. Time periods of significant events that tend to repeat themselves are long-term trends, business cycles, seasonal differences, and even trading-day effects (days that particularly affect a variable, such as the occasional occurrence on a long holiday within a period to be predicted). Figure 7-6 graphically displays the characteristic, long-term trend line, the shorter-term (usually three- to seven-year) business cycle fluctuations, and the seasonable fluctuations occurring within each year. The model's predictions are frequently achieved by multiplying variables using the equation

$$Y = T + C + S + I$$

where *T, C,* and *S* stand for trend, cyclical, and seasonal effects and *I* stands for irregular effects (some, usually unpredictable, one-time, special event). Various methods are used to adjust for trading-day effects, with the simplest method being to adjust the predictive data before performing any calculations; thus, the trading-day variable is not included in the foregoing equation. For example, assume that a major trade show occurs on either the last two days of June or the first two days of July. If one attempts to predict for an upcoming month of June during which the trade show will not take place, the data for each June in previous years are adjusted to remove the effects of the trade show before any calculations are performed.

Interestingly, like exponential smoothing, moving average, and simple trend analysis methods, time series uses only data for the variable to be predicted. However, its greater predictability in many situations results from partitioning the data in accordance with the recurring cyclical, seasonal, trend, and trading-day events; that is, the effects of many other variables are brought to bear on time-series predictions.

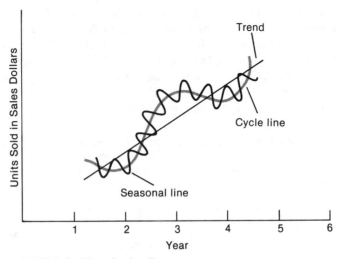

FIGURE 7-6   Time-Series Components

TABLE 7-11 ARIMA Software

IBM-mainframe [S/370 & up]
   Informetrica, Ltd. — AMS-FS
      "Time-series forecasting for high volume applications. Features census XII seasonal adjustment, Box-Jenkins for short term forecasting and trend projections for medium and long term applications." Sold 6 since 1975.
IBM PC-MS/DOS
   Automatic Forecasting Systems, Inc. — Autobj, AutoBox, Boxx, EZF, MTS, SimBoxJ
      [SimBoxJ] "Generates from 1 to 5 discrete time series. Calculates data by multiplying random numbers and user-specified Box-Jenkins equation. Handles univariate transfer function, single intervention and Vector ARIMA models." Sold 36 since 1985. Cost $195.
   Lionheart Press, Inc. — Sales and Market Forecasting
      "Apple Macintosh; PC-MS/DOS compatible . . . Shows how to use forecasting techniques incuding Box-Jenkins ARIMA models and how to relate company time-series to economic time-series. Provides selection of US Department of Commerce time-series so techniques can be learned using real-life data." 1,000 sold since 1984. Cost $145.

Source: Reprinted by permission of Ziff-Davis Publishing Company. From *Data Sources,* 1st Edition 1990 [New York: Ziff-Davis Publishing Company, 1990], pp. J-277–J-278.

We will not dwell further on this basic time-series model as it is covered in most college statistics courses; rather, we turn our attention to a group of time-series models that are receiving increasing use in industrial marketing.

ARIMA (or Box-Jenkins Models) ARIMA (autoregressive-integrated-moving average), or Box-Jenkins, models evaluate trend, cyclical, seasonal, and even trading-day effects but have a sounder statistical foundation than do other simpler methods of performing time-series analysis.[47] (See Table 7-11.) Although their effectiveness has been shown to depend upon the variables forecasted (for some variables, other methods have been shown to be superior), particular studies have shown that AR-IMA models (1) provide better forecasts than do management experts in 30 out of 40 forecasts,[48] (2) yield better forecasts than do exponential smoothing and other models,[49] and (3) perform better (by a factor of 2 to 1) than do large econometric models.[50] Because of the long-term buyer-seller relationship, industrial forecasters are in a better position to obtain data for several past periods, making ARIMA models more appropriate for industrial than consumer forecasting. Customarily, 35 or more periods of past data are needed, though at least 50 are recommended.

[47]This discussion is based on Spyros Makridakis, Steven Wheelwright, and Victor McGee, *Forecasting Methods and Applications* (New York: John Wiley & Sons, Inc., 1983), pp. 356–359.

[48]Kenneth Lorek, Charles McDonald, and Dennis Patz, "A Comparative Examination of Management Forecasts and Box-Jenkins Forecasts of Earnings," *The Accounting Review* (April 1976), pp. 321–330.

[49]V. A. Mabert, "Statistical versus Sales Force—Executive Opinion Short-Range Forecasts: A Time Series Analysis Case Study," *Decision Science* 7 (1976), pp. 310–318.

[50]Thomas Naylor, Terry Seaks, and D. W. Wichern, "Box-Jenkins Methods: An Alternative to Econometric Models," *International Statistical Review* 40:2 (1972), pp. 123–137.

VENTURE ANALYSIS

Essentially, venture analysis measures the relationships among many factors expressed in mathematical terms for the purpose of predicting the future. The underlying rationale is that if [1] for all new products introduced over a substantial period of time there is a strong relationship between demand levels and the specific variables considered during the early period of a product's life, and if [2] this relationship persists, the probable market activity for future new products can be estimated from corresponding early-period variable. From these interacting relationships, reliable output can be generated that includes aggregate demand, levels of demand at various points in time, prices throughout the product's life cycle, upper and lower limits of profits that can be expected over its life, and comparable analysis as programmed into the model.

Once the foregoing venture analysis program is operational, a market researcher can sit at a computer terminal and call in the program. The researcher will then supply various estimates as they are called for by the computer, including the estimated size of the target group, recent product trial rates, repeat purchases, the promotional budget, size of investment, target rate of return, product price, and gross profit margin. The computer will process this information and print out a forecast for the next few years of the total number of customers, company market share, price[s], period profits, and discounted cumulative profits. The market researcher can alter various input estimates and readily ascertain the effect of the altered data on sales and profits. Also, the individual can perform the analyses deemed necessary for the new product under study.

The values of the key input variables and their uncertainty profiles are functions of many factors. For example, revenue is a function of selling price, total market, market share, and the like. In turn, these factors may be interrelated; for example, market share is a function of selling price, total market is a function of selling price, selling price may be related to manufacturing costs, manufacturing costs may be a function of quantity manufactured, which is related to market size, and so on. In essence, this . . . venture analysis model is a management laboratory in which marketing management can experiment, before the fact, with a variety of alternatives and, at the same time, support the market research decision-making process.

Source: Reprinted with permission of Robert Thierauf, *Decision Support Systems for Effective Planning and Control* (Englewood Cliffs, N.J.: Prentice-Hall, Inc., 1982), pp. 324–326.

The label for this group of models, "Autoregressive-integrated moving average" is derived from three factors. First, these models use linear regression to regress present Y values against lagged Y values. Regressing Y on previous Y's leads to the term autoregressive and the equation

$$Y_t = a + b_1 Y_{t-1} + b_2 Y_{t-2} + e_t$$

which bears a strong resemblance to our previous linear regression formula. Table 7-12 shows the meaning of Y_t, Y_{t-1}, and Y_{t-2}; that is, each term refers to an entire column of data.

Second, these models also use a type of moving average (though not in the conventional sense) that is developed through the equation

$$Y_t = a + b_1 e_{t-1} + b_2 e_{t-2} + e_t.$$

where Y, a, and b have the same meaning as in linear regression but the linear regression X is replaced with e. The e term represents how different each actual Y value is from the regression line, say, a little above or a little below it. The regression line depicts where Y should be, or the average value of Y, so that how the actual *Y's move* around that line of *averages* is represented by the series of related and dependent e terms in the equation; that is, they provide a moving average.

Third, the term "integrated" refers to combining previous levels of Y with the present level. If we subtract Y from the previous period from Y for the present period, we have integrated the two and found the difference. It is not always necessary to find this difference. It is only found when a plotted time series does not have a consistent mean or variance or both. Finding the differences and plotting it allows one to determine if inconsistent means and variances can be made consistent over time, referred to it as "stationary." If, after finding differences between present *Y's* and *Y's* lagged one time period, we still have not achieved stationarity, we then integrate (or subtract *Y's*) lagged two periods. Seldom does the researcher have to consider more than two lag periods.

Although a complete ARIMA model would be one that included autoregression, moving averages, and differencing, the term ARIMA is commonly used to refer to models dealing only with subparts of the complete model (such as moving averages or autoregression) but that use the statistical methods of development characteristic of ARIMA models.

Performing ARIMA forecasting involves a three-stage method of development that includes (1) identification (identifying the model to be examined initially, such

TABLE 7-12 Autoregression Columns

Time Periods	Original Y Data	One Time Period Lag	Two Time Period Lags
1	45	—	—
2	43	45	—
3	40	43	45
4	36	40	43
5	35	36	40
6	31	35	36

as an autoregressive versus a moving-average model), (2) estimation (estimation of parameters), and (3) diagnostic checking (determining if the model is adequate). The researcher must make certain decisions at each of these three stages. Those decisions can vary considerably, depending on the Y variable data. Due to the wide variability in the decisions, it is not possible to discuss them here; however, the references previously given in this discussion, as well as the users' guides provided with ARIMA software should effectively guide the researcher through the process.

The advantages and disadvantages of prediction methods discussed to this point often lead industrial organizations to utilize more than one and often several of the methods. "Venture Analysis" is a software program that integrates several of the concepts discussed to this point and that provides a level of predictive sophistication that can only be achieved with our modern technology.

PRESENTING THE FINDINGS

In very recent years computer systems have come to play a new and important role in presenting research findings. To understand that role, perhaps we should first explain that when information systems were first computerized, the role of the computer was essentially to speed up information handling. These systems, referred to as *management/marketing information systems (MIS)*, used computers to store, perform calculations on, and provide retrieval of data. Thus, they were "backward-looking" systems because they involved accumulating data for various periods of time, entering them into the computer system, and then generating periodic reports of past events.[51]

Current computerized systems enable managers to call on computers to produce analyses of research findings, to provide real-time information (information stored into a computer as the information becomes available), and to be what may be termed "forward looking." For example, these systems allow managers to ask questions such as, "What will result if we increase the price of a particular product 10 percent?" called, "what-if" questions. In other words, computerized systems can now access computer decision-making programs, data bases, historical and current status reports, projected reports, and even recommended courses of action. (See Figure 7-7). They can also forecast changes in sales, profits, market share, operating costs, and competitor reactions, as well as other environmental reactions that might occur.[52] These, more advanced computerized systems are called *decision support systems (DSS)*, because, as their name implies, they directly support the managers' decision making. In doing so, they not only perform all these analyses, but they present them through terminals at the desks of decision makers. Decision makers can, thus, call for various analyses using what-if questions, be presented the research results via terminal, and on the bases of the results, immediately adjust

[51]Thierauf, *Decision Support Systems,* p. 19.
[52]Alter, *Decision Support Systems,* pp. 11–12.

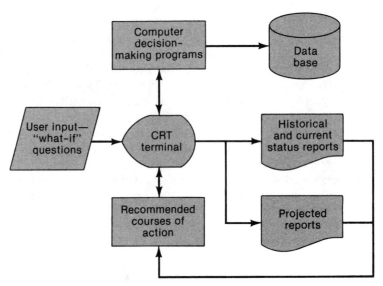

FIGURE 7-7 **Interactive Decision-Making Process of Decision Support Systems**

Source: Reprinted with permission of Robert Thierauf, *Decision Support Systems for Effective Planning and Control* [Englewood Cliffs, N.J.: Prentice-Hall, Inc., 1982], p. 27.

their requests for further research using other what-if questions. Such rapid analysis and presentation of the findings add greatly to the flexibility and potential of decision making.

Decision Support Systems.   To illustrate how DSS performs, we can use *response curves,* one of the tools used by DSS. (See Figure 7-8.) Figure 7-8 indicates that as the number of sales people increases from 10 to 20 to 30, sales will change from some reference period by multiples of .5, 1.0, and 1.3. If, for example, the company's sales during reference period 19xx were $500,000, and the firm increases the size of its sales force from 20 to 30, its sales would be forecasted to be 1.3 × $500,000, or $650,000.

DSS response curves can also utilize empirical data (real data, obtained through sampling and/or company records) to evaluate sales force size, territorial design, and sales effort. Since decisions regarding sales force size, territorial design, and sales effort are interrelated, DSS—which has capabilities of examining interrelationships—is extremely useful. DSS response curves are also used to examine individual customers, groups of customers, salespersons' characteristics, company products, competitive products, and competitors' reactions.

Decision support systems are intended to "be able to reflect the way managers think, be flexible and adaptive through ease of modification, support managers in a complex process of exploration and learning, and evolve to meet changing needs,

FIGURE 7-8 Sample Response Curve

Source: Adapted from and reprinted with permission of Steven Alter, *Decision Support Systems: Current Practice and Continuing Challenges* (Reading, Mass.: Addison-Wesley Publishing Co., 1980), p. 11.

knowledge and situations.''[53] In effect, decision support systems offer a great advance in the performance of research and the presentation of research findings.

Executive Information Systems. Though only a handful of software suppliers presently offer Executive Information Systems (EIS), users find them very promising. EIS are intended to make great amounts of current information attractively available to top management. Rather than DSS future-oriented types of information, EIS present current information; EIS then answer ''What is'' questions rather than the ''What if'' questions typically answered by DSS. EIS information can be supplied from internal organization sources as well as by commercially supplied secondary information sources. To make the use of such systems attractive to top management, access to information is provided through such devices as the computer mouse and touch-screen programs that can quickly access a variety of menu possibilities. These devices pull up reports, graphs, and summarizes in formats that top managers prefer, and information that can be even more closely examined for more detail. These systems are not intended to replace DSS, but to enhance it by tailoring voluminous amounts of existent data in ways that top managers prefer, and then making it exceptionally easy to retrieve that data. The manager who can determine how the company is doing compared to other firms shown through an on line database can better make future-oriented DSS decisions.[54]

---

[53]P. Keen and G. Wagner, ''DSS: An Executive Mind-Support System,'' *Datamation* (November 1979), p. 117.

[54]Mary Lou Jordan, ''Executive Information Systems Make Life Easy for the Lucky Few,'' *Computerworld* (February 29, 1988), pp. 51–57.

LOOKING BACK

Market opportunities are assessed through marketing research. As with conventional research, the process begins with defining the problem and establishing research objectives. However, because industrial marketers deal with concentrated markets with limited numbers of technical, knowledgeable people, and because of limited research budgets, industrial marketing research has its own peculiarities.

Industrial marketing researchers usually use secondary rather than primary data. Secondary data sources have proliferated in recent years, particularly computer on-line data bases. SIC codes are used to classify many industrial data; however, the codes pose many problems, and these problems are compounded in governmental secondary sources because they are frequently outdated.

Primary data are mainly gathered through surveys. These are almost always unstructured and nondisguised because of the close personal relationships prevalent in the industrial area; however, customers are often reluctant to be candid when supplying information. Gathering primary data through group surveys, usually performed only with the researcher's organization, is most accurate when simple averages of individual estimates are used.

Due to wide swings in industrial sales, caused by derived demand, data analysis methods that involve more than one variable, such as multiple regression and time series, are more useful than are simple methods such as trend analysis and exponential smoothing. Decision support systems that take advantage of several computer capabilities have become increasingly popular in performing industrial research in recent years.

QUESTIONS FOR DISCUSSION

1. Given the accelerating pace of worldwide change, discuss the feasibility of long-range forecasts (two years or longer).
2. What might be done to improve the SIC code system?
3. What are the advantages and disadvantages of salespersons providing research information?
4. How might a decision support system be made to perform sales force scheduling?
5. Discuss the advantages of qualitative research over quantitative research.
6. Discuss how industrial marketing research might be involved in government Star Wars contracts.
7. Discuss possible advantages of computer-based MRP systems to marketing managers.
8. Find an index in the *Business Conditions Digest* that, when lagged, enables you to predict production of synthetic rubber and rubber products (rubber and tires and tubes). Tell why you believe the index to be a good predictor.

SUGGESTED ADDITIONAL READINGS

ALTER, STEVEN, *Decision Support Systems: Current Practice and Continuing Challenges* (Reading, Mass.: Addison-Wesley Publishing Co., 1980).

BERRY, DICK, "Inside the Art of Regression-Based Sales Forecasting", *Business Marketing* (June 1984):100–111.

BOLFING, CLAIRE P., and SANDRA L. SCHMIDT, "Utilizing Expert Database Services," *Industrial Marketing Management* 17 (1988), pp. 141–150.

COURETAS, JOHN, "Counting Smokestacks, Census Help for Marketers," *Business Marketing* (January 1984):86–88.

HOGARTH, ROBIN, and SPYROS MAKRIDAKIS, "Forecasting and Planning: An Evaluation," *Management Science* 27: 2 (February 1981):115–138.

KOTLER, PHILIP, "A guide to Gathering Expert Estimates," *Business Horizons* (October 1970):78–87.

SCHERER, RON, "'Information Boutiques,'—Intelligence for a Price," *U.S. News & World Report* (May 20, 1985):72–73.

SOVNER-RIBBLER, JUDITH, "Which Database Solves which Marketing Problem?" *Sales & Marketing Management* (July 1988):53–55.

WALLACE, KATHLEEN M., "The Use and Value of Qualitative Research Studies," *Industrial Marketing Management* 13 (1984): pp. 181–185.

WHITE, RON, "The Online Access Guide," *Online Access* (September-October 1987):58–64.

CHAPTER 8

Industrial Market Segmentation, Target Marketing, and Positioning

Successful industrial marketing strategy rests on the marketer's ability to identify, analyze, and evaluate attractive market segments. Effective market selection is necessary if the firm is to allocate its resources so that those markets served contribute to the achievement of organizational objectives. In this chapter, then, we discuss

1. Market segmentation and its benefits, requirements, and cost.
2. How industrial marketers can go about segmenting the industrial market.
3. The need for evaluating potential segments to choose target markets effectively.
4. Market coverage strategies.
5. The importance of developing effective positioning strategy.

Few firms have the resources to pursue actively all potential markets, "nor could they justify doing so on a return-on-investment basis."[1] Thus, the task facing the industrial marketer is to identify, evaluate, and choose those markets in which it can compete most effectively. In choosing markets to serve, however, the firm is not only choosing its customer base, it is choosing the competitive, technical, political, and social environments in which it will compete. This is not an easy decision to reverse. As Raymond Corey points out,

[1]Andris A. Zoltners and Joe A. Dodson, "Market Selection Model for Multiple End-Use Products," *Journal of Marketing* 47 (Spring 1983), pp. 76–88.

Having made the choice, the company develops skills and resources around the markets it has elected to serve. It builds a set of relationships with customers that are at once a major source of strength and a major commitment. The commitment carries with it the responsibility to serve customers well, to stay in the technical and product-development race, and to grow in pace with growing market demand.[2]

Market choices, then, must be based on an evaluation of the company's distinctive competencies and differential advantages in the areas of marketing, manufacturing, and technical strengths.

MARKET SEGMENTATION

As Figure 8-1 outlines, market segmentation is the first in a series of steps that ultimately enables a firm to maximize the return on its investment. Attractive market segments must be identified and evaluated, target markets selected, and decisions made as to how the firm will compete in those markets before positioning and marketing mix strategies can be developed.

Industrial customers, like consumers, differ in their needs, resources, and buying attitudes. A practical approach to understanding these differences is to identify variables by which potential buyers can be segmented. Market segmentation strategy, then, is undertaken to identify groups of firms whose purchasing requirements and responses to marketing programs are similar. Market segmentation, however, is not the same as target marketing. Market segmentation strategy is the process of dividing a market into distinct groups of buyers whose marketing responses to products and/or marketing mixes may be similar. Thus, the firm (1) identifies different ways to segment the market, (2) develops profiles of each resulting segment, and (3) evaluates each segment's attractiveness. Target marketing, on the other hand, is "the act of evaluating and selecting one or more of the market segments to enter."[3]

Benefits of Market Segmentation

Unfortunately, market segmentation in the industrial arena has not been pursued as vigorously as it has in the consumer arena because of the difficulties involved. Not only is there great diversity among end-users and the end-uses that exist for many industrial products, but differences also exist in product application, customer characteristics, buying practices, and benefits sought. This makes it very difficult for organizations to compare different segments on the basis of a few simple criteria. The task of market segmentation is also complicated by the purchasing decision process within organizations—a process that normally involves several individuals

---

[2]E. Raymond Corey, "Key Options in Market Selection and Product Planning," *Harvard Business Review* (September–October, 1975), pp. 119–128.

[3]Philip Kotler, *Marketing Essentials* (Englewood Cliffs, N.J.: Prentice-Hall, Inc., 1984), p. 162.

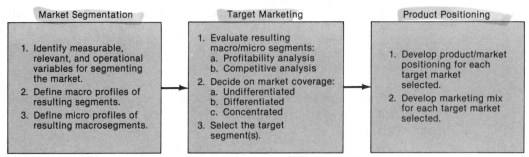

FIGURE 8-1 A Market Segmentation and Product Positioning Model

Source: Adapted from Philip Kotler, *Marketing Management: Analysis, Planning, and Control,* 5th ed., [Englewood Cliffs, N.J.: Prentice-Hall, Inc., 1984], p. 251. Reprinted by permission.

with different backgrounds and job responsibilities.[4] Thus, grouping potential customers into segments whose responses to marketing programs will be similar is not an easy task. However, due to tougher competition and changing customer needs, some of the larger industrial and high-tech organizations are now beginning to utilize segmentation strategies. Moore Corporation, a business forms marketer, and Unisys Corporation, a computer manufacturer, for example, are now developing and executing segmentation strategies. They have found that despite the difficulties involved market segmentation has three distinct advantages:[5]

1. The seller is in a better position to spot and compare marketing opportunities.
2. The seller can create separate marketing programs aimed to meet the needs of different buyers.
3. The seller can develop marketing programs and budgets based on a clearer idea of the response characteristics of specific market segments.[6]

Effective industrial market segmentation, then, enables the marketer to examine and evaluate the needs of each potential segment against competitors' offerings to determine the extent of each segments' satisfaction. Where current satisfaction is relatively low, marketing opportunities may exist. Further, once attractive markets are identified and chosen, marketing programs can be developed and resources allocated more efficiently so that the desired results are achieved.

[4]See: Cornelis A. de Kluyver and David B. Whitlark, "Benefit Segmentation for Industrial Products," *Industrial Marketing Management* 15 (1986), pp. 273–286; and Jean Marie Choffray and Gary L. Lilien, "Industrial Market Segmentation by the Structure of the Purchasing Process," *Industrial Marketing Management* 9 (1980), pp. 331–342.

[5]Kate Bertrand, "Harvesting the Best," *Business Marketing* (October 1988), pp. 44–46.

[6]Philip Kotler, *Marketing Management: Analysis, Planning, and Control,* 3rd ed. (Englewood Cliffs, N.J.: Prentice-Hall, Inc., 1976), p. 144.

Requirements for Effective Market Segmentation

While there are a number of approaches to segmenting the industrial market, to be useful, the variables that are selected for analysis must be:

Measurable — Information on the variables of interest should exist and be obtainable either through secondary or primary information sources.

Relevant — The variables chosen should impact on decision making for a significant number of potential customer groupings and relate to important differences across customer groups regarding responses to different marketing programs.

Operational — The variables chosen for evaluation among customer groups should be related to differences in customer requirements and buying behavior. They should indicate marketing approaches with respect to products, pricing, communication, or distribution.[7]

The purpose behind segmenting the industrial market is to enable the marketing firm to allocate its resources more effectively to maximize return on investment. Thus, not only should the resulting market choices be sufficiently large and profitable to warrant attention, they should be different enough to enable distinctive marketing programs.

It should be noted, however, that market segmentation is not always practical, particularly when the market is composed of oligopsonistic buyers, a single large customer, or when the "market is so small that marketing to a portion of it is not profitable."[8]

Market Segmentation Involves Costs.   Market segmentation strategy involves costs in obtaining and analyzing data, and in developing and implementing separate marketing and manufacturing plans to serve segments effectively. Market segmentation efforts, then, must result in sufficient additional sales volume and profits to justify its costs.[9] Thus, before embarking on a segmentation analysis, some estimation of the costs versus the benefits must be made.

BASIS FOR SEGMENTING INDUSTRIAL MARKETS

There is no magic formula for segmenting the industrial market. In approaching this task, the marketer will have to try different segmentation variables, either alone

[7]Frederick E. Webster, Jr., *Industrial Marketing Strategy* (New York: John Wiley & Sons, Inc., 1979), pp. 74–75.

[8]Shirley Young, Leland Ott, and Barbara Feigin, "Some Practical Considerations in Market Segmentation," *Journal of Marketing Research* 15 (August 1978), pp. 405–412.

[9]Thomas V. Bonoma and Benson P. Shapiro, "Evaluating Market Segmentation Approaches," *Industrial Marketing Management* 13 (1984), pp. 257–268.

UNISYS: LINING UP BUSINESS TARGETS

Rapidly changing technologies, shifting customer needs, and increasing competition in almost every part of the computer industry have forced Blue Bell, Pennsylvania-based Unisys Corporation, to segment its markets, which include workstation and mainframe computer users, by what it calls a "line of business" approach.

"You have to understand what's driving change in the customer's business and ask, 'Why are they buying this stuff?'" says Richard Williams, Unisys' vice president of marketing strategy and development. So Unisys looks at the end user. The needs of a bank are different from the needs of the motor vehicle department or a plastics plant. In putting that knowledge to work, Unisys segmented the market into six commercial and governmental clusters: the industrial and commercial markets, financial services, the communications and airlines markets, the public sector, the federal government, and the defense department. Each of those clusters is further segmented. For example, the public sector market is comprised of four groups: state and local agencies, educational institutions, health care providers, and utility companies. Each of these groups is again split. The health care group, for instance, includes hospitals, health maintenance organizations, and private practices.

In implementing its marketing segmentation strategy, Unisys reorganized its direct salespeople according to the industries they covered, launched a lead-sharing program to boost the success of its resellers in vertical market, advertised heavily in vertical business publications, and launched a third-party program to develop industry-specific products and services. For example, by signing a product development and marketing agreement with Jack Henry & Associates, a software developer in the financial market, a software program was adapted to handle all the operations needed to run a small bank.

Source: Kate Bertrand, "Harvesting the Best," *Business Marketing* (October 1988), pp. 44–46. Reprinted by permission.

(which may be sufficient in some cases) or in combination. For segmentation variables to be meaningfully evaluated, however, they must be based on characteristics that are easily identified, understood, and discernible.[10] While consumer markets are typically segmented on the basis of demographic or psychographic variables, industrial marketing segmentation is approached on the basis of what has been termed macro- and microsegmentation. *Macrosegmentation* approaches the task on the basis of differences between industries and organizations, such as size, geographic location, or product application. *Microsegmentation* approaches it on the basis of the differences in criteria that are more directly related to the purchasing decision-making process and behavior of those individuals involved in the decision-

---

[10]Robert E. Krapfel, Jr., and Darlene Brannigan-Smith, "An Experimental Approach to Segmenting Buyers of Marketing Research," *Industrial Marketing Management* 14 (1985), pp. 27–34.

making units.[11] Because of the fundamental differences between organizational and individual buyer behavior, Wind and Cardozo have recommended that market segmentation be approached in two stages: (1) identify meaningful macrosegments and (2) subdivide those macrosegments into meaningful microsegments.

MACRO VARIABLES

Table 8-1 lists some of the macro variables that industrial marketers can use to identify and evaluate potentially attractive markets during the first stage of market segmentation. Most of those variables are not difficult to identify and are easily obtained through secondary sources of information such as trade directories and publications, general business magazines and directories, government reports, and market research companies as well as company sources of information.

TABLE 8-1 Some Macro Variables Used to Segment the Industrial Market

Variables	Examples
Industry	Agriculture, mining, construction, manufacturing, transportation, wholesale, retail, finance, services
Organizational characteristics	
Size characteristics	Size of customers' parent company, size of customers' business, and number of plants sold
Plant characteristics	Size of customers' plant, age of customers' plant, inventory turn-over, and degree of automation
Location	Distance from plant, state of plant, and suburban/urban/rural location
Economic factors	Cyclicality of customers' industry
Customers' industry	Growth rate of industry and customers' growth stage within the industry; ultimate customer of customers' product
Competitive forces	Degree of competition in customers' industries, ease of entry into customers' industries, and ease of customer switching
Purchasing factors	Decentralized versus centralized, and number of levels of purchasing authority
End-use markets	Residential/commercial contractors, coal/ore miners, foresters, federal/state highway maintenance departments, banks/insurance/brokerage houses
Product application	Small appliance, computer, television, and airplane manufacturers

Source: Norman Wiener, "Customer Demographics for Strategic Selling," *Business Marketing,* [May 1983], pp. 78, 80, 82. Reprinted by permission.

[11]See Yoram Wind and Richard N. Cardozo, "Industrial Marketing Segmentation," *Industrial Marketing Management* 3 (1974), p. 155; Richard N. Cardozo, "Segmenting the Industrial Market," in Robert L. King, ed., *Marketing and the New Science of Planning* (Chicago: American Marketing Association, 1968), pp. 433–440; and Ronald E. Frank, William F. Massy, and Yoram Wind, *Market Segmentation* (Englewood Cliffs, N.J.: Prentice-Hall, Inc., 1971), Chap. 4.

Industry Characteristics

Many firms produce products and services that can be targeted to different, even dissimilar, industries. For example, computer manufacturers can market their products to such diverse industries as health, finance, manufacturing, and retailing. For these marketers, effective market segmentation and subsequent marketing programs will rest on a clear understanding of the similarities and differences between these industries. For example, while retailers, banks, and hospitals will have some common needs with respect to computers, many of their requirements will be markedly different, as will their attitudes and approaches toward purchasing.

Significant differences may also be present within an industry. Consider, for instance, the sale of computer equipment and software programs within the finance industry. While commercial banks, stock brokerage houses, savings and loan associations, and insurance companies are all part of the finance industry, their product and service requirements with respect to terminals, data handling, and software programs will be considerably diverse. Thus, in some instances, further subdividing of individual industries may be necessary to obtain a more detailed segmentation scheme.[12]

Organizational Characteristics

Demographics. Industries and organizations within industries, like consumers, have different demographic characteristics. Larger organizations, like larger families, have different purchasing requirements (e.g., volume purchasing, normally accompanied by quantity discounts) and will respond differently to marketing programs than will smaller firms that purchase in smaller quantities. Thus, when companies are segmented on the basis of size, larger producers may want to avoid small firms because their low volume needs cannot be served profitably. On the other hand, smaller producers may want to avoid large companies because their volume requirements exceed production capacities.

Customer location can also be an important segmentation variable. In the industrial market, for example, on-time delivery is an important factor in serving customers. Thus, due to effects on inventory, transportation, and warehousing, marketers may want to avoid those customer markets that are located too far away or are too dispersed. Location also affects sales force organization and deployment. Borg-Warner, for instance, which produces mechanical seals for slurry coal pipelines, would want to provide more coverage in those areas where coal mines are concentrated.

Decentralized versus centralized procurement is another important macrosegmentation variable due to the influence it can have on the purchasing decision. As

[12]Benson P. Shapiro and Thomas V. Bonoma, "How to Segment Industrial Markets," *Harvard Business Review* (May–June 1984), pp. 104–110.

discussed in Chapter Five, when purchasing is centralized, the purchasing managers' power and specialization, the criteria emphasized, and the composition of the buying center are strongly affected. Thus, purchasing factors provide a good base for isolating specific needs and marketing requirements of individual organizations within industries and enable the marketer to organize the sales force to serve chosen customers better within markets (e.g., national versus local account sales force organization).

Segmenting organizations by demographics is crucial in deciding which markets to serve and in the development of marketing strategy for the long run as well as the short run. And, as Table 8-1 outlines, organizational demographic analysis can also include evaluating plant characteristics, economic factors, industry forces, and competitive forces as well as organizational size, location, and purchasing variables. *Business Marketing,* a well-known trade publication, for instance, points out that organizational demographics is an important tool in selling business to business and that too few industrial marketers make use of these important variables in developing and implementing their strategies.

When customer demographics are analyzed in conjunction with potential sales and profitability, a firm gains valuable information that can be applied to the development of long-range as well as short-range strategy. (See Table 8-2.)[13] For example, when customers are segmented on the basis of decentralized versus centralized purchasing factors, the firm might want to organize its selling approach to serve national accounts versus local accounts. Further, when sales personnel are more aware of the unique demographic traits of their respective customer base, they are in a better position to approach or serve those accounts on the basis of their distinctive differences.

End-Use Markets. Many firms also produce products and services that can be offered to a multitude of end-use markets. For example, International Harvester manufactures such heavy-duty equipment as wheel loaders, excavators, off-highway trucks, and long skidders. These various equipments, for instance, can be marketed to residential and commercial contractors, coal and ore miners, foresters, and federal and state highway maintenance departments. Banks and other commercial lending institutions also offer a multitude of end-use services to such markets as mining, agribusiness, construction and engineering, and shipping and marine. "Such opportunities differ in different markets and since the future of a multi end-use product or service is tied to the future of its market,"[14] market segmentation via the end use of products by market is a key component in identifying attractive markets to serve.

Product Application. Many products are used in several different ways. For instance, small electrical switches are used in the production of small household appli-

---

[13]Norman Wiener, "Customer Demographics for Strategic Selling," *Business Marketing* (May 1983), pp. 78, 80, 82.

[14]Zoltners and Dodson, "A Market Selection Model," pp. 76–88.

TABLE 8-2 Applications of Customer Demographic Analysis

Long-Range Applications	Short-Range Applications
Determine critical factors, and establish a profile of the potentially profitable customer.	Establish minimum order sizes.
Evaluate new sales territories for future sales development.	Establish cold-customer prequalifications criteria.
Evaluate customer potential for proposed new plant sites.	Evaluate sales territory potentials.
Assess the company's long-term vulnerability to business economic cycles.	Determine specific factors for poor sales and profit performance by individual sales reps.
Determine the form of the selling organization.	Determine which accounts to relinquish to competitors.
Evaluate the customer base for a proposed acquisition within the same industry.	Appraise monthly or quarterly performance of sales territories and sales managers.
Determine target industries for future product and sales development.	
Evaluate the quality of the company's current sales force.	
Evaluate a competitor's customer base.	

Source: Norman Wiener, "Customer Demographics for Strategic Selling," *Business Marketing*, (May 1983), pp. 78, 80, 82. Reprinted with permission.

ances, computers, televisions, and even jumbo jets. Thus, markets can be segmented on the basis of product application. The SIC system and related secondary data sources discussed in Chapter 7 can be useful in segmenting the market by product application as well as end use.

MICRO VARIABLES

Macrosegmentation facilitates the identification of industry, organizational, end-use markets, or product applications variables that are similar across industries. Microsegmentation, as Table 8-3 indicates, allows the marketer to subdivide further those segments through the identification and evaluation of specific organizational, purchasing, and individual criteria that are more directly related to the purchasing decision. To isolate those variables effectively, however, it is often necessary to gather primary information—either through the company sales force or by conducting special market studies.

Organizational Variables

Purchasing Situation/Phase.   As discussed in Chapter 4, marketing strategy, particularly communication strategy, is significantly affected by the type of purchasing situation customer firms are facing and where they are in the purchasing decision

TABLE 8-3 Microsegmentation Variables

Variables	Examples
Organizational variables	
Purchasing situation/phase	New task, modified or straight rebuy; stage in the purchasing, decision process
Customer experience stage	Product life-cycle stages (i.e., introduction, growth, and maturity) as it relates to customer adoption process (i.e., early and late adopters)
Customer interaction needs	Dependence on supplier in implementing decision-making process or supplier's knowledge compared to customer's knowledge
Product innovativeness	Innovative firms versus followers
Organizational capabilities	Extent of operating, technical, or financial capabilities
Purchase situation variables	
Inventory requirements	Material requirement planning or just-in-time systems
Purchase importance	Degree of perceived risk (i.e., cost, usage factors, or time)
Purchasing policies	Market-based prices, bids, or leasing preferences
Purchasing criteria	Supplier reputation, technical services, reliability, flexibility, etc.
Structure of the buying center	Key influencers and decision makers (e.g., engineering, marketing, plant managers, and R&D)
Individual variables	
Personal characteristics	Demographics (e.g., age and experience), personality, non-task motives, perceptions, and risk takers/avoiders
Power structure	Collaboration, compromise, avoidance, or coalition formation

process. In the new task situation, for instance, the firm's ability to penetrate the market will depend on its ability to assist in problem solutions, to provide information to key decision makers, and to work with customers through all phases of the purchasing decision process.[15] On the other hand, in a straight rebuy purchasing situation, out suppliers must be capable of convincing customers that it is worth reevaluating current suppliers by offering superior product advantages or significant price differences. Thus, segmentation across the Buygrid continuum (see Chapter Four) is an important micro step in examining buyers' purchasing needs, information requirements, and the structure of the buying center and interaction patterns.

Customer Experience (or PLC Considerations).[16]   When customers are unfamiliar with products (product introduction), they tend to assign purchasing responsibility to those persons within the firm who are competent in dealing with the uncertainties involved. They also tend to be attracted by "a bundle of vendor supplied benefits

---

[15]Richard N. Cardozo, "Situational Segmentation of Industrial Markets," *European Journal of Marketing* 14 (1980), pp. 264–276.

[16]F. Stewart DeBruicker and Gregory L. Summe, "Make Sure Your Customers Keep Coming Back," *Harvard Business Review* (January–February 1985), pp. 92–98.

WHY MICROSEGMENTATION? POTENTIAL CUSTOMER ORGANIZATIONS DIFFER IN THEIR COMPOSITION OF BUYING CENTERS

Potential customer organizations differ in their need specification dimensions'—that is, in the dimensions they use to define their requirements. They also differ in their specific requirements along these dimensions.

Potential customer organizations differ in the composition of their buying centers—in the numbers of individuals involved, their specific responsibilities, and in the way they interact.

Decision participants, or individual members of the buying center, differ in their sources of information as well as in the number and nature of the evaluation criteria used to assess product alternatives.

Source: Jean-Marie Choffray and Gary Lilien, "Assessing Response to Industrial Marketing Strategy," *Journal of Marketing* (April 1978) pp. 20–31. Reprinted by permission of the American Marketing Association.

---

and proven technology.''[17] As they become more familiar with product application, however, they tend to shift purchasing responsibility to functional specialists or purchasing agents who are more price sensitive, and supplier support programs begin to decline in value, opening the door to out suppliers. Thus, the level of customer experience, as Table 8-4 shows, not only affects the composition of the decision-making unit and the decision-making process, it also affects marketing strategy considerations for current as well as potential customer firms.

While customer experience can evolve with the product life cycle, "the transition from inexperienced to experienced customer often takes place independent of product maturation."[18] Since, as DeBruicker points out, product benefit patterns are identifiable and predictable as customers move from product inexperience to product experience, market segmentation by customer experience level can provide a basis for further refinement of microsegments.

Customer Interaction Needs.   Where complex or strategically important products, such as computer hardware and software or capital goods, are concerned, final purchasing decisions often depend on the buyer's response to the seller's marketing stimuli during the decision-making process. Since product packages must be adapted to customer needs, the buyer-seller relationship often involves considerable interaction. The duration and involvement of that interaction will depend on whether buyers are capable of determining their own needs or are dependent on suppliers. Buyers who are uncertain of their needs will exhibit different sets of problems and behaviors and desire considerably more supplier interaction. In the case of com-

[17]Ibid.
[18]Ibid.

TABLE 8-4 Effects of Customer Experience in the Engineering Plastics Industry

	Customer Groups	
	Inexperienced	Experienced
Decision-making unit	Applications engineers	Purchasing agents
Decision-making process	New task, two years	Routine repurchase, four to five per year
Marketing policy areas		
Dominant produce benefits	Technical assistance, applications support	Performance, availability, price
Price/value considerations	Enhanced competitive position	Low cost
Sales program	Account management via industry specialists	Field sales on geographic basis
Key success factors	Account management and technology	Low cost of goods sold, low or parity prices

Source: Reprinted by permission of *Harvard Business Review*, "Make Sure Your Customers Keep Coming Back," by F. Stewart DeBruicker and Gregory L. Summe, January–February 1985. Copyright © 1985 by the President and Fellows of Harvard College; all rights reserved.

puters, for instance, when buyers are capable of determining their own needs, the purchasing decision process will be shorter, and buyers will be less dependent on suppliers' knowledge and support. Thus, market penetration will consume considerably less resource allocation than when buyers are more dependent on suppliers.[19] Microsegmentation on the basis of different needs during the interaction process, then, can be a useful tool to marketers of complex products.

Customer Benefits. Benefit segmentation—identifying similar user needs and product attributes within groups of potential customers—can provide a detailed and multifaceted picture of customer needs. Such identification is useful for product design, pricing, distribution, and marketing support decisions. It also affords a look at competitive offerings in terms of their technical sophistication and service requirements, thereby alerting the firm to potential weakness in technology or marketing skills, or to gaps in the existing product line. In fact, according to some authorities, segmentation by benefits sought is frequently more relevant in industrial markets than segmentation on some purchase characteristic, particularly among firms in such basic industries as steel forging.[20]

[19]Jan B. Vollering, "Interaction Based Market Segmentation," *Industrial Marketing Management* 13 (1984), pp. 65–70.

[20]Cornelis A. de Kluyver and David B. Whitlark, "Benefit Segmentation of Industrial Products," *Industrial Marketing Management* 15 (1986), pp. 273–286; and Mark L. Bennion, Jr., "Segmentation and Positioning in a Basic Industry," *Industrial Marketing Management* 16 (1987), pp. 9–18.

Product Innovation.   According to recent studies, considerable differences exist in the buying needs and practices of organizations that are innovative product leaders as opposed to those that are followers.[21] For example, high-technology component purchase decisions in the instrument manufacturing industry tend to be influenced by current product innovation practices. As Table 8-5 shows, buying center structure and degree of interaction differs during the initiation and implementation stage of new product development as well as between innovative leaders and followers. For instance, an examination of Table 8-5 shows that innovator firms tend to adopt rather loose (LOW) structures during the initiation phase and tight (HIGH) structures during the implementation phase of the product development process. Positional (followers) firms, on the other hand, tend to adopt relatively tight (HIGH) structures during the implementation phase, loosening their structures during the implementation phase (MEDIUM to LOW).

Such findings have an important impact on how a particular firm might pursue a product innovator versus a follower firm. The more open (loose structured) way of doing business during the initiation phase for innovative firms would suggest, for suppliers of advanced component products, that people within the firm are more ready for information with respect to new component possibilities. It would also suggest that purchasing decision influence is likely to be spread across a wide range of people involved in the buying center during the early phases of the purchasing decision process (the initiating phase).

Once a product is under development (moved into the implementing phase), the potential for influencing the decision process will have diminished since "deviations will be accepted only in exceptional circumstances."[22] Thus, reaching decision makers and influencers in innovative firms will require informal contact with a wide range of persons during the initiating stage, becoming more difficult as decision making within a prospect firm progresses, eliminating certain alternatives from further consideration (the concept of creeping commitment discussed in Chapter Four).

In contrast, because of the tightly held structures of positional firms during the initiation phase of product development, the chance of influencing purchasing decisions during the early phases of the decision process through informal contact may be difficult. Thus, formal sales presentations will most likely be required to market to those firms that are followers, and as they move into the implementation stage, more time may be required of sales personnel in attempting to reach influencers now operating under a more relaxed system of management.

High-technology products also tend to diffuse (move through their life cycle) in some segments more rapidly than in others. Thus, in addition to determining the necessary strategy to reach resulting segments, "microsegmentation on the basis of organizational innovativeness enables marketers to identify those segments that should be targeted first when new products are introduced."[23]

[21]Frederick A. Johne, "Segmenting High Technology Adopters," *Industrial Marketing Management* 13 (1984), pp. 59–63.

[22]Ibid.

[23]David T. Wilson, "Industrial Buyers' Decision Making Styles," *Journal of Marketing Research* 8 (November 1971), p. 433.

TABLE 8-5 Typical Structures Used for Innovation Purposes

	Firms in the Innovative Mode [N = 8]		Firms in the Positional Mode [N = 8]	
	For Initiating	For Implementing	For Initiating	For Implementing
Specialization: functional	Medium [−, 8, −]* Marketing and engineering departments are involved.	High [7, 1, −] All departments are involved in product development tasks.	Low [−, 4, 4] One department is looked to for initiatives.	Low [−, 6, 2] Engineering and/or production are asked to get on with it.
Formalization: written communication	Low [−, −, 8] The spoken word is used predominantly.	High [6, 2, −] Progress is monitored in writing written proposals.	High [8, −, −] Certain persons are asked to submit orally.	Medium [2, 4, 2] Progress is frequently reported.
Standardization: consistency in control	Low [1, 5, 2] Guidance is given in very general market terms.	High [4, 4, −] A development manual is used to monitor progress.	High [8, −, −] Guidance is given in product class terms.	Low [1, 1, 6] Different criteria are used to monitor progress.
Centralization: power retention by CEO	Medium [−, 8, −] The CEO delegates authority for initiation within a strategy.	High [7, 1, −] The CEO exercises tight control.	High [7, 1, −] CEO monitors closely new product ideas.	High [4, 4, −] CEO or his deputy monitor progress.
Stratification: status differentials	Low [−, 2, 6] Status differentials are frequently ignored.	High [4, 3, 1] Status differentials are maintained.	High [4, 4, −] Status differentials are maintained slightly less.	Medium [2, 5, 1] Status differentials are maintained.

Specialization—the degree of division of labor.
Formalization—the extent to which communication is in writing.
Standardization—the consistency and frequency in reviewing tasks.
Centralization—the degree of power retained by chief executive.
Stratification—the degree of status differentials.
Note: The phase of *initiation* includes idea generation, screening, and concept testing. The phase of *implementation* includes development, test marketing, and commercialization.

*To be read, of the eight firms, none was scored high, eight were scored medium, one was low in terms of functional specialization.

Source: Reprinted by permission of the publisher from "Segmenting High Technology Adopters," by Frederick A. Johne, *Industrial Marketing Management* 13 (1984), pp. 59–63. Copyright © 1984 by Elsevier Science Publishing Co., Inc.

Organizational Capabilities. Organizations can also be segmented on the basis of their operating, technical, or financial capabilities. For example, companies that operate on tight inventories may be more attracted by supplier delivery capability. On the other hand, where financial capabilities are weak, supplier discounts may be more important than supplier delivery factors. Technical strength or weakness can also be an important segmentation variable. For instance, chemical industry firms that are technically weak "traditionally depend on suppliers for formulation assistance and technical support."[24]

Purchase Situation Variables

Individual organizations also vary considerably in their philosophies and approaches to purchasing requirements. While the organization of the purchasing function (macrosegmentation) will influence the size and operation of buying center involvement, other factors, such as inventory requirement needs (MRP and JIT), the importance of the purchase, general purchasing policies, purchasing criteria, and the structure of the buying center, may also be useful microsegmentation variables.

Inventory Requirements. As discussed in Chapter Five, manufacturers who utilize MRP and JIT inventory systems have a definite impact on industrial marketing programs. Not only are they more technical and financially oriented in their approach to buying, but the scope of their responsibility is considerably broader. Marketing to these organizations not only requires a sales force that is highly adept in negotiating and human relations skills, it requires that suppliers be highly capable of delivering defect-free products, on time, on a regularly scheduled basis. Segmentation, then, on the basis of inventory requirements is another important consideration. Where suppliers are not capable of meeting customers' inventory requirements, those firms should not be considered as a viable target market.

Purchase Importance. When products are applied differently across organizations, classifying them on the basis of their perceived importance may be particularly useful. For instance, the risks involved in the purchase of heavy-duty grease used by an original equipment manufacturer (OEM) as a lubricant in sealed bearings will be perceived differently than if it is purchased by users to keep handcarts running smoothly. The OEM's grease purchase is to enhance the salability of the end product; the user's is to maintain production. Thus, while both buyers will perceive a degree of risk in the purchasing situation, the importance of the purchase will differ considerably.

The perceived importance of the purchase (the degree of perceived risk in the purchasing situation) for some product categories can have a direct influence on the size, composition, or behavior of the decision-making unit; the greater the importance, the greater the number of individuals and departments involved, as well as

---

[24]Shapiro and Bonoma, "How to Segment Industrial Markets," pp. 104–110.

SEGMENTATION ON THE BASIS OF CUSTOMER SERVICE LEVELS

Traditionally, since the early 1970s, distribution service has been seen as an augmented part of the product offering; thus, customer service levels emerge over time to meet corporate objectives. But customer service represents a potent force in competitive strategy, and one way to obtain a competitive advantage is to redevelop and tailor customer service mixes to meet market needs.

The idea that customers will react in different ways to changes in service levels is nothing new. Indeed there has been a good deal of research which advocates the segmentation of a firm's customers using the service level expected by different groups of customers. Customers' perceptions with respect to service needs differ. Indeed, within a given market, different customer types may also have different priorities in relative importance of activities. It is therefore of great importance for a company planning to enter a market to investigate the service levels expected by different customer types before developing its customer service offering. . . . This is particularly important when one realizes that customer service is an integral part of the product offering and possesses demand-generating properties in the same way as other factors in the marketing mix.

Source: Norman E. Marr, "The Impact of Customer Services in International Markets," *International Journal of Physical Distribution and Materials Management* 14, 1 [1984], pp. 33–40. Reprinted by permission of MCB University Press Ltd., Bradford, West Yorkshire, England.

organizational levels. Where multiple influencers, departments, or organizational levels are involved, the more extensive the marketing effort must be to provide assurance that the offering will satisfy organization needs.[25]

Purchasing Policies. Potential customers may also be segmented on the basis of whether they prefer agreements based on supplier cost (automobile producers for example, or large retailers such as Sears, Wards, and J. C. Penney), market-based price, or bids. In the area of government, or quasi-government organizations, for instance, bidding is an important consideration in obtaining contracts because these organizations prefer to purchase on the basis of price competitiveness. On the other hand, some organizations may prefer leasing to outright purchasing when the purchase under consideration can be treated as an expense.[26]

Purchasing Criteria. Purchasing criteria also differ across organizations, product categories, and situations. Lehmann and O'Shaughnessy have identified five types of criteria that will vary in their degree of importance, depending on the purchasing situation. (See Table 8-6.) For instance, where products are standardized, economic

[25]Cardozo, "Situational Segmentation of Industrial Markets," pp. 264–276.
[26]Shapiro and Bonoma, "How to Segment Industrial Markets," pp. 104–110.

TABLE 8-6 Categories of Buyers' Choice Criteria

Criteria	Explanation
1. Performance criteria	These criteria evaluate the extent to which the product is likely to maximize performance in the application(s) envisaged for it.
2. Economic criteria	These criteria evaluate the anticipated cost outlays associated with buying, storing, using, and maintaining the product.
3. Integrative criteria	These criteria evaluate the willingness of suppliers to cooperate and go beyond minimal standards in providing services to integrate their efforts in accordance with the buyer's requirements.
4. Adaptive criteria	These criteria evaluate the extent to which the buying firm may have to adapt its plans to accommodate uncertainty about the capability of the supplier to meet the buyer's requirements for production and delivery.
5. Legalistic criteria	These criteria evaluate the impact on the buying decision of legalistic or quasi-legalistic constraints (e.g., government regulations, company policies and practices).

Source: Donald R. Lehmann and John O'Shaughnessy, "Decision Criteria Used in Buying Different Categories of Products," *Journal of Marketing,* 38 (April 1974), pp. 36–42. Reprinted by permission of the American Marketing Association.

criteria tend to dominate. Since nonstandardized, complex, or novel products appear to generate a degree of uncertainty with respect to product application, performance criteria dominate. Depending on organizational capabilities, in some instances, service factors may dominate over technical capabilities. Thus, markets can also be further segmented on the basis of the purchasing criteria employed by buyers across organizations.[27]

Structure of the Buying Center. Organizations can also be segmented on the basis of involvement in the purchasing decision process. As discussed in Chapter Five, buying center involvement often includes personnel from such areas as marketing, engineering, and purchasing. When involvement patterns are isolated, it can lead to the identification of meaningful microsegments. For example, Choffray and Lilien identified four distinct microsegments in their analysis of the commercial air-conditioning market.

As Table 8-7 shows, important differences in buying center involvement were noted across each microsegment. For instance, in microsegment 1, plant managers and top managers were involved in most decision phases as compared to production engineers and HVAC consulting engineers in microsegment 3. Additionally, Choffray and Lilien found that those companies that fell in microsegment 4 tended to be "smaller, more satisfied with their current air-conditioning system, and more concerned with the economic aspects of industrial air conditioning," and relied

[27]Donald R. Lehmann and John O'Shaughnessy, "Decision Criteria Used in Buying Different Categories of Products," *Journal of Marketing* 38 (April 1974), pp. 36–42.

TABLE 8-7 Average Number of Decision Phases in Which Each Category of Participants Is Involved

	Microsegment			
	1	2	3	4
Production engineers	1.91	1.54	4.39	4.67
Plant managers	4.39	0.57	1.57	2.83
Financial controllers	1.13	0.50	0.69	0.50
Purchasing deparment personnel	1.43	0.71	1.79	0.79
Top management	2.91	3.68	1.45	1.29
HVAC/engineering firms	1.48	2.89	3.30	0.62
Architects and building contractors	1.35	2.25	1.64	0.70
A/C equipment manufacturers	0.35	0.68	0.36	0.29

Note: For ease of interpretation, the two large entries in each segment are underlined.

Source: Reprinted by permission of the publisher from "Industrial Market Segmentation by the Structure of the Purchasing Process," by Jean-Marie Choffray and Gary L. Lilien, *Industrial Marketing Management*, 9 (1980), pp. 331–41. Copyright © 1980 by Elsevier Science Publishing Co., Inc.

more on external sources of expertise. In contrast, firms within microsegments 2 and 3 tended to be larger and more confident of their own engineering capabilities.[28] Thus, while it is difficult to focus on the structure of the purchasing process because the collection and analysis of data are not only difficult but time consuming and potentially costly,[29] where possible, it does enable the marketing firm to adjust marketing communication strategy to better address the needs and requirements of each microsegment.

Individual Variables

Personal Characteristics. Purchasing decisions are ultimately made by the individuals within the organization. While decisions are influenced by organizational variables and policies, it is possible to segment the industrial market by the characteristics of individuals involved in the purchasing situation (e.g., demographics, personality, nontask motives, individual perceptions, and risk management strategies). For example, Krapfel and Brannigan-Smith have found that experience (measured in years of experience in market research positions) was significantly related to buyer's price sensitivity.[30] Also, some buyers are more willing to take risks, whereas others avoid them. Willingness to take risks, however, appears to be directly related to personality variables such as intolerance of ambiguity or self-confidence.[31] Fur-

[28]Choffray and Lilien, "Industrial Market Segmentation by the Structure of the Purchasing Process," pp. 331–342.

[29]Krapfel and Brannigan-Smith, "An Experimental Approach," pp. 27–34.

[30]Ibid.

[31]Shapiro and Bonoma, "How to Segment Industrial Markets," pp. 104–110.

ther, some buyers are more influenced by the need for social relationships than are others and, thus, tend to be more interested in maintaining those relationships than switching suppliers.

While data in this area are difficult to obtain, when buyers can be classified on the basis of personal characteristics, it can be quite useful, particularly for sales people who interact extensively with potential buyers. Thus, it is worthwhile for the marketer to implement a formal sales information system to ensure that sales people gather and transmit data for use in developing segmentation strategies along personal factors.

Power Structures.   As discussed in Chapter Five, individuals within organizations tend to hold reward, legitimate, or expert power. The use of power will also differ across organizations, as well as individual functional areas and buying situations. For instance, one company may have a powerful engineering department that strongly influences purchase decisions, another a powerful financial unit. Since strategies for resolving conflict can involve collaboration, compromise, avoidance, or coalition formation (particularly where power is diffused), where appropriate, it is useful to segment on the basis of power, enabling better refinement of marketing communication strategy to address those in power and determine conflict resolution needs of individual buyers.

Market Segmentation: A Step-by-Step Process

As previously mentioned, market segmentation involves definite costs. "The more a market is segmented, the more expensive it is."[32] Thus, the degree of market segmentation (moving from macro to the three levels of micro segmentation) depends on how detailed customer knowledge must be for effective use. As the marketer moves from macrosegmentation into microsegmentation, more intimate knowledge of potential market segments is required. While macro variables are relatively easily obtained from available secondary data sources, such is not the case with micro variables.

In the industrial market, it is often necessary to implement a research study to determine which buyer attributes at the micro level best define segment differences. Further, as segmentation moves from an examination of organizational variables, to an examination of purchase situation variables, to an attempt to identify and examine individual variables, more and more intimate contact with prospects becomes necessary. Therefore, as Bonoma and Shapiro argue, market segmentation should begin with macro variables, working inwardly (see Figure 8-2) to the more intimate areas only if necessary. That is, once it is clear that the segmentation scheme is "good enough," further segmentation should not be undertaken.

[32]Bonoma and Shapiro, "Evaluating Market Segmentation Approaches," pp. 257–268.

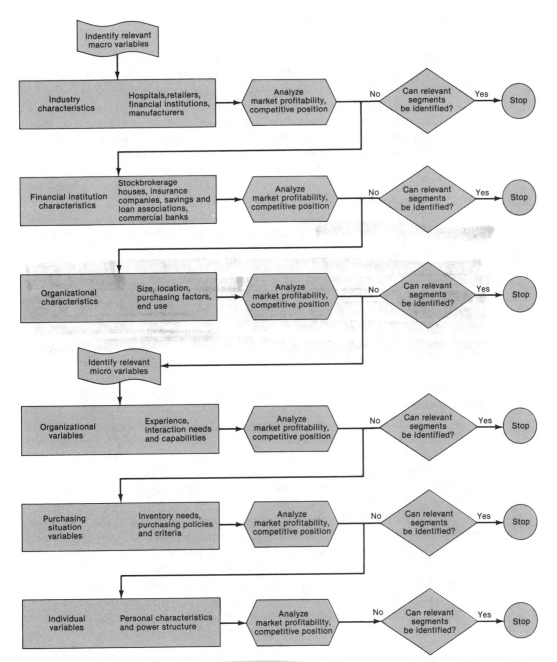

FIGURE 8-2   A Process of Industrial Market Segmentation Strategy for a Manufacturer of Computer Software

EVALUATING POTENTIAL SEGMENTS

Market segmentation merely identifies potential opportunities and the most attractive markets that a firm can serve effectively with its limited resources. Thus, before target markets can be chosen, the potential profit and competitive situation of the various segments must be evaluated. The relationship between marketing strategy and company performance in a competitive market must not be overlooked. Identified market segments will not be equally profitable; neither will potential customers within a segment. Chosen markets, as well as customers within those markets, must be served at a reasonable cost to the firm. Additionally, for some segments, competitors will be in a stronger position than the firm, others will be weaker. Where competitors are weak, it may be easier to lure customers away.

Market Profitability Analysis. In analyzing the profitability of any potential market segment, it must be remembered that four different elements are involved: (1) market potential, which refers to the most optimistic estimate of the amount of product that an entire market will purchase in a given time period; (2) sales potential, which is the most optimistic estimate of a company's share of market potential in a given time period; (3) sales forecast, which is the estimate of a company's expected sales in a given time period; and (4) profitability, which is the difference between potential revenue and the cost of serving and maintaining customers.

As Table 8-8 outlines, numerous methods exist for measuring market potential within any given market segment. Along with regression and time-series analysis, discussed in Chapter Seven, which are quantitative techniques, qualitative techniques may be employed. When markets are clearly defined, it is easier to acquire and examine historical data by the various statistical methods available.

While quantitative techniques are generally based on available data, qualitative techniques rely on informed judgment and rating schemes. Thus, when data do not exist, management may call on the sales force, top-level executives, or distributors to exercise their knowledge with respect to the market and customers in an effort to estimate market potential.

Once market and sales potentials are estimated, but before a sales forecast can be made, it is necessary to determine the firm's ability to access customers. Accessing customers within a particular segment is dependent on the firm's proposed marketing program as well as competitors' positions within the segment.

Attracting and maintaining additional market segments is not without costs. Ordinarily, because market segments will differ in their marketing responses, different marketing programs will have to be developed. Thus, before individual segment profitability can be determined, the costs associated with such factors as communication strategy (sales force deployment and advertising campaigns), product strategy (the development of new or variant products), pricing strategy (special quantity discounts or other incentive programs), and logistics strategy (inventory, warehousing, or inventory changes) must also be considered.

**TABLE 8-8 Forecasting Methods Available for Profitability Analysis
of Product/Market Segments**

	Description	Typical Application
Qualitative methods		
Delphi	A panel of experts via questionnaires project their best estimate of future sales. Rounds continue until mean converges. Information available to some experts and not others is passed on to other experts to increase forecasting ability.	Forecasts of long-range and new product sales, forecasts of margins.
Panel consensus	Panels are based on the assumption that several experts can arrive at a better forecast than can one person. No secrecy is involved, and communication is encouraged.	Forecasts of long-range and new product sales, forecasts of margins.
Historical analogy	Comparative analysis of the introduction and growth of similar new products to base forecasts on similar patterns.	Forecasts of long-range and new product sales, forecasts of margins.
Sales force composite	Sales people estimate future sales based on their knowledge of market, customers, and competitors.	Forecasts of short- and long-range sales, new product sales, territory, and customers.
Quantitative methods		
Trend projections	Past trends, based on historical data, are projected into the future so that seasonal/irregularities are eliminated.	Production and inventory control, forecasting of margins and other financial data.
Regression analysis	Relates sales to other economic, competitive, or interval variables such as marketing programs using least squares techniques.	Forecasts of sales by product classes, forecasts of margins.
Correlation analysis	Relates demand of one or more independent variables to product under consideration.	Forecasts of sales by product classes, forecasts of margins.
Input/output analysis	Analysis of interindustry flow of goods or services in the economy. Shows flow of inputs that must occur to obtain certain outputs. Requires considerable effort and cost to be used effectively.	Forecasts of company sales and division sales for industrial sectors and subsectors.
Econometric models	Integrates a system of interdependent regression equations that describes some sector of economic activity.	Forecasts of sales by product classes, forecasts of margins.

Competitive Analysis. "The success of any marketing strategy depends on the strength of the competitive analysis on which it is based.[33] Thus, profit potential as well as the ability to penetrate a particular market segment depends on a careful analysis of the strengths and weaknesses of existing or potential competitors—both domestic and foreign. In evaluating market segments, then, the firm should seek answers to such questions as: "Who are the target competitors?" "What are the target competitors' strategic weaknesses?" and "What are the design vulnerabilities of the target competitors?"[34]

In formulating strategy, current and future competitors' abilities to respond must be evaluated. This entails an assessment of their strengths and weaknesses in the areas of manufacturing, R&D, finance, technical service, sales force, advertising, distribution, organizational design, and support systems (e.g., planning, control, and reward systems). "Competitors are in business to defend or take market share from the organization, and their ability to do so varies with their individual strengths and weaknesses."[35]

DECISION SUPPORT SYSTEMS AND THEIR USE IN MARKET SEGMENTATION

Decision support systems (see Chapter Seven) can also be used for identifying and evaluating alternative market segments.[36] They can assess the extent to which different groupings of market segments meet organizational objectives. For example, Zoltners and Dodson point out that markets can be identified and evaluated on the basis of numerous performance attributes deemed important to management (i.e., growth potential, sales revenue, net income, ROI, and cash flow). Other variables of interest might include timing of production (which may vary by end-use market), cyclical demand (cyclical and countercyclical firms can be grouped to provide stable demand), inflation vulnerability, technological strength, and competitive strength. Much of the necessary data can be obtained from secondary sources (e.g., historical sales volume, cost and profitability by market, demographics, industry and market demand), and knowledgeable people within the firm may be called on to estimate competitive intensity or technological vulnerability.

While the variables used are stated in terms of quantitatively measurable performance factors, it should be noted that, while analysis may appear to point out market segments that are optimal choices in view of the variables chosen, many relevant variables that are qualitative in nature and, thus, nonmeasurable may also

[33]Bruce D. Henderson, "The Anatomy of Competition," *Journal of Marketing* 47 (Spring 1983), pp. 7–11.

[34]Ian C. MacMillan and Patricia E. Jones, "Designing Organizations to Compete," *The Journal of Business Strategy* 5 (Spring 1984), pp. 11–26.

[35]Ibid.

[36]Zoltners and Dodson, "A Market Selection Model," pp. 76–88.

have a significant influence on the final choice. Thus, resultant markets must also be established "on the basis of intuitive criteria as well as quantifiable criteria."[37]

The decision support system evaluates data for various combinations of markets and in various ways determines which group best fits management's objectives. The system can, for example, construct a group of markets that has the least total amount of deviation from the firm's quantitative objectives (i.e., most closely approximates the firm's desired production capacity, profit level, and stability of demand).

Once the system presents this portfolio of markets, it can be evaluated by management on the basis of "nonquantifiable and nonmeasurable" criteria. For example, should management arbitrarily decide that a particular segment should be added to the portfolio, the system can be instructed to add it and reevaluate the new portfolio.

When a firm is faced with evaluating several market segments on the basis of numerous objectives, the decision support system can be a valuable tool for decision making.

TARGET MARKETING

Market segmentation and profitability analysis allow the marketer to determine where opportunities exist, how marketing strategy may be developed, and which segments are profitable. Once accomplished, however, decisions must be made as to which segments will be served; that is, "targeted." This is partially determined by whether marketing strategy can treat segments as if they are similar or different. Three alternative market selection strategies are available regarding these segment similarities and differences: undifferentiated, differentiated, and concentrated.[38]

Undifferentiated Market Selection. When the products or services produced by an organization are relatively standardized and sold in a horizontal market (i.e., potential markets exist in a broad spectrum of industries), an undifferentiated marketing strategy may be the most appropriate choice. Undifferentiated refers to the fact that the firm ignores segment differences and develops a single marketing program that will focus on what is common to all buyers within the market in the hope of appealing to the broadest number possible. For example, manufacturers of operating supplies such as lubricants may market their products to all types of manufacturing facilities since product usage varies little by customer type.

While undifferentiated marketing is defended on the basis of cost economies, it must be remembered that "there is no such thing as a commodity. All goods and

---

[37]Ibid.

[38]See Philip Kotler, *Marketing Management: Analysis, Planning, and Control,* 5th ed. (Englewood Cliffs, N.J.: Prentice-Hall, Inc., 1984), p. 267; and Robert W. Haas, *Industrial Marketing Management,* 2nd ed. (Boston: Kent Publishing Co., 1982), p. 110.

services are differentiable."[39] To persist and survive, a firm must have a unique advantage over all others who compete in the market place. For example,

> On the commodities exchanges . . . dealers in metals, grains, and pork bellies trade in totally undifferentiated generic products. But what they "sell" is the claimed distinction of their execution—the efficiency of their transactions in their clients' behalf, their responsiveness to inquiries, the clarity and speed of their confirmations, and the like. In short, the offered product is differentiated, though the generic product is identical.[40]

Undifferentiated marketing strategy exposes an organization to competitive attack by firms that do differentiate. Customers do not simply buy physical products. When delivery expectations or supplier flexibility is erratic or only partially fulfilled, customers have not received the "augmented" product they expected and may turn to other sources. Thus, when highly similar products are marketed, organizations must take steps to ensure that other marketing mix factors differentiate them from competitors.

Differentiated Market Selection. A firm may also choose to offer its products or services to a number of diverse segments whose needs, product usage, or market responses are appreciably different. Differentiated marketing strategy, to meet the differences among target markets, however, increases overall costs to such areas as product development and modification, production, marketing, and administration. The objectives behind this type of strategy are to attain higher sales, a deeper position within each market segment, and greater company identification by developing separate marketing strategies for each market chosen.

Concentrated Market Selection. Even though a number of diverse segments exists whose needs could be satisfied through product and market variations, when company resources are limited, the firm may choose to go after a large share of one or a few markets. When marketing strategy is well conceived, it is possible for the firm to achieve a strong market position within the chosen market(s) as well as operating economies. As a firm increases its knowledge of the segments' marketing responses and tailors its strategy to serve them better than competitors, it also increases its reputation in the marketplace, thereby achieving a stronger market position. Operating economies accrue due to specialization in production, distribution, and promotion.

[39]Theodore Levitt, "Marketing Success Through Differentiation of Anything," *Harvard Business Review* (January–February 1982), pp. 83–91.
[40]Ibid.

NICHE MARKETING IS GAINING FAVOR

Niche marketing takes the market segmentation of the 1960s one step further. In fact, it is by definition a process of finer and finer market segmentation . . . moreover, it's a strategic approach to marketing which is gaining favor among business and industrial product and service marketers.

. . . Similar to the way in which some consumers prize a toothpaste more for its teeth-whitening ability than for, say, its decay preventative qualities, different groups of industrial and business product buyers have different needs for the same type of product. . . . For example, in the industrial and commercial lighting field, some buyers will be more concerned with reliability of the product while others put greater emphasis on energy efficiency [long-term cost], as a third group emphasizes low price [acquisition cost] as its primary buying interest. . . . Nor are important factors solely part of the product itself. A vendor's delivery reliability, service support and overall image, for example, can be more important than physical product characteristics or price for certain buyers.

Therefore, the task facing . . . business/industrial product marketers . . . is one of identifying the niches in which a company competes best, then creating products and a marketing presence in those niches which beats the competition.

. . . Most package goods marketers have learned the value of niche marketing. But only recently are business/industrial marketers adopting niche strategies. . . . Increasingly, they are realizing that technology, direct selling and price alone are not enough to succeed. The marketplace is teaching them that few, if any, manufacturers can be all things to all buyers.

Source: Joseph F. Barone, "Niche Marketing: What Industrial Marketers Can Learn from Consumer Package Goods," *Business Marketing*, November 1984, pp. 56, 58, 62. Reprinted with permission.

Niche Marketing

Niche marketing is a process by which a firm segments the market into finer, more homogeneous clusters than that which is normally approached under traditional segmentation strategies.[41] For instance, Coca Cola has segmented its market into four distinct niches: regular Coke drinkers, diet Coke drinkers, caffeine-free Coke drinkers, and diet caffeine-free Coke drinkers. Thus, niche marketing enables an organization to provide products (or product versions) to buyers who are seeking products that are specifically tailored to their individual desires and preferences. And it is "a strategic approach to marketing which is gaining favor among business and industrial product and service marketers."[42]

[41]Joseph F. Barone, "Niche Marketing: What Industrial Marketers Can Learn from Consumer Package Goods," *Business Marketing* (November 1984), pp. 56, 58, 62.

[42]Ibid.

Industrial marketers are coming to realize that technical innovation, price, or direct selling are not enough to succeed in today's competitive marketplace. Thus, many industrial marketers are beginning to monitor current and potential users in a particular market to determine (1) if a trend or concern is emerging that may be creating a niche within which they can compete successfully by developing a new product, or by promoting an existing product in a new way; or (2) if the market can be further subdivided into large enough niches to make it worthwhile to promote a unique application for an existing product.

Niche marketing is an approach to market segmentation that is being driven by both the industrial marketer and the market due to today's ability to process information quickly. That is, because of the availability of information, today's buyers are more knowledgeable about the products that are available to them, and manufacturers, armed with an unprecedented amount of market information, are better able to identify market needs and create marketing mixes to meet those needs. For example, the growing concerns of electronic equipment manufacturers regarding proprietary designs created a demand for customized chips—a concern to which the semiconductor makers responded by developing design centers and software to enable customers' engineers to design all or part of a chip themselves. Thus, while the concept of niche marketing is similar to market segmentation, when a firm attempts to further its segmentation strategy along the basis of specific needs of potential markets, such as reliability, speed, or heat-generation needs in the semiconductor market, niche marketing enables the firm to fine tune its positioning and marketing strategy to reach potentially unsatisfied markets more effectively and profitably than competitors.

PRODUCT POSITIONING

Regardless of the type of market coverage chosen, the firm must develop and communicate, for every market selected, a positioning strategy that will clearly differentiate it or its products from competitors. Regardless of competitors' strengths or weaknesses, each competitor operating within chosen markets will occupy some distinct position in the minds of prospective customers.

> Positioning starts with a product. A piece of merchandise, a service, a company, an institution, or even a person. . . . But positioning is not what you do to a product. Positioning is what you do to the mind of the prospect. That is, you position the product in the mind of the prospect.[43]

Success in any market, whether consumer or industrial, depends on the firm's ability to create a position in the mind of the prospect. This is accomplished through

---

[43]Al Ries and Jack Trout, *Positioning: The Battle for Your Mind* (New York: Warner Books, 1982).

careful manipulation of the marketing mix variables based on the firm's distinctive competencies and differential advantages.

Positioning strategy in the industrial market, however, is more difficult and subtle than in the consumer market. The difficulty arises for two reasons: (1) lack of adequate marketing research support and (2) in many cases, a lack of understanding of positioning principles. That it is more subtle than in the consumer market occurs because of the differences in the way positioning strategy is communicated. In the consumer market, positioning strategy is primarily accomplished through advertising. In the industrial market, it is accomplished through personal selling, publicity, and trade shows, as well as advertising, and through the company's performance—both with respect to customer service and product performance.[44] Consequently, very few industrial organizations purposefully employ positioning strategy.

If a firm is to differentiate its market offering from those of competitors in such a way as to take advantage of its distinctive competencies and gain a differential advantage, however, it must develop a unique position within the market. For example, although market growth in the CAD/CAM (computer-aided design and manufacturing) systems slowed between 1982 and 1983 (dropping from a 35 percent growth rate to 33 percent), Intergraph, an Alabama-based hi-tech company, increased its market share from 13 percent to 15 percent by positioning itself as a "technology-driven" firm that talks to people about their applications problems in a technological environment. The key to its success was the formation of a group of application specialists in such areas as plant design, electronics, and architecture who approached the market on the basis of application needs versus industry attributes. Working with sales people, application specialists called on customers to provide advice on specific applications and explain how Intergraph's software systems could solve their individual problems.[45]

While positioning strategy in the consumer market is normally applied along the lines of functional or psychological product attributes, in the industrial market, there are several variables that may be used in developing positioning strategy. In addition to product variables (e.g., features, reliability, quality, and price), a firm may be able to position itself on the basis of superiority in pre- and postsale service capabilities; on its capability of solving customer problems; on its ability to teach and help customers; or on its capabilities in developing new methods and technologies. For instance, Foxboro positions itself on the basis of helping customers to make more and better for less through its expertise in the area of process management and control. (See Figure 8-3.)

Before embarking on a positioning strategy, several questions must be asked, for once developed, the firm must be committed to the strategy. While the questions

[44]Dick Berry, *Industrial Marketing for Results* (Reading, Mass.: Addison-Wesley Publishing Co., 1981), pp. 23–24.

[45]"Intergraph Gains Share by Aiming At Applications," *Sales and Marketing Management* (January 16, 1984) pp. 21–22.

FOXBORO CONTROLLED PROCESSING CONVERTS CACAO BEANS INTO CHOCOLATE SWEETS.

Turning cacao beans into chocolate, bauxite into aluminum or making sea water potable requires many stages of precisely controlled processing. Process Management and Control is the system Foxboro offers its customers to help them make more and better for less. We do this with the world's broadest range of process controls, from single instruments to completely computerized installations.

We are acutely aware of the need to conserve natural resources and maximize the use of power and water. Not only do we help reduce waste in raw materials, but we also participate in reclamation and recycling programs involving rubber, paper, glass and metal containers.

Foxboro is a worldwide company with design, engineering, manufacturing and training facilities wherever customers are located. They can be sure we will stay with them all the way. That's a sweet and comforting thought. The Foxboro Company, Foxboro, MA 02035, U.S.A.

Cacao Beans, Ecuador

FOXBORO

Thompson Candy, Meriden, Connecticut USA

FIGURE 8-3   An Example of Industrial Positioning Strategy. Through its advertisements, Foxboro positions itself as "helping customers make more and better for less."

Source: Courtesy of PALM•DEBONIS•RUSSO•INC. Advertising and Public Relations, Bloomfield, CT.

may be simple to ask, they are difficult to answer and often require the firm to evaluate carefully its differential advantages with respect to competitors.[46] Specific questions that the firm should address include

1. What position do we own? In other words, positioning strategy begins with determining what is already in the minds of prospects because it is much easier to work with what is already there than it is to develop an entirely new strategy.

2. What position do we want to own? This involves the firm in attempting to develop a position that will best serve it over the long term. While it is possible to compete successfully with an industry leader, attempting to compete head on with IBM, for instance, as RCA, General Electric, and Honeywell have discovered, is not possible. The better strategy is to determine what position is already owned by the firm in the minds of prospects and then relate them to a new position. RCA, for instance, is a leader in the field of communications. If it had attempted to position its computer line in such a way that it related to its expertise in the area of communications, RCA may have been able to take advantage of the position it already owned.

3. Whom must the firm outgun? This involves the firm in thinking about positioning strategy from the point of view of its competitors. Positioning strategy must be selected in an area that no one else already owns.

4. Once chosen, can the firm stick it out? In today's vastly changing marketplace, it is important for the firm to determine its basic position and be prepared to stick it out. A winning positioning strategy is cumulative—a strategy that takes advantage of advertising and personal selling over the long term. IBM has been solving customer information processing problems for years. Rarely, according to Rise and Trout, should a firm change its basic positioning strategy.

5. Does the firm match its positioning strategy? EDS, for instance, positions itself as a conservative firm that is capable of solving "large-scale business, industry, and government applications" problems by "providing hardware, software, and data processing professionals who design, install and operate large-scale business information systems."[47] One ambitious woman who presented a college recruiter with a resume that started out with the words, "An Uncommon Resume from an Uncommon Lady," found her resume tossed aside and herself escorted out of the recruiter's temporary office. In determining positioning strategy then, the firm must be able to match its advertising, sales, and support personnel to its stated position.

LOOKING BACK

If marketing strategy is to be successful, the firm must identify markets that it can serve effectively with its limited resources. Industrial customers, whether commercial, institutional, government, or distributors, differ in their needs, resources, buying attitudes, and practices. To understand those differences and to identify attractive market segments that can be served effectively, and are not being handled well by competitors, industrial marketers must undertake market segmentation.

[46]Ries and Trout, *Positioning: The Battle for Your Mind.*
[47]*CPC Annual, A Directory of Employment Opportunities for College Graduates, 1985/86* (Bethlehem, Pa.: College Placement Council, Inc., 1985), p. 136.

While several variables exist for segmenting the industrial market on both macro and micro factors, to be useful, they must be measurable, relevant, and operational. Further, because of the costs involved, before segmentation strategy is undertaken, it must be determined if segmentation is justified. Additionally, since the more a market is segmented, the more costly it becomes; thus, segmentation should begin with macro variables, working inwardly to micro variables, only if more detailed knowledge is needed for effective use.

Since market segmentation is undertaken merely to pinpoint potential opportunities within the most attractive markets, before target markets are actually chosen by the firm, identified segments must also be evaluated with respect to their profitability—the cost of serving and maintaining them as it relates to the potential sales revenue they may generate. In analyzing the profitability of any segment, competitive strengths and weaknesses, as well as their ability to respond to a given marketing strategy must also be evaluated.

The decision as to which markets can be served and how they will be served rests on company resources, product/market homogeneity, the stage of the product life cycle, and competitors' marketing strategies. Thus, in choosing target markets, the firm must also decide whether it will use an undifferentiated, differentiated, or concentrated market selection strategy. Once chosen, before marketing strategy can be developed, decisions must be made with respect to how the firm will position itself within the marketplace.

With an understanding of strategic industrial marketing and planning, the resources available for assessing marketing opportunities, and how industrial marketers should approach the identification of attractive market segments that can be served with its limited resources, we shall now turn to the specifics involved in developing the marketing mix variables.

QUESTIONS FOR DISCUSSION

1. To ensure its future viability, a business offering a multiple end-use product or service must assess the ability of each of its current or prospective markets to contribute to the goals and objectives of the business. If this is true, how would you assess current and prospective customers' ability to contribute to organizational objectives?

2. It has been proposed that purchasing decisions involved with complex industrial products "can be segmented on the basis of the amount of conflict associated with each decision." If this is true, then conflict would depend on the role of those involved in the decision process. How would you proceed to examine the roles of individuals involved in the purchasing decision across organizations?

3. There are definite costs involved in obtaining necessary data, and in developing a multiplicity of plans to serve each resultant segment effectively. How does the amount of segmentation affect the cost of segmentation?

4. "Any product or service can be differentiated, even the commodity that seems to differ from competitors' offerings only in price." Do you agree?

5. Which characteristics of the decision-making unit should the marketer take as a basis for

segmentation, age, number of persons involved, or the pattern of involvement in the buying decision process?

6. One industrial marketer recently observed, "I can't see any basis on which to segment my market. We have 15 percent of the market for our type of plastics fabrication equipment. There are 11 competitors who serve a large and diverse set of customers, but there is no unifying theme to our customer set or to anyone else's." Is that knowledge a basis for segmenting the industrial market?

7. How does customer experience versus inexperience affect marketing segmentation strategy?

8. Successful industrial market segmentation may often depend on the marketer's ability to identify key characteristics influencing purchasing preferences. Is it possible, then, to identify key characteristics along the variables of age and experience of key decision makers?

SUGGESTED ADDITIONAL READINGS

BARONE, JOSEPH F., "Niche Marketing: What Industrial Marketers Can Learn from Consumer Package Goods," *Business Marketing* (November 1984):56, 58, 62.

BONOMA, THOMAS V., and BENSON P. SHAPIRO, "Evaluating Market Segmentation Approaches," *Industrial Marketing Management* 13 (1984):257–268.

CARDOZO, RICHARD N., "Situational Segmentation of Industrial Markets," *European Journal of Marketing* 14 (1980):264–276.

CHOFFRAY, JEAN-MARIE, and GARY L. LILIEN, "Industrial Market Segmentation by the Structure of the Purchasing Process," *Industrial Marketing Management* 9 (1980): 331–342.

DEBRUICKER, F. STEWARD, and GREGORY L. SUMME, "Make Sure Your Customers Keep Coming Back," *Harvard Business Review* (January–February 1985):92–98.

HENDERSON, BRUCE D., "The Anatomy of Competition," *Journal of Marketing* 47 (Spring 1983):7–11.

JOHNE, FREDERICK A., "Segmenting High Technology Adopters," *Industrial Marketing Management* 13 (1984):59–63.

LEHMANN, DONALD R., and JOHN O'SHAUGHNESSY, "Decision Criteria Used in Buying Different Categories of Products," *Journal of Purchasing and Materials Management* (Spring 1982):9–14.

LEVITT, THEODORE, "Marketing Success Through Differentiation of Anything," *Harvard Business Review* (January–February 1982):110.

SHAPIRO, BENSON P., and THOMAS V. BONOMA, "How to Segment Industrial Markets," *Harvard Business Review* (May–June 1984):104–110.

VOLLERING, JAN B., "Interaction Based Market Segmentation," *Industrial Marketing Management* 13 (1984):65–70.

WIENER, NORMAN, "Customer Demographics for Strategic Selling," *Business Marketing* (May 1983):78, 80, 82.

YOUNG, SHIRLEY, LELAND OTT, and BARBARA FEIGIN, "Some Practical Considerations in Market Segmentation," *Journal of Marketing Research* 15 (August 1978):405–412.

ZOLTNERS, ANDRIS A., and JOE A. DODSON, "A Market Selection Model for Multiple End-Use Products," *Journal of Marketing* 47 (Spring 1983):76–88.

PART FOUR

Formulating Product Planning

ROLM'S UNNECESSARY BUT LUCKY PRODUCT DECISION

Co-founder Kenneth Oshman, 44, of Rolm Corp.—a classic Silicon Valley success, acquired last year by IBM for $1.9 billion—believes a chief executive's job is to peer intently three to five years into the future, looking for problems. In 1971 the first flicker of an adverse change in Rolm's environment galvanized him into furious activity. Rolm was then a fast-growing $1.5-million-a-year maker of heavy-duty computers, 60% of which were sold to the military—'not a totally rational customer,' Oshman recalls. That year, as he began to worry that the market for his specialized product would soon be saturated at around $15 million in annual sales, the Navy announced plans to use only one standard computer design, with specifications identical to a machine made by Sperry Univac. Oshman scrambled to find a second, related product line.

"Well," remarked two employees, "there's always the computerized telephone business. . . ." Oshman decided to investigate.

After several months of study and the hiring of a technical expert and a marketing veteran . . . Oshman believed Rolm could develop digital switching equipment much more sophisticated than the equipment AT&T and a handful of competitors were supplying to businesses. What big companies really wanted, Rolm's talks with potential customers found, was a phone system that would route calls over the cheapest available lines, monitor phone use to control costs, and make it easy to let employees keep the same phone number when they changed offices—tasks made to order for a computer-controlled system. The same system could solve Rolm's service problem by having a built-in diagnostic capability that would pinpoint malfunctions on its own.

"As the Boston Consulting Group would tell you," says marketing vice president Richard Moley, 45, "the last thing you ever do is go into a new market with a completely new product." That's true—if you don't want to take the risk of building a giant new business. In this case the product worked, customers bought it, and in nine years Rolm grew at an annual compound rate of 57% to the $660 million in annual sales it reached just before IBM acquired it.

And the premises that set this whole beautifully logical process in motion turned out to be completely wrong. The military-specification computer market did not stop at $15 million a year but grew to an estimated $200 million, of which Rolm today has around half. And the Navy began to loosen its single computer standard in 1976. Says Oshman: "I'd rather be lucky than right."

Source: Reprinted by permission of the publisher, Fortune magazine, "How Top Managers Make a Company's Toughest Decision," March 18, 1985, pp. 52–57.

Industrial product strategy involves the most crucial decision making of any area of the marketing mix. And Rolm's product decision illustrate the phenomenal growth that can be achieved when the right products are maintained or developed. In this section, then, we cover the various considerations that must be examined if existing products and product lines are to be managed effectively and how new product development is used to ensure continued growth of the firm. Although we make no suggestions regarding the area of pure luck, we hope that it will accompany your strategic product decisions.

CHAPTER 9

Developing Product Strategy

Successful marketing strategy centers on two essential elements, products and markets. While distribution, promotion, and pricing decisions must be carefully conceived in relation to the overall marketing plan, it is the product offer that must ultimately satisfy customer needs. Product decisions also tend to be the riskiest variable in the marketing mix, and when ill conceived, they can be costly. New product design, development, and introduction are a costly venture, entailing company commitment and risk. Further, due to the increased pace of technological change, products can become obsolete before the firm has recouped all its development costs. This chapter, then, focuses on

1. The need to understand products from the industrial customer's point of view.
2. Product strategies over the industrial product life cycle.
3. Managing the industrial product line.
4. The difference between marketing products and systems.
5. The special problems and strategic alternatives involved in the marketing of professional services.

Unquestionably, product decisions are the most important and complex decisions facing management. They affect factors both external and internal to the firm. It is the product that is the principal component through which the firm aligns its resources with the market environment to achieve organizational objectives. Product decisions also dictate distribution requirements, establish promotion needs, and set the limits on what can be done with price—factors that comprise the total market offer.

Within the firm, product decisions are the elements that bind together the diverse interests of the various functional departments. It is research and development, engineering, manufacturing, inventory control, technical services, and marketing working together that create and deliver the total product offering to the marketplace.

In developing product strategies, an organization has two primary goals: (1) to ensure that the product mix (all the products marketed by the firm) is in accord with overall organizational and marketing objectives and (2) to set guidelines for developing product lines and items. Because product strategy decisions often involve modifying, adjusting, or altering current products and developing new ones, product strategies affect the organization as a whole. The modification of an existing product or the development of a new one, for example, can have a direct influence on the sales performance of other products in the line, affecting profits as well as production.[1] Thus, product strategies have an impact on the entire organizational system, requiring an integrated effort for successful product planning.

WHAT IS AN INDUSTRIAL PRODUCT?

Product decisions ultimately rest on the marketer's understanding of what constitutes a product for a particular market. Thus, before discussing the issues involved in developing industrial product strategies, the concept of what an industrial product is should be understood. The concept of a product to the buyer is multidimensional, involving more than its physical properties. From the buyer's perspective, a product is a combination of basic, enhanced, and augmented properties.

Basic Properties. Basic properties are those that constitute the generic product and connote the various benefits sought by buyers and influencers. A "forklift" is a specific generic product that will be thought of by alternative purchasers as providing different benefits.

Enhanced Properties. Generic products are made differentiable by adding enhanced properties. These properties are physical additions or deletions to the generic product and include features, styling, and quality. For example, a purchaser of computers will expect to obtain the basic properties of a computer from most computer sources and will, therefore, base the ultimate buying decision on enhanced properties, such as ease of use, availability of software, and the ability to tie into existing equipment. A deletion involves enhancing a product by removing properties, such

---

[1]William Lazer and James D. Culley, *Marketing Management* (Boston: Houghton Mifflin Co., 1983), p. 476.

PURCHASING AGENTS SEEK TO ENSURE COMPATIBILITY ACROSS COMPUTER SYSTEMS

As office products and systems buyers increase their purchasing responsibilities, they are determined to see that money is spent "more wisely and more effectively than ever before. That means buyers will be clamping down on equipment purchases which don't fit into their company's office automation strategy. It also means they'll pay ever greater attention to precisely matching equipment to user needs."

At the top of the list is standardizing product brands, particularly through negotiating and more fully utilizing national agreements, and making sure that only compatible, upgradeable equipment is bought. . . . We're trying to make sure that the equipment we buy today can be easily upgraded and expanded to meet the needs of tomorrow.

. . . To convince local divisions to standardize, Allied provides centralized training at its Morristown, N.J., corporate headquarters to do two things: [1] familiarize users with the equipment, and its productivity-improving possibilities; and [2] demonstrate the importance of buying standard, compatible equipment in order to easily access corporate data bases and exchange editable documents between systems.

Source: Reprinted from *Purchasing* magazine, "Purchasing Gets Tough on Standardization," May 23, 1985, pp. 79–80. Copyright © by Cahners Publishing Company, 1985.

---

as IBM's unbundling of word processing equipment to make that equipment less expensive and user specific. In developing or modifying a product, decisions must center on the enhanced properties the buyer is actually purchasing. To the potential buyer, a product is a complex package of problem-solving capabilities.

Augmented Properties. Augmented properties are those additional benefits connoted in the purchase of a particular product. These are usually intangible benefits and include training, technical assistance, availability of spare parts, maintenance and repair services, assurance of supply, warranties, delivery capabilities, and financing terms. Seldom do industrial buyers purchase only on the basis of basic and enhanced product characteristics. As Theodore Levitt has pointed out,

> Competition is not between what companies produce in their factories, but between what they add to their factory output in the form of packaging, services, advertising, customer advice, financing, delivery arrangements, warehousing, and other things that people value.[2]

In developing and implementing product decisions, the industrial marketer must be astutely aware of what comprises the total product package in the minds of prospective buyers. This is not an easy task.

---

[2]Theodore Levitt, *The Marketing Mode* (New York: McGraw-Hill Book Company, 1969), p. 2.

PRODUCT AUGMENTATION VIA APPLICATIONS EXPERTISE

To compete in the highly competitive computer market, where products are quite similar and purchase decisions are no longer based on just technical product capability, Apple Computer adopted a product augmentation strategy. By developing extensive software programs for particular customer applications, and offering training, product maintenance, and related support, Apple Computer has survived while others, unprepared for a shift in customer needs, fell victim to the industry shakeout of the mid-1980s.

Source: Reprinted by permission of the *Harvard Business Review.* Excerpt from "Make Sure Your Customers Keep Coming Back," by F. Stewart DeBruicker and Gregory L. Summe, January–February 1985, pp. 92–98.

Economic conditions, business strategies, customers' wishes, competitive conditions, and much more can determine what sensibly defines the product. . . . What's "augmented" for one customer may be "expected" by another; what's "augmented" under one circumstance may be "potential" in another.[3]

Product strategies, then, must result from a careful assessment of opportunities (Chapter Seven), an evaluation of competitive strengths and weaknesses, and market analysis and selection (Chapter Eight).

PRODUCT STRATEGY INVOLVES CONTINUAL CHANGE

Product offerings are designed to satisfy customer needs. Thus, any change in customer needs must ultimately result in changes in the firm's product offering if the firm is to continue to satisfy its customer base. Customer needs change as their environments change. For instance, firms in the semiconductor industry refurbish their plants every two or three years to keep pace with rapidly changing technology. Every time there is a significant increase in the number of circuits on a single chip, more elaborate production equipment is needed.[4] Thus, technological changes can require product modification or make existing products obsolete as customers revise their operating procedures to meet their new needs. Changing laws, politics, or economics can also affect customer needs, which in turn can have a direct effect on product requirements, bring about product obsolescence, lead to new product opportunities, or affect customer expectations in other areas that comprise the product offering.[5]

[3]Theodore Levitt, "Marketing Success Through Differentiation of Anything," *Harvard Business Review* (January–February 1982), pp. 83–91.

[4]"Chip Wars: The Japanese Threat," *Business Week* (May 23), 1983.

[5]Gordon E. Greenley, "Tactical Product Decisions," *Industrial Marketing Management* 12 (1983), pp. 13–18.

The sales and profits of a product also tend to change over time as the product moves through its life cycle. As a product reaches maturity (the point of market saturation), decisions must be made as to whether it should be modified to maintain a market position or be withdrawn from the market. Because most products eventually reach the decline stage, new products must be developed to replace those that are phased out if the firm is to maintain and increase its profitability.

Product strategy issues, then, involve a continuous process of evaluating product/market positions to determine (1) whether changes are needed in current products and (2) whether products should be added or dropped.

INDUSTRIAL PRODUCT MANAGEMENT

The development of product strategies evolves around establishing product policies, setting product objectives, modifying existing products, providing needed pre- and postsale servicing and technical services, searching for new product additions, phasing out old products, and maintaining the proper product mix. To ensure that the "necessary plans, decisions, and commitments made throughout a company effectively meet the changing needs of the marketplace,"[6] industrial firms require that their product managers have more experience than consumer product managers. Some firms adopt a type of dual management approach that organizationally overlaps market and product managers.

Product Manager Differences

While product management in the industrial market is, in many ways, similar to such management in the consumer market, recent studies have pointed out some interesting differences between the positions and those filling them. For instance, industrial product managers are responsible for 50 percent more products than are consumer product managers. Industrial product managers also have greater responsibility for forecasting sales, setting product objectives, product planning, and pricing, and are more involved in production planning. They are also responsible for determining which market a product will enter, controlling product conceptualization, initiating product changes and reengineering decisions, and determining when products should be deleted and phased out.[7] In addition, as Table 9-1 points out, they are more experienced (reaching their position from sales or engineering), have longer tenure with the firm, have less formal education, and are older than their consumer counterparts. It would appear, then, that industrial product managers

[6]B. Charles Ames, "Dilemma of Product/Market Management," *Harvard Business Review* (March-April 1971), pp. 66–145.

[7]See Robert W. Eckles and Timothy J. Novotny, "Industrial Product Managers: Authority and Responsibility," and William Theodore Cummings, Donald W. Jackson, Jr., and Lonnie L. Ostrom, "Differences Between Industrial and Consumer Product Managers," *Industrial Marketing Management* 13 (1984), pp. 71–75, 171–180.

TABLE 9-1 Background Variables of Industrial versus Consumer Product Managers

	Consumer Product Manager	Industrial Product Manager
Average years of age	32.90	38.37
Average years with firm	6.02	9.15
Average years as a product manager	5.14	4.65
Average products managed	6.20	8.61
Average years of education	17.64	16.46

Source: Reprinted by permission of the publisher, adapted from "Differences Between Industrial and Consumer Product Managers," by William Theodore Cummings. Donald W. Jackson, Jr., and Lonnie L. Ostrom, *Industrial Marketing Management*, 13 (1984), pp. 171–180. Copyright © 1984 by Elsevier Science Publishing Co., Inc.

have greater technical responsibilities, but less formal education, so that additional on-the-job experience is a necessity.

A survey of the supervisors of Australian industrial product managers indicated that they felt their product managers played more important roles than consumer product managers in (1) assessing market size, (2) analyzing competitor activity, (3) making projections of competitors' market shares, and (4) monitoring external environmental developments likely to have an impact on product performance.[8] The researchers believed that these "analysis/forecasting roles" of external developments were likely more important because of the large effects derived demand can have on industrial production and the more limited secondary market-research information in the industrial area. If these findings can be generalized and applied to the United States, one implication that would follow would be that the industrial product manager needs to develop good competitive intelligence and forecasting skills, and to keep a close watch on external environmental events.

Product versus Market Management

When a company has a series of different products that are sold into one market, product managers are commonly used. This allows managers to concentrate on decision making relative to the products. However, when a single product or line of similar products is sold to several, very different markets, market managers are used, since they can concentrate on decision making aimed at meeting the needs of the different markets. These two categories, product versus market, simply allow managers to concentrate on those areas where the differences are the greatest: products or markets.

[8]P. L. Dawes and P. G. Patterson, "The Performance of Industrial and Consumer Product Managers," *Industrial Marketing Management* 17 (1988), pp. 73–84.

Product/Market Management Systems. When a variety of products is sold into multiple markets, the firm is faced with a dilemma. If product managers are used, they are likely to concentrate on their existing products rather than on serving the markets more effectively. On the other hand, the utilization of market managers can lead to a focus on their respective markets' needs. To overcome this dilemma, a growing number of industrial firms utilize a product/market organizational system. Under this type of organization, market managers are responsible for understanding the needs of the market and determining how the firm can be more responsive, while product managers retain responsibility for their product lines.[9]

Product/market management systems, however, inevitably lead to conflict as each respective manager strives to fulfill his or her area of responsibility. Product managers concentrating on selling and improving products, but, giving insufficient attention to the peculiarities of different markets, may find market managers pointing out that competitors will better meet the needs of individual markets. Market managers, on the other hand, concentrating on the desires of their individual markets, may bring about product marketing changes that are beneficial to their markets, but not for the product in the majority of markets. Although these diametrically opposed areas of concentration by the two classifications of managers will inevitably lead to conflict, the conflict can be a positive force when properly managed. It is the head of marketing who has the responsibility of assuring that the conflict is turned into a positive force.

The head of marketing must clearly define the roles of the two different types of managers. Ames has concluded that the basic roles of industrial product and market managers, operating under the product/market management system, should include those activities outlined in Table 9-2. Once roles are defined, it is the head of marketing who must assure that the managers work together in a participative manner. Most important, it is the head of marketing who is vested with the responsibility of synthesizing the efforts of the two manager classifications to capture the best of both perspectives. The intent of such a system is to inspire these managers to work together in a symbiotic manner for the good of the organization, choosing the action that is best for the firm as a whole, whether that decision emphasizes a product or a market point of view.

INDUSTRIAL PRODUCT LIFE-CYCLE ANALYSIS

A widely used concept for determining appropriate product strategies is the product life-cycle (PLC) theory. According to the theory, products tend to go through different cycles, or series of stages, that begin when they are introduced and end when they are removed from the market. Because each stage is affected by different competitive conditions, each stage requires different marketing strategies if sales and profits are to be efficiently realized. While the PLC concept is a familiar one and

[9]This section is based on Ames, "Dilemma of Product/Market Management."

TABLE 9-2 Product versus Market Manager Roles

Market Manager Roles
1. Develop an understanding of customer and end-user operations and economics to determine how existing product/service package can be improved to provide a competitive edge.
2. Identify related products and/or services that represent attractive opportunities for profitability.
3. At regular intervals, summarize for top management the most attractive opportunities in the marketplace. Recommend strategy to capitalize on them.
4. Develop a reputation for industry expertise among key customer and end-user groups. Bring know-how to bear on negotiating major orders and the training and development of sales people.

Product Manager Roles
1. Protect the pricing integrity of products. See that pricing policies and practices in one market do not jeopardize the company's position or profit structure in another.
2. Maintain product leadership by making certain that product design, cost, and performance characteristics are not only responsive to customer needs in all markets, but are also not inadvertently altered to meet the needs of one market at the expense of the company's position in another.
3. Ensure that product is responsive to market needs while protecting the engineering and production process from becoming cluttered with a proliferation of small-lot, custom, or special orders.
4. Ensure that production scheduling and capacity are intelligently planned to meet current and anticipated aggregate demand of various markets profitably.
5. Provide in-depth technical and/or product knowledge required to support selling efforts on major and complex applications.

is given a place of prominence in marketing textbooks, most discussions involve products in the consumer market. This has resulted in a simplistic view of the PLC concept and hampered its use as a valuable planning tool for industrial marketing. Consequently, its use in the industrial market has received limited attention. In fact, it has been criticized many times for its lack of relevance to business marketing.[10]

As Figure 9-1 shows, the general PLC model is shown as an S-shaped curve that portrays the sales and profit history of a typical product.

Applying the PLC Theory to Industrial Product Strategies

Although PLC analysis has received limited attention in developing industrial marketing strategy, it is a useful concept. As Smallwood has pointed out,

The maturation of production technology and product configuration along with marketing programs proceeds in an orderly, somewhat predictable course over time with

[10]Robert D. Buzzell, "Competitive Behavior and Product Life Cycles," in John S. Wright and Jack L. Goldstucker, eds., *New Ideas for Successful Marketing* (Chicago: American Marketing Association, 1966), p. 47.

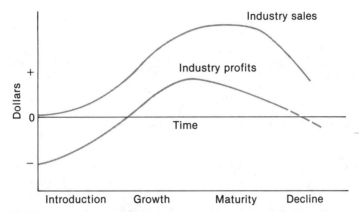

FIGURE 9-1 A General Model of the Product Life Cycle

the merchandising nature and marketing environment noticeably similar between products that are in the same stage of their life cycle. Its use as a concept in forecasting, pricing, advertising, product planning, and other aspects of marketing management can make it a valuable concept, although considerable amounts of judgment must be used in its application.[11]

Thus, although many doubts and criticisms have been noted regarding the usefulness of the product life cycle, it should be remembered that its usefulness results from viewing it as a dependent variable rather than a determining one. "Marketing strategies should be directed not at the stage of the life cycle but at the factors that govern it."[12] PLC analysis enables marketers to determine where a product is in its life cycle and to develop appropriate marketing strategies aimed at those governing factors.

Industrial Product Life-Cycle Strategies

Introduction Stage. Product acceptance, during the introductory stage of an industrial product, is considerably different from what is generally experienced in the consumer market.[13] While some products are rapidly accepted, others are accepted very slowly and entail considerable market development before reaching an appreciable growth stage. Hand-held electronic calculators, for instance, replaced mechanical calculators practically overnight whereas electric typewriters took over two decades (1926–1940) to achieve market acceptance. As Figure 9-2 indicates, product strategies during the introduction stage, as well as other stages of the PLC, are

---

[11]John Smallwood, "The Product Life Cycle: A Key to Strategic Marketing Planning," *MSU Business Topics* (Winter 1973), p. 35.

[12]Lazer and Culley, *Marketing Management,* p. 465.

[13]Chester R. Wasson, "The Importance of the Product Life Cycle to the Industrial Marketer," *Industrial Marketing Management* 5 (1976), pp. 229–308.

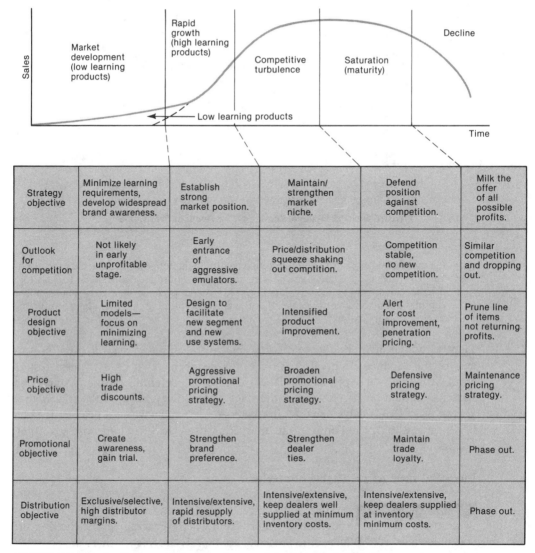

	Market development (low learning products)	Rapid growth (high learning products)	Competitive turbulence	Saturation (maturity)	Decline
Strategy objective	Minimize learning requirements, develop widespread brand awareness.	Establish strong market position.	Maintain/ strengthen market niche.	Defend position against competition.	Milk the offer of all possible profits.
Outlook for competition	Not likely in early unprofitable stage.	Early entrance of aggressive emulators.	Price/distribution squeeze shaking out comptition.	Competition stable, no new competition.	Similar competition and dropping out.
Product design objective	Limited models— focus on minimizing learning.	Design to facilitate new segment and new use systems.	Intensified product improvement.	Alert for cost improvement, penetration pricing.	Prune line of items not returning profits.
Price objective	High trade discounts.	Aggressive promotional pricing strategy.	Broaden promotional pricing strategy.	Defensive pricing strategy.	Maintenance pricing strategy.
Promotional objective	Create awareness, gain trial.	Strengthen brand preference.	Strengthen dealer ties.	Maintain trade loyalty.	Phase out.
Distribution objective	Exclusive/selective, high distributor margins.	Intensive/extensive, rapid resupply of distributors.	Intensive/extensive, keep dealers well supplied at minimum inventory costs.	Intensive/extensive, keep dealers supplied at inventory minimum costs.	Phase out.

FIGURE 9-2 Dynamic Competitive Strategy and the Market Life Cycle

Source: Reprinted by permission of the publisher, from "The Importance of the Product Life Cycle to the Industrial Marketer," by Chester R. Wasson, *Industrial Marketing Management* 5 (1976), pp. 299–308. Copyright © 1976 by Elsevier Science Publishing Co., Inc.

strongly affected by the rate of product acceptance. Thus, as Wasson points out, we need some means of predicting the rate of product acceptance before we can develop product strategy.

What influences product acceptance? Product acceptance in the industrial market is affected by how the product fits into the buyer's total use system. Generally, use systems involve other products, other persons, and a developed system of what Wasson terms "habitual skills," skills that are accompanied by (1) perceptions of the expected satisfaction sources, (2) perceptions of the social role of the user in relation to the product, and (3) perceptions of the value of a given kind of satisfaction.

Habit systems, once developed, are not easily changed. The reason for the slow acceptance of the electric typewriter, which was not revolutionary but merely evolutionary (since there was little change in the composition of the keyboard and it operated in a similar manner to a manual one), was due to the inability of users to break old habits and develop new ones. Electric typewriters required a change in the positioning of the user's fingers. Rather than rest the fingers on the keyboard, as typists had been trained to do on manual typewriters, all fingers had to be kept off the keys of the electric typewriter until ready to strike. To adjust to the newer form of typing, then, typists had to undergo a lengthy period of spoiled work until the old hand-resting habit was broken. Thus, product acceptance was quite slow until typists began to be trained on electric typewriters, developing an entirely new habit.

On the other hand, since the use of calculators required neither skill nor speed for job success, and since operational changes were made mostly in terms of the mechanism under the housing, the electronic calculator achieved ready acceptance. Thus, products that fit into the industrial buyer's use system or habitual skills are adopted more rapidly than those that require changes.

When products have the potential for rapid acceptance (entail a low level of learning), the marketer must be prepared to meet vigorous competition. As Figure 9-2 indicates, when the potential for rapid acceptance exists, planning should focus on keeping well ahead of entering competition. With slowly accepted products (products that require a high level of learning), marketing strategy should focus on market development.

Growth Stage. As a product begins to enter the rapid growth stage, the emphasis on product strategy shifts to improving product design, improving distribution service, and lowering price as increasing product demand, accompanied by accumulated production experience, begins to lower cost substantially. As market demand increases, product design and other aspects of the product offering must be changed to meet both low end and premium market segment needs. Further, when product availability is weak, competitors are encouraged to enter the market. Unfortunately, however, too many firms tend to overlook the need to lower price as costs decrease. When prices are lowered as costs decrease, experience has proven that entering competitors are not as strong as when price is allowed to lag decreases in cost.

Maturity Stage. By the time market demand reaches the maturity stage, industrial buyers have found suppliers whose offerings satisfy their needs fairly well and are "neither searching for new suppliers nor paying much attention to promotion of other offerings." Marketing strategy, therefore, should be directed toward keeping current users satisfied and looking for opportunities to find new buyers or enter new markets through product modification and changes in other marketing mix variables. It should be noted, however, that unless buyers perceive substantial benefits in product modification, increases in promotional efforts alone are seldom effective.

Decline Stage.   Changes in customer desires as well as changes in the state of the art that create better substitute offerings eventually bring about a decline in the sales and profits of every product. When a product enters the decline stage, the marketer is faced with the choice of phasing the product out or embarking on a milking strategy in which marketing expenses are sharply reduced to increase current profit margins.

Locating Industrial Products in Their Life Cycles

Where a particular product is in its life cycle is dependent on numerous factors, such as industry profits, the rate of change in industry sales growth, and the total number of units purchased. While a number of methods are available for locating a product in its life cycle, Clifford has suggested using accounting information for this purpose. The steps he proposes are

1. Develop trend information for the past three to five years on unit and dollar sales, profit margins, total profit contribution, return on investment, market share, and prices.
2. Examine recent trends in the number and nature of competitors, their market share rankings, and their product performance advantages.
3. Analyze short-term competitive tactics such as recent new product introduction or plant expansion announcements.
4. Obtain and analyze historical information of the life cycles of similar or related products.
5. Project product sales for the next three to five years based on steps 1 through 4 and estimated profit ratios for each of those years. (Profit ratios tend to improve as products enter the growth stage, begin to deteriorate as they approach maturity, and then drop dramatically as they approach obsolescence in the decline stage.)
6. Estimate the number of profitable years remaining in the product's life cycle, and, from the preceding analysis, fix the product's position on its life-cycle curve.[14]

DEVELOPING PRODUCT STRATEGIES
FOR ESTABLISHED PRODUCTS

Industrial product strategies deal with such important issues as which products should be continued, which should be phased out, the number and diversity of prod-

---

[14]Donald K. Clifford, Jr., "Managing the Product Life Cycle," *The McKinsey Quarterly* (Spring 1965).

ucts to be offered, and product innovation. Thus, the firm must make decisions with respect to individual product items (a specific product version), product lines (a group of related products), and its overall product mix (all the items and lines marketed).

Product Evaluation Matrices

Once the necessary data have been collected and analyzed to determine where products are in their life cycle, the product manager can use these data to determine appropriate strategies for all product items within a product line. When historical and projected figures on industry sales, company sales, market shares, and profits are combined into a comprehensive *product evaluation matrix,*[15] such as that shown in Figure 9-3, a product or group of products can be analyzed with respect to where they have been and where they might go. For example, product A, shown in Figure 9-3, was in a growth industry for three of the last four years. In 1983, it was in a growth industry and had an average market share, and its profits were on target. But, in 1987 (the current year), it is in a stable industry, with declining sales, a marginal market share, and below-average profits. Product B, on the other hand, has been in a growth industry, with market share moving from average to dominant, while meeting its profit objectives for the last two years.

In analyzing the current position of products A and B, the marketing manager is in a better position to determine which strategy is appropriate for the products within the line. To improve product A's market position, the marketing manager might consider product modification or improvement, targeting new market segments, or even deleting the product from the line. The strategy for product B, of course, would be aimed toward maintaining its favorable market position.

Strategic alternatives for a particular product or for the entire line might include[16]

1. Maintaining the product and its marketing strategy in the present form.
2. Maintaining the present form of the product but changing its marketing strategy.
3. Changing the product and altering the marketing strategy.
4. Dropping the product or the entire product line.
5. Adding one or more new items into a line or adding new product lines.

Before deciding on the appropriate future strategy for products A and B, the product manager can simulate market conditions by projecting competitive behavior in relation to alternative strategies through DSS (discussed in Chapters Seven and Eight) and plot them on the matrix.

---

[15]Yoram Wind and Henry J. Claycamp, "Planning Product Line Strategy: A Matrix Approach," *Journal of Marketing* 40 (January 1976), pp. 2–9.

[16]Ibid., p. 8.

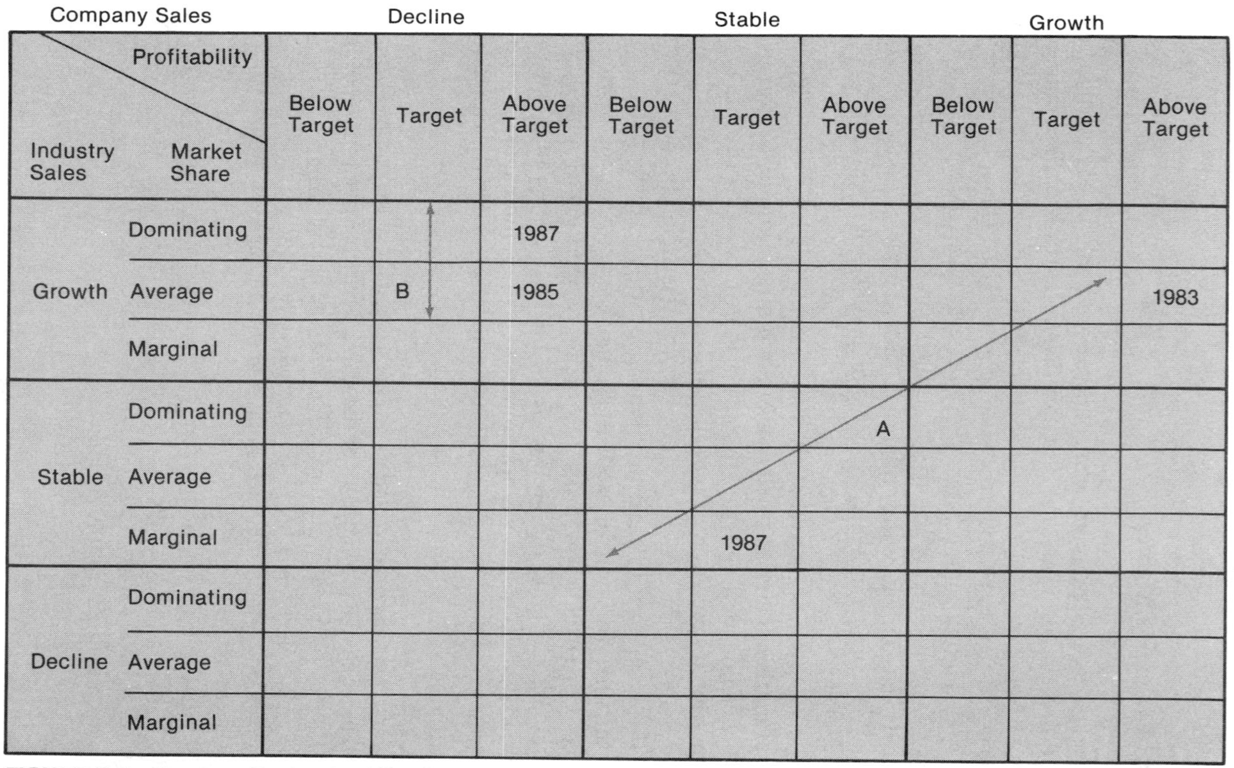

FIGURE 9-3 Product Evaluation Matrix

Industry Sales	Market Share	Decline — Below Target	Decline — Target	Decline — Above Target	Stable — Below Target	Stable — Target	Stable — Above Target	Growth — Below Target	Growth — Target	Growth — Above Target
Growth	Dominating		B	1987						1983
Growth	Average		B	1985						
Growth	Marginal									
Stable	Dominating									
Stable	Average									
Stable	Marginal					1987				
Decline	Dominating									
Decline	Average									
Decline	Marginal									

Company Sales / Profitability (column group header); arrow A extends diagonally from Stable (Below Target) toward Growth (Target).

Source: Adapted from Yoram Wind and Henry J. Claycamp, "Planning Product Line Strategy: A Matrix Approach," *Journal of Marketing*, January 1976, p. 5. Reprinted by permission.

Perceptual Mapping in Product Evaluation

Industrial marketers now use computer programs to perform perceptual mapping evaluation.[17] Perceptual mapping is a widely used technique for examining the relative strengths and weaknesses of a product compared to competitors'. While many programs are little more than cross-tabulations, others are capable of portraying complex, derived relationships. These programs enable the marketer to map the perceptions of different groups of buying influencers, such as top management, compared to engineers, compared to researchers, and do so across customer groups.

Perceptual mapping generates three important types of information that are highly useful in developing marketing strategy: (1) the position of competing brands relative to one another, (2) the position of brands, or product options, with respect to their attributes, and (3) the position of product attributes compared to each other.

How perceptual mapping works can best be illustrated through an example. Let us assume that a company produces brand X of chemical analysis (a product/process similar to photographic filming) and the company wishes to improve its competitive position in the market. Through discussions with current and potential customers, the company's sales and technical support people generate a list of eighteen product attributes that buyers use to evaluate its own and competitors' chemical analysis (see Table 9-3). By interviewing a sample of 300 customers and having them rate each product/process on the eighteen attributes, the company (via a computerized perceptual mapping program) generates the perceptual map of brands and attributes shown in Figure 9-4.

The closer two brands are to each other, the more similar and competitive they are perceived to be by buyers. Thus, in Figure 9-4, the old position of brand X is

TABLE 9-3 Perceptual Attributes for Evaluating Suppliers in the Chemical Analysis Industry

1. Accurate process readings	10. Highly sensitive process readings
2. Clear, sharp results	11. Cost
3. Cost/performance ratios	12. Pricing flexibility
4. Pleasantness of sales people	13. Knowledgeability of sales people
5. Technical support	14. Flexible delivery
6. On-time delivery	15. Good return policy
7. Fast processing of results	16. American versus foreign technology
8. High-tech company image	17. "Status image"
9. Heaviness of advertising	18. Usage by major customers

Source: Hugh J. Devine, Jr., and John Morton, "How Does the Market Really See Your Product? Diagnosing Your Product Position with Perceptual Mapping," *Business Marketing,* July 1984, pp. 70, 74, 78–79, 131. Reprinted by permission.

[17]Hugh J. Devine, Jr., and John Morton, "How Does the Market Really See Your Product? Diagnosing Your Product Position with Perceptual Mapping," *Business Marketing* (July 1984), pp. 70–131.

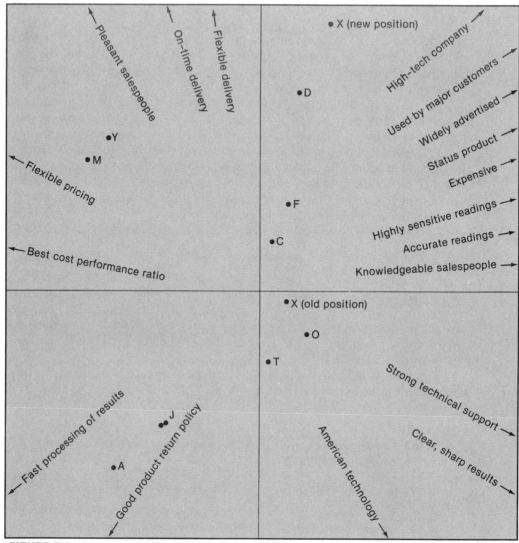

FIGURE 9-4   Perceptual Map of Vendors and Attributes in the Chemical Analysis Industry

Source: Hugh J. Devine, Jr., and John Morton, "How Does the Market Really See Your Product? Diagnosing Your Product Position with Perceptual Mapping," *Business Marketing,* July 1984, p. 79. Reprinted by permission.

perceived by buyers to be quite similar to brands O and T. We can assume, then, that brand X competes most heavily with O and T. On the other hand, the farther two brands are from one another, the less similar and the less competitive they are perceived to be. The new position of brand X, for instance, is perceived as offering a product quite different from O and T; that is, brands O and T are perceived as fulfilling a different set of needs than is brand X.

Figure 9-4 not only shows the competitive position of suppliers' brands in the chemical analysis market but also how they stand with respect to the eighteen attributes. Brands Y and M, for instance, have the strongest position on flexible pricing and pleasant sales people, while brands C and F excel in the areas of highly sensitive and accurate readings and knowledgeable sales people.

When attributes are located in close proximity, they may have similar meanings. For instance, some suppliers are characterized as high-tech firms that offer a "status product" or process that is highly valued by major purchasers. These products/processes, as Figure 9-4 indicates, tend to be heavily advertised and offer sensitive and accurate *readings,* and price may be the factor that links these attributes together. In a market where performance is important, but difficult to measure, a high price, then, may promote an image of high quality.

In analyzing brand X's old position relative to competitors', then, it is obvious that it has no outstanding strengths. It is perceived to fall in the center of the matrix, offering adequate but unexceptional delivery on all product/process attributes. Thus, if it is to experience an increase in market share, the company must differentiate itself from competitors. For instance, by improving its research and development staff, offering new software and a microprocessor-based system for more sensitive customer on-site analysis, adding sales and support personnel, revitalizing customer interfaces, and increasing advertising efforts and price to reflect these changes, brand X can be repositioned into the northeast corner of the map (see Figure 9-4).

New Product Opportunity Analysis.   Perceptual mapping can also be used to identify new product opportunities. If the company with brand X is looking for an opportunity to develop a new product, current and potential customers can be asked to rank their ideal product attributes and how well current suppliers' products meet those attributes. For example, if the positions currently occupied by brands C and F in Figure 9-4 were vacant, the opportunity would exist to develop a product to fill that void.

PRODUCT REVITALIZATION DECISIONS

When a product's profit margin, sales volume, or market share falls below expectations, management has two options: either revitalize it or eliminate it.[18] Before a revitalization decision can be made, however, the cause of the product's unsatisfactory performance must be pinpointed and alternative corrective actions examined. Thus, product revitalization decisions involve identifying weak products and searching for alternative actions to restore product performance to acceptable levels. Where no corrective actions are feasible, or the product's situation fails to justify

---

[18]George J. Avlonitis, "Revitalizing Weak Industrial Products," *Industrial Marketing Management* 14 (1985), pp. 93–105.

further improvements and investments, further investigation should be undertaken to determine the consequences of eliminating the product.

Identifying Causes of Poor Product Performance

Avlonitis, in a recent study of 20 industrial firms, found that management tends to identify poor product performance on the basis of profitability factors (e.g., product cost structure, production methods, and product design). Thus, when products deviate from some established performance measure, accountants and/or engineers are requested to measure the total costs associated with the product, analyze the product's design and production method, and make recommendations regarding the feasibility of reducing the product's cost. However, when opinions of causes of poor product performance are sought from the sales force, a more revealing picture of the product's market situation is developed (e.g., competitive activities and customer requirements).

Once product performance deviations from established norms are identified and analyzed, it is often discovered that weak product performance is seldom the result of one single factor. Rather it generally results from a variety of factors that are frequently interrelated. Table 9-4 shows the range of reasons cited by respondents as the cause of unsatisfactory product performance.

Identifying Alternative Corrective Actions

According to Avlonitis's study, alternative corrective actions may involve (1) cost reductions, (2) product modifications, (3) price change considerations, (4) promotion change considerations, or (5) channel change considerations. The majority of

TABLE 9-4 Statements Explaining the Unsatisfactory Performance of Specific Products Studied

Statement	No. of Companies Citing
Uncompetitive price	7
Production problems (e.g., inferior technology, hard to assemble)	6
Not mass product, uneconomic batches	6
Too costly to produce and market	5
High costs to manufacture	5
Overengineered	4
Competitors dominated the market	4
Customer requirements not as expected	2
Low selling price	2.

Source: Reprinted by permission of the publisher from "Revitalizing Weak Industrial Products," by George J. Avlonitis, *Industrial Marketing Management,* 14 (1985), pp. 93–105. Copyright © 1985 by Elsevier Science Publishing Co., Inc.

TABLE 9-5 Alternative Corrective Actions Cited by 20 Sample Companies

Corrective Actions	No. of Companies Citing
Product modifications [mainly for cost-reduction purposes]	15
Increase in the product's price	9
Product improvement	7
Decrease in the product's price	6
Development of new markets	3
Increased promotional expenditure	2
Increased effort of sales force	2
Changed channels of distribution	1

Source: Reprinted by permission of the publisher from "Revitalizing Weak Industrial Products," by George J. Avlonitis, *Industrial Marketing Management,* 14 [1985], pp. 93–105. Copyright © 1985 by Elsevier Science Publishing Co., Inc.

the respondents indicate that the first step is to search for alternative means of reducing costs through product redesign or modification, improved parts and materials sourcing, or investment in capital equipment, tooling, and plant. The most popular corrective action pursued, however, as Table 9-5 indicates, is product modification through value analysis to (1) reduce cost by eliminating waste, allowing for greater pricing flexibility or (2) improve product quality, features, or style to meet customer requirements.

Product Elimination Decisions

In the industrial market, product elimination decisions center on marketing and financial considerations.[19] In a recent study of more than 100 engineering firms, it was found that whether a product is eliminated depends on its contribution to overhead, its effect on the profitability and sales of other products, and its effect on customer relationships. However, when product elimination tends to affect production capacity, or results in a need to find an appropriate substitute for customers, product elimination depends on whether a new product is available to replace the one under evaluation and on the product's importance to company activities. (See Table 9-6.)

When a product represents from 15 to 30 percent of a firm's resources and sales turnover, it is necessary to determine the effects of the product's elimination on the sales of other products, customer relationships, manufacturing, and the ability of other products to take its place. Thus, product elimination decisions center on (1) new product potential; (2) customer relationships, (3) the impact on profit

[19]See George J. Avlonitis, "Product Elimination Decision Making: Does Formality Matter?" *Journal of Marketing* 49 (Winter 1985), pp. 41–52; and Avlonitis, "Advisors and Decision-Makers in Product Eliminations," *Industrial Marketing Management* 14 (1985), pp. 17–26.

TABLE 9-6 Product Elimination Evaluation Factors

Product's elimination effect upon
1. Full-line policy
2. Corporate image
3. Sales of other products
4. Customer relationships
5. Profitability of other products via manufacturing overhead allocation
6. Profitability of other products via selling overhead allocation
7. Profitability of other products via distribution and overhead allocation
8. Fixed and working capital
9. Employee relationships
    New product potential
    Reallocation of resources
    Release of executive time
    Existence of substitutes
    Competitive moves
    Organized intervention

Source: Reprinted by permission of the publisher from "Product Elimination Decision Making: Does Formality Matter?" by George J. Avlonitis, *Industrial Marketing Management*, 14 [1985], pp. 41–52. Copyright © 1985 by Elsevier Science Publishing Co., Inc.

and sales of other products, (4) the corporate image, (5) employee relationships, and (6) competitors' moves. The importance of these factors during the product elimination evaluation process, however, varies with the type of industry, the number of products manufactured, and the nature of competition.

SYSTEMS MARKETING

Theodore Levitt points out that buyers no longer seek to purchase a product for its own value.[20] Rather, they prefer to buy a package of interrelated products and services from a single supplier versus making numerous individual decisions pertaining to several products and needs. Thus, many sellers have adopted the practice of *systems marketing*. In systems marketing, the supplier not only sells a system of interrelated products, but a system of operating procedures, management routines, inventory control, and other service components to meet buyers' needs. For example, IBM includes maintenance, emergency repairs, and training services in some of its systems.

Systems marketing may involve (1) product systems, composed of capital

[20]Theodore Levitt, "After the Sale Is Over," *Harvard Business Review* (September–October 1983), pp. 87–93.

KIERULFF ELECTRONICS EXPANDS ITS SYSTEMS BUSINESS

In 1980, systems sales were about 2 percent of Kierulff Electronics' total sales. By 1985, they were 20 percent and expected to increase—good news for small-volume buyers who were once at a disadvantage, unable to purchase systems from large equipment manufacturers. Now, thanks to Kierulff and other electronic parts distributors like Arrow Electronics and Hamilton Avnet, small-volume buyers are realizing the advantages of "one-stop shopping, improved inventory management, better credit terms, and faster delivery."

Systems selling is also an advantage for major manufacturers who "can't or won't deal with" the numerous smaller firms. Although Hewlett-Packard is currently refusing to sell through distributors, Kierulff is representing such firms as AMD, AT&T, Control Data Corp., Data General, Tandon, RCA, TI Systems, Data Products, and Quine.

A big part of Kierulff's marketing strategy is providing technical service and advice to buyers on how to design the best system. To accomplish this, Kierulff publishes a designer's guide to assist system planners in choosing compatible parts and alternatives, conducts technical seminars where designers and planners learn how to assemble and choose computer systems, loans systems to prospective customers for evaluation testing, and has set up 30 hands-on systems centers where buyers can actually use systems. As part of its systems marketing, "Kierulff passes on manufacturing warranties, and also offers a disk drive alignment and repair through Metermaster."

Source: Reprinted from *Purchasing* magazine, Jack F. Russell, "Kierulff Leads Ducommun's Charge into the Systems Business," *Purchasing,* May 9, 1985, p. 108A27. Copyright © by Cahners Publishing Company, 1985.

---

goods and the supplies that are used in operating the equipment, (2) systems contracting, which involves the selling of a computerized order processing routine for low-value, repetitive maintenance, repair, and operating (MRO) supplies, and (3) service systems, which involve integrated and balanced methods of delivering services, such as information processing or management consulting, to help customers manage their businesses better. Thus, systems marketing consists of a set of products, products and services, or services that are customized and packaged into a system solution.[21]

Systems Marketing is Service Marketing. The essence of systems marketing is that the firm is offering more than a product and the accompanying services. Systems marketing is the marketing of a service, a service that is personalized and tailored to meet individual customer needs. Thus, the vendor "becomes the customer's con-

---

[21]Albert L. Page and Michael Siemplenski, "Product Systems Marketing," *Industrial Marketing Management,* 12 (1983), pp. 89–99.

sultant,'' focusing the firm's expertise on a wide range of customer problems to solve their needs. For example, before selling and installing pollution control equipment, the marketer would perform a confidential, analytical survey of customer operations to determine the extent to which the customer needed to control air, water, or solid-waste pollution. Once the need were determined, the marketer would work with the customer to develop a system that (1) meets all pertinent codes, (2) fits the operating demands of the customer's existing and planned facilities, and (3) represents the most reliable system needs at minimum cost.[22]

The Elements of Systems Marketing

The most important characteristic of a good system is that it solves customer problems. This requires (1) identifying those problems in financial terms (i.e., what a problem is costing the customer), (2) developing and quantifying a profit-improvement solution to customer problems, and (3) accepting the management of and responsibility for the performance of the system.[23] Before the expertise, hardware, and services that comprise an effective system can be developed, customer needs must be thoroughly understood. This requires an understanding of customer operations and involvement with a wider range of buying influencers and decision makers than in the marketing of products.

Systems marketing is based on the foundation of the marketing concept. It recognizes that customers do not buy products; they buy benefits, and when the value satisfactions sought are provided, they are willing to pay for them. For instance, to solve customer MRO sourcing problems, Standard Register sells business forms for virtually every printed product use (e.g., W-2 forms; forms for purchasing and billing; forms that can be used with computers, typewriters, and accounting machines; single-copy forms; multiple-copy forms; and pressure-sensitive labels) to its 100 largest accounts who spend over $100 million per year on Standard's forms.[24]

Effective systems marketing requires greater responsibility to the customer than does product marketing. In general, systems marketers are responsible for

1. Developing the general systems design for a broad set of product/market systems needs.
2. Analyzing the needs of the individual customer.
3. Determining the best solution for individual customers.
4. Installing and ensuring timely delivery.
5. Debugging the system.
6. Assisting in the conversion to a new system where one existed in the past.

[22]Mack Hanan, James Cribbin, and Jack Donis, *Systems Selling Strategies* (New York: AMA-COM, 1978), p. 7.

[23]Ibid., p. 1.

[24]Rayna Skolnick, "Standard Register Sells in Top Form," *Sales and Marketing Management* (October 11, 1982), pp. 49–52.

7. Maintaining and, when needed, updating the system.
8. Guaranteeing that the system will perform adequately.[25]

Benefits of Systems Marketing

Systems selling provides the vendor and the customer with benefits that are not normally realized under the product marketing approach. When properly conceived, it enables a supplier to differentiate its offering from those of competitors in a manner that is more profitable to both the vendor and buyer. Under the concept of systems marketing, the vendor produces and supplies all the major parts and services needed by customer firms. This results in increased revenues from tie-in sales of related products; reduced unit costs through common advertising, sales promotion, and increased productivity of the sales force and other channel members; and brand loyalty once a system is installed. Because competitive replacement can often be a costly undertaking, as long as the system continues to meet the buyer's needs, replacement seldom occurs. Customers, on the other hand, experience reduced costs in the development and procurement of a system, in the constant sourcing of suppliers (system contracts are normally in effect for one year), and in the reduction of inventory costs through the provision of efficient service.

PROFESSIONAL SERVICE MARKETING: PROBLEMS AND STRATEGIES

Compared to a few years ago, when most providers of professional services relied on their country club connections and reputations to obtain business, today's professionals are actively involved in the marketing of their services:

> Newsletters, press releases, and other public relation tools are widely used by accounting, law, architectural, engineering, and management consulting firms. And, in a less visible way, professional service firms of all types and sizes are employing marketing research and strategic planning with increasing frequency.[26]

The marketing of professional services, however, presents a unique set of problems, problems that require a different marketing approach. As Table 9-7 points out, services are (1) intangible—they cannot be seen, tasted, felt, heard, or smelled before they are purchased; (2) inseparable—they cannot be separated from their source; (3) heterogeneous—service quality depends not only on the provider, but when and where they are provided; and (4) perishable—they cannot be saved and

---

[25]Page and Siemplenski, "Product Systems Marketing."

[26]Paul N. Bloom, "Effective Marketing for Professional Services," *Harvard Business Review* (September–October 1984), pp. 102–110.

TABLE 9-7 Unique Service Features, Resulting Marketing Problems, and Suggested Marketing Strategies

Unique Service Features	Resulting Marketing Problems	Suggested Marketing Strategies
Intangibility	1. Cannot be stored. 2. Cannot be protected through patents. 3. Cannot be readily displayed or communicated. 4. Prices are difficult to set.	1. Stress tangible cues. 2. Use personal sources more than nonpersonal sources. 3. Simulate or stimulate word-of-mouth communications. 4. Create strong organizational image. 5. Use cost accounting to help set prices. 6. Engage in postpurchase communications.
Inseparability	1. Consumer involved in production. 2. Other consumers involved in production. 3. Centralized mass production of services difficult.	1. Emphasize selection and training of public contact. 2. Manage consumers. 3. Use multisite locations.
Heterogeneity	1. Standardization and quality control difficult to achieve.	1. Industrialize service [standardizing certain common services]. 2. Customize service.
Perishability	1. Services cannot be inventoried.	1. Use strategies to cope with fluctuating demand. 2. Make simultaneous adjustments in demand and capacity to achieve closer match between the two.

Source: Valarie A. Zeithaml, A. Parasuraman, and Leonard L. Berry, "Problems and Strategies in Services Marketing," *Journal of Marketing,* 49 (Spring 1985), pp. 33–46. Reprinted by permission of the American Marketing Association.

stored. Each of these characteristics, as further outlined in Table 9-7, requires a different approach in developing industrial marketing strategy.

Product Intangibility

The most critical distinction between industrial products and services is that services are performances rather than objects.[27] Thus, they must be evaluated and purchased on either "credence" or "experience" qualities. Credence qualities involve obtaining service purchasers' faith in the competency of those who sell services. Experience

---

[27]See John E. Bateson, "Do We Need Service Marketing?" in *Marketing Science Institute Report #77-115* (Coral Gables, Fla.: Academy of Marketing Science in Cosponsorship with the School of Business, University of Miami, 1977); and O. C. Ferrel, S. W. Brown, and C. W. Lamb, Jr., eds., *Theoretical Developments in Marketing* (Chicago: American Marketing Association, December 1979), pp. 131–146.

qualities, on the other hand, refer to the fact that most customers must evaluate service companies on the basis of experience, since they lack the necessary technical skills to otherwise assess service providers' capabilities.[28]

Not only are credence and experience attributes needed to assist in the purchase decision, they are also needed after the sale is made. Few laypersons are able to determine whether an audit has been performed thoroughly, a building designed safely, or a case pleaded properly.[29] Thus, it is difficult for customers to conceptualize what is being offered or evaluate what they received once the purchase was made. Because of this, they tend to look for "tangible evidence of the intangible" in evaluating the service. Marketing strategy must take this into consideration. Not only must industrial marketers clarify their service offering for customers, they must assist customers' attempts to evaluate them by "providing tangible surrogate features whenever possible."[30]

Recent evidence indicates that industrial organizations attempt to enhance the tangibility of their service offering by carefully selecting and training customer contact personnel, by encouraging their customers to tell others about their services, and by gearing their marketing programs to project a specific company image. One accountant, for instance, states that it is important "to do things like setting out accounts neatly and carefully, answering letters promptly and making sure you look as if you are totally familiar with the client's affairs."[31]

Overcoming Buyer Uncertainty. To overcome buyer uncertainty in the purchase and evaluation of professional service, Bloom suggests that personal contacts, public relation activities, advertising, and service delivery be designed to educate clients on[32]

1. When they should seek professional services.
2. Which attributes to consider in evaluating different providers.
3. How to communicate their concerns, desires, or other issues to professionals.
4. What they can realistically expect providers to accomplish.

Product Differentiation.[33] Professional service firms face a more difficult task in differentiating their product offering than do product marketers. How does one differentiate an accounting audit, management analysis and advice, or an executive search service from those offered by competitors? While some providers of services attempt to use clever titles, such as TRAP (Touche Ross audit process) and STAR

[28]Valarie A. Zeithaml, A. Parasuraman, and Leonard L. Berry, "Problems and Strategies in Service Marketing," *Journal of Marketing* 49 (Spring 1985), pp. 33–46.

[29]Angela M. Rushton and David J. Carson, "The Marketing of Services: Managing the Intangibles," *European Journal of Marketing* 19:3 (1985), pp. 19–39.

[30]Ibid.

[31]Bloom, "Effective Marketing for Professional Services."

[32]Ibid.

[33]Ibid.

(statistical techniques for analytical review) to differentiate their offerings, the most useful approach is achieved through researching potential market segments.

When service providers research potential market segments and pinpoint the attributes that clients use to differentiate one service from another, they are in a better position to establish their firm as a possessor of the desired attributes. Once market needs are known, a service marketer might differentiate the firm's offering by emphasizing

1. More experience, specialization, credibility, and contacts.
2. Better solutions to problems and superior procedures.
3. Personal involvement by high-level professionals.
4. Easy access to services.
5. On-time completion of work.
6. The use of state-of-the-art support equipment like computers, communications systems, and testing devices.
7. Easy-to-understand reports, presentations, and invoices.
8. Frequent follow-up contacts to ensure satisfaction.

Inseparability of Production and Consumption

Services are first sold, then produced and consumed simultaneously. Thus, the buyer's perception of both the firm and the quality of the service rendered depends on the interaction that takes place between the buyer and the seller during the service encounter (i.e., the face-to-face interaction between a buyer and a seller in a service setting).[34] Not only is the perception of quality received dependent on the effectiveness of the person rendering the service, it is determined, in part, by the customer. For example, the quality of tax advice provided depends to some degree on the information provided by the customer. In attempting to achieve greater control, then, industrial marketers must be aware of the importance of effectively managing the human element.

Product Heterogeneity

Services are not only rendered by different individuals within a firm, but individual performance also tends to fluctuate from day to day.[35] Thus, in the performance of services, a high potential for variability exists, making standardization of delivery extremely difficult. Quality in service delivery, however, must be carefully guarded. Since word of mouth is an essential ingredient in communicating a professional service firm's offering, a bad experience on the part of buyers can severely affect a

---

[34]Michael R. Solomon, Carol Surprenant, John A. Czepiel, and Evelyn G. Gutman, "A Role Theory Perspective on Dyadic Interactions: The Service Encounter," *Journal of Marketing,* 49 (1985), pp. 99–111.

[35]Zeithaml, Parasuraman, and Berry, "Problems and Strategies in Service Marketing."

firm's business. While consistent quality is difficult to achieve, industrial marketers appear to be quite marketing oriented in their attempts to influence customers favorably in such ways as contacting customers after their purchase to ensure satisfaction, choosing personnel carefully, and regularly collecting information on customer needs.[36]

Product Perishability

The most troublesome area in the marketing of industrial services is the fact that they cannot be mass produced and stored. Thus, strategies for coping with fluctuating demand are difficult to develop. When demand is low, industrial service firms attempt to increase business by calling on customers. According to Aquila, the major objective in the marketing of a CPA program is to motivate and assist personnel in the development of new business and the retention of current clients.

> Growth is a major objective of most CPA firms. To support and complement this goal, the marketing program needs to teach people to be attuned to new business opportunities which present themselves during the normal course of the day. . . . Too often, accountants simply are afraid to ask for referrals from satisfied clients, so the marketing staff must groom them in developing empathy for clients, appreciating their problems, and asking them for referrals.[37]

To handle peak demand, service firms cross-train employees, have employees work overtime, hire extra part-time employees, and encourage customers to use services during nonpeak periods. While some service firms may take care of their regular customers first, allowing new customers to wait (or even turn away business), "demand for services must be met or lost" or the firm will miss the chance of earning increased revenues.[38]

Communicating the Service Offering

While approximately 14 percent of the nation's lawyers and several CPA firms use advertising to reach potential clients, the use of advertising to communicate with potential markets by service providers has two important limitations.[39] First, many service users are unaccustomed to seeing or hearing advertising for professional services and they may not accept it. They may even interpret it negatively, perceiving that the firm lacks competency if it has to advertise. Second, because professional service firms usually need to reach only a very narrow audience and with compli-

---

[36]August J. Aquila, "Marketing of Accounting Services Hinges on Referrals, Service Expansion, Communications," *Marketing News,* April 27, 1984, p. 3.

[37]Ibid.

[38]Kenneth P. Uhl and Gregory D. Upah, "The Marketing of Services: Why and How Is It Different?" in Jagdish N. Sheth, ed., *Research in Marketing* 6 (Greenwich, Conn.: JAI Press, Inc., 1983), pp. 231–257.

[39]Solomon et al., "A Role Theory Perspective on Dyadic Interactions."

cated explanations of their service, advertising is often not worth the expense involved—even if it may appear to be acceptable. For these reasons, most professional service organizations are leery of the results that may be achieved through advertising.

Despite these problems, however, some professional firms are quite successful in their use of advertising. For instance, one CPA firm that used advertising as its only means of developing business reported an increase in billings from $8,000 to $1.75 million over a four-year period. When used properly and prudently, then, advertising can be a viable means of reaching potential markets.[40] This means that the service provider must identify target audiences, reach them through low-cost advertising in specialized publications or direct mail, and monitor the results. Only by carefully tracking the number of inquiries and their receptivity to the professional's sales call can the marketer fine tune the firm's advertising program to achieve desired results.

Whether or not a firm uses advertising, personal selling plays a major role in the marketing of professional services, and consideration should be given to having it performed by those who will provide the service. In general, clients prefer to be courted by those who actually perform the service. Finding professionals who can sell the service as well as provide it, however, is a difficult task. Many architects, accountants, lawyers, and other professionals have no desire to take on the selling task, viewing it as "too commercial, too demeaning, and too difficult." Further, when an emphasis is placed on selling, it "can demoralize highly competent practitioners, who may seek employment at another firm where they merely have to practice their profession."

What steps can a firm take to overcome these problems? First, during the recruitment and hiring process, they should consider the candidates' potential selling skills. Second, sales training programs that teach basic selling skills can be incorporated into staff development programs. And, third, management can encourage selling by making it financially and professionally rewarding (e.g., providing bonuses, raises, promotions, and other rewards to those who bring in and retain valuable clients).

LOOKING BACK

Because of the complexity involved in developing industrial product decisions, and the impact they have on the entire organization, product development, modification, or deletion strategies involve an integrated effort across functional departments. In contrast to consumer product managers, industrial product managers have considerably more responsibility and are more involved in production decisions. In setting product objectives and strategies, however, they, like their con-

---

[40]Bloom, "Effective Marketing for Professional Services."

sumer counterparts, must be aware of how prospective buyers perceive a product. The concept of a product to the industrial buyer is multidimensional, involving basic, enhanced, and augmented properties.

In formulating product strategies, the industrial marketer must also be aware of how low- versus high-level learning products impact marketing strategies across the industrial product life cycle. When products require a low level of learning, rapid market acceptance can be expected. Thus, the marketer must be prepared to meet vigorous competition. When they require a high level of learning, marketing strategy should focus on market development.

To manage the product line, industrial marketers can utilize product evaluation matrices and perceptual mapping to determine the most appropriate strategies for products and lines. Product matrices enable the marketer to track where a product is in its life cycle. When combined with perceptual mapping, the positions of competing brands and attributes can be identified. Both matrix evaluation and perceptual mapping are useful in deciding whether to reposition or drop an existing product or to add a new product.

Systems marketing is becoming an increasingly vital strategy for differentiating a firm's product offering from competitors'. Under the concept of systems marketing, the firm offers more than a product; it offers customers a personalized service that is tailored to meet individual customer needs. While systems marketing requires greater responsibility to the customer, it provides additional benefits to both the firm and the customer.

In marketing professional services, the marketer must be aware that they present unique problems that require a different marketing approach from the marketing of products. Because they are intangible, inseparable, heterogeneous, and perishable, buyers must evaluate them on both credence and experience qualities. Thus, marketing strategy must be built around educating buyers to overcome buyer uncertainty, enhancing the tangibility of the service being offered, maintaining product quality, and managing fluctuating demand.

QUESTIONS FOR DISCUSSION

1. Due to the increased emphasis on product planning, promotion, and profitability, many industrial firms have introduced product management. However, findings indicate that, compared to consumer product managers, most industrial product managers reach their position from sales or engineering. Discuss how your knowledge of industrial marketing and product strategy could assist you in entering this area directly. What might your responsibilities be in this market compared to your counterpart in the consumer market?

2. Chester Wasson has pointed out that industrial marketers "must be aware of the real differences in rapidity of market acceptance and of the consequent differences in product life cycles" when developing product strategies. Discuss these differences and how they affect industrial marketing strategy.

3. According to Rink and Dodge, "Different personnel sales skills, qualities, and motiva-

tion are optimum for the various phases of industrial product life cycles.'' How would you identify where a product is in its life cycle and what are these different personnel requirements?

4. Avlonitis has pointed out that weak product revitalization decisions and product elimination decisions ''represent the key alternative courses of action that a company can undertake in response to either current or projected unsatisfactory product performance.'' Thus, he concludes that these decisions must be considered together. Explain why you would agree or disagree.

5. In the area of systems marketing, explain why the components of the system and the system itself should or should not be standardized.

6. ''Systems contracting has some extremely important strategic marketing implications for both the industrial distributor and manufacturer of MRO (maintenance, repair, operating) items.'' How can purchasing systems contracting improve marketing opportunities for industrial distributors and manufacturers of MRO supplies?

7. Explain why marketing strategy should differ for services because services are performances rather than objects.

8. According to Theodore Levitt, ''During the era we are entering the emphasis will be on systems contracts, and buyer-seller relationships will be characterized by continuous contact and evolving relationships to affect the system.'' Explain why you agree or disagree and the implications of your belief.

SUGGESTED ADDITIONAL READINGS

AVLONITIS, GEORGE J., ''Revitalizing Weak Industrial Products,'' *Industrial Marketing Management* 14 (1985): 93–105; and ''Product Elimination Decision Making: Does Formality Matter?'' *Journal of Marketing* 49 (Winter 1985): 41–52.

BLOOM, PAUL N., ''Effective Marketing for Professional Services,'' *Harvard Business Review* (September–October 1984): 102–110.

CUMMINGS, THEODORE, DONALD W. JACKSON, JR., and LONNIE L. OSTROM, ''Differences Between Industrial and Consumer Product Managers,'' *Industrial Marketing Management* 13 (1984): 171–180.

DREYFUSS, JOEL, ''What Do You Do For An Encore?'' *Fortune* (December 19, 1988): 111–119.

ECKLES, ROBERT W., and TIMOTHY J. NOVOTNY, ''Industrial Product Managers: Authority and Responsibility,'' *Industrial Marketing Management* 13 (1984): 71–75.

GREENLY, GORDON E., ''Tactical Product Decisions,'' *Industrial Marketing Management* 12 (1983): 13–18.

LAMBKIN, MARY and GEORGE S. DAY, ''Evolutionary Processes in Competitive Markets: Beyond the Product Life Cycle,'' *Journal of Marketing* (July 1989): 4–20.

LEVITT, THEODORE, ''Marketing Success Through Differentiation of Anything,'' *Harvard Business Review* (January–February 1982): 83–91.

LEVITT, THEODORE, ''After the Sale is Over,'' *Harvard Business Review* (September–October 1983): 87–93.

PAGE, ALBERT L., and MICHAEL SIEMPLENSKI, ''Product Systems Marketing,'' *Industrial Marketing Management* 12 (1983): 89–99.

RINK, DAVID R., and H. ROBERT DODGE, ''Industrial Sales Emphasis Across the Life Cycle,'' *Industrial Marketing Management* 9 (1980): 305–310.

RUSHTON, ANGELA M., and DAVID J. CARSON, "The Marketing of Services: Managing the Intangibles," *European Journal of Marketing* 19: 3 (1985): 19–39.

SCHEIDT, MARSHA A., I. FREDERICK TRAWICK, and JOHN E. SWAN, "Impact of Purchasing Systems Contracts on Distributors and Producers," *Industrial Marketing Management* 11 (1982): 283–289.

WASSON, CHESTER, R., "The Importance of the Produce Life Cycle to the Industrial Marketer," *Industrial Marketing Management* 5 (1976): 299–308.

ZEITHAML, VALARIE A., A. PARASURAMAN, and LEONARD L. BERRY, "Problems and Strategies in Service Marketing," *Journal of Marketing* 49 (Spring 1985): 33–46.

CHAPTER 10

Strategic Innovation
and
New Product Development

The new product development process has always been a challenging task at best, one that tests a company's market knowledge, technical competence, and financial strength, as well as its willingness and ability to compete. As markets in the 1990s exhibit increased global competition and faster rates of technological change, both governments and business managers will place great emphasis on R&D, new products, and technological innovation.[1] Firms that do not create new products, or at least respond effectively to the creations of competitors, will find themselves obsolete in an unsympathetic marketplace. In this chapter, we shall examine

1. How a firm can generate new ideas.
2. The impact of innovation on a firm's competitiveness.
3. Innovation applied to manufacturing and marketing.
4. Organizational factors affecting new product success.
5. Marketing's role in the development process.

Developing and marketing new products is a costly venture that entails commitment and risk. Research indicates that approximately thirty to thirty-five percent

[1]Robert G. Cooper, "New Product Success in Industrial Firms," *Industrial Marketing Management* 11 (1982), pp. 215–223.

of all industrial products that reach the market fail during the introductory stage.[2] We shall examine some of the major causes of product failure.

Innovation does not stop with the creation of new products. Firms must also upgrade their production techniques and marketing methods to remain competitive. In fact, American firms are losing more business to foreign competition due to production and marketing shortcomings than to a lack of product creativity.[3] We shall examine this phenomenon along with possible remedies.

WHAT IS A NEW INDUSTRIAL PRODUCT?

Booz, Allen & Hamilton have identified six categories of new products in terms of their newness to the company and to the marketplace:[4]

1. **New-to-the-world products**—new products that create an entirely new market.
2. **New product lines**—new products that allow a company to enter an established market for the first time.
3. **Additions to existing product lines**—new products that supplement a company's established product lines.
4. **Improvements in/revisions to existing products**—new products that provide improved performance or greater perceived value and replace existing products.
5. **Repositionings**—existing products that are targeted to new markets or market segments.
6. **Cost reductions**—new products that provide similar performance at lower cost.

In general, a firm will usually pursue a mix of these new products. Research indicates, however, that only ten percent of new products are new to the world. These products represent the greatest risk because they are new to both the company and the market. One study of products introduced during the late 1970s yielded the distribution shown in Figure 10-1.

WHO DREAMS UP NEW PRODUCTS?

New product ideas come from a variety of sources, both inside and outside the company. Within the firm, ideas can come from manufacturing, sales, engineering, and management personnel, as well as formally structured development groups. Outside sources include distributors, independent researchers, competitors, government agencies, and existing or potential customers.

[2]C. Merle Crawford, *New Products Management,* 2nd ed. (Homewood, Ill.: Richard D. Irwin, Inc., 1987), p. 21.

[3]C. Jackson Grayson, Jr. and Carla O'Dell, *American Business: A Two-Minute Warning* (New York: The Free Press, 1988), pp. 256–57.

[4]*New Product Management for the 1980s* (New York: Booz, Allen & Hamilton, 1982).

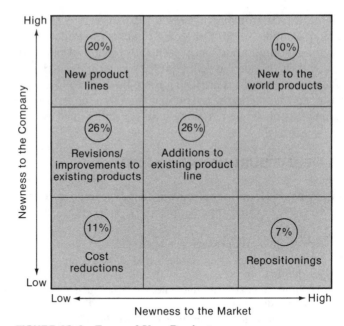

FIGURE 10-1   Types of New Products

Source: *New Products Management for the 1980s* (New York: Booz, Allen, & Hamilton, 1982). Reprinted by permission.

INTRAPRENEURSHIP AT 3M

About 30 years ago, a 3M Co. technician had a great idea: Why not make an extra-wide sheet of adhesive that could be used as a drape during surgery?

Hospitals liked the sound of the product. It was inexpensive and it could attach easily to a patient's body, eliminating the need for the traditional 'tents' of draping used in surgery.

3M liked the idea too. Shortly, the St. Paul, Minn.-based company was manufacturing the drapes.

Subsequently 3M moved more aggressively into the health care industry, and today the health care products and services group accounts for a substantial portion of the company's $1.3 billion life sciences sector, says a spokesman.

The man with the idea for the surgical drapes and the company's ensuing surge into health care is Lewis W. Lehr, now chairman of the board. He was practicing what's now commonly known as intrapreneurship—or intracorporate enterpreneuring.

Source: Peter Finch, "Intrapreneurism: New Hope for New Business," *Business Marketing*, July 1985, pp. 32–40. Reprinted by permission.

New Product Ideas from Within the Company

"Intrapreneuring is arguably surpassing 'excellence' as the hottest topic (of the year)."[5] Intrapreneuring is the process of encouraging and enabling employees to develop new product ideas and to follow them through to commercial profitability.

Companies encourage intrapreneuring by giving employees freedom to develop their ideas. They are encouraged to act as entrepreneurs and are not required to turn their projects over to others, but are allowed instead to make major decisions themselves.[6] They are given resources to use as they choose, even being allowed to go outside the company or their particular division for additional resources. They are not called down for working in areas organizationally assigned to others. They are given time and money to pursue their product developments and are allowed to take risks and make mistakes in the process. They are encouraged to make small accomplishments and are not required to achieve sizable gains. Finally, they are allowed to work in small teams composed of people throughout the organization.

Because of these many freedoms, intrapreneuring violates many bureaucratic principles and practices. Therefore, without top management support it will have little hope for success.

New Product Ideas from Customers

If a firm believes in the marketing concept, all new product ideas will be aimed at satisfying some market need. Thus, producers should be anxious to receive product ideas from customers who recognize a specific need and request a solution. Research findings are mixed on this subject. Some studies indicate that industrial firms use customer ideas in developing new products; others indicate that they do not. A possible explanation may stem from the fact that it takes a long while to develop a product from an original idea. By the time the idea becomes a functioning reality, the originator has been forgotten, or the developing company feels a sense of ownership and no longer gives credit to the originator.[7]

Customer Needs and Technology Efforts. New product development can be inspired by technological change as well as customer need. However, product development should not lead to companies emphasizing either a technological focus or a customer focus. The emphasis should be placed on achieving the proper coordination between the two areas.[8]

[5]Peter Finch, "Intrapreneurism: New Hope for New Business," *Business Marketing* (July 1985), pp. 32–40.

[6]Ibid.

[7]See Leigh Lawton and A. Parasuraman, "The Impact of the Marketing Concept on New Product Planning," *Journal of Marketing* 44 (Winter 1980), pp. 19–25; and Eric von Hippel, "Successful Industrial Products from Customer Ideas," *Journal of Marketing* 42 (January 1978), pp. 39–49.

[8]Roland W. Schmitt, "Successful Corporate R&D," *Harvard Business Review* 63 (May–June 1985), pp. 124–128.

An effective R&D program must be based on several directing inputs. First, it should be concerned with satisfying the needs of specific customers or markets. Very few firms, however, have the capability, or even the desire, to satisfy all the diverse needs in their target markets. Thus, a set of criteria must be developed to screen for desirable business opportunities, and some individual or group must be assigned this screening responsibility.

Second, an R&D program should be aimed at satisfying "generally known" needs in the target market(s). For example, all customers want computers that will handle more data more quickly and at less cost. These needs may also be described as *latent,* not having been satisfied by any other source. Satisfying latent needs gives the firm the prestige of being first and a lead over competition in developing production volume and efficiency.[9]

Third, an effective R&D program should also attempt to expand upon those technologies that represent the firm's strengths. One of the factors leading to a product's potential success is the utilization of technology that has already been proven in the manufacture of other products.[10] Technologies can become obsolete, however, just as products do. For example, between 1960 and 1983, the semiconductor industry rendered obsolete five basic fabrication technologies and countless minor variations of these.

Thus, it is necessary to evaluate which customer needs will be considered, to choose a technology capable of satisfying those needs, and to recognize when the technology and needs are no longer compatible.

Satisfying the Changing Needs of Key Customers. Industrial marketers must be especially sensitive to the changing needs of industry leaders, particularly if the industry is an oligopoly. When a few companies represent the bulk of an industry's buying power, a supplier cannot afford to dissatisfy, let alone ignore, their needs.

Current industry leaders do not always remain dominant, however. Geographic areas such as Silicon Valley contain many firms that have been in business less than five years but already possess considerable buying power. Consequently, industrial marketers not only face the challenge of satisfying current industry leaders, but must also identify and penetrate future leaders. This penetration is difficult because future leaders often emerge in conjunction with, or because of, new technologies. Their needs may be incompatible with a potential supplier's current capabilities. Suppliers willing and able to satisfy these new needs strengthen their own industry position.

---

[9]Von Hippel, "Successful Industrial Products from Customer Ideas."

[10]Robert G. Cooper, "The Dimensions of Industrial New Product Success and Failure," *Journal of Marketing* 43 (Summer 1979), pp. 93–103; also Cooper, "Predevelopment Activities Determine New Product Success," *Industrial Marketing Management* 17 (1988), pp. 237–247.

INNOVATION AND COMPETITIVENESS

As we enter the last decade of the twentieth century, it might be beneficial to analyze where American industry stands internationally in regard to technology, innovation, and overall competitiveness. Only through such an analysis can we fully understand the impact of technology and innovation on a firm's competitive position. To make this analysis, we must consider several associated factors and establish some relationships.

An Historical Perspective of Productivity

Productivity is a good starting point, because it defines what level of output competing firms (or nations) are able to achieve with a given input level, or, more simply put, what they can do with what they have. Grayson and O'Dell, in a book obviously aimed at removing any complacency in the minds of American industrialists, provide an excellent long-range perspective on this issue.[11]

Based on gross domestic product per employee (GDP/employee), the United States is still ahead of nine other industrialized nations (see Table 10-1). Two other aspects must be considered, however, before this lead can be properly evaluated.

First, the United States is the third nation since 1700 to lead the world in productivity. The Netherlands led during the eighteenth century. Nations were not industrialized in today's sense of the word, but the Dutch surpassed other European

TABLE 10-1 Real Gross Domestic Product per Employee

	1986 U.S. Dollars	Rating U.S. = 100	Growth Rates 1973–86
United States	$37,565	100.0	.5%
Canada	$35,670	95.0	1.2%
Netherlands	$32,415	86.3	.7%
France	$31,667	84.3	2.2%
Italy	$31,216	83.1	1.6%
Belgium	$30,543	81.3	2.0%
Germany	$30,390	80.9	2.2%
Norway	$30,114	80.2	2.4%
United Kingdom	$26,448	70.4	1.5%
Japan	$25,882	68.9	2.8%

Source: C. Jackson Grayson, Jr. and Carla O'Dell, American Business: A Two-Minute Warning, [New York: The Free Press, 1988], p. 39.

[11]Grayson and O'Dell, *American Business.*

nations in textile production, shipbuilding, insurance, banking, and international trade. Italian manufacturers in Genoa, Milan, and Venice decried the "cheap" Dutch textiles that invaded and took over their home markets.

As a result of the Industrial Revolution, the United Kingdom assumed productivity leadership by 1790. Throughout most of the nineteenth century, the United Kingdom was the financial and technological powerhouse of the world. The British dominated the coal, iron, and cotton cloth markets, and London became its financial center.[12]

Although their lead had begun to decline during the 1850s, the United Kingdom in 1870 enjoyed about the same position that the United States has today, as Table 10-2 indicates. By the 1890s, however, the United Kingdom lost its lead to the United States and became a relatively weak follower in this century. There were a multitude of reasons for this decline, many beyond the scope of this text, but it was not due to a falloff in British creativity. One of the primary factors was the ability of the United States to mass produce, at lower cost, products that were invented by the British.

The second significant aspect of the current United States leadership is the relative productivity growth rates of the nine nations between 1973 and 1986. As shown in Table 10-1, the United States ranks dead last in productivity improvement during this time interval. Table 10-2a shows the shift in the rankings between 1870 and 1986 using the United Kingdom as the standard. The British fell from first to ninth place because of their dismal productivity growth. Table 10-2b shows what shift would occur if the 1973–86 growth trends were to continue until 2006. The potential results are ironically similar—so is the cause. International competitors are copying American ideas, improving them, manufacturing them rapidly at low cost and high quality, and beating us in the marketplace.[13] Grayson and O'Dell attribute this productivity slowdown to five underlying causes:

1. The United States had very little international competition from 1946 through the 1960s. We enjoyed what Lester Thurow termed an "effortless superiority."
2. A complacency was spawned by affluence. A desire for "the good life" continued to grow, but the willingness to make sacrifices for it diminished.
3. Government programs and policies in the 1960s and 1970s gave higher priority to equity and social justice than to productivity and efficiency.
4. Both government and business neglected the "human dimension." Government underinvested in education; business viewed its work force as a production variable, not a partner in the planning process.
5. Both the economy and the population are aging. The daring, vitality, and goal orientation of youth are being replaced by a desire for security and the status quo.[14]

[12]Ibid., p. 54.
[13]Ibid., p. 256.
[14]Ibid., pp. 69–75.

TABLE 10-2 Relative Levels of Productivity

10-2a	1870	United Kingdom = 100	1986
UNITED KINGDOM	100	United States	142
Belgium	93	Canada	135
Netherlands	93	Netherlands	123
United States	88	France	120
Canada	76	Italy	118
Italy	55	Belgium	116
Germany	54	Germany	115
France	53	Norway	114
Norway	50	UNITED KINGDOM	100
Japan	21	Japan	98

10-2b	1986	United States = 100	2006*
UNITED STATES	100	France	118
Canada	95	Norway	117
Netherlands	86	Germany	113
France	84	Belgium	109
Italy	83	Canada	109
Belgium	81	Japan	108
Germany	81	Italy	103
Norway	80	UNITED STATES	100
United Kingdom	70	Netherlands	90
Japan	69	United Kingdom	86

*if 1973–86 productivity growth trends continue

Source: C. Jackson Grayson, Jr. and Carla O'Dell, American Business: A Two-Minute Warning, (New York: The Free Press, 1988), p. 86.

It must be emphasized that the productivity trends do not constitute a prediction. In fact, one can already find indications that there will be some significant improvements in American productivity levels during the 1990s. We will return to this encouraging point shortly.

The Relationship of Innovation to Productivity

If we interpret innovation narrowly to mean only *the creation of new things,* then its relationship to productivity is weak. However, innovation should also denote *new and better ways* of doing what has been done before. Besides the creation of new products, innovation also involves designing products that can be produced more efficiently, devising methods to improve the overall manufacturing process, and even increasing the effectiveness of the marketing and distribution functions.

When viewed from this perspective, innovation can be seen as not only an element of productivity but also a significant contributing cause.

The Relationship of Innovation to Competitiveness

A direct relationship seems evident, whether we view innovation as the creation of new products or as an improved method of producing and delivering current products to customers. If a new product gives increased satisfaction to some target market (although many do not), the producer should be in a stronger competitive position. In the same vein, if two firms supply similar products, the one with a more consistent and higher quality, a lower cost, and a more dependable delivery cycle should end up with the lion's share of the market.

The electronics industry, and the semiconductor segment in particular, serves as an excellent example of both issues. We will use this industry as our analytical framework. At first sight, this may appear to be a very limited perspective, but a closer view should reveal how broad-based it really is.

THE IMPACT OF TECHNOLOGY

The Vacuum Tube

The American electronics industry stemmed from two American inventions—De Forest's triode vacuum tube and the Hazeltine feedback amplifier circuit. The combination of these two technologies paved the way for several major industries: radio broadcasting, wireless telegraphy, and long-distance telephone service. In turn, these industries spawned a host of other component and end-product industries. Edison's phonograph was dramatically improved, the initial research began in video transmission, and the fledgling aircraft industry had the electronic tools necessary to make commercial flight safe and profitable. In the 1940s, vacuum tubes became the primary components of the first computers.

Vacuum tubes had several inherent shortcomings. They generated heat, which had a negative effect on their reliability, and their power requirements put an excessive drain on batteries. Moreover, their size affected the bulk and weight of the end products. All three factors had a negative affect on portable and airborne applications.

The Microelectronic Revolution

In the 25-year span between 1948 and 1973, the electronics industry was changed dramatically by three more American inventions: the transistor, the integrated circuit, and large-scale integration.

The Transistor.   Scientists at Bell Telephone Labs announced their major invention in 1948. Because these miniscule devices simultaneously solved the problems of limited reliability, excess size, and power drain, transistors rapidly supplanted vacuum tubes in a multitude of portable and airborne applications. Moreover, they paved the way for a broad spectrum of new end products that could capitalize on their form and function.

A Redistribution of Market Power.   When BTL announced the transistor, three firms—RCA, GE, and Sylvania—held a combined seventy percent of the $500 million vacuum tube market. Their reaction to the transistor was mixed.

RCA was the leading producer of radio receivers and transmitting equipment as well as the owner of the National Broadcasting Company (NBC). General Electric was also a major producer of radio equipment and a myriad of other electrical products. Sylvania, which began as a light bulb producer competing with GE, diversified into vacuum tubes and then purchased a radio manufacturer to give it a toehold in the equipment market. Thus, while the transistor represented exciting opportunities for Sylvania's equipment divisions, it also posed a very serious threat to the company's tube business. Consequently, when BTL offered licenses in 1953 to any interested firm for $25,000, the three tube companies responded, but mounted only cursory developmental efforts in this new technology.

Three other firms took a far more enthusiastic and aggressive position. Texas Instruments, only a $19 million firm in 1953, saw the opportunity for tremendous growth. Motorola, heavily involved in consumer radios and two-way communication equipment, wanted to diversify into the component market, supported by the guaranteed volume of their own sizeable in-house requirements. Raytheon, a leading producer of airborne equipment and hearing aids, saw transistor technology as a means of improving its equipment performance. These three firms, plus Fairchild Camera and Instrument, were the leading semiconductor producers in 1960. It should be noted that Sony, despite strong resistance from the Japanese government, also bought a BTL license in 1953.

The Integrated Circuit.   Two scientists, Jack Kilby at TI and Robert Noyce at Fairchild, working independently but concurrently, developed a means of incorporating a number of transistors, diodes, resistors, and capacitors within a single chip of silicon. In effect, an entire circuit was contained in this chip (hence the name integrated circuit).

Kilby's breakthrough was announced first, but Noyce developed an improved "planar" process and applied for a patent within five months of TI's 1960 application. After TI had filed a lawsuit, the courts decided that Kilby and Noyce should be considered to be co-inventors, and that any firm desiring to produce these new devices would require licenses from both TI and Fairchild. Nippon Electric (NEC), Hitachi, and Sony were among a number of Japanese firms that applied for licenses.

This new device transformed circuits into simple components. Engineers who had previously spent their time designing circuits could now work at the system level. This fact alone increased engineering productivity, but integrated circuits (ICs) had an even greater impact on small companies with limited R&D budgets. As ICs continued to grow in complexity (that is, as more functional circuitry was added to one chip) and to decrease in cost, it became easier for these small firms to jump into a product market by simply buying the proper ICs and/or copying a competitor's electronic hardware. This also meant that remaining competitive in any market would require the constant updating of a product's electronic content.

Large-scale Integration.   Noyce and several other key executives at Fairchild left to form a new firm, Intel, with the intention of concentrating on complex ICs. They quickly developed several memory ICs with a capacity of 1K (more precisely, 1024 bytes, or characters). While working under contract to a group of Japanese calculator firms who wanted a family of custom ICs, Intel designers found that they could not meet the prescribed space limitations with individual chips. They decided to put all the functions on one chip of silicon. Their successful outcome was a microprocessor, sometimes called a "computer on a chip." The Japanese firms were skeptical about the device and gave Intel the right to market what eventually became the 8080—the heart of the first microcomputers and an industry standard.

With the microprocessor and the early memory chips, Intel essentially created a breakthrough in large-scale integration. During the 1970s and early 1980s, Intel and a few other IC manufacturers managed to quadruple the capacity of memory chips every few years (4K, 16K, 64K, 256K, and 1 Meg). By 1988, development work had started on a 4 Meg (4,000,000 byte) chip. Several Japanese producers played major roles in this sequential development process.

Further Change in Market Power.   In 1970, ICs comprised only fifteen percent ($300 million) of a worldwide two-billion-dollar semiconductor market. Discrete devices (transistors, diodes, and so on) constituted the balance. By 1980, the semiconductor market grew to thirteen billion dollars, with ICs comprising seventy percent. Once again, the market power base had changed. Texas Instruments and Motorola were the leading producers. Intel joined the leadership ranks, but Fairchild and Raytheon slipped badly. Asian and European manufacturers held about one-third of the market.

During the 1980s, even more dramatic shifts occurred. By 1988, the worldwide semiconductor market grew to $45 billion. Moreover, Japanese producers captured fifty percent of the market for the first time, while American producers dropped from sixty-five to approximately forty-five percent. Japanese firms (NEC, Toshiba, Hitachi) occupied the top three positions, the leading American firms (Motorola, TI, Intel) were in the next three slots, followed by three more Japanese firms plus a Dutch/American conglomerate (Phillips/Signetics). The development work of the Japanese in large-scale integration paid off handsomely as the microcomputer market mushroomed and the demand for ever-larger memory chips seemed insatiable.

Foreseeing Some Trends, Missing Others

In a special 1980 issue entitled "The Reindustrialization of America," *Business Week* observed

> Barring some spectacular breakthrough, the most significant driving forces in high technology for the balance of this decade will be continuations of two current trends in electronics. First is the steep decline in the price of computing power. Second, and linked to the first, is the spread of the microprocessor into an ever-widening array of products. . . .
>
> Microelectronics will be the keystone technology not only because it is the world's fastest-growing industry. Even more potent than its sheer dollar volume is its pervasiveness. There will be few markets where "dumb" products can long compete against more sophisticated, computerized units. . . .
>
> [In addition, with] computer-aided design (CAD) and computer-aided manufacturing (CAM), it will be progressively less expensive for companies to . . . not only turn out new product designs much faster, but also . . . to make sure that the designs provide quality and reliability as well as the lowest possible manufacturing costs.[15]

Business Week's predictions proved to be quite accurate. Semiconductors, particularly microprocessors and memory chips, have indeed permeated virtually every segment of the electrical and electronic industries. In addition, a wide variety of previously mechanical ("dumb") products have been converted to electronics, everything from hand held "pinball" machines to automated process-control systems. Table 10-3 provides a partial indication of microelectronic pervasiveness.

THE DIFFUSION OF INNOVATION

Three key factors triggered this dramatic change in market composition. First, as *Business Week* correctly foresaw, microelectronic "building blocks" have made the production of even complex electronic systems rather simple. And as stated earlier, a firm with limited technological expertise and a minimal development budget, but armed with the right components, can become an instant competitor.

Second, with the addition of computer technology and creative personnel, aggressive competitors can improve the design of the innovator's product or devise a method to produce it more consistently and economically. Japanese firms have been particularly adept in this area of innovation. For example, Sharp Electronics devotes a significant amount of R&D activities to automated design (CAD) and manufacturing (CAM) technologies. It's results are recognized worldwide as models for low-cost design and high-volume production efficiency.[16] In the same vein, Sony made

---

[15]"Technology Gives the U.S. a Big Edge," *Business Week* (June 30, 1980), pp. 102–106.

[16]William J. Spencer and Deborah D. Triant, "Strengthening the Link Between R&D and Corporate Strategy," *The Journal of Business Strategy* (January–February 1989), pp. 38–42.

TABLE 10-3 Some Common Microelectronic Applications

Generic Category	Specific Examples
Automotive controls	dashboard information, comfort controls, engine controls (fuel, ignition, exhaust), brake system, diagnostic systems
Banking	automatic cash tellers, electronic fund transfers, credit card systems, check readers
Computers	magnetic disc and drum controls, memories, central processors, intelligent terminals, optical and laser readers, multiplexors
Consumer entertainment	radios, TV sets, video and audio recorders, still and movie cameras, video games, TV satellite dishes
Design and engineering	computer-aided design (CAD), computer-aided engineering (CAE)
Domestic controls	washers, dryers, sewing machines, microwave and convection ovens, blenders, thermostats, alarm systems, light dimmers
Manufacturing	measuring and test equipment, process monitoring and control, robotics, machine tool controls, computer-aided manufacturing (CAM)
Medical systems	body scanners, heart pacemakers, diagnostic and patient monitoring systems, electronic aids for speech, sight, and hearing impairment
Office productivity	data and word processing, electronic files, dictation equipment, electronic mail, copiers, printers, retrieval systems
Personal activities	computers, watches, calculators, copiers
Telecommunications	data and voice transmission, mobile and portable phones, telephone system exchanges, facsimile equipment, paging and answering devices

a commercial success of the audiotape and videotape recorder technologies that Ampex originated. Table 10-4 lists some of the more significant products that were invented in the United States and later copied by foreign manufacturers. Not only have American producers lost worldwide market share, they are losing their domestic markets as well (shades of Italian producers and imports of 18th century Dutch textiles!). Ironically, the 1980 *Business Week* article mentioned earlier was entitled "Technology Gives the U.S. a Big Edge."

Third, firms that intend to be major players in the broad-based electronics market of the twenty-first century are developing vertically integrated technological capabilities. In other words, they already are, or are taking steps to become, self-sufficient in the component, end-product, production equipment, and control sys-

TABLE 10-4 Import Penetration Into U.S. Product Markets

Products	1987 Mkt $ Mill	Import Share of U.S. Market			
		1970	1975	1980	1987
U.S.-INVENTED TECHNOLOGIES					
Computers	$53,500	1%	3%	4%	26%
Semiconductors	$19,100	11%	29%	35%	36%
Color TV	$14,050	10%	20%	40%	90%
Videotape recorders	$2,895	90%	90%	99%	99%
Telephones	$2,000	1%	5%	12%	75%
Phonographs	$630	10%	60%	70%	99%
Audiotape recorders	$500	60%	90%	90%	100%
Machine tool controls	$485	1%	3%	21%	65%
OTHER BASIC U.S. INDUSTRIES					
Motor vehicles & parts	$278,975	17%	19%	21%	28%
Apparel	$57,350	5%	8%	14%	32%
Footwear	$11,000	15%	21%	37%	62%
Farm machinery	$10,745	8%	11%	15%	20%

Source: For U.S.-invented technologies: "Back to Basics," Business Week, June 16, 1989, p. 17. Data: Commerce Department.
For other industry data: U.S. International Trade Administration, Industrial Outlook, annual issues.

tem technologies necessary to ensure "world class" costs and quality. These firms, which exist in every industrialized country, include Siemens of West Germany, Philips of Holland, Olivetti of Italy, Thomson-CSF of France, Northern Telecom of Canada, and a host of Japanese firms—Fujitsu, Hitachi, Mitsubishi, Matsushita, NEC, Sharp, Sony, and Toshiba.

Technology Can Help to Alter the Trends

Elements of this same microelectronic revolution can play a significant role in altering some of the current trends, particularly the declining market shares of American producers. Ford Motor Company provides an excellent example.

Ford decided in 1982 that quality improvement was only one of their challenges—their product lines also needed a major redesign to give them greater physical appeal. The Taurus and Probe were to be the symbols of corporate resurgence. When the Taurus was introduced in 1985, Ford's share of the U.S. new car market was only 18.8%. By the first quarter of 1989, that share widened to 23.4%, the company's strongest showing since 1978.

To meet this greater demand, output of cars and trucks from North American plants had to be increased by more than 700,000 units. But after seeing their volume plunge by forty-nine percent between 1978 and 1982, Ford was very reluctant to build new factories. However, one relatively small plant was built in Mexico with a

73,000-car capacity. Second shifts were added in two other plants, increasing their output by about 140,000. The remainder of the added output, more than 500,000 vehicles, resulted from increased production efficiency in existing plants.[17] In 1988 alone, Ford reduced manufacturing costs by $1.2 billion, thus becoming the nation's most profitable auto producer.

During this same time period, IBM stopped buying printers for their personal computers from Seiko Epson Corp. Originally, IBM felt that they could not improve on Epson's costs, which stemmed, in part, from an assembly time of only thirty minutes. Yet in 1985, IBM launched its Proprinter line from an automated Kentucky factory that can produce almost 500,000 printers a year, with an assembly time of only 3 minutes.[18]

Texas Instruments did equally well with an infrared gun sight supplied to the Pentagon. Assembly time was reduced eighty-five percent, the number of parts seventy-five percent, and the number of assembly steps seventy-eight percent.[19]

NCR Corporation designed an electronic cash register that snaps together without nuts, bolts, or rivets. An NCR manufacturing engineer performed this task in less than two minutes—blindfolded.[20]

Design for Manufacturability and Assembly (DFMA). All of these examples have one thing in common: Manufacturers utilized relatively inexpensive computer software programs developed by Boothroyd Dewhurst Inc., a small New England firm founded by two British professors who emigrated to the United States after their ideas were ignored by British industry.

Boothroyd emphasized the basic concept that design decisions can have significant economic implications. Although design itself may be a minor factor in the total cost of a product, the design process determines between seventy and ninety-five percent of all costs. Moreover, changing a design after it reaches the production line costs ten times as much as catching it on the drawing board—and one hundred times as much if the change is made in the middle of the production cycle. The National Science Foundation began supporting Boothroyd's research in 1977. Industrial firms began adding their support in 1978, led by AMP, Inc., and soon joined by Digital Equipment, GE, Westinghouse, Xerox, IBM, TI, and Ford.[21]

Necessary Changes in Research Methods and Goals

While technology can provide significant opportunities for innovation and increased productivity, additional changes are required before American producers can take full advantage of these opportunities.

[17]"How to Teach Old Plants New Tricks," *Business Week* (June 16, 1989), p. 130.

[18]"Pssst! Want a Secret for Making Superproducts?" *Business Week* (October 2, 1989), pp. 106, 110.

[19]Ibid.

[20]Ibid.

[21]Ibid. See also "Smart Factories: America's Turn?" *Business Week* (May 8, 1989), pp. 142–45, 148.

A Series of Small Steps.   Researchers in many American industries have traditionally concentrated on "major breakthroughs." They have sought to create technologies and products that represent a quantum leap beyond that which exists. According to the research director of NEC Corporation, Japanese innovation "is the result of tiny improvements in a thousand places." A Japanese applied chemist adds, "Real industrial innovation . . . spans the search for new materials, process technology, successful manufacturing schemes, and successful marketing." As a result, American homes are filled with Japanese consumer electronic products that are the result of continuous improvements in cost and performance.[22] As discussed earlier, American breakthrough inventions created many of these markets; the Japanese style of innovation eventually captured them.

Research as a Team Effort.   Virtually all studies of new product successes and failures have found that early interaction of R&D, engineering, manufacturing, and marketing personnel is essential to success.[23] Innovative firms assemble teams that bring these diverse disciplines together in the earliest stages of a project. However, the team concept does not fit well into traditional companies organized by function. These firms still cling to the "bucket brigade" approach. Research develops an idea that is passed on to engineering for design. Manufacturing gets a list of specifications, with no prior discussion, and tries to figure out the best way to make the thing. Marketing is eventually given the responsibility for finding customers for something that nobody wants.[24]

R&D Linked to Corporate Strategy.   R&D and corporate strategy should benefit from a natural synergy: (1) both involve extended time horizons; (2) each is mutually concerned with maintaining long-term corporate strengths; and (3) both provide future business opportunities. Despite these commonalities, there often exists a wide chasm between the two functions. This problem can usually be alleviated by opening regular lines of communication. Corporate planners gain a better understanding of technology and its impact while R&D adds a stronger and more perceptive marketing orientation to its efforts.[25]

PRODUCT DEVELOPMENT STRATEGY

New product development strategy begins with an unsatisfied need. As Peter Drucker has pointed out, most successful new products are geared toward some specific application, some known need. Thus, "the innovation that creates new us-

---

[22]"Nurturing Those Ideas," *Business Week* (June 16, 1989), pp. 106–7.

[23]See David A. Boag and Brenda L. Rinholm, "New Product Management Practices of Small High-Technology Firms," *Journal of Product Innovation Management* 6 (1989), pp. 109–122; also Cooper, "Predevelopment Activities . . .", p. 239; and Peter L. Link, "Keys to New Product Success and Failure," *Industrial Marketing Management* 16 (1987), pp. 109–118.

[24]"Nurturing Those Ideas," p. 107.

[25]Spencer and Triant, "Strengthening the Link . . .", p. 41.

ers and new markets should be directed toward a specific, clear, and carefully designed application.[26] The marketing department must provide this direction.

The New Product Development Process

As a product evolves from an idea to a commercial reality, it passes through a series
of stages. In total, these stages comprise the "new product development process."
This process involves three questions that must be considered in sequence: (1) Is
there a market for the idea? (2) Can the idea be transformed into a physical product?
and (3) Can the physical product be manufactured and marketed profitably?[27]

Each of these questions gives rise to a set of criteria that must be weighed to
arrive at a final decision. The first question involves market criteria, the second,
product or technology criteria, and the third, financial criteria. Table 10-5, though
not intended as an all-inclusive list, indicates the type and range of these criteria.

Marketing Implications.   Several important points arise as a result of these questions and the resulting criteria. As suggested before, product development should
center on customer needs. If a customer is the source of the product idea, the first
question has been answered. If the idea stemmed from in-house technical efforts,
market research must take place as early as possible in the development process.[28]

TABLE 10-5 Product Evaluation Criteria

A. Market criteria
1. Present size
2. Growth potential
3. Current or new customers
4. Amount of competition
5. Strength of competition
6. Price consciousness
7. Technical service required
8. Present channels suitable
9. Variety of end-uses known
10. Impact on present products

B. Product/technology criteria
1. Degree of innovation
2. Differential advantages
3. Lead time over competition
4. Patentable product/process
5. Estimated product life
6. Amount of research know-how
7. Experience with technology
8. Technical feasibility
9. Competing technologies
10. Other resources needed

C. Financial criteria
1. Initial investment
2. Expected sales revenue
3. Profit-to-sales ratio
4. Estimated ROI
5. Manufacturer's cost-to-price ratio
6. Expected cash flow
7. Payback period
8. Net gain/loss on other products

[26]Peter E. Drucker, "The Discipline of Innovation," *Harvard Business Review* 63 (May–June
1985), pp. 67–72.

[27]Ilkka A. Ronkainen, "Criteria Changes Across Product Development Stages," *Industrial Marketing Management* 14 (August 1985), pp. 171–178.

[28]Cooper, "Predevelopment Activities," p. 239.

Various studies yield similar but differing lists of reasons for new product failures. But, as Crawford suggests, virtually all of these reasons fall into three broad categories: (1) no real need for the product exists, (2) the product fails to meet the need adequately or has offsetting deficiencies, and (3) some significant aspect of the marketing strategy is mishandled or flawed.[29]

These reasons for product failure clearly imply that it is necessary to have a complete and objective definition of customer needs. Industrial firms are often tempted to limit the need definition to the anticipated capability of the final product; that is, "If we can't make it, they don't need it!"

A third implication is that the dominant criteria will change throughout the new product development process. Although some will quarrel with the sequence of the criteria established by the questions, particularly the trailing position of financial criteria, unless a firm identifies an attractive market whose needs can be adequately satisfied, financial analysis becomes a fruitless exercise.

ORGANIZING FOR EFFECTIVE PRODUCT DEVELOPMENT

A firm has a choice of organizational structures. Each choice presents certain strengths and limitations, and the type best suited for a given firm will depend upon the firm's size, resources, and degree of innovativeness. Before selecting any option, however, the firm should ponder several issues that will have an impact on the R&D process.

An Atmosphere that Encourages Risk-Taking and Innovation

Many business organizations are risk-averse. To such firms, innovation means change, and change means unnecessary risk. Their product development activity is likely to be, at most, a defensive response to the innovations of more aggressive competitors. They fail to recognize, or refuse to accept, that change externally induced by competition can be more harmful than internally-generated change.

Even firms that are willing to accept the potential risks of innovation may unwittingly create an environment hostile to such innovation. For example, undue emphasis on short-term profits often restricts projects that do not promise fast results. Employees get the message that "status-quo" thinking is rewarded. Such an attitude not only limits innovation but jeopardizes long-term profits.

A 1988 study of 897 American companies in forty industry groups sought to determine whether any correlation existed between company performance—measured by profit margins, return on assets, and productivity per employee—and the level of R&D spending per employee. To approximate the real-world lag, company perform-

---

[29]C. Merle Crawford, "New Product Failure Rates—Facts and Fallacies," *Research Management* (September 1979), pp. 9–13.

ance in 1987 was measured against average R&D spending from 1983 through 1986. No significant correlation was found between R&D spending and return on assets, but the correlation with productivity was well beyond 99.9 percent, and the correlation with profit margins was in excess of 99.5 percent.[30]

It must be noted that practical comparisons between companies in different industries cannot be made. Firms in industries with evolving technologies, for example, will normally spend more for R&D than those in old-line businesses. It should also be noted that some researchers question whether R&D is a leading indicator of sales and profits or vice versa; that is, whether firms spend more as a result of growing profits. The analyst who conducted the referenced survey feels quite certain that R&D spending, particularly in high-tech industries, is the driving force for sales and profits, not the beneficiary.

Every Product Should Have a Champion

The term "product champion" (or its equivalent) appears with increasing frequency in business literature and is a concept to which business practitioners are affording greater weight. Some see this champion as a company-oriented manager who inspires subordinates to find better ways of doing things.[31] Others describe a champion in somewhat begrudging terms as

> . . . the zealot or fanatic in the ranks . . . not a typical administrative type . . . apt to be a loner, egotistical and cranky. But he *believes* in the specific product he has in mind.[32]

Theodore Levitt sees the champion in the context of creativity and innovation, which functions he feels are often confused.

> Creativity is thinking up new things. Innovation is doing new things. . . . Ideas are useless unless used. . . . there is no shortage of creativity or creative people in American business. The shortage is of innovators. . . . Creative people tend to pass the responsibility for getting down to brass tacks to others. . . . The scarce people are the ones who have the know-how, energy, daring, and staying power to implement ideas. . . . Creativity without action-oriented follow-through is a barren form of behavior.[33]

As part of their comparison of a dozen major American and Japanese firms, Peters and Waterman analyzed twenty-four major busines innovations, such as GE's un-

---

[30]"R&D in 1988," *Business Week* (June 16, 1989), pp. 178-9.

[31]Grayson and O'Dell, *American Business,* p. 239.

[32]Thomas J. Peters and Robert H. Waterman, Jr., *In Search of Excellence: Lessons from America's Best-Run Companies* (New York: Harper and Row, 1982), p. 208.

[33]Theodore Leavitt, "Ideas are Useless Unless Used," *Inc* (February 1981), p. 96, as cited by Peters and Waterman.

TABLE 10-6 The Impact of a Product Champion on Development Success

	Project Successes			*Project Failures*		
	Championed	*No Champion*	*Total*	*Championed*	*No Champion*	*Total*
United States	8	1	9	2	3	5
Japan	6	0	6	1	3	4
Total	14	1	15	3	6	9

Source: Adapted from Thomas J. Peters and Robert H. Waterman, Jr., In Search of Excellence, (New York: Warner Books, 1984), p. 204.

successful venture into computers and its success in engineered plastics such as Lexan. As Table 10-6 indicates, fifteen of the innovations were successful, and fourteen of these had champions. Of the nine failures, only three were championed. It is interesting to note that, despite the frequently cited collectivist approach in Japan, the American and Japanese results are quite similar.[34]

Centralized Versus Decentralized R&D

Firms can either centralize or decentralize their R&D activity. As Figure 10-2 depicts, a functional compromise is often made. Theoretical or basic research is conducted at the corporate level, with the results distributed to all operating divisions; applied product research is carried out in the appropriate product divisions. Some firms even use separate terminology, referring to centralized R&D and decentralized product development or product engineering.

This centralization of basic research has several advantages. First, research scientists are freed from the time constraints and pressures of a line operation, and are thus provided with an atmosphere more conducive to creative effort. Second, it brings all basic research into a centralized location, making it more visible to all operating divisions while encouraging synergistic exchange of ideas. Third, it allows operating divisions to pick up any new technology that will enhance their business. Scientists are notorious for holding off on the application of theoretical research because "it isn't perfected yet."

Centralization of basic research, however, can have a major drawback. As discussed earlier, R&D must be more closely aligned with the strategic direction of the firm. Unless provided with at least broad guidelines, research scientists could spend too much of their efforts in technologies that are not readily applicable to

[34]Peters and Waterman, *In Search of Excellence,* p. 204.

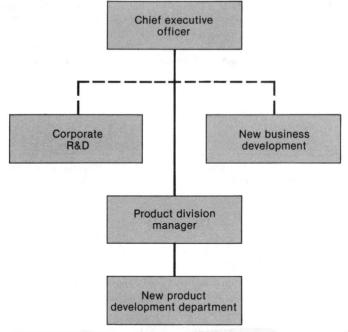

FIGURE 10-2   Product Development Centers

the firm's strategic thrust.[35] To counteract this possibility, top management should provide scientists with the necessary commercial guidance and review their research activities on a regular basis (either quarterly or semiannually). This review process will also enhance communication by providing management with a better understanding of technology and giving R&D a stronger market orientation.[36]

New Business Development Department.   As we have already established, innovation is not always technical. A firm might be interested in finding business opportunities with no direct relation to its current products, but which can provide desirable, synergistic effects (as when General Motors bought Electronic Data Systems in order to gain greater expertise in computer-aided design and manufacturing). Since product divisions normally lack the interest and expertise to search for such opportunities, management establishes a staff department to perform this task (see Figure 10-2 again). This department would probably also coordinate any mergers or acquisitions.

[35]Spencer and Triant, "Strengthening the Link . . .", p. 41.
[36]Ibid.

ORGANIZATIONAL ALTERNATIVES FOR NEW PRODUCT DEVELOPMENT

New Product Committee

When a company does relatively little innovating, it would derive insufficient benefit from a full-time new product operation. In such cases, new product ideas that originate anywhere in the organization are examined, evaluated, funded for development, or cancelled, by a committee. This group is usually established by top management and includes managers from engineering, manufacturing, marketing, and finance. This committee meets at whatever interval is appropriate to handle the workload (usually monthly). The primary strengths of a committee are: (1) members view each other as experienced equals and work fairly well toward a balanced, consensus opinion; (2) bureaucratic delay is minimized since the members usually report directly to top management; and (3) additional members can be added and then dismissed as needed, keeping the overall committee at an effective size.

On the negative side, committee members are not development specialists, and tend to view development as secondary to their daily operating problems and decisions. Given this attitude, they may indeed reach a consensus decision, but one of questionable strategic value. Further, with corporate managers sitting in at irregular intervals, none of the committee members is likely to take a strong leadership position. There is no product champion.

Task Force

The task force is similar to a new products committee in that its members come from the various departments and serve on a part-time basis. For that reason, the task force leader must struggle for the time and commitment of members and overcome the loyalty they feel to their departments.

The task force is different than the committee in that it deals with only one development project. Thus, if there is more than one project at any time, there will be multiple task forces.

Task forces can be very effective or ineffective. In their search for excellent companies, Peters and Waterman found that the most effective task forces had a number of common characteristics:

1. Membership limited to ten or less; all necessary participants included, but bureaucratic stagnation minimized.
2. Reporting level and seniority of task force members proportional to the importance of the project.
3. The group's tenure rarely lasted beyond six months.
4. Voluntary membership; results usually stem from people who feel strongly about the problem.

5. No "staff" assigned; paperwork kept informal and minimal.
6. Management expects at least preliminary results within three months.[37]

A task force with these characteristics is more likely to provide a tight link with corporate strategy and create an atmosphere conducive to innovative action.

New Product Development Department

A firm continually engaged in technological innovation will often establish a new product development department and delegate its manager substantial authority to oversee the complete development function from idea generation to commercialization. This department will have its own engineering and cost accounting operations, at least a pilot line production capacity, and often a specialized marketing function. The manager also has the authority to call upon whatever additional talents that may be required to bring a product to market. Eventually, the product is turned over to some other line operation for full-scale production.

   The new product development department can devote all its efforts to the development of one or two products at a time, while also accumulating considerable expertise. However, there is one potential flaw that can be critical. Unless the department continues with the product at least into pilot production and through the final commercialization stage, it can lose touch with the realities of the marketplace. Consequently, products may begin to lose their customer orientation: benefits may be compromised for increased short-term profits. In short, the entire development process may become inward-looking and self-serving. Constant and open communication with other functional areas, particularly the sales department, is necessary if this problem is to be avoided.

Product Manager

Whether a company leans toward the permanence and expertise of a new product department or the flexibility and spirit of a task force, somehow it must interweave the needs of the market with its technological capabilities and financial resources. As we discussed before, the developing product needs a champion. Although the new product department has a manager, this individual is usually too burdened with organizational responsibilities to act with the freedom and initiative of a champion. And the task force, by virtue of its ad hoc nature, has no natural leader.

   Some firms attempt to "create" a champion. They seek out someone who has technical competence, market knowledge, strong interpersonal skills, and a goal-oriented nature. These skills and traits define a well-qualified product manager. Product managers can be selected from any functional area, but come most frequently from marketing.

   Some companies, particularly in high-tech industries, fear that a marketing

---

[37]Peters and Waterman, *In Search of Excellence,* pp. 129–30.

person will either lack the technical competence to make realistic product evaluations, or be too "customer oriented" to make unbiased business decisions. An engineer with some market experience, such as an application engineer, is the most frequently chosen alternative. Research personnel are usually considered too far removed from the business activities to be effective in this position, while manufacturing personnel often lack both in-depth technical knowledge and marketing experience.

These trade-off considerations only serve to emphasize the range of skills and experience necessary to enable someone to function effectively as an industrial product manager. Regardless of their background specialization, it is imperative that product managers function with an objective, broad-based perspective. An "ideal" candidate often has a technical undergraduate degree, an MBA, and several years' experience selling and/or designing similar products.

Product Managers Versus New Product Development Managers. A lively debate continues as to whether product managers should have responsibility for ongoing products as well as new product development. Compelling arguments can be constructed for and against a combined responsibility. These arguments parallel the strengths and weaknesses of product committees and separate product development departments. Product committees, though aware of current market conditions, suffer because members are often distracted by other responsibilities. New product departments, conversely, have no distractions but can lose touch with market dynamics because of their isolation from customers and competition.

Personal experience and observation leads us to believe that the most effective product manager is one who can devote sufficient time to the development process, but whose decisions are based on firsthand knowledge of current market conditions. The critical issue is having an individual with sufficient experience, drive, and creativity, supported by an adequately-sized staff, to cope with the combined, but synergistic, responsibility. And even these conditions are inadequate without the full and active support of a top management that is sensitive to the organizational dynamics of new product development.[38]

The Venture Team

This form of development organization, which evolved during the 1960s, is the most autonomous of all those discussed. It is also the most expensive. Like the task force, its members are drawn from various disciplines within the company. Unlike the task force, the members divorce themselves from their original duties and work full-time on the development project. A study of ninety-eight venture teams indicated some typical characteristics:

[38]Crawford, *New Products Management,* p. 481.

1. They are organizationally separated from the rest of the company.
2. Members are recruited from all relevant functional areas.
3. Existing lines of authority within the company may not apply to venture teams.
4. Team managers report to top management and have authority to make major decisions.
5. The team is free of deadlines and remains intact until the project is completed.
6. Freedom from time pressures fosters creativity and innovativeness.[39]

Venture teams usually exist in larger companies and work on major projects that are not readily assignable to any operating division. In this sense, they are similar to new business development units, although the latter entities usually concentrate on business aspects rather than the associated technology. At the completion of their projects, venture teams are often spun off into new operating departments or even separate subsidiaries.

The freedom and authority level of the venture team can trigger some serious interorganizational conflicts. To prevent such conflicts, top management must ensure that the resources allocated and attention given to the venture team and operating divisions are reasonably balanced. On the positive side, venture teams can develop technological opportunities of a magnitude unattainable through other organization forms.

An Overview of Organization Forms

All of the alternative organizations serve the same basic purposes: (1) to free general managers from direct involvement in the new product development process, (2) to bring together the multifaceted talents and inputs necessary for the success of the process, and (3) to separate the process, when possible and practical, from the pressures and distractions of ongoing business operations.

Given the complexity of this process and its potential impact on the growth and profitability of the firm, however, top management can neither delegate its ultimate decision making nor assume a disinterested "rubber stamp" posture regarding new product choices and strategy. This does not mean that senior officers should approve data sheets, price schedules, or advertising campaigns. It does mean that top management retains the responsibility to ensure that each new product strategy has a positive impact on corporate goals. For example, a skimming price strategy probably will not jibe with an objective of maximized sales growth. Similarly, each new product strategy should be compared with existing product strategies. This comparison is particularly critical when the firm is divided into autonomous product divisions, each with its own product development program.

---

[39]Richard M. Hill and James D. Hlavacek, "The Venture Team: A New Concept in Marketing Organization," *Journal of Marketing* 36 (July 1972), pp. 44–50.

THE NEW PRODUCT DEVELOPMENT PROCESS

Although authors differ in the titles they give the various stages, the fundamental concepts involved vary only slightly. Potential product ideas must be generated, screened by criteria of importance to the firm, and converted into physical products. While R&D is performing the physical conversion, marketing personnel test the product concept for market acceptance and gather data for the formal business plan. For our discussion of this interlocking process, we shall consider seven stages: (1) idea generation, (2) screening, (3) idea evaluation, (4) preliminary business analysis, (5) product development and testing, (6) formal business planning, and (7) commercialization.

It should be emphasized that many firms, particularly smaller ones, either have no formal development process or follow one that is at best haphazard. Given the substantial costs involved in product development and the even greater costs associated with market failures, this cavalier approach would appear both dangerous and foolhardy.

Research studies consistently show a strong correlation between the formalization and proficiency of the development process and subsequent product success.[40] The early stages are particularly critical. These include initial market research, idea screening, technical evaluation, and preliminary business analysis. The composite evidence forces two conclusions. First, successful firms spend more time and resources in these early stages. Second, the typical Japanese firm prepares much better than its American counterpart.[41]

Idea Generation

We do not devote space to the many and diversified methods of idea generation (such as brainstorming and attribute listing) since they are covered quite well in principles of marketing texts. Also, it has been our personal observation that most manufacturers of industrial products suffer not from a shortage of ideas but from the challenge of separating the good ideas from the bad. Instead, in this section we reemphasize two points introduced earlier. First, any initial product idea should be aimed at solving a specific problem or providing definitive customer benefits. Second, the idea should support and enhance the firm's overall strategic thrust.

So that the idea will support a strategic thrust, business objectives and marketing strategy must precede product development; that is, the firm must first decide what business it wants to be in and what quantitative goals it seeks to achieve. These goals determine the screening criteria to be used in evaluating product ideas. For example, in the 1960s Texas Instruments set several underlying criteria for all new

---

[40]See *New Product Management for the 1980s;* also Boag and Rinholm, "New Product Management Practices."

[41]Cooper, "Predevelopment Activities," p. 239.

semiconductor products. Each had to be capable of sustaining a fifteen percent compound growth rate over its life cycle while generating a twenty-five percent pre-tax return on assets. In addition, aside from those products aimed at duplicating competition, new products had to stem from unique design or fabrication techniques that would afford a differential cost and/or performance advantage. The growth criterion forced marketing personnel to search out the most promising business opportunities; the demand for differential advantage minimized "me-too" design efforts, while increasing the probability that products would be aimed at providing a measurable satisfaction level in specific applications; and the profitability criterion served as the cornerstone for financial analysis.

Idea Screening

The primary purpose of the screening stage is twofold: (1) to try to eliminate those ideas that are likely to fail (no market need, competition already better, investment level prohibitive) and recognize those with promising potential and (2) to optimize the remaining stages of the development process.

We say "try to eliminate and recognize potential failures and successes" because the market failure rate referenced earlier (25 to 30 percent) clearly indicates that losers get through the screening process. How many good ideas are dropped for lack of support at this stage is unknown, but the figure is influenced by the risk-taking attitude of the firm as well as the expertise and objectivity of those responsible for the screening.

It is important that the output of the screening stage (the number of ideas sent forward) be within the firm's ability to act. As we suggested previously, most firms are not limited by the input of product ideas; they are limited by resources (time, money, personnel) as to how many of these ideas can be developed into physical products and successfully commercialized.

Idea Evaluation

Ideas that pass the screening stage require further evaluation. Those with an internal origin must be checked for market need and volume potential. If the idea stemmed from a recognized market need or a specific customer request, the feasibility of creating a physical product must still be established. When product ideas satisfy both market and technical criteria, they should be rank-ordered. This ranking will vary with the firm's marketing strategy and business conditions. For example, priority may be given to strengthening the firm's market position, increasing sales volume, improving profits, diversifying the business portfolio, or simply broadening the product line.

Marketing/Engineering Agreement.   As suggested earlier, this evaluation stage is critical. Moreover, it involves bringing two separate elements into accord: customer satisfaction and technical feasibility. Crawford refers to this process as creating a *protocol* or basis of agreement.[42]

Two aspects of this agreement are particularly important. First, marketing should describe their requirements in terms of customer benefits or performance characteristics, not product features. In other words, they should describe the product in terms of what it does rather than what it is. In addition, these benefits are subdivided into three categories: essential, desirable, and trade-offs. Essential benefits cannot be compromised; they represent the product's primary advantage. Desirable benefits remain so only if they do not detract from the essentials. For example, miniaturization is desirable only if it does not detract from product reliability or ease of use. Trade-offs are benefits that impact each other negatively. Price and overall performance level are common trade-offs, and these must often be negotiated before the development process is completed.

The second important aspect of the agreement concerns the limits of marketing's inputs. These inputs should be based on specific knowledge of customer needs, competitors' capabilities, and general market conditions. In other words, marketing provides information that deals with its area of expertise. The description of the physical product should be limited to those features necessary for customer satisfaction or competitive positioning (indicating, for example, the product must weigh less than x pounds or be smaller than y cubic inches). Engineers should have the freedom to utilize technology in whatever fashion will optimize performance and profitability. The agreement is put in writing and tends to protect engineers from constant changes in performance goals, as well as giving marketing assurance that the eventual product will meet the original goals.

Preliminary Business Analysis

At this point in the process (which may be three to six months after an inital brainstorming session), the firm should have enough information about customers, competitors, volume potential, tentative pricing, technology, investment level, and estimated production cost to make a first-pass financial analysis. Financial criteria (see Table 10-5) are utilized to determine whether or not the product idea should become a physical entity.

The conversion of an idea into a physical product can represent a significant portion of the total development cost, particularly for firms that require an elaborate pilot facility to prove production feasibility. In these instances, the preliminary business analysis is of major consequence. Other firms, whose development costs are relatively insignificant, may choose to skip this stage entirely on the basis that most of the numbers come from conjecture, forecast, and guesswork. Some research, however, indicates that managers consider financial criteria the most important screening factors and are not likely to ignore them at this point.[43]

---

[42]Crawford, *New Products Management,* pp. 246–49.

[43]Robert G. Cooper and Ulrike de Brentani, "Criteria for Screening New Industrial Products," *Industrial Marketing Management* 13 (1984), pp. 149–156.

GUIDELINES FOR MARKETING NEW PRODUCTS IN THE PETROLEUM MARKET

"It appears that many of the individuals involved in the development of new high tech products have more of an engineering, as opposed to business, orientation. There seems to be more of an emphasis on 'technical push' rather than 'marketing pull' in the development of new high tech products. An unfortunate consequence of this situation is that more of a product orientation (i.e., 'Build a Better Mousetrap' concept) rather than a market need orientation is being followed. Too many new high tech products reach concept and prototype development without ever answering the question of what market need will it fulfill. Thus, several marketing guidelines or insights are suggested to facilitate new product development in the industrial market:

1. Will the new product provide benefits that will fulfill a need?
2. Has the market been analyzed to ascertain what product or products the proposed innovation would be competing with or attempting to replace?
3. Have potential product benefits been identified and analyzed with respect to advantages/ disadvantages or problems/opportunities inherent in the market that could be capitalized on?
4. Have environmental constraints such as EPA laws or regulations been considered, which may need altering to facilitate market acceptance?"

Source: Reprinted by permission of the publisher from "Guidelines for Marketing a New Industrial Product," George H. Lucas, Jr., and Alan J. Bush, *Industrial Marketing Management,* 13 (1984), pp. 152–161. Copyright © 1984 by Elsevier Science Publishing Co., Inc.

In either case, firms often face limited resources, forcing them to drop some otherwise promising projects. Combining the business analysis with other selection criteria provides the firm with a means of choosing the best projects for further development, while the other projects are either dropped or are put on indefinite hold.

The two preceding paragraphs are based on the assumption that product ideas are truly innovative. If, on the other hand, the ideas are merely revisions of earlier developments (the industrial version of "new and improved"), the financial data would be mostly factual and the decisions relatively simple.

Product Development and Testing

Several important events will occur during this stage. The R&D department will convert the product idea into a physical reality, proving technical feasibility; the manufacturing department, at least on a limited volume basis, will confirm or negate its ability to reproduce the product within the cost estimates and performance guidelines previously established; and the marketing department, once functional samples are available, will approach selected customers to verify that the product's attributes do indeed satisfy specific application requirements. It is also important to reaffirm the market potential that was estimated earlier. During an extended development process, such as one that consumes a year or more, significant changes can occur in manager and economic conditions, competitive capabilities, and customer priorities. A product idea that was very promising a year ago may be virtually obsolete today.

Designing to Cost Goals. Another aspect of the development stage is particularly important to marketers of industrial products. Given the pragmatic and profit-oriented nature of industrial buying decisions, price plays a major role. As opposed to consumer goods such as designer jeans or automobiles, industrial products afford little status or ego satisfaction to justify a higher price. Consequently, price should be as important a design criterion as product performance or quality. Many firms, however, allow price to be a random effect rather than a specific goal. Costs are allowed to drive selling price rather than a target selling price dictating a maximum acceptable cost. An example may help to clarify this point.

Suppose that the XYZ company is developing a computer-controlled, multi-head drill press capable of productivity and accuracy levels that are unobtainable with current equipment on the market. The firm has surveyed the market and found that customers are willing to pay approximately $5,000, a 20 percent premium over the price of conventional drill presses. XYZ can normally generate an acceptable profit by doubling its direct labor and material cost to establish an original equipment manufacturer (OEM) sales price.

The preferable approach in this instance would be to set a $2,500 labor and material cost goal along with essential performance criteria. Engineering and manufacturing personnel would know how much latitude was available to them from a cost standpoint to achieve the necessary performance. The approach used by many firms, however, stresses the performance criteria without establishing cost limits. Under these conditions, XYZ engineers might design an excellent product that meets or exceeds all essential specifications. Unfortunately, the cost ends up at $3,500, dictating an OEM price of $7,000. This price will significantly reduce market demand and potential profits, essentially negating the financial data generated in the preliminary business analysis. In other words, the information that indicated the project should move forward is no longer used. Now, instead of enjoying the fruits of their labor, the firm will expend wasted effort to determine "who was wrong."

Test Marketing. The test marketing of new industrial products centers on the evaluation of the product by major potential users. This means that sales people must identify these firms and then interact with individuals who make the buying decisions as well as the technical personnel who will actually evaluate the product. Given the oligopolistic nature of most industries, acceptance of a product by relatively few users can often assure its success. For example, if IBM, Apple, Compaq, and AT&T were all to approve the use of a new disk drive in their personal computers, the disk drive manufacturer would not have to worry about keeping the production line running. In fact, having sufficient capacity to satisfy the combined requirements of these firms might be a problem.

Acceptance of a new product by major users, as pointed out in Chapter Nine, is neither automatic nor a rapid process regardless of the product's merits. A new component, for example, may require redesign of the end equipment to make full use of the cost or performance advantage. The equipment manufacturer (OEM) may not have personnel immediately available to do the redesign work. The production manager may convince other decision makers that it would be unwise to disrupt the smooth-running production line, since potential cost savings could be offset by lower product quality or reduced yields (due to the impact of change on production workers). Even if the decision is reached to make the necessary changes on a limited quantity basis, final approval may rest on the results of field tests. In other words, test marketing of the component could hinge on test marketing of potential buyers' end equipment.

The foregoing comments do not mean to imply a gloomy prospect for new industrial products. On the contrary, if a product addresses an important need and satisfies it well, market acceptance will probably follow. The time delay, however, can easily stretch into months. Hence, the new product supplier may face an extended period during which productive capacity is in place but no sizable demand develops. Since some customers will have purchased limited quantities for evaluation purposes, the subsequent delay gives the impression of a market failure, that is, a very brief growth followed by decline. Actually, the growth phase of the product life cycle has not yet begun.

Formal Business Planning

Upon completion of product development and testing, the firm has determined both technical and production feasibility along with current market demand and time/volume projections. A formal business plan can now be established. This plan should include quantification of all relevant financial criteria to determine whether the physical product can be manufactured and marketed profitably.

Controlling Product Introduction. In addition to a financial plan, a marketing plan must be developed that spells out and coordinates all the tactical programs that lead up to the introduction of the new product. (Although major customers have already been approached and sampled during the market testing stage, the product has not yet been formally introduced to the overall target market.) Pricing must be established, an advertising program developed, the sales force trained, distributor inventories put in place, and so forth.

An example of a planning checklist for new product introduction is shown in Table 10-7. While this list is not complete and will vary appreciably with product, industry differences, and variations in company policies, it points out two important factors. First, there is a broad range of activities, extending beyond the marketing department, that must be coordinated. Second, the sequencing of activities, time

TABLE 10-7 New Product Introduction Planning Checklist

	Area/Person Responsible	Prior Task	Time Required (weeks)
Product (Manufacturing Dept.)			
M1. Order production equipment	Manufacturing, Purchasing	—	13
M2. Hire needed production workers	Manufacturing, Personnel	—	3
M3. Install production equipment	Manufacturing	M1	2
M4. Initiate pilot production run	Manufacturing	M2–3	2
M5. Determine specification yields	Manufacturing	M4	1
M6. Compute costs	Cost Accounting	M5	1
M7. Begin volume production	Manufacturing	M6, S4	1
Product (Engineering Dept.)			
E1. Analyze specification yields	Product Engineering	M5	2
E2. Complete evaluation tests	Quality Control	M5	5
E3. Finalize specifications (with Marketing Dept.)	Product Engineering Product Manager	E1–2	2
E4. Provide data sheet information	Product engineering	E3	1
Sales Force			
S1. Hire required sales people	Sales Manager	—	3
S2. Complete product training	Product Manager	S1, E4	2
S3. Contact major potential users to determine demand	Sales Force	S2, A6	3
S4. Prepare initial sales forecast	Sales Force	S3, P4	1
S5. Establish annual sales quotas	Sales Manager	S4	1
Advertising/Promotion			
A1. Establish total budget	Product Manager	—	2
A2. Complete space ad layouts	Advertising Manager	A1	4
A3. Select appropriate media	Product/Advertising Manager	A1	1
A4. Establish space ad scheduling	Product/Advertising Manager	A1	2
A5. Run initial ads	Advertising Manager	A2–4	1
A6. Prepare and print data sheets	Product/Advertising Manager	E4	3
A7. Prepare and mail direct mailers	Product/Advertising Manager	A6	2
Distribution			
D1. Compose distributor agreement	Marketing Manager	—	1
D2. Analyze need for distributors by market area	Sales/Product Manager	S3	3
D3. Select and sign distributors	Sales Manager	D1–2	2
D4. Obtain initial stocking orders	Sales Force	D3, P5	2
D5. Ship stocking orders	Manufacturing	D4, M4	1
D6. Train distributor personnel	Sales Force	D5	3
Pricing			
P1. Analyze production costs	Product Manager	M6	1
P2. Analyze competitors' prices	Product Manager	—	1
P3. Estimate demand elasticity	Product Manager	S3	1
P4. Establish OEM pricing	Product Manager	P1–3	1
P5. Establish distributor pricing	Product Manager	P4	1

CRITICAL PATH: A VITAL PLANNING TOOL FOR INTRODUCING NEW PRODUCTS

"The new product development process contains a number of steps from the inception of an idea through the actual introduction of the new product, first internally to the organization and ultimately externally to the chosen target markets. Errors at any of these stages are costly and debilitating to the organization. The closer to the 'completed end' of the process, however, the greater the risk as the firm has invested considerable time, dollars, and effort in the new product. Failure at the market introduction point is generally acknowledged to translate to heavy financial loss, tremendous man-hour loss, and possible design/concept loss to competition . . .

"The critical path method [CPM] is a planning tool that is suited for the announcement/introduction phase planning requirements of new industrial products . . .

"The critical path method has been applied to the development and marketing of new products of all types including automobiles and computer programs. Since the technique requires establishment of project objectives and specifications, it is advantageous to planning. It requires that the marketing manager clearly identify what is important and what must be accomplished."

Source: Reprinted by permission of the publisher from "Critical Path Method for Introducing an Industrial Product," Glenn R. Dundas and Kathleen A. Krentler, *Industrial Marketing Management,* 11 [1982], pp. 125–131. Copyright © 1982 by Elsevier Science Publishing Co., Inc.

requirements, and individual responsibilities must be established. Some firms refer to these checklists as "What, When, Who," or "W3" forms. Organizations use this information to create some type of control mechanism to track the introduction process through the sequence of activities and call attention to potential delay problems.

Critical Path Method (CPM). One of the most challenging tasks in new product introduction is coordinating the activities of multiple, independent departments and keeping these activities on schedule. For example, the sales force cannot be trained in the details of the new product until a data sheet has been developed by engineering, but the engineers will not establish specifications before they receive yield information from the production department. Pricing also depends upon this yield information, and without pricing, distributors will not place orders for their initial inventories.

As Figure 10-3 shows, CPM graphically displays the various sequences in-

FIGURE 10-3   A Critical Path Network. *Note: Circled numbers and letters* represent production activities, namely, M = manufacturing, E = engineering, S = sales, A = advertising, P = pricing, D = distribution; *uncircled numbers* represent weeks estimated to complete; *tinted line* represents critical path.

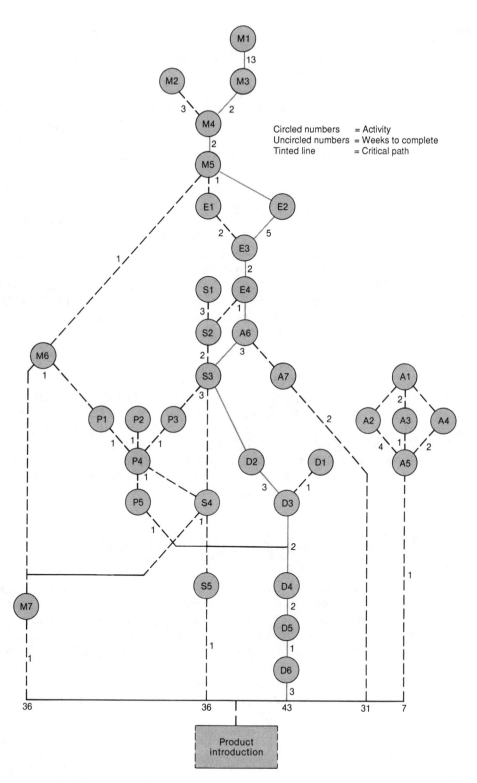

Circled numbers = Activity
Uncircled numbers = Weeks to complete
Tinted line = Critical path

volved in the introduction process along with the time estimated for completion of each task. The critical path is that sequence of tasks or activities that consumes the greatest amount of time. Other paths, requiring less total time, could incur slippage without affecting the introduction date. With CPM, program coordinators know which tasks must be monitored closely and who is responsible for their completion.[44]

Other Control Techniques. Depending on the complexity of the scheduling task facing the firm, control mechanisms can range from a simple bar chart on a single sheet of paper to a complex computer program. PERT (Program Evaluation and Review Technique) is an example of a sophisticated, computerized control system designed to monitor a complex development process. PERT was originally devised by the U.S. Navy to monitor the design and development process of the Polaris missile and submarine. No other scheduling system in use at the time could satisfactorily track the thousands of interrelated activities.

Programs as complex as PERT are not commonly used in conjunction with commercial products. The firm, in effect, must weigh the cost of scheduling delays against the cost of the system designed to prevent such delays.

Commercialization

A product is commercialized when it is formally introduced to a target market. Viewed from another perspective, commercialization is the implementation of a tactical marketing program. This implies that all the action items associated with market communication, product distribution, and customer support activities will be triggered. Weaknesses, or failure to act, in any of these areas can undermine the entire program. An untrained or uninformed sales force, lack of introductory advertising, failure to stock distributors adequately, or an understaffed customer service organization could prove disastrous.

LOOKING BACK

No manufacturer will enjoy continued market success without upgrading the cost-effectiveness and performance capability of its product line. Such upgrading, unfortunately, often obsoletes existing products. But the firm has only two choices: obsolete its own products or be obsoleted by competition. New product ideas can be generated by the market (either customers or competitors) or by various groups within the firm, including top management, R&D personnel, and the marketing department. When the idea originates externally, the firm must determine whether it has the technology, resources, and motivation to respond. Not all business opportunities justify product development. When the idea originates internally, the firm

---

[44]See, for instance, Glenn R. Dundas and Kathleen A. Krentler, "Critical Path Method for Introducing an Industrial Product," *Industrial Marketing Management* 11 (1982), pp. 125–131.

must verify that specific needs, capable of generating sufficient volume, exist in the market. Otherwise, a product idea that is very exciting technologically may become a commercial failure.

Innovation does not end, however, with the creation of a new product. Creative firms can and do lose market share to imitators who find better and less costly methods of production, distribution, and marketing.

The criteria used to decide which product ideas to pursue should stem from the marketing strategy, which, in turn, is based on corporate objectives. Thus, the product development process becomes an organized, logical extension of strategic planning rather than a haphazard, expedient response to changes in either market conditions or the firm's technological capability.

Regardless of the organizational structure chosen to carry out the development process, top management should be guided by three primary principles: (1) creativity thrives only in an atmosphere that encourages risk-taking and innovation, (2) every product idea needs a "champion" who is committed to its success, and (3) successful development depends on a coordinated team effort involving all relevant business functions.

The overall product development process consists of an interrelated series of stages, during which the product is transformed from an abstract idea into a physical entity. The firm will sequentially seek answers to three fundamental questions. Is there a market for the idea? Can the idea be transformed into a physical product? Can the physical product be manufactured and marketed profitably? Thus, successful commercialization will depend on customer needs, market conditions, technological feasibility, and profit potential. Although concerned individuals within the firm (top management, engineers, manufacturing personnel, financial analysts, and marketers) must decide how to answer the three questions, both customers and competitors will act as prominent decision influencers.

QUESTIONS FOR DISCUSSION

1. A major manufacturer of medical equipment approaches one of its suppliers with specifications for a precision switch that has been tentatively designed into a new blood analyzer. The switch supplier thinks existing technology can be utilized but has not previously produced a device with such close tolerances. What information and assurances should the switch supplier have before embarking on a full-scale development program?

2. If the idea for this precision component had originated within the switch manufacturer's product development group, how would this fact alter the need for information? Does this change the likelihood that the product can be successfully and profitably marketed?

3. "A firm is much better off if the majority of its new products originate internally. As long as the technology is 'state of the art,' and the products are priced aggressively, there is bound to be a ready market." Respond to this statement.

4. Which is more important: creating a constant flow of new products or continually updating and improving the current product line? Explain your answer.

5. Given the challenge American electronic firms face in trying to regain market position, what specific tasks would you assign to the marketing department? To R&D? To Manufacturing?

6. Describe the major strengths and weaknesses of new product committees and new product departments. Which is your personal preference and why?

7. What generalized but significant comments should be made about all forms of new product development organizations?

8. Explain the relationship between new product development and strategic planning. Should one precede the other? Why?

9. We discussed an agreement that should be reached between marketing and engineering personnel before the product idea is converted into a physical entity. What elements or factors should be included in this agreement? Why is an agreement necessary?

10. "Price should drive cost instead of cost dictating price." Explain the meaning and implications of this statement.

SUGGESTED ADDITIONAL READINGS

COOPER, ROBERT G., AND ULRIKE DE BRENTANI, "Criteria for Screening New Product Ideas," *Industrial Marketing Management* 13 (1984):149–156.

CRAWFORD, C. MERLE, *New Products Management,* 2nd ed. (Homewood, Ill.: Richard D. Irwin, Inc., 1987).

DRUCKER, PETER F., "The Discipline of Innovation," *Harvard Business Review,* 63 (May–June 1985):67–72.

FINCH, PETER, "Intrapreneurism: New Hopes for New Business," *Business Marketing* (July 1985), pp. 32–40.

GRAYSON, C. JACKSON, JR. AND CARLA O'DELL, *American Business: Two-Minute Warning* (New York: The Free Press, 1988).

"INNOVATION IN AMERICA," *Business Week,* Special Issue (June 1989).

SCHMITT, ROLAND W., "Successful Corporate R&D," *Harvard Business Review* 43 (May–June 1985):124–128.

SPENCER, WILLIAM J. AND DEBORAH D. TRIANT, "Strengthening the Link Between R&D and Corporate Strategy," *The Journal of Business Strategy* (January–February 1989):38–42.

PART FIVE

Formulating Channel Strategy

IMPERSONAL DECISIONS ABOUT PERSONAL COMPUTERS

When marketing strategies for personal computers were originally devised, it seemed a logical conclusion that traditional consumer channels should be utilized. The hardware and software of the late 1970s was best suited for playing a friendly game of chess, destroying alien spaceships, or balancing the family budget, so firms like Apple, Commodore, and Texas Instruments headed for the major department stores, discount chains, and mass merchandisers. But, to paraphrase the title of an old movie, a funny thing happened on the way to the marketplace.

As more sophisticated hardware and software became available, customers rushed to buy this new and exciting electronic marvel. Many of the customers, however, were business people, not typical consumers. They wanted to play "what-if" forecast simulations, balance a complex business budget, or "destroy" their competitors. They were less interested in getting double their money back if dissatisfied than in doubling their productivity. They wanted some helpful suggestions from an applications specialist rather than a friendly smile from a sales clerk. In short, they wanted the type of pre- and postsale service they were used to getting in the office or factory.

Suddenly, channel strategy was no longer simple and obvious. Consumers would, of course, expect to visit a retail outlet to buy their PC. But would business people do the same? Or would they expect sellers to come visiting them, as was usually the case in industrial transactions? Would business buyers purchase from retailers, or would they expect to buy from wholesalers (with the implication of price discounts)? Since the preponderance of larger business computers were sold directly, manufacturer to user, could distributors and/or sales agents be found who were experienced and technically competent enough to handle this type of business?

The preceding situations and questions are representative of those faced whenever a firm prepares to market a new industrial product. The questions usually fall into three basic categories. First, what service enhancements will the customer expect in addition to the product itself? Second, should the firm provide any or all of these services? And, third, are outside agents available who are capable of providing the services that the firm does not supply?

In the next two chapters we will address these questions. In Chapter Eleven we discuss channel intermediaries, their relative strengths and weaknesses, and the services they normally provide. Chapter Twelve covers the total physical distribution function, all the interrelated activities that are involved in moving a product from the point of manufacture to the place it is used, balancing cost-effectiveness against customer satisfaction.

CHAPTE

Marketing Channel Participants

The industrial firm seeking a distributor or manufacturers' representative will face decisions and pitfalls similar to those encountered by the lonely single in search of a mate. For even though channel members remain independent of the manufacturer, free to seek their own goals and profits, both parties agree to work together for common goals and even greater profits than either could achieve independently. And, as is true of individuals, these business partners will have a greater likelihood of success the more their values, priorities, and "life-styles" are similar. This chapter discusses

1. The internal and external factors that indicate that a marketer should probably use distributors.
2. The services that industrial customers require of distributors.
3. The characteristics that a marketer should consider in choosing a distributor.
4. The circumstances that dictate the use of manufacturers' reps (or other sales agents) instead of an employee sales force.
5. The steps that the industrial marketer must take to ensure that indirect channels are effective.

Just as manufacturers can be classified as large or small, innovative or traditional, venturesome or conservative, and oriented toward quality or price, distributors and manufacturers' representatives are differentiable by these same characteristics. The stereotypical image of a large, innovative, well-managed manufacturer being forced to use small, unimaginative, poorly run intermediaries (middlemen), who sell primarily on price, is just that—a stereotype that simply does not reflect modern realities.

In this chapter, then, we will attempt to establish a realistic profile of industrial middlemen as they exist and function in today's marketplace. Distributors will be examined first, followed by manufacturers' representatives and several specialized forms of middlemen.

WHY USE DISTRIBUTORS?

It would be unusual if a manufacturer did not ask this question at some point, particularly when struggling with a strategic marketing decision involving profitability, growth, market share, or competition. Regarding profits, manufacturers will often view distributors as a cost rather than a contribution to profits. After all, distributors demand a profit margin, which means that the manufacturer must sell to them at a price lower than would be realized by selling direct. And it is "common knowledge" that distributors are only interested in serving markets that the manufacturer has developed, so they make no effort to develop either new markets or new product applications in existing markets. But the worst situation involves market share and competition. Distributors traditionally sell not only complementary products, but also identical products from competing manufacturers. So indeed, why use distributors?

Critical Functions and Weaknesses

A manufacturer should really ask this question prior to developing marketing strategy, but not before pondering several other equally significant questions. First, the manufacturer should ask what marketing functions, such as quick delivery or exceptional service, will be critically important to the success of the marketing strategy. Such functions require special attention to achieve superb performance. Second, which of these functions involves a weakness in the firm either in the form of scarcity (e.g., financial resources, manpower, expertise, or time) or opportunity trade-offs (i.e., would assets be better utilized elsewhere)? Finally, if such weaknesses exist, can these critical functions be performed efficiently and cost effectively by an outside agency?

If a manufacturer views distributors in this context, the probability is much greater that any decision made will be more realistic, objective, and unbiased. Distributors will be evaluated for what they can contribute, not for what they will cost. They will be seen as valuable partners in a joint marketing venture instead of opportunities profiting from the efforts of the manufacturer. All this assumes that they do indeed have something to contribute.

TABLE 11-1 Why Industrial Firms Choose Their Distributors

Reason	1980 [%]	1981 [%]	Category
1. Dependable local service	30%	40%	1
2. "One-stop shopping" for most requirements	23	27	2,3
3. Keeps an inventory for us	19	25	2
4. Prompt telephone service	34	25	1
5. Immediate availability on variety of parts	22	22	2,3
6. Consistently low-priced	14	22	4
7. Keeps in-depth inventory of specialized parts	20	20	2,3
8. Expedites factory for us	25	20	1
9. Good technical support	13	18	5
10. Offers blanket contracts	18	16	4
11. Always ships accurately	12	14	1
12. Can suggest cost-effective alternative items	7	14	4,5
13. More inventory than others	15	13	2
14. Ships faster than others	12	8	1
15. Consistently ships complete orders	5	8	1,2
16. Liberal credit policy	5	5	4
17. Consistently supplies proper quantities	5	5	1
18. Various services offered	1	3	6
19. Gives premiums with orders	1	1	4
Grouped by category			
1. Dependable service	43.8	39.2	
2. Inventory level	37.0	37.6	
3. Product line breadth	23.1	22.5	
4. Price	16.0	19.0	
5. Technical capability	7.1	10.5	
6. Variety of services	0.4	1.0	

Source: Adapted from *Electronic Buyers' News*, December 1981.

Customer Expectations

Both formal academic research and less formal industry surveys indicate that industrial buyers are very concerned with the "nuts and bolts" of marketing—customer service. In fact, Perreault and Russ have concluded that industrial buyers consistently rate distribution service second only to product quality as a factor influencing their buying decision.[1]

To discover why industrial firms choose particular distributors, *Electronic Buyers' News* ran replicate surveys of their readership (1980 and 1981). The results of the surveys are shown in Table 11-1. Where responses could have multiple implications, we have listed them under two categories. The replies are consistent with

---

[1]William D. Perreault, Jr., and Frederick A. Russ, "Physical Distribution Service in Industrial Purchasing Decisions," *Journal of Marketing* 40 (April 1976), pp. 3–10.

other research findings. Buyers are clearly more concerned with service than with price, and they gauge the quality of service by prompt and accurate communications coupled with adequate inventories. They also do not expect distributors to be the primary source of technical assistance. A manufacturer's sales force plays this role.

In times of excess supply, customers usually experience little difficulty in getting timely shipment of products. However, they do run across some distributors who cut back on inventory levels or sell at uncompetitive prices in an attempt to shore up eroding profits. Overall, though, the idea of local service, provided consistently and dependably, remained the primary reason that buyers did business with a particular distributor.

Distributors Are True Middlemen

Distributors are often perceived by manufacturers and industry observers primarily as customer agents. Thus, manufacturers fear that distributors will lack the commitment to carry out critical marketing tasks. Table 11-2 lists the more significant distributor functions. We can analyze these functions as though they were two-sided coins. One side benefits the seller (product manufacturer), while the other side benefits the buyer (product user). Thus, each time a distributor serves a customer well, the cause of the product manufacturer is served equally well.

Successful distributors may indeed appear to be customer oriented because of their emphasis on service. They, too, read the results of industry surveys and act accordingly. However, distributors are only as strong as the product lines they carry. They neither create nor produce these products. Desirable franchises are essential to a distributor's success. Therefore, only a naive middleman would ignore the necessity to satisfy suppliers as well as customers.

Manufacturers who view distributors as being overly customer oriented usually fall into one of two categories. Either their product lines have failed to generate a desired level of interest in the marketplace, or their own commitment to customer service is less than optimal.

TABLE 11-2 Distributors Serve Buyers and Sellers

Seller Benefit	Buyer Benefit
1. Carry inventory	Provide fast delivery
2. Combine supplier outputs	Provide product assortment
3. Share credit risk	Provide local credit
4. Share selling task	Assist in buying decisions
5. Forecast market needs	Anticipate needs
6. Provide market information	Provide product information
7. Enhance customer service	Enhance customer service

DUAL-CHANNEL STRATEGIES

The majority of manufacturers serving industrial customers utilize both direct and indirect channels of distribution, or stated another way, they sell through a company-employed sales force as well as through industrial distributors and manufacturers' representatives. As with any generalized statement, this one has some exceptions. For example, some firms use manufacturers' reps exclusively rather than their own sales force for reasons we discuss later.

So that we may analyze the quantitative aspects of this dual-channel strategy, we have selected seven industry segments with associated data from their wholesale sales volumes for 1972, 1977, 1982, and 1987, and their 5-year growth rates over this time span. These data will serve as background information for our analysis. As a benchmark for comparison, wholesale trade for all durable goods (SIC 50) excluding automobiles (SIC 5012) grew at an annual rate of 6.1 percent from 1982 to 1987. This figure would roughly approximate the growth of the industrial market.

The seven segments listed in Table 11-3 were chosen for specific reasons:

1. They include both "smokestack" and high-tech industries.
2. They cover capital equipment as well as component parts.
3. They have experienced considerably different growth rates.
4. Most sales are made to industrial customers.

Regarding the fourth reason, there are various other industry segments wherein a portion of the wholesale trade volume involves industrial customers (commercial enterprises, government agencies, and institutions), but most of the total volume goes through the wholesaler-retailer channel to consumers. This is true, for example, of motor vehicles (SIC Code 5012), furniture (5021), electrical appliances (5064), and hardware (5072). Including such segments, then, would bias the picture in favor of indirect distribution since the bulk of consumer-directed products flow in this manner.

Indirect versus Direct Distribution

Researchers regularly conclude that distributors are more readily acceptable to both suppliers and customers when (1) the product is relatively simple and inexpensive, (2) the customer's total buying potential is modest, and (3) the overall market is made up of many customers geographically dispersed.[2]

---

[2]Donald M. Jackson, Robert F. Krampf, and Leonard J. Konopa, "Factors That Influence the Length of Industrial Channels," *Industrial Marketing Management* 11 (1982), pp. 263–268. See also Donald M. Jackson and Michael F. d'Amico, "Products and Markets Served by Distributors and Agents," *Industrial Marketing Management* 18 (February 1989), pp. 27–33.

TABLE 11-3 Sales and Growth Rates for Selected Industries: 1972–1987

Industry	SIC Code	Sales ($ billions)				Growth per Year		
		1972	1977	1982	1987	1972–77	1977–82	1982–87
All metals	5051	$40.5	$70.1	$87.8	$101.1	11.6%	4.6%	2.9%
Electrical apparatus	5063 #	$28.4	$36.5	$54.0	$65.9	5.1%	8.1%	4.1%
Electronics	5065	$8.3	$15.6	$40.4	$71.1	13.5%	21.0%	12.0%
Commercial/office equipment	5081	$12.7	$27.4	$64.5	$121.9	16.6%	18.7%	13.6%
Office eqpt.	5044 *	—	—	—	$27.8	—	—	—
Computers/software	5045 *	—	—	—	$84.5	—	—	—
Other comm'l eqpt.	5046 *	—	—	—	$9.6	—	—	—
Construction/mining equipment	5082	$8.0	$17.7	$19.3	$24.0	17.2%	1.7%	4.5%
Industrial equipment	5084 #	$17.1	$40.3	$68.6	$64.9	18.7%	11.2%	−1.1%
Industrial supplies	5085	$16.5	$28.9	$39.8	$41.8	11.9%	6.6%	1.0%
TOTAL		$131.5	$236.5	$374.4	$490.7	12.5%	9.6%	5.6%

*SIC code 5081 was subdivided into codes 5044, 5045, and 5046 for 1987 statistics. The 1987 figure for 5051 is the sum of the subdivisions shown for growth comparison.

#In 1987, the data for "electrical measuring and testing equipment" was transferred from 5063 to 5084 ($6.5 billion in sales). The figures shown above ignore this transfer for the sake of more accurate growth comparisons.

Source: Adapted from U.S. Department of Commerce, Census of Wholesale Trade for 1972, 1977, 1982, and 1987, Vol. 1, Summary and Subject Statistics (Washington, D.C.: U.S. Government Printing Office, 1976, 1981, 1984, 1989).

Smokestack industries (basic metals, industrial supplies) presumably involve products of less technical complexity than high-tech products such as monolithic memories and microprocessors (included in electronics) and computers (formerly part of SIC 5081, now listed separately as SIC 5045). Hence there would be greater use of distributors in selling these simpler products.

However, capital equipment involves a much higher average price than do components or supplies, and purchases are made less frequently, two conditions that usually suggest managerial decision making and direct-channel selling. This suggests that manufacturers of construction/mining and other costly equipment are more likely to use direct selling than are producers of industrial supplies.

The occasion of an industry slump (such as experienced during 1982–87 in most industries, particularly SIC codes 5084 and 5085) can also affect the involvement of middlemen in both directions. On one hand, manufacturers will try to reduce overhead by eliminating the fixed expense of a sales force in favor of the constant and predictable cost-to-sales ratio of indirect distribution. On the other hand, the critical need to increase market share can convince many manufacturers that they require the greater control and commitment of direct sales.

Actual Market Circumstances

Table 11-4 presents the distribution of wholesale trade volume across the three major channels: manufacturers' sales offices (their own sales personnel), distributors, and independent sales agents (manufacturers' representatives). This information will allow us to compare theory and intuition against actual market data.

These seven industries have as many differences as commonalities; nevertheless, distributors' share of the trade has at least remained steady in all industries and increased notably in some. Even the ten-year decline in SIC 5065 was reversed. Two market conditions during the 1982–87 time period probably contributed to this result. First, a slower market growth threatened sales revenues and prompted manufacturers to reach as broad a customer base as possible. Simultaneously, severe price competition caused lower profit margins and necessitated cost reductions wherever possible, including in sales expenses. Many manufacturers saw distributors as a logical solution to this two-pronged problem.

It is interesting to compare the electronics industry (5063) with industrial supplies (5085). Both industries had fairly constant channel percentages from 1972 to 1982 and then exhibited significant increases in distributor shares. This phenomenon is certainly not the result of industry similarities. Electronics underwent a series of major technological changes during this period, while the supplies industry remained relatively constant and unsophisticated. Moreover, the growth in electronics was double the industrial average; the supplies industry stagnated.

The industrial supplies data present a "textbook" story. Distributors theoretically gain their greatest importance in a slow-growth, mature market for unsophisti-

TABLE 11-4 Share of Wholesale Trade by Channel: 1972, 1977, 1982, 1987 (percentages of total)

Industry	SIC Code	Mfrs' Sales Offices				Distributors				Mfrs' Reps			
		1972	1977	1982	1987	1972	1977	1982	1987	1972	1977	1982	1987
All metals	5051	56.6	51.1	45.4	34.7	35.0	41.3	49.0	59.3	8.4	7.6	5.6	6.0
Electrical apparatus	5063	31.3	40.6	45.4	29.3	60.7	46.7	40.8	54.3	8.0	12.7	13.8	16.4
Electronics	5065	38.9	38.1	39.9	32.6	31.3	25.9	32.0	47.1	29.8	36.0	28.1	20.3
Commercial/office equipment	5081	67.4	65.8	63.3	51.7	27.3	29.7	32.8	44.9	5.3	4.5	3.9	3.4
*Office equipment	5044	—	—	—	34.6	—	—	—	61.7	—	—	—	3.7
*Computers/software	5045	—	—	—	62.1	—	—	—	35.8	—	—	—	2.2
*Other comm'l. eqpt	5046	—	—	—	10.0	—	—	—	77.0	—	—	—	13.0
Construction/mining equipment	5082	23.6	27.9	27.4	25.3	73.4	69.8	70.3	72.5	3.0	2.3	2.3	2.2
Industrial equipment	5084	36.2	33.0	29.4	23.4	47.9	51.9	57.3	62.7	15.9	15.1	13.3	13.9
Industrial supplies	5085	45.4	46.0	42.6	35.5	47.1	45.6	49.5	57.9	7.5	8.4	7.9	6.6
Weighted Average†	—	50.9	45.0	42.2	35.9	39.2	44.1	47.4	54.4	9.9	10.9	10.4	9.7
Unweighted Average#	—	45.9	42.3	40.1	33.2	43.0	45.3	49.2	57.0	11.1	12.4	10.7	9.8

*SIC code 5081 was subdivided into codes 5044, 5045, and 5046 for 1987 statistics.

†The weighted average is the total channel sales divided by total wholesale trade for that year.

#The unweighted average is simply the arithmetic mean of the seven industry percentages.

Source: Adapted from U.S. Department of Commerce, Census of Wholesale Trade for 1972, 1977, 1982, and 1987, Vol. 1, Summary and Subject Statistics [Washington, D.C.: U.S. Government Printing Office, 1976, 1981, 1984, and 1989).

cated products.[3] However, the electronics data clearly indicate that distributors are not discarded solely on the basis of product complexity, technological change, or market growth. This fact is further supported by SIC 5051, which was dominated by computers and peripheral hardware, software, photocopy and microfilm equipment. In this composite industry, the distributor share actually increased as products became more complex. It is reasonable to assume, however, that the lower absolute distributor share in both 5065 and 5045, compared to other industries, correlates to greater product complexity and changing technology.

Thus, market data substantiates theory regarding (1) less use of direct sales given product simplicity and (2) increased use of distributors in mature markets. However, the data for SIC 5082 opposes the theory that the largest portion of equipment with higher price tags is sold directly. Moreover, distributors can and do play a significant role in the sale of complex, evolving technologies.

The interrelation of sales through a firm's sales force and independent sales agents (reps) will be discussed later, at which point we will also cover the appropriate columns in Table 11-4.

CHOOSING THE RIGHT DISTRIBUTOR

When a manufacturer decides to utilize independent distributors, this initial decision prompts several other choices regarding the potential relationship. The manufacturer must also decide (1) what marketing functions will be assigned to or shared with distributors; (2) what portion of the product line will be sold through this channel; (3) what size and type of distributor should be chosen; (4) should exclusive or multiple distribution be used; (5) how should the selling function be divided between distributors and the company sales force; and (6) what policies must be spelled out to ensure an effective, profitable, mutually satisfying relationship.

Assigning Marketing Functions

Almost invariably a distributor will be expected to carry local inventory sufficient to serve the market. In addition, the manufacturer will often divide existing and potential customers into two broad categories: those that will be sold directly via the company sales force, except for emergency shipments that the distributor will make, and those that will be served almost entirely by the distributor, except for occasional technical support provided by the manufacturer.

As one might expect, customers that are handled directly tend to be larger and fewer in number. In effect, most manufacturers "high spot" target markets with

---

[3]See Jackson and d'Amico, "Products and Markets Served," p. 33; also see Gul Butaney and Lawrence H. Wortzel, "Distributor Power Versus Manufacturer Power: The Customer Role," *Journal of Marketing* 52 (January 1988), pp. 52–63; also Frank V. Cespedes, "Control vs. Resources in Channel Design: Distribution Differences in One Industry," *Industrial Marketing Management* 17 (August 1988), pp. 215–27.

their direct sales force. The remaining accounts are assigned to the distributor, or perhaps allocated, if more than one distributor is franchised in a given geographic market. This latter approach can become rather sticky, since a manufacturer cannot legally restrain a distributor from selling to any customer.

Along with inventory and sales responsibilities, the distributor will be expected to assume credit liability for those customers who buy through distribution. This often relieves the manufacturer of a problem disproportionate to the sales volume involved. While one cannot make a sweeping generalization, there is normally a greater likelihood of assuming bad credit risks when dealing primarily with small firms.[4]

Other responsibilities, such as repairs, in-warranty service, local advertising, trade show participation, and new product sampling may also be assigned to distributors, but these tend to be quite product specific. Inventory maintenance, selling, and credit risk assumption are universal.

Product Line Coverage

Fragmented Channels.   Manufacturers will sometimes decide to fragment the channeling of their overall product line. They usually reach this decision on the premise that portions of the product line are aimed at different market segments and, hence, require different distributor groups. For example, Texas Instruments markets semiconductor devices through electronic parts distributors who deal primarily with original equipment manufacturing (OEM) customers. However, to market calculators effectively, TI franchises distributors who deal primarily with retailers.

As a general rule, though, marketers are wise to minimize the fragmentation of their product lines. Within the bounds of practical application, customers will more likely use the complementary products of a manufacturer (products that are demanded jointly) when these products are available from a single source. And, as shown in Table 11-1, one of the primary benefits customers seek from distributors is "one-stop shopping."

Specialized Products.   The major exception to the sourcing of a complete product line through distributors is custom-designed or single-customer products. The average distributor lacks the technical competence to negotiate complex specifications with industrial users. Thus, it is better for the marketer to handle these matters directly. Moreover, customer engineering departments have a habit of redesigning special products from time to time, which can leave the distributor with a useless inventory of expensive parts that no one wants, including the manufacturer. Therefore, it usually makes for better control, communication, and relationships to sell specialized products direct.

---

[4]James A. Narus, N. Mohan Reddy, and George L. Pinchak, "Key Problems Facing Industrial Distributors," *Industrial Marketing Management* 13 (1984), pp. 139–147.

Distributor Size

Some manufacturers are unaware that this topic represents a major decision; others make the decision, but traumatically and subjectively. If all distributors were indeed the stereotypical $1 to 2 million, ten-employee, single-location type of operation, this decision would be relatively simple. But, as shown in Table 11-5, such is not the case.

The seven industries previously analyzed in Tables 11-3 and 11-4 included 59,632 distributors in 1982. If these firms were analyzed as one group, we could correctly state that the "average" distributor has sales revenue of $3.0 million, employs 14.8 people, and does business from a single stocking location (1.2 actually). When we purposely segregate the fifty largest distributors in each industry (or a total of 350 for the seven industries), several facts emerge that are of critical importance to any marketer setting up a distribution channel.

These top 350 distributors are, on average, $158 million organizations, each employing over 400 people and operating from 15 stocking locations—each of which generates almost $11 million in sales. As Table 11-5 shows, all these numbers dwarf the comparable figures for the remaining distribution houses. Of even greater importance to manufacturers, these top distributors enjoyed 31 percent of the total distribution business and had a significant cost advantage over their smaller competitors.

This combined volume and cost-effectiveness suggests several associated points. First, these firms can afford to carry a larger and more complete inventory for better customer service. Second, with lower selling costs, they can either generate higher profits to support complementary services or pursue increased sales with more aggressive pricing. In addition, given their size and relative success in their

TABLE 11-5　Comparison of Top 50 Distributors vs. All Others, Selected Industries, 1982

	Top 50	Others
Average sales/firm (millions)	$157.5	$2.1
Number of locations/firm	14.6	1.2
Sales/location (millions)	$10.8	$1.8
Employees/firm	410	13
Sales/employee (thousands)	$384.2	$165.1
Relative cost of sales*	.43	1.00
Employees/location	28.2	10.8
Number of firms	350	59,282
Percent of total firms	.6%	99.4%
Percent of total sales	31.1%	68.9%

*Reciprocal of relative sales/employee ($165.1/$384.2 = .43)

Source: Adapted from U.S. Department of Commerce, 1982 Census of Wholesale Trade, Industry Series (Washington, D.C.: U.S. Government Printing Office, 1984).

marketplace, they can regularly attract franchises for those product lines most in demand by industrial users.

These strengths, however, are a mixed blessing to any marketer seeking to establish a distribution channel or improve upon an existing one—particularly if the manufacturer's product line commands only a weak market share. While the distributor's strengths, if conscientiously applied, could undoubtedly help to increase that market share, the manufacturer must question whether these strengths will indeed be applied to a secondary line, and if applied, who will have control of channel strategy.[5]

Manufacturers do have the alternative, of course, to select one or more of the many small distributors. Perhaps such firms will, through solid effort, commitment, and enthusiasm, produce outstanding results. Moreover, manufacturers are more likely to retain strategic control.[6] There might also be greater compatibility between two smaller firms trying to battle the industry giants together. While this begins to sound like a most promising scenario, there remains the unfortunate possibility that these smaller firms can also fail together, lacking the strength to offset or compensate for each other's weaknesses. As was suggested earlier, the choice of distributors can be a very traumatic experience.

Distributor Type

Even though all distributors perform the same primary functions (carrying inventory, selling, and providing credit), the relative importance and effort they assign to each will vary. There is also notable variation in the types of customers pursued, the emphasis placed on price, the number of product lines carried, and the relative amount of time spent on creative versus maintenance selling. Thus, manufacturers must choose not only the distributor's size (assuming options are available), but also the type of business being conducted.

This latter choice harks back to the basic questions that marketers must answer before establishing a channel strategy, namely: "What marketing functions are critical to the success of strategy?" and "Which of these functions can best be performed by an outside agency?" Obviously, if a marketer sacrifices some degree of control by shifting responsibilities outside the firm, there should be reasonable assurance that the contracted functions will be well performed. And, since distributors can be categorized by their specific strengths and areas of concentration, there is no reason to make this choice a coin-tossing exercise.[7]

[5]I. David Ford, "Stability Factors in Industrial Marketing Channels," *Industrial Marketing Management* 7 (1978), pp. 410–422. See also Butaney and Wortzel, "Distributor Power vs. Manufacturer Power," pp. 60–61.

[6]Peter R. Dickson, "Distributor Portfolio Analysis and the Channel Dependence Matrix: New Techniques for Understanding and Managing the Channel," *Journal of Marketing* 47 (Summer 1983), pp. 35–44. See also Cespedes, "Control vs. Resources," pp. 222–26.

[7]See Thomas L. Powers, "Industrial Distribution Options: Trade-offs to Consider," *Industrial Marketing Management* 18 (August 1989), pp. 155–61; also Louis W. Stern and Frederick D. Sturdivant, "Getting Things Done," *Harvard Business Review* 65 (July–August 1987), pp. 34–41.

Why a Particular Distributor Is Chosen. In 1979 the American Supply and Machinery Manufacturers' Association (ASMMA) hired a research firm to determine the answers to several important questions:[8] (1) Which type of distributor is most effective in selling a product line? (2) What amount and type of market coverage do they provide? (3) What sales and inventory support can manufacturers realistically expect from distributors? Table 11-6 shows the summary results of this survey, which include several important implications for marketers who use or plan to use distributors.

TABLE 11-6 Profile of Industrial Distribution ASMMA 1979 Survey, Summary Report

	Technical Specialists	General-Line Distributors	Inventory Specialists
1. Number of lines	Less than 40	Over 100	Less than 20
2. % sales from top three lines	70% +	Under 40%	80% +
3. % of total cost spent on selling	37%	32%	26%
4. % of total cost spent on inventory	42%	42%	63%
5. % of sales effort put on primary/ secondary/ tertiary product lines	45/45/10%	72/27/1%	90/10/0%
6. % of revenue obtained from primary/secondary/ tertiary product lines	55/40/5%	64/26/10%	90/10/0%
7. Selling role and market coverage	a. Primary lines sold on repeat buys to large/medium customers.	a. Primary/ secondary lines both for repeat buys to large/medium customers.	a. Stress large-customer contract business.
	b. Secondary (new) lines used to create markets.	b. Limited effort to sell small customers.	b. Aggressive pricing.
	c. Ignore small customers.	c. Some small customer "call-in" orders.	c. Ignore small/medium customers.
8. High-volume/low-profit contract business	Only 10% of total; not low bidders.	About 30%, mostly in multiproduct "system" sales.	About 50%, actively pursue with price/inventory.

Source: An industry survey conducted by Frank Lynn & Associates, Inc., and sponsored by the Distribution Trends Committee, American Supply and Machinery Manufacturers Association, Inc., *Summary Report* [Cleveland, Ohio, 1979].

[8]Frank Lynn & Associates, Inc., *Profile of Industrial Distribution 1979: Summary Report* (Cleveland, Ohio: American Supply and Machinery Manufacturers Association, Inc., 1979).

Market/Customer Coverage.   Marketers who are concentrating their direct sales effort on major potential customers would like to see distributors actively soliciting business from the remainder of a geographic market, including the smaller potential customers. The survey reveals, however, that both technical and inventory specialists also direct the majority of their sales effort toward larger potential customers, ignoring the smaller ones. Only general-line distributors expend any effort in this area, and this effort is spotty at best.

Clearly, then, a small manufacturer with resources too limited to hire a sizable sales force, and with an equally limited market acceptance, will have to consider space advertising (advertising in trade or business publications), direct mail, and other communication techniques to generate a broad base of customers. Another viable alternative might be the use of reps. We will return to this point later.

Another survey, which studied the buying habits of more than 300 OEM firms in the electronics industry, might help to explain distributors' concentration on larger customers. Customers were asked to quantify their total purchases and the percentage they placed with distributors. Their answers were grouped into six segments, as shown in Table 11-7. The data would appear to contradict a basic channel theory that distributor participation decreases as the customer's buying potential increases.

Actually, there is no contradiction of theory regarding the *percentage* of total dollar purchases going through indirect channels. However, the falloff in percentage is more than offset by the relative increase in total dollar potential of larger accounts, *up to some level.* As a consequence, distributors can realize greater sales volume and potential profit—for the same amount of effort and inventory investment—by concentrating on at least medium-sized customers. For example, given the data in Table 11-7, a distributor can average twice as much in sales concentrating on customers whose purchases are in the range of $1 million to $2.499 million as

TABLE 11-7   Distributor's Participation in Industrial OEM Purchases

Total Purchases [$000]	% of Total	Distributor Amount [$000]	Midpoint [$000]
< 250	75–100%	< 250	125
250–499	50–80	125–400	262
500–999	30–60	150–600	375
1,000–2,499	15–35	150–875	512
2,500–4,999	5–15	125–750	437
5,000–10,000	0–5	0–500	250

Source: E. G. Brierty, "Survey of Midwest Industrial OEM Customers, Purchases of Electronic Components Through Distribution," September 1976. Previously unpublished.

compared to expending the same effort on those with potentials in the $250,000–499,000 range.

Most certainly, the percentages and related dollar potentials shown in Table 11-7 will vary with product, economic conditions, customer buying philosophy, distributor service image, and myriad other factors. But there is a strong likelihood that the same general results would occur across a range of products and markets, as implied by the ASMMA survey.

Market Development. The ASMMA survey results also imply rather strongly that distributors do not, as a general rule, engage in market development activity, preferring to direct their sales effort toward product markets that have already been developed. (The authors corroborated these findings in other industries.) Thus, manufacturers cannot rely on distributors to share the market development burden, except for the partial effort expended by technical specialists. A more realistic expectation for distributors would be that they provide the types of postdevelopment service that customers normally demand from them (review Table 11-1).

Product Concentration. Manufacturers who have not yet established a reputation within their target market are at a disadvantage when trying to develop demand for a new product. Unless the product exhibits a distinct technological advantage, technical specialists will be reluctant to take it on as a market development tool. Inventory specialists will view it as a secondary product at best and give it less than ten percent of their effort. General-line distributors might be interested, but the product line then becomes only one of more than 100 separate lines vying for attention and sales effort. We can see, then, why manufacturers often use multiple channels to reach their markets effectively. Distributors can and do perform certain marketing tasks quite well. Other tasks they perform poorly or not at all.

Exclusive or Multiple Distribution

Manufacturers selling into industrial market segments will usually let the size and dispersion of a given geographic market determine the number of distributors that they will franchise. Distributors often start out being market specialists, but over time develop more into product specialists. For example, electronic parts distributors in the 1950s did over half their business with radio and TV service dealers. The replacement of defective vacuum tubes alone accounted for 25–35 percent of total sales dollars. With the advent of new technologies, particularly semiconductors and computers, two significant changes took place.

First, due to the dramatic increase in component reliability (transistor failure rates were only 1/100 that of vacuum tubes), the replacement market dwindled. Second, partly due to component reliability, but also the result of electronic systems capabilities, many industrial operating functions previously performed with mechanical equipment were converted to electronics. However, relatively few industrial equipment and supplies distributors (SIC codes 5084 and 5085) began to carry electronic components. Rather, distributors in SIC code 5065 found themselves serving a much broader and more diversified group of customers, with the open encouragement of both manufacturers and industrial users. For example, if a steel company needed replacement parts for its computer-controlled rolling mill, it went to a hardware distributor for mechanical parts and an electronics distributor for electronic components and subsystems. It was a natural evolution that all parties seemed to accept readily.

Therefore, a marketer's decision regarding the number of distributors to use is primarily based on the size of a market and the market share held by channel members. If one distributor is clearly dominant in a market with a relatively low potential, the choice of exclusive distribution would be quite logical. However, in major market areas (often coincident with major population centers), multiple distribution is a common strategy.

Problems to Avoid.   A manufacturer should be wary of two potential problems. First, franchising too many distributors in any market simply makes the product line undesirable to all. There is no magic answer to how many is too many.[9] It will relate to industry norms and the distributor's expectation of potential sales. For example, if the majority of manufacturers in a given industry use three to five distributors to serve the greater Los Angeles area, then one would probably be insufficient and seven would be too many. From the distributor's standpoint, primary product lines in that same industry might be generally defined as those producing at least $100,000 in annual sales. It would not be prudent, then, to franchise four distributors in a market with a $200,000 potential, unless the manufacturer was willing to occupy a secondary position (with secondary attention) for an indefinite period.

The second potential problem involves the mixture of distributors in multiple distribution markets. For example, a manufacturer might consider the mix of a general-line house and an inventory specialist, feeling that this combination would ensure the broadest possible market coverage. The generalist could be expected to cover smaller customers with a comprehensive product package, while the specialist would pursue major potentials on a concentrated, price-aggressive basis. On the surface, this would seem to be an excellent strategy and might work out that way. However, if the two houses meet too often as competitors for business at medium-size accounts, and the specialist consistently undercuts the generalist's prices, there will surely be trouble at the OK Corral. A marketer cannot always prevent such problems or even foreseen them, but careful analysis during the channel formation stage is well worth the effort.

Distribution Policies

The formulation of an effective and workable distributor franchise agreement represents a real challenge to a manufacturer. Some firms will sin by excess, trying to

[9]"J & J Tears a Strip off," *Sales and Marketing Management,* May 14, 1984, p. 32.

cover every last detail and contingency that might crop up over the next decade; others sin by defect, leaving too many important variables to chance. The happy compromise will do three things: (1) spell out the respective duties of both parties to each other and to their common market, (2) recognize the rights of both parties and show how these will be protected, and (3) by virtue of the points elaborated, attempt to foresee major potential conflicts and resolve them beforehand.

The compilation of an all-inclusive list of items to address in a distributor agreement is virtually impossible because many important items are product or market specific. However, Table 11-8 attempts to set forth some issues that are likely to affect manufacturer-distributor relationships in a variety of industries.

Duties and Goals. Since there is a broad range of activities that might be assigned to a distributor, and manufacturers differ in their desire or willingness to delegate these activities, the marketer must detail, quite clearly, this sharing of responsibility. Besides a clarification of duties, the marketer must also explain the major elements of the marketing strategy as they pertain to the distributor, such as the principal target segments, the approximate market share desired, the relative emphasis on price, the degree of product innovation to be expected, and the level of customer service required. These strategic positions cannot be left to inference or individual interpretation.

A large portion of channel conflict can be traced back to ambiguity and incompatibility between the goals of the manufacturer and those of the distributor. A skimming strategy, for example, will be subverted by a distributor who emphasizes low prices instead of superior service. A broad customer base will not result through distributors who concentrate on the same key customers that the manufacturer intends to serve directly. A manufacturer seeking increased market share requires distributors who are equally dissatisfied with their own competitive position. There is no reason for ambiguity, and it is much better that incompatibilities arise during initial channel negotiations, when they might be resolved, rather than later, when they can impair the entire strategic approach.

Rights and Protection. We stated at the beginning of this chapter that channel participants remain independent business organizations, even though both parties recognize benefits to be derived from working together. While this might sound like an elaboration of the obvious, some marketers give the impression that they are concerned solely with their own needs and desires. And, on the other side, some distributors imply by their actions that customers are important, but suppliers are only a necessary evil. Therefore, the wise and prudent marketer will take the first step toward the prevention of false impressions by exhibiting an understanding of both sides of the proposed relationship.

For example, by stressing product innovation, marketers will often engage in self-obsolescence. This means that portions of a distributor's inventory can suddenly become worthless. Unless manufacturers are willing to assume some financial liability, distributors must choose between carrying a level of inventory too low to

TABLE 11-8 Issues to Address in Distributor Franchise Agreements

I. Duties of both parties
  A. Distributor
     1. Carry sufficient inventory to satisfy market needs.
     2. Help to disseminate new product information and samples.
     3. Extend competitive credit terms to customers.
     4. Use pricing to stimulate market growth while maintaining reasonable profit margins.
     5. Utilize co-op advertising programs to enhance market share.
     6. Pass along any market information indicating business opportunities and/or problems.
     7. Provide manufacturer with a list of current customers by product segment.
     8. Follow up on all customer leads provided by manufacturer.
  B. Manufacturer
     1. Provide products with a quality and innovation level necessary to meet market penetration plans.
     2. Make these plans known to distributor so that joint efforts can be coordinated and conflicts avoided.
     3. Provide distributor buy prices (costs) that allow competitive market pricing plus reasonable profits.
     4. Devise promotional programs to stimulate market interest.
     5. Supply distributor personnel with adequate training, guidance, and written information.
     6. Handle all stocking orders on a timely basis.
     7. Refer to distributors those customer orders that fall within "protected quantity" levels.
     8. Keep the distributor informed regarding those customers being handled directly.
II. Rights/protection of both parties
  A. Distributor
     1. Right to return obsolete inventory to manufacturer provided inventory mix and level was previously approved.
     2. Protection against arbitrary decision by manufacturer to make any distributor customer a "house account."
     3. Protection against arbitrary addition of distributors provided market penetration goals have been met.
     4. Inventory cost protection if manufacturer reduces market price.
  B. Manufacuturer
     1. Any proprietary information given to distributor for guidance or coordination purposes will be safeguarded.
     2. Distributor will not use price in such a way as to be a disruptive market influence.
     3. Protection against distributor arbitrarily adding competing product lines.
     4. Distributor will not use co-op advertising funds to promote products outside the manufacturer's product line.

serve customers properly and running the risk of severe profit erosion.[10] As a consequence, many manufacturers agree to accept the return of obsolete inventory for full credit, provided the distributor has exercised reasonable judgment by carrying a level of inventory commensurate with the desired service level and market potential.

As we discussed earlier, marketers commonly use multiple distributors in ma-

---

[10]Narus, Reddy, and Pinchak, "Key Problems," p. 143.

jor market areas. This practice is obviously self-serving. By the same type of reasoning, distributors regularly carry competing product lines to satisfy a range of customer preferences. While neither party is completely satisfied with these conflicts of interest, they must both accept the situation as a market reality. Nevertheless, each wants some control over potential alterations after the franchise agreement is in effect. Thus, marketers want "veto power" over the distributor's desire to increase the number of competing lines, while distributors want the same prerogative regarding the addition of distributors within the served market.[11]

Franchise agreements commonly include a 60- or 90-day cancellation clause, with either party having the right to cancel for "just cause." The addition of distributors or competing lines is a frequent reason for this clause being exercised.

MANUFACTURERS' REPRESENTATIVES

Reps Compared to Distributors.   Manufacturers' reps share relatively few characteristics with distributors. Both distributors and reps are independent entrepreneurs, and both are primarily selling organizations. Beyond these factors, however, differences abound. Distributors buy and stock inventory, which they resell at prices of their own choosing. Reps, as sales agents, do not buy the products they sell, rarely carry inventory, and sell at prices dictated by the manufacturer. Distributors, as previously mentioned, also regularly sell competing products, whereas reps will handle complementary products, but not competing lines. And, although both emphasize the selling function, reps are more likely to develop new markets and applications through a combination of persuasive selling skills and technical competence. Part of this technical competency stems from the fact that reps usually handle only five to eight product lines that they learn fairly well. Distributors, however, handling 50 to 100 different product lines, cannot be expected to provide a customer with much more than catalog information. Finally, a product manufacturer will frequently use more than one distributor in a geographic market. Reps, with rare exception, operate under an exclusive franchise in their assigned territory.

Although reps are usually described as an indirect marketing channel, this designation can be misleading. Distributors are indeed an indirect channel, because they purchase products made by a manufacturer and resell these products to various customers. The products do not flow directly from maker to user. That same manufacturer may sell part of its output directly to other customers. Customer contacts, negotiations, and follow-ups may be handled by company-employed sales personnel, independent reps, or a combination of both. In this context, reps are not really an indirect channel, but a substitute or alternative for a direct sales force. What is important is an understanding of the marketing roles performed by distributors and reps, not their semantic definitions.

[11]Ibid.

What to Expect from a Rep

Reps have been described as the purest form of sales practitioner. Indeed, operating as they do with no assets other than personal skills, rewarded on straight commission (no sales, no income), and subject to the whims of both suppliers and customers, they are certainly not lacking in self-confidence and motivation. In addition, given any reasonable success, a rep also evidences product and market knowledge, customer acceptance, and the ability to compete.[12] In short, the rep would appear to offer all the traits that a corporate sales manager seeks in employees, but cannot always find or afford.

As one might expect, firms are likely to opt for reps instead of a company sales force when experiencing some sort of financial constraint, such as limited resources, disappointing cost/sales ratios, or a declining market potential. Since reps are paid on a straight commission basis, the marketer will not face fixed personnel expenses without sales, and once sales start to flow, the cost/sales ratio will be predictable and fixed at the commission rate.

Even though start-up firms might have the financial ability to hire and support their own sales force, they can still benefit from a rep organization's established market presence and customer rapport. In addition, the complementarity of the rep's other lines often serves as an indirect door-opener for the new line, an advantage the manufacturer would not have selling directly. Finally, an established rep firm will provide a level of experience, professionalism, and cohesiveness that the manufacturer would have difficulty matching with new sales force hires. These factors will prompt many firms to begin their sales efforts with reps, even though they intend to hire a sales force eventually.

Potential Problems in Dealing Through Reps

Lack of Control. A reason frequently given by manufacturers who do not use reps, and a common complaint by those who do, is the lack of control over reps' activities.[13] Neither group perceives open rebellion, but it is a fact that independent enterpreneurs are not as easy to direct and control as company employees. Some manufacturers go a step further and state that reps are also more difficult to motivate.[14]

Not all manufacturers, however, lay blame for these problems completely at the feet of their reps. As one firm, which has been quite successful in selling through

---

[12]Harold J. Novick, "The Case for Reps vs. Direct Selling: Can Reps Do It Better?" *Industrial Marketing Management* (March 1982), p. 90.

[13]"Why We Don't Use Sales Reps," *Sales and Marketing Management* (July 9, 1979), p. 32; see also Edwin E. Bobrow, "Suddenly, an Urge to Boost Their Potential," *Sales and Marketing Management* (June 7, 1982, Special Report).

[14]Bobrow, "Suddenly an Urge to Boost."

reps, expressed its feelings, "Too many of us expect the rep to do all the work in return for his commission."[15] This spokesperson could well have been thinking that manufacturers often expect more from reps than they would from their own sales force.

For example, reps often complain about being loaded down with excessive missionary sales, market research, credit and collection problems, and similar tasks that subtract from their productive selling time and do not generate commissions. Yet, if the offending firm had a company sales force, one of the primary concerns would be keeping sales people free of tasks that do not produce sales. For instance, product managers would perform the preliminary missionary work and market research (perhaps aided by a research department or outside agency), a credit department would worry about delinquent payments, and customer service people would take care of routine paperwork and follow-up. Moreover, the rep's sales skills and customer contacts will not substitute for desirable products, competitive prices, and effective advertising. Without these prerequisite tools, the world's greatest salesperson will be ineffective.

Competing Product Lines.   Marketers must also remember that they face competition at two levels when selling through reps.[16] Not only do they face competition from other manufacturers' product lines, they also face the competition of other firms selling products through the same reps. In this instance, they are competing for time and attention. Theoretically, a rep with five complementary product lines might spend 20 percent of his or her effort on each line. In reality, this situation rarely occurs. As any logical and goal-oriented individual does, the rep allocates time and effort in proportion to results obtained. As one firm becomes responsible for an increasing share of the rep's sales, it will place greater demands on the rep for time and attention, and the rep finds it very tempting to oblige. Thus, products, prices, promotion, and supportive services are essential not only to attract customers, but also to motivate reps who sell to those customers.

Franchise Agreements for Reps

Many of the comments made earlier regarding distributor franchise agreements apply equally to rep agreements. Since the functions of a rep and a distributor differ, however, the agreements will emphasize different operational details. For example, since the rep is acting as the duly authorized sales agent of the manufacturer, the laws of agency apply. Therefore, if for no other purpose, the manufacturer would want an agreement that clearly spells out the range and limitations of the rep's delegated authority. But, in addition to legal considerations, the critical need to spell

---

[15]Earl Hitchcock, "What Marketers Love and Hate About Their Manufacturers' Reps," *Sales and Marketing Management* (September 10, 1984), pp. 60–65.

[16]Ibid.

out shared or mutual responsibilities as well as individual rights and protections still exists.

PARTICIPATION OF REPS IN THE INDUSTRIAL MARKET

In 1984, an estimated 45,000 to 50,000 U.S. manufacturers, plus some unknown number of foreign suppliers, were selling through reps.[17] And a 1982 survey placed the number of reps being utilized at approximately the same level.[18] About 60 percent of those reps, or 30,000, operated in the industrial market.

Not unlike distributors, reps are often stereotypically defined, especially as to how and where they function. They are usually pictured as handling the products of smaller manufacturers, or serving larger manufacturers only in secondary markets. Their tenure with the smaller manufacturer is described as short and tenuous, for as the business increases, the manufacturer will "grow out of" the relationship and hire its own sales force.

Large Manufacturers Also Use Reps.   When viewed as generalized comments, these descriptive observations of reps are reasonably accurate. However, not all firms using reps are small. Manufacturers like National Semiconductor, ITT, Corning, Monsanto, Teledyne, and Mobil Oil are included. Nor are the relationships always short. National Semiconductor began using reps in the early 1960s when the firm's total sales were less than $50 million. It continues this practice in the 1980s, even though it has become a billion-dollar manufacturer.

A review of Table 11-4 might help to put the rep's participation into perspective. In these seven selected industries, reps are responsible for about 10 percent of total industry sales, and this percentage has been relatively constant since 1972. We can see, however, that the participation level varies considerably among industries. Although no known research has been published to explain why this variability exists, one can make conjectures as to plausible reasons.

In the electronics industry (SIC 5065), rep participation is the highest. This could be the result of many small, specialized U.S. manufacturers (plus an increasing number of foreign suppliers) competing for market share. These firms lack the financial resources, market acceptance, or breadth of line to support their own sales force. On the other hand, the computer/software industry (SIC 5045) and the construction/mining industry (SIC 5082) are dominated by large firms that employ their own sales personnel. These groups include firms such as IBM, Xerox, Hewlett-Packard, Caterpillar, and Tenneco. Perhaps two points would best summarize the situation: (1) those firms that represent the bulk of industrial wholesale trade dollars have opted to use their own sales force rather than reps, but (2) indirect sales, the combined total of distributors and reps, is the dominant industrial channel.

[17]Ibid.
[18]"Special Report," *Sales and Marketing Management* (June 7, 1982).

OTHER CHANNEL PARTICIPANTS

Distributors and reps are by far the predominant middlemen in the industrial market. There are, however, several other categories that play lesser roles. Brokers and value-added resellers are two examples.

Brokers.   These commissioned middlemen may represent a seller or buyer or both. The term of service is usually shorter than that of the rep; it may only be a "one-shot" relationship. Brokers are often involved in the buying and selling of surplus inventory. For example, a manufacturer of military equipment may have its contract cut short and may be left with an unneeded stock of component parts. The firm will likely be advised by the contracting agency that it will be reimbursed for the unusable parts, but first, a reasonable effort should be made to recover some part of the cost. The firm then turns to a broker who is commissioned to "find a home" for the surplus inventory. The broker may know of another industrial user who needs the parts or a distributor who normally sells this type of product. The broker then negotiates a deal that is mutually satisfactory to buyer and seller.

Value-Added Resellers (VARs).   This is not a new category of middlemen, but one that has gained greater prominence since the 1970s because of the computer industry. Computer manufacturers also refer to them as OEMs to differentiate them from industrial end users. These middlemen are usually specialists dealing with a particular market segment (retailers, banks, accounting offices, medical labs, etc.). They gather together the separate products of individual firms and design an operating system tailored to the needs of their specialty market. With computers becoming increasingly pervasive, peripheral equipment more diversified, and specific applications more demanding, VARs provide a very valuable service to both buyer and seller.

MAINTAINING INDIRECT CHANNEL EFFECTIVENESS

The manufacturer will not always be the dominant member of a marketing channel. Specific industry situations bear this out. For example, each of the ten largest electronic parts distributors had 1989 sales volumes in excess of $250 million. The largest, Avnet, Inc., sold $1.47 billion. The top ten captured sixty-five percent of the national market, and Avnet alone controlled seventeen percent.

An "average" manufacturer with total sales, direct and indirect, in the $10 to 20 million range would have little success trying to dictate Avnet's strategies and tactics. Yet every manufacturer, regardless of size, must assume the responsibility for its own marketing strategy, including the choice of channels. Unless the firm can produce a desirable product that satisfies some target market, there is no need for a channel of distribution. Once the product and market exist, the firm must see to it that the chosen channels enhance the product's value in the eyes of potential customers. To ensure that channel participants will provide this enhancement, the firm must supply several essential ingredients.

Realistic Goals.   No distributor or rep is attracted to a manufacturer producing inferior or uncompetitive products. Almost equally unattractive is the manufacturer with unrealistic goals for a desirable product—the manufacturer who wants a 30 percent market share in six months, when reality would suggest 15 percent in two years.

Therefore, objectivity must be an ingredient of any successful channel strategy. This objectivity should encompass not only quantitative goals, but also the level of commitment expected from middlemen and the factory support necessary to earn it.

Two-Way Communications.   Virtually every industrial survey aimed at identifying and eliminating channel problems includes poor communications at or near the top of the list. Ironically, manufacturers and middlemen express the same sentiment with equal vehemence. Middlemen complain, for example, that manufacturers do not clarify their goals or intended support efforts, and manufacturers are unhappy because distributors and reps do not willingly discuss their customer plans and results.

Like the chicken and the egg dilemma, this one must also have a beginning. The manufacturer that gives evidence of recognizing the middleman as a marketing partner will more likely be treated the same. A sharer of proprietary information will probably receive similar information in return. Treating constructive criticism with respect, and effective action, will increase the flow of information (and may even reduce the amount of trivial complaints).

The establishment of a distributor and/or rep council is an excellent first step in creating an effective two-way communication flow. This allows management personnel to meet informally, on an equal footing, to discuss mutual goals and problems. Proprietary information is more likely to be exchanged and respected in this type of forum.

Essential Training.   The word "essential" indicates both importance and variability. Reps do not (or should not) require sales training, but they will certainly require training in new products and will benefit from greater knowledge of product competition and market or industry trends. Distributors often require some assistance in training new sales people in effective selling techniques and need "highlight" training in products. In addition, smaller distributors can use (and, if it is presented properly, will appreciate) business training. This may include inventory control, handling accounts receivable, pricing for profitability, or analyzing customer potentials.

The important point is that marketers can either sit back and bemoan the "lack of capability and professionalism" they perceive in middlemen, or they can take constructive steps to remedy deficiencies. Obviously, only the latter approach will improve channel effectiveness to the benefit of the manufacturer.

Compatibility. As we suggested earlier, the compatibility of channel partners is critical. This includes compatible positions regarding the importance of growth, pricing philosophy, target markets, and customer service levels. Incompatibility in size may prove inevitable, depending on the availability of distributors or reps. But the other issues are independent of size, and a suitable choice should be available to the marketer willing to devote sufficient time and energy to the search.

Compensation and Support. Too often manufacturers worry more about the cost of their selected channels than the benefits provided. A controller once asked, "A 6 percent commission is okay for the rep selling $100,000, but suppose he lucks out and sells $1 million. What do we do then?" He was advised, "Don't worry about the rep, just have fun counting your $940,000!"

A manufacturer must again use objectivity when evaluating the functions performed by middlemen. Presumably, the middleman can perform both effectively and efficiently; otherwise, the manufacturer has made a poor choice. If the choice is correct, the compensation should realistically reflect the costs and benefits involved. Unless this is true, the distributor will sell competing products, and the rep will concentrate on the complementary lines.

Middlemen, even when compensated fairly, do not perform all the functions necessary to make the channel strategy a success. For example, product innovation, quality control, advertising, and competitive pricing are still required. These responsibilities, along with a segment of customer service and inventory maintenance, fall to the manufacturer. Thus, the manufacturer's overall image in the market depends upon the service provided by middlemen, but the middleman's ability to serve customers depends on the manufacturer's support. It is truly a partnership.

LOOKING BACK

Most manufacturers, after evaluating their own capabilities and the service requirements of potential customers, decide to channel at least part of their product sales through distributors. Although this indirect channel costs the manufacturer some degree of control, the loss is offset by the benefits of localized service and inventory, plus the synergy of associated product lines that the distributor can offer.

Industrial distributors vary widely in size, market coverage, and operating philosophy; thus, they may be completely out of sync with the manufacturer's attitude toward price selling, attention given to smaller customers, or willingness to develop new markets. And, although multiple distribution is commonplace in major markets, problems can also arise if the distributors chosen prove to be more competitive than complementary. These facts indicate that problems more serious than partial lack of control can occur if distributors are not selected carefully.

To offset some of these problems, both distributor and rep franchise agreements should clearly define the primary duties and responsibilities, as well as the rights and protection, of both parties. If marketers expect to gain optimal middleman cooperation, they must first provide evidence that they perceive middlemen as partners.

The basic differences between distributors and reps indicate the division of functions that might be made when both types of middlemen are utilized.

The primary responsibility for channel success lies with the manufacturer. Thus, manufacturers must recognize those functions that cannot be delegated to middlemen and perform them at a level at least equivalent to that expected from the other channel members.

QUESTIONS FOR DISCUSSION

1. "The typical manufacturing firm is neither organized nor motivated to perform the tasks normally assigned to distributors." Explain why you agree or disagree with this statement.

2. If you were appointed the general manager of a distributorship, given the customer demands and supplier expectations discussed in this chapter, what goals and objectives would you establish for the firm? How would you rank them?

3. Assume that you are the marketing manager for some manufacturer. The product and market served may be any you choose. Describe the characteristics and strengths you would most desire in a distributor and the weaknesses you would want to avoid.

4. Given the product/market scenario you chose for the preceding question, enumerate the most important issues you would include in your distributor franchise agreement, and explain their importance.

5. What, in your opinion, are the primary advantages and disadvantages of a company sales force versus the use of manufacturers' reps or other sales agents?

6. If, as an industrial marketing manager, you had chosen to sell through a combination of distributors and reps, explain how and why you would subdivide the duties between these two groups.

7. With reference to the preceding question, would the use of a company sales force and distributors make the division of responsibilities easier or more difficult? Explain your answer.

8. In what areas of activity and attitude is it most essential that manufacturers be compatible with their distributors? with their reps?

SUGGESTED ADDITIONAL READINGS

BUTANEY, GUL, AND LAWRENCE H. WORTZEL, "Distributor Power Versus Manufacturer Power: The Customer Role," *Journal of Marketing* 52 (January 1988):52–63.

CESPEDES, FRANK V., "Control vs. Resources in Channel Design: Distribution Differences in One Industry," *Industrial Marketing Management* 17 (August 1988):215–27.

DICKSON, PETER R., "Distributor Portfolio Analysis and the Channel Dependence Matrix: New Techniques for Understanding and Managing the Channel," *Journal of Marketing* 47 (Summer 1983):35–44.

HITCHCOCK, EARL, "What Marketers Love and Hate About Their Manufacturers' Reps," *Sales and Marketing Management* (September 10, 1984):60–65.

NARUS, JAMES A., N. MOHAN REDDY, AND GEORGE L. PINCHAK, "Key Problems Facing Industrial Distributors," *Industrial Marketing Management* 13 (1984):139–147.

NOVICK, HAROLD J., "The Case for Reps vs. Direct Selling. Can Reps Do It Better?" *Industrial Marketing Management* 11 (1982):90.

STERN, LOUIS W., AND FREDERICK D. STURDIVANT, "Getting Things Done," *Harvard Business Review* 65 (July–August 1987):34–41.

CHAPTER 12

Marketing Logistics: Physical Distribution and Customer Service

Regardless of the channels utilized, unless products are delivered in the right amount, at the right time, and in proper condition, buyers will not hesitate to switch suppliers. However, suppliers must be able to furnish this service at a cost that still allows them a satisfactory profit margin. Thus, manufacturers invest substantial resources in physical distribution systems that provide a satisfying level of customer service at an affordable cost. This chapter discusses

1. The importance of logistics in a marketing strategy.
2. The role of physical distribution and customer service.
3. Methods used to optimize customer service levels and reach desired profit goals.
4. Difficulties involved in optimizing customer service.

Customer service is a crucial element in any marketing strategy. Industrial customers depend on consistent deliveries to maintain production flow. Shutting down a production line due to a parts shortage results in a sizeable financial loss. Thus, as mentioned in Chapter Eleven, industrial buyers rank dependable service second only to product quality and more important than price when selecting suppliers.[1]

Logistical marketing activities—transportation, inventory availability, ware-

---

[1]William D. Perreault, Jr., and Frederick A. Russ, "Physical Distribution Service in Industrial Purchasing Decisions," *Journal of Marketing* 40 (April 1976), pp. 3-10.

housing, materials handling, and order processing—can also have a significant impact on customer costs and operations. Poor service in any area can cause delayed or inconsistent deliveries, forcing customers to carry larger safety stocks, to develop secondary sources of supply, or to utilize another source entirely to ensure a smooth-running, cost-effective operation.

Thus, the typical firm finds that the most effective logistical system is one that balances overall performance against total cost. Rarely will either lowest total cost or highest service performance be the best logistical strategy.[2]

THE RELATIONSHIP OF LOGISTICS AND PHYSICAL DISTRIBUTION

The term "logistics" originated in the military. In fact, Webster's dictionary gives the definition as "the aspect of military science dealing with the procurement, maintenance, and transportation of military matériel, facilities, and personnel." The unprecedented problems faced by Allied armed forces during World War II led to the

---

LOGISTICS SOFTWARE BOOMS AT DISTRIBUTION SHOW

Judging from the buyer interest at the second annual Distribution Computer Expo, . . . 'business logistics' is emerging as one of the hottest segments of the marketing software industry. . . . Some 95 vendors of software, time-sharing and consulting services played to a robust audience of 1,400 marketing executives bent on automating the information that accompanies goods in shipment from manufacturer through distributor to dealers and end users.

. . . Although the two-year-old Chicago show is not the biggest in the logistics field, its growth reflects expectations that logistics software and information services will grow to a $200 million business, from $40 million, in 'several years.'

. . . Logistics, a low-visibility but obviously critical backroom function for manufacturers, is a $500 billion business in the United States alone. . . . Managing the information portion of it quickly and accurately is an important part of logistics success.

For example, Geisco systems either customized or off-the-shelf linked field sales people with regional offices, headquarters and distribution points to facilitate quick deliveries, accurate price quotations, inventory and production scheduling and customer inquiries.

Source: Daniel C. Brown, "Logistics Software Booms at Distribution Show," *Business Marketing,* July 1984, pp. 19, 33. Reprinted with permission.

---

[2]Donald J. Bowersox, David J. Closs, and Omar K. Helferich, *Logistical Management,* 3rd ed., (New York: Macmillan Publishing Company, 1986), p. 30.

development of distribution systems that were quite remarkable for their time. Today, manufacturers use modern revisions to serve worldwide product markets.

In the business arena, logistics refers to the interrelation and management of all the activities (see Table 12-1) involved in making products and raw materials available for manufacturing and in providing finished products to customers when, where, and how they are desired. This requires the management of two primary product flows: physical supply and physical distribution. Physical supply (also called materials management) involves all those activities necessary to make production inputs (raw materials, component parts, and supplies) available to the manufacturing process. Physical distribution encompasses those tasks necessary to deliver the completed product to customers or channel intermediaries. These flows must be coordinated to meet delivery requirements of customers. However, while physical supply is certainly important, it is more the responsibility of production and purchasing. Thus, in this chapter, we focus on logistical activities involved in physical distribution, which is a responsibility of marketing. It is the physical distribution side of the logistical function that interacts with the customer's physical supply system. To support the customer's manufacturing process, suppliers must develop the logistical capability to respond to their needs. Failure to provide timely inputs to the production process can cost thousands of dollars in lost production time.

TABLE 12-1 Typical Logistical Activities

Key Elements	Supporting Activities
1. Transportation	1. Warehousing
a. Mode and carrier selection	a. Space determination
b. Carrier routing	b. Warehouse configuration
c. Vehicle scheduling	c. Stock layout and placement
2. Inventory management	2. Materials handling
a. Stock-level policies	a. Equipment and personnel
b. Short-term sales forecasting	b. Order picking procedures
c. Product mix by location	c. Stock storage and retrieval
d. Stocking locations	3. Protective packaging
3. Customer service	a. Design for handling
a. Determine customer needs	b. Design for storage
b. Analyze customer response to service	c. Design for protection
c. Set customer service levels	4. Production scheduling
4. Order processing	a. Aggregate volume forecasts
a. Sales order-inventory interface	b. Sequence and timing of production
b. Order information transmittal	5. Information maintenance
c. Ordering rules	a. Collection and storage
	b. Data analysis

Source: Adapted from Ronald H. Ballou, *Business Logistics Management: Planning and Control,* 2nd ed. (Englewood Cliffs, N.J.: Prentice-Hall, Inc., © 1985), pp. 7–8.

PHYSICAL DISTRIBUTION AND MARKETING STRATEGY

Industrial marketers can use logistics to create a competitive advantage in the marketplace.[3] Thanks to the computer, most organizations have become more sophisticated and effective in their problem-solving techniques. For example, both manufacturers and resellers have installed inventory control systems that can analyze demand trends, recalculate minimum-maximum quantity levels, and automatically issue necessary purchase orders or cancellations.

Faced with the necessity of reducing costs wherever possible, many businesses are lowering their holding costs by reducing inventory levels, seeking better utilization of their facilities, and becoming more efficient in materials handling. By establishing an efficient physical distribution system capable of providing quick, reliable delivery, the industrial marketer can pass on substantial savings to customers and gain a competitive advantage.

The importance of physical distribution and its ultimate impact on marketing objectives, however, depends on the type of product being marketed, the needs of the customer, and the structure of the distribution channel. Where products are used as inputs in the manufacture of other end products, buyers normally face a wide range of problems, including storage, stock control, order processing, and traffic management. Thus, suppliers of component parts frequently face challenging logistical performance demands from their customers. Suppliers of heavy equipment, on the other hand, are more concerned with the problems of meeting scheduled delivery dates than with the maintenance of a finished goods inventory and, therefore, tend to have relatively low logistical service requirements.

The effectiveness of physical distribution also has a dramatic impact on the ability of distributors and resellers to serve end markets. When manufacturers' delivery service is erratic, middlemen are forced to carry higher inventory levels or face stockouts, which can result in the loss of customers. Thus, their costs, as well as their ability to provide adequate product availability, are directly influenced by the physical distribution system.

THE TOTAL-COST APPROACH

The objective of an efficient physical distribution system is to minimize the costs involved in storing products and moving them from the point of production to the point of purchase within a specified level of customer service. Management of logistical activities, then, focuses on two essential variables: (1) total distribution costs and (2) the level of service provided to customers. The logistics system must result in a combination of costs and service levels that maximize profits to the firm and

---

[3]H. Jay Bullen, "New Competitive Selling Weapon—Physical Distribution Management," *Sales and Marketing Management,* May 8, 1985, pp. 41–42.

to channel members. Logistical costs in industrial markets vary considerably, depending on the nature of the product and the level of service. At the manufacturing level, logistical activities may consume as much as twenty-five percent of every sales dollar.[4]

Interactive Costs. The total-cost approach to logistics management is based on the premise that a firm should consider as a lump sum the costs of all the activities involved in physically moving and storing materials and products when it attempts to establish specific customer service levels. The costs of logistical activities interact, often in an inverse manner. For instance, a policy of maintaining low inventory levels to reduce holding costs can result in stockouts and backorders, special production runs, costly air-freight shipments, or even lost customers. When logistical activities are evaluated individually on their ability to achieve a given management objective, suboptimization often occurs. The total-cost approach seeks to achieve efficiency of the *entire system,* not just one specific activity. Thus, all cost items should be considered simultaneously, including the cost of lost sales that may result when service levels are too low.

Evaluating Cost Trade-offs. Cost trade-offs are not limited to any specific activity. They occur among all logistical activities. For example, Xerox once had forty sales branches stocked with complete inventories of supplies, including parts and chemicals, for their copying machines. When an investigation disclosed that only twenty percent of the items were ordered regularly, the firm decided to stock only those few items locally and consolidate the remaining inventory in selected regional warehouses. It was further recommended that goods be shipped from regional warehouses to sales branches overnight via air freight to maintain customer service. Management had never considered air freight as a normal transportation method because of its expense, failing to weigh that cost against the cost of maintaining multiple warehouses. Xerox is reported to have saved millions of dollars, in spite of increased transportation costs, by closing thirty-three warehouses.[5]

Hammond Valve Company's experience, on the other hand, was just the opposite. By opening six additional warehouses, it was able to cut total order cycle time from six weeks to two days. While overall logistical costs increased, they were more than offset by additional sales revenue due to the improved customer service level, so total profits went up.[6] Obviously, then, each aspect and level of logistical activities must be evaluated in relation to the revenue generated from the desired customer service level.

[4]Douglas M. Lambert and James R. Stock, "Strategic Planning for Physical Distribution," *Journal of Business Logistics* 3:2 (1982), p. 42.

[5]"New Strategies to Move Goods," *Business Week* (September 24, 1966), p. 119.

[6]Cited in Martin Zober, *Principles of Marketing* (Boston: Allyn & Bacon, Inc., 1970), p. 455.

WHAT IS CUSTOMER SERVICE?

The key to customer service is understanding the customer and the customer's perceptions. It doesn't matter what a supplier does in the area of customer service; it only matters what customers think the supplier does. If a company gives twenty-four hour delivery service, but its customers think it is 36-hour delivery, the relevant delivery time is thirty-six hours. If a company provides free trips for customers' purchasing personnel, but the purchasing department would prefer a lower price, the free trips are not a customer service.

. . . Customer service is presumed to be a means by which companies attempt to differentiate their product, keep customers loyal, increase sales, and/or increase profits. Thus, customer service is not just an outcome of business activities; it can be a managed element of that business.

Source: Frances Gaither Tucker, assistant professor, Department of Marketing, Syracuse University School of Management, "Need for a More Accurate and Reliable Measure of Customers' Opinion Regarding Customer Service," *Logistics Issues for the 1980's,* ed. by Messo Nishi, Logistics Resource, Inc., sponsored by Leaseway Transportation (Shaker Heights, Ohio: Corinthian Press, 1983), pp. 191–198. Reprinted with permission.

CUSTOMER SERVICE

Customer service presents a supplier with a classic cost/benefit trade-off decision. An improved service level will probably increase sales revenue, but it will likely increase costs also. But what about the potential impact on pricing? For example, from the customer's perspective, a reduction in order-cycle time (the elapsed time from placement of the order to receipt of delivery) justifies a lower buffer inventory and reduces holding costs. Consistent, on-time delivery performance by a supplier permits a routine, lower-cost purchasing process and greatly reduces the danger of production shutdowns. As discussed in earlier chapters, industrial buyers determine the value of a product not just by its invoice price, but by its total use cost. Therefore, when customers receive a higher level of service, resulting in lower use cost, they are more receptive to paying a higher price.

In effect, the selling firm should look at customer service not as a generated cost per se, but as an essential and contributory part of the total marketing mix. Economists like to remind us that there is no free lunch. We would also do well to remember that there are no free marketing tools.

Determining Customer Service Levels

Determining the level of customer service requires consideration of all those activities involved in filling orders and keeping customers happy. The service elements most frequently cited as important to buyers are shown in Table 12-2. Note the

TABLE 12-2 Relative Importance of Customer Service Elements

Element	Description	Importance to customers of Manufacturers	Resellers
1. Product availability	Most common measure; the percent of items shippable from stock.	42.7	43.1
2. Order cycle time	Elapsed time from placement of order until receipt of shipment.	19.4	25.5
3. Information support	Timely and accurate answers regarding inventory levels, order status, etc.	12.4	11.8
4. System flexibility	Ability to handle unusual situations, emergencies; to expedite and substitute.	11.6	10.1
5. Malfunction handling	Ability to rectify problems quickly (errors, delays, damage, claims, etc.)	8.0	7.2
6. Postsale support	Efficiency in providing technical support, repairs, spare parts, etc.	5.1	2.3
7. All other		.8	0.0
Total points		100.0	100.0

Source: Adapted from Bernard J. LaLonde and Paul H. Zinszer, *Customer Service: Meaning and Measurement* (Chicago: National Council of Physical Distribution Management, 1975), p. 118; also Bernard J. LaLonde, *The Distribution Handbook,* (New York: The Free Press, 1985), p. 244.

distinct similarity between the items shown here and the reasons given by industrial buyers for their use of distributors (Table 11-1). This similarity suggests two associated ideas: (1) distributors play a vital role in providing ultimate customer service levels, and (2) customers perceive the service provided by this indirect channel as being more consistent and effective than what they would obtain directly from the manufacturer.

Customer service has traditionally been a frustrating area to analyze because of the difficulties involved in establishing an all-inclusive statement of standards. As noted by a National Council of Physical Distribution Management task force, "No apparent means exist to specifically measure customer service performance in a total sense. Therefore, individual 'elements' must be defined and measured."[7] Customer service elements actually occur in three stages: (1) before the transaction (preaccount servicing, assistance in problem solution and product specifications),

[7]James C. Johnson and Donald F. Wood, *Contemporary Physical Distribution and Logistics,* 3rd ed., (New York: Macmillan Publishing Company, 1986), p. 69.

(2) as part of the transaction, (the speed and efficiency with which a supplier fills and delivers orders), and (3) after the transaction has been completed (the provision of technical services, training, and support materials).[8]

The customer's point of view should be the base for establishing customer service levels. Not all customers require the same level. As discussed previously, purchasers of heavy machinery generally have lower service needs than do those who buy component parts. The level of service also depends on the aspects of service that are most important to the customer; however, service levels cannot be set on customer desires alone. Management must also consider the nature of the competitive environment and its own profit goals.[9]

The Competitive Environment.   The competitive environment relates to industry service standards. Customers form expectations based on what they view as "normal" within their industry. When services are lower than those offered by competitors, sales will be lost unless some other element of the marketing mix offsets the deficiency. On the other hand, when customers neither expect nor value a given service, a supplier would be foolish to offer it.

When there are many competing products that perform basically the same task, good service is an essential competitive tool. However, when the product is a highly desired innovation with minimal competition, a high level of customer service may not be required.

Profitability.   The major criterion for evaluating the appropriate customer service level is profitability. The higher the level of service, the greater the costs involved. Rapid air freight to ensure fast delivery increases transportation rates. Therefore, the sales and cost impact of various service levels must be analyzed, both from the firm's perspective and the customer's.

Information must be developed on alternative service levels and resultant sales revenues. Figure 12-1 shows that profit contribution varies with the level of service. In the illustrated graph, at the present level of service, approximately seventy-three percent, profits are suboptimal. Between the seventy-third and eighty-fifth percent service levels, sales will increase faster than costs, generating additional profits. Beyond eighty-five percent, marginal costs increase faster than sales, with a resultant loss of profit. Thus, in this case, the optimal service level is at eighty-five percent. How much a firm should invest in customer service, however, can be determined only by studying the specific conditions in its industry and by assessing customer expectations.

Assessing and Optimizing Customer Service Requirements

The effectiveness of customer service policies depends on the customer's definition of desired service. Too often firms set service levels much higher than customers

[8]Ibid., pp. 69–70.
[9]Ibid., pp. 84–85.

How Much Should You Spend to Improve Service?

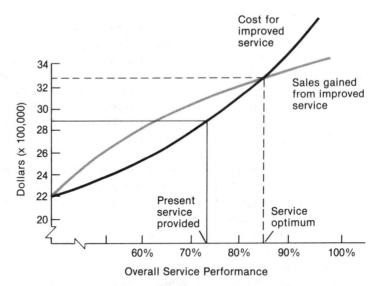

FIGURE 12-1 Cost Service Relations. How much should a firm spend on customer service to gain extra sales? Graph shows how much a typical firm can improve its share of market for each $100,000 spent. Indicated too is the point of diminishing returns, at which additional expenditures will exceed the value of increased sales. Although the graph suggests a breakpoint of about 85 percent, a company can determine its own figure only by studying specific conditions in its field. The nature of the product, geographic circumstances, transport characteristics, and other factors all affect optimum service point.

Source: Illustration from *Traffic Management* Magazine, September 1982, p. 55. Reprinted by permission.

require. Surveys indicate that customers often prefer a lower, but more reliable service level than what is normally offered.[10] Thus, customer service levels can be optimized by (1) researching the customer's needs, (2) setting service levels that realistically balance revenues and expenses, (3) making use of the latest technology in order processing systems, and (4) measuring and evaluating the performance of individual logistical activities.[11]

Customer Service Audits. Quantitative and qualitative information pertaining to the target market's perceptions of and desires for service can be obtained through

[10]Robert E. Smith, "How Much Service Do Customers Really Want?" *Business Horizons* (April 1978), p. 26.

[11]James R. Stock and Douglas M. Lambert, *Strategic Logistics Management,* 2nd ed., (Homewood, Ill.: Richard D. Irwin, Inc., 1987), p. 146.

an audit.[12] Not only does an audit evaluate existing services, but it also provides a benchmark for establishing effective customer service policies. Shifts in inventory policies, transportation modes, and warehouse locations have a direct effect on both channel members and end users. Customer service audits provide a viable means of assessing, and where necessary, redirecting, customer service strategy to emphasize those aspects that are important to customers or that represent uncompetitive performance.

This is another area in which distributors and reps can provide valuable information. Since they handle complementary, and even competing, product lines, they are in a better position to evaluate the various service levels available to customers and to assess the impact that each level has on sales volume.

The Impact of Logistical Service on Channel Members

Logistical service levels affect the relationship between the manufacturer and customer as well as the operations of channel members. Inefficient service to middlemen either increases their costs, by forcing them to carry higher inventory levels, or results in stockouts, leading to a loss of business. Poor logistical support in the channel negates the marketing effort of the firm by constricting potential sales and antagonizing middlemen. One study estimated that a five percent reduction in service at this level can result in a twenty percent decrease in sales to end markets.[13] Both the length and consistency of the order-cycle period affect the level of distributor inventories, which generally represent their highest asset investment and largest distribution expense. Distributors will not remain loyal when logistical service adversely affects their service to end users. To ensure an adequate level of logistical service to middlemen, information systems should provide realistic sales forecasts, and

---

THE COSTS OF NOT KNOWING YOUR COSTS

When suppliers "blissfully ignore" relevant costs, or underestimate costs, they may be "rejecting profitable alternatives to their present distribution systems."

For example, customer service standards can be maintained by using premium transportation from fewer distribution centers. The increased transportation costs are traded off against reduced inventory-carrying costs and reduced warehousing costs. To know exactly what the tradeoff is, though, you have to know what all these costs are.

Source: Denis Davis, "The Costs of Not Knowing Your Costs," *Distribution*, January 1984, p. 86. Reprinted with permission.

---

[12]Ibid., pp. 131–136.

[13]B. J. LaLonde and P. H. Zinszer, *Customer Service: Meaning and Measurement* (Chicago: National Council of Physical Distribution Management, 1976), p. 77.

where possible, inventory control systems should be linked to the manufacturer's information system.

IDENTIFYING COST CENTERS

Logistics management includes the integration of relevant cost centers so that the level of logistical service desired by customers and middlemen can be provided at the lowest possible cost. Management must consider both the operating costs and investment level associated with each level of customer service.

Total-cost analysis begins with the identification of relevant cost centers (i.e., transportation, warehousing, inventory, materials handling, and order processing). Depending on the firm's situation and customer needs, individual cost centers will vary in importance. Thus, the objective of total-cost analysis is to (1) identify the costs by activity center, (2) evaluate these costs in terms of a desired level of customer service, and (3) seek trade-offs between and among the various activity centers so that a possible cost increase in one activity is more than offset by a reduction in another.[14]

Cost Trade-offs. Cost trade-offs are possible within a single activity center. For instance, in the area of transportation, there are modal alternatives (rail, motor carrier, water, air, or pipeline.) Trade-offs can occur at two levels. The first trade-off concerns the type of mode selected, such as motor carrier over rail. Once a mode has been selected, trade-offs are possible within that mode, such as the use of leased versus company-owned trucks.

Of equal importance is the trade-off between and among activity centers. The number and location of warehouses, for example, affect inventory levels, transportation, materials handling, and order processing. Table 12-3 shows the results from several studies of logistical costs. Although the distributions vary, transportation, inventory carrying costs, and warehousing consistently account for the major portion.

While trade-offs within an activity center are relatively easy to identify, measuring trade-offs between and among centers is more difficult. Therefore, total-cost analysis begins with the identification of relevant cost centers.

Transportation

The single most important (and generally the most expensive) activity function in physical distribution is the shipment of goods to customers and/or middlemen. Depending upon the factors of speed, dependability, availability, and cost, product movement may be accomplished via air freight, rail, motor carrier, water, and, for some products, pipeline. Table 12-4 indicates how the five primary transportation modes have changed over the past five decades in terms of their relative shares of intercity freight.

[14]Bowersox et al., *Logistical Management,* p. 301.

TABLE 12-3 Examples of Logistical Cost Distribution

	Transportation	Inventory Carrying	Warehousing	Other
1. Composite 1976 [a]	35%	28%	18%	19%
2. Composite 1984 [b]	45	20	20	15
3. Electronics [c]	24	19	24	33
Machinery & tools	45	10	20	25
Chemicals & plastics	44	11	23	22
All manufacturers	46	10	26	18
Industrial resellers	22	52	11	15
Consumer resellers	33	35	17	15

Sources:
a) Herbert W. Davis & Co., "Survey of Selling Costs," *Sales & Marketing Management* [April 1976].
b) Adapted from *Davis Database*, a newsletter published by Herbert W. Davis & Co., Englewood Cliffs, N.J., [October 1984] as cited in Johnson and Wood, *Contemporary Physical Distribution and Logistics*, p. 106.
c) Adapted from LaLonde and Zinszer, *Customer Service: Meaning and Measurement* as cited in Ronald H. Ballou, *Business Logistics Management*, 2nd ed., [Englewood Cliffs, N.J.: Prentice-Hall, Inc., 1985] pp. 16–17.

TABLE 12-4 Distribution of Intercity Freight by Transportation Mode

Year	Railroad	Truck	Waterway	Pipeline	Air	Ton-miles [billions]
1940	61.3%	10.0%	19.1%	9.5%	—	618
1960	44.1	21.7	16.7	17.4	0.1	1,314
1980	37.5	22.3	16.4	23.6	0.2	2,487
1985	36.4	24.8	15.5	22.9	0.3	2,458
1987	36.8	25.1	15.6	22.2	0.3	2,640
Preliminary						
1988	37.0	25.2	15.5	21.9	0.3	2,793

Source: Frank Smith, *Transportation in America*, 7th ed., [Westport, CT: Eno Foundation for Transportation, 1989], p. 7.

Air Freight. Air freight is by far the most expensive mode of transporting freight (see Table 12-5). It is also the fastest from airport to airport, although this time advantage is often decreased by weather delays, terminal congestion, and/or the need to use other modes between airports and points of origin and destination. Its use is determined by unique circumstances rather than product categories.

Highly perishable goods (fresh seafood, cut flowers) are regularly shipped by air, as are emergency shipments of other products. Air freight is also used to ship products with a high value per density or weight in order to reduce overall logistical costs. For example, for a few hundred dollars, microprocessors worth thousands of dollars can be delivered overnight, reducing the backup inventory level from days to hours.

Truck. Since 1940, the trucking industry has increased its share of total intercity freight shipments (in terms of ton-miles) from ten percent to twenty-five percent. Trucks transport over seventy-five percent of all agricultural product tonnage, plus a wide variety of manufactured products, including most consumer goods.

Trucks compete favorably with air carriers for any size shipment transported up to one thousand miles. They also outperform railroads on shipments under ten thousand pounds transported five hundred miles or more.[15] The 3.8 million miles of highway in the United States allow trucks to reach many locations not served by other transportation modes. The 42,500 miles of the interstate system, while only one percent of total highway mileage, carry more than twenty percent of all auto and truck traffic.[16]

Rail. Railroads specialize in transporting raw materials, such as metallic ores, coal, gravel; unprocessed agricultural products; scrap; and automobiles. The bulk

TABLE 12-5 Relative Modal Costs (in Cents per Ton-mile)

Year	Railroad	Truck	Waterway	Pipeline	Air Freight
1970	1.4	8.5	0.30	0.27	21.9
1975	2.0	11.6	0.52	0.37	28.2
1980	2.9	18.0	0.77	1.00	46.3
1985	3.04	22.9	0.80	1.22	48.6
1987	2.73	22.0	0.74	1.11	42.5

Source: Frank Smith, *Transportation in America,* 7th ed., [Westport, CT: Eno Foundation for Transportation 1989], p. 12.

[15]Stock and Lambert, *Strategic Logistics Management,* pp. 176–177.
[16]Johnson and Wood, *Contemporary Physical Distribution and Logistics,* p. 112.

of rail shipments is in carload (CL) quantities, usually 30,000 pounds or more. In 1984, the average rail shipping rate was 3.1 cents per ton-mile, reflecting the efficiency of transporting commodities in bulk quantities. However, while railroads transported about fifty percent more tonnage than trucks did in 1984, the trucking industry received seven times more revenue.[17]

Pipeline. Transportation by pipeline is rather limited in adaptability. Products that are normally moved by pipeline include crude oil, refined petroleum, and natural gas. Almost ninety percent of all petroleum products are transported by this method.[18] By means of what are termed "slurry pipelines," other products such as coal may also be shipped. To accomplish this, coal is ground into a powder, which is then mixed with water and sent through the pipeline. Other products that are adaptable to this method include limestone, sulfur, potassium chloride, iron ore, and waste commodities.[19]

Intermodal Transportation. In addition to the individual forms of transportation modes available, a combination of two or more modes may be used. The major feature of intermodal transportation is the free exchange of equipment between modes. For example, transoceanic shipping containers are transferred to domestic airlines, or highway truck trailers are carried on railroad flatbed cars. Trailer on flat car (TOFC), or "piggyback," is by far the most common form of intermodal

---

DEREGULATION HAS IMPROVED AIR-FREIGHT FORWARDING SERVICE

Deregulation has created new price and service packages. Before the Deregulation Act, passed in 1978, air-freight forwarders were limited to the use of commercial carriers for moving freight. With deregulation came the freedom to fly anything anywhere, along with the opportunity to own and operate aircraft. Now, companies like Emery and United Parcel own their own aircraft fleets. Thus, they are able to offer same-day delivery, next-day delivery, and second-day delivery—a graduated level of service and prices, due to the removal of tarrif-filling requirements. The removal of geographic restrictions on air-freight pickup and delivery zones has also led to door-to-door service. Truckers can now carry freight far beyond an airport's boundaries. True air-truck intermodalism is emerging, whereby the truck performs far-ranging pickup and delivery service and the aircraft provides the linehaul.

Source: H. Harrington, "Freight Forwarders: Living with Deregulation . . . and Liking It," *Traffic Management,* November 1984, pp. 57–58, 62–64. Reprinted with permission.

---

[17]Ibid., p. 106.

[18]The American Waterways Operators, Inc., *Big Load Afloat* (Washington, D.C.: U.S. Inland Water Transportation Resources, 1965), p. 15.

[19]Johnson and Wood, *Contemporary Physical Distribution and Logistics,* pp. 120–121.

transportation service. This method is used to transport truck trailers over longer distances than trucks normally haul. The cost of this service is less than for trucking alone, and it provides the shipper the convenience of door-to-door service.

Freight Forwarders. Freight forwarders, because they consolidate shipments to get lower rates for their customers, are considered transportation middlemen. Transportation rates on less than truckload lots (LTL) or less than carload lots are often twice as high on a per unit basis as are TL or CL shipments. Freight forwarders charge less than the higher rate but more than the lower rate. In many instances, freight forwarders provide faster and more complete service than does a carrier.

State and Federal Regulation of Carriers

Decisions regarding the mode of transportation to use are also affected by the legal form of carriers—the extent to which the carrier's operation is subject to state and federal regulation. At present, there are four legal forms of transport: (1) common, (2) contract, (3) private, and (4) exempt.[20]

Common Carriers. Common carriers are licensed to operate only within specific geographical areas and may transport either specialized commodities, such as petroleum products and household goods, or general commodities. They must assume full responsibility for safe delivery of all shipments, at reasonable rates, and their services must be available to all shippers without discrimination. Virtually all railroads are common carriers, but common carriers also exist in other forms of transportation.

Contract Carriers. Contract carriers offer a specialized service to a limited number of firms, carry a restricted range of commodities, and serve a limited number of geographical points on a contractual basis. Contracts specify in detail the compensation rate to the carrier, the service to be rendered, and the carrier's financial liability in case of performance failure. Contract carriers are legally obliged to render service only to those customers with whom they have contracts, and the rates charged vary with the volume of traffic the shipper can offer. Thus, transportation costs on shipments are entirely variable. Additionally, due to the contractual arrangement between the carrier and the shipper, the service tends to be more personalized than that afforded by common carriers. Contract carriers are fairly extensive in the trucking and water carrier industries.

Private Carriers. Transportation facilities owned or leased by the shipper are referred to as private carriers. Since the services of privately owned or leased transportation modes are not sold outside the company, no regulation is needed.

[20]Ibid., pp. 173–175.

Exempt Carriers. Many carriers are exempt from regulation by the Interstate Commerce Act either geographically, for certain commodities, or because of the nature of the shipper association. Within certain zones or areas, as defined by the Interstate Commerce Commission, anyone may perform transportation service without price regulation restraints for commodities that are specifically exempt from regulation, such as agricultural products. In general, exempt carriers offer lower rates than common or contract carriers. However, since very few commodities receive exempt status, the exempt carrier is not a viable alternative for most shippers.[21] Certain shipper associations, such as agricultural cooperatives, retail cooperatives, and machine parts manufacturers' cooperatives, are also exempt.

Criteria for Selecting the Mode of Transportation

Transportation costs are directly affected by the location of the firm's warehouses, plants, and customers, and the level of customer service goals. The selection of individual carriers, however, is based on delivery performance—speed of service, dependability of delivery, and capability in accommodating the goods to be shipped—as well as the cost of the service.[22] Table 12-6 compares the five transportation modes on important operating characteristics.

Speed and Availability of Service. As mentioned previously, speed of service (i.e., the elapsed time to move products from one facility to another) is often more important than the cost of service. While slower modes involve lower transportation costs, they result in lower service levels. Thus, a firm must evaluate not only individual

TABLE 12-6 Comparison of the Five Modes of Transportation

Operating Characteristic	Transportation Mode				
	Rail	Highway	Water	Pipeline	Air
Speed	3	2	4	5	1
Availability	2	1	4	5	3
Dependability	3	2	4	1	5
Capability	2	3	1	5	4
Frequency	4	2	5	1	3

Source: Donald J. Bowersox, David J. Closs, and Omar K. Helferich, *Logistical Management,* 3rd ed., [New York: Macmillan Publishing Company, 1986], p. 166.

[21]Stock and Lambert, *Strategic Logistics Management,* p. 200.
[22]Bowersox et al., *Logistical Management,* p. 166.

transportation modes, but also various intermodal combinations. Availability is the ability of a mode to serve any given pair of locations. This factor will also, in many instances, necessitate intermodal combinations, particularly the use of trucks (in addition to rail, air, or water transport) for pickup and final delivery.

Dependability of Service.   Dependability of service refers to the ability of the carrier to deliver a product on time and in good condition. Dependability is at least as important as speed.

Carrier Capability.   The capability of the carrier to physically accommodate the size and weight of the product being shipped must also be considered. While barges have the capability of transporting the Saturn rocket because of their size, trucks are limited by state and federal weight restrictions.

Frequency of Service.   Frequency refers to the number of scheduled movements. Pipelines are best because of their continuous operation between two points. Trucks and air freight are next in line.

Transportation decisions depend on a number of interrelated factors: unit value of the product, predictability of demand, savings in transit time, the cost of the transport mode, related impact on inventory costs, and desired customer service levels. Table 12-6 shows the trend and magnitude of relative modal costs. The significant differences among the five modes is obvious. However, these differences cannot be analyzed properly except in the context of total logistical costs and customer service.

Transportation modes and specific carriers are normally selected on the basis of overall efficiency—the lowest rate for a desired delivery performance. Perhaps five percent of the time, customer orders will require speedier handling to meet unexpected changes in production rates or to replace defective parts. More frequently, higher transport cost will be used to offset even greater inventory carrying cost.

Warehousing

Significant opportunities for cost savings, without lessening customer service, exist in the area of warehousing. Decisions regarding the location of warehouse facilities have a tremendous impact on a firm's sales volume and distribution costs. When warehouses are properly deployed, customer delivery service can be improved, or transportation costs reduced, or both. The major problem in determining the number and location of warehouses is that the important factors to be considered (markets, customers, sources of supplies, transportation, and other distribution costs) are in a constant state of flux.

The objective of warehouse location decisions is to improve customer service and/or reduce costs. Thus, warehouses must be located so that the flow of goods to the market will be efficient and timely. For instance, if short order-cycle time is necessary (as is usually true for repair, maintenance, and operating supplies), warehouses are usually located in key markets to avoid costly order processing and premium air freight transportation.

Both the number and location of warehouses are influenced by the channel of distribution. When manufacturers' representatives are employed, it is usually necessary to support their selling function with strategically located inventories. In contrast, when industrial distributors are utilized, their stocking function eliminates or greatly reduces the need for company-operated warehouse locations.

Private or Public Facilities. Warehouse space may be owned, rented, or leased. When space is owned or leased, it is classified as "private warehousing." When rented space is utilized, it is referred to as "public warehousing." The chief advantage of private over public warehousing is total control of operations and personnel. Thus, from a customer service perspective, private warehousing generally provides a higher level because specialized equipment and facilities can be utilized, and company personnel are more familiar with the firm's products, customers, and service goals. While the investment in capital can be substantial, private facilities also provide operating cost advantages when they are used close to capacity. The main disadvantage of private warehousing is its inflexibility. When sales fluctuate, or demand shifts to another market area, they must either be operated at a loss or closed.

The most significant advantage of public warehousing is that it does not require the firm to commit a large sum of money. Since no fixed investment is required, a firm can increase or decrease usage in a given market, or move into or out of any market quickly. Thus, when demand is erratic or low in a given market, or sales volume is seasonal, public warehousing is an economical means of providing product availability. Public warehousing can also be used to supplement or replace distributors in a market, as well as to support the sales force or manufacturers' representatives. A major disadvantage, however, is that operating costs tend to be higher due to the inclusion of a profit factor, selling and advertising costs, and a premium to cover unused space.

Many public warehouses have begun to offer a variety of logistical services to their clients besides physical handling and storage. For example, Distribution Centers, Inc. (DCI), which operates out of Columbus, Ohio, maintains warehouse facilities in a number of major markets. DCI will repackage products to end users' order, label, and arrange for local delivery. DCI can also link its computer with the manufacturer's to facilitate order processing and inventory updating.[23] Table 12-7 lists factors to consider when choosing a public warehouse.

Warehouse Site Location. Warehouses should be situated so as to provide the desired level of customer service at the least cost of distribution. Warehouse location decisions are generally approached from a macro and micro perspective. Macro

---

[23]Michael D. Hutt and Thomas W. Speh, "Realigning Industrial Marketing Channels," *Industrial Marketing Management* 12 (July 1983), pp. 171–177.

TABLE 12-7 Factors Influencing the Choice of a Public Warehouse

How do you go about selecting a public warehouse? In a technical paper recently published by the Warehousing Education and Research Council, William R. Folz, senior vice president of Tri-Valley Growers, offers some tips on finding the right facility. The following recommendations are excerpted from his paper.

1. First, review the reasons for your requirement. Examine why you want to use a public facility.

2. Develop a list of warehouses you want to contact.

3. Contact each warehouse by phone and set up a personal visit. Consider the following points during the visit:

a. Housekeeping. Develop a perception of what the facility looks like every day. Is there an ongoing plan for good sanitation?

b. Equipment. Review equipment age, maintenance, number of makes, and equipment selection. A high percentage of old equipment may mean increased downtime and maintenance costs. A good maintenance program is a must. Keep in mind that the existence of a high number of makes may indicate a lack of purchasing strategy. Also, note whether the kind of equipment you require is readily available.

c. Operations control. Study the procedures that the warehouse uses to control costs and improve efficiency.

d. The facility. The building should be well maintained and meet your needs in terms of sprinklers, rail siding, dock doors, etc.

e. Management clerical procedures. Review administrative and clerical controls and procedures for inventory management, customer service, claims, shipment logs, etc.

f. Insurance. Know your insurance needs and inquire about the operator's coverage.

g. Proximity to rail yard/major highways. Study the facility's transportation access.

4. Obtain outside references. Talk to other users of a facility and ask their opinions of the services provided.

5. Ask about the warehouse's financial condition. If you're potentially a large customer, you can demand financial information and the operator probably will provide it.

Source: "How to Choose a Public Warehouse," *Distribution,* September 1984. Reprinted with permission.

considerations involve geographical choices of location, whereas micro considerations examine economic and legal factors within specific geographical areas.[24] From the macro perspective, warehouses may be (1) market positioned, (2) production positioned, or (3) intermediately positioned.[25]

Market-Positioned Warehouses.   Market-positioned warehouses are located close to final customers to maximize customer service levels. This type of warehouse location strategy is influenced by such factors as order-cycle time, order size, and the cost and availability of transportation.

Production-Positioned Warehouses.   These warehouses are located in close proximity to production facilities or sources of supply. While this type of location strategy does not

[24]Stock and Lambert, *Strategic Logistics Management,* p. 313.

[25]Edgar M. Hoover, *The Location of Economic Activity,* (New York: McGraw-Hill Book Company, 1948), p. 11, as cited in Stock and Lambert, *Strategic Logistics Management,* p. 313.

provide the same level of service that can be offered through market-positioned warehouses, production-positioned warehouse locations serve as collection points for products that are manufactured at a number of different plants. Factors influencing location close to production include product perishability, a very broad product line, multiple production sites, and advantageous transportation consolidation rates (TL and CP shipments).

Intermediately Positioned Warehouses. When a firm must offer a relatively high level of customer service and has a variety of products being produced at several plant locations, warehouses can also be located somewhere between customer and producer. Customer service levels for intermediately positioned warehouses are typically lower than market-oriented facilities and higher than production-positioned facilities.

Site location strategies, however, also include consideration of local economic and legal aspects. When a firm is leaning toward private warehousing, the following factors must be considered:

1. The quality and variety of transportation carriers serving the site.
2. The quality and quantity of labor.
3. Labor rates.
4. The cost and quality of industrial land.
5. The potential for expansion.
6. The tax structure.
7. Building codes.
8. The nature of the commodity environment.
9. The cost of construction.
10. The cost and availability of utilities.[26]

Factors to be considered when public warehousing is desirable are outlined in Table 12-7.

Inventory

The quality of inventory management has a significant impact on a firm's ability to serve customers well, but at a reasonable cost. Inventories act as a buffer against supply and demand uncertainties and as an economic trade-off to transportation, production, and other conflicting costs. Production and demand are rarely in perfect balance. Operating deficiencies, such as delayed shipments or inconsistent carrier performance, occur. And, because of machine breakdown or a sudden surge in their own market demand, industrial customers cannot always predict their requirements with certainty. Therefore, finished goods inventories are an essential part of any customer service system.

[26]Stock and Lambert, *Strategic Logistics Management,* p. 315.

Determining the level of inventory that will optimize customer service while minimizing cost requires full knowledge of inventory carrying costs and total system costs.[27] Inventory carrying costs impact both the number of warehouses used and transportation mode choice. Low carrying costs lead to more warehouses and slower, cheaper modes of transportation.

Inventory Carrying Cost.   Inventory carrying cost usually represents one of the highest costs in the logistical system and includes a number of different elements. These elements are subtle and difficult to comprehend, however, since they are not grouped together but are spread throughout the firm's accounting system. In fact, many firms do not calculate carrying cost directly, but use estimates or traditional inventory benchmarks.[28]

Inventory carrying cost is usually stated as a percentage of the total inventory value. For example, a carrying cost of twenty-five percent means that the cost of carrying one unit in stock for one year is twenty-five percent of the unit's value. This cost can range from thirteen to thirty-five percent, depending on the type of product, and can be considerably higher when all relevant inventory-related costs are included.[29] Thus, it is dangerous to use inventory trends or averages to compute carrying cost. Instead, each firm must determine its own percentage and attempt to minimize it.

Inventory costs should include only those costs that vary with the level of inventory and can be grouped into four basic categories: (1) inventory acquisition costs; (2) inventory service costs, such as property taxes and insurance; (3) storage space costs; and (4) inventory risk costs, including damage, pilferage, obsolescence, and relocation costs.

Optimizing Inventories

Being out of inventory can be costly. Customers grow disenchanted and turn to competitors. But carrying an inventory large enough to fill every order from stock can also be very costly. There is no hard-and-fast rule governing the percentage of orders that should be filled from stock. Most industrial marketers who deal with a broad, diversified product line accept the 80/20 axiom. This generalized principle states that approximately eighty percent of all sales will be generated by only twenty percent of the product line. Therefore, those products should represent a disproportionate share of the inventory to ensure that a minimal number of orders will be lost because of poor availability.

ABC Analysis.   This technique allows the identification of those items with the largest sales payoff. Inventory items are classified in three groupings: high dollar volume (A), moderate dollar volume (B), and low dollar volume (C).[30]

---

[27]Ibid., p. 354.
[28]Ibid., p. 358.
[29]Denis Davis, "Distribution Warehousing," *Distribution,* June 1984, pp. 65–66.
[30]Stock and Lambert, *Strategic Logistics Management,* pp. 420–422.

When the annual usage of inventory items is listed in descending order of dollar volume, as shown in Table 12-8, it becomes readily apparent how few items account for the preponderance of sales volume. The average sales price of an item does not automatically determine its classification. Many low-priced items will be classified A because of their high volume usage, whereas expensive items may generate very low volume. Through ABC analysis, suppliers can reduce inventory costs by cutting back on slow-moving items, while concentrating inventory dollars in fast movers. For example, when Kaman Bearing & Supply Corporation discovered that over half its assets were tied up in inventory, it overhauled the entire inventory system. With the assistance of ICPMG Peat Marwick, a cost-effective, computerized inventory control system that utilized ABC analysis was installed. Through accurate status reports on inventory levels plus improved sales forecasts, Kaman can now set product-by-product service levels that eliminate unnecessary inventory.[31]

Determining Inventory Levels. The goal of inventory planning is to find and maintain that level that provides the desired customer service at the least total cost in physical distribution. To accomplish that end, physical distribution managers, using sales forecasts and movement analyses, must determine how much inventory to keep on hand and when those stocks should be replenished to achieve the most economic cost. To obtain the lowest overall cost, managers must strike a balance between order processing costs and inventory carrying costs. The cost of restocking field warehouses typically includes (1) the cost of transmitting and processing the inventory transfer, (2) the cost of handling at the shipping and receiving points, (3) transportation costs, and (4) the cost of associated documentation.[32]

TABLE 12-8 ABC Analysis

Item	Sales	Percentage of Total Dollars	Percentage of Items	Item Category
1	$22,000			
2	20,000	51.5%	25%	A
	$42,000			
3	10,000			
4	8,000			
5	6,000			
6	4,000	34.4	40	B
	28,000			
7	5,000			
8	3,000			
9	2,000			
10	1,500	14.1	35	C
	11,500			

[31]Lisa Harrington, "Better Management Means Lower Costs," *Traffic Management* 21 (November 1982), p. 43.

[32]Stock and Lambert, *Strategic Logistics Management,* p. 404.

There are two basic approaches used to determine the best inventory policy. One is the economic order quantity model (EOQ), which is used under conditions of continuous, constant, and known rates of demand. The other is the fixed-order-quantity model, which is used when demand is uncertain.

The EOQ Model. The cost trade-offs involved in determining the most economical order quantity, given demand certainty, are shown graphically in Figure 12-2.

After determining the EOQ and dividing the annual demand by this quantity, both the size and frequency of the minimal-cost order will be known. The EOQ can be found through the following formula.[33]

$$EOQ = \frac{\sqrt{2PD}}{CV}$$

where

P = the ordering cost (dollars per order)
D = annual demand or usage (number of units)
C = annual inventory carrying cost (as a percent of product value or cost)
V = average cost or value of one unit of inventory

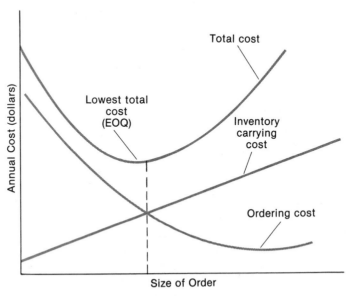

FIGURE 12-2 Cost Trade-Offs Required to Determine the Most Economic Order Quantity

[33]Ibid., p. 405.

If

$$V = \$100 \text{ per unit}$$
$$C = 25\%$$
$$P = \$40$$
$$D = 4{,}800 \text{ units}$$

then

$$\text{EOQ} = \frac{\sqrt{2(\$40)\ (4800)}}{(.25)\ (\$100)}$$

$$= \frac{\sqrt{384{,}000}}{25}$$

$$= 124 \text{ units}$$

THE SAD FATE OF THE EOQ FORMULA

One of the casualties of MRP thinking, indicates Ollie Wight, is the Economic Order Quantity (EOQ) formula. EOQ formulas, he says, are at best, a crude method of sizing order quantities to an imprecise understanding of what will be needed to meet manufacturing plans. With MRP, "we don't need an artificial mechanism, because we have real schedules with real numbers.

"If you asked 100 purchasing people how they use EOQ formulas, 98 of them would laugh at you. The other two would be right out of school where they still talk of such animals.

"In any case, the idea of the formula isn't bad if that's all you've got to work with. The trouble is that EOQs don't work that well in real life.

"I'll show you what I mean. First let's have Q stand for quantity; I for unit carrying costs; A for annual usage; and C for the purchase order cost. Most basic EOQ formulas are based on the principle of balancing inventory cost with the ordering cost. Like this:

$$\frac{QI}{2} = \frac{AC}{Q}$$

"On the inventory side, we're saying that whatever I order, I'll have half of that on hand, so we divide by 2.

"Now when we cross multiply we get:

$$Q^2 = \frac{2AC}{I}$$

Solving for Q we get:

$$Q = \frac{\sqrt{2AC}}{I}$$

"So far, everything is very logical. Now, here's what's wrong. First, no one knows what the cost of holding money is. Interest rates is only part of the cost. Next we are working from a forecast that is probably wrong. Then, the formula assumes a linear usage and linear costs. This just doesn't happen that often in real life.

"A really hard cost to plug into the formula is the ordering cost. What is it? Do we take something as ridiculous as the purchasing department's budget divided by the number of purchase orders issued? Or do we plug in some equally slippery number?

"My point is this: the EOQ formula says the key issue is how much you order. MRP says the key issue is scheduling to get the material at the right time. If your manufacturing process is held up waiting for a particular shipment, you've tied up a lot of inventory in spite of your EOQ formula. A good MRP system can provide better inventory control."

Source: Reprinted from Purchasing magazine, "The Sad Fate of the EOQ Formula," Purchasing, July 1982, p. 65. Copyright © by Cahners Publishing Company, 1982.

Although the EOQ model has received widespread attention and is broadly used in industry, its application under conditions of uncertain demand is restricted by its underlying assumptions:

1. The rate of demand is continuous, constant, and known.
2. Lead time is a constant or known.
3. Price is constant and is independent of order quantity or time.
4. All orders are filled (no stockouts permitted).
5. There is no inventory in transit.
6. There is no interaction between different items in inventory.
7. The planning horizon is infinite.
8. Capital funds are unlimited.

Fixed-Order-Quantity Model. Rarely does a firm know with certainty what demand to expect for its products. Order-cycle and transit times are not consistent. As a result, suppliers normally maintain additional inventory as safety stock, particularly for fast-moving products, to avoid lost sales. Fixed-order-quantity models (also termed min-max inventory models) enable the manager to concentrate on *when* to order. Through previous analysis of demand rate and necessary lead time (order-cycle time for replenishment stock), the manager knows the inventory level necessary for customer demand and the point at which replacement stock should be ordered.

For example, assume that a distributor sells an average of 1,000 gizmos per month, carries a maximum inventory equal to two months' demand, and never wants inventory to drop below two weeks' demand. In addition, the supplier's quoted delivery time is currently two weeks after receipt of order (ARO). From these data, we know the min-max inventory points are approximately 500 and 2,000 units, respectively. With lead time running two weeks, an order will have to be placed when the inventory level drops to 1,000 units (four weeks before stockout, or 250 units/week times 4). But what quantity should be ordered? Not 1,000. By the time delivery is made, two weeks later, inventory will be down to 500 units. So the manager ordes 1,500. If lead time changes to three weeks, the replacement order will still call for 1,500 units, but will be placed when the inventory level reaches 1,250. (Think it through.)

Computer Simulation. Computer simulation or statistical techniques, such as IBM's inventory management program and control technique (IMPACT), are used to determine the amount of safety stock necessary to satisfy a given level of customer demand. IBM's IMPACT model is used by firms that are mainly concerned with the distribution phase of their production/distribution systems, such as wholesalers, retailers, and suppliers of basic materials.[34] The primary objective of IMPACT is to provide inventory control rules that minimize cost. Its main advantage is that it forces management to (1) forecast demand, (2) determine the required safety stock for a specific level of customer service, (3) determine the order quantity and time for reorder, (4) consider the effects of freight rates and quantity discounts, and (5) estimate the expected results of the inventory plan. Users of the IMPACT system claim that it

1. Reduces inventory costs because inventory size is reduced with no loss in service to customers, or service levels have increased with no additional inventory.
2. Improves overall management control because the specific rules and objectives are consistent and easily revised, the effectiveness of the system can be measured, customer service is more stable, unprofitable product lines and slow-moving items are readily identified, and the cost output from the program is valuable for profit analysis and planning.

Whatever system is applied, it must be applied cautiously and will depend on the cost and service trade-offs involved. Inventory decisions must be based on cost/service and transportation/warehousing trade-offs. Analysis of product turnover and customer usage dictate the specific inventory, transportation, and warehousing policies to be implemented.

Order Processing

An essential aspect of logistical coordination is an efficient order processing system. Physical distribution starts with the receipt of a customer order and ends when the customer receives the shipment. Order processing functions include (1) a credit check by the credit department, (2) crediting the salesperson with the sale, (3) re-

[34]Ibid., pp. 424–428.

cording the transaction in the accounting department, (4) contacting the warehouse nearest to the customer to arrange for shipment, (5) updating the firm's master inventory controls, and (6) translating shipping documents into an invoice and a permanent sales record.[35] An efficient system should also include communicating with customers as to expected arrival dates, anticipated delays, incomplete orders and/or substitutions, or any impending changes in price.

Materials Handling

The cost-effectiveness with which inventory will be physically handled in warehouses and elsewhere depends on a variety of factors: absolute volume and the degree to which it fluctuates, relative space and labor costs, and the ability to minimize idle time, overtime, breakdowns, breakage, and errors. The efficient use of mechanized handling equipment (forklifts, hoists, handtrucks, conveyors, computer-aided stocking, and retrieval equipment) can also help to minimize costs.

THE OVERALL CONTRIBUTION OF MARKETING LOGISTICS

An effective logistics system plays an essential role in the overall marketing strategy of the firm, particularly in maintaining a favorable customer perception of the firm's service capability and attitude. The effectiveness of logistical activities establishes the level of customer service. For example, the availability of products is largely determined by company inventory and storage policies, while delivery reliability is largely the result of efficient order processing and carrier selection. Thus, when used effectively, a well-designed logistics system can be an invaluable selling tool. Further, the ability to meet customer service needs is prerequisite to maintaining long-term customer relationships.

The actual effectiveness of marketing logistics, however, depends on four basic factors. First, the marketer must recognize that the ability of the firm to provide a high level of customer service is of great concern to many customers, and those customers should be informed of the firm's ability to meet their needs in a straightforward, realistic manner whenever possible. Specific information pertaining to product packaging, material handling, order processing, transportation modes, and normal delivery times and their variability must be transmitted to customers. Second, sales people must listen to customers to determine their service needs, demonstrate an understanding of those needs, and relate to customers what the company is capable of doing in meeting those needs. Third, procedures to meet emergency situations, such as the shipment of rush orders or critical parts, must be developed and communicated to customers. Fourth, sales people must be capable of explaining any available service options and their price differentials to customers. The crucial

[35]Ibid., p. 505.

point is that the marketer be fully aware of the capabilities of the distribution system, integrate these capabilities into the overall marketing strategy, and communicate the results to customers.

LOOKING BACK

Marketing logistics alone do not determine the effectiveness of a marketing strategy, but while a highly effective and competitive system will improve any strategy, an inefficient system will reduce a brilliant strategy to mediocrity.

A logistics system is the interrelation of all those activities (inventory control and storage, order processing, material handling, transportation, and customer communications) that move products efficiently and cost-effectively from a point of manufacture to the end user. The combination of these activities is commonly referred to as *customer service.*

Every activity has a cost, but not every one has a value—to every customer in every market. Therefore, a firm will wisely survey its target markets to identify those services with the highest value to the majority of customers, thus providing some reasonable assurance of optimizing the return on its logistics investment.

Optimizing the return will involve cost trade-offs not only within operating departments, but across departmental lines. Therefore, strategic logistical decisions will have to be made at middle to upper management levels. These decisions will include the level of customer service, normal and emergency transportation modes, number and type of warehouses, and overall inventory level.

Given the increasing complexity of modern logistics systems and the broadening of product lines, a firm (if it has not already done so) should give serious consideration to one other cost, namely, the cost of computerizing the entire system. The inaccuracies, slow response, cost, and relative inflexibility of a manually controlled system make the trade-off decision rather straightforward.

QUESTIONS FOR DISCUSSION

1. Marketing logistics entails a variety of activities, all aimed at providing products to customers on a timely basis. Describe these activities and show how they are all interrelated.
2. Each logistical activity has associated costs, but a purposeful cost increase in one area might actually reduce the cost of the entire system. Explain this apparent contradiction.
3. Certain market conditions increase the pressure on a supplier to maintain a competitive logistics system. Describe some of these conditions and explain why they have such an impact.
4. What factors should a firm evaluate in determining what level of customer service to offer and which elements to emphasize?
5. What modes of transportation would best serve the following situations and why:
   a. Shipping iron ore from the Mesabi Range in northeastern Minnesota to steel mills in Gary, Indiana?

      b. Shipping $100 microchips from a semiconductor plant in Texas to distributors in New York, Chicago, and San Francisco?

      c. Shipping auto air conditioners from a factory in Ohio to an automotive assembly plant near Los Angeles?

      d. Shipping head lettuce from the San Joaquin Valley to markets in the Midwest? To Seattle?

6. What factors should a firm consider in deciding
      a. Where to locate warehouses?
      b. Whether to operate its own or use public facilities?

7. How can a firm determine "the right amount" of inventory to carry in stock?

SUGGESTED ADDITIONAL READINGS

BULLEN, H. J., "New Competitive Selling Weapon—Physical Distribution Management," *Sales and Marketing Management* (May 8, 1985):41–42.

HARRINGTON, LISA, "Better Management Means Lower Costs," *Traffic Management* 21 (November 1982):43.

HUTT, MICHAEL D., AND THOMAS W. SPEH, "Realigning Industrial Marketing Channels," *Industrial Marketing Management* 12 (July 1983):171–177.

LAMBERT, DOUGLAS M., AND JAMES R. STOCK, "Strategic Planning for Physical Distribution," *Journal of Business Logistics* 3:2 (1982):42.

SMITH, ROBERT E., "How Much Service Do Customers Really Want?" *Business Horizons* (April 1978):26.

PART SIX

Formulating Marketing Communication Planning

CHARLES WANG DOESN'T WING IT ON CUSTOMER SATISFACTION

Discussing his family's immigration to the United States in 1952, Charles Wang said, "You hear stories about people coming to this country with two suitcases. I'm not sure if we had both." Today, as C.E.O. of the largest independent computer software company in the world, Computer Associates, Mr. Wang carries more luggage to everyday company meetings than the cargo of his immigrant parents of yesteryear.

One of his customer ideas gives insight into the explanation of his success—in order to fulfill customer needs, he goes much farther than most companies are willing to go. His salespeople distribute forms requesting information regarding customer desires. Those ideas are then submitted to customer groups to determine the extent of market desires.

In order to ultimately fulfill customer needs, Mr. Wang will lead in-house developments of new products or ask his employees to locate present suppliers of desired products. He will frequently purchase those suppliers. During the last seven years, Computer Associates has purchased about eighteen companies or products at a cost of over $1.5 billion.

A major reason for Mr. Wang's success is unquestionably his well-conceived plan to fulfill customer needs. It surpasses competitors' maneuvers by not only mandating written surveys of customer needs, but by committing considerable funds for the development of new products to fill those needs, and, even more inspiring, by purchasing other suppliers' products or even entire competitive companies.

Source: Sue Kapp, "A Fast Breaker," *Business Marketing,* September 1989, pp. 12–16. Reprinted with permission.

Successful communication strategy depends on the industrial marketer's understanding of its role in the marketing mix. While advertising and sales promotion are important communication tools, due to the complexity and sophistication of many industrial products, systems, and applications, and the uniqueness of buying situations, personal selling is a primary contributor to industrial marketing success. In this section, then, we discuss how industrial marketers go about developing and managing an effective, efficient professional sales force and how advertising and sales promotion are used to supplement, support, and reinforce the selling effort.

CHAPTER 13

Developing the Industrial Sales Force

Salesmanship, according to Irving Shapiro, is "the art of successfully persuading prospects or customers to buy products or services from which they can derive suitable benefits."[1] Successfully persuading today's buyers, however, requires the capability of analyzing buyers' and potential buyers' needs to communicate effectively the firm's offering, skills in interpersonal relations to deal with the diversity of personalities encountered, and the ability to negotiate over areas of differences to bring about a mutual satisfaction of the goals of both the buyer and the seller. The purpose of this chapter, then, is to discuss how sales managers can develop and direct an efficient, professional sales force by

1. Effectively selecting and hiring potentially successful sales people.
2. Utilizing sales training as a means of maximizing the full potential of sales people.
3. Using methods of directing the sales force to produce the most favorable results.
4. Developing compensation packages and other incentives to achieve the greatest amount of sales force motivation.

As many successful salespeople will tell you, selling is a personally rewarding career opportunity. Not only does it offer the career person a lucrative income and

---

[1] Irving J. Shapiro, *Marketing Terms,* 3rd ed. (West Long Branch, N.J.: S-M-C Publishing Co., 1973), p. 147.

WOMEN IN INDUSTRIAL SALES

More and more women are moving into industrial sales, taking on positions that were once exclusively men's. They're selling everything: steel, lumber, heavy machinery, and high-tech computer systems. While they are still a minority, many of them are making great inroads, particularly in the area of computer sales. At Xerox and Computer Sciences, a California-based corporation, for instance, they represent more than one-fourth of the sales force.

Regardless of the problems they face, such as role reversal, sexual overtures, and loneliness during travel, they continue to prove their ability. Women are mastering the intricate knowledge of complicated product lines and are selling and servicing their accounts as well as, if not better than, their male counterparts. And according to D.D. Miller, board chairman of Rumrill-Hoyt, Inc., "women are often better sales representatives then men. . . . Women are often far better prepared, far more organized, and do a far better follow-up job, and think a lot faster on their feet than do their male counterparts."

Although women were still reporting that they were often objects of sexual advances and had difficulty in learning to pick up the tab for drinks and meals courteously when entertaining clients, . . . it seems the main obstacle they have not yet overcome is the feeling of isolation and vulnerability when on the road. Walking into a lounge for a drink, eating in a restaurant, or being in an airport alone at an odd hour still seems to be very uncomfortable to many females. And until they learn to handle it, their advancement up the ladder may be difficult. Divisional directors, for instance, can spend from three to six weeks on the road.

Source: See Robert N. Carter and Milton R. Bryant, "Women as Industrial Sales Representatives," *Industrial Marketing Management,* 9 (1980), pp. 23–26; "On the Job with a Successful Xerox Saleswoman," *Fortune,* April 30, 1984, p. 102; and "A Women's Place Is on the Sales Force," *Sales and Marketing Management,* April 1, 1985, pp. 34–37.

---

career path (see Figure 13-1), but it provides a springboard for those who wish to advance into management positions. According to a recent survey, nearly half of this nation's top CEOs have business degrees, with very nearly equal proportions coming from each major business degree. For example, thirteen percent hold marketing degrees.[2]

According to the U.S. Labor Department, by the year 2000 approximately 1.5 million people will be employed in industrial sales.[3] The greater portion of these people will come from the field of marketing. In fact, estimates are that nearly sixty percent of all marketing graduates begin their careers in sales.[4] And, with sales

[2]Louis E. Boone and David L. Kurtz, "CEOs: A Group Profile," *Business Horizons* (July–August 1988), pp. 38–42.

[3]*Occupational Projections and Training Data,* 1980 Edition, Bulletin 2052, U.S. Department of Labor, Bureau of Labor Statistics (September 1980), pp. 44–47.

[4]Louis E. Boone and David L. Kurtz, *Contemporary Marketing,* 5th ed. (Chicago: The Dryden Press, 1986), p. 437.

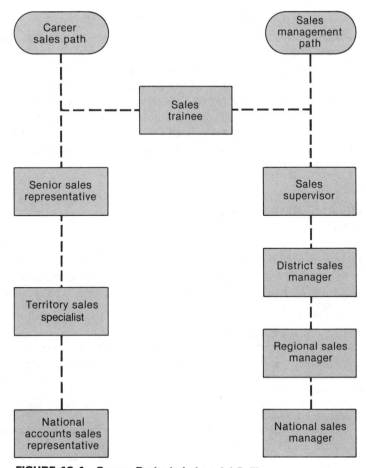

FIGURE 13-1   Career Paths in Industrial Selling

Source: Vincent L. Pesce, Jr., "Careers in Technical Sales and Marketing," *Graduating Engineer,* Spring 1980, p. 105.

compensation ranging from $18,000 to $110,000, more and more women are choosing industrial sales as their career.[5]

Professional salespeople, those people who choose to stay in selling, however, are unique, different from other people. They have particular and even peculiar desires—desires that somehow set them apart from other members of the corporate firm. These uniquely different individuals are often difficult to find. Thus, conventional methods of personnel selection can too frequently lead one with hiring authority to make a suboptimal selection of a salesperson in the industrial arena. Professional salespeople, the people who are vital to the firm in developing and carrying on the long-term buyer-seller relationship, are motivated by means other than those

---

[5]"User's Guide," *Sales and Marketing Management* (February 20, 1989), p. 8.

that inspire the more conventional corporate employee. Table 13-1 capsulizes one outstanding salesperson's perception of what makes a successful salesperson. It portrays that person as a very special type of individual.

To cultivate a professional sales force with such enviable attributes from among the masses of more ordinary people, sales managers must be especially thoughtful in developing procedures that differentiate among applicants for sales positions. Then, to develop their full potential, sales managers must tailor training programs so that they provide not only the usual selling skills but also additional human relations and negotiating skills, skills that are so necessary in the long-term buyer–seller interface.

SELECTING AND RECRUITING INDUSTRIAL SALESPEOPLE

In selecting and hiring salespeople, any or all of the conventional selection steps can be employed. As Table 13-2 shows, the personal interview, personal history application evaluation, and personal reference check are the most commonly used

TABLE 13-1 The Salesman*

Usually has no one he's trying to impress. He feels his production speaks for itself.

Gives a straight answer under all circumstances, even if he knows the boss really wants to hear something else.

Would like to get involved in the "big picture" to an extent, but will not lose any sleep if he is not asked to participate.

Prefers "action oriented" direction, rather than coffee-klatch philosophizing.

Does not get involved with internal political movements.

Almost always looks to his peer group for the acknowledgment of his personal contributions, rather than to the "titled ones."

Is not afraid to ask for suggestions from people in other departments, as long as the suggestions will help him accomplish his goals.

Feels he is a crusader for the company's cause.

Truly feels that he has more insight into the customer's needs and wants than anyone else (including the president).

Normally more than happy to give field input but must first feel that the request is genuine.

Is the type of person who truly recognizes the help given by people in all departments to properly service the customer.

Advocates internal communication either directly or by phone and has very little use or respect for type-written memos.

His competitive drive comes naturally and he shows a great deal of genuine enthusiasm for a common cause that he believes makes sense.

Feels all customers are important.

*A profile of an individual who wants to be referred to as a "salesman" (or even as a "peddler," for that matter).

Source: Nick DiBari, "Marketing vs. Sales! Is There Really a Difference?" Sales and Marketing Management, September 10, 1984, p. 52. Reprinted with permission.

TABLE 13-2 Percentages of Small and Large Firms That Extensively Use the Following Selection Tools

Selection Items	Percentage of Small Firms	Percentage of Large Firms
Personal interviews	91%	96%
Application blanks	73	70
Personal reference checks	70	62
List of job qualifications	34	45
Job descriptions	30	51
Psychological tests	22	32
Credit reports	15	36

Source: Reprinted by permission of the publisher from "A Survey of Sales Management Practices," by Alan J. Dubinsky and Thomas E. Barry, *Industrial Marketing Management,* 11(1982), pp. 133–141. Copyright © 1982 by Elsevier Science Publishing Co., Inc.

methods of selecting sales personnel. In fact, over ninety percent of all businesses use personal interviews.[6]

Primary Selection Criteria

Generally, organizations tend to evaluate three criteria when searching for sales personnel: motivation, human relations skills, and job knowledge. In searching for industrial salespeople, sales managers should also look for individuals who have technical backgrounds and abilities in performing negotiations.

In the area of industrial selling, it is quite common to consider a candidate's technical background to determine how well that person can meet the demands for technical knowledge. Individuals with good technical skills are better able to identify buyer problems and suggest solutions—an increasingly important consideration in industrial selling.

Due to the nature of the buyer–seller interface, which typically requires negotiating sizable purchases and the maintenance of favorable intercompany relationships over long periods of time, industrial salespeople must possess good human relation skills and negotiating abilities. Not only does IBM, for example, look for people who are highly motivated with good communication skills, it looks also for candidates who have technical abilities or aptitudes. Thus, all candidates for a selling position with IBM are required to take the Information Processing Test to determine if they possess the ability to learn and/or understand technical information.[7]

---

[6]Alan Dubinsky and Thomas Barry, "A Survey of Sales Management Practices," *Industrial Marketing Management,* 11 (1982), pp. 133–141.

[7]"The IBM Salesperson Is King," *Sales and Marketing Management* (December 3, 1984), p. 39.

Personal Interviews

The primary method used to determine if a candidate is motivated, has good human relations skills, and has the ability to learn the necessary technical, selling, and negotiating skills is the personal interview. Numerous studies, however, have shown that its validity (ability to determine what it is intended to determine) is lower than other selection techniques.

Multiple and Panel Interviews.   To overcome the weakness in the personal interview, many companies are turning to multiple or panel-type interviews. Multiple interviews involve interviewing the candidate at different times with various company individuals. In the panel interview, the candidate appears before a diverse group on just one occasion. Both techniques, however, help in reducing biases that can occur when only one interviewer is involved. They also provide a better means of determining the technical skills of interviewees.

Patterned or Structured Interviews.   The most successful interviewing method is the patterned or structured interview, which involves constructing questions beforehand and asking all interviewees those same questions. This technique allows interviewers to compare responses among candidates. During the interview, for example, candidates can be asked open-ended questions (questions that cannot be answered by a simple "yes" or "no"). Since open-ended questions begin with words like who, what, why, where, when, and how, they force the interviewee to reveal more of his or her thought processes. Thus, they are more valuable than are less thought-provoking, closed-ended questions.[8]

Problem-solving questions are also used to reveal reasoning abilities and are useful in determining a candidate's technical capabilities. Such questions involve the candidate in a situation that must be analyzed and responded to. For example, the candidate might be asked: "What would you do if a buyer made several appointments to meet with you but was never in her office when you arrived?"

Realistic Job Previews.   Increasingly, companies are using "realistic job previews."[9] This type of interview involves informing the candidate about the difficulties as well as the favorable aspects of the position. Many companies also allow the candidate to spend a day in the field, making sales contacts with a company salesperson. Realistic job previews enable a candidate to feel that he or she has contributed more in making the decision to join the company; that is, he or she "owns" the decision. Individuals who believe that they make decisions (versus being "sold") tend to attempt to prove that they made the correct decision.

---

[8]Thomas Stroh, *Managing the Sales Function* (New York: McGraw-Hill Book Company, 1978), p. 228.

[9]Leonard Sayles and George Strauss, *Managing Human Resources* (Englewood Cliffs, N.J.: Prentice-Hall, Inc., 1981), p. 176.

Auditioning.   Since the recessionary years of the early 1980s resulted in eliminating many executive positions, a new slant on hiring has come into use: auditioning.[10] Auditioning is intended to ensure, through on-the-job observance, that new executives will be capable. This practice generally involves placing a candidate in a prospective position for just three to six months. The time limit is strictly adhered to. At or before the end of the period a decision is made regarding hiring the executive.

One can easily rationalize how auditioning can be most stressful. Candidates feel obliged to "prove out," and to do so during that very short three- to six-month time period.

However, auditioning does enable the executive to receive a salary, often higher than salaries of peers, since usually no fringe benefits are given during the auditioning period. Auditioning also can allow the truly capable executive to outshine his or her lesser counterparts whereas other selection methods are generally less predictive regarding who will do best.

DEVELOPING PROFESSIONAL SALESPEOPLE

Salespeople must be provided with the necessary training if they are to perform at their full potential. The importance of sales training in developing the industrial sales force is exemplified by the considerable amount of money expended on it. In the area of consumer sales training, for instance, the average amount spent on each industrial salesperson in 1988 was $22,236, compared to $11,617 for consumer salespeople. Industrial salespeople also spend more time in training: an average of eight months for sales trainees versus five months for consumer sales trainees.[11] To prevent salespeople from becoming stale or outdated, ongoing training should also be provided. Unfortunately, however, experienced industrial salespeople are often the forgotten members of the selling team.[12]

> Industry has done a magnificent job of continuing the training and development of the new sales trainee, of sales management, of middle management, and of upper management, but little has been produced and directed to the specific needs of the person on the firing line.

Recurring training throughout the salesperson's selling career not only rejuvenates their self-motivation, it is also necessary as new products are developed and when environmental changes occur, such as new competition or new ways of doing things.

---

[10]Arthur Bragg, "A New Twist: 'Auditioning' for a Job?" *Sales and Marketing Management* (July 1988), pp. 30–35.

[11]"1988 Survey of Selling Costs," *Sales and Marketing Management* (February 20) 1989, p. 23.

[12]David Arthur Stumm, *Advanced Industrial Selling* (New York: AMACOM, 1981), p. ix.

TRAINING ISN'T MICRO AT IBM

"The importance of education to IBM shows up clearly in some simple numbers. On any given day, 18,000 of its 390,000 employees take part in some kind of formal education event—in a classroom, through self-study, or via computer-based training. IBMers around the world complete a staggering five million student days per year, giving each one an average of about twelve days. The yearly education budget of $900 million includes the costs of the people, equipment, and facilities needed to deliver the training but does not include the salaries of the people being trained."

Source: Patricia A. Galagan, "IBM Gets Its Arms Around Education," *Training & Development Journal,* January 1989, pp. 34–41. Copyright © 1989, American Society for Training and Development. All rights reserved. Reprinted with permission.

The Use of Learning Theory in the Training of Professional Salespeople

Training industrial sales people involves learning theory that is applicable to collegiate learning, as well as learning that is not.[13]

Motivation. The most important element of learning theory is the motivation to learn. The college student who has been turned off by a particular instructor knows the difficulties of attempting to master that instructor's course material. While newly hired salespeople tend to be motivated to learn, long-time employees can have difficulties. Thus, it is absolutely essential that the person doing the training is adequately prepared and capable.

Involvement. Learning theory also requires that salespeople be involved in learning activities. In the specialized area of industrial sales, salespeople can participate in most phases of learning through role playing involving sales presentations, human relations skills, and negotiating. While role playing has been criticized for creating an unreal situation, it is very effective for simulating different kinds of sales situations, allowing enthusiastic participants to get into the game and develop their full potential. This type of "learning through performing" is often extended into the field by dividing the training into small segments and encouraging salespeople to put their learning to use with actual customers during intervals between training segments.

Feedback. Salespeople must also be provided with positive feedback when they use their newly learned materials on the job. Meaningful feedback should also be provided in classroom exercises. The value of immediate, positive reinforcement,

---

[13]This section is based on Sayles and Strauss, *Managing Human Resources,* pp. 205–207.

at a level appropriate to the accomplishment, has been well proven by behavioral psychologists. In this regard, sales work exercises and role playing are particularly conducive to positive reinforcement when trainers make use of videotapes and recordings of participants' performances. When video cameras or other playback equipment is utilized, participants are able to view their behavior in various selling situations, learning more about their actions or potential actions in dealing with customers.

Experienced Versus Inexperienced Salespeople. Experienced salespeople often have difficulties digesting or accepting new concepts because of previous training and experience. New material often seems to be in conflict with what they believe to be true. For that reason, some sales managers tend to hire inexperienced salespeople rather than cope with the confusion experienced salespeople feel when being trained in a new company. These feelings of discomfort, however, are generally of little consequence when compared to the considerable potential these experienced salespeople bring to their new positions.

Accelerated Learning. A recent trend in training is accelerated learning. The principles of accelerated learning involve (1) being positive and accepting; (2) providing a natural, comfortable, and colorful setting; (3) exalting rather than trivializing trainees; (4) helping people eliminate or reduce any fears, stresses, or learning barriers; (5) being supportive of both trainer and trainee; (6) providing a multidimensional approach to learning; (7) accommodating different learning styles, speeds, and needs, rather than forcing people, assembly-line fashion; (8) making learning fun rather than overly serious or solemn; (9) providing for group-based learning; and (10) presenting material pictorially as well as verbally.[14]

Accelerated training seems to parallel the current flow of managerial thought; that is, it uses theories that study what makes a good manager good. It emphasizes principles of positive reinforcement, the foundation of many developing management-marketing programs. The commitment to making training a positive learning experience is certainly a valuable addition to previous learning theory.

Who Should Train?

To a large degree, successful training depends on the capabilities of those persons doing the training. Training is a specialized skill, and care should be taken in choosing those who are to do the training. The three most popular types of sales trainers are (1) the sales manager, (2) an experienced salesperson, and (3) training specialists.

Sales Managers as Trainers. When sales managers are given the obligation of training new salespeople, several advantages accrue. The salesperson's immediate super-

[14]Mary Jane Gill and David Meier, "Accelerated Learning Takes Off," *Training & Development Journal,* January 1989, pp. 63–65.

DIGESTIBLE TRAINING PROGRAMS CAN INCREASE SALES

Richardson Brothers, a Wisconsin furniture manufacturer, attributes a 41 percent sales incrase to Step into Your Future. Step into Your Future is a sales training and consulting company that tailors programs for its clients. For a sum of $45,000 Richardson increased sales by $2.6 million over a six-month period. The program, which contained 6 hours of videotape, 16 hours of audiocassettes, and a 240-page training manual, was tailored into "digestible" hourly segments followed by a week of on-the-job practice for Richardson's 36 sales people. Dealers too purchased the program for $550 and, in return, increased their sales by an average of 60 percent.

Source: See "Richardson's 'Digestible' Program," *Sales and Marketing Management,* September 10, 1984, pp. 28, 30.

---

visor acquaints him or her with precisely what he or she will be evaluated on in the future, the trainee gains the experience of preparing for a sales presentation and meeting with the sales contact along with the experienced sales manager, and the sales manager, having firsthand experience with the trainee, can pinpoint the salesperson's strong and weak points so that future areas of developmental needs can be anticipated. Sales managers, however, have busy schedules, are afraid of destroying the formal supervisor/subordinate relationship, and lack knowledge of learning theory. Trainees are also often more concerned with impressing the supervi-, sor than learning.[15]

Experienced Salespeople as Trainers.   Some organizations, with limited formal training programs, place new salespeople in the hands of experienced salespeople to acquire additional "on-the-job training." While experienced sales personnel can provide excellent guidance, they generally do not. Numerous reasons account for this. For one, experienced salespeople often view the additional training load adversely because it is seen as something for which they are not getting paid and because they tend to perceive the trainee as a potential competitor. Additionally, experienced salespeople often have different backgrounds from new salespeople. Most important, though, they lack the necessary training skills.[16]

Training Specialists.   While more expensive, and often resented by sales managers, the use of training specialists from within or outside the firm is a fairly common practice, both in consumer and industrial sales. However, these individuals may not be up to date in the sales methods being employed by a particular company, or in

[15]Ibid., pp. 199–200.
[16]Ibid., p. 200.

different geographical or product areas, and they often lack realistic field selling experience.[17]

Using Combinations of Trainers. By combining training methods, many of the foregoing problems may be avoided. For example, training specialists can handle the basic training and sales managers the advanced training. Training specialists can also conduct training for sales managers so that those managers can become more capable trainers of their sales force. Of course, company size, the quality and number of sales personnel, and the cost of the various alternatives will influence such decisions. For example, IBM found that its cost of training a student for one day was $350 if the training was done in one of its educational institutes, $150 if done in a class at a plant site, $125 if in a class in a plant site taught by satellite, or $75 if the learning involved only self study.[18]

AREAS OF SALES TRAINING

Areas of sales force training and the emphasis given each area depend on the company and its goals, the products involved, the marketing environment, and the experience and previous training of the sales personnel. Typical areas of sales training are listed in Table 13-3. It appears, however, that too few industrial firms devote adequate attention to training in the areas of human relations and negotiating skills.

One compilation of seven years of industrial-buyer opinions regarding important characteristics of salespeople is shown in Table 13-4. It is interesting to note that while product knowledge is an important factor, buyers are more interested in the ability of salespeople to follow through with the sale and in their willingness to support the buying firm's position within their respective sales firms.

Company Knowledge

A salesperson is more likely to perform better in two of the most important selling attributes in Table 13-4, which are listed as points 1 and 3, thoroughness and follow-through and buyer support, when properly trained with respect to company-specific factors. Such training should enable better follow-through and enhance the salesperson's ability to support the buyer's position. It should also build company loyalty and increase morale, factors that result in reduced turnover.

Company knowledge enhances the salesperson's awareness of company policies as they relate to such factors as product quality, service, and integrity, as well as whom to contact within the firm to get things accomplished on behalf of cus-

---

[17]Ibid.

[18]Patricia A. Galagan, "IBM Gets Its Arms Around Education," *Training & Development Journal* (January 1989), pp. 34–41.

HOW RAYTHEON PLUGS IN ITS SALES FORCE

"The hottest trend for the computer in sales and marketing stems not from its 'number-crunching prowess' but from its ability to speed communications between field salespeople and the home office. This helps eliminate 'telephone lag,' provides up-to-the-minute information on the status of customer orders and deliveries, lops off the bulk of administrative paperwork chores, and circumvents time-zone roadblocks when salespeople need vital information fast.

"At Raytheon . . . a computerized sales communication and information management system 'has increased the salesperson's selling time significantly.' . . . Because he is able to gather the data for a customer call regardless of where he is located, he spends much less time in the office.

"The system, called Unity, is comprised of portable workstations (Unity 100) that the division's salespeople carry in their briefcases. . . . The workstations can be put to various uses while the salesperson is calling on a customer. For one thing, he can give a detailed report as of the previous midnight on the status of orders and ship dates. The boost in selling time has produced 'an increase of 5% to 10% in the average salesperson's productivity.'"

Source: "How Raytheon Plugs in Its Sales Force," *Sales and Marketing Management,* December 3, 1984, pp. 62, 63. Reprinted with permission.

---

tomers.[19] It also enhances the salesperson's ability to handle correctly the bureaucratic plague of properly performing paperwork (developing expertise in such skills as writing orders and preparing expense vouchers). Many companies, including Raytheon, are turning to portable computers and software programs to help salespeople with this chore.

Product Knowledge

Table 13-4 indicates that product knowledge ranks second in importance in the buyer's mind and that it affects other attributes that buyers seek in sales people. Because

TABLE 13-3 Typical Areas of Sales Training

	Examples
1. Company-specific knowledge	Customer service levels and policies
2. Product knowledge	Product applications and customer benefits
3. Industry and market trends	Business cycle effects on purchasing
4. Competitive knowledge	Strengths, weaknesses, and competencies
5. Selling skills	Prospecting, qualifying, and closing

[19]C. Robert Patty, *Managing Salespeople,* 2nd ed. (Reston, Va.: Reston Publishing Company, 1982), p. 235.

TABLE 13-4 Outstanding Salesperson Characteristics

	Average Percent Mentioned
1. Thoroughness and follow-through	65.0
2. Knowledge of his/her product line	58.9
3. Willingness to go to bat for the buyer within the supplier's firm	54.3
4. Market knowledge and willingness to keep the buyer posted	40.6
5. Imagination in applying his/her products to the buyer's needs	23.1
6. Knowledge of the buyer's product line	18.3
7. Diplomacy in dealing with operating departments	16.3
8. Preparation for well-planned sales calls	12.4
9. Regularity of sales calls	8.7
10. Technical education	7.4

Source: Reprinted by permission of the publisher from "What Buyers Like from Salesmen," by Alvin J. Williams and John Seminerio, *Industrial Marketing Management*, 14, (1985), pp. 75–78. Copyright © 1985 by Elsevier Science Publishing Co., Inc.

of the importance of product knowledge, accompanied by the accelerating nature of technological change, many industrial suppliers provide ongoing or continuous product training.[20] Further, given the buyer–seller interface, the greater the product knowledge of the salesperson, the more effectively the salesperson can participate in that interface. Product knowledge enables salespeople to use "imagination in applying products to buyer's needs."

Industrial training programs must be thorough in their coverage of product features, applications, and customer benefits, including how products are used in buyers' production processes, buyers' end products, and how the supplying firm's products can mitigate production or other problems better than competing products. Thus, product training must also be related to competitors' products, including their pricing strategy relative to such factors as quantity discounts, FOB pricing, and financing.

Industry and Market Trend Knowledge

The purpose behind training in industry and market trends is to develop salespeople who are knowledgeable about current business conditions within specific industries

[20]Gordon R. Storholm, *Sales Management* (Englewood Cliffs, N.J.: Prentice-Hall, Inc., 1982), pp. 156–157.

and markets of the vendor. Such knowledge enables salespeople to understand current trade practices, such as a recent reduction in inventory levels in response to increased interest rates. It also ensures that salespeople are aware of usable specifics concerning buyers, such as who makes buying decisions, who potential influencers are, how often buyers reorder, and the location and size of customer firms. Sales managers who advocate that sales people document their experiences with customer firms also find that they have a valuable base for training and supervising new sales personnel.

Training with respect to customer markets should involve both present and potential markets as well as market trends. When salespeople are knowledgeable with regard to the firm's markets and industries, it greatly enhances their self-confidence as well as their potential for making additional sales. Further, when salespeople are apprised of downward trends industrywide, they tend not to become as discouraged when they personally experience decreasing sales results.

Competitive Knowledge

To be effective, salespeople must be aware of competitors' distinctive competencies, their strengths and weaknesses, and any major threats with which they may be faced. Salespeople must also be aware of how competitors employ their marketing mixes. Only then will they have the foundation for determining how buyers perceive competitors, how their own firm's marketing mix stacks up against competitors', and how they can overcome competitive situations. Referring again to Table 13-4, competitive knowledge, coupled with industry and market knowledge, puts the salesperson in the best position to "keep the buyer informed"—the fourth-ranked characteristic of importance to buyers.

Ethics Are Important Too. Ethics, or moral standards of conduct, however, must not be overlooked. A recent nationwide study of CEOs indicated that seventy-one percent of them "put integrity at the top of a list of sixteen traits most responsible for enhancing an executive's chances for success."[21] For example, salespeople must know the acceptable limits of criticizing competition. Criticizing competitors has been shown to be one of the least desirable salesperson characteristics in the eyes of buyers.[22] An acceptable rule is that salespeople have the right to point out their products' advantages over those of their competitors but not to "denigrate or downgrade" unfairly the competitors' products.[23] Buyers frequently seem to have an inherent dislike for the overly critical salesperson.

Ethical considerations are even more difficult when selling internationally; thus, we will devote additional discussion to ethics when we cover international industrial marketing.

---

[21]"Profiles in Leadership," *Management Review* 76 (May 1987), p. 8.

[22]Larry Giunipero and Gary Zenz, "Impact of Purchasing Trends on Industrial Marketers," *Industrial Marketing Management* 11 (1982), pp. 17–23.

[23]Storholm, *Sales Management,* p. 159.

TABLE 13-5 Presentation Points to Remember

Your presentation has to be believed, agreed with, and acted upon.	Personalize your presentation.
One way to gain the prospect's attention is to dramatize the product value.	Slant your presentation to your prospect's self-interest.
Your presentation produces orders when it is built around buyer benefits.	Choose impact words with motivation strength.
The sale is seldom closed unless your prospect has confidence in the proposition.	Achieve credibility. Bring on your evidence and testimonials.
Speak the prospect's language. It's a sure way to build confidence.	The ideal presentation uses both emotion and logic.
In motivating the prospect to take action and give you the order, it's very important that you take the initiative.	Be an assistant buyer who stays in front of decision makers with a strategy you believe in.

Source: See Roger Staubach, Jack Kinder, Jr., and Garry Kinder, "Secrets of Making *Good* Presentations," *Marketing Times,* March/April 1983, pp. 20–23.

Sales Skills Knowledge

Selling skills in the industrial market can parallel those in the consumer market, as is often the case when selling operating supplies. Selling skills can also differ considerably, as is often the case when selling capital equipment. In selling capital equipment a salesperson may work with a buyer for months, even years, before closing a sale. Where selling situations involve items of lesser importance, such as supplies, industrial salespeople may need to employ only the rudimentary skills involved in the selling processes (see Table 14-1, Chapter Fourteen). Table 13-5, however, reflects one team of expert sales people's perception of some of the finer selling points that should be remembered when preparing for a sales presentation.

Professional Selling Styles. In the industrial arena, depending upon the demands of the profession, one of several selling styles may be of importance. These styles are being referred to as technical, consultative, negotiating, systems, and team.[24]

> *Technical styles* require the ability to solve customer problems through the use of the salesperson's technical background and knowledge. In actuality, then, technical selling involves the selling of a service as well as a product because of the problem-solving nature of the sales process. In fact, many technical salespeople have degrees in engineering or some other scientific discipline.
>
> *Consultative styles* require excellent writing and verbal communication skills as well as analytical abilities because of the need to reach and solve problems of decision makers at very high levels of customer organizations. This is so because consultative

[24]See, for instance, Michael D. Hutt and Thomas W. Speh, *Industrial Marketing Management* (Chicago: The Dryden Press, 1981), p. 344; and Gordon Storholm and Louis C. Kaufman, *Principles of Selling* (Englewood Cliffs, N.J.: Prentice-Hall, Inc., 1985), pp. 53–54.

selling frequently involves the selling of services such as management consulting or executive search, large-scale computer system, or corporate pension plan. Thus, people involved in this area of selling must be capable of becoming an expert on the client's business operation to deal with the upper levels of management over protracted periods of time.

Negotiating styles involve the ability to maximize benefits for both the buyer and seller during the transaction period to ensure that both parties form a mutually beneficial partnership.

Systems styles require the ability to analyze a prospect's business or information needs and make recommendations as to a package of goods and/or services to fulfill those needs, such as a training program for the prospect's employees, redesigned operating procedures, or maintenance arrangements.

Team selling styles involves the ability to work with other functional experts within the selling firm who are more capable of matching the specialized knowledge or requirements of the buying firm.

Developing Human Relations and Negotiating Skills

Industrial selling often involves devoting considerable time in identifying and building relationships with key influencers and decision makers. This often involves a series of calls over an extended period (perhaps a year or two). During these calls, salespeople attempt to identify and reach key influencers within prospective customer firms and accumulate the respect and confidence of those influencers. This often involves going out of their way to obtain information and concessions from people within their firm, displaying creativity and initiative in their sales presentations and follow-through—skills that far surpass those customarily found in the consumer market. Thus, salespeople must be highly adept in the use of human relations and negotiating skills.

Human Relations Skills. As Stumm points out, the major difference between success and failure in the area of selling depends on the salesperson's ability to deal with the different personalities of the buyers they encounter.[25]

> People do not react to an objective world, but to a world they have fashioned for themselves out of their own unique, individual perceptions and assumptions about the world. Sales people, like all the rest of us, can readily be trapped by these assumptions into misleading, misdirected, and ineffective selling efforts.

The decisions that buying influencers make are ultimately influenced by their personalities (which includes their motivations, attitudes, knowledge, and skills), the environment within which they work, the nature of their job, and the rewards associated with their performance. In attempting to uncover buying motives, then, the salesperson must also recognize "that there is always a relationship between the variables of the individual's total, if faulty, awareness and the variables of his

[25]Stumm, *Advanced Industrial Selling*, p. 1.

environment."[26] Rarely are buying decisions made on cold logical reasoning. In fact, studies have shown that we tend to make decisions based on our personal perception of the situation and then use logic and reasoning to justify those decisions. Therefore, successful selling is directly related to the salesperson's ability to relate to the emotional needs of the customer. This requires the use of interpersonal skills in relating to potential buyers—the ability to apply psychology in dealing with potential buyers. Sales training, then, must also include teaching salespeople to be good listeners and questioners, and how to be sensitive to the needs of others.

Negotiating Skills. In the industrial market, emphasis on "mutual dependence" during negotiation is more important than is emphasis on "self-interest," which is frequently associated with basic selling techniques. The emphasis in basic selling skills is on achieving benefits for the seller, with too little regard for the benefits to be gained by the buyer. Because of the importance in building a long-term buyer–seller relationship, coupled with increasing worldwide competition, the fundamental goals of negotiation have been moving away from those involved with self-interest toward those involved with mutual advantage and mutual survival. Not too long ago training in negotiations would have been built on such rules as "always concede something in return for a concession," "try to make your concessions smaller than the other party's," "never be the first party to concede," and "make several small concessions and immediately attempt to obtain a major concession."

The Japanese buyer–seller interface helps to explain the current perspective of mutual interdependence. The Japanese buyer typically relies on only one firm to supply all quantities of a particular input. Thus, supplier and buyer work together, and the supplier is counted on to deliver a quality product in a way that will minimize the buyer's inventories. That is, Japanese buyers and sellers interact in much the same manner as divisions within a company interact—as if their interests, their mutual well-being, is of concern to both and together they compete against the world.

As more United States businesses adopt just-in-time and materials requirement planning to meet increasing domestic and international competition, their negotiating relationships will also reflect this concern. Banting and Dion have found that exploitative and adversarial negotiating strategies are the exception rather than the rule. Adversarial strategies tend to impede negotiation and the development of productive buyer–seller relationships.[27] Thus negotiation strategies should center on developing synergistic effects between firms by jointly utilizing the distinctive competencies and comparative advantages of each rather than their individual self-interests.

Successful negotiation consists of three important stages: (1) preparing for negotiating, (2) establishing fundamental attitudes, and (3) conducting the negotiations.

[26]Ibid.

[27]Peter M. Banting and Paul A. Dion, "The Purchasing Agent: Friend or Foe to the Salesperson," *Journal of the Academy of Marketing Science* 16 (Fall 1988), pp. 16–22.

TRAINING SPECIALISTS TEACH SALESPEOPLE HOW TO SELL

GET OFF the stage, Willy Loman. A smile and a shoeshine won't do it any longer. The fast-talking, yarn-spinning, hard-drinking peddler belongs to the past. Today's sales training teaches the salesperson to be a good listener and questioner, sensitive to the needs of others, knowledgeable about his products, more an adviser than a hustler. . . .

At least that's the high road to selling taught by the three major purveyors of sales training to American business. *Fortune* recently sampled short sales courses offered by the three: Xerox Learning Systems of Stamford, Connecticut, part of Xerox Corp.; Wilson Learning Corp. of Eden Prairie, Minnesota, a subsidiary of publisher John Wiley & Sons; and Forum Corp. of Boston, a $16-million-a-year company that specializes in management and sales training. . . .

All three courses stressed a high-principled style of selling that favors a close, trusting, long-term relationship over the quick sell. The approach works best for sales representatives who deal with customers on a continuing basis rather than in one-shot visits or phone calls. . . .

The courses are lively two- or three-day affairs. . . . The reading comes not in heavy tomes but in breezy pamphlets with a lot of empty space on the pages. Students can't lapse into the usual classroom stupor of school and college: at any moment, they may be called on to act in an improvised sales skit or analyze the mistakes in video shows produced for the courses. A well-polished instructor keeps the class on its toes by orchestrating an entertaining mixture of video material, lectures, reading, quizzes, and role-playing—with no segment dragging on too long.

Preparing for Negotiations.[28]   The first step in preparing for negotiation is to develop strategies for conducting the negotiating. This entails gathering as much information as possible on the matter to be negotiated. During this stage, it is important to evaluate the firm's strengths and weaknesses relative to the buyer, as well as potential competition in terms of the upcoming negotiations. Salespeople must be prepared to discuss the relevant issues under consideration so that the basic interests of both parties can be served. When salespeople are knowledgeable on where the firm stands on the issues, they are in a better position to make any necessary concessions or to pursue alternative courses of action.

One valuable tool that can be used in preparing for this stage is product performance analysis (PPA) as discussed in Chapter Four. Not only can PPA be used to identify key influencers and their respective information needs, it can also be used to determine where the negotiating firm stands relative to the buyer's as well as competitors' strengths and weaknesses.

---

[28]This section is based on David D. Seltz and Alfred J. Modica, *Negotiate Your Way to Success* (New York: The New American Library, Inc., 1980).

To provide a favorable atmosphere for negotiating, arrangements should be made to hold negotiations in a fitting location, one without distractions, preferably with a seating arrangement that reflects equality of status for both parties, and at a time that is convenient to both. A formal atmosphere accompanied by formal conduct on the part of both parties tends to reflect mutual respect and is beneficial to negotiators. Negotiators usually bring written documents, charts, and sometimes experts in a particular field to reflect their preparation for and involvement in the negotiations.

Establishing Fundamental Attitudes.[29]   The second important element in successful negotiation is the establishment and continuation of favorable negotiating attitudes. Negotiators often spend considerable time in defining a problem and its subproblems to establish several instances of agreement and, thus, a favorable relationship before discussing points of conflict. It is important, then, that the stage is set for favorable negotiations. This can be done by bringing up the negative as well as the positive aspects that might be incurred by both parties as a result of decisions to be reached during negotiations. Salespeople should make known their company's degree of concern and commitment in resolving the issues.

Conducting the Negotiations.   During the negotiations, salespeople should focus on the basic interests of one another rather than on positions or personalities. Creative and objective methods of satisfying those positions should be pursued. During negotiations, questions rather than statements are of value since questions often facilitate learning and give the other party little or nothing to find fault with. It is worthwhile to break issues into subparts that can be easily understood and discussed.

Salespeople should always have an alternative method of resolving a problem, or be ready to leave the negotiations and pursue the alternative should the negotiations degenerate sufficiently in terms of their company's interests. Since negotiating is such an important aspect in the area of industrial marketing, more on the subject will be covered in Chapter Sixteen. Table 13-6 summarizes these important aspects of negotiation.

DIRECTING (MOTIVATING) THE SALES FORCE

Many industrial salespeople experience considerable stress because their jobs seem to have very few "average" days, but instead seem to be composed of extremes, either very good or very bad days. It is not unusual for industrial salespeople to become depressed by the solitude of on-the-road days and in-the-motel nights. Further, in industrial sales, where salespeople are committed to customer satisfaction, they can also become frustrated in their attempts to perform the often conflicting

---

[29]See Robert Fish and William Ury, *Getting to Yes* (Boston: Houghton Mifflin Co., 1981).

TABLE 13-6 Elements of Good Negotiating Strategy

Steps	Elements

Prepare for negotiating	Gather information on buying organization and competitors; know where each party stands.
	  Arrange for favorable negotiating atmosphere.
	  Use graphs and charts where possible.

Establish attitudes	Define problem and subproblems.
	  Discuss negative and positive aspects.
	  Express degree of commitment.

Conduct negotiations	Focus on both parties' interests.
	  Ask questions, avoid statements.
	  Break issues into subparts.
	  Have alternatives for solving problems.
	  Be prepared to stand your ground.

role of satisfying needs of both buyers and sellers. Because of these considerations, many industrial sales managers find that their most important function is that of attempting to renew their salespeople's motivation.

Motivating Theories

Directing "is concerned with stimulating members of the organization to undertake action consistent with the plans."[30] As a function performed by industrial sales managers, directing is generally perceived to be synonymous with motivating. Motivation theories are generally divided into two groups: content theories, which describe the internal drives or needs of individuals, and process theories, which describe the reasoning processes involved in motivation.

Content Theories. Two popular content theories are those developed by Abraham Maslow and Frederick Herzberg. Maslow discussed a hierarchy of needs and hypothesized that individuals progressed through physiological, safety and security, social, esteem, and self-actualization levels of needs.[31] The hierarchy's ultimate need, self-actualization, is defined as involving fulfilling one's true potential and growth, that is, being all that one can be. Herzberg theorized that people are not motivated by salary, work conditions, job security, and other external considerations, but instead are motivated by achievement, recognition, responsibility, advancement, and growth opportunities, that is, feelings of self-accomplishment.[32]

[30]R. Wayne Mondy, Robert E. Holmes, and Edwin B. Flippo, *Management: Concepts and Practices* (Boston: Allyn & Bacon, Inc., 1980), p. 13.

[31]Abraham Maslow, *Motivation and Personality* (New York: Harper & Bros., 1954).

[32]Frederick Herzberg, "One More Time: How Do You Motivate Employees?" *Harvard Business Review* (January–February 1968), pp. 53–62.

Process Theories.   One popular process theory is *expectancy theory,* which is expressed by the formula:[33]

$$\text{motivation} = E\text{-}P \times P\text{-}O \times \text{valence}$$

where

$E\text{-}P$ = a person's perceived probability of *performing* a task given he or she puts in the effort to do so

$P\text{-}O$ = a person's perceived probability of obtaining an *outcome* (such as a reward) given that he or she does perform the task

valence = the anticipated value (satisfaction or dissatisfaction) one perceives he or she will obtain from an outcome

Another process theory, *attribution theory,* holds that individuals are motivated or demotivated as a result of their perceptions regarding who is in control or responsible for their actions. It stipulates that those who perceive themselves to be in control tend to be motivated, while those who perceive someone else to be in control are not motivated. One study of two groups of school children, for instance, showed that those praised but not paid continued to work on a puzzle during their free time, while those who were paid (thus, perceiving someone else to be in control) did not work during their free time even though they had also been praised.[34]

Implications for Sales Management.   Expectancy theory implies that sales managers must consider ways to increase the salesperson's perception of probabilities in both *E-P* and *P-O* areas. Studies have shown that improved communications, training, co-workers, and previous experiences can lead people to believe that if they put in the effort they can do the job and that they will receive the rewards.[35,36] The model also implies that people will be motivated by different and unique considerations. Some people will need more training than others to increase their belief that their attempts will in fact lead to accomplishments. Others, with higher levels of self-confidence, will need considerably less training.

The outcomes that individuals attempt to achieve will also have considerable variability. While one salesperson may press harder to receive a promotion to impress a spouse, another may press harder simply to receive recognition from a sales manager. Such variability in outcomes desired implies that the sales manager who develops personal job relationships with his or her sales people will be more successful.

[33]Lyman W. Porter and Edward E. Lawler, *Managerial Attitudes and Performance* (Homewood, Ill.: Richard D. Irwin, Inc., 1968), pp. 329–331.

[34]Edward Deci, "Paying People Doesn't Always Work the Way You Expect It To," in Organ, ed., *The Applied Psychology of Work Behavior,* pp. 175–181.

[35]Fred Luthans, *Organizational Behavior* (New York: McGraw-Hill Book Company, 1985), pp. 211–212.

[36]Porter and Lawler, *Managerial Attitudes and Performance,* p. 273.

Attribution theory relates well to the theories of Maslow and Herzberg. Individuals who believe that they are personally responsible for their accomplishments will, in the Maslow framework, have an increased sense of self-esteem and an increased sense of self-actualization. According to Herzberg, individuals who believe that they are personally responsible for accomplishments will have an increased sense of achievement, recognition, responsibility, advancement, and of growth opportunities.

It is difficult to escape the realization that industrial salespeople, who spend so much of their time on the road working without supervision, will usually perceive themselves to be in control of their own actions and not only motivated thereby, but also resentful of any attempts to deprive them of that personal control. A marketing vice president at Du Pont indicated that firm's use of this concept when he said, "The company's salesperson . . . may bring in the director of production or even a vice president when he makes a sales call, but the salesperson is the one who calls the shots. Nothing happens at that account without his say-so."[37]

Trust, Subtlety, and Intimacy.   Interestingly, the foregoing motivational theories relate well to current popular theories regarding Japanese management. One popular Japanese management theorist maintains that American managers must be more trusting, subtle, and intimate in regard to their subordinates.[38] In discussing "trust," he suggests that American managers should more closely approach the Japanese practice of placing great trust in subordinates. By "subtlety" he means that managers should become more knowledgeable about the individual differences and peculiarities of their subordinates. By "intimate" he means that managers should encourage the development of personal friendships in the workplace.

Ambiguity and Indirection.   Two other authorities on Japanese management also advocate the use of ambiguity and indirection by management so as to allow subordinates to save face and to have more involvement in decision making.[39]

Trust, subtlety, and intimacy, as well as managing through ambiguity and indirection, all tend to allow a salesperson to feel increased esteem and self-actualization (steps in Maslow's hierarchy), increased feelings of achievement, recognition, responsibility, and growth (in agreement with Herzberg's theories) and to feel that they are more in control of their own actions (as attribution theory recommends).

Drama, Symbols, and Love.   There is a plethora of excellent new books reemphasizing many of the thoughts already discussed here. For example, Tom Peters and Nancy Austin wrote that workers need to be liberated, involved, accountable and allowed to reach their potential.[40] At the same time many of these new books also

---

[37]"At Du Pont Everybody Sells," *Sales and Marketing Management,* December 3, 1984, p. 33.

[38]William Ouchi, *Theory Z* (Reading, Mass.: Addison-Wesley Publishing Co., 1981), pp. 5–10.

[39]Richard Pascale and Anthony Athos, *The Art of Japanese Management* (New York: Simon & Schuster, Inc., 1981), pp. 101–106.

[40]Tom Peters and Nancy Austin, *A Passion for Excellence* (New York: Warner Books, Inc., 1985).

emphasize new slants on older methods. For example, Peters and Austin stress that a supervisor should be more of a leader than a manager and should use symbols, drama, and vision. These new slants are inspiring in that they often rekindle drive in leaders, giving them a chance to experiment with something; thus the many new writings in the leadership/management field should not be ignored. However, we do warn that cassette-tape summaries of books can short circuit much of their inspirational potential.

EFFECTIVE USE OF SALES COMPENSATION

During the early years of the twentieth century, money was believed to be *the* motivator. Since then considerable research and increases in our standard of living have caused many people to wonder if money is indeed the primary motivator. Attribution theory, for example, indicates that money, in some instances, can be a demotivator. It is interesting to note, however, that in 1988 the average amount spent on compensation and field expenses to support one salesperson in the field was $87,500—a sufficiently sizeable amount to indicate that business perceives money to be a prime motivator in the area of selling.[41]

Monetary Compensation

These differences of opinion can be partially reconciled if we realize that money motivates an individual to work in three different ways. First, a sufficiently high salary can motivate one to accept a job offer. Many students who believe it is money that motivates them to work may in fact only be feeling motivated to take a job offer because of money; they may feel little motivation to work once they are on the job.

Second, money motivates an individual to keep a job. Individuals so motivated, however, usually perform only the minimum amount of work necessary to keep from being fired. The exception occurs when they are also motivated by some other consideration, such as Protestant work ethic conditioning, which causes them to believe that they should contribute an "honest day's work for an honest day's pay."

Straight salaries can be thought of as providing this type of motivation and are often used as a basis of sales compensation because they give the salesperson a sense of security. In addition, they are easy to understand and administer, remain constant (to the benefit of the company) as sales increase, and reduce salesperson resistance to direction from sales managers requiring performance of nonselling activities, such as reporting customer responses to product surveys or making missionary sales calls.[42] The important realization is, that in this instance, money alone

---

[41]"Survey of Selling Costs," *Sales and Marketing Management,* February 20, 1989, p. 8.

[42]Douglas J. Dalrymple, *Sales Management: Concepts and Cases* (New York: John Wiley & Sons, Inc., 1982), p. 294.

motivates the individual to expend only the minimal effort necessary to retain the job.

Finally, money can motivate an individual to perform something more than the minimal job retention amount of work. For this type of motivation to exist, however, the money paid must depend upon the amount or quality of work performed. Such a tie between work effort and money received is characteristic of sales compensation programs.

Herzberg's contention that people are not motivated by salary can be equated with these three ways in which money motivates. Most U.S. workers are paid straight salaries that motivate them only to accept jobs and display some minimal performance level to retain those jobs. However, industrial sales compensation plans are frequently constructed with the intention of providing the third type of motivation.

Straight Salaries, Commissions, and Bonuses.   Table 13-7 depicts the tendency of companies to pay sales personnel on the basis of both a straight salary and either a bonus or commission tied to the salesperson's accomplishments.

As Table 13-7 indicates, only fourteen percent of industrial companies pay sales compensation in the form of a straight salary. The majority of industrial companies (86 percent) use money as a motivator that is tied to the work involved by compensating salespeople through commissions, or through a combination of straight salary plus commission and/or bonus. In fact, the two most popular compensation plans are "salary plus commission" and "salary plus bonus." A commission is a predetermined percentage of sales, or profits, and is usually paid on a

TABLE 13-7 Percentages of Companies Using Various Compensation Plans in 1988

Method	Industrial Products	Consumer Products
Straight salary	14%	12%
Straight commission	19	21
Salary plus commission	28	26
Salary plus bonus	26	32
Salary plus commission & bonus	10	5
Total	100%	100%

Source: Adapted from "Methods of Compensation by Industry Group," *Sales and Marketing Management,* February 20, 1989, p. 20. Reprinted with permission.

monthly basis. On the other hand, a bonus is a discretionary amount of money, usually paid for the achievement of goals, and is paid less frequently—on a quarterly, semiannual, or yearly basis.

Commissions and Bonuses as Motivators. Both commissions and bonuses are used to motivate salespeople. Commissions can be adjusted as a proportion of total compensation to provide increased or decreased motivation. For instance, a marketer who increases commission payments from ten to thirty percent of the salesperson's total compensation does so in expectation of adding increased motivation. Commissions are also more easily explained to salespeople than are bonuses. Since they are paid on a more frequent basis than are bonuses, they also tend to strengthen the perceived relationship between increased performance and reward (expectancy theory).

Bonuses are usually determined more subjectively and are frequently based on the accomplishment of various tasks, such as improved customer relations, obtaining new accounts, feedback reports regarding customer needs, or increased sales. Bonuses facilitate motivation with regard to the many nonselling activities that are important in industrial marketing, as well as sales activities. While widely used, however, there are various drawbacks to the system. For instance, because they are usually determined more subjectively than commissions, salespeople tend to question whether they are determined fairly. Additionally, the infrequent payment of bonuses makes it more difficult for the salesperson to perceive the relationship between performance and reward.[43]

Secrecy versus Openness in Pay Differentials. Because of the tendency for salespeople to condemn as unfair subjective methods of determining compensation, one study has found that it is best to keep compensation differentials secret from sales people, even though such secrecy reduces the motivational potential of bonuses.[44] If sales force pay differentials are to be made public in attempting to motivate sales people, objective versus subjective criteria must be employed when determining the differentials, and, according to another study, salespeople should have some input into determining the objective criteria.[45]

Industrial salespeople, who are called upon to perform many and varied tasks, can certainly be expected to be capable of comprehending and evaluating even the more complicated methods of bonus determinations; secrecy is not essential if objectivity is maintained, no matter how complicated objective formulas may be.

[43]Ibid., pp. 297–300.

[44]Charles M. Futrell, "Disclosing Sales Force Pay Increase," *Industrial Marketing Management,* 8 (1979), pp. 301–304.

[45]Edward Lawler, "Merit Pay: An Obsolete Policy?" in J. Richard Hackman, Edward Lawler, and Lyman Porter, eds., *Perspectives on Behavior in Organizations* (New York: McGraw-Hill Book Company, 1983), pp. 305–310.

Incentive Programs as Motivators

Sales managers often use the term "incentive program" to describe an array of motivational schemes other than those involving monetary compensation. Such incentive programs usually involve contests. Due to the strong American enculturation of competitiveness, contests tend to yield excellent motivational results. They also add an element of recognitional "stroking," an important element, since employees in the United States too frequently display a lack of fulfillment in their self-esteem needs.[46]

Signode's programs illustrate several important considerations regarding nonmonetary compensation. Incentives should be tied to specific sales objectives, such as opening new accounts. When incentives are tied to general objectives, such as increasing overall sales, sales people tend to concentrate on high-priced, large-volume items at the expense of other products. General objectives also tend to favor sales people with seniority who have established clientele to the detriment of new sales people. Incentive programs must offer some motivation for everyone and be designed so that they provide more bang for the buck than other types of compensation.

Use Appropriate Motivational Frills. Nonmonetary compensation programs should also have the appropriate motivational frills. Thus, they should be designed so that they have clever and exciting themes, are colorfully reinforced, are used frequently, and are varied often. Prizes should be intriguing and inspiring. A highly intriguing but inexpensive prize can provide inspiration that far surpasses that of a much more costly bonus. Several companies have been formed to effect just this end. For example, GoldChex, travelers' checks issued by a company in Cincinnati, come in $25 and $50 denominations and can be used to cruise on sixteen different shipping lines, to charter a yacht, to fulfill a baseball fantasy, to rent a car, or to stay at 190 different hotels or seven hundred KOA campsites around the United States.[47] Such checks, issued for varying amounts, allow the salespeople to accumulate them until they have acquired sufficient amounts to take a vacation of their own design.

Nonmonetary incentive programs provide an increasingly vast array of opportunities for inspiring salespeople, an array limited only by the imgination of individuals in companies that choose to use them, but an array of programs that provide more motivation for the dollar than salaries, commissions, or bonuses. They provide an opportunity that few companies can afford to overlook. And the more time spent in designing an incentive program, the better the results tend to be.

[46]Mason Haire, Edwin Ghiselli, and Lyman Porter, *Managerial Thinking* (New York: John Wiley & Sons, Inc., 1966), p. 89.

[47]Al Urbanski, "A Shopper's Guide to Incentive Travelers Checks," *Sales and Marketing Management* (September 10, 1984), pp. 106–108.

HOW SIGNODE MOTIVATED ITS SALES FORCE WITH NONMONETARY INCENTIVES

In the late 1970s when the economy began to grow sluggish, it became increasingly difficult for salespeople at Signode Corporation to earn their usual bonus levels. To supplement the salary-plus-bonus compensation of its 280 sales personnel, Signode implemented a series of nonmonetary incentive programs. Initially, a free trip to Hawaii was offered, followed by a program called "Sell-a-Bration," which offered a choice of gifts ranging from $250 to $300 for renewing former accounts and opening new ones. Within 60 days, 39 percent of the sales force had qualified for the gifts.

Signode also developed its "Share the Action" program, awarding $5.00 Sears, Roebuck gift certificates to district sales managers and order entry clerks, as well as the sales force, for meeting quotas. These awards, incidentally, had the added benefit of being tangible items, serving as continual reminders of each person's accomplishments. To involve the whole family, catalogs of prizes were sent home and newsletters were launched to publicize successful winners.

Source: See "Signode Corp. Gets Salesreps Out of Their Slump," *Business Marketing,* July 1983, pp. 53–56.

Contemporary Challenges.   As industrial companies face increasingly punishing competition, growing litigation, higher costs, input shortages, and a plethora of other contemporary problems, they are devoting increased attention to revamping sales-force compensation. The intent is to fine-tune compensation packages so that they are harmonious with marketing goals and objectives.

One writer explains that some companies increase the commission rate on one product line if a specified goal on a second line is met, some reward the rep with increased commissions if goals are met in two (or more) product lines, and some base commissions on the achievement of multiple quotas.[48] Also, companies "segment volume;" that is, they vary commissions in order to motivate the development of more desired market segments, such as increasing sales in new industries or sales to new versus present customers.[49]

Pitney Bowes, for example, runs a two-tier program that involves a trip to Hawaii for those in the top tier and various smaller incentives for those in the second tier. To qualify for the tiers, salespeople meet quotas for both existing and new customers. Additionally, Pitney Bowes has tailored its sales managers' compensation to necessitate their reaching an overall sales goal, "say 105 percent of quota,"

---

[48]Stockton B. Colt, Jr., "Improving Sales Productivity: Four Case Studies," Sales & Marketing Management (May 1989), pp. 10–12.

[49]Leslie Brennan, "Promoting Quality Sales Through Incentives," *Sales & Marketing Management* (May 1989), pp. 64–72.

as well as inspiring a given percentage of their reps to achieve superior perform-ance.[50] Some companies tailor their compensation to boost quality sales. USAA, for example, bases thirty-five percent of its commissions on how well sales reps handle correspondence, phone conversations, and accurately quote prices.[51] In an effort to quell litigation and enhance customer rapport, Dun & Bradstreet now uses customer satisfaction surveys to establish a portion of its sales compensation.

Corporate America is expending considerable effort in developing compensa-tion plans that enhance the achievement of corporate goals and objectives. These and other such contemporary precision-designed compensation programs are not happenstance occurrences, but increasingly mandatory necessities.

LOOKING BACK

Selecting and hiring salespeople involves more than the usual selection procedures. Due to the nature of industrial sales, sales managers must look for technical, human relations, and negotiating skills. Several interviewing methods, such as multiple, panel, patterned, or structured interviews, as well as realistic job previews enable sales managers more effectively to find those uniquely different individuals who make the best industrial salespeople.

Once selected, salespeople must be given the opportunity to develop to their full potential through company, product, competitive, and industry and market spe-cific training. In addition to training in selling techniques, industrial salespeople must also be trained in human relations and negotiating skills. Such training en-hances the salesperson's ability to understand and meet the needs of both buyers and sellers. Care, however, must be taken in selecting those who are to do the training. Marketers may choose sales managers, experienced salespeople, or training special-ists as sales force trainers. While each choice will have advantages, the disadvantages must also be considered. Whoever is chosen to supervise sales force training must be aware of learning theory that emphasizes that to learn, people must be motivated, involved, and given immediate, positive feedback.

Directing the sales force involves both content and process theories of motiva-tion. Since salespeople spend much of their time working without supervision, a sales manager might want to consider using trust, sympathy, and intimacy, as well as ambiguity and indirection, in directing the sales force. Both monetary and non-monetary forms of compensation can be used effectively as a motivator when they are tied directly to selling as well as nonselling objectives.

[50]Ibid.
[51]Ibid.

QUESTIONS FOR DISCUSSION

1. In hiring and selecting salespeople, it is well to remember that "About eighty percent of the industrial buyers are male and it is possible that the sex role stereotypes that are common in our culture may work to the disadvantage of saleswomen." Do you agree?

2. Traditional measures are inadequate to evaluate the short-term productivity of the sales process because many nonselling activities, performed as part of the job, may not result in any measurable sales output until months or years later. Discuss.

3. "The manager gave me specific instructions about how to handle a particular customer. I carried out those instructions. But when the customer contacted my boss he made a change and handled the situation entirely differently." In this situation, was the sales manager a good motivator?

4. Older workers have greater pride in job accomplishment, the moral importance of work, and the Protestant ethic. Thus, older people make better salespeople. Do you agree?

5. It has been suggested that the practice of sales management has resembled the practice of medicine by tribal witch doctors with the sales manager relying on large doses of folklore, tradition, and personal experience in directing and motivating sales representatives. How can Herzberg's theory rectify this situation?

6. How can a sales compensation plan be designed to consider both management's and the sales force's objectives?

7. In many organizations salespeople do not know if rewards are based on performance because they often do not know how their peers are evaluated and rewarded. Is this a good practice?

8. What special skills or motivations explain the high school dropout who earns more by selling than we pay the president of the United States? Can any of those skills be taught through sales force training?

SUGGESTED ADDITIONAL READINGS

BERL, ROBERT, TERRY POWELL, AND NICHOLAS C. WILLIAMSON, "Industrial Salesforce Satisfaction and Performance with Herzberg's Theory," *Industrial Marketing Management* 13 (1984):11–19.

BERTRAND, KATE, "The 12 Cardinal Sins of Compensation," *Business Marketing* (September 1989):51–58.

BRENNAN, LESLIE, "Promoting Quality Sales through Incentives," *Sales & Marketing Management* (May 1989):64–72.

CARDOZO, RICHARD AND SHANNON SHIPP, "New Selling Methods Are Changing Industrial Sales Management," *Business Horizons* (September–October 1987):23–28.

DARMON, RENE Y., "Compensation Plans that Link Management and Salesman's Objectives," *Industrial Marketing Management* 11 (1982):151–163.

DECI, EDWARD, "Paying People Doesn't Always Work the Way You Expect it To," in Dennis Organ, ed., *The Applied Psychology of Work Behavior* (Plano, Tex.: Business Publications, Inc., 1983):175–181.

FUTRELL, CHARLES M., "Disclosing Sales Force Pay Increases," *Industrial Marketing Management* 8 (1979):301–304.

HENDRICKSON, JOHN, "Getting Close to the Business," *Training & Development Journal* (February 1989):68–70.

HERZBERG, FREDRICK, "One More Time: How Do You Motivate Employees?" *Harvard Business Review* (January–February 1968):53–62.

LINKEMER, BOBBI, "Women in Sales: What do They Really Want?" *Sales & Marketing Management* (January 1989):61–68.

PASCALE, RICHARD, AND ANTHONY ATHOS, *The Art of Japanese Management* (New York: Simon & Schuster, Inc., 1981).

CHAPTER 14

Planning, Organizing, and Controlling the Selling Function

While some industrial organizations are quite successful in reaching their markets through advertising alone, particularly small suppliers of MRO items, personal selling constitutes a major force in the marketing of industrial goods and services. For most products such as office equipment and word processing, building materials, and capital equipment, or services such as management consulting, computer systems, and corporate pension plan investments, it requires the expertise and knowledge of well-trained sales people to link the firm's offering to the needs of the marketplace. While advertising and sales promotion are important tools for communicating a firm's image and product or service capability, rarely can they close a sale or create a competitive edge. In this chapter, then, we discuss the importance of

1. The sales force in industrial marketing strategy.
2. Planning and organizing the selling effort to produce an effective and efficient professional sales force.
3. The use of control methods to ensure that the selling effort is achieving the desired results.

A firm selling in the industrial market has the choice of using its own sales force, manufacturers' representatives, distributors, or dealers. Whatever choice is made will depend on the nature and composition of the market, the types of prod-

---

WHAT BUYERS WANT FROM SALES PEOPLE

There is a substantial amount of agreement among respondents that a good salesman is: [1] one who is thoroughly informed about his products and his company; [2]
one who has a good technical background and grasp or knowledge of production
problems; [3] one who is well-versed in his customer's needs and business requirements; and [4] one whose personality characteristics meet the buyers' ideas concerning the attributes of an efficient salesman.

Source: "What Factors Affect Industrial Buying Decisions," by Bertrand Klaus, Ph.D., executive vice
president, Forbes Marketing Research, New York, *Industrial Marketing,* May 1961, pp. 33–35. Reprinted
by permission.

---

ucts marketed, and the company's objectives and financial capabilities. Regardless
of the method chosen, personal selling, whether by the manufacturer, the distributor, or the dealer, is the principal means by which industrial marketers reach organizational customers. It is the industrial salesperson who "is the company" (provides
the company image), who communicates the company's product/service capability
from the customer's point of view, and who handles the lengthy transactions characteristic of industrial marketing. Two primary reasons account for this heavy reliance
on person selling.

First, compared to the consumer market, the number of potential customers
in the industrial market is relatively small, easily identified and located, and the
dollar value of sales is comparatively large. Second, many purchasing agents prefer
to buy from sales people who have direct access to individuals within the vendor
organization and who can secure immediate solutions to their problems. Industrial
problems are often complex, require technical solutions, and must be supported by
pre- and postsale services. These two primary reasons for relying on industrial selling have been around for a very long time. To appreciate this you might enjoy
comparing the insert, "What Buyers Want from Sales People," with Table 13-4 in
the previous chapter. The insert, a direct quote written in 1961, bears criteria re-
markably similar to those in Table 13-4, which resulted from a recent compilation
of surveys made over a seven-year period.

ACTUALIZING THE MARKETING CONCEPT

Sales people play a greater role in actualizing the marketing concept in the industrial
market than they do in the consumer market. This is so because of the necessity
of making many mutual adjustments while working through the decision processes
involved in buying and selling over long periods of time. And, as industrial buyers
face increasing competition and shorter deadlines, industrial marketers must discover more effective ways to meet their needs. It is the salesperson, working in

conjunction with engineering and manufacturing, who offers the potential for developing the necessary creativity to satisfy customer needs. For example, one customer's yearly inventory costs were reduced 35 percent. By analyzing the customer's usage and discovering how, in several instances, two or three different inserts could be replaced by one common part, the customer's inventory of inserts was reduced from 400 to 200 individual parts. Such attempts to find ways to incorporate a single input into multiple products are becoming increasingly important. Not only are Intel's microprocessors the brains of IBM's Personal Computer, they are also the brains of its Displaywriter word processor and Datamaster small business computer.[1]

Sales people offer more than physical products; they provide recommendations, technical assistance, and ideas for improving production processes. In turn, they communicate specific buyer needs back to the various functional areas of their own organizations.

To actualize the marketing concept effectively, however, sales people must be well-trained experts in areas involving the choice and applications of products. They must be conveyors of confidence, capable negotiators, and coordinators who are able to bring about changes in accordance with product specifications, affect delivery dates, provide technical services, and even affect price.

Sales Force Automation (SFA)

Sales Force Automation, popularly called "SFA," is making such an impact on enhancing the abilities of salespeople to actualize the marketing concept that a brief mention of it should be made here.

The founder of a leading market research and consulting group, Howard Anderson, states that SFA includes "everything from software to cellular phones to voice mail to artificial intelligence. It means using these tools to make the salesperson more productive, help the manager manage the sales force more effectively, and make relations with customers more profitable."

He exemplifies this by stating that "The salesperson now has data on customer usage that wasn't available before. He can use the data to help the customer buy smarter. He'll go in and say, 'Ms. Customer, you're buying product XYZ in ten gallon drums. Based on your growth and usage, you should be buying it in one hundred gallon drums starting in June. To take advantage of the larger drums, you should buy the proper forklifts now. As a result, you will save $28,000 in one year.'"

Mr. Anderson then explains that the salesperson will also be able to ". . . reinforce that proposal with desktop publishing software that will show graphically how the savings will come about." He concludes that "Selling will never be the same."[2]

[1]Standout Sellers Are Named by Buyers," *Purchasing,* August 19, 1982, p. 98; and "IBM and Intel Link up to Fend off Japan," *Business Week* (January 10, 1983), pp. 143, 149.

[2]Thayer C. Taylor, " 'Selling Will Never Be the Same,' " *Sales & Marketing Management* (March 1989), pp. 48–53.

In support of industry's growing usage of SFA, one research company points out that the sales of SFA equipment (in millions of dollars) totalled 8.4 in 1984, 176.7 in 1989, and will total 883.8 in 1994.[3]

THE INDUSTRIAL SELLING ENVIRONMENT

Industrial sales people operate in a complex environment. The foundation for understanding that environment and the problems encountered lies in the areas of organizational buying and buyer behavior (Chapters Four and Five). Perhaps if Apple had understood organizational buying and buyer behavior, it would have gotten off to a better start and not had to redesign its approach. Most sales people, however, respond to this environment through planning, executing, and controlling their sales efforts. In performing these functions they face three primary tasks: (1) identifying buying center members and what and who influences their behavior, (2) making the sales presentation, and (3) developing and maintaining customer rapport.

Identifying Buying Center Members

As Figure 14-1 shows, before an effective sales presentation can be made, industrial sales people must create an atmosphere of professionalism and establish credibility relative to their companies, their product lines, and themselves. However, what might be considered professional and/or credible to purchasing agents often differs from what engineers or production people perceive to be so. Therefore, different communication strategies often have to be developed. Not only must industrial sales people recognize individual needs in developing communication strategies, but organizational and departmental needs as well. And these three sets of needs must be considered concurrently in making a sales presentation. The first task in the selling process, then, is to identify buying center members and what and who influences their behavior.[4]

As discussed in Chapter Five, expectations and needs of buying center members stem from a variety of influences, both organizational and environmental. The key to understanding those needs lies partially in the underlying orientation of the buying firm. If a firm's members are homogeneous in nature, for example, if they all tend to be technically oriented, as they are in the high-tech areas, then they are likely to have similar backgrounds, educations, and experiences. Individual departmental and organizational goals will more likely be similar and integrated. Thus, differences between groups and individuals will tend to be minimized, and sales people can expect product or service attributes to be evaluated similarly by various

[3]Market Intelligence Research Co., Sales Automation Software Markets: 1984–1994, in "SFA Software to Top $100 Million in 1989," *Sales & Marketing Management* (March 1989), pp. 85–86.

[4]The discussion in this section is based on Richard E. Plank and William A. Dempsey, "A Framework for Personal Selling to Organizations," *Industrial Marketing Management* 9 (1980), pp. 143–49.

Dimension 1: Selling

A. Setting the stage
   1. Mood, professionalism
   2. Credibility
   3. Communication level(s)
B. Determining buyer(s)' needs
   1. Organizational needs
   2. Individual needs
   3. Departmental needs
C. Presentation
   1. Stage 1—Develop interest
   2. Stage 2—Demonstration
   3. Stage 3—Handle objections, close, or conclude
D. Exit

Buyer–Seller Dyad

A. Buying group identification
B. Influence pattern identification
C. Organizational factor identification
D. Environmental factor identification

Dimension 2:   Organizational
Buying Environment

FIGURE 14-1   Functions of Industrial Selling

Source: Reprinted by permission of the publisher from "A Framework for Personal Selling to Organizations," by Richard E. Plank and William A. Dempsey, *Industrial Marketing Management,* 9 (1980), pp. 143–149. Copyright © 1980 by Elsevier Science Publishing Co., Inc.

buying center members. On the other hand, a low degree of similarity among buying center members can lead to goal conflicts, causing products or services to be evaluated on significantly different attributes. Before a salesperson can create an atmosphere of professionalism and establish credibility, he or she must determine what differences exist among individuals, departments, and organizations.

Industrial sales people use their experience with the buying firm, along with questioning and observing, to identify buying center members and predict influence and conflict resolution patterns. While these patterns may be understood in one firm, they will be different for other similar firms, and they will tend to differ even more between firms in different industries.

Making the Sales Presentation

Before a sales presentation can be made, a great deal of planning must take place. Prospects must be identified, access to buying center members must be gained, and the sales presentation must be carefully developed to meet the needs of potential buyers. Selling is a process of logical steps that are designed to achieve a specific predetermined result, steps that begin with finding prospects and end with maintaining a continuing favorable relationship with the buying organization.

Identifying Prospects. An essential part of the selling process (see Table 14-1) is identifying prospective customers. Rarely can an organization rely on its current customer base to achieve growth objectives let alone sustain its current market share. For one reason or another, customers are lost. Thus, prospecting is essentially a future-oriented task that provides both the company and the salesperson with (1) future sources of sales revenue, (2) a more productive selling environment, and (3) better use of the limited time available for selling.[5] Identifying prospective customers, then, is an important part of the selling process.

A wide variety of sources are used by industrial sales people to identify customer prospects. These include, along with personal observation and referrals, company-generated sources that are discussed in Chapter Fifteen such as media advertising, trade shows, direct mail, and telemarketing. Experienced sales people, however, are aware that prospecting activities must be maximized. That is, prospects must be identified as to their need for the product or service, their eligibility to purchase, and their authority to buy.

Industrial customers purchase to save money, make money, or facilitate the running of a business. Need alone, however, is not sufficient for a firm to qualify as a potential customer. In the resellers' market, for instance, buyers are assigned budgets that limit the amount of dollar purchases they can make within a specific time period. Thus, the salesperson who sells to retailers must be aware of whether the potential prospect is "open to buy." If current funds have been expended, even though the status changes constantly, more merchandise cannot be purchased.

In almost every area of industrial selling, then, sales people must establish and follow an orderly procedure for identifying potential customers. This entails (1) setting quantitative objectives for prospecting (i.e., the number of qualified new accounts to be called on); (2) allocating time for prospecting (i.e., setting time aside from other sales demanding areas such as selling and servicing existing accounts, attending sales meetings, and the completion of administrative tasks); (3) systematizing the prospecting plan (i.e., classifying accounts by geography, sales volume potential, type of business, and type of product they might purchase); and (4) evalu-

---

[5]Gordon Storholm and Louis C. Kaufman, *Principles of Selling* (Englewood Cliffs, N.J.: Prentice-Hall, Inc., 1985), p. 94.

TABLE 14-1 The Selling Process

	Examples
1. Searching for and identifying organizations and individuals who might be potential customers.	Screening potential prospects against evaluative and qualifying criteria
2. Making the approach	Getting the interview and opening the sale
3. Qualifying prospect	Determining the needs of the prospect
4. Making the sales presentation	Demonstrating company's ability to satisfy customer needs, may include demonstrating the product
5. Answering objections	Anticipating unresolved problem areas
6. Closing the sale	Asking for the order, includes avoiding overselling after the prospect has agreed to purchase
7. Following up	Maintaining a continuing favorable relationship with the buyer

ating the results (i.e., analyzing which prospecting techniques worked best to discard those which are not producing qualified prospects).[6]

Gaining Access to Buying Center Members. Before sales people can actually make a sales approach, they must obtain as much information as possible on individual prospects. If a salesperson makes a sales presentation without adequate knowledge of whom to reach within a prospect firm, its problems, needs, personalities, and influence patterns, serious errors can be made. The key element in making a sale is the ability to satisfy the prospect's needs. To avoid serious blunders, then, industrial sales people often make several preliminary calls on prospect accounts. Most industrial sales "result from the cumulative effort of many calls."[7] Further complicating the selling task is the fact that sales people must work through their initial contacts, normally purchasing agents, to gain access to other decision makers.

The Sales Presentation. The purpose of the sales presentation is to provide prospects with specific information, to educate them about the firm's product or service offer, to answer questions, or to solve problems. The key to successful selling rests on the salesperson's ability to recognize and respond to customer needs. This requires a sensitivity to the variation between buying organizations and among buying center members within individual organizations. Rarely, however, are prospects convinced to buy on a single call. Before a sale can be made, buyers must be sold on

---

[6]Danny N. Bellenger and Thomas N. Ingram, *Professional Selling* (New York: Macmillan Publishing Company, 1984), pp. 139–142.

[7]Clifton J. Reichard, "Industrial Selling: Beyond Price and Persistence," *Harvard Business Review* (January–February 1985), pp. 127–133.

the fact that they want to do business with the firm. Thus, they must be convinced
that they will be supplied efficiently and that their business will be handled compe-
tently. Seldom can this be accomplished within a few calls. Rather, it may require
numerous sales calls to different individuals within the buying organization over a
long period of time.

Developing and Maintaining Customer Rapport

The importance of developing and maintaining customer rapport varies considerably in the industrial market and is dictated by the nature of the buyer-seller interface and the size of transactions that take place. For some selling functions, it assumes no greater importance than in the consumer market. In others, it becomes a
way of life. In these latter instances, building harmonious relationships with customers consumes considerably more time and effort, requiring special skills beyond
making simple sales presentations. These skills have been labeled human relations
and negotiating skills. For a very long while, many marketers have believed that
sales people succeed or fail due to the nature of their interaction with people. According to a 1959 study sponsored by *Steel Magazine,* "There is no such thing as a
cold, rational, dispassionate buyer who buys solely on merit." While industrial sales
people must understand customer procedures, methods, and manufacturing processes, and the products they represent, their knowledge does not stop there. It
must be applied in terms of people. Thus, sales people must continually study their
customers as individuals, understand what motivates them, how they react to others,
and how they react in conflict situations.[8]

    Negotiating skills underscore the reality that industrial selling requires ongoing
cooperative efforts between buyers and sellers rather than occasional sales presentations. Over the lengthy selling process, sales people must be capable negotiators in

[8]David Arthur Stumm, *Advanced Industrial Selling* (New York: AMACOM, 1981), pp. 113–114.

SOFTWARE THAT PROBES THE PSYCHOLOGY OF MAKING A SALE

Imagine calling on a customer again and again, getting near a sale, and then being unable to close. What's the salesperson's standard tactic at that point? It's probably to make another call.

That is, unless the salesperson has two advantages: a microcomputer and a software program called Sales Edge. Created by the Human Edge Software Corp. of Palo Alto, Cal., the Sales Edge is a $250 "expert system" designed to help salespeople close those elusive deals by matching the psychological traits of buyer and seller.

Instead of trudging back to the potential customer's office yet again, only to take a similar sales approach, the rep equipped with the Sales Edge first spends about 10 minutes at the computer terminal. There, he or she answers a number of multiple-choice and "agree-or-disagree" questions about the customer: Is he or she outgoing, conservative, aggressive, polite, shy, etc.?

Those answers are then compared and contrasted with information the salesperson has already entered about himself or herself—a one-time process that takes about 20 minutes and includes about 80 "agree-or-disagree" items such as "I usually arrive early for work," "I like being feared by other employees" and even "a strong defense is necessary for America's survival."

In a few minutes, a detailed sales strategy, from opening presentation to the close, is displayed. "You are competitive, so open with a neutral posture," reads a portion of one example. "You focus on the big picture, while Mr. M [the customer] observes details. Mr. M gets anxious when pressed to make a decision, so concentrate on one detail at a time to relax him."

Source: Peter Finch, "How Computers Are Reshaping the Sales Process," *Business Marketing,* June 1985, pp. 108–111. Reprinted by permission.

---

such areas as postsales services and maintenance, product specifications, delivery dates, and pricing. Unfortunately, however, while major corporations are emphasizing negotiation skills in the development of their purchasing people, the art of negotiation in the development of professional sales people continues to be a neglected area.[9] The fundamental skills of selling involve the application of psychology in dealing with people as well as the ability successfully to reach an agreement that is satisfactory to both the seller and the buyer.

Dyadic Interaction.   The environment of industrial selling is a dyadic interaction that consists of a process of exchange between the buyer and the seller.[10] In return for the reward of a specific sale, the salesperson exchanges information and assistance in solving a buyer's purchasing requirements. The image that each party devel-

---

[9]Ibid.

[10]Thomas V. Bonoma and Wesley Johnston, "The Social Psychology of Industrial Buying and Selling," *Industrial Marketing Management* 7 (July 1978), pp. 213–223.

ops for the other during this exchange process is important in establishing the boundaries of the purchasing interaction. Both the salesperson and the buyer have plans, goals, needs, and intentions that are often negotiable and serve as the starting point for the exchange process. According to Stumm, organizational buyers have three needs to fill:

1. **The needs of the job function.** Sometimes these needs are part of the buyer's function to be an "engineer" or a "purchasing agent." More often the need the buyer is dealing with is part of a plan or some item required to fill another job need.
2. **The needs of the organization.** These are needs having to do with the goals and objectives of the company, including needs to reduce costs or increase sales.
3. **Personal needs.** These include needs for self-growth, promotion, security, and recognition.[11]

Thus, friendship, trust, and cooperation must be developed over time for a mutually satisfactory sale to take place.

MANAGING THE INDUSTRIAL SALES FORCE

Competitive survival in the industrial market depends on an aggressive, well-trained professional sales force. Today's marketplace demands sales people who are keenly sensitive to customers' needs and equipped with the technical knowledge and necessary communication skills to operate efficiently and effectively to the mutual advantage of both sellers and buyers. The function of sales management, then, is to ensure that the industrial sales force is managed so that it is responsive to market conditions and requirements in a way that generates maximum profits to the firm.

While sales force management has been defined as planning, directing, and controlling the selling effort,[12] for the purposes of our discussion, we shall divide it into two areas, strategy and administration. Strategy involves planning, organizing, and controlling; administration involves such considerations as recruiting, selecting, training, determining compensation, motivating, and directing the sales force. The remainder of this chapter is devoted to strategy. Administration was discussed in Chapter Thirteen.

The discussion of strategy in terms of its component parts of planning, organizing, and controlling is intended to explain such areas as how sales potential is determined for effective deployment of the sales force, how sales force assignments are established to maximize efficiency in the selling effort, and how sales force activities are evaluated and adjusted to produce an efficient and effective professional sales force.

---

[11]Stumm, *Advanced Industrial Selling,* p. 3.

[12]Committee on Definitions, American Marketing Association, *Marketing Definitions* (Chicago: American Marketing Association, 1960), p. 20.

PLANNING FOR SALES FORCE DEPLOYMENT

Effective utilization of sales force effort is extremely important if maximum sales are to be achieved in a cost-effective manner. The cost of maintaining a single sales rep in the field now averages $840 per week.[13] Lodging alone costs $455 each week. And costs aren't plummeting; Gurney's Inn in Montauk, N.Y., will cost from $250 to $310 per night.[14] And, to help you view this with realism, according to a McGraw-Hill survey, the average salesperson spends only thirty-nine percent of his or her time in front of prospects. Travel and waiting time consume thirty-two percent; reports, paperwork, and sales meetings twenty-four percent; and service calls five percent.[15]

Traditionally, sales managers have attempted to improve sales effort effectiveness through administrative functions, tending to neglect efforts to improve sales force deployment strategy.[16] Perhaps one reason for this neglect is the complex nature of sales deployment analysis. Deployment refers to decisions regarding the size of the sales force, territorial design, and the organization and allocation of the selling effort. As David Hughes has pointed out, "Sales managers should not be recruiters and cheerleaders but business managers of territories, districts, and regions."[17]

While many methods of deploying the sales force are available, such as work load analysis and return on time invested, over the last decade several sales force decision models have been developed that make the task of sales force deployment more manageable. However, several problems exist with these models. They require the collection and processing of large amounts of data, many are applicable to specific types of selling situations, and often management does not understand or trust the ability of computers to handle the mathematical formulations required for analyses.[18] One recent survey of computer use in performing nine sales-force functions indicated that computers were least used for sales force deployment. Only seventeen percent of firms surveyed used them for this purpose.[19] Typical approaches to sales force deployment analyses and decisions are shown in Figure 14-2.

Regardless of the method chosen, effective deployment of the industrial sales force involves

[13]"Compensation and Expenses," *Sales & Marketing Management* (February 20, 1989), p. 45.

[14]"Metro Market Profiles," *Sales & Marketing Management* (February 20, 1989), p. 93.

[15]See C. Robert Patty, *Managing Salespeople,* 2nd ed. (Reston, Va.: Reston Publishing Company, 1982), p. 149.

[16]Raymond LaForge and David W. Cravens, "Steps in Selling Effort Deployment," *Industrial Marketing Management* 11 (1982), pp. 183–192.

[17]G. David Hughes, "Computerized Sales Management," *Harvard Business Review* (March–April 1985), pp. 102–112.

[18]See Cravens and LaForge, "Salesforce Deployment Analysis," and LaForge and Cravens, "Steps in Selling Effort Deployment."

[19]"How the Game Will Change in the 1990s," *Sales & Marketing Management* (June 1989), pp. 52–61.

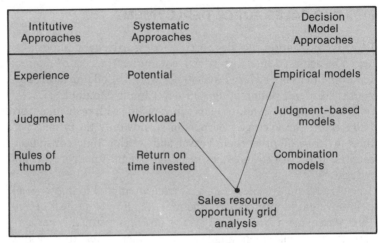

FIGURE 14-2   Typical Sales Force Deployment Analyses Approaches

Source: Reprinted by permission of the publisher from "Steps in Selling Effort Deployment," by Raymond LaForge and David W. Cravens, *Industrial Marketing Management,* 11 [1982], pp. 183–194. Copyright © 1982 by Elsevier Science Publishing Co., Inc.

1. Estimating total market sales potential by geographic regions and customer type.
2. Adjusting these estimates to reflect the company's sales potential.
3. Compiling these adjusted estimates into sales estimates for specific customers in geographical areas.
4. Evaluating trends that may affect potential sales.
5. Determining how many sales people will be needed to bring about projected sales, referred to as work load analysis.
6. Assigning sales people to territories and customers.

Estimating Company Sales Potential

When sales managers reach the point of estimating company sales for their areas of responsibility, total market potential has usually been projected by forces higher up in the organizational hierarchy. Thus, they normally work with macro estimates of potential sales that must be adjusted if they are to be useful in planning for sales force deployment.

Adjusting Market Potential.   Sales managers are in charge of what is almost always that group of people most capable of adjusting a market sales forecast, sales people. For example, discussions with sales people might indicate that different-size companies have different levels of commitment to their existing suppliers so that very large companies, which purchase greater amounts, are not as likely as smaller companies to switch to a new supplier. Other sources, however, include knowledgeable people in the industry, discussions with knowledgeable people within the firm, secondary information sources, and clues often provided by the original market potential forecast.

For purposes of illustrating how sales managers adjust a market potential, let us assume that a firm is considering market expansion through the cultivation of new customer accounts whose total market sales potential (shown in Table 14-2) has been estimated. Discussions with the sales force indicate the maximum portion of company sales that can be obtained from the market potential (column 1 of Table 14-2) within a specific geographical area from four different customer account groups, A, B, C, and D. As Table 14-2 indicates, when each customer group's total potential purchases are multiplied by the sales force's projections, column (2) × column (3), the resulting figures are the company's sales potential. The probability of obtaining the maximum sales potential, column (4), however, must also be considered. One way of accomplishing this task is through *expected value analysis*.

Expected Value Analysis. Expected value analysis involves adjusting the company sales potential by considering the probability of obtaining sales within prospective customer groups. This requires that sales people further adjust their projections by estimating the probability of obtaining sales within the various customer groups. The different customer group potentials can then be multiplied by these probabilities; column (4) × column (5) in Table 14-3. Column (6), "Expected Value," reflects the forecasts of projected sales, forecasts that have been adjusted downward to reflect the maximum percentage of total sales that the company might be able to obtain and the probability that the company will obtain sales within the different customer groups.

Evaluating Strategy Choices. Expected value is not equivalent to a company sales forecast. A vendor will frequently estimate that it will not obtain the full sales potential because of such reasons as a limited number of sales people or inadequate promotional funds. Such factors lead it to estimate the actual anticipated sales, the company sales forecast, as something less than the company sales potential. Multi-

TABLE 14-2 An Adjusted Market Potential for Potential Customer Groups

[1] Customer Group	[2] Market Sales Potential	[3] Maximum Portion Vendor Potential	[4] Projected Company Potential [2] × [3]
A	$1,000,000	50%	$500,000
B	500,000	80	400,000
C	250,000	100	250,000
D	75,000	67	50,000

TABLE 14-3 An Expected Value Analysis

[1] Customer Group	[2] Market Sales Potential	[3] Maximum Portion Vendor Potential	[4] Company Sales Potential [2] × [3]	[5] Probability of Obtaining Sales	[6] Expected Value [4] × [5]
A	$1,000,000	50%	$500,000	35%	$175,000
B	500,000	80	400,000	60	240,000
C	250,000	100	250,000	75	187,500
D	75,000	67	50,000	20	10,000

plying sales potential by the probability of obtaining an account, on the other hand, is primarily used for comparison between prospective customer groups and will seldom, if ever, equal the sales forecast. Expected value analysis, then, is a useful tool for comparing possible alternative choices of action. For example, analysis of Table 14-3 indicates that customer group B is a better prospect than is group A. Even though A group's total purchases are higher than are those of B, the expected value of purchases from group B and even group C is greater. Therefore, the sales manager, in this case, would develop a program to pursue groups B and C rather than A or D. Firms that have been in operation for some time use this method with the awareness that their previous experience and sales force feedback enhance its accuracy.

The Heavy Half.   In the industrial market, a small number of customers tend to buy large amounts of a company's product or service. In fact, many firms have discovered that sixty-five to eighty percent of their business comes from fifteen to twenty percent of their customers.[20]

Expected value analysis helps in identifying the "heavy half" of prospects that make up or can make up the greater volume of company sales. Once identified, the major portion of the selling effort can be concentrated on these higher-volume accounts. This does not imply that lower-volume accounts should be ignored. It merely indicates that greater attention should be given to customers who have higher purchase potentials. For instance, less face-to-face selling time can be allocated to lower-volume accounts, or inside salespersons may be utilized to make the necessary contacts via telephone (usually termed "telemarketing").

Work Load Analysis

Once potential sales volume has been estimated, it is necessary to determine the number of people needed to perform the selling function. Work load analysis is defined as the amount of work assigned for completion within a given time period.

---

[20]Dubinsky and Hansen, *California Management Review* (Winter 1981), pp. 86–95.

INSIDE SALES PEOPLE SUPPORT OUTSIDE SALES PEOPLE VIA TELEMARKETING

As single-family housing starts decline, Georgia-Pacific focuses its forest product lines on local apartment building booms, do-it-yourself home centers, office buildings, factories, California vineyards, and New York furniture factories. It's not just selling two-by-fours now, it's selling mixed truck loads of lumber, plywood, and other building materials.

To keep up with changing markets, Georgia-Pacific added roofing materials, metal siding, and prefabricated fireplaces—and, as each market changes, sales people attend company-sponsored product education programs. But, even that isn't enough. Without its inside sales people, Georgia-Pacific's 145 semiautonomous sales teams wouldn't be able to keep up with their promises. It's the inside sales people who maintain customer ties through telemarketing. While these inside sales people receive no commission, through incoming lines, WATS lines, and USA WATS lines they keep in constant contact with customers, monitoring their changing needs.

Source: See "Georgia-Pacific Blazes Trails," *Sales and Marketing Management,* December 3, 1984, p. 36.

To perform work load analysis, sales managers must first determine how many sales calls each salesperson can make in a given period of time, say, in one year. This requires an estimate of

1. The number of selling days available per sales person during the period.
2. The average travel time between customers.
3. The length of time the average sales call will require per customer.
4. The number of calls to be made per customer during the period.[21]

Estimating the number of selling days available is not difficult. Sales managers simply arrive at the number of selling days available for the time period under consideration by deducting weekends, holidays, vacation time, estimated days off due to illness, and the number of days to be set aside for sales people to attends sales meetings or trade shows or engage in other nonselling activities.

The time that a salesperson can spend with a prospect or customer, however, depends on the amount of travel time between customers. Thus, the number of days available for selling must be reduced by the number of days spent in travel during the year. For instance, in Table 14-4, given that 221 days are available for selling, a salesperson who travels 10,000 miles each year, averages fifty miles per hour, and

---

[21]The following discussion is based on Patty, *Managing Salespeople,* pp. 156–157, and Charles E. Bergman, "All out for Productivity," *Sales and Marketing Management* (March 14, 1977), pp. 52–59.

TABLE 14-4 Net Sales Days per Year Given Various Travel Mileages

Business Travel Miles per Year [000s]	Total Sales Days	Less: Travel Days	Net Sales Days
10	221	25	196
20	221	50	171
30	221	75	146
40	221	100	121
50	221	125	96

Source: Adapted from C. Robert Patty, *Managing Salespeople,* 2nd ed., 1982. Reprinted by permission of Reston Publishing Company, a Prentice-Hall Company, 11480 Sunset Hills Road, Reston, Va. 22090.

works eight hours a day uses twenty-five days per year just for travel—leaving only 196 days of actual selling time.

Actually, the mile-per-hour average will vary considerably. A salesperson driving in a heavily populated city may average less than twenty miles per hour, while one driving large distances between customers in sparsely populated regions may average fifty-five miles per hour. In estimating such averages, then, salesperson input is essential. One pharmaceutical salesman, for instance, stated that he was able to cover 700 miles a day. "I would fly to a town like Guyman in western Oklahoma. Then I would take my Honda out of the airplane and visit all my customers."[22]

Estimating the Number of Sales Calls That Can Be Made. Once the number of days a salesperson will actually spend in selling has been determined, it is possible to estimate the number of calls that can be made during those days (in this case, 196). This is accomplished by estimating the average number of hours needed per successful sales call—hours spent with the customer, including waiting time. Depending on the type of account and the number of influencers to be reached, different amounts of time must be set aside for the actual sales call.

It is not difficult to determine the number of calls that can be made in 196 eight-hour days. The sales manager simply multiplies the number of days times eight hours and divides the result by the average length of a sales call.

As Table 14-5 depicts, it is important to estimate accurately the average length of sales calls. For example, if sales calls average one hour for the salesperson who travels 10,000 miles per year, but an inaccurate estimate of two hours per call is made, the estimated number of salespersons needed will double.

[22]Max Nichols, "New Products, Sales Approach Build T. E. Williams," The [Oklahoma City] *Journal Record* (March 14, 1984), pp. 1–2.

TABLE 14-5 Number of Sales Calls Given Various Lengths per Call

Business Travel Miles per Year [000 days]	Net Sales	Average Length of Call [hours]			
		1	2	3	4
10	196	1,568	785	523	392
20	171	1,368	684	456	342
30	146	1,168	587	389	292
40	121	968	484	323	242
50	96	768	384	256	192

Source: Adapted from C. Robert Patty, *Management Salespeople*, 2nd ed., 1982. Reprinted by permission of Reston Publishing Company, a Prentice-Hall Company, 11480 Sunset Hills Road, Reston, Va. 22090.

Return on Time Invested

Even though estimates of sales people needed are accurate, the work load analysis may not be financially profitable to the company. Sales managers must also be concerned with whether the various considerations (customer accounts and length and number of sales calls, for example) offer potential profitability. More specifically, they must be concerned with whether the cost of each call will be greater than expected profits.

When the cost of making sales calls is less than expected profits, it becomes profitable to make calls. When costs exceed profits, more efficient use of the sales force should be considered. The cost of maintaining a salesperson in the field can be considerable. The average cost of making a sales call in 1983 was estimated to be $205.40.[23] Actually, sales call costs vary, depending on the size of the sales force. Sales forces of 100 or more averaged $137.10, while those under 10 averaged $290.70.[24] Costs per sales call are usually estimated by dividing the number of calls a salesperson makes into his or her total direct sales cost (compensation plus auto, travel, and entertainment expenses). If, for example, a salesperson makes 1,500 calls a year, and has total direct costs of $90,000 a year, the cost per call is $60.00.

Determining ROTI. One method used to determine the profitability of sales force allocation is called return on time invested (ROTI). How return on time invested is determined is illustrated in Table 14-6, which assumes a work load plan for accounts A through D, from Table 14-2. You will note that the number of accounts per account group, column (1), the planned calls for each account for the period, column (1) × (2), and the average cost per call, $205.40 for this example, column (4), have been used to determine the total cost of servicing each account group.

[23]"1984 Survey of Selling Costs: Something Old, Something New," *Sales and Marketing Management,* (February 20, 1984), pp. 12–17.
[24]Ibid.

TABLE 14-6 Calculating Return on Time Invested *

Customer Group	[1] Number of Accounts	[2] Frequency per Account	[3] Total Planned Calls	[4] Average Cost per Call	[5] Cost for Group	[6] Company Sales Potential	[7] Gross Margin	[8] ROTI
A	14	9	126	$205	$25,880	$ 500,000	$100,000	3.86
B	35	5	175	205	35,945	400,000	80,000	2.23
C	13	3	39	205	8,010	250,000	50,000	6.24
D	17	4	68	205	13,967	50,000	10,000	.72
	79		408		$83,802	$1,200,000	$240,000	2.8

where

Column 3 = column [1] × column [2]
Column 4 = Average cost of a sales call for 1983 = $205.40 [from previous discussion]
Column 5 = column [3] × column [4]
Column 6 = company sales potential from Table 14-2, column [4]
Column 7 = .2 of projected company sales
Column 8 = column [7]/column [5]

*Totals differ due to rounding.

Source: Adapted from C. Robert Patty, *Managing Salespeople*, 2nd ed., 1982. Reprinted by permission of Reston Publishing Company, a Prentice-Hall Company, 11480 Sunset Hills Road, Reston, Va. 22090.

It is possible to determine the ROTI for each account group by dividing gross margin, column (7), by the total cost of serving each account, column (5). Expected gross margin in this example is 20 percent of projected sales. When ROTI is below "1," the planned work load is unprofitable; above "1," it is profitable.

For example, analysis of Table 14-6 indicates that while overall ROTI for the work load plan is 2.86, not all account groups are equally profitable. The calculations regarding potential account groups and the frequency and length of average sales calls, given projected sales, have led to a plan that is not entirely profitable. Account group D is not profitable enough to warrant an average of four calls per account. In view of this, the estimates should be pared by either reducing the number of calls or by eliminating the account group. If, for instance, sales calls are cut to 2 per account in group D, total sales call costs would amount to $6,983 (34 × $205.4), and the ROTI would then be 1.43 ($10,000/$6,983). This, as well as other possibilities, should be explored with sales force personnel.

The Sales Resource Planning Grid

A useful technique for improving deployment effort is the *Sales Resource Planning Grid,* which is similar in many respects to the grids used for analyzing strategic business units discussed in Chapter Nine.[25] Instead of analyzing a portfolio of SBUs, a portfolio of planning and control units (PCUs) is analyzed. A PCU may consist of products, prospects, customers, territories, or districts. While work load and ROTI analysis are useful, they do not provide for an analysis of all the relevant variables (e.g., salesperson's selling time, number and length of sales calls, and number of sales people) across all PCUs. A major consideration in the allocation of sales force deployment "is the opportunity available from the PCU." Thus, the grid is useful for assessing whether sales force deployment decisions are optimal across PCUs.

When PCUs are analyzed via the Sales Resource Planning Grid (see Figure 14-3), current deployment and potential benefits from redeployment can be measured. In assessing a PCU's opportunity, the following factors, in addition to those factors considered under work load and ROTI analysis, are taken into consideration:

1. Factors external to the firm including environmental and competitive variables.
2. Target market characteristics including account dispersion, servicing requirements, and other relevant characteristics.
3. Organizational factors such as marketing effort and management capabilities.
4. Salesperson factors including characteristics and behavior (effort, quality).

The most important aspect of analyzing PCUs is that it enables sales managers to determine whether the firm has employed the correct number of sales people, whether territories are organized into appropriate sales districts, whether accounts

[25]Cravens and LaForge, "Salesforce Deployment Analysis."

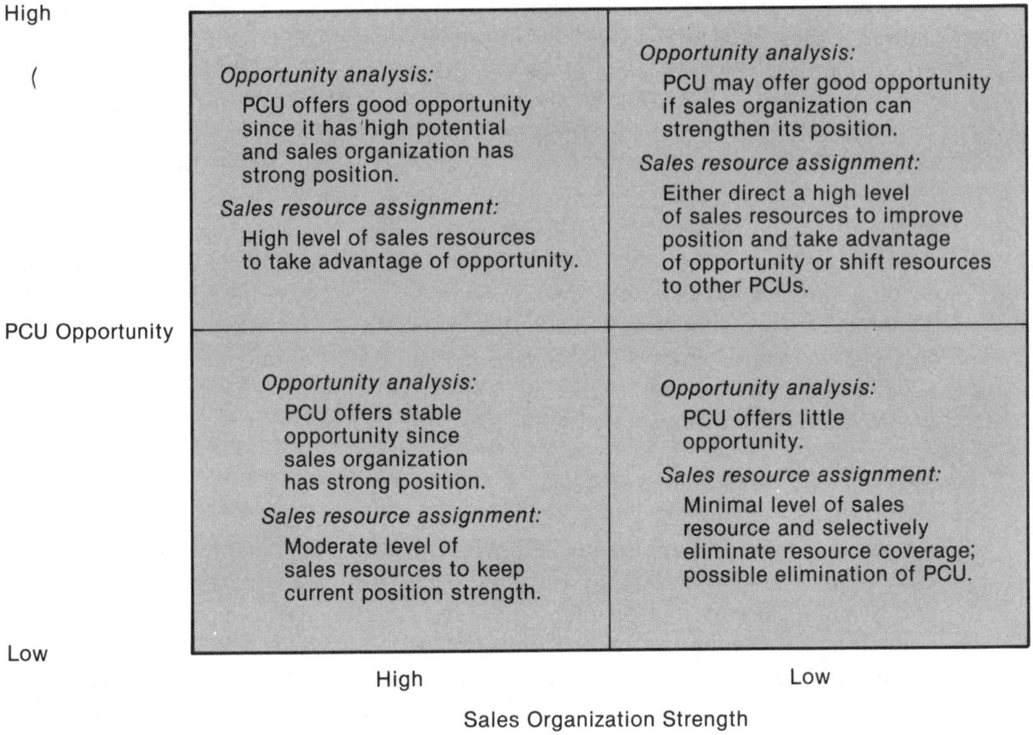

High

(

	Opportunity analysis: PCU offers good opportunity since it has high potential and sales organization has strong position. Sales resource assignment: High level of sales resources to take advantage of opportunity.	Opportunity analysis: PCU may offer good opportunity if sales organization can strengthen its position. Sales resource assignment: Either direct a high level of sales resources to improve position and take advantage of opportunity or shift resources to other PCUs.
PCU Opportunity	Opportunity analysis: PCU offers stable opportunity since sales organization has strong position. Sales resource assignment: Moderate level of sales resources to keep current position strength.	Opportunity analysis: PCU offers little opportunity. Sales resource assignment: Minimal level of sales resource and selectively eliminate resource coverage; possible elimination of PCU.

Low

      High   Low

Sales Organization Strength

FIGURE 14-3   Sales Resource Opportunity Grid

Source: Reprinted by permission of the publisher from "Steps in Selling Effort Deployment," by Raymond LaForge and David W. Cravens, *Industrial Marketing Management,* 11 [1982], pp. 183–194. Copyright © 1982 by Elsevier Science Publishing Co., Inc.

are receiving the correct number of sales calls, and whether territories are designed so as to provide equal opportunity for all sales people.

ORGANIZING THE SALES FORCE

To accomplish planning and organizing in the ever-changing selling environment, industrial marketers organize their sales forces by territory, product, customer, and function.[26] (How sales force personnel are categorized is shown in Table 14-7.)

However, as Table 14-8 shows, territory structures or some combination of product, customer, and territory specialization are the most popular forms of sales force organization. How the sales force is organized, however, depends on (1) the nature and length of the product line, (2) the diversity of market segments served,

[26]Arthur Meridan, "Optimizing the Number of Industrial Salespersons," *Industrial Marketing Management,* 11 (1982), pp. 63–74.

TABLE 14-7 Classifications of Sales Personnel

Account representatives	Sales people who call on customers who are already established.
Detail salespersons	Sales people who provide details relative to promotional activities. Such a salesperson might visit the offices of medical doctors and attempt to inform them of the specific possibilities of a new drug. These sales people seldom get credit for a sale; instead, the credit usually goes to a middleman.
Sales engineers	A title that was originally bestowed to increase esteem of those who held it is that of "sales engineer." This title has come to signify that the salesperson has technical know-how relative to the construction and/or application of the product. Salespersons in such areas as heavy machinery, electronic parts and equipment, and raw materials often bear this title.
Nontechnical industrial products sales repre- sentatives	Individuals who sell nonsell, nontechnical, tangible products, such as floor wax.
Service salespersons	Service salespersons are in the business of selling services, that is, intangibles. They may sell such things as management consulting and advertising. There is also the "missionary salesperson" classifi- cation, which was discussed and defined earlier in this text.

Source: Reprinted by permission of the publisher from "Optimizing the Number of Industrial Salespersons," by Arthur Meridan, *Industrial Marketing Management,* 11 (1982), pp. 63–74. Copyright © 1982 by Elsevier Science Publishing Co., Inc.

TABLE 14-8 Percentage of Small and Large Firms that "Extensively Use" the Following Organization Practices

	Percentage of	
Organization Items	*Small Firms*	*Large Firms*
Organization of sales force by territorial/geographical specialization	68%	75%
Organization of sales force by combination of product class, customer class, or territorial geographical specialization	41	60
Organization of sales force by product class specialization	41	30
Organization of sales force by customer class specialization	19	38

Source: Reprinted by permission of the publisher from "Survey of Sales Management Practices," by Alan J. Dubinsky and Thomas E. Barry, *Industrial Marketing Management,* 11 (1982), pp. 133–141. Copyright © 1982 by Elsevier Science Publishing Co., Inc.

(3) the role of intermediaries in the marketing program, (4) the structure of competitors' sales forces, and (5) the nature of buying behavior encountered in each market segment.

Organization by Territories.   Territorial-structured sales forces are structured on the basis of defined geographical areas. For instance, one salesperson might have Ohio, Indiana, and Illinois while another has Arizona and Nevada as his or her territory. The major advantages of such organizational structures are reduced travel distance and time between customers and the familiarity that sales people obtain with customers and prospects within their territorial area. A major disadvantage is that sales people must be capable of performing all the selling tasks across the firm's products and customer base.

Organization by Products.   Product-structured sales forces are those in which groups of salespersons specialize in a specific category of products, a few products, or only one product. This approach is often used when products are technically complex or significantly different from each other, as with different types of telephone services. Thus, sales people tend to become product experts and more adept at meeting customer needs as well as identifying and communicating with buying influencers. Product-oriented sales forces, however, are more costly to develop. Therefore, sales and profit potential of the various products represented must justify individual selling attention for a firm to organize along product lines. Product specialization, however, can also lead to duplication of effort across customer accounts.

Organization by Customer Groups.   Customer-structured sales forces are built on the basis of serving different categories of customers within specific industries. The wide diversity of customers in the industrial market raises the need for this type of organization, and categories are often determined by the customer's end market (i.e., industrial—commercial, institutional, or government—or consumer). Organization by customer (or industry) enables sales people to learn of and respond to the specific needs of buying influencers within the accounts they service. For this type of organizational structure to be profitable, however, market segments must be sufficiently large enough to warrant such a specialized focus.

Organization by Function.   The function structure is a special form of organizing by product. It is sometimes desirable when products are highly complex or extremely costly in nature. It involves structuring the sales force to provide advice to different operational entities within the customer's organization, for example, selling computers that will be used by accounting, research and development, manufacturing, and marketing. It can involve sales force composition so as to include individuals with varying backgrounds (called team selling), which allows them to associate easily with different personnel within the buying organization's hierarchy.

Organizing to Serve National Accounts

Over the last decade, emphasis on serving national accounts has increased. While the designation of "national account" will vary from seller to seller, they are generally considered to be very large and important customers, with centralized purchasing units that buy or coordinate buying for decentralized units, with operations in more than one geographic lcoation that consume the supplier's products.[27] Selling to such firms, according to a recent survey, frequently involves

1. Obtaining acceptance or specification of the company's products at the customer's headquarters.
2. Maintaining customer relations at various levels in the customer's organization.
3. Negotiating long-term sales contracts.
4. Ensuring superior customer service.[28]

Such activities require a wide range of selling effort that often involves other company personnel besides the salesperson. Thus, many organizations serving national accounts often employ team selling.

Team Selling. Team selling combines the efforts of sales people with other personnel from the firm to provide a specialized, yet unified, sales coverage. For example, engineers from both the seller's and the buyer's organization may negotiate over complex product specifications, logistics personnel on storage, and shipping requirements, while marketing research people interlock their expertise to ensure market acceptance of the buyer's end product. Thus, team selling provides a method for responding to the complex requirements involved in selling to large national accounts by including the efforts of multiple divisions in the selling company in the selling effort.

Organization. How the efforts of a national account program are organized and structured varies. In some firms, sales managers have line authority over a large, geographically dispersed sales and support team; in others, they may simply coordinate the efforts of sales and support personnel. Regardless of the type of organization, the objective of a national account program is to become the preferred or sole supplier of large or potentially large complex accounts.[29]

[27]Roger M. Pegram, *Selling and Servicing the National Account* (New York: The Conference Board, 1972).

[28]Ibid., pp. 24–53.

[29]Benson P. Shapiro and Rowland T. Moriarty, "National Account Management: Emerging Insights," Report No. 82–100 (Cambridge, Mass.: Marketing Science Institute, 1982).

Changing Organizational Structure

Organization represents an arrangement of activities that are directed to achieve company objectives. Objectives, on the other hand, guide a firm's strategies, which in turn determine its activities. Therefore, when a firm changes its objectives or strategies, it often becomes necessary to redesign the organization of the sales force. For example, to achieve its objectives of selling highly complex technical automated office products while lowering overall selling costs and getting greater productivity out of its sales people, Xerox is reorganizing its sales force.[30]

Xerox's present sales force, which is specialized by product offering (printing systems, office systems, information processing systems, facsimile, and sales engineering) will be restructured into what it terms a general-line concept to serve specific customer groups. That is, rather than selling products in specialized areas, Xerox's sales force will eventually sell related products to specific customers. National accounts will be serviced by national account managers and major accounts (accounts that represent a significant amount of potential business versus accounts that are both large and complex) will be serviced by major account managers, while standard commercial accounts will be serviced by account representatives. Although Xerox has had national account managers for several years, for the first time they will have complete control. While sales people from office, printing, and information processing systems made individual calls on national accounts, competing with each other as well as the account manager, under the new structure, national and major account managers will lead a team of representatives who will support the selling effort for their individual products.[31]

Assigning the Sales Force to Territories

If all individuals were of equal ability and all territories of equal potential, sales people could be assigned to territories on the basis of random selection. However, sales people are never of equal ability nor are territories of equal potential. In the creation of territories, these differences can be accounted for by assigning territories of lower potential to the more capable sales people, assuring that final incomes will be on a parity. The problem with this approach is that capable sales people can become discouraged and resign.

When territories of higher than average potential are assigned to the more capable salespersons, they usually achieve extraordinarily higher incomes, which, of course, discourages salespersons of lesser capabilities. The best solution lies in creating territories of equal potential, recognizing that sales people are not equally capable, and letting the more able stand out as those who attain above-average sales and earnings. While this will result in slightly lower short-term profits, over the long run

---

[30]Storholm and Kaufman, *Principles of Selling,* p. 295.

[31]"Xerox's Sales Force Learns a New Game," *Sales and Marketing Management* (July 1, 1985), p. 48.

it will result in higher profits since it elicits the best efforts of the entire sales force, rather than overrewarding some and frustrating others.[32]

Personalities Affect Customer Relations. In assigning sales territories to sales people, it is wise to consider the effect that a salesperson's personality attributes have on customers. Territories differ in their distribution of large versus small accounts and some sales people are good at handling small accounts, others at handling large accounts. Some territories will also have different concentrations of industries, and sales people tend to vary in their knowledge regarding industries. Because of their education, backgrounds, and experience, some sales people will also be more effective in one part of the country than in another. For reasons of this nature, sales managers must look beyond average sales data and a territory's potential in determining assignments to different territories.[33]

Buyer-Seller Interactions. The need for sales managers to take into consideration characteristics of sales people and customers centers on important elements in the buyer-seller relationship. It has been theorized that two elements strongly influence the quality of interaction between a seller and a buyer: the content of information and the style in which that information is exchanged.[34]

Content refers to the variables of interest that brought the two parties together, such as the offering or negotiating of a set of product-specific attributes and the expectations of the parties relative to those attributes. Thus, content of communication centers on performance attributes of products or services as well as individual needs, such as social, organizational, or emotional. Style refers to the format, ritual, and mannerisms that buyers and sellers use in their personal interactions.

According to the theory, three styles of interaction may be adopted: (1) task oriented, which is highly purposeful, (2) interaction oriented, which involves socializing and personalizing, and (3) self oriented, which is a preoccupation with one's own self-interest.

It is hypothesized that successful interaction occurs only when buyer and seller are compatible in both content and style of communications. As you can observe in Figure 14-4, an ideal transaction requires compatibility in both style and content, and incompatibility in both these dimensions results in no transaction. In fact, incompatibility in these two dimensions may lead to distrust or unfavorable word of mouth concerning one another.

When content is compatible and style is incompatible, the interaction process might even be terminated, or, if a sale does result, negative feelings can remain. If

---

[32]Philip Kotler, *Marketing Decision Making: A Model Building Approach* (New York: Holt, Rinehart and Winston, 1971), p. 378.

[33]Ibid.

[34]See Jadish N. Sheth, "Buyer-Seller Interaction: A Conceptual Framework," in B. B. Anderson, ed., *Advances in Consumer Research,* Vol. III (Cincinnati: Association for Consumer Research, 1976), pp. 133–144.

	Compatible Style	Incompatible Style
Compatible Content	Ideal transaction	Inefficient transaction
Incompatible Content	Inefficient transaction	No transaction

FIGURE 14-4 Style versus Content

Source: Adapted from Jagdish N. Sheth, "Buyer-Seller Interaction: A Conceptual Framework," in B. B. Anderson, ed., *Advances in Consumer Research,* Vol. III [Cincinnati, Ohio: Association for Consumer Research, 1976], p. 383. Reprinted with permission.

the buyer and seller are compatible in style but not in content, the process may either cease, or both parties might attempt to alter one another's product expectations through further negotiations.

This theory highlights the importance of considering salespersons' characteristics when assigning them to territories and/or customers. When incompatibility centers on content, adjustments can be made in the firm's product/service offering. However, when incompatibility centers on style, corrective action might include changing the salesperson's territory, modifying his or her selling approach through training, or changing recruiting and selecting strategies.

Territory Sales Response. One model that emphasizes the compatibility between the salesperson and the customer, and also incorporates a number of other techniques that are worthwhile in the area of organizing, is called PAIRS (Purchase Attitudes and Interactive Response to Salesmen).[35] Key elements of this model are shown in Table 14-9.

When PAIRS is used, sales managers define the selling skills deemed important in dealing with a particular customer or customer groups and develop a salesperson's effectiveness index. Each salesperson is rated on the characteristics considered to be important on a "1" (extremely poor) to "10" (excellent) scale. These skills are then weighted as to their relative importance to each customer category. The important point with the PAIRS approach to assigning territories is that it recognizes that different skills may be required for different customer markets or customer types.

Route Analysis

Organizing also involves routing sales people through their territories. Careful scheduling of each salesperson's route can produce substantial cost-saving benefits.

[35]A. Parasuraman and Ralph L. Day, "A Management-Oriented Model for Allocating Sales Effort," *Journal of Marketing Research* 14 (February 1977), pp. 22–33.

TABLE 14-9 Key Elements of PAIRS

1. On a territory by territory basis, customers who are similar in their responses to selling effort are classified into mutually exclusive and exhaustive groups of approximately equal sales potential.
2. The impact of the selling effort on a customer is perceived as being dependent upon the selling ability of the sales personnel as well as the number of sales calls made. Therefore, sales managers rank salespeople on such characteristics as education, knowledge of company products, personality traits or other attributes that they deem essential to the selling job.
3. Planning periods are divided into periods of time based on the average length of the purchase cycle rather than weekly, monthly, etc.
4. Variations in the time per sales call for different customers are utilized rather than a stated average.
5. The expected total volume of sales from each customer type is specified in terms of potential dollar revenue.

Source: Reprinted by permission of the American Marketing Association from "A Management-Oriented Model for Allocating Sales Effort," by A. Parasuraman and Ralph L. Day. *Journal of Marketing,* 14 [February 1977], pp. 22–23.

For instance, when driving patterns were analyzed, one firm reduced sales force travel by 15,000 miles per year while increasing sales calls per salesperson by eight per week.[36]

The increased cost of gasoline has brought about the use of management science techniques to schedule and route sales people with a minimum expenditure of time and money. A variety of techniques is available for determining the best routes, such as linear programming, integer programming, nonlinear programming, heuristic programming, and branch and bound methods. While a discussion of these complex procedures is beyond the scope of this book, they all provide good solutions to the problem. A disadvantage of their usage, however, is that they all require complicated computations of travel cost between cities to find the optimal routing. One simple way to plan travel routes for the sales force is shown in Table 14-10.[37]

CONTROLLING SALES FORCE ACTIVITIES

Controlling is defined as regulating activities. Once planning and organizing have been accomplished, it is necessary to examine results to determine if objectives are being accomplished. When there are significant variances between planned and actual results, adjustments must be made to bring about desired results.

Sales managers cannot control all activities since sales force activities are too numerous and vary considerably in importance. Thus, attention should be given to

[36]*Sales and Marketing Management* 126:3 (February 23, 1981), p. 24.
[37]C. Robert Patty, *Managing Salespeople,* 2nd ed. (Reston, Va.: Reston Publishing Company, 1982), pp. 158–59.

TABLE 14-10 Routing Sales People Without Simulated Computer Models

1. Obtain a detailed map of each salesperson's territory.
2. Mark the map to show the location of each account or account group. Use different colors for each.
3. Look for natural clusters.
4. Consider designing routes that begin and end near the salesperson's home (or the office if he or she checks there when beginning and completing a route).
5. Consider designing routes that periodically place the salesperson within visiting distance of important customers during routes that are very long timewise.
6. Consider scheduling as few nights and especially weekends away from home as possible.
7. Place transparent acetate or tracing paper over the territory and experiment by drawing various alternative routes until the best possible route is found.

Source: See C. Robert Patty, *Managing Salespeople,* 2nd ed. (Reston, Va.: Reston Publishing Co., Inc., 1982), pp. 158–159.

those activities that are strategically important and those that are inconsequential should be ignored. Managing several sales people involved in numerous activities, however, can be very painstaking, even when the inconsequential activities are ignored. One solution, which has been a commonplace answer to this problem, is the use of "management by exception."

Management by Exception

Management by exception involves analysis of only those results that are unusually unfavorable or unusually favorable—that is, controlling only the exceptional performances. For example, if 95 percent of the time each salesperson sells between $10,000 and $20,000 a week, management would step in only to analyze the performance of a salesperson who happened to sell less than $10,000 or more than $20,000. When a particular salesperson's sales fall above the norm, management would want to determine how those sales were achieved to pass the information along to other sales people or to verify that short-term profits were not being made at the expense of a long-term customer relationship. When sales fall below the norm, management would want to determine why. Market conditions may have deteriorated, or the salesperson could have a personal problem, need retraining, or just lack motivation.

Control Charts. Managers customarily set their management-by-exception range at 95 percent and only become involved in controlling when there are exceptions above and below that range. The 95 percent range is arrived at by first finding the average and the standard deviation of sales, and then adding and subtracting two standard deviations from the average. The resultant interval is used to represent the 95 percent range. For example, if sales over the last six months averaged $15,000, and the standard deviation was $2,500, management can construct a "control

TABLE 14-11 Management By Exception Control Chart

		1	2	3	4	5	6	7	8	9	10	11	12	13	14
Upper Control Limit	$20,000									X					
plus one standard deviation		X					X								
Average	[$15,000]									X				X	
						X									
minus one standard deviation															
		X	X											X	
Lower Control Limit	$10,000														
	Week	1	2	3	4	5	6	7	8	9	10	11	12	13	14

chart," shown in Table 14-11, to show the upper and lower limits for each salesperson.

Control charts enable managers to post individual sales on a regular basis (usually weekly). Controlling actions can then be taken when sales fall above or below the control limits. Posting is usually done by a clerk or computer and management is notified only when control limits have been exceeded.

Numerous statistical methods are used in management by exception, ranging from simple tests to determine differences between means, to complicated methods such as regression analysis and analysis of variance. All these techniques are worth consideration by managers who want to control on the basis of probabilities rather than "off the cuff." Control charts, however, are commonly used since mathematical computations are not too difficult and the chart itself it easily understood—both by the sales manager and the salesperson. It is far easier to read a graphic display than a column of numbers.

Control charts can be used to reflect whatever sales managers are interested in observing: the number of new customers added, the volume of new products sold, or the size of expense vouchers.

Management by Objectives

The effectiveness of both planning and organizing depends on the involvement of the sales force. An excellent tool for involving sales people as well as for evaluating them, and one that facilitates planning and organizing, is called management by objectives, or MBO.

MBO involves superior-subordinate interaction in the establishment and evaluation of objectives. By allowing sales people to participate in setting goals, such as the level of sales revenues per week or the number of new customers to be contacted per week, they not only become more involved, they become more motivated to achieve the prescribed goals. MBO as a control tool, however, takes effect before and during the work; control charts become effective after some measurable work has been performed. In this sense, MBO, when properly utilized, offers the potential of reducing the number of problems that could be reflected later in the control charts.

Key Elements of MBO.   MBO programs include two key elements: "(1) specific objectives, best expressed in quantitative terms with target due dates, and (2) subordinate participation in the process of goal setting and review."[38]

Considerable thought must go into the formulating of objectives to ensure that both company and individual objectives are realistic. Objectives should be ranked in order of importance, be consistent, be quantified whenever possible, and have specific completion dates. It is up to the sales manager, working with individual sales people, to see that their respective objectives are formulated so that they can be measured and that they represent company objectives as well as individual objectives. Additional characteristics of well-formulated objectives are listed in Table 14-12.[39]

Making MBO Work.   While MBO is widely used by sales managers as well as other managers, it does have some limitations. First, for MBO to work, it requires a commitment of the sales manager's time. Second, unless the program is taken seriously and objectives are adhered to by the sales manager, sales people will become skeptical of the program. And, third, it is often difficult to establish quantitative objectives for some selling tasks. Thus, MBO works best when objectives are placed in writing, when control measurements (such as control charts) reflecting progress toward objectives are regularly updated, and when sales managers constantly reaffirm their support and interest in the program. To build and actuate an effective program, sales managers must have a participative management style if sales people are to develop a belief that they "own" the objectives and work toward reaching those objectives.

THE FUTURE OF SALES FORCE STRATEGY

Increasing international competition, rapid technological change, and soaring costs are three primary causes of potentially dramatic changes in the industrial sales force of the 1990s. The former governor of Colorado, Richard Lamm, illustrated increasing competition by pointing out that when he graduated from high school in 1953, the United States produced eighty percent of the world's automobiles and ninety

[38]Edwin B. Flippo and Gary M. Munsinger, *Management,* 5th ed. (Boston: Allyn & Bacon, Inc., 1982), p. 91.
[39]Ibid., p. 94.

**TABLE 14-12 Additional Characteristics
of Well-Formulated Objectives**

1. The total set of objectives for a job should be limited in number.
2. Each objective should be stated in highly specific terms.
3. Objectives should be set for outputs or results rather than processes.
4. Objectives should be challenging, yet attainable.
5. Objectives for one job should be coordinated with those of related jobs.

Source: See Edwin B. Flippo and Gary M. Munsinger, *Management*, 5th ed. [Boston: Allyn & Bacon, Inc., 1982], p. 91.

percent of its televisions, and "made in Japan" meant "junk." However, when his son graduated from high school in 1986, the United States was producing less than thirty percent of the world's automobiles and TVs, and "made in America" often meant "poor quality."[40] Technological developments leading to SFA have only just begun to have an impact on sales force operations, and the increasing pace of technological change will accentuate that impact. Soaring costs, meanwhile, require buyers to demand increasing, faster, and more imaginative sales assistance. Additionally, the average cost of a field sales call ranges between $200 and $225, and "with four to 4.5 calls needed to close an average industrial sale, costs of obtaining an order may reach four figures."[41] These dramatic changes have stimulated an increasing advocacy of intrapreneurial philosophy and structural changes in the industrial sales force.

Intrapreneurial Philosophy

Many marketers are beginning to view the present S.W.O.T. (strengths, weaknesses, opportunities, and threats) approach to strategy as primarily reactive. They see it as one that primarily encourages responses to environmental change. On the other hand, the entrepreneurial approach is seen as encompassing the dimensions of innovativeness, risk-taking, and proactiveness. One authority explains that the entrepreneurial firm is one that "engages in product-market innovation, undertakes somewhat risky ventures, and is first to come up with 'proactive' innovations, beating competitors to the punch."[42]

Gifford Pinchot III developed the word "intrapreneurship" as a shorthand for "intra-corporate entrepreneurship."[43] An intrapreneur is thus a person within a

[40]Richard D. Lamm, "Crisis: The Uncompetitive Society," in Martin K. Starr, ed., *Global Competitiveness* (New York: W.W. Norton & Co., 1988), pp. 12–42.

[41]Richard Cardozo and Shannon Shipp, "New Selling Methods Are Changing Industrial Sales Management," *Business Horizons* (September/October 1987), pp. 23–28.

[42]Miller, D., "The Correlates of Entrepreneurship in Three Types of Firms," *Management Science* 29 (1983), pp. 770–791, in Michael H. Morris, Duane L. Davis, and Jane Ewing, "The Role of Entrepreneurship in Industrial Marketing Activities," *Industrial Marketing Management* 17 (1988), pp. 337–346.

[43]"Secrets of Intrapreneurship," *Inc.* (January 1985), pp. 69–76.

large organization who plays the role of an entrepreneur: one who asks, "What would I do in this situation were I an entrepreneur?"[44]

Intrapreneurship is, thus, an attempt to inspire and maintain a decision-making spirit and determination in the employees of a large corporation. To do this effectively, top management must advocate and continuously support the intrapreneurial philosophy. Once this is accomplished management should establish a means of (1) soliciting creative/innovative ideas, as well as a means of screening those ideas; (2) giving innovators freedom from traditional organizational constraints in order to pursue their ideas; and (3) rewarding the innovators.[45] Establishing the theoretical framework and performing the steps can be very difficult, though very rewarding, and can cause major adjustments in sales-force operations.

Sales Force Structure

Research indicates that increased specialization of sales personnel is reducing the number of sales generalists; that communications are increasing between units involved with different business functions; and computers and technology are enabling specialization, as well as adding to the improved communications.[46] Cardozo and Shipp interpret these changes to mean small accounts will increasingly be handled through telemarketing, as will medium-account prospecting, qualifying, servicing and reordering. They further envision national account managers coordinating more with other functional areas in order to specialize the servicing of very large accounts. They thus predict a much smaller role for the present generalist salesperson, that of making presentations to and closing selling contacts with medium-size accounts.

As these various structural changes are made and are coupled with increasing use of the intrapreneurial approach, both marketing managers and salespeople are being required to change. National account managers are being required increasingly to use interpersonal relations skills. Sales managers are required to be more supportive, participative, and flexible. Salespeople are realizing that they must be more flexible, innovative, thorough, and knowledgeable. At the very least, the synergistic effects of both structural and intrapreneurial change promise to make the selling function highly volatile and of considerable interest to observe, and enjoyable as a vocation.

LOOKING BACK

The role of the sales force in actuating the marketing concept makes it the primary emphasis in the industrial marketer's promotional mix. That the sales force plays

[44]Ibid.

[45]Erik G. Rule and Donald W. Irwin, "Fostering Intrapreneurship: The New Competitive Edge," *The Journal of Business Strategy* (May/June 1988), pp. 44–47.

[46]Cardozo and Shipp, "New Selling Methods," pp. 23–28; and Andrew Parsons, quoted in Thayer C. Taylor, "How the Game will Change in the 1990s," *Sales & Marketing Management* (June 1989), pp. 52–61.

such a principal role in promotion depicts a major difference between industrial and consumer marketing and mandates the necessity of understanding the environment within which sales people operate and the functions of sales management. How effective, efficient, and professional sales people operate in their environment depends on how well they are managed.

Sales management involves two primary areas: developing strategy for effective deployment of the sales force, and administration of sales personnel. Sales force administration (e.g., recruiting and training sales personnel) was discussed in Chapter Thirteen. Strategy involves the management functions of planning, organizing, and controlling the selling effort.

Planning is the decision-making process involved with choosing among alternative courses of action that the sales force might pursue. It involves considerations as to sales potentials and service requirements for individual customers within a firm's target market and how the sales force can best be deployed to provide optimal service to customers with varying requirements. Sales deployment analysis utilizes such tools as expected value analysis, work load analysis, and return on time invested to ensure that the sales effort is deployed in such a way as to maximize sales in a cost-effective manner.

Organizing is the decision-making process involved with establishing relationships among the factors and resources of an organization. A sales force must not only be properly structured, but its members must also be logically categorized according to their functions and assigned to customers and territories that maximize their sales and service efforts.

Controlling involves the regulating of activities in accordance with the goals and objectives of an organization. Since the detailed performances of all sales personnel in their many activities cannot be efficiently monitored and controlled by management, management by exception is often employed to monitor and control the unusual performances. Management by objectives is a means of control that enlists the support of sales personnel in the self-control of their activities. It offers the added advantage of inspiring or initiating control before activities are begun as well as during the performance of selling and servicing duties.

QUESTIONS FOR DISCUSSION

1. If sales or marketing managers allow their people to think that they are not on the same team, the results could be disastrous. Do you agree?
2. To discharge the selling function best, a salesperson must understand the nature of personal selling and how it relates to organizational buying behavior. One common method used in selling is AIDA; that is, first attain the buyer's *attention,* develop *interest,* kindle *desire,* and induce *action* to buy. Given the environment of industrial selling, is such an approach to selling effective?
3. Important, but difficult, questions for many sales organizations are: "How good is the current deployment of selling effort?" "What type of sales productivity improvement might we expect from formal deployment analysis?" and "Where are our best opportunities for increasing sales productivity by improving deployment?" Discuss the various

deployment methods available and decide which would offer the best answer to these questions.

4. How can sales managers measure the productivity of nonsales activities and use these measures to evaluate overall job performance in the short term?

5. Prior to being transferred from the New York/New Jersey area, Sarah Jones was a top-notch salesperson who consistently exceeded her quota. However, shortly after her transfer to the Kansas/Oklahoma territory, her sales fell considerably below her average, and within six months she left the company. Discuss the factors that could have contributed to Sarah's downfall.

6. Industrial firms may organize the sales force around territories, products, customers, and functions. Discuss the possible advantages or disadvantages of each type of sales force organization.

PROBLEMS FOR REVIEW

1. Fortel, Inc., a manufacturer of electronic components, is contemplating expansion into a new geographical area. In analyzing the annual market potential for the area by potential customer accounts, Fortel has estimated the following:

Customer Group	Market Potential
A	$1,500,000
B	2,000,000
C	1,750,000

Discussions with experienced sales people and other personnel within the company indicate that the maximum sales portions the company could obtain from each customer group are as follows: 35 percent from group A, 40 percent from group B, and 25 percent from group C. What are the projected company sales potentials for each customer group?

2. Further discussions with sales people have led to the conclusion that the firm has a 35 percent probability of actually obtaining sales from group A, 15 percent from group B, and 50 percent from group C. What is the expected value for each customer group? Which group should be given top priority? How might this expected value compare to a chance in a lottery game?

3. To cultivate accounts from the customer groups in Problems 1 and 2, it has been decided that group A, which consists of 10 potential customers, will require 4 calls per customer per year over the next 6 months; group B, which consists of 15 potential customers, 6 calls; and group C, which consists of 22 customers, 8 calls. Given that the average sales call costs Fortel $225 and the company's gross margin is 20 percent, calculate ROTI. Would you now change the Problem 2 decision you made regarding which group should be given priority? Explain why you would or would not.

SUGGESTED ADDITIONAL READINGS

"America's Best Sales Forces," *Sales & Marketing Management* (June 1989):31–48.

BONOMA, THOMAS V., and WESLEY JOHNSTON, "The Social Psychology of Industrial Buying and Selling," *Industrial Marketing Management* 7 (July 1978):213–223.

CRAVENS, DAVID W., and RAYMOND W. LAFORCE, "Salesforce Deployment Analysis," *Industrial Marketing Management* 12 (1983):179–192.

FALVEY, JACK, "Compare Football to Selling? Nonsense," *Sales & Marketing Management* (January 1989):15–17.

KELLEY, BILL, "Ideal Selling Jobs," *Sales & Marketing Management* (December 1988):26–31.

LAFORGE, RAYMOND, and DAVID W. CRAVENS, "Steps in Selling Effort Deployment," *Industrial Marketing Management* 11 (1982):183–192.

LEIGH, THOMAS W. and PATRICK F. MCGRAW, "Mapping the Procedural Knowledge of Industrial Sales Personnel: A Script-Theoretic Investigation," *Journal of Marketing* 53 (January 1989):16–34.

REICHARD, CLIFTON J., "Industrial Selling: Beyond Price and Persistence," *Harvard Business Review* (March–April 1985):127–133.

STUMM, DAVID ARTHUR, *Advanced Industrial Selling* (New York: AMACOM, 1981).

SUAREZ, EDWARD A., "Results Will Sell Marketing," *Business Marketing* (April 1989), pp. 52–54.

WORTMAN, LEON A., "Meet the 'Hot Shot,'" *Business Marketing* (August 1988):62–68.

CHAPTER 15

Managing Advertising, Sales Promotion, and Publicity Strategy

While personal selling is the dominant tool in most industrial marketers' communication strategy, advertising, sales promotion, and publicity also play important roles. Properly planned and controlled, they can enhance the company's image, build recognition for its products and services, reach unknown or inaccessible buying influencers, and generate new sales prospects. The purpose of this chapter is to discuss

1. How promotional variables other than personal selling enhance the effectiveness of the firm's overall communication strategy.
2. Industrial advertising media options.
3. What decision factors are crucial in the effective development of advertising, sales promotion, and publicity programs in the industrial marketing.

To position itself in the rapidly expanding software market as a producer of reliable products, Hunter and Ready embarked on a "get a bug if you find a bug" promotional campaign. (See Figure 15-1.) Over a six-month period, customers were offered a free, discontinued model of a Volkswagen "bug" or $1,000 cash for every bug (programming error) users found in the company's VRTX microprocessor operating system. To reach engineers, advertisements were run in *Electronics, Electronic*

Get a bug if you find a bug.

Show us a bug in our VRTX® real-time operating system and we'll return the favor. With a bug of your own to show off in your driveway.

There's a catch, though.

Since VRTX is the only microprocessor operating system completely sealed in silicon, finding a bug won't be easy.

Because along with task management and communication, memory management, and character I/O, VRTX contains over 100,000 man-hours of design and testing.

And since it's delivered in 4K bytes of ROM, VRTX will perform for you the way it's performing in hundreds of real-time applications from avionics to video games.

Bug free.

So, to save up to 12 months of development time, and maybe save a loveable little car from the junkyard, contact us. Call (415) 326-2950, or write Hunter & Ready, Inc., 445 Sherman Avenue, Palo Alto, California 94306.

Describe your application and the microprocessors you're using—Z8000, Z80, 68000, or 8086 family. We'll send you a VRTX evaluation package, including timings for system calls and interrupts. And when you order a VRTX system for your application, we'll include instructions for reporting errors.*

But don't feel bad if in a year from now there isn't a bug in your driveway.

There isn't one in your operating system either.

HUNTER ◆ READY
VRTX
Operating Systems in Silicon.

*Call or write for details. But, considering our taste in cars, you might want to accept our offer of $1,000 cash instead. (c) 1983 Hunter & Ready, Inc.

FIGURE 15-1   Sales Promotion Can Be Very Effective in the Industrial Market

Source: Courtesy of Ready Systems of Sunnyvale, CA.

Design, and *Computer Design.* Prior to the campaign, the company had relied on company-written technical articles and publicity to establish a name in the industry.[1]

Obviously, advertising, sales promotion, and publicity play an important role in the promotional mix of Hunter and Ready, as well as other industrial marketers. While personal selling is often the most important aspect of the industrial marketer's communication strategy (due to the technical complexity of many products and the extensive negotiation process involved in the selling of industrial goods), advertising, sales promotions, and publicity also play a critical role in the development of communication strategy. Advertising, for instance, is used to lay a foundation for the sale by providing information on the company and its products and by reaching unknown or inaccessible buying influencers. Sales promotion, in the form of trade shows and specialty advertising, also supplements the selling effort in a variety of ways. Trade shows, for instance, are not only used to create awareness and generate sales leads, they can also reduce the number of sales calls required to close a sale.[2] And publicity, because of its high credibility, is "one of the most important sources of information used by industrial customers" in their buying decisions.[3]

Advertising, sales promotion, and publicity, however, must be coordinated with personal selling efforts so that they contribute to the effectiveness of communication strategy. Rarely can they substitute for an effective sales call. Advertising, sales promotion, and publicity are primarily used to create awareness, enhance the company's reputation, disseminate information on products, or generate leads for sales people. Thus, it is important for industrial marketers to understand how these variables support the selling function and what is important in formulating and developing an effective communication program.

THE USE OF ADVERTISING IN THE INDUSTRIAL MARKET

Rarely is advertising employed by itself in the industrial arena. The complexity of most industrial products, coupled with buyers' expectations and unique information needs, requires personal contact. It is not possible, however, for sales people to make contact with all the various individuals who may be involved in a purchasing decision. In fact, studies have indicated that on the average for every ten buying influencers, a salesperson reaches only three to four.[4] Not only is industrial advertising an effective means of reaching inaccessible or unknown buying influencers, it

[1] Eddy Christman, "Ads Pay to Get the Bugs Out," *Business Marketing* (October 1983), pp. 11–40.

[2] Richard K. Swandby and Jonathan M. Cox, "Trade Show Trends: Exhibiting Growth Paces Economic Strength," *Business Marketing* (May 1985), pp. 50–56.

[3] Jerome D. Williams, "Industrial Publicity: One of the Best Promotional Tools," *Industrial Marketing Management* 12 (1983), pp. 207–211.

[4] Richard Manville, "Why Industrial Companies Must Advertise Their Products," *Industrial Marketing* (October 1978), p. 47.

creates awareness, enhances the effectiveness of the sales call, increases the overall efficiency of the selling effort, and is an important ingredient in creating and maintaining demand at the distributor level.

Reaching Buying Influencers

It is not uncommon for industrial sales people to be unaware of individuals within a firm who may be in a position to exert influence on a purchasing decision. This is particularly true when deploying a new salesperson or when calling on a new customer for the first time. Also, for various reasons including the inability to get past purchasing agents, buying influencers are often inaccessible to sales people. Executive turnover is a never-ending problem. Buying influencers are constantly moving out of their areas of responsibility, moving up in the organization, or changing jobs. These influencers, however, do read trade magazines and general business publications and can be reached through advertising. Additionally, through requests for further information called for in ads, unknown influencers often identify themselves, making it possible for sales people to contact them.

Creating Awareness

Industrial advertising is an effective means of creating awareness of the industrial supplier, as well as the supplier's market offering. As discussed in Chapter Four, buyers normally select a supplier after moving through several phases of the purchasing decision process. These phases include (1) recognizing a need, (2) determining characteristics and quantitites of a needed item, (3) describing those characteristics and quantities, (4) searching for and qualifying sources, (5) acquiring and analyzing proposals, and (6) evaluating proposals and selecting suppliers. Effective industrial advertising creates awareness or alerts potential purchasers to problems within their operations (phase 1) and identifies the supplier's company and its products as offering possible solutions to those problems (phases 2 and 4), which helps to assure that the advertiser is given favorable consideration when specifications are written and suppliers are selected (phases 3 and 6).

Enhancing the Sales Call

Effectively planned advertising enhances the sales call by arousing interest in the supplier's offering and by helping to create supplier preference.[5] When buyers are aware of a company, its reputation, its products, and its record in the industry, sales people are more effective. In fact, according to one study, when buyers are exposed to a firm's industrial ads, their opinion of the firm improves, dollar sales per call

---

[5]Joseph C. Siebert, "Advertising and Selling Objectives for Industrial Markets," in T. C. Coram and R. W. Hill, eds., *New Ideas in Industrial Marketing*, (London: Staples Press, 1970), p. 209.

are higher, and the firm's sales personnel are rated considerably higher on product knowledge, service, and enthusiasm.[6]

Increasing Overall Sales Efficiency

For some industrial producers, particularly producers of industrial supplies, advertising may be the only way of efficiently reaching broad groups of buyers. Additionally, because little or no product differentiation exists between many industrial supplies, marketers of such products frequently need to remind users and potential users of their firms' unique capabilities (dependability and reliability of service, for example) or make them aware of new products and services.

The cost of reaching large numbers of buyers through personal contact cannot only be prohibitive, but unjustifiable. The average yearly cost of maintaining just one salesperson in the field is $87,500. This includes average compensation of $64,000 and average field expenses of $23,500.[7] When one considers that advertising has the potential of reaching a large portion of the market at a relatively inexpensive cost, it is easy to see why it is difficult to justify the use of personal selling in all cases. For instance, according to a recent survey conducted by *Business Marketing* (see Table 15-1), the *adjusted* cost per thousand reached by Minolta, IBM, and Toshiba in the same issue of *Time* magazine ran from $49.71 to $51.78—as little as

TABLE 15-1 Survey Results of Advertising Effectiveness

	Minolta [Spread]	IBM [Single Page]	Toshiba [Two-thirds Page]
% Involved	92%	72%	46%
% Fleeting glance	8	20	32
% Missed ad	—	8	22
% Missed advertiser name	53	76	74
% Involved who saw advertiser name	46	24	20
Return on investment			
Magazine rate base	4,500,000	4,500,000	4,500,000
% Involved who saw name	48%	24%	20%
	(2,070,000)	(1,080,000)	(900,000)
Approximate cost per ad	$102,900	$60,525	$46,600
Adjusted cost per thousand	$49.71	$56.04	$51.78

Source: Joan Treistman, "Where the Reader Eye Roams," *Business Marketing,* April 1984, pp. 110–116. Reprinted with permission.

[6]John E. Morrill, "Industrial Advertising Pays Off," *Harvard Business Review* 48 (March–April 1970), pp. 4–14.

[7]"User's Guide," *Sales & Marketing Management* (February 20, 1989), p. 8.

50 cents per person reached. (The *adjusted* cost per thousand reached was based on the percentage of readers that not only became involved with the advertisement (92 percent for Minolta, 72 percent for IBM, and 46 percent for Toshiba), but remembered the advertiser's name (46 percent for Minolta, 24 percent for IBM, and 20 percent for Toshiba).[8]

Supporting Channel Members

Manufacturers who use middlemen must support those intermediaries' efforts by ensuring that end markets are aware of their products. While middlemen are interested in the producer's support activities, resellers, because they are positioned so closely to ultimate consumers, are even more concerned with consumer acceptance. They will also want to know what profit they can expect on a product, and what the producer is doing in the way of consumer advertising and other promotional support activities. Rarely can a sales force be deployed to reach all potential distributors and resellers often enough to meet all these information needs. Industrial advertising, then, frequently provides an economical and efficient supplement to personal selling in providing information to distributors and resellers, as well as end markets.

INDUSTRIAL ADVERTISING MEDIA

While some industrial advertisers use traditional consumer media when they serve their advertising objectives, their choices generally center on whether to use print media (business magazines, trade publications, and industrial directories), direct marketing (direct mail, telemarketing, catalogs, and data sheets), or some combination thereof.

General Business and Trade Publications

General business and trade publications are classified as either horizontal or vertical.[9] Horizontal publications deal with specific functions, tasks, or technologies and cut across industry lines. Vertical publications are directed toward a specific industry and may be read by almost anyone from the person on the assembly line to the company president. The choice of one or the other, or both, is dictated by the desire to penetrate a particular industry, reach common influencers across industries, or optimize the goals of reach and frequency.

[8]Joan Treistman, "Where the Reader Eye Roams," *Business Marketing* (April 1984), pp. 110–116.

[9]Courtland L. Bovee and William F. Arens, *Contemporary Advertising* (Homewood, Ill.: Richard D. Irwin, Inc., 1982), pp. 688–689.

TABLE 15-2 Top Ten Specialized Business Publication Advertisers

Company	Ad Expenditures [in millions]
1. AT&T Co	16,507
2. Du Pont Co	12,537
3. Hewlett-Packard Co	11,594
4. General Electric Co	10,936
5. General Motors Corp	9,658
6. NEC Corp	9,446
7. IBM Corp	8,926
8. 3M Co	8,886
9. Tektronix Inc	7,754
10. Motorola Inc	7,071

Source: MMS-Rome Reports and *Business Marketing.* Reprinted with permission.

Table 15-2 lists the ten leading specialized business publication advertisers in the United States and these firms' expenditures for 1987. Notice that AT&T held the No. 1 spot, spending $16.5 million in specialized business publications. According to *Business Marketing,* advanced-technology marketers dominate business and industrial advertising spending. Of the top twenty business advertisers in 1987, fifteen marketed computers, electronics equipment, sophisticated office products, or related technologies. Eight of the companies listed in the top ten in Table 15-2 belong in the advanced, high-tech arena.[10]

General business publications (e.g., *Fortune, Business Week,* and *The Wall Street Journal*) tend to be read by business professionals across all industries because of their general business editorials. Specialized business publications, such as *Advertising Age, Purchasing,* and *Chemical Week* are targeted to individuals across industries who have responsibility for a specific task or function such as advertising or purchasing, or who are interested in a particular technology such as chemicals. Industrial publications, such as *Consulting Engineer* and *Electronic News* address the information needs of readers with specialized knowledge in technical areas such as engineers and electricians and also cut across industries. However, other specialized

[10]Advanced-Tech Marketers Dominate Ad Spending," *Business Marketing* (July 1988), pp. 68.

business publications—*Iron Age* and *Steel,* for example—are targeted to individuals in a specific industry.

Directory Advertising

Every state has an industrial directory, and there are also a number of private ones. One of the most popular industrial directories is the New York-based *Thomas Register,* which generates "$400 million in daily direct response sales or about $102 billion a year for its advertisers."[11] The *Thomas Register* consists of nineteen volumes, containing 60,000 pages of 50,000 product headings and listings from 123,000 industrial companies selling everything from copper tubing to orchestra pits. Although there are similar publications, such as Sweet's architectural catalog, the *Register* has practically no competition.

One of the *Register*'s biggest users is General Electric, which buys as many as 300 sets a year, diverting some to its overseas divisions. In fact, the *Register* estimates that as many as 30,000 sets are in use overseas, many of which have been distributed by departments of commerce and state. Thus, many inexperienced American manufacturers have been able to develop some international business.[12]

The main advantage of directory advertising is that it is a highly credible medium, and for many buyers, their basic purchasing tool. One disadvantage is that unless buyers purchase directories for use, advertising in this medium is not seen.

Consumer Media

Consumer media, in spite of wasted circulation, can be very effective because it tends to experience a minimum of competition from other industrial advertisers. Since the message exposure occurs away from the office, it also experiences less competition from the receiver's other business needs. According to Sarah Lang, an account executive for Wight, Collins, Rutherford, and Scott, a London-based advertising agency, "TV is the medium for reaching small businessmen, who are a mass audience. . . . It is also the most effective for shifting attitudes, which is the job we have to do."[13] Where market coverage is limited geographically, consumer media may also provide an excellent way of reaching a market. One industrial supplier of food equipment, for example, has been quite successful in his use of television for generating sales inquiries. When it was discovered that the average sales call cost $200, he began to advertise heavily on television, and backed it with direct mail and classified ads in local newspapers and a 24-hour, toll-free answering service.[14]

[11] *"Thomas Register* Ranks as King of Catalogs," *Advertising Age* (March 7 1985), p. 54.

[12] Ibid.

[13] "Ad Rates," *Business Marketing* (April 1988), p. 38.

[14] Joseph Bohn, "Food Equipment Maker Tries Local Television," *Business Marketing* (June 1983), p. 12.

Direct Marketing

In addition to trade magazines and general business publications, industrial marketers also utilize various other vehicles, such as direct mail, telephone, catalogs, and data sheets, to reach their markets. In fact, with the increasing sophistication of computer technology, industrial marketers are "turning to direct mail as never before."[15] For example, Xerox has more than tripled its sales for low-end products through the use of direct mail. Additionally, numerous industrial marketers are also making more use of the telephone as a means of enhancing the efficiency of their overall communications program.

Direct Mail. Direct mail is an especially useful tool that is frequently employed in conjunction with, or as an alternative to, business or trade publication advertising. When carefully conceived, because of its potential to gain the reader's full attention, direct-mail advertising can provide a greater impact than can an advertisement in trade or business publications.

Direct mail offers the advertiser numerous advantages over the use of business or trade publications. Advertising messages can be developed and targeted toward a precisely defined market to introduce a new product, promote the corporate image, support the sales force, or communicate with industrial distributors. It is relatively low in cost, highly selective, and flexible with regard to timing, and it offers considerable space for telling the "full story."

There are, however, definite disadvantages in using direct mail. Direct mail can be extremely wasteful if prospects are not clearly identified. It is also often

---

THREE ESSENTIALS FOR USING TELEVISION AS AN INDUSTRIAL ADVERTISING MEDIUM

1. Prospects must be concentrated geographically.
   TV can't be used like a business publication. On the average, it can run up to $200,000 for a 60-second spot on "60 Minutes." Contrast this to $200–300 for a local spot.

2. The sales pitch must be boiled down to "one simple, compelling, human message."
   It should be simple because there is time for only about 65 words in a 30-second spot. Thus, the sales proposition must be single-minded and worthwhile. Don't view the prospect as a "technological sponge." His job is not his life. He's subject to emotional appeals, too.

3. Complement television with other basic promotional tools.
   A combination of TV and print is more effective than is either one alone. Publicity can be more valuable than both. Publicity plus TV plus print plus direct mail is better yet.

   Source: Jeffrey W. Kaumeyer, "When Should Business/Industrial Advertising Use Broadcast TV?" *Business Marketing,* April 1985, pp. 106–112. Reprinted with permission.

---

[15]Peter Finch, "The Direct Marketing Data Base Revolution," *Business Marketing* (August 1985), pp. 34–35, 44–47.

TELEMARKETING MEANS A DISCIPLINED APPROACH

"Telemarketing" in the true sense of the word means a disciplined approach to the telephone, a rigorous application of controls with much more sophistication than simply calling up a customer to chat about Marge and the kids. Telemarketing must be as carefully designed and implemented as space advertising, direct mail, or trade show programs.

Personnel must be trained and they must keep regular call records. . . . Both activities are essential for campaign quality control if the telephone is to achieve its full potential as a marketing tool. This means following . . . structured, pretested scripts when talking with prospects and customers. Experienced supervisors should monitor operators' calls, inbound and outbound, on a periodic basis. And, as with any marketing program, companies should set specific cost and performance objectives, then compare results to those objectives.

Source: Murray Roman and Bob Donath, "What's Really Happening in Business/Industrial Telemarketing," *Business Marketing*, April 1983, pp. 82–90. Reprinted with permission.

---

thought of as "junk mail" and tends to be tossed aside without ever being read. It may also never get past the secretary to the intended recipient. To avoid these problems, direct-mail programs should be carefully conceived and directed toward a specific target audience whose names, job titles, or functions are known.

It is relatively easy to develop mailing lists that contain the names, titles, and functions of the audience to be reached. Mailing lists can be secured from trade publications, industrial directories, mailing list houses such as Dun & Bradstreet's Marketing Services Division or National Business Lists, lists obtained through trade show leads, and the company's own marketing information system. When obtaining mailing lists from outside sources, however, care should be taken to make certain that the lists are up to date.

Telemarketing. According to recent studies, approximately 20 percent of the industrial firms in the United States, including Xerox, IBM, and NCR, use telemarketing to generate nearly $100 billion in yearly sales.[16]

Telemarketing is a marketing communications tool that employs trained specialists who utilize telecommunications and information technologies to conduct marketing and sales activities. These activities may be through incoming calls (calls originating with the customer) or outgoing calls (calls originating with the company). Most organizations utilize both. It is interesting to note, however, that outgoing telemarketing offers the largest future growth potential as the cost of face-to-face sales continues to increase.[17]

---

[16]S. Bower, "Telemarketing: An Intimate Instrument," *European Research* 71 (May 1987).

[17]Judith J. Marshall and Harrie Vredenburg, "Successfully Using Telemarketing in Industrial Sales," *Industrial Marketing Management* 17 (1988), pp. 15–22.

The use of telemarketing, which is increasing at the rate of twenty-five percent a year, is viewed as a means of complementing, rather than replacing, face-to-face selling. According to one study of 249 industrial sales and marketing managers, the major uses of telemarketing are (1) to qualify sales leads, 73.6; (2) support field sales representatives, 73.2; (3) generate sales leads, 73.1; and (4) to handle marginal accounts, 70.0.[18] (The numbers above indicate the percentage of firms studied that used telemarketing for the reasons given.) When used effectively, however, telemarketing also enhances the effectiveness of publication and direct-mail advertising. When a toll-free number is included in print and direct-mail advertising, prospects can easily respond and get immediate information while the advertised message is still fresh in their minds.

Successful telemarketing, however, requires specific goal setting, clearly established target markets, and careful planning. The major reasons attributed to failure in the use of telemarketing, according to Benein, are (1) lack of commitment, (2) improper facilities, (3) lack of formal scripts, and (4) poor human resource planning.[19]

Table 15-3 shows how success in telemarketing is determined by the extent of

---

DATA SHEETS THAT SELL

1. Include as much technical information as possible. Data sheets should answer all the customer's questions. When the information isn't there, the data sheet is worthless.

2. Good product data sheets explain and highlight technical features to show the customer what benefits he'll receive when he buys the product.

3. Use photographs. Nothing beats photographs for establishing what something looks like and how it works.

4. Use competitive data sheets to help customers make the comparisons between products.

5. Use $8\frac{1}{2}''$ × 11" pages so the data sheet doesn't get lost at the bottom of the file folder.

6. Know your reader. Make the content and technical depth of your data sheet compatible with the background and buying interests of your readers.

7. Know where in the buying process the data sheet fits in. Know the environment in which it will be used. Will there be advertising support, public relations, distributors, sales people, catalogs, brochures, direct mail, and word of mouth?

8. Ask for customers' help in preparing the data sheet.

9. Use one writer for the entire project: the ads, the public relations, and the highly technical sheets.

10. Figure out how many people you would like to have read the data sheet, and multiply the number by four to arrive at the number of sheets needed.

Source: See "Data Sheets That Sell," *Sales and Marketing Management,* May 14, 1984, pp. 45–46.

---

[18]Ibid.

[19]R. L. Benein, "The Trouble With (Some) Telemarketers," *Business Marketing* 80 (August 1986).

TABLE 15-3 Extent of Planning for Telemarketing

	Very Successful	*Moderately Successful*	*Not Very Successful*	*Total*
		[n = 249]		
Specific Goals Had Been Set	80.6%	75.9%	59.8%	71.0%
Specific Goals Were Not Set	19.4%	24.1%	40.2%	28.9%
$\chi^2 = 10.7\ P = .005$				
Had Formulated Clear Cut Plan	81.7%	56.9%	57.4%	66.3%
Little or No Planning Done	18.3%	43.1%	42.6%	33.7%
$\chi^2 = 15.9\ P = .000$				

Source: Reprinted by permission of the publisher. From "Successfully Using Telemarketing in Industrial Sales," Judith J. Marshall and Harrie Vredenburg, *Industrial Marketing Management,* 17, 1 (1988), pp. 15–22. Copyright © 1988 by Elsevier Science Publishing Co., Inc.

goal setting and planning. Of the very successful firms, 80.6 percent had set specific goals that included the number and type of accounts to be called, the number of calls to be placed per hour, and dollar sales to be aimed for.[20]

Catalogs and Data Sheets. Catalogs and data sheets are an important part of a firm's promotional effort because of their unique ability to support the selling function. Industrial customers use catalogs to compare products, product applications, and prices of potential suppliers. Rarely, however, are catalogs alone used to make a purchasing decision. They merely provide buyers with a basis of comparison with other companies' products once a decision has been made to purchase a particular product. When properly prepared and effectively distributed, however, catalogs can speed up the purchasing process by providing information, securing recognition for the company, and additional opportunities for business. Catalogs also support the efforts of distributors because it is not always possible for them to carry in inventory all the items a manufacturer supplies. Thus, most manufacturers provide their distributors with loose-leaf catalogs so that noninventoried items can be located and ordered quickly from the catalog.

Data sheets provide detailed technical information on such things as product dimensions, efficiencies, performance data, and cost savings and, thus, are an important complement to the personal selling effort. Sales people seldom have all the answers that technical buyers require. Further, buying decisions are often made when a salesperson is not present. When data sheets are prepared so that key selling points and technical information are presented in a clear, persuasive, credible manner, they can be powerful sales tools. Data sheets should include enough technical

[20]Marshall, "Successfully Using Telemarketing in Industrial Sales," *Industrial Marketing Management,* 17:1 (1988), pp. 15–22.

and product performance information to assist customers in their decision making and should be left by sales people with the appropriate decision makers.

THE USE OF SALES PROMOTION IN THE INDUSTRIAL MARKET

In addition to advertising, sales promotion, in the form of trade shows, premium incentives, and specialty advertising, plays an important part in the overall communication strategy of an industrial firm.

Trade Shows

For many industrial companies, trade show exhibits are a major part of their marketing communication activities and are used to support both selling and other marketing activities.[21] Depending upon the size of the firm, yearly trade show participation can range from six to twelve a year, or more. Caterpillar, for example, exhibits at more than forty-five conventions and expositions a year.[22] And, according to one source, a company may allocate as much as 35 percent of its annual promotional budget to trade show expenditures.[23] As shown in Table 15-4, trade shows offer manufacturers, as well as distributors and other vendors, an opportunity to display their products or describe their services to customers, distributors, suppliers, and the press. Not only do trade shows enhance the firm's ability to increase overall company awareness and generate sales leads, they are an effective means of:

Reaching a relatively large audience. Trade show attendance can range from as little as 2,343 for the Midwestern Telecommunications Showcase, to over 70,000 for the NRA Restaurant, Hotel-Motel shows held in Chicago during 1984.

Reducing the number of sales calls needed to close a sale. A recent study, conducted for the Trade Show Bureau, found that it requires an average of less than one sales call (.8) to close a trade show lead because more than half the purchases are made either by phone or mail after the show. In contrast, according to a McGraw-Hill study, it takes an average of 5.1 sales calls to close an industrial sale.[24]

The effective use of trade shows, however, depends on the role they are to play in the overall promotional mix and how well trade show objectives are established. While they can be very effective, trade shows can also be a costly means of communicating with the market. The average cost per visitor reached, including personnel travel, living and salary expenses, and preshow promotion costs for 1985-

[21]Thomas V. Bonoma, "Get More Out of Your Trade Shows," *Harvard Business Review* (January-February 1983), pp. 75-83.

[22]J. Edward Roberts, "Training Trade Show Salespeople: How Caterpillar Does It," *Business Marketing* (June 1988), pp. 70-73.

[23]Bonoma, "Get More Out of Your Trade Shows."

[24]Swandby and Cox, "Trade Show Trends."

TABLE 15-4 Shows Surveyed in 1987

Show	Location	Registered Attendance
National Retail Merchants Association	New York	9,516
National Association of Home Builders	Dallas	30,330
Communication Networks	Washington, D.C.	12,096
USTA Eastern Telecommunications Show-case	Indianapolis	5,191
National Roofing Contractors Association	New York	4,608
World of Concrete	Houston	13,194
SAE International Congress and Exposition	Detroit	24,086
CONEXPO	Las Vegas, Nev.	95,412
National Spring Design Engineering	Chicago	17,729
Pittsburgh Conference	Atlantic City	15,242
Association of Operating Room Nurses	Atlanta	7,164
INTERFACE	Las Vegas, Nev.	9,371
AFS CASTEXPO	St. Louis	6,376
FOSE/FOSE Software/FOSE Computer Graphics	Washington, D.C.	7,831
Federation of American Societies for Experimental Biology	Washington, D.C.	10,107
American College of Cardiology	New Orleans	10,268
American Society of Microbiology	Atlanta	7,457
AIChE Petrochemical Expo	Houston	6,088
National Association of Broadcasters	Dallas	15,688
AWS Welding	Chicago	12,705
ROBOTS 11 Exposition	Chicago	9,829
Super Market Industry Exposition	Chicago	7,831
Offshore Technology Conference	Houston	25,832
International Programmable Controllers Conference	Detroit	9,010
TELOCATOR	Phoenix, Ariz.	956
NCGA's Computer Graphics Conference and Exposition	Philadelphia	20,647
Association for Information & Image Management	New York	12,541
NRA Restaurant, Hotel-Motel Show	Chicago	77,321

Source: Jonathan M. Cox, Ian K. Sequeiro, and Lori L. Bock, "Show Size Grows; Audience Quality Stays High," *Business Marketing* (May 1988), pp. 84–88.

1987 was $116.00.[25] This was up thirty-six percent over the 1984 average. Thus, the effectiveness of trade shows depends on understanding the role they should play in the total marketing communications program and carefully developing trade show strategy. Not only must the marketer set specific trade show objectives, he or she

[25] Jonathan M. Cox, Ian K. Sequeiro, and Lori L. Bock, "Show Size Grows; Audience Quality Stays High," *Business Marketing* (May 1988), pp. 84–88.

must specify the target market to be reached, the results to be expected, and how funds are to be allocated.

Setting Specific Objectives. Specific objectives are important for deciding which shows to attend, what should be achieved at shows, and how much of the promotional budget to allocate for trade show expenses.

To support selling objectives, trade shows are useful for identifying prospects; gaining access to key decision makers; disseminating information on products, services, and company personnel; and actually selling products. To support nonselling objectives, trade shows are a viable vehicle for obtaining information on and encouraging interest of suppliers, gathering information regarding competitors' proposed products and prices, influencing distributors, testing and evaluating customer reactions to products, and maintaining and enhancing corporate morale.

Reaching the Target Audience. In considering the cost of visitor reached, it is important for the firm to participate in those shows that will be frequented by members of its target audience. Unfortunately, since the demise of the *Business Publications Audit*'s Exposition Audit Service in December 1980, trade show exhibitors "have lacked a comparable audit service independent of promoters' attendance figures and classification of registrants" for identifying and profiling trade show participation.[26]

IXO HAS ONE-DAY GIVEAWAY

In response to its one-day marketing blitz in which $750,000 worth of giveaways were distributed to 1,000 CEOs, IXO, a manufacturer of computer equipment, received more than 200 inquiry letters, several hundred telephone calls, and 1,200 response cards.

The objective of the giveaway program was to sell large quantities of telecomputers to each CEO's company. Hand-held telecomputers and a copy of that day's *Wall Street Journal* containing a three-page advertisement announcing the system were delivered to each CEO. When operated, the $500 units greeted each executive by name, allowed them to access their company's stock quotation from Dow Jones, and to try out simulated transactions such as making airline reservations or banking deposits.

The $750,000 retail value of the giveaway, according to IXO's president, was "far cheaper, and more effective than attempting to reach those executives through in-person sales calls." From the company's point of view, the promotion was cost effective . . . "when you're selling a half-million dollar system, you don't need a whole lot of sales to break even."

Source: Richard Esposito, "It Pays to Give Product Away," *Industrial Marketing*, April 1983. Reprinted with permission.

---

[26]John Couretas, "Too Few Care About Trade Show Audits," *Business Marketing* (November 1983), pp. 118, 120.

Thus, most exhibitors are now relying on registration cards to determine trade show participation and develop a profile of show attendees. Other methods include an examination of past trade show effectiveness, such as the number of qualified leads, the number of leads converted to sales, and the number of key prospects reached.[27]

Without credible information on trade show participation, marketers run the risk of bringing in products that are too sophisticated for the audience, sending the wrong people to the show, or even setting up the wrong-sized exhibit. Thus, to plan their trade show strategy to fit the needs of their target audience, many marketers also conduct a preshow survey of target prospects to determine (1) which shows they plan to attend and (2) what they hope to gain from attending.

Allocating Funds. As exemplified by Hunt Chemical's trade show strategy, the trade show budget may not only call for an allocation of funds for actual show exhibits, it may include advertising before and during the show, a preshow direct-mail campaign, and a relevant giveaway. How much should be allocated for trade show expenses, then, depends on the objectives as well as the strategies for achieving the objectives.

Premiums, Incentives, and Specialty Advertising

While promotional contests and giveaways are quite common in consumer marketing, they are also used, though less frequently, in industrial marketing. When properly conceived, as the IXO example illustrates, they tend to be quite successful. In contrast to premiums which are items of value and normally closely related to the products they are intended to sell, specialty advertising consists of useful, low-cost giveaways such as calendars, ballpoint pens, cigarette lighters, baseball caps, or other gifts given to prospects by salespersons. Since the item will have the firm's name and address on it somewhere, and possibly contain an advertising message, it is also classified as an advertisement.

Care must be taken regarding the manner in which specialty advertising is distributed so that the offering will be neither misunderstood nor offensive.[28] For instance, specialty items can be included as part of a proposal (the memo pad on which it is written, or the binder in which it is contained) or offered to several members of the buying firm (e.g., desk calendars or pens). When offered to a prospect, they should be presented in a way that does not appear to apply pressure or obligate the prospect.

THE USE OF PUBLICITY IN THE INDUSTRIAL MARKET

Publicity, because of its high credibility and low cost, is a highly effective promotional tool. When favorable editorial material about a company or its products is

---

[27]Ibid.

[28]George M. Zinkham and Lauren A. Vachris, "The Impact of Selling Aids on New Prospects," *Industrial Marketing Management* 13 (1984), pp. 187–193.

placed in the media, it generates sales leads and brings about better relationships with customers. Evidence indicates that industrial customers rate technical editorial material in trade journals as an important source of information in the buying process.[29] Thus, technical articles, frequently referred to as "signed articles" in trade publications, are excellent vehicles for reaching industrial customers. While the term "technical article" includes all types of technical publicity (e.g., feature articles written by the publication's staff and interviews of key industry personnel), a signed article is an article with the byline (name) of the author and thus gives authenticity to the product.

Sophisticated industrial buyers, who evaluate and analyze proposals to meet product requirements, engage in considerable search activity to determine product characteristics and identify potential sources of supply as they move through the purchasing decision process. Part of that search includes information gathered from trade publications: information that is perceived as coming from a highly credible source. Industrial buyers recognize that most editors of trade journals have technical knowledge in the field and are able to evaluate the usefulness of information for their readers. Therefore, when industrial buyers read about a product in the editorial

TABLE 15-5 Four Good Reasons for Using Signed Articles in Industrial Promotion

1. Signed articles help to improve a company's technical image and to presell products.	An effective and inexpensive way to demonstrate technical competency. Approaches customers via a credible route. Stimulates customer interest via education and a fresh awareness of company capabilities.
2. Signed articles extend the reach of sales engineers.	Helps to reach buying influencers not normally contacted. Approaches influencers in a credible way because they are published by a third party. Gives reasons for contacting a particular buying influencer. Backs up salesperson and continues to sell in salesperson's absence.
3. Signed articles are an important source of information to customers.	Highly important as a source of information to customers. Only handbooks are regarded as a more important source of information by buyers. Rank ahead of catalogs, advertising, conferences, and other promotional variables.
4. Signed articles appear in publications that are well read by industrial customers.	Ninety-eight percent of all buying influencers at every level read one or more articles in issues of interest. High probability of reaching top executives.

Source: Reprinted by permission of the publisher, adapted from "Industrial Publicity: One of the Best Promotional Tools," by Jerome D. Willams, *Industrial Marketing Management,* 12 [1983], pp. 207–211. Copyright © 1983 by Elsevier Science Publishing Co., Inc.

[29]Based on Jerome D. Williams, "Industrial Publicity: One of the Best Promotional Tools," *Industrial Marketing Management* 12 (1983), pp. 207–211.

section of a trade journal, they tend to believe that the editor has deemed the product worthy of special consideration. The benefits of using signed articles are outlined in Table 15-5.

While publicity is free, it does have costs associated with obtaining space in the publication; that is, someone has to write the article or prepare the news release and arrange for it to be placed in the right publication. However, these costs are in no way comparable to the cost of actual advertising, which can amount to as much as $3,000–4,000 for a one-page, one-time, black and white ad.[30] Generally, publicity represents about 10 percent of a firm's total promotional budget.

In designing an effective publicity program, the industrial marketer must be aware of the fact that publicity is most effective when it is used to complement the total promotional program.

DEVELOPING THE INDUSTRIAL PROMOTIONAL PROGRAM

Today's economic conditions call for careful consideration of the elements that are essential in developing an effective communication program—whether it is industrial or consumer oriented. Promotional variables must be artfully integrated if communication objectives are to be achieved most effectively.

Many of the principles that are followed in developing consumer advertising programs are not only applicable but are necessary in developing an effective industrial promotional program. The objective of industrial advertising, for instance, is to communicate something about the company and its products. It should be designed, then, to enable the company and its sales people to become favorably known to current and potential customers, to convey specific and technical information regarding the characteristics of a particular product(s), to help sales people in their selling effort, to motivate distributors of industrial goods, and to reach those who either directly or indirectly influence the buying of industrial goods.

An effective advertising program is built around careful consideration of advertising objectives, the advertising budget, the target audiences to be reached, and the message strategy.

Advertising Objectives

The first step in developing an effective advertising plan begins with the formulation of advertising objectives. Advertising objectives, however, cannot be formulated in isolation. They must be formulated on the basis of the firm's overall corporate and marketing objectives. In the development of corporate objectives, a company sets the direction for its desired business performance. Once established, management

---

[30]Courtland L. Bovee and William F. Arens, *Contemporary Advertising* (Homewood, Ill.: Richard D. Irwin, Inc., 1982), p. 685.

chooses the strategies and actions necessary to achieve those objectives. Figure 15-2 depicts how communication strategies evolve from corporate objectives.

Marketing objectives indicate what is to be accomplished through advertising to achieve corporate objectives. For instance, if the corporate objective is to increase return on stockholders' equity by five percent, the marketing objective may be to increase sales by thirty percent. The advertising objective, then, should be stated in terms of increasing product knowledge, or in terms of generating sales leads.

Advertising objectives should never be stated in terms of increasing sales. While increased sales are usually the ultimate objective desired, it is difficult, if

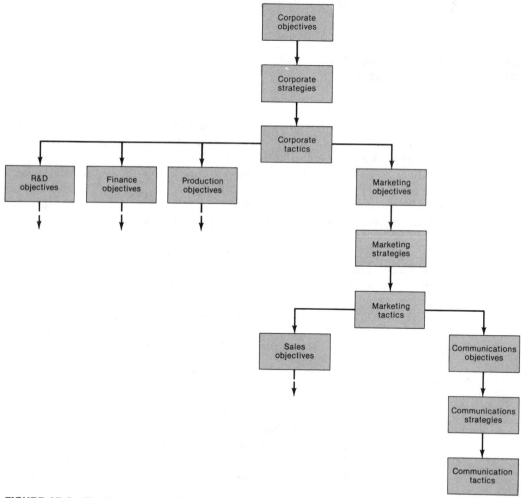

FIGURE 15-2   The Promotional Planning Process

Source: Robert A. Kriegel, "Anatomy of a Marketing Communications Plan," *Business Marketing*, July 1983, pp. 72–78. Reprinted with permission.

not impossible, to link advertising directly to sales. Personal selling, price, product performance, competitive actions, and other factors, such as increased consumer demand for end products, also affect sales levels. Thus, pinpointing the impact of advertising on sales is a difficult job indeed.

Whatever the marketing objective, to set the direction for creating, coordinating, and evaluating the entire promotional program, advertising objectives must specify exactly what is to be accomplished in terms of the marketing objective, and they must be stated in specific, measurable, realistic, and obtainable terms that delineate what is to be accomplished within a specific period of time, for example,

> Increase XYZ chemical process user (the existing market) awareness of Acme's dependable product capabilities from twenty-five percent to forty-five percent in eighteen months beginning January 1, 19XX.

APPROPRIATING ADVERTISING FUNDS

Since industrial advertising accounts for fourteen percent of all American advertising spending, it is an important element in the marketing budget. Research suggests, however, that industrial marketers have tended to rely on arbitrary methods for developing promotional budgets.[31] The appropriation of funds for advertising involves considerations of the cost of purchased space or time in advertising media (including the cost of direct mail) and the cost of producing the advertisements that appear in the purchased media over a specific time period, generally one year. An advertising budget, on the other hand, details how advertising dollars are to be expended from monies appropriated for advertising for individual campaigns by media, by time frames, by market segments and audiences, and by geographic areas.[32]

To ensure that expenditures budgeted for advertising can be effectively monitored, advertising appropriations should not include trade shows, catalogs, or other promotional outlays. These outlays should be monitored separately to evaluate their individual effectiveness. Table 15-6, while slightly outdated, indicates how the average industrial firm invests its promotional budget. To monitor the effectiveness of these promotional expenditures, promotion funds should be appropriated and budgeted separately. An advertising appropriation should not be a "catch-all" for other promotional expenses.

As Table 15-7 shows, advertising appropriations are approached in a variety of ways depending on the philosophy of the particular company. While some firms use such computer simulations for experimenting as ADVISOR (see Table 15-7), others use a variety of other methods. Computer models are built on a series of

[31]James E. Lynch and Graham J. Hooley, "Advertising Budgeting Practices of Industrial Advertisers," *Industrial Marketing Management* 16 (1987), pp. 63–69.
[32]Ibid.

TABLE 15-6 Methods Used to Set Advertising Budgets*

	Use Regularly [%]	Have Tried It [%]	Heard Of But Never Used [%]	Never Heard Of or No Reply [%]
What we can afford	54.1	15.7	9.5	20.7
Objective and Task	39.8	13.0	17.7	29.5
Percentage of Expected Sales	33.0	15.4	29.1	22.5
Experimentation	7.3	17.9	37.7	37.1
Desired Share of Voice	5.7	10.9	31.1	52.3
Accept Angry Proposal	4.6	24.3	35.7	35.4
Match Competition	4.3	13.7	48.7	33.2

*Number of industrial marketing companies = 560.

Source: Reprinted by permission of the publisher, adapted from "Advertising Budgeting Practices of Industrial Advertisers," by James E. Lynch, *Industrial Marketing Management,* 16 [1987], pp. 63–69. Copyright © 1987 by Elsevier Science Publishing Co., Inc.

situations such as the life-cycle stage of the product, frequency of purchase, market share, concentration of sales, profit patterns, and controlled advertising experiments. In addition to the "what can we afford method," two other conventional appropriation techniques used by industrial advertisers are the rule-of-thumb and the objective-task techniques.[33]

TABLE 15-7 ADVISOR: Variables Affecting Advertising and Promotional Budgeting

1. Product life cycle	As the PLC progresses, the ratio of marketing expenditures [advertising and personal selling] to sales [M/S] decreases. Advertising expense to sales ratio [A/S] behaves differently: early in the PLC it is high, tending to decrease as the PLC progresses.
2. Purchase frequency	The M/S ratio is not affected by purchase frequency. The greater the purchase frequency, however, the higher the advertising-to-marketing-expense ratio [A/M ratio]. As a result, purchase frequency has a positive effect on the A/S ratio.
3. Product variables	Products that are high in quality, unique, or strongly identified with the company have a high A/M ratio because of their worth in advertising. Thus, the A/S ratio is also larger.
4. Market share	As market share increases, M/S and A/S ratios tend to decrease.
5. Customer concentration	As sales are concentrated with fewer larger customers, the M/S ratio declines.
6. Customer base	As the number of customers increases, all three ratios [M/S, A/M, and A/S] increase.

Source: Adapted from "The Advisor Project: A Study of Industrial Marketing Budgets," by Gary L. Lilien and John D. C. Little," *Sloan Management Review,* 17, 3 [Spring 1976], pp. 24–25. Reprinted with permission.

[33]Vincent J. Blasko and Charles H. Patti, "The Advertising Budgeting Practices of Industrial Marketers," *Journal of Marketing* 48 (Fall 1984), pp. 104–110.

Rule of Thumb.   A rule of thumb relates advertising expenditures to some other measure of company activity in a consistent way. For instance, funds can be allocated on the basis of past sales (two percent of sales, say, to advertising) or on the basis of industry averages. Such rule of thumb methods for appropriating advertising dollars are quite common in industrial marketing, particularly where advertising is a relatively small percentage of the total communication budget.

The problem with this method of allocation is that it violates the basic marketing principle that marketing activities stimulate demand and thus sales. When advertising dollars are fixed as a percentage of sales, for instance, advertising increases when sales increase and decreases when sales decrease. Thus, this method ignores all other business conditions that might be suggesting a totally opposite strategy.

Objective Task.   Recent studies suggest that the popularity of the "objective-task" method for setting the industrial advertising budget is increasing, moving from a fourth or fifth ranking in popularity in the 1970s to second in the 1980s.[34] The objective-task technique is a relatively logical method for establishing the advertising allocation in that the steps involved (see Table 15-8) in developing the advertising program formulate the bases for appropriating advertising funds. The costs involved in implementing the advertising program become the basis for determining the advertising appropriation. In developing the appropriation, the company's financial position is also considered. If the appropriation appears to be too high, the objectives

TABLE 15-8 Steps in the Objective-Task Method of Appropriating Advertising Funds

	Examples
1. Determine marketing objectives	Introduce a new product, increase market share or sales
2. Determine advertising objectives	Increase product awareness, generate sales leads
3. Determine audiences to be reached	Engineers, production, purchasing
4. Determine reach, frequency, and continuity needs (communication objectives)	How wide is the market, how often must the message be repeated to have impact, and how long will it be necessary to run the campaign to achieve the desired results
5. Determine appropriate media to reach audiences	Business or trade publications
6. Establish other promotional support needs	Publicity, incentives, data sheets
7. Determine control measures	Pre- and posttesting
8. Estimate necessary promotional funds to achieve media and communication objectives	Computer simulation of media costs

[34]Lynch, "Advertising Budgeting Practices of Industrial Advertisers," *Industrial Marketing Management* 16 (1987), pp. 63–69.

may be scaled down and strategies adjusted accordingly. Program results are also monitored in light of appropriate revisions for the next planning period.

The important aspect of the objective-task method is that it forces the firm to think in terms of objectives and whether they are being accomplished. The major drawback of the task method, however, lies in the difficulty of determining in advance the amount of funds that will be needed to reach specific objectives. Further, while techniques for measuring advertising effectiveness are improving, they are still not sufficient in many areas. As these techniques become more exact, though, advertisers are using this method more and more.

DEVELOPING MESSAGE STRATEGY

Message strategy specifies how advertising objectives are to be achieved by defining the theme for the communication program and the company image (positioning) desired in the marketplace. When industrial buyers make purchases, though, they are buying physical products, they are in a deeper sense purchasing problem-solving benefits and abilities to improve operations. Thus, industrial advertising must provide the reader with useful information regarding these intangible benefits. Additionally, industrial buying criteria generally center on technical rather than emotional issues:

> Unlike the consumer marketplace, where products, services and even the ads themselves often must promise satisfaction for strong emotional desires, the context of business/industrial advertising is the reader's work. He needs to make correct decisions heavily dependent on performance and value facts. Although emotions such as fear, anxiety, frustration and status attainment can play a large role in a business buyer's mind, those desires to achieve are best served and those fears are best assuaged by the performance and value benefits attached to a business decision.[35]

Advertising messages must be formulated on the basis of how the supplier's product(s) can assist in solving customer problems and relate to the needs of the particular target audience. Research, however, has indicated that many industrial advertisers do not understand the major considerations that influence their markets.[36]

Identifying Audience Needs. Determining the requirements of the audiences to be reached is the key element in developing message strategy. As Table 15-9 indicates, information needs and responses will vary across influencers. For instance, in one study of industrial cooling system purchases, operating cost and energy savings were of major concern to production engineers, while heating and air-conditioning con-

[35]"Our Choice: 1984's Best Business/Industrial Print Ad," *Business Marketing* (January 1985), pp. 114–128.

[36]Gordon McAleer, "Do Industrial Advertisers Understand What Influences Their Markets?" *Journal of Marketing* 38 (January 1974), pp. 15–23.

TABLE 15-9 A Guide to Developing Creative Advertising According to Social Style

	Driver*	Expressive†	Amiable‡	Analytical§
Approach should be	Straightforward, structured	Highly creative, imaginative	Strongly people-oriented	Detailed, orderly
Copy style should be / Emphasize product [or service]	Concise, right to the point Benefits that directly affect costs, production, profitability; speediness of results; avoid lengthy process explanation	Stimulating, rousing Innovations; features that are exclusive or unusual: "Sizzle," not the steak"; status and recognition gained from the decision	Friendly, conversational Features that minimize chance and risk, improve safety, help people	Precise Features with detail and data; process integrity
Impress them with	Short-term results, "bottom-line" expectations	Testimonials from well-recognized sources; short-term results	Buyer-seller "partnerships": proof of claims, testimonials, vendor service orientation Superiority of the process	Logic, long-term as well as short-term results, tangible proof of claims, testimonials of authorities
For action, offer them	Choices, options, custom design to their specs	Incentives, chance for personal recognition, speed of results	Guarantees, assurances, service, and support	Complete proposals, service, proof of salesperson competency

*Has above-average assertiveness and below-average responsiveness.
†Has above-average assertiveness and above-average responsiveness. ‒
‡Has below-average assertiveness and above-average responsiveness.
§Has below-average assertiveness and below-average responsiveness.

Source: Robert A. Kriegel, "Does Your Ad Talk the Way Your Prospect Thinks?" *Business Marketing,* July 1984, pp. 86–98. Reprinted with permission.

sultants were more concerned with plant noise levels.[37] To reach the production engineers, then, message objectives might have been stated in terms of "Advertise Acme Widget's economical operating cost and maintenance advantages compared to the XYZ product."

Keep the Message to Important Specifics. Many industrial advertisers attempt to cover too much in their advertising messages. Industrial buyers tend to purchase on the basis of a few specifics. Thus, advertising messages should be developed around what is *really* important, emphasizing the major concerns of the audience as they relate to their business needs or objectives.[38] Table 15-10 emphasizes the ingredients that are essential to successful industrial advertising.

Advertising messages can be developed around case histories, testimonials, short stories, audience participation, or straight exposition.[39]

Case Histories. Case histories use the experience of the user and show readers how they can benefit by purchasing from the supplier. This approach is quite useful when an audience can be reached through very specialized trade journals since readers tend to share common experiences.

Testimonials. Testimonials are similar to case histories except that those giving testimonials are usually chosen from well-known companies.

TABLE 15-10 Copy Chasers Criteria

1. The successful ad has a high degree of visual magnetism.
2. The successful ad selects the right audience.
3. The successful ad invites the reader into the scene.
4. The successful ad promises a reward.
5. The successful ad backs up the promise.
6. The successful ad presents the selling proposition in logical sequence.
7. The successful ad talks "person to person."
8. Successful advertising is easy to read.
9. Successful advertising emphasizes the service, not the source.
10. Successful advertising reflects the company's character.

Source: "Our Choice: 1984's Best Business/Industrial Print Ad," *Business Marketing,* January 1985, pp. 114–128. Reprinted with permission.

[37] Jean-Marie Choffray and Gary L. Lilien, "Assessing Response to Industrial Marketing Strategy," *Journal of Marketing* 42 (April 1978), pp. 20–39.

[38] Joseph A. Bellizzi and Julie Lehrer, "Developing Better Industrial Advertising," *Industrial Marketing Management* 12 (1983), pp. 19–23.

[39] See Frederick R. Messner, *Industrial Advertising* (New York: McGraw-Hill Book Company, 1963), pp. 102–103.

Short Stories.   While research has shown that only a small percentage of industrial companies use the strictly comparative format of advertising,[40] when communication strategy is enhanced through comparison to competitors, short stories are often effective.

Audience Participation.   Audience participation is a unique way to get readers involved in the advertising message. This approach involves asking readers to complete quizzes or mathematical calculations to obtain some of the message's information.

Straight Exposition.   The most commonly used message approach, one that is generally respected by industrial buyers, is the straight exposition. This approach uses a straightforward narration regarding the company's product and its uses.

In developing the advertising message it must be remembered that buyers tend to screen out messages that are inconsistent with their attitudes, needs, and beliefs. They also tend to interpret information so that it conforms to their beliefs. Thus, unless the message is carefully designed around the needs of the target audience, it will be disregarded or improperly interpreted.

DEVELOPING THE MEDIA PLAN

An effectively developed media plan in the industrial market involves consideration of (1) the number of different target audiences to be reached (reach), (2) the number of times they should be reached for the message to have impact (frequency), (3) the length of time the campaign is to run (continuity), (4) media selection, and (5) scheduling.

Reach.   In the typical industrial purchase, multiple buying influencers are involved: influencers with unique information needs and interests who read different types of publications. To reach these buying influencers with a message that addresses their needs, different message strategies must be developed and delivered through media that addresses their interests.

Frequency.   One-time ads are generally ineffective as several exposures are necessary before a message has an impact. As the number of message exposures increases, both the number of individuals who remember it and the length of time they can recall it increases. However, overexposure of a message can be wasteful. When an audience experiences wear-out effects, it tends to tune out the message. In justifying the media plan on the basis of frequency, then, media planners must assume some response function that relates to the number of exposures.

[40]Thomas H. Stevenson and Linda E. Swayne, "Comparative Industrial Advertising: The Content and Frequency," *Industrial Marketing Management* 13 (1984), pp. 133–138.

Continuity. When the same message is repeated over and over for a long period of time and has both long continuity and high frequency, wear-out effects can be severe. In developing message strategy, then, the advertiser may want to build in variety yet maintain the overall theme and positioning strategy. For example, the Borg-Warner campaign in Figure 15-3 has been running for more than five years. While the theme "Watch Borg-Warner" is continuously maintained, as noted, advertisements feature different product categories and different advertising messages. Determining the best mix of reach, frequency, and continuity is directly related to media selection and scheduling.

Media Selection

Selection of the appropriate media focuses on the target audience to be reached, the ability of the media to reach the audience, and the efficiency with which the media can be utilized to maximize reach, frequency, and continuity goals within budgetary constraints.

Media selection also depends on whether the advertiser wishes to penetrate a particular industry or cut across various industries. It would make little sense to pay the higher costs of advertising in publications read in several industries than the lower costs charged by publications directed at only those few industries in which the advertiser's product is used. On the other hand, where many industries are potential users, and the functional areas of key buying influencers are not well defined, publications that cut across industries and functional areas can produce the best results.

Circulation, Editorial Content, and Cost. Selection also depends on circulation, editorial content, and the cost of advertising space. Thus, media planners must carefully assess these variables. To define the audiences of particular publications accurately, media planners use the circulation audits of business publications. Three organizations, the Audit Bureau of Circulation, the Business Publications' Audit of Circulations, and the Verified Audit Circulation Corporation, also audit the circulation, via SIC codes, of their member businesses. Business publications are also listed by such services as the *Standard Rate and Data Service's Business Publications* and the *Business Publication Rates and Data Directory,* which provide information on editorial content, advertising rates, closing dates for ad placements, and circulation figures.

Controlled Circulation. Business and trade publications are circulated on a paid basis or a controlled basis. When a publication is available on a paid basis, the recipient pays the subscription price to receive it. Controlled circulations are free and are mailed to a selected list of individuals, chosen by the publisher on the basis of their unique position to influence purchase decisions. To qualify, recipients must designate their profession or occupation, their job title, function, and purchasing responsibilities. Thus, users of controlled circulation publications can more accu-

Want to see water where it almost never rains?

Borg-Warner submersible pumps help bring vital irrigation water 5000 feet, almost a mile, straight up from beneath arid desert sands. That's today's Borg-Warner. Diversified for financial stability. A company worth watching.

© 1983 Borg-Warner Corporation

Watch Borg-Warner

For an annual report call 312-322-8680.

FIGURE 15-3   An Excellent Example of How Continuity of Theme Can Be Carried While Maintaining the Same Positioning Strategy—"Watch Borg-Warner"

Source: Courtesy of Borg-Warner Corporation, Chicago, IL.

Want to see more coal brought to the surface for less?

Borg-Warner mechanical seals help coal slurry pipelines transport more coal with less water and greater reliability for increased mine production. That's today's Borg-Warner. Diversified for financial stability. A company worth watching.

 BorgWarner

Watch Borg-Warner

© 1984 Borg-Warner Corporation.

For an annual report, call: 312-322-8680.

FIGURE 15-3 (cont.)

Want to see the Father of our country around for your grandchildren?

Borg-Warner air conditioning systems keep the temperature and humidity constant to help preserve the historic paintings at the National Gallery of Art. That's today's Borg-Warner. Diversified for financial stability. A company worth watching.

Watch
Borg-Warner

For an annual report call 312-322-8680.

FIGURE 15-3   (cont.)

rately evaluate which target markets their publications reach and whether their advertising dollars are being properly expended.

Scheduling

Scheduling in business or trade publications depends on whether they are monthlies, weeklies, or dailies. If the media plan incorporates the use of a daily, a weekly, and a monthly publication, scheduling of advertising inserts to achieve frequency objectives might, for example, require six inserts per year in the monthly, twenty-six inserts per year in the weekly, and fifty-two inserts per year in the daily.

Scheduling also depends on the objectives of the advertising program. If the advertising objective is to achieve recognition, scheduling might call for a steady year-round campaign. For advertising to achieve recognition, it takes time. If it is to introduce a new product, scheduling might call for heavier advertising at the beginning of the campaign with periodic pulsing at regular intervals throughout the year to keep influencers reminded of the product's existence.

EVALUATING THE ADVERTISING PLAN

To ensure that advertising objectives are being achieved and that money is being spent wisely, the effectiveness of the advertising program must be evaluated. Various elements of the advertising plan can be measured before and after the advertising plan is implemented. Measuring the effectiveness of the message before it is implemented is called *pretesting*. By pretesting particular elements of the plan, the advertiser can discover what is or is not effective, correct the ineffective elements, and avoid costly errors.

Determining the effectiveness of the plan after it has been implemented is known as *posttesting*. While posttesting is generally more costly and time consuming than pretesting, it can provide useful guidelines for future advertising programs. It also permits the advertiser to measure the effectiveness of the plan under actual market conditions. The effectiveness of an advertising plan depends on how well it reaches the intended market and whether the message had an impact on the market. Thus, advertisers are generally concerned with the areas shown in Table 15-11.

The Need for Preplanning. Evaluating the effectiveness of the advertising plan involves careful consideration of the elements to be evaluated, the data to be collected, and how the data are to be analyzed. Thus, it must be determined in advance what is to be measured, how it is to be measured, and what techniques are to be used.

For example, while it is very difficult for IBM to measure whether advertising goals have been attained, because the name IBM washes over all its advertising, IBM develops its advertising program by first researching specific market areas, establishing advertising objectives based on research findings, and then pre- and

TABLE 15-11 Primary Areas of Advertising Evaluation

	Pretesting	*Posttesting*
Markets	Tests advertising message strategy against various target audiences to measure reaction.	Determines extent to which campaign succeeded in reaching target market. Measures changes in awareness.
Motives	Determines why buyers behave as they do and what product benefits appeal to them.	Measures effect of motives [i.e., did purchase occur?].
Messages	Determines what the message says and how well it is said—includes copy, headlines, illustrations, and typography.	Determines if ad was seen, remembered, believed.
Media	Determines the best combination of media to reach target market; includes space and time elements—usually done through computer simulation.	Determines whether media used was effective in reaching audience.
Scheduling	Determines the aspects of reach, frequency, and continuity.	Determines if scheduling was effective.
Budgeting	Determines the optimum level of expenditures—usually done through computer simulation.	Evaluates effectiveness of budgeting stragtegy.
Overall Results		Evaluates whether objectives were achieved. Determines whether to continue, what to change, and how much to spend in the future.

posttesting the effectiveness of its program.[41] How IBM assesses its business-to-business advertising is shown in Figure 15-4.

How advertising is evaluated depends on the specific objectives of a given advertising campaign. How well they are conceived and executed, however, depends on the sophistication of those people who are responsible for the planning and evaluation of advertising. Frequently, outside research professionals are utilized to develop field studies. Many industrial firms are also finding that advertising agencies are not only helpful in planning the campaign, but also in conducting advertising research.

Industrial Advertising Agencies. A number of advertising agencies have begun to specialize in the area of industrial advertising. The number of agencies that offer services on a per job basis has also increased. These agencies assist the industrial advertiser with various aspects of the communication plan. In addition to preparing advertisements and conducting research, they assist in coordinating the advertising program with other marketing efforts by providing assistance in the design of sales promotion material and publicity releases. The top ten ranked business/industrial advertising agencies are listed in Table 15-12.

[41]Byron G. Quann, "How IBM Assesses Its Business-to-Business Advertising," *Business Marketing* (January 1985), pp. 106–112.

HOW IBM EVALUATES THE EFFECTIVENESS OF ITS ADVERTISING STRATEGY

IBM develops its advertising program by first researching specific market areas, establishing advertising objectives based on research findings, and then pre- and post-testing the effectiveness of its program. For instance, when IBM discovered that its leading position in the typewriter market was being challenged, advertising objectives were developed to maintain the IBM typewriter as the preferred typewriter in the minds of buyers—an existing preference uncovered through research. To reach both decision makers and influencers (secretaries) both television and print media were utilized, and communication strategy was developed to capitalize on the "preference" theme. Through post-testing of advertising recall on the print ad shown below, IBM was able to measure the impact of its media and communication strategy. The ad received the highest day-after recall score (59) compared to IBM's normal day-after recall score (29) and the industry norm (23).

Source: Byron G. Quann, "How IBM Assesses Its Business-to-Business Advertising," *Business Marketing,* January 1985, pp. 106–112. Reprinted with permission.

THE INTEGRATED PROMOTION PLAN

The basic elements essential in a well-conceived industrial communication plan have been discussed individually to this point. However, these elements must be artfully integrated if communication objectives are to be achieved most effectively. Once the various strategies have been conceived, action plans must be developed (preferably

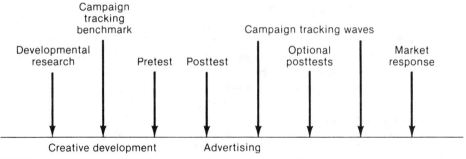

FIGURE 15-4   IBM's Campaign Research Measurement Model

in writing) so that the various individuals involved can carry through with their areas of responsibility in implementing the plans.

Individuals in industrial advertising departments typically have greater participation in the actual creation and placement of promotional strategy than do those in consumer organizations. This is because most industrial advertising and sales promotion is noncommissionable to advertising agencies—direct mail, catalogs, and trade show exhibits, for example.[42] Additionally, industrial advertising tends to be technical, and this generally requires that experts within the firm prepare copy and other artwork, including graphs and tables.[43]

TABLE 15-12   The Ten Top-Billing Business/Industrial Advertising Agencies

Rank	Agency	Gross Business Billings (millions)
1	Doyle, Dane, Bernbach	$165.4
2	Marsteller	160.0
3	Bozell & Jacobs	155.0
4	Doremus & Company	152.9
5	HBM/Cramer, Inc.	90.0
6	Muir Cornellus Moore, Inc.	71.3
7	Needham Harper & Steers	70.0
8	N. W. Ayer Incorporated	69.4
9	Fletcher/Mayo/Associates	65.7
10	Rolf Warner Rosenthal	50.0

Source: "Top Business/Industrial Ad Agencies," *Business Marketing,* September 1984, p. 149. Reprinted with permission.

[42]Bovee, *Contemporary Advertising,* p. 686.
[43]Ibid., p. 689.

A well-written action plan, as developed in Table 15-13 should cover specifically what is to be communicated, when it is to be communicated, and through what media it is to be implemented. It should also include all promotional plans (publicity, trade shows, giveaways, and data sheets) that are intended to be a part of the overall promotional strategy.

A communication action plan that is well written helps the person responsible for its development to illustrate the value of the plan to management in a professional manner. Once approved, it is more easily understood and implemented by all individuals involved in the program.

TABLE 15-13 Anatomy of a Marketing Communication Plan

Marketing objective	Increase Acme's market share in the industry from 12% to 18% over the next 12 months, beginning January 19xx.
Advertising objectives	Increase awareness in existing market of Acme Widgets from 35% to 55% over the next 12 months.
	Create awareness in new market of Acme Widgets from 0% to 20% over the next 12 months.
Target market and audience	Widget processing industry, plant engineers, product designers, and purchasing agents.
Communication strategies	
Advertising	Prepare advertising copy to emphasize the production and purchasing benefits of one source of Widget product applications. Develop headline and illustrations to draw attention to the problems of multiple sourcing.
	Run six two-page, four-color spreads every other month in *Widgeting World*.
	Run one-half page black-and-white ad each month in *Widget Product News* offering free technical manual "Widgeting Cross Sectional Dimensionality." Insert "800" toll-free number. Run 4 four-color spread in June, July, September, and October issues of *ABC Monthly Roundup* and *ABC Process Times* announcing widgeting "breakthrough" cost superiority, without maintenance or quality deficiency, compared to ABC process. Emphasize Acme Widget new wider size range, technical top line, and free offer of Widgeting Versatility technical manual.
Direct Mail	Rewrite "The Acme Widget Advantage" product brochure, emphasizing new wider range of sizes. Complete rewrite, editing, approval, and production by March 20, 19xx.
	Mail brochure and letter to customer list in April 19xx, and to sales department's "hit list" the same month.
	Distribute brochure in bulk to district sales offices and distributor list in February.
Telemarketing	Hire telemarketing consultant in January to set up incoming telephone program. Complete upgrade by March.
Sales promotion	Schedule trade show for new market prospects for July 19xx at Cleveland Widget Expo. Promote trade show through invitations mailed with technical manual to new market sales leads. Complete invitation and trade show sched-

TABLE 15-13   (Continued)

	ule outline by March 31. Complete trade show planning by June 15. Offer free "Widgeting Versatility" manual in nine fractional ads, April through December, in *Production Unlimited* and *Factory Engineering Extra*, inserting "800" toll free phone number. Run same ad in *Perfect Plant* postcard mailing in September.
Publicity	Write and distribute press release and product brochure to *Widget Industries'* editorial department in January, emphasizing user and purchasing benefits of new larger-size range of Acme Widget Line.
	Distribute technical manual and press releases with a short synopsis to *Factory Engineering* editorial department in June.
	Research and write application case history, emphasizing the role of the wide range of widget sizes available from single-source Acme, for presentation to editor of *Widgeting World* in April for possible late spring or early summer publication.

Source: Adapted from Robert A. Kriegel, "Anatomy of a Marketing Communications Plan," *Business Marketing,* July 1983, pp. 72–78. Reprinted with permission.

LOOKING BACK

Advertising, sales promotion, and publicity play an important part in the communication strategy of industrial marketers. These variables, however, must be carefully coordinated with personal selling if they are to contribute to the overall effectiveness of communication strategy.

Industrial advertising is used to reach unknown or inaccessible buying influences, to create awareness of the company, to enhance the sales call, to increase the overall effectiveness of the selling effort, and to support distributors' effort. While media usage generally differs from that used in the consumer market, the same principles apply in developing advertising and other promotional strategy.

The various reasons for using sales promotion and publicity and how they complement advertising as well as the selling effort were pointed out. Effective use of these variables, however, requires a well-thought-out, integrated communication program. That program begins with carefully developed advertising objectives that must be formulated from corporate and marketing objectives in such a manner as to set the direction for creating, coordinating, and evaluating the entire promotional program. Unless target markets are carefully identified, it is unlikely that communication and media strategy will attain the results desired. Once strategies are developed, based on the desired objectives, marketers can then decide on the appropriations necessary to carry through. Advertising and promotion strategy must also be evaluated and controlled, making adjustments where necessary.

QUESTIONS FOR DISCUSSION

1. In an attempt to measure the effectiveness of advertising on the advertiser's sales force, Motor City marketers conducted research on several midwestern manufacturers' sales staffs. While the majority of respondents were kept apprised of advertising objectives and programs, only 31 percent stated that their companies solicited their advice regarding advertising. Express your point of view, pro or con, about sales people's involvement in advertising programs.

2. One top industrial marketing CEO consistently had the bad habit of cutting advertising budgets, even though he had, on several occasions, been presented with evidence of a solid link among advertising, market awareness, preference, share of market, and profit. Each time this occurred, he would staunchly maintain his skepticism—even in the face of such evidence of the power of advertising as the Morrill study, which showed that the average industrial firm can increase its market share by 30 percent when it backs up the sales force with advertising. He would always lean back, reflect on the range of his product/market situations, and say, "That's only true sometimes." Can you come up with some arguments to change his mind?

3. Most companies spend the bulk of their advertising effort in developing direct mail, trade shows, and advertising. The lowly data sheet is often created as an afterthought. Should this be the case?

4. Sales and profitability are the measures of effectiveness that advertisers are ultimately interested in, but sales depend upon so many things that it is often difficult to isolate the unique effect that advertising has on sales while controlling for other extraneous variables, such as level of economic activity. Discuss possible ways to measure the effectiveness of advertising.

5. What can the industrial marketer do to get important or valuable technical information published in several competing publications to reach the various markets of interest?

6. The promotional strategy to a managerial audience should be different from one targeted to operating engineers. Do you agree?

7. Industrial buyers are usually serious, interested, and experienced in the products they purchase; therefore, technical wording is common. However, industrial advertising should be more than just technical language. Do you agree with this?

8. Many industrial marketers who have embraced the use of trade shows come away from them feeling as though they have been hustled. This appears to be due to the fact that little has been done to develop a measure of their effectiveness. Develop a plan for evaluating the benefits of a trade show.

SUGGESTED ADDITIONAL READINGS

BELLIZZI, JOSEPH A. and ROBERT E. HITE, "Improving Industrial Advertising Copy," *Industrial Marketing Management* 15 (1986):117–122.

BONOMA, THOMAS V., "Get More Out of Your Trade Shows," *Harvard Business Review* (January–February 1983):75–83.

CHAKRABART, ALOK K., STEPHEN FEINMAN, and WILLIAM FUENTEVILLA, "Targeting Technical Information to Organizational Positions," *Industrial Marketing Management* 11 (1982):195–203.

COURETAS, JOHN, "Study to Measure Ads' Effect on Sales Force," *Business Marketing* (May 1984):8–34.

KRIEGEL, ROBERT A., "Anatomy of a Marketing Communications Plan," *Business Marketing* (July 1983):72–78.

LYNCH, JAMES E. and GRAHAM J. HOOLEY, "Advertising Budgeting Practices of Industrial Advertisers," *Industrial Marketing Management* 16 (1987):63–69.

MARSHALL, JUDITH J. and HARRIE VREDENBERG, "Successfully Using Telemarketing in Industrial Sales," *Industrial Marketing Management* 17 (1988):15–22.

MEHR, HOWARD, "Finessing the Competitive Press," *Business Marketing* (November 1983): 112–116.

SWAYNE, LINDA E. and THOMAS H. STEVENSON, "Comparative Advertising in Horizontal Business Publications," *Industrial Marketing Management* 16 (1987):71–76.

WILLIAMS, JEROME D., "Industrial Publicity: One of the Best Promotional Tools," *Industrial Marketing Management* 12 (1983):207–211.

ZIEGENHAGEN, M. E., "When Management Doesn't 'Believe' in Advertising," *Business Marketing* (July 1984):81–84.

ZINKHAM, GEORGE M., "Rating Industrial Advertisements," *Industrial Marketing Management* 13 (1984):43–48.

ZINKHAM, GEORGE M., and LAUREN A. VACHRIS, "The Impact of Selling Aids on New Prospects," *Industrial Marketing Management* 13 (1984):187–193.

PART SEVEN

Formulating Pricing Policies

GENERAL DYNAMICS' $425 MILLION WRITE-OFF

On April 29th, 1957, Frank Pace smiled as the board of directors of General Dynamics overwhelmingly elected him president and chief executive officer. Well dressed, personable, and unquestionably intelligent, he had been pulled into the company just three years earlier. Pace did have a rather flawless record, albeit one which was not entirely business oriented. He had been more involved in public life. He had graduated from Princeton, earned a law degree from Harvard in 1936, had risen through the Washington bureaucracy to Director of the Budget under Harry Truman, and had gone on to become Secretary of the Army just before the Korean War.

Pace reflected many of the traits of the good federal official. He was an excellent public speaker, considerate and reflective in his thinking, not given to extremes, and quite willing to involve subordinates in decision making.

His predecessor, one Jay Hopkins, the man who had built General Dynamics into the biggest manufacturer of weaponry in the world, a man recognized for his "brilliance and audacity in finance," was not ecstatic over Pace's election. Ellsworth Alvord, a director of General Dynamics and close friend of Hopkins, is recalled to have said, " . . . this took all the fight out of him," The next day Hopkins entered the hospital, and one day later, he was pronounced dead.

Frank Pace took command. All too quickly, however, Pace was challenged with problems faced by General Dynamics' Convair Division. That division had estimated that 257 of its first jet aircraft could be sold over the next ten years for a potential profit of $250 million, and that at worst, the company would lose only $30 to $50 million if the venture failed. Shortly after production had begun, an engineer from Convair's purchasing division, while totaling the various construction costs, discovered that the costs of parts and material alone came to more than the selling price of the planes. When he presented his figures to higher Convair management, pointing out that even after excluding the $75 million research and development costs and the additional 30% labor costs incurred by Convair, the company was losing money with each plane it produced, he was fired. Two years later, however, when the accuracy of his figures proved to be correct, he was reinstated.

Convair continued to produce the aircraft but soon realized that its break-even costs were not realistic. Over a two-month span, it raised the break-even quantity from 68 to 74 planes. Ultimately, the break-even quantity would be raised to a total of 200 in the 880 and 990 series. By 1958, total orders for the 880s amounted to only 44, while only 32 of the 990s had been ordered.

In February 1962, with only 66 880s and 23 990s actually sold, General Dynamics was forced to write off $425 million in losses. Banks which had lent money to General Dynamics began demanding bank "scrutiny of the company's divisional budgets, the pledging of its government accounts receivable, a bank veto on sale of leaseback arrangements, an end to further borrowing, and a two-year moratorium on dividends." Frank Pace told a reporter, "If you don't think it twists my insides to see what has happened to General Dynamics, you are very wrong. You must know what this kind of a defeat does to a man who has been successful."

Jay Hopkins, looking down from his big corporation in the sky, said simply, "I told you so; pricing is more difficult than you can perceive."

Source: Reprinted by permission of *FORTUNE* magazine. Excerpted from "How a Great Corporation Got Out of Control: The Story of General Dynamics, Parts I and II," by Richard Austin Smith (January–February 1962), pp. 64, 120. Copyright © 1962 Time Inc. All rights reserved.

In the next two chapters, we shall examine various pricing strategies over a range of market conditions. We shall see that a firm must analyze not one, but three, factors in every pricing decision—customer demand, competition, and costs: These factors are inseparably intertwined and, unfortunately, often contradictory with regard to pricing strategy.

Chapter 16

Price Determinants: Customers, Competition, and Costs

Industrial buying decisions are typically more pragmatic and "fact oriented" than are similar decisions made by consumers. This does not say that industrial decisions are completely emotionless, nor consumer decisions based solely on ego and status needs. However, industrial products have a direct impact on the profits of both buyer and seller. Price thus becomes a pivotal issue, with each party considering multiple factors to determine the relative importance of price in a specific negotiation. The purpose of this chapter, then, is to discuss

1. How price interacts with other marketing variables.
2. The factors that influence pricing strategy.
3. The range of pricing policies necessary to serve multiple markets.
4. The impact of price on profitability.

Pricing is an indispensable part of industrial marketing strategy. It must be carefully interrelated to the firm's product, distribution, and communication strategies. The industrial marketing manager has the challenging responsibility of blending the various elements of the marketing mix to ensure that the total offering is not only responsive to the needs of the market, but also provides a return consistent with the firm's profit objectives. This is not an easy task.

From a marketing perspective, price represents the value customers place on a product at some point in time, but diverse groups of customers will perceive prod-

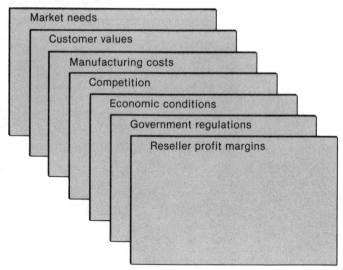

FIGURE 16-1   Price Constraints

uct value differently. They may also place different values on the various attributes that comprise the product offering, such as durability, innovative design, or ease of use. Further complicating the marketer's task is the fact that pricing decisions must also consider costs, market demand, competition, and governmental regulations. Additionally, pricing decisions influence channel decisions and relationships because they affect the profit margins of distributors, the commissions of manufacturers' representatives, and in turn, the price to industrial end users and ultimate consumers. Figure 16-1 depicts these multiple and conflicting price constraints.

Assessing all these areas is quite difficult. Seldom is there enough time and information. The competitive and economic environments can change unexpectedly. However, for a firm to survive in today's turbulent market, the industrial marketer must base pricing strategy upon sound criteria, operating both proactively and reactively. The marketer must not only anticipate future contingencies and constraints, but also respond quickly and effectively to competitive actions.

PRICE: A CRUCIAL ELEMENT IN PRODUCT STRATEGY

For two reasons, price must be viewed as a part of the product offering as well as a separate element in the marketing mix. First, from the buying firm's perspective, it is the cost that must be weighed against product quality, delivery, and supplier service. Second, from the seller's point of view, the price charged determines the profitability of the product and provides the margins necessary to support other aspects of the product offering, such as postpurchase service and technical assistance.[1]

To the industrial buyer, price is only one determinant of the economic impact that a product will have on the firm. Buyers are concerned with the "evaluated" price of a product, that is, the total cost of owning and using the product. Such costs include, in addition to the seller's price, transportation charges, the cost of installing capital equipment, inventory carrying costs for parts and material, possible obsolescence (due to engineering process changes), order processing costs, and less apparent costs such as production interruption caused by product failure, late delivery, or poor technical support.[2] This distinction between cost and price is important and should not be overlooked by the industrial marketer. Price merely measures the amount of the customer's capital investment; cost is a reflection of a product's efficiency.[3] A high price may be offset by cost savings in the use of a product, while a low price may lead to higher operating expenses, shorter product life expectancy, and other increased costs.

FACTORS THAT INFLUENCE PRICING STRATEGY

There is no simplistic approach to the industrial pricing decision. Rather, this decision hinges on multiple factors, and consideration must be given to the interaction of (1) customer demand, (2) the nature of derived demand, (3) competition, (4) cost and profit relationships, (5) the market's reaction to and perception of price, and (6) government regulation. Each of these dimensions is independently and jointly significant in the pricing decision.

Customer Demand

As discussed in Chapter 1, the demand for virtually all industrial products is derived from the demand and production of some consumer end product. As a result, industrial buyers are more concerned with the questions of whom to buy from and why than whether or not to buy (this ignores, of course, the "make-or-buy" decision). In turn, the industrial marketer usually worries more about influencing the more immediate industrial demand than about stimulating demand in the consumer market.

However, the industrial market is diverse and complex. A single product may be used in many different applications and have varying usage levels across individ-

---

[1]Frederick E. Webster, Jr., *Industrial Marketing Strategy* (New York: John Wiley & Sons, Inc., 1979), p. 135.

[2]Benson P. Shapiro and Barbara B. Jackson, "Industrial Pricing to Meet Customer Needs," *Harvard Business Review* (November–December 1978), pp. 119–127.

[3]George Risely, *Modern Industrial Marketing* (New York: McGraw-Hill Book Company, 1972), p. 189.

ual firms and market segments. The importance of the product to buyers' end products may also vary. For these reasons, potential demand, sensitivity to price, and potential profitability differ across market segments. In setting price to influence demand, therefore, industrial marketers must understand how products are used, recognize the potential customer benefits, examine the cost of owning and using the products, and determine product values from the customer's perspective.

Analyzing Customer Benefits.   In evaluating competing suppliers, organizational buyers assess the benefits of each supplier's total offering in relation to the price quoted. However, the various buying-decision influencers within the firm emphasize different benefits and, thus, do not all value the product identically. Product benefits may be functional, operational, financial, or personal.[4]

Functional benefits involve product design characteristics, aspects that might be particularly attractive to technical personnel. Operational benefits focus on product attributes such as reliability and consistency and are usually deemed important by manufacturing and quality control people. Financial benefits center on favorable credit terms and cost-saving opportunities that are important to purchasing managers and comptrollers. Personal benefits involve such factors as reduced risk, organizational status, and the personal satisfaction of doing a job well. These benefits might impact the decision of any influencer.

Analysis of potential customer benefits begins by focusing on the attributes of a physical product (horsepower or yards of earth moved per hour) as well as the elements of the augmented product (delivery, financing, or technical support). Analysis of all potential benefits enables the marketer to view the product from the customer's perspective, evaluate competitive strengths more objectively, and identify unique market opportunities.

While it is relatively easy to analyze physical product benefits, augmentation benefits may be more difficult to define. However, because many competing industrial products are virtually identical in physical attributes and are purchased to customer specifications, a firm may be able to differentiate its product only by the type of services offered.

Analyzing Customer Costs.   In addition to weighing benefits, organizational customers assess the costs associated with owning and using the product. By applying *life-cycle costing,* a method that calculates the total cost of a purchase over its life span, the buyer evaluates all relevant costs.[5] Maintenance, repair, operating costs, and useful product life are included in life-cycle costing analysis.

Effective cost analysis should also include less obvious costs such as product failure or potential production delays, particularly when these events represent unacceptable risks that customers will pay a price premium to avoid.

[4]Shapiro and Jackson, "Industrial Pricing to Meet Customer Needs," pp. 119–127.
[5]Robert J. Brown, "A New Marketing Tool: Life Cycle Costing," *Industrial Marketing Management* 8 (April 1979), pp. 109–113.

WHY UNITED BOUGHT BOEING'S 720s

One of the primary reasons United Airlines decided to buy Boeing 720s over Convair 880s was that the 720s' lower operating costs per passenger-mile made them a better buy, even though each 880 initially cost $200,000 less. Since United was one of Convair's three primary target customers, their purchase of 720s reduced Convair's market potential from 110 to only eighty planes.

Source: See Richard Austin Smith, "How a Great Corporation Got Out of Control: The Story of General Dynamics, Part II," *Fortune*, February 1962, p. 120.

Price Sensitivity. Product value is related to the buyer's sensitivity to price. Price sensitivity varies with purchasers, over time, and from one set of circumstances to another. For instance, the buyer who can pass on the cost of a purchase (to a subsequent customer) is less likely to be price sensitive than one who cannot. Product price may be less important to engineers than performance variables, less important than reliable delivery to manufacturing personnel, and less important than supplier innovation to top management.

The price of the product in relation to the total cost of producing an end product can also influence a buyer's sensitivity to price, as can the uncertainty that accompanies a switch from a proven source to a new supplier. Therefore, price differences must be significant enough to overcome a buyer's anxieties about product quality, service, and reliability of unknown suppliers before they will switch from a known, dependable source of supply.[6]

The Nature of Derived Demand

Derived demand means that sales to an original equipment manufacturer (OEM) ultimately depend on the level of customer demand for products that the OEM makes. Total quantity demanded by the OEM for component parts, raw material, capital equipment, and ancillary services will increase only as a result of increased purchases by end-product users. Because of the relatively distant relationship between an industrial supplier and ultimate consumer, what was a direct relationship between price and quantity demanded in the consumer market becomes an indirect and often reversed relationship. For the supplier, a number of nonprice contingencies can work to reverse the theoretical price/quantity relationship.

Consider the following scenario. A supplier to a large, quality-oriented OEM reduces price in an attempt to increase its share of business. Instead, its volume declines further. The OEM has had reservations about the supplier's product and sees the price reduction as confirmation of inferiority. Less technically oriented ultimate consumers might not have had the same reservations.

---

[6]Wroe Anderson and Paul E. Green, *Planning and Problem Solving in Marketing* (Homewood, Ill.: Richard D. Irwin, Inc., 1964), pp. 249–251.

BOEING'S 720s HAD TIME-PROVEN ENGINES

One of the reasons that United Airlines chose Boeing's 720 over Convair's 880 was that the 720 had time-proven Pratt & Whitney engines, while the commercial performance of the 880's General Electric engines was "an unknown quantity." United Airlines' technical people were apprehensive, though United's passengers had no such concern. United also opted to purchase from Boeing, the in supplier, while United's customers simply wanted to fly the friendly skies.

Source: Richard Austin Smith, "How a Great Corporation Got Out of Control: The Story of General Dynamics, Part II," *Fortune*, February 1962, p. 120.

Competition

Existing and potential competition inevitably affects pricing strategy by setting an upper limit. Research indicates that "competitive-level pricing" is regarded by the majority of firms as the most important pricing strategy.[7] The amount of latitude a firm has in its pricing decision depends largely on the degree to which it can differentiate its product in the minds of buyers. As previously discussed, price is only one element of the buyer's cost/benefit analysis. A product that is differentiated by its functional design, the supplier's reputation for dependable service, or technical innovation can command a higher price.

Pricing strategy is also influenced by the anticipated reactions of competitors to pricing decisions. In contemplating price changes, therefore, competitive responses must be considered. Price reductions on products that are relatively undifferentiated are generally met immediately by all suppliers, resulting in little shift in market share. However, this is not always the case. Table 16-1 depicts those factors that determine a competitor's ability to react to a price reduction.

Price Leadership.   When initiating price increases, the marketer must predict how competitors will react. A price increase that is not followed by competitors will most likely lead to a loss of market share. For competitors to follow a price increase, they must believe that (1) total demand will not be reduced by the increase, (2) other major suppliers will also follow the increase, and (3) the initiator of the price increase is acting intelligently and in the best interest of all suppliers.

Most major industries are oligopolistic (for example, basic metals, chemicals, glass, automobiles, electronic systems, and machine products). When a firm operates in such an industry and is not a dominant source, it normally cannot induce its major competitors to follow a price increase. On the other hand, a price reduction often brings swift reaction, even an undercutting. Market leaders can usually induce

---

[7]John G. Udell, *Successful Marketing Strategies* (Madison, Wisc.: Mimir Publishers, Inc., 1972), p. 109.

**TABLE 16-1 Factors That Determine a Competitor's Ability
to React to a Price Reduction**

Costs	A major factor affecting competitive reaction to a reduction in price is cost. Where costs are relatively high in comparison to price, lowering price may eliminate profit. Thus, a competitor may respond with aggressive promotional effort rather than a price reduction to maintain market share. In the short run, if variable costs can be covered, price reductions may be met. Knowledge of competitors' costs, therefore, is extremely important. Estimating competitors' cost structures is important not only in gauging their willingness to respond to price reductions or increases, but also in predicting where prices might go in the future.
Time to react	The speed with which competitors can react to a price change influences their ability to respond. In general, competitors can react immediately. However, when a price reduction is made possible by a change in production techniques or product design, competitors may need time to bring about similar changes. When this is true, the short-run impact on the price cutter's sales volume may be substantial.
Existing commitments	Existing commitments to other groups or classes of products may prevent competitors from meeting price changes, particularly when such a move might bring the product in question into competition with similar products in the line. For instance, a price reduction on a "quality" item may cause it to replace a "standard" item. The existence of a substantial unsold inventory will also slow down a competitor's response.
Relative sales volume	A small supplier may be able to reduce price without its larger competitor meeting the price change. The absolute loss in total revenue to the large firm could outweigh the value of the small amount of business to be retained by meeting the price change. Such instances are not unusual in industrial marketing.
Existing operating capacity	When firms are operating at full capacity or have substantial backorders to keep them operating for an extended period, they have little to gain in meeting price reductions. In fact, when market demand taxes existing capacity, firms are more often inclined to increase price.

Source: E. Raymond Corey, *Industrial Marketing: Cases and Concepts,* 2nd ed., Copyright © 1976, pp. 157–178. Adapted by permission of Prentice-Hall, Inc., Englewood Cliffs, N.J.

their competitors to follow both price increases and reductions. Because total demand for industrial goods is often inelastic due to its derived nature, market volume is not increased by price reductions, but an individual firm's market share will certainly suffer unless it remains price competitive.

Price leaders cannot always dictate prices in the market. Since the general price level tends to reflect both supply and demand pressures, leaders have only limited power; however, the price leader does act as the dominant reference point among competing sellers. This does not imply that other firms do not influence price levels.

Smaller firms can develop technologically superior products or innovative marketing programs that impact pricing strategies for all competing firms.

Cost and Profit Relationships

While competition sets the upper limits on price, costs set the lower limits. Therefore, it makes little sense to develop pricing strategy without considering the costs involved. However, many organizations tend to set prices based on their costs alone, adding some acceptable increment for profit. Such an approach does have advantages. First, it is relatively simple to calculate. Second, for a low-cost producer, cost-plus pricing can be a very competitive strategy. The trade-off for such simplicity, however, may be lost profits—profits that are sacrificed due to the difference between what customers are charged and what they would be willing to pay. Cost-plus pricing fails to consider the customer's perception of value, the degree of differentiation from competition, and the interaction of volume and profit. Since costs vary over time and fluctuate with volume, they must be considered in relation to demand, competition, and the market share objectives of the firm. Marketing, production, and distribution costs are all relevant to the pricing decision.

As Table 16-2 indicates, the total cost of a product is made up of multiple elements that react differently to changes in the quantity produced. Properly identifying and classifying these separate costs is an essential step toward making profitable pricing decisions. The marketing manager should determine which costs are volume dependent, which products or markets generate the costs, and where opportunities for additional profits might exist.

When fixed costs make up a large portion of total cost, prices must be set to maximize the use of operating capacity. Until fixed costs are covered, a firm is losing money. Once covered, each incremental sale can contribute to profits. On the other hand, when variable costs are relatively high, pricing to maximize the contribution margin (selling price minus variable costs) is crucial to profitability. Break-even analysis, a method of determining quantity levels of production that are necessary to cover fixed and variable costs, is discussed in Chapter Seventeen.

Under certain conditions, a firm may elect to price at less than full cost (that is, not counting those costs, direct and indirect, that are traceable to a particular activity). For example, during a recession a firm with high fixed costs may set price to cover variable costs and make some contribution to fixed costs to keep its plant in operation. This is often called "survival" pricing. Such pricing strategy may also be used in the short run to secure an exceptionally large order, to penetrate a specific customer, or to gain market share. In these instances, it is "preemptive" or "predatory" pricing, and may be illegal. If an irate competitor were to allege, and subsequently prove in court, that the price cutter's primary purpose was the reduction of competition, the offending firm could be found in violation of the Sherman Antitrust Act, the Clayton Act, and/or the Robinson-Patman Act (depending on the exact nature of the preemptive pricing).

Over the short run, when a firm has excess capacity, management tends to

TABLE 16-2 Cost Classifications

Fixed costs	Costs that remain constant over a reasonable range of output. Rent, insurance payments, and managerial salaries are typical examples. As volume increases, the average fixed cost per unit will decrease, since the total cost is being spread over a greater unit volume.
Variable costs	Costs that fluctuate in direct proportion to the level of output. Production materials and direct labor fall in this category. The average variable cost per unit is usually quite high for the first few units produced. As production and marketing efficiencies increase, the variable cost per unit declines, eventually reaching a low point, which indicates the optimal production level from the standpoint of costs. Beyond the optimal volume point, variable cost per unit will again rise as inefficiencies develop.
Semivariable costs	Costs that fluctuate with changes in output but not in direct proportion to quantities produced. These costs have both a fixed and a variable component. Equipment repair and maintenance costs are typical examples.
Direct costs	Fixed and variable costs that are directly related to a specific product or market (e.g., advertising, selling expense, and freight).
Indirect costs	Fixed or variable costs that can be associated with and indirectly assigned to a product or market. Production overhead, quality control, and customer service are usually considered indirect costs.
Allocated costs	Costs that support a number of activities but cannot be objectively assigned to a specific product or market. These costs are usually allocated across business segments by some arbitrary criterion such as sales volume or generated work load. Administrative overhead, institutional advertising, and corporate legal expenses are allocated costs.
Sunk costs	The costs of resources already acquired whose total will be unaffected by alternative decisions.

ignore allocated costs so long as the pricing received for an additional order covers more than its direct cost and makes a contribution to overhead. However, over the long run, all costs must be covered if the firm is to survive. The industrial firm that views its costs in these various categories adds increased dimensions and valuable new perspectives to its decision making.

Marginal Costs and Revenue. To develop a profitable pricing strategy, the price setter must also understand the concept of marginal revenue and cost. Theoretically, the firm should continue to increase sales and production volume as long as the total cost of producing the last unit does not exceed its selling price. (Remember, as discussed in Table 16-2, that the variable component of unit cost will bottom out at some volume level and then begin to rise, sometimes rather steeply, due to decreased efficiencies.) In practice, it can be quite difficult to determine actual cost trend lines, as opposed to spurious aberrations, and even more difficult to maintain sales at the optimum level. Moreover, the marginality theory must be balanced against the learning curve concept, which holds that the firm's variable costs will decline as quickly (or as slowly) as total volume accumulates. If the firm forsakes business opportunities based on current costs, and these opportunities are seized by a more aggressive competitor (whose current costs might be equal), the competitor will drive its costs down more quickly and eventually be in a position to command industry pricing—and profits. This subject is discussed further under "Cost Behavior over Time."

Estimating Cost.   Price setters can use two different sources of information in estimating costs: accounting records plus engineering and manufacturing estimates. Accounting records on cost are useful where past experience can be applied to the pricing decision. Engineering and manufacturing estimates are used when no cost precedent exists. Based on knowledge of the production technology involved and the product specifications set by engineering, cost estimators determine the optimal input combinations to produce any given output. Costs are then formulated by multiplying each input by its price. Engineering estimates are very useful for determining the costs of new products where historical data necessary for statistical cost analysis are unavailable.[8]

If enough information can be gathered via historical records, multiple regression analysis can be used to aid the estimation process. This approach is particularly useful when products share production and/or marketing costs. Once the total-cost function has been estimated, then marginal cost, the cost influence of order size or multiple product mix, and other factors can be extrapolated. Importantly, total-cost curves for the construction of break-even charts can be determined.[9]

Cost Analysis

The cost of producing and distributing a product establishes the floor for the contemplated price. If these costs are not at least covered, losses will be incurred. But which costs should the price setter consider? We have already discussed that fixed

---

GENERAL DYNAMICS WENT FOR DOUBLE OR NOTHING

General Dynamics' Convair Division, attempting to overcome losses on the 880 jet series, went "for double-or-nothing" by signing an ill-fated contract to build twenty five long-range 990 series jets for American Airlines. "Yet nobody knew how much it [990] would cost because its costs were figured on those of the 880, which were still on the rise and unpredictable."

Source: See Richard Austin Smith, "How a Great Corporation Got Out of Control: The Story of General Dynamics, Part II," *Fortune*, February 1962, p. 120.

---

[8]Kristian S. Palda, *Pricing Decisions and Marketing Policy* (Englewood Cliffs, N.J.: Prentice-Hall, Inc., 1971). Chap. 2.

[9]Ibid., pp. 16-23.

and variable costs are the major concerns, but the specific type and level of cost to be used as the basis for unit price is subject to change, depending upon the situation under which price is to be determined. Therefore, care must be exercised to ensure that relevant costs are considered, that is, those costs that bear directly upon the decision at hand. Perhaps an example will show how such costs change and exemplify the concept of relevant costs.[10]

Assume that a manufacturer is contemplating the development, production, and sale of a thermoforming mold (a mold used to make plastic containers). We will call the firm Thermo-Molds, Inc. (or TMI, for short). The proposed addition to the existing line will require the purchase of new production machinery as well as the hiring of a production supervisor, several semiskilled machine operators, and one more salesperson to call on distributors. Since there is executive slack, no addition to the TMI management core is foreseen—a situation that would change if yearly volume exceeds 150,000 units. The firm will spend $50,000 to promote the product in various trade magazines, and it will spend $10,000 training the production supervisor and salesperson. Table 16-3 shows the purchase of new machinery for $120,000, plus the promotion and training costs, or a total investment of $180,000 to be written off by straight-line depreciation over a five-year period at $36,000 a year. (The discrepancy between this approach and standard accounting procedures will be discussed later.) Table 16-4 shows the fixed expenses, direct and indirect, as well as the variable expenses per unit for estimated yearly volumes of 75,000, 100,000, and 150,000.

An examination of Table 16-4 raises the question of which is the appropriate unit cost to use as a floor for the price: $2.27, $1.94, or $1.60? Obviously, there is no single, "natural" cost. Cost depends on the predicted volume of sales, and this volume accumulated over time will, per the learning curve, result in still lower costs. However, predicting the sales volume is only one of three basic difficulties encountered in determining a relevant cost for pricing purposes.

Another difficulty is the estimation of variable and semivariable costs as a function of volume. Although Table 16-4 shows these costs to be constant between 75,000 and 150,000 units per year (roughly 6,000 to 12,000 per month), variable costs are not constant over the full range of output, but first decline, then reach a

TABLE 16-3 Capital Investment

New machinery	$120,000
Initial promotional expense	50,000
Training of supervisor	5,000
Training of sales people	5,000
Total investment	$180,000

[10]Ibid.

TABLE 16-4 Unit Costs at Yearly Volumes of:

	75,000	100,000	150,000
Fixed expense			
Supervisor's salary	$ .26	$ .20	$ .13
Salesperson's salary	.20	.15	.10
Tax and insurance	.03	.02	.01
Depreciation	.48	.36	.24
Cost of capital	.36	.27	.18
Total fixed unit cost	$1.33	$1.00	$ .66
Variable expenses			
Direct labor	$ .45	$ .45	$ .45
Direct materials	.35	.35	.35
Factory supplies	.05	.05	.05
Inventory carrying charges	.09	.09	.09
Total variable unit cost	$ .94	$ .94	$ .94
Average total unit cost	$2.27	$1.94	$1.60

low point, and finally increase as output is expanded (the U-shaped economy-of-scale curve). Figure 16-2 displays this phenomenon.

A third difficulty in attempting to determine relevant cost involves the inclusion or exclusion of certain cost items. Should "depreciation" include noncapital items, and should "cost of capital" be included as we have done in Table 16-4? In our TMI example, total investments amounted to $180,000. To raise these funds, investors or lenders must receive a return on their investment—either through dividends or interest. Assuming a 15 percent rate of return, as was done in Table 16-4, the cost of capital is $27,000 ($180,000 × .15), or 36, 27, and 18 cents per unit at the three production levels.

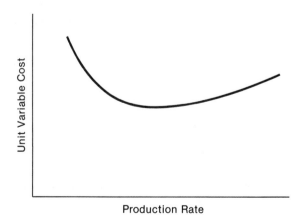

Production Rate

FIGURE 16-2   Economies of Scale

Consider also the promotional expense and training cost that were included in Table 16-3. The accountants at TMI would not capitalize such expenses, holding that only tangible assets should be included. However, the interest and goodwill that the promotion creates with distributors continues to bring in revenues over the long run just as the machines do. The cost of training invested in "human capital" also produces returns over the long run. Therefore, these investments should be treated as depreciation charges to provide a better estimate of the true profitability of the project, even though they may not be entered in the legal accounts of the firm.

Whether fixed costs should be included in the pricing decision depends on the situation under consideration. Suppose that TMI is successfully marketing the molds at an annual rate approaching 100,000 units for an average price of $2.85, and sales begin to fall off. If the opportunity arose to sell an additional 20,000 units to a foreign buyer for $1.35 each, should the offer be accepted? The answer lies in an analysis of fixed and variable costs. Fixed costs will exist whether or not this particular order is accepted. If the variable costs associated with the order are covered, any excess revenue can be applied to fixed costs, thereby increasing net profits (or decreasing net losses if the firm is currently unprofitable). The contribution margin (i.e., sales revenue minus variable costs) of the proposed offer is

20,000 units at $1.35	$27,000	
Less: Total variable cost	18,800	[@ $.94/unit]
Contribution margin	$ 8,200	

In the TMI example, the price decision centers around the introduction of a new product. Unless the firm expects to recover all costs incurred, including fixed costs, there is no point in going through with product development. None of the costs should be incurred. Thus, in the long run, all the costs are variable in the sense that all can be avoided or incurred. But in ongoing, short-run situations, fixed costs will be incurred whether or not a particular decision is made. For example, a decision to increase plant capacity would involve the variable costs of doing so, while the fixed costs of the existing plant would be unaffected by the decision. Thus, the test of cost relevance hinges on whether the cost changes with the contemplated decision. If it does, it should be included as a cost that is relevant to the pricing decision.

Cost Behavior over Time: The Learning Curve

The "learning curve" (or "experience curve" as some prefer to call it) has become one of the most researched and analyzed strategic concepts since it was originally championed by the Boston Consulting Group in 1972.[11] One research team states that few strategic concepts have gained wider acceptance than the notion underlying the experience curve, that value-added costs (excluding inflation) decline systemati-

[11]Staff of the Boston Consulting Group, *Perspectives on Experience*, (Boston: Boston Consulting Group, Inc., 1972).

cally with increases in cumulative volume.[12] Another researcher says it has become a central concept in corporate strategic planning.[13] Even an avowed critic accepts the basic concept of production volume rising and costs falling concurrently, while rejecting the idea that the former is the primary cause of the latter.[14] Another critic feels that there are a number of circumstances under which an aggressive pricing strategy based on the learning curve would be doomed to failure.[15] In short, there is an ongoing debate as to whether the learning curve (L-C) is a valuable strategic tool or a flawed source of misdirection.

The Basic Concept. Before considering the opposing schools of thought, we should have a more precise definition of the learning curve. The phenomenon was first recognized in the early 1950s by Boeing. They discovered that the number of hours required to build aircraft decreased about twenty percent each time cumulative production doubled. Many other firms that have actively employed the L-C concept (including General Motors, General Electric, IBM, and Texas Instruments) found that not only did labor hours decrease, but other volume-related cost factors (scrap materials, defective parts, machine down-time, procurement costs, distribution costs, and even marketing expenses) decreased as well. The Boston Consulting Group found similar results in such diverse industries as chemicals, paper, steel, electronics, knitwear, and mechanical goods.

Hence, it was postulated that variable or volume-dependent costs (in constant dollars) decline by a predictable and constant percentage each time cumulative volume is doubled. This percentage will vary among product categories from ten to thirty percent, with fifteen to twenty percent the most common range. It might be noted that one of the authors, while utilizing the L-C concept to make some very effective and profitable pricing decisions, witnessed a reasonably constant decline in variable costs of a semiconductor product line from a cumulative volume of less than 100,000 units to more than a billion. This increase took place over a multi-year period and represented a doubling of cumulative volume more than thirteen times!

Important Distinctions. Three additional points should be emphasized. First, the learning curve is a volume-dependent, not a time-dependent, phenomenon. Thus, as a product line matures, it takes longer to realize any given percentage of cost reduction. This has led some to erroneously surmise that the *rate of cost reduction* declines. This is not so. It simply takes longer to achieve the same ten, fifteen, or twenty percent reduction. Second, the cost savings are definitely not limited to the

---

[12]George S. Day and David B. Montgomery, "Diagnosing the Experience Curve", *Journal of Marketing* 47 (Spring 1983), pp. 44–58.

[13]Marvin B. Lieberman, "The Learning Curve, Diffusion, and Competitive Strategy," *Strategic Management Journal* 8 (September 1987), pp. 441–452.

[14]William W. Alberts, "The Experience Curve Doctrine Reconsidered," *Journal of Marketing* 53 (July 1989), pp. 36–49.

[15]Thomas T. Nagle, *The Strategy and Tactics of Pricing*, (Englewood Cliffs, N.J.: Prentice-Hall, Inc., 1987), pp. 225–227.

production process. Managerial decision making, product and process designs, and distribution systems, as well as marketing programs and tactics, can all become more cost effective. Third, the L-C concept is not the same as "economies of scale." It deals with the accumulation of quantity over time and is independent of the rate of production. In effect, it shows the evolution of variable costs. Contrariwise, economies of scale show the impact that different levels of production have on unit costs at a specific time.

Figure 16-3 should help clarify this last point. Curves A, B, and C each show a variation of unit costs over a range of production rates (hypothetically, from one hundred to one thousand units per week). Curve A shows the level of these costs after a cumulative output of 10,000 units. Curve B spans the same range of production rates, but shows how the entire curve falls after cumulative output reaches 20,000 units (double the level for curve A). How many weeks were required to reach this cumulative quantity is irrelevant. Curve C repeats the story after 40,000 units, or double the level of curve B. In short, the shape of the curve shows the impact of production rates while the distance between the curves shows the impact of learning or experience.

Strategic Use of the Learning Curve. The learning curve is frequently considered in conjunction with a market penetration strategy. An industrial firm, aiming for a dominant position in a new product-market segment, adopts an aggressive pricing

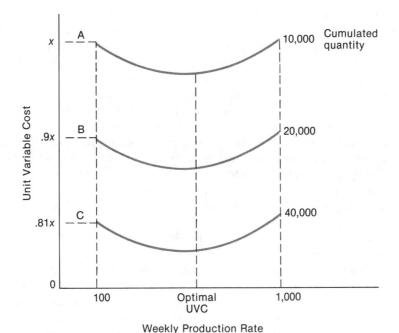

FIGURE 16-3 Learning Curve Impact on Economies of Scale

policy. Theoretically, this price will speed up market growth as well as discourage some potential competitors from entering the market. However, it is fallacious to assume that all firms utilizing the L-C concept as a strategic tool do so in the form of predatory pricing.

If a firm feels confident that the target market will grow at a satisfactory rate and its position in this market will be strong without aggressive pricing, the L-C cost reductions can be used for other desirable purposes:

1. to cover sunk costs more quickly
2. to enhance marketing efforts in this market
3. to develop new market opportunities
4. to increase R&D expenditures
5. to raise needed working capital
6. to expand production capacity

It is also important to remember that an effective pricing strategy, as we discussed earlier in this chapter, must be based on external factors in addition to costs. The ratio of demand to supply, the number and strength of competitors, the relative impact of pricing on derived demand, and the ability of the product to satisfy market needs must all be part of the pricing decision. Firms that myopically base their pricing solely on costs plus some magic multiplier rarely survive in today's competitive international markets.

The Current Debate. Part of the controversy regarding the usefulness and reality of the learning curve stems from the problem researchers face in trying to develop empirical evidence, either pro or con. It is extremely difficult to obtain detailed data on volume-cost relationships for specific products from individual firms. Most firms guard such data very closely and will not reveal it to anyone without proof of "a need to know." Consequently, most research must be based on "substitute" information, either industry- or firm-specific prices or computer-simulated cost data.

Industry-wide data is of very little value for several reasons. Published price schedules bear little relationship to the prices negotiated on major contracts. Various competitors operate under different pricing strategies. So-called "average prices" usually refer to a relatively heterogeneous mix of products. And, as discussed above, there is no automatic relationship between price and current costs. The last point alone makes the analysis of individual firms, without their explicit cooperation, rather questionable.

Barring specific product-firm volume and cost data, one is left with the apparent consistency of price-volume trends across a wide variety of American industries. During the 1980s, Japanese manufacturers have provided rather clear evidence that they, too, recognize and use the L-C concept. When asked about the apparent "dumping" of memory chips by Japanese producers, Paul Ely, president of Convergent Technologies, said, "We don't have any right to complain about the Japanese companies using tactics [such as learning-curve pricing] that we invented." Unfortunately for American producers, the Japanese can use these tactics even more effectively because they run their manufacturing operations far more efficiently. This leads us to a significant factor associated with the L-C concept.

Opportunities Must Be Capitalized. In rebutting what he terms the "experience curve doctrine," Alberts makes several incisive and accurate observations:

1. innovations (involving the operator, management, and processes) are a significant source of cost reductions
2. most innovations do not "just pop up" as the result of volume increases, but must be made to happen by a perceptive management
3. the degree to which opportunities for innovation are recognized and exploited within the firm depends on:
    a. volition (desire to innovate),
    b. imaginativeness (creative intelligence),
    c. drive (ability to pursue goals effectively).[16]

Whether these observations rebut the L-C concept or simply add a very important qualification is less important than the caveat they present to managers. We believe it is a reasonable paraphrase to say that learning or experience makes it easier to spot opportunities, but like the horse led to water, the firm and its managers must want to seize the opportunity. As we discussed in Chapter 10, the Japanese provide an excellent example of this issue. In countless instances, they have taken products that were invented elsewhere and, by innovating the product, the process, or the marketing strategy, have gained market dominance. The originating firm had equal, if not greater, opportunity to innovate but failed to do so. While we debate strategic concepts, international competitors are capitalizing on them.

When this topic was initially covered in Chapter 10, we emphasized that price should be one of the critical design criteria for any new product. A firm with the proper market orientation will determine what customers want in terms of product performance, as well as the price they are willing to pay, *before* it begins the physical development phase of the new product development process. A target resale price then dictates the upper acceptable limit for costs, rather than costs being allowed to fall where they may, resulting in a resale price well beyond the market's willingness to pay.

Many industrial products that fail because of uncompetitive pricing are not the result of inferior engineering design or inefficient production techniques. Instead, either the marketing department does not specify price-performance relationships or the input is ignored. As a consequence, the value perceptions of customers are essentially omitted from the design equation. High-technology firms that place undue emphasis on a product's physical attributes are particularly prone to make this fatal mistake.

---

[16]Alberts, "The Experience Curve Doctrine Reconsidered," p. 41.

Government Influences

Government's primary influence on pricing strategy is in the area of legislation. Sections 1 and 2 of the Sherman Antitrust Act specifically forbid agreements among suppliers to fix prices in industry. Violators of this act may be fined, imprisoned, or both, in addition to having to pay treble damages to injured parties. The Clayton Antitrust Act (Section 2) and the Robinson-Patman Act also prohibit price discrimination among similar buyers of identical products. Section 2(a) through 2(f) of the Robinson-Patman Act specifically relate to price differences and price concessions being offered to competing manufacturers and distributors.

Pricing to drive out competition, geographic price discrimination, and general price discrimination are also prohibited by the Bonah-Van Nuys Amendment, Section 3, of the Robinson-Patman Act. The widespread use of discounts and rebates in the industrial market, therefore, dictates that marketing managers be well aware of these acts in establishing list and net pricing strategy.

PRICING STRATEGIES

Pricing strategies must be conceived in relation to overall business objectives and marketing strategy. The success of any business depends on a blend of long-run profit, growth, and survival objectives. Price, because of its influence on unit sales volume and profit margins, affects long-run profit objectives. By contributing to a positive cash flow, price helps to finance growth objectives. And maintaining profitability through sound pricing practices is necessary to ensure the firm's survival over time. It should be recognized, however, that a diversified firm with multiple product lines can have several pricing strategies in operation at one time. They must be consistent with one another as well as with overall marketing strategy.

New Product Introduction

Activities associated with the development and marketing of a new product (research, planning, testing, and market introduction) represent a substantial investment that the firm must eventually recover. How fast a firm should attempt to recover its investment, however, depends on the nature of the product and its projected life span, the strength of potential competition, the type of demand, and the financial strength of the company. Generally, two broad strategies are available in pricing a new product: (1) market skimming—setting an artificially high price that the market will not be able to sustain in the long run—and (2) market penetration—setting price at or near the level it would eventually reach after competition developed.[17]

---

[17]Joel Dean, "Pricing Policies for New Products," *Harvard Business Review*, November 1980, pp. 45–53. See also: David V. Lamm and Lawrence C. Vose, "Seller Pricing Strategies: A Buyer's Perspective," *Journal of Purchasing and Materials Management* 24 (Fall 1988), pp. 9–13.

Market Skimming Strategy. A market skimming strategy, charging an artifically high price and then gradually reducing it over time, has the advantage of generating greater profits per unit earlier than would be possible with a lower price. If development and marketing costs can be recovered before competitors enter, surplus earnings can be used for product improvement and expansion into large-volume markets, thus reducing the average cost of producing. Unless late-arriving competitors achieve a real breakthrough in product design or processing, they will be at a cost disadvantage relative to the innovative firm.

The greatest disadvantage to market skimming is that the high margins attract competition. A firm that has a successful price skimming strategy can expect competitors to introduce similar products. Therefore, skimming is more effective when the product has strong patent protection, or other barriers to market entry exist, such as complex technology or high capital requirements. Other conditions that favor price skimming are listed in Table 16-5.

Market Penetration Strategy. Penetration pricing is based on the assumption that demand for the product is highly elastic. By setting a relatively low price, the firm hopes to stimulate market growth and capture a large share of it. The advantage is that penetration pricing tends to discourage competition, because there is less opportunity to reap an unusually high return on investment. Penetration pricing may also be used to achieve economies of scale. By seeking a dominant market share, a firm may increase both its scale and efficiency of operation, realizing lower production costs than competitors—by moving down the learning curve more quickly—and, thus, greater potential profits.

There are, however, two primary disadvantages to penetration pricing. First, a larger volume must be sold before start-up costs are recovered. Thus, short-run profits are sacrificed to gain market share and long-run profits. Second, although the absolute magnitude of profits could be higher than that realized with a skimming strategy, the profit ratios (the return on assets or investment, or the profit on sales) could be lower. Firms that judge their success on these ratios will be reluctant to use a penetration strategy. Conditions favorable to penetration pricing are outlined in Table 16-6.

Skimming and penetration pricing strategies are only guides and cannot be applied in all situations. Some situations will require that an intermediate price be

TABLE 16-5 Conditions Favoring Price Skimming

1. Product has a strong patent protection or other barriers to market entry.
2. Genuine product innovation that is likely to represent substantial value to potential users.
3. Buyers who are willing to pay a premium to enjoy the product's benefits.
4. A relatively short life span, so that a quick recovery of investment is essential.
5. Potential competitors are relatively weak or distant in time.
6. Uncertainty concerning the market's price sensitivity. Should the initial price prove to be in error, the firm can always lower price, whereas a low price may be difficult to raise.

TABLE 16-6 Conditions Favorable to Penetration Pricing

1. The market appears to be highly price sensitive.
2. Unit cost of production and distribution fall with accumulated output.
3. Strong potential competitors exist who are seeking new profitable ventures.
4. The firm's primary goal is significant market share rather than maximized short-term profits.
5. The product has hidden or subtle benefits that will become obvious only after use.
6. The sale of complementary products will also increase.

set, somewhere between a high or low initial price. The choice of an appropriate pricing strategy for new products is dependent upon the firm's objectives, the relevant customer segments, the impact of price on the actions of present and future competition, cost considerations, and appropriate distribution strategies.

Product Life-Cycle Considerations

During the course of an industrial product's life cycle, the competitive situation and market demand level will vary greatly. The product itself, along with promotion and distribution, must change accordingly. In like manner, for price to remain an effective marketing tool, it must be constantly monitored and adjusted when appropriate.[18]

Growth. During the product growth stage, when more customers develop a use for the product and competitors are able to offer substitutes, price will take on more importance in the purchasing decision. However, in an expanding market, suppliers tend to emphasize nonprice factors as their primary selling points. The exceptions are those firms dedicated to the learning curve concept and desirous of achieving a dominant market share. During this stage the desire for multiple sources of supply by industrial buyers will cut into the innovator's volume. In general, the price in this stage falls below the introductory level.

Maturity. By the time a product enters the maturity stage, the level of competition has peaked, and product differentiation is minimal. Consequently, although buyers will still insist on product quality and service dependability, price considerations will heavily influence their buying decisions. And since a supplier can increase volume in a flat market only by cutting into the market share of competitors, price wars become commonplace.

Decline. Since many competitors will have already left the market, particularly those with heavy emphasis on growth strategies, the decline stage *can* be a fairly

[18]Richard M. Hill, Ralph S. Alexander, and James S. Cross, *Industrial Marketing*, 4th ed. (Homewood, Ill.: Richard D. Irwin, Inc., 1975), pp. 209–210. See also Nagle, *The Strategy and Tactics of Pricing*, pp. 144–152.

profitable one for the remaining suppliers. Assuming a firm has developed a very positive image by providing a quality product, competitively priced, dependably shipped, and consistently serviced, there is no reason why profits must erode completely in the decline stage. Industrial firms, both sellers and buyers, realize the necessary relationship between production volumes and incurred costs. Within reason, the well-accepted firm can increase prices during the decline stage and maintain an acceptable profit level, as long as some segments of the market continue to feel a need for the product and will adjust their value perceptions to match the required selling price.

Flexible Pricing Strategy

In the past, the pricing structure of most large industrial firms has been rather rigid. Price was established by adding a traditional markup to costs, by following the industrial leader, or by aiming for some predetermined return on investment. However, since the early 1970s, American firms have faced a pricing environment that included several recessionary periods, price controls introduced by President Nixon, double-digit inflation, stagnant demand, and intense competition from abroad.

The need to adapt to such a dynamic environment has brought about flexibility in pricing and a willingness to cut prices aggressively to hold market share. Smaller firms are not consistently willing to play "follow the price leader." On the contrary, many smaller companies have successfully undercut the price leader. For example, when Owens-Illinois, a giant in the glass container industry, attempted to raise beer bottle prices 4.5 percent in May 1980, its smaller competitors won orders from major brewers by offering volume discounts.[19]

Flexible pricing strategy, that is, the willingness to adjust prices or profit margins on specific products when market conditions change, is now common in industrial marketing. However, price flexibility does not always mean a change in list prices. Escalator clauses to protect against inflation, quantity discounts to entice major users, and emphasis on nonprice factors can each contribute to strategic flexibility.

PRICING POLICIES

Because industrial products are sold to different types of customers who buy in different quantities and are located in different geographical regions, pricing policies involve adjustments to the base price to account for these differences. The most important price to organizational buyers is the net price. Net price refers to the list price less allowances for various cost-significant concessions made by the buyer, such as volume purchases. List price is the published figure distributed to all customers, regardless of their type or classification. List pricing is used by manufac-

[19]*Business Week* (September 21, 1984), p. 109.

turers for two primary reasons. First, the many products that are described in a catalog preclude the printing of a new catalog each time the price of one or more items is adjusted. Second, list pricing provides a common base from which a wide variety of discounts can be subtracted.

Discount Pricing

Discount pricing involves a deduction from the published price list to (1) account for the cost and benefits of dealing with different classifications of customers, (2) encourage customers to buy in large volumes, and (3) encourage rapid payment by customers.

Trade Discounts.   Trade discounts are used by manufacturers to account for benefits derived from dealing with various groups of customers or middlemen. Discounts afforded to distributors should cover the operating costs they incur in providing sales effort and associated services (local inventory, customer credit, and technical support) and allow them a reasonable profit margin. Discounts to OEMs can be justified on the basis of their high-volume purchasing and lower marketing expense/ sales ratio. In establishing trade discounts, however, care must be taken. A variance in discounts given to basically the same types of customers can amount to price discrimination, a violation of the Robinson-Patman Act. Trade discounts, therefore, must be nondiscriminatory and cost-justified, with a reasonable trade-off for the benefits they induce.

Quantity Discounts.[20]   To encourage volume purchasing and maintain buyer loyalty, quantity discounts are given for the volume of goods purchased either on individual orders or a series of orders over a longer period of time, usually one year. These discounts are termed noncumulative and cumulative, respectively. Cumulative discounts have the effect of "locking in" a customer's purchases for an extended period, thus reducing both marketing expense and competitive pressure, while providing a smoother, more cost-effective production flow. Noncumulative discounts tend to encourage larger individual orders, which reduce costs of storage, order processing, and delivery for the seller.
  So long as quantity discounts are available to all customers and are cost-justified, they do not constitute a violation of the Robinson-Patman Act. However, if the discount granted is not equal to or less than the savings gained by doing business on the increased quantity, both buyer and seller can be charged with violation of the act.

Cash Discounts.   To encourage rapid payment and allow for a better cash flow, cash discounts are typically granted in the industrial market. A discount of 2/10,

---

[20]Hill, Alexander, and Cross, *Industrial Marketing*, pp. 332–334. See also Kent B. Monroe, *Pricing: Making Profitable Decisions* (New York: McGraw-Hill, Inc., 1979), pp. 172–178.

net thirty results in the customer deducting two percent if payment is made within ten days of the invoice date; otherwise, the gross bill is due and payable within thirty days. Cash discounts, however, can present a problem for the marketer when large buyers pay their bills well beyond the ten-day period, but still deduct the cash discount. This practice is especially prevalent during periods of high interest rates. Whether a marketer can correct this problem depends on the power of the firm in the buyer-seller relationship. The Robinson-Patman Act compounds the problem by stipulating that the same terms must be offered to all buyers, large and small.

Geographical Pricing

Geographical factors are an important concern in pricing decisions because shipping costs may impact the ultimate price to be paid by buyers and the ability of the selling firm to remain competitive in discount markets. Thus, decisions must be made on how these costs will figure into the overall price structure the firm uses.

Basically, the selling firm has three options in handling shipping costs. These are described in Table 16-7. When the seller concentrates on local markets or sells products wherein shipping charges are minimal compared to product value (precious metals and microprocessors), these costs are a minor issue. However, unlike consumers buying at various local retailers, industrial buyers are often involved with multiple suppliers located at various distances from the delivery point. Moreover, many products (basic metals, unsophisticated capital equipment, and shelving) have a high weight-to-value ratio so that shipping charges are a significant part of the combined product-transportation cost.

The seller must weight the importance of covering costs, by passing them on to the customer, against the need to be competitive in distant target markets. If there

TABLE 16-7 Alternative Means of Handling Shipping Costs

F.o.b. Factory. Buyer selects mode of transportation and pays all costs. Seller's invoice price is the same to all customers, regardless of distance. However, more distant customers have a higher total product cost because of transportation charges.

F.o.b. Destination or Uniform-Delivered Pricing. Seller ships via the most economical mode but absorbs all of the shipping charges. [Buyer can dictate a premium mode but will pay the difference in charges.] Both the invoice price and total product cost are the same for all customers. Since the seller's potential profits are reduced by absorbing these added costs, this is not a viable pricing strategy when the cost per unit shipped is significant in relation to product price. Uniform-delivered pricing is legal as long as all customers are charged the same product price for like quantity and quality.

Freight-Absorption Pricing. Seller absorbs a portion of the transportation charges to distant markets depending on the competitive environment. Seller evaluates the strength of important competitors in specific markets, the charges they levy based on distance/cost factors, and acts accordingly. The magic phrase in this strategic approach is "Ok to meet, but can't beat" competition. This allows the seller to stay within the legal boundaries of the Robinson-Patman Act.

is a significant product differentiation, the seller may gamble that buyers will ignore a difference in shipping charges. In the case of basic commodities with little or no difference from competition, however, this gamble could be foolhardy.

PRICING FOR PROFITS

Although some critics would argue to the contrary,[21] the goal of most business organizations is to maximize long-term profits.

> Profit maximization has many dimensions, and one of the most important of these is time. The firm must decide when to realize profits. Maximizing current-period profits is seldom the same as maximizing the present discounted value of a stream of profits over time. If a firm discounts future profits at a very high rate, then the firm's managers will choose to wring the highest possible profits out of the market in the current period, perhaps by a policy that emphasizes high product prices in price-inelastic markets. Such a policy will induce entry by competitors and will reduce profits in future time periods. Alternatively, a longer time horizon and lower discount rate will often lead to a policy of greater market penetration and lower prices. This strategy will not maximize current-period profits, but can increase the size of the future profit stream and discourage potential competitors. Which strategy the firm chooses will depend upon management's beliefs regarding the magnitude and regularity of future profits as well as upon the firm's rate of discount.[22]

Pricing decisions, then, are influenced by both short-term conditions and possible long-term consequences. For instance, should the price of a new product be set at a level high enough to attract competitors into the market, potential profits over the long run could be considerably less than if the price had been set lower to accelerate growth and discourage competition. On the other hand, pricing decisions are often influenced by the need to achieve an early payback of the firm's product development costs, and this short-term goal takes precedence over any longer-term considerations. This is particularly true when the product's lifetime is unpredictable or of estimated short duration.

Pricing decisions, however, cannot rest on demand and cost relationships, product line considerations, or long-term profit goals alone. They must also support the firm's marketing objectives and correlate with any unique market situations that may exist (for example, price leadership patterns, reciprocity relationships with major customers, and the bargaining power of oligopsonistic buyers).

Clearly, it is not always possible to analyze all the variables affecting the pricing decision. It is essential, therefore, to determine which variables are most important to the particular decision at hand and then analyze and respond to these. Thus, pricing decisions depend as much on the price setter's ability to extract qualitative and quantitative information as on the use of sophisticated statistical techniques.

---

[21]James V. Koch, *Industrial Organization and Pricing* (Englewood Cliffs, N.J.: Prentice-Hall, Inc., 1974), Chap. 3.

[22]Ibid., p. 46.

While specific, quantitative solutions should be sought—the price setter is often "forced to rely heavily on rough data, broad impressions, and logic rather than on numerical computations."[23] The risks involved, however, in pricing without carefully studying the interrelation of demand, costs, and competition can be disastrous, particularly in the pricing of new products. Such a situation appears to have contributed substantially to the estimated $425 million loss incurred by General Dynamics in the ill-fated Convair 880 and 990 jet series.[24] Thus, while the price of a particular product or service, given the competitive situation, cannot exceed the value of its benefit to the buyer, neither can it fall below the cost to the seller.

LOOKING BACK

Price setting in today's environment calls for a proactive approach to pricing. Industrial marketers must base pricing decisions on current market information, monitor competitor and customer responses, and carefully analyze their pricing decisions.

Profitable pricing decisions, however, rest on a clear understanding of two important variables, cost and demand. Cost is a function of demand, and that demand is a function of the customer's "perceived value" of the product. Thus, in setting price, the firm cannot ignore costs and profits, but the market-oriented firm will have a target price driving costs rather than costs driving price. This is true not only when establishing price for the first time, but throughout the life of the product. In addition, costs will change over the product life cycle, as will customer demand and competitive pressures. Hence, marketers must anticipate the changing role and importance of price.

While price is a prime determinant of the manufacturer's profit, it also impacts the profit margins and commissions of middlemen. Manufacturers cannot ignore the functions performed on their behalf by middlemen or fail to compensate for them adequately.

Because the success of any business depends on the attainment of long-run profit objectives, which are directly influenced by price, pricing strategies must be viewed as more than just part of the marketing mix. They are the financial framework for the firm's overall business objective.

QUESTIONS FOR DISCUSSION

1. Of all the factors that influence pricing strategy, which ones do you consider the most important? How would they impact the setting of price?
2. What factors make it difficult for competitors to react to a price change?
3. The proper identification of costs is the first step toward making a profitable pricing decision. Do you agree or disagree with that statement? Explain your answer.

[23]Alfred R. Oxenfelt, *Pricing Strategies* (New York: AMACOM, 1975), p. 15.

[24]Richard Austin Smith, "How a Great Corporation Got Out of Control: The Story of General Dynamics, Part II," *Fortune* (February 1962), p. 120.

4. How does the learning curve concept influence the setting of price?
5. Discuss the various ways a manufacturer's pricing strategy can impact an industrial distributor.
6. In introducing a new product, price may be set high or low. Under what circumstances should price be set high? When should it be set low?
7. Price should only be changed as a reactionary measure. Do you agree with that statement? If so, why? If not, how would you inititate a proactive pricing strategy?
8. What factors make it difficult to determine cost?
9. Do you agree that the cost of capital (interest on borrowed funds) is a part of the product cost?

SUGGESTED ADDITIONAL READINGS

ALBERTS, WILLIAM W., "The Experience Curve Doctrine Reconsidered," *Journal of Marketing*, 53 (July 1989): 36–49.

BROWN, ROBERT J., "A New Marketing Tool: Life Cycle Costing," *Industrial Marketing Management* 8 (April 1979): 109–113.

DAY, GEORGE S., and DAVID B. MONTGOMERY, "Diagnosing the Experience Curve", *Journal of Marketing* 47 (Spring 1983): 44–58.

KOCH, JAMES V., *Industrial Organization and Prices* (Englewood Cliffs, N.J.: Prentice-Hall, Inc., 1974).

LIEBERMAN, MARVIN, B., "The Learning Curve, Diffusion, and Competitive Strategy," *Strategic Management Journal* 8 (September 1987): 441–452.

OXENFELT, ALFRED R., *Pricing Strategies* (New York: AMACOM, 1975).

PALDA, KRISTIAN S., *Pricing Decisions and Marketing Policy* (Englewood Cliffs, N.J.: Prentice-Hall, Inc., 1971).

SHAPIRO, BENSON P., and BARBARA B. JACKSON, "Industrial Pricing to Meet Customer Needs," *Harvard Business Review* (November–December 1978): 119–127.

CHAPTER 17

Pricing Decision Analysis

The industrial marketer cannot make intelligent price decisions without analyzing costs in relation to projected sales volume and long-term profit goals. Also, the marketer must study the needs and positional strengths of the customer, as well as the strengths and weaknesses of competition, and develop strategic approaches in the important areas of negotiation and bidding. A program might also be devised to offer leasing in addition to outright sale. After reading this chapter, you should understand

1. The use of break-even analysis and learning curves to determine the effect of price on cost, volume, and profit.
2. The value and application of return-on-investment pricing.
3. The use of expected payoff analysis when initiating or responding to price changes.
4. The development of strategic models for competitive bidding.
5. The factors that determine a firm's negotiating position.
6. The role of leasing in pricing strategy.

Pricing decisions involve balancing the effect of price on short-term profits versus the effect on long-term volume and subsequent cost reductions. These effects should be analyzed during the development and prior to the introduction of a new product, when initiating a price change, and when responding to competitors' actions. Profitability analysis, normally referred to as break-even analysis, is an important first step in looking at the impact of pricing decisions.

BREAK-EVEN (OR PROFITABILITY) ANALYSIS

Price should not be set without first determining what will happen to profits at various price levels. To do otherwise is to tempt disaster as was the case with the Convair jet series. A common financial tool used to determine the level of sales required to cover all relevant fixed and variable costs is break-even analysis, sometimes referred to as profitability analysis. This process also indicates the impact different pricing strategies will have on profit margins and identifies the minimum price below which losses will occur.

Obviously, to employ break-even analysis, the marketer must know the fixed and variable costs of producing and marketing a product. As discussed in Chapter Sixteen, these costs are not always easily determined. Although fixed costs generally remain constant as volume increases, this is only true for so long as output can be expanded without associated increases in administrative personnel, plant size, depreciation, debt-service costs, and other fixed costs. Also, the distinction between fixed and variable costs is not always clear. To compound the problem, the economies of scale curve shows that variable costs do not increase linearly with increases in production.

Break-even calculations are often heavily weighted by historical data, but such data should be adjusted to reflect current realities. Projected costs, not their historical counterparts, are the critical elements in the pricing decision process, and the industrial marketer should expend the necessary effort to forecast future costs by drawing on learning curve patterns. Marketers must also constantly monitor the level of market demand and the pricing strategies of competition. Even though these are uncontrollable variables, they have a significant impact on the firm's break-even point and pricing flexibility.

Break-even Quantity and Contribution Margin

A firm's profitability can be expressed by the equation

$$Y = PX - VX - F$$

where

Y = profit
X = number of units produced/sold
P = price per unit
V = variable cost per unit
F = total fixed costs

By definition, the breakeven point occurs where total revenues equal costs, or

$$PX = VX + F$$

By solving for X, we find the break-even point.

$$X = \frac{F}{P - V}$$

Note that the expression $P - V$ is the *contribution margin,* that is, the amount (if any) by which the selling price of a unit exceeds its variable cost and contributes toward fixed costs. Therefore, at the break-even point, the contribution margin multiplied by the unit volume equals total fixed costs. We will return to this important concept shortly.

Once demand has been estimated, and possible price levels forecasted, total revenues and costs at different sales volumes can be estimated and displayed on a break-even chart, such as the one shown in Table 17-1. Figure 17-1 depicts this same information graphically.

In the TMI example covered in Chapter Sixteen (see Tables 16-3 and 16-4), the company's fixed costs were $180,000, and its variable costs were constant at $.94 per unit. More realistically, unit variable costs will change with volume, so that all three unit financial quantifiers (fixed and variable cost and price) will be "moving targets" in the analysis to determine optimal price-cost-volume level. By the way, we are assuming production volume to be identical to market demand.

In the break-even analysis shown in Table 17-1, unit variable cost is $1.10 for an output of 60,000 units; it reaches a low of $.90 from 110,000 to 120,000 units and begins to climb again above 120,000 units. It should be noted in Table 17-1 and

TABLE 17-1 Break-even Analysis for TMI (units and dollars in thousands)

Unit Price	Market Demands [000]	Total Revenue [000]	Unit Variable Cost	Total Variable Cost [000]	Fixed Cost [000]	Total Cost [000]	Total Profit [000]	
$3.80	60.0	$228.0	$1.10	$66.0	$180.0	$246.0	$(18.0)	
3.50	70.0	245.0	1.05	73.5	180.0	253.5	(8.5)	
3.25	80.0	260.0	1.00	80.0	180.0	260.0	.0	Minimum B/E point
3.05	90.0	274.5	.97	87.3	180.0	267.5	7.2	
2.85	100.0	285.0	.94	94.0	180.0	274.0	11.0	
2.65	110.0	291.5	.90	99.0	180.0	279.0	12.5	
2.58	115.0	296.7	.90	103.5	180.0	283.5	13.2	Optimal point
2.50	120.0	300.0	.90	108.0	180.0	288.0	12.0	
2.40	130.0	312.0	.94	122.2	180.0	302.2	9.8	
2.30	140.0	322.0	.97	135.8	180.0	315.8	6.2	
2.20	150.0	330.0	1.00	150.0	180.0	330.0	.0	Maximum B/E point
2.15	160.0	344.0	1.05	168.0	180.0	348.0	(4.0)	
2.10	170.0	357.0	1.10	187.0	180.0	367.0	(10.0)	
2.05	180.0	369.0	1.15	207.0	180.0	387.0	(18.0)	

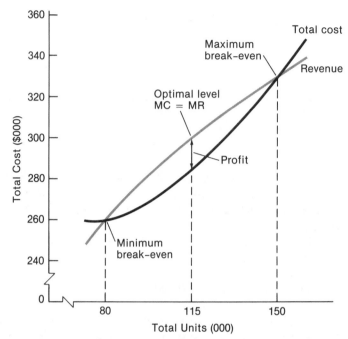

FIGURE 17-1   Break-even and Optimal Profit Analysis Graph

Figure 17-1 that two break-even points occur. The minimum point represents the "critical mass" quantity necessary (at the price the market is willing to pay) to generate revenue dollars equal to total incurred fixed and variable costs. In Table 17-1, this point is 80,000 units at $3.25 each. The maximum point occurs where revenue and total costs are again equal.

We can verify the dual break-even points by analyzing the contribution margin. At 80,000 units, the contribution margin (revenue − variable cost) is $2.25 ($3.25 − $1.00), which generates $180,000, the exact amount of total fixed costs. At 150,000 units, the contribution margin is only $1.20, but multiplied by the larger quantity, this again produces $180,000. Thus, we can see that internal and external factors conflict in the establishment of pricing. A price that generates a larger contribution margin has a restrictive impact on market demand. Lowering the price to increase demand also reduces the contribution margin.

In examining the break-even data, we find that the optimal price for the firm to charge is $2.58. At this price, estimated sales volume is 115,000 units, generating $296,700 revenue, total costs of $283,500, and profits of $13,200. At any volume above or below this level, profits decline. This leads to the concept of marginality.

Marginal Costs and Revenues

If the next increment in market demand is analyzed (115,000 to 120,000), we find that marginal costs are greater than marginal revenue. For 5,000 units, total costs increase $4,500, or 90 cents per unit, while revenue goes up only $3,300, or 66 cents per unit. Profits necessarily decline. If we make a similar analysis of the 110,000–115,000 increment, we find a cost increase of $4,500 again, but a revenue increase of $5,200 or $1.04 per unit. Profits are increasing. Therefore, it can be stated that a firm should continue striving for increased volume as long as marginal revenue exceeds marginal costs, in other words, as long as *total profits increase.* Thus, the most important analytical data in Table 17-1 are contained in the total profit column.

Where price is eventually set will still depend on the marketing objectives of the firm. If TMI establishes an objective of market penetration, it could set a price as low as $2.20, still covering current costs, but capturing a larger portion of the market than would have been the case at a price of $2.58. The significance of this "penetration pricing" strategy will be discussed shortly. On the other hand, if the firm had an objective of market skimming, it would be concerned with generating maximum short-term profits. Hence, assuming market response to price (demand elasticity) has been correctly analyzed, a price of $2.58 would be the optimal market skimming price.

RETURN-ON-INVESTMENT PRICING

A widely used method of setting price in the industrial market is return-on-investment pricing (sometimes referred to as target return or capital asset pricing). To understand return-on-investment pricing, it is helpful to examine the concept of return on investment (ROI), which refers to the amount of profit earned on the dollars invested by the firm during a finite time period, usually one year. It is expressed as[1]

$$\frac{profit}{investment} = \text{return on investment} \qquad (17\text{--}1)$$

This simple equation can also be developed using the two equations "profit margin" and "investment turnover," which are

$$\frac{profit}{sales} = \text{profit margin} \qquad (17\text{--}2)$$

and

$$\frac{sales}{investment} = \text{investment turnover} \qquad (17\text{--}3)$$

[1]Glenn A. Welsch, *Budgeting: Profit Planning and Control* (Englewood Cliffs, N.J.: Prentice-Hall, Inc., 1964), p. 261.

When these two equations are multiplied, we have

$$\text{profit margin} \times \text{investment turnover} = \text{return on investment} \quad (17\text{--}4)$$

In the TMI example, capital investment was $180,000. If the firm chooses to charge a price of $2.58 on an expected demand of 115,000 units, expected profit will be $13,200. With these figures in mind, the firm's return on investment can be determined by using Equation 17–1,

$$\text{return on investment} \quad \frac{\$13,200 \ (\text{profit})}{\$180,000 \ (\text{investment})} = 7.3\%$$

or by developing Equations 17-2 and 17-3, and then combining them as in Equation 17-4:

$$\text{profit margin} = \frac{\$13,200 \ (\text{profit})}{\$296,700 \ (\text{sales})} = 4.45\%$$

$$\text{investment turnover} = \frac{\$296,700 \ (\text{sales})}{\$180,000 \ (\text{investment})} = 1.65$$

so that

$$\text{return on investment} = 4.45\% \times 1.65 = 7.3\%$$

These last three equations illustrate that ROI is a direct function of profits and investment level, but is also related to sales volume. Both sales volume and profits are a function of price. Hence, ROI pricing simply sets a price level that will generate some target return, given the demand curve and costs previously estimated.

Returning to the TMI example, let us assume that before the start of production, management decides that the molds will eventually have to generate at least a 12 percent ROI. Given the investment of $180,000, this means an annual profit goal of at least $21,600. Referring again to the break-even chart, Table 17-1 (as the TMI marketing manager would do), we find that this profit level cannot currently be obtained at any sales volume between the two break-even points.

The TMI marketing manager would now have the choice of being conservative by recommending a price around $3.00, thus allowing the opportunity to double check demand elasticity and keep production commitments low. There is also the opportunity to "go for broke" by pricing at $2.40 or less and hoping that market demand will at least equal the forecast. Finally, short-term profits as well as return on investment can be maximized (assuming that all the estimates and forecasts are correct) by setting the price at $2.58.

Studies have shown that this type of price determination is one of the most common methods used by industrial organizations operating in oligopolistic markets.[2] There are several justifications for this widespread usage. First, in the typical large industrial firm, multiple profit centers exist, each with their own ROI goals, dependent upon the relative degree of risk involved in their individual projects or businesses. Investments involving greater risks are required to project higher rates of return before they are undertaken. The projected ROI will later serve as a yardstick for measuring accomplishments over the life of the business. Second, the projected ROI necessary for the undertaking of investment projects is reflected directly in the price of the products to be marketed, thus adding internal consistency to pricing strategies.[3]

Also, as discussed earlier, the computations for ROI pricing involve profits, sales volume, and total investment. Thus, the decision maker is less prone to make judgments based on more restrictive financial criteria, such as expense/sales ratios or absolute profit dollars. Quite frequently managers attempt to improve profits by raising prices or cutting costs, while giving no concern to market demand or the level of investment already made.

Finally, ROI pricing is particularly suited to industrial oligopolies in that it is based on standard costs and volumes estimated for lengthy time periods. Over a year, actual costs may fluctuate considerably. But by using estimated cost as a standard, firms are able to hold prices relatively constant. Such stability is conducive to oligopolistic markets where firms customarily want to avoid price competition. It is also conducive to the long-term buyer-seller interface that characteristically exists in the industrial market.

LEARNING CURVE EFFECTS ON PRICE ANALYSIS

The basis elements of the learning curve concept were described in Chapter Sixteen. Restated simply, if a product is manufactured and sold on a continuous basis, unit costs will decline as cumulative quantity increases. It would follow, then, that unit costs will decline more rapidly if the rate of production is greater. (For clarification, it should be emphasized that fixed costs will normally not be impacted by the learning curve, only those costs that are volume dependent or variable.)

As stated earlier, learning curves with slopes of 85 percent are quite common. This means that variable costs will decline 15 percent each time accumulated volume doubles. Table 17-2 illustrates this point, using slopes of a conservative 90 percent and a more optimistic 80 percent.

Table 17-2 assumes that the variable cost per unit shown in the TMI example (94 cents in Table 16-4) holds for a production rate of 100,000 units per year and resulted from the "learning" that took place during the production of the first 100,000 units. It then shows what this cost and the costs for other production rates

---

[2]Otto Eckstein, "A Theory of the Wage-Price Process in Modern Industry," *Review of Economic Studies* 31 (October 1964), pp. 267–287.

[3]Ibid., p. 269.

TABLE 17-2 **Change in Variable Unit Costs versus Production Level
(80% and 90% Learning Curve)**

Cumulative Quantities [000]	Production Level L. C. Slope	80		100		115		130		150	
		90%	80%	90%	80%	90%	80%	90%	80%	90%	80%
100.0		1.00	1.00	.94	.94	.90	.90	.94	.94	1.00	1.00
200.0		.90	.80	.85	.75	.81	.72	.85	.75	.90	.80
400.0		.81	.64	.76	.60	.73	.58	.76	.60	.81	.64
800.0		.73	.51	.69	.48	.66	.46	.69	.48	.73	.51
1,600.0		.66	.41	.62	.39	.59	.37	.62	.39	.66	.41

will be after the cumulative production of 200,000, 400,000, 800,000, and 1,600,000 of units with learning curves of 90 and 80 percent. Note, first, that costs decline at a constant *percentage.* Therefore, the *absolute* decline is steadily decreasing (the result of a constant percentage being applied to an ever-smaller number). Second, remember the difference between the learning curve and economies of scale as was discussed in Chapter Sixteen. Economies of scale refers to the relative production efficiency at different quantity levels *at any given point in time.* The learning curve

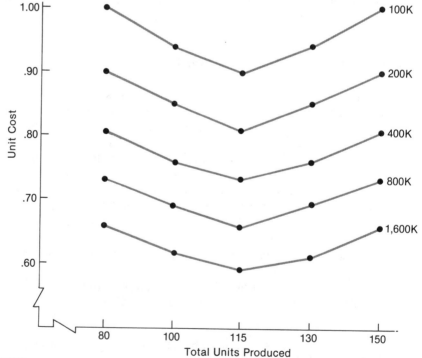

FIGURE 17-2 **Graphic Representation of Variable Unit Costs versus Production Level at 90 Percent Learning Curve**

shifts the EOS curve downward with the accumulation of quantity. This relationship is shown graphically in Figure 17-2 for a 90 percent slope only.

Finally, note here that the *entire* EOS curve shifts downward. In other words, "learning" helps the firm in three ways:

1. For any given price, profits are increased.
2. The minimum break-even quantity is reduced, giving the firm greater protection against major market erosions.
3. The maximum break-even quantity is increased, allowing the firm to capitalize on major market expansions.

This leads us to a reconsideration of TMI's pricing options and an analysis of the importance of market share. Our previous break-even analysis showed that TMI would maximize short-term profits by establishing a $2.58 selling price and producing at an annual rate of 115,000 units. But this analysis ignores time-related factors. For example, if TMI reduced its price to $2.20, and indeed increased its annual volume to 150,000 units, it would only break even by *current* cost standards. But in less than three years, it will produce more than 400,000 units, and unit variable cost at a 150,000 run rate will drop from $1.00 to $.81 even with a conservative ninety percent learning curve. Table 17-3 shows that profits will rise from a break-even level to $28,500, more than double the firm's current optimal profits at the 115,000 unit run rate. Return on investment will also rise to 15.8 percent, exceeding management's target.

Of equal importance is the fact that TMI would like to maintain a leadership position in its market. If it can hold onto the largest market share, it will obviously move down the learning curve faster than any competitor. Therefore, all other things being equal (technology, production techniques, and efficiency), its variable costs will be lower than those of competition.

Competition might decide to "buy into" the market by cutting price. If this should happen, TMI will be in a strong cost position to compete on price. Or, given its leadership position, it can shift emphasis to nonprice factors (product quality, technical assistance, promotion, and delivery dependability) to retain market share. As we have stated repeatedly, a firm will not rise or fall on price alone. The entire marketing mix must be optimized for customer satisfaction. But the quicker a firm moves down the learning curve, the more profits it will generate at any given volume and price, and the more discretionary dollars it will have to develop the most effective marketing mix.

A significant cautionary note must be added regarding the learning curve. To take full advantage of the cost-saving opportunities, a firm must have a steady production flow that is uninterrupted by shutdowns, major technology changes, or changeovers in personnel. Labor costs for the first Convair 880 were $500,000 and were projected to drop to $200,000 by the fortieth or fiftieth plane produced. Howard Hughes, the purchaser of the first 880s, impounded the initial four planes, locked them in a hangar guarded by his men, and held up delivery of the next thirteen planes still under construction. Convair moved the thirteen uncompleted planes

TABLE 17-3 Profit Impact of the Learning Curve (90 Percent Slope)

Cumulative Volume [000]	Market Unit Demand [000]	Unit Price	Total Revenue [000]	Unit Variable Cost	Total Variable Cost [000]	Fixed Cost [000]	Total Cost [000]	Total Profit [000]	B/E Price
100.0	80.0	$3.25	$260.0	$1.00	$ 80.0	$180.0	$260.0	$ 0.0	$3.25
	100.0	2.85	285.0	.94	94.0	180.0	274.0	11.0	2.74
	115.0	2.58	296.7	.90	103.5	180.0	283.5	13.2	2.47
	130.0	2.40	312.0	.94	122.2	180.0	302.2	9.8	2.32
	150.0	2.20	330.0	1.00	150.0	180.0	330.0	0.0	2.20
	180.0	2.05	369.0	1.15	207.0	180.0	387.0	[18.0]	2.15
200.0	80.0	3.25	260.0	.90	72.0	180.0	252.0	8.0	3.15
	100.0	2.85	285.0	.85	85.0	180.0	265.0	20.0	2.65
	115.0	2.58	296.7	.81	93.2	180.0	273.2	23.5	2.38
	130.0	2.40	312.0	.85	110.5	180.0	290.5	21.5	2.23
	150.0	2.20	330.0	.90	135.0	180.0	315.0	15.0	2.10
	180.0	2.05	369.0	1.04	187.2	180.0	367.2	1.8	2.04
400.0	80.0	3.25	260.0	.81	64.8	180.0	244.8	15.2	3.06
	100.0	2.85	285.0	.76	76.0	180.0	256.0	29.0	2.56
	115.0	2.58	296.7	.73	84.0	180.0	264.0	32.7	2.30
	130.0	2.40	312.0	.76	98.8	180.0	278.8	33.2	2.14
	150.0	2.20	330.0	.81	121.5	180.0	301.5	28.5	2.01
	180.0	2.05	369.0	.93	167.4	180.0	347.4	22.4	1.93
800.0	80.0	3.25	260.0	.73	58.4	180.0	238.4	21.6	2.98
	100.0	2.85	285.0	.69	69.0	180.0	249.0	36.0	2.49
	115.0	2.58	296.7	.66	75.9	180.0	255.9	40.8	2.23
	130.0	2.40	312.0	.69	89.7	180.0	269.7	42.3	2.07
	150.0	2.20	330.0	.73	109.5	180.0	289.5	40.5	1.93
	180.0	2.05	369.0	.84	151.2	180.0	331.2	37.8	1.84

onto an open field. Months later, when Hughes was financially able to take delivery, the planes (then water-damaged from exposure) had to be completed. The original construction crews had been cut back, and many new workers had to be hired and trained. The value of the learning curve had been lost. On top of this, the weathered planes had to be hand-finished on the field, and as one vice president put it, "It took a real expert to diagnose the exact state of completion of each plane. . . . For instance, we had to work with a stack of blueprints to decide whether the wiring was nearly finished, just begun, or had to be completely changed. Do you continue wiring? Do you rip it out?" One month later, Convair's president, Jack Naish, resigned.[4]

EXPECTED PAYOFF ANALYSIS

Pricing decisions are not over when a firm sets its prices. As discussed in Chapter Sixteen, a number of circumstances will arise calling for the firm to reconsider its pricing decisions. Prior to initiating a price change, however, the reactions of buyers, competitors, distributors, and government must be carefully weighed. The price setter must somehow integrate expectations and uncertainties regarding the responses of these parties into a logical pattern for decision making. The use of expected payoff analysis lends itself well to this type of decision making, since it requires the careful gathering of relevant information on the possible outcomes that might result from a price change and forces knowledgeable executives to assign subjective probabilities to those outcomes.[5]

Initiating a Price Change

How expected payoff analysis is used in making pricing decisions for established products can be illustrated by returning to TMI again. Let us assume that the firm introduced the product at $2.58 and did indeed enjoy a demand of 115,000 units. Let us further assume that now, one year after TMI's product introduction, another firm is offering a similar product at the same price. The sales manager of TMI estimates that the potential market demand during the coming year could reach 200,000 units due to the presence of dual sources plus movement of the product into its growth stage.

To hold market leadership, TMI is considering a price cut. From previous break-even analysis (Tables 17-1 and 17-3), management knows that price can be reduced to $2.20 before the firm will begin to lose money. The marketing manager narrows the decision set to three options: (1) maintain price at $2.58, (2) reduce price to $2.40, or (3) reduce price to $2.20. Given these options, a team of experi-

[4]Richard Austin Smith, "How a Great Corporation Got Out of Control, Part II," *Fortune* (February 1962), p. 120.
[5]Paul E. Green, "Bayesian Decision Theory in Pricing Strategy," *Journal of Marketing* (January 1963), pp. 5–14.

enced sales and production managers assigns probabilities to the occurrence of various events as a result of the three options. Table 17-4 outlines the three possible decision options. The expected payoffs for the proposed pricing decisions are outlined in Table 17-5.

Since the expected payoff for option 2 is $13,940 and only $7,600 for option 3, maintaining the current $2.58 price yields the greatest profit ($23,500) and would appear to be the obvious choice. However, TMI must weigh the benefits of short-term profits against growth potential, market share, and long-term profits. They must also consider whether the higher price will attract other competitors into the market.

The use of expected payoff analysis involves assumptions regarding the probable reactions of competition, along with the effect on market demand, subsequent production output, variable unit costs, and profit. Once the effect of a price change on sales volume has been estimated, it is not difficult to determine changes in production costs and profits due to shifts in volume produced. It is more difficult to assess the qualitative aspects of price changes. Will competition view the move as the logical result of lower costs or as the start of a price war? Will lower price generate a higher market volume, or will industrial demand be constrained by an unchanged consumer demand for the end products? Will the Justice Department

TABLE 17-4 Decision Options for Proposed Price Change

Option 1—Maintain price at $2.58
   If price is maintained at $2.58, there will be no change in annual sales volume or costs, and profits will remain at $23,500.
Option 2—Reduce price to $2.40
   a. Given a 40% probability that competition will not react, unit sales volume should increase to 130,000, and unit variable cost will increase to 85 cents. Total revenue will be $312,000, total cost $290,500, and profits $21,500.
   b. Given a 30% probability that competition will match the price reduction, sales volume should increase to 125,000 units, and unit variable cost will rise to 84 cents. This situation would yield revenue of $300,000, total cost of $285,000, and $15,000 profit.
   c. Given a 30% probability that competition will undercut price to $2.30, sales volume would stay at 115,000 units, and unit variable cost at 81 cents. This would yield $276,000 revenue, $273,150 total cost, and a profit of $2,850.
Option 3—Reduce price to $2.20
   a. Given a 20% probability that competition will not react to the price reduction, sales volume should increase to 150,000 units, and unit variable cost rise to 90 cents. Total revenue would then be $330,000, total cost $315,000, and profit $15,000.
   b. Given a 40% probability that competition will exactly match the price reduction, sales volume should increase to 140,000 units, and unit variable cost rise to 87 cents. Total revenue would be $308,000, total cost $301,800, and profit $6,200.
   c. Given a 30% probability that competition will reduce price to only $2.30, unit sales volume should increase to 145,000, and unit variable cost rise to 89 cents. This would yield total revenue of $319,000, total cost of $309,000, and a profit of $10,000.
   d. Given a 10% probability that competition will undercut price to $2.10, unit sales volume would still increase to 125,000, and unit variable cost rise to 83 cents. Total revenue would now be $275,000 and total cost would be $283,800, causing a loss of $8,800.

TABLE 17-5 Expected Payoffs for Price Change Options

Option 1—Maintain $2.58 price and profits of $23,500
Option 2—Reduce price to $2.40

Possible Reactions	New Volume [000]	Estimated $ Revenue [000]	New Unit Variable Cost	Total $ Cost [000]	Estimated $ Profit [000]	Probability Outcome	Expected Payoff [000]
No reaction	130.0	$312.0	$.85	$290.5	$21.5	.40	$8.60
Match	125.0	300.0	.84	285.0	15.0	.30	4.50
Drop to $2.30	115.0	276.0	.81	273.2	2.8	.30	.84
							$13.94

Option 3—Reduce price to $2.20

Possible Reactions	New Volume [000]	Estimated $ Revenue [000]	New Unit Variable Cost	Total $ Cost [000]	Estimated $ Profit [000]	Probability Outcome	Expected Payoff [000]
No Reaction	150.0	$330.0	$.90	$315.0	$15.0	.20	$3.00
Match	140.0	308.0	.87	301.8	6.2	.40	2.48
$2.30	145.0	319.0	.89	309.0	10.0	.30	3.00
$2.10	125.0	275.0	.83	283.8	[8.8]	.10	[.88]
							$7.60

view the proactive move of an industry leader as an illegal attempt to restrain competition? These potential outcomes must also be weighed, but are not easily quantified.

The important point in using payoff analysis is that it provides an approach for considering the effects of alternative choices in the face of uncertainty and forces management to apply its judgment quantitatively rather than making a subjective, "shoot from the hip" decision. In the process, it provides a quantitative analysis, interrelating multiple alternatives, that would be virtually impossible to perform intuitively.

COMPETITIVE BIDDING

In the industrial market, a significant volume of purchasing is transacted through competitive bidding rather than on the basis of a price list. Government agencies and most public institutions are required to purchase through the bidding system. Industrial buyers also use competitive bidding as a means of exploring and determining price levels when purchasing nonstandardized materials, complex fabricated products on which design and manufacturing methods vary, and items made to their specification that do not have an established market price.[6,7]

[6]Stuart F. Heinritz and Paul U. Farrell, *Purchasing Principles and Applications* (Englewood Cliffs, N.J.: Prentice-Hall, Inc., 1976), p. 198.
[7]J. H. Westing, I. V. Fine, and Gary J. Zenz, *Purchasing Management* (New York: John Wiley & Sons, Inc., 1976), p. 198.

Competitive bidding may be either closed or open. Closed bidding starts with a formal invitation to potential suppliers to submit written, sealed bids. At a preestablished time, all bids are opened and reviewed. Open bidding is more informal in that suppliers may make a series of oral or written offers up to a specified date. When products or services of competing suppliers vary substantially, or when specific requirements are hard to define precisely, open bidding is more commonly used because it allows for deliberation between buyers and suppliers throughout the bidding process.

Developing bids is a costly and time-consuming process, and the profitability of potential contracts will depend on the firm's technical expertise and past experience. While the awarding of bids is highly dependent on price, the low bidder does not always get the contract. In some cases, contracts are awarded to the "lowest responsible bidder." This means that the award is made on the basis of the bidder's ability to deliver as promised, the purchaser's past experience with the bidder, or an assessment of the bidder's technical, financial, and management capabilities. Therefore, carefully developed strategy is necessary in the competitive bidding environment. Bidding strategy consists of two stages, prebid analysis and bid determination.[8]

Prebid Analysis

Prebid analysis requires a precise definition of company objectives, an analytical approach for screening alternative bid opportunities, and a method for assessing the probability of success for a particular bidding strategy.

Company Objectives.   Decisions as to whether to bid or not begin with a clear understanding of company objectives at the time of a bid invitation. Objectives may focus on profit maximization, gaining market entry, or keeping the plant operating and the labor force intact. Whatever the objectives, they assist the firm in deciding what types of business to pursue, when to bid, and the level of pricing to use. For example, to make some contribution to overhead and/or keep its labor force intact for the short run, a firm may bid at a level close to its variable costs.

Screening Bid Opportunities.   The use of a screening procedure to evaluate alternative contracts is crucial and has greatly improved the bidding success of many industrial firms.[9] Three stages are involved in the screening process: (1) an identification of criteria deemed important in evaluating contracts, (2) a measure of their relative importance, and (3) an evaluation of the bid opportunity.

To assess the value of various bids, marketing managers must consider factors such as plant capacity, competition, delivery requirements, and profits. While the nature and number of criteria to be considered in the prebid analysis will vary by

[8]Stephen Paranka, "Competitive Bidding Strategy: A Procedure for Pre-bid Analysis," *Business Horizons,* June 1974, p. 39.

[9]"Evaluation System Boosts Job Shop's Bidding Average," *Steel* (September 21, 1964), p. 47.

firm and by industry, plant capacity is usually a very important factor in deciding whether or not to respond to a bid opportunity. For instance, if a company is at ninety-five percent capacity, it may not be too eager to respond to a bid that would require twenty percent more capacity. The firm might bid regardless, but its figures would reflect the costs of the additional production capacity. On the other hand, if production facilities were underutilized by fifty percent, the firm would most likely want the contract at virtually any price above variable cost.

Also crucial to effective prebid analysis is knowledge regarding the number of potential competitors and the probable range of their bids. However, this information may be quite difficult to obtain, particularly by a firm that is relatively inexperienced in the bidding process. Other factors that a firm might wish to analyze would be its degree of experience with this or similar products and the likelihood of follow-up business opportunities.

Bid Determination

Once it has been determined that a desirable bid opportunity exists, the probability of winning the contract at various prices must be estimated to determine the bid price. The optimal bid price is dependent upon perceptions of how competitors might bid, the profit to be expected if the bid is accepted, and the probability that the contract will be won. A high bid with a large expected profit has a low probability of being accepted. Conversely, a low bid that offers little or no profit has a high probability of being accepted. Several quantitative approaches can be used to determine prices in a competitive bidding situation, the most common of which are probability models. These models provide the marketer with an objective procedure for evaluating potential profits and success probabilities of different pricing alternatives by drawing on historical data and assumptions as to how competitors will behave. Such models also force managers to quantify what otherwise might be only vague intuitive feelings.

The key objective in probabilistic bidding models is to determine the optimum level of profit (or contribution to profit and overhead) if a bid is accepted and the likelihood of its acceptance. An optimum bid is one that offers the highest expected payoff. It would maximize $E(X)$ as expressed in the equation[10]

$$E(X) = P(X)Z(X)$$

where

X = amount of the bid
$Z(X)$ = profit of bid if accepted
$P(X)$ = probability of a bid of X being accepted
$E(X)$ = expected profit of a bid of X

[10]Wayne J. Morse, "Probabilistic Bidding Models: A Synthesis," *Business Horizons* (April 1975), pp. 67–74.

How this model is used to determine a bid price is illustrated here. We assume that company A is considering bidding on a contract to be awarded to the lowest bidder. Company A has three competitors, companies B, C, and D, and wishes to determine the probability of its bid being the lowest. To accomplish this, company A must (1) gather historic information on relationships between its estimated direct costs and B, C, and D's bids on similar projects (shown in Table 17-6) and (2) analyze the data to determine the probabilities that its competitors will submit bids at various levels above A's estimated direct costs. The results are shown in Table 17-7.

Since the contract is to be awarded to the lowest bidder, if the contemplated bid is stated as a percentage of estimated direct costs, the probability that competitors will submit a bid higher than any given percentage of A's estimated direct cost is also the probability that A will be awarded the contract. Accordingly, from Table 17-7 we can determine the probability that a bid will be successful based on the number of times competitors bid higher in the past. (Company A assumes, by the way, that they will be awarded at least part of the contract if a competitor ties their low bid.)

If A submits a bid of 125 percent of its estimated direct costs, then, as Table 17-7 indicates, there is a 77 percent probability that the bid will be lower than B, C, or D's bid ($.90 \times .95 \times .90 = .7695$.) If A submits a bid of 115 percent of estimated direct costs, its bid would almost certainly be lower than its competitors. However, a bid of 115 percent provides little contribution to profit and overhead.

As previously stated, the optimum bid is the bid that has the highest expected payoff. We can determine the optimum bid by multiplying the contribution margin on each bid by the probability that the bid will be accepted. Thus, if company A is considering bids of 120, 125, and 130 percent of estimated direct costs, the optimum bid is 125 percent:

$$(.855)(20\%) = 17.1\% \text{ for 120 percent}$$
$$(.727)(25\%) = 18.2\% \text{ for 125 percent}$$
$$(.472)(30\%) = 14.2\% \text{ for 130 percent}$$

A bid of 125 percent of estimated direct costs has the highest expected payoff (18.2%). As the number of competitors increase, the probability that a given bid will be accepted, or lower than all competitors', decreases. This does not necessarily mean that the optimum bid will be lower.[11]

When a bidder is totally new to a market, or is not familiar with the past strategies of specific competitors, or lacks historic data that is applicable to a given bid situation, there may be no choice but to make the best possible intuitive guess.

[11]See ibid.: Franz Edelman, "Art & Science of Competitive Bidding," *Harvard Business Review* 45 (July 1965), pp. 53-66; Arleigh W. Walker, "How to Price Industrial Products," *Harvard Business Review* 45 (September–October 1967), pp. 125–132; and Stephen Paranka "The Pay-off Concept in Competitive Bidding: A Way to Improve the Bidding Record," *Business Horizons* (August 1969), pp. 77–81.

TABLE 17-6 Relationship of B, C, and D's Bid to Company A's Estimated Direct Cost

Project	A's Direct Cost	B's Bid Amount	B's Bid Percent of A's Direct Cost	C's Bid Amount	C's Bid Percent of A's Direct Cost	D's Bid Amount	D's Bid Percent of A's Direct Cost
1	$59,000	$73,750	125%	$74,930	127%	$70,800	120%
2	28,000	41,160	147	39,200	140	39,760	142
3	30,000	43,200	144	45,000	150	43,800	146
4	3,000	47,520	132	48,240	134	46,082	128
5	21,000	34,440	164	34,020	162	33,180	158
6	15,000	23,250	155	24,000	160	24,300	162
7	20,000	29,800	149	30,400	152	30,000	150
8	30,000	39,900	133	38,100	127	37,500	125
9	42,000	60,900	145	58,800	140	59,640	142
10	22,000	29,700	135	28,600	130	28,160	128
11	70,000	99,400	142	102,200	146	98,000	140
12	32,000	53,760	168	52,480	164	53,120	166
13	8,000	12,080	151	12,160	152	12,000	150
14	47,000	64,860	138	61,100	130	62,980	134
15	10,000	12,000	120	12,200	122	11,500	115
16	50,000	72,500	145	71,500	143	69,000	138
17	25,000	33,750	135	35,000	140	33,000	132
18	40,000	62,800	157	64,000	160	61,600	154
19	65,000	88,400	136	89,700	138	88,400	132
20	15,000	19,800	132	19,500	130	20,100	134

Source: Adapted from Wayne J. Morse, "Probabilistic Bidding Models: A Synthesis," Business Horizons, April 1975, pp. 67–76. Reprinted with permission.

TABLE 17-7 Probability of Underbidding Competitors

Bid as % of Estimated Direct Cost	No. of High Bids			Probability of Underbidding*			Probability of Winning*	Contribution Margin [%]**	Expected Payoff of Bid [%]***
	B	C	D	B	C	D			
110	20	20	20	1.00	1.00	1.00	1.000	10	10.0
115	20	20	19	1.00	1.00	.95	.950	15	14.2
120	20	20	19	.95	1.00	.90	.855	20	17.1
125	18	19	17	.90	.95	.85	.727	25	18.2
130	18	14	15	.90	.70	.75	.472	30	14.2
135	13	13	12	.65	.65	.60	.254	35	8.9
140	11	9	9	.55	.45	.45	.111	40	4.5
145	7	8	7	.35	.40	.35	.049	45	2.2
150	5	6	4	.25	.30	.20	.015	50	.7
155	3	4	3	.15	.20	.15	.004	55	.2
160	2	2	2	.10	.10	.10	.001	60	.1
165	1	0	1	.05	.00	.05	.000	65	.0

*The probability of winning (or the probability of the bid being accepted) is found by multiplying the probabilities of underbidding each one.

**The contribution margin is the difference between the bid price and the estimated direct costs.

***The expected payoff (optimum bid) is found by multiplying the contribution margin by the probability of winning.

Source: Adapted from Wayne J. Morse, "Probabilistic Bidding Models: A Synthesis," *Business Horizons,* April 1975, pp. 67–76. Reprinted with permission.

Published information of awards made on similar projects sometimes provides helpful guidance. Trade association information regarding industry profitability and/or capacity utilization can also suggest a ballpark price. But there is obviously no satisfactory substitute for relevant and quantitative data. As was true of price determination models, the primary advantage of bidding models is that they substitute quantification, where available, for intuitive guesswork.

PRICE NEGOTIATION

Price negotiation is typical in industrial marketing, particularly in complex buying situations where buyers and sellers make a number of proposals and counterproposals before a price is agreed upon. In this sense, negotiation and open bidding are virtually synonymous. Most major purchases by institutions, government agencies, and commercial businesses are negotiated. Not only price, but service, delivery, technical assistance, product characteristics, and quality are commonly negotiated.

The process of negotiation may begin with a quotation or a bid that is later modified to reflect the pertinent requirements of the buying company and the special strengths of the seller. In the case of open bidding, negotiations are often carried on simultaneously with a number of suppliers until enough information has been exchanged to allow for a competitive bid.

Negotiation is almost always employed in the selling and purchase of a new product due to the uncertainties involved. With little or no experience in manufacturing or estimating costs of such products, sellers often prefer to negotiate rather than volunteer a fixed price.

Many industrial buyers also prefer to negotiate price, believing that negotiated prices are closer to the "right" price than original quotations. Buyers characteristically have specific goals in mind when negotiating with prospective suppliers. These goals, while subject to some flexibility, are based on a careful examination of the buying firm's needs and alternatives. The industrial marketer, therefore, must be prepared for shrewd bargaining, particularly where price is concerned.

Compared to Convair's 880, the new 990 "had a bigger wing area . . . a fuselage ten and a half feet longer, weighed over 50,000 pounds more, required an enlarged empennage (tail assembly), a beefed-up landing gear, greater fuel capacity, stronger structural members, and was supposed to go 20 mph faster." Many of these changes had been imposed upon Convair by American Airlines' "hard-bargaining" C. R. Smith. "But Smith hadn't stopped with just designing the 990; he designed the contract too, using all the leverage Convair's plight afforded him. In it he demanded that Convair guarantee a low noise level for the plane, finance the 990s' inventory of spare parts until American actually used them, and accept, as American's $25- million down payment, twenty-five DC-7s,"—which Convair found it could not sell for even $500,000 each.[12]

The successful negotiation of a contract requires skill, experience, and preparation on the seller's part. Like a good trial lawyer, the industrial marketer must analyze the firm's strengths and weaknesses compared to potential competition, the factors most important to the buying firm, future growth opportunity, and projected profitability.

Negotiation between buyer and seller involves some form of bargaining strategy that is influenced by the relative strengths of the parties. In general, there are four types of negotiating strategies:[13] (1) a *negotiated strategy* in which buyer and seller have a close match of strengths and will negotiate a price that would be fair to both parties, (2) a *dictatorial strategy* in which the buyer is weak relative to the seller and the seller will attempt to set a price that is most favorable to his or her firm, (3) a *defensive strategy* in which the seller is weak relative to the buyer, and (4) a *gamesmanship strategy* in which both parties are weak and will play "hide and seek" to arrive at price. Figure 17-3 illustrates the relationship among these four strategies.

[12]Smith, "How a Great Corporation Got Out of Control," p. 120.
[13]See Subhash C. Jain and Michael V. Laric, "A Framework for Strategic Industrial Pricing," *Industrial Marketing Management,* 8 (1979), pp. 75–80.

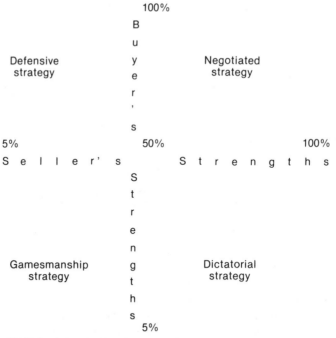

FIGURE 17-3 Pricing Strategy Quadrangle

Source: Reprinted by permission of the publisher from "A Framework for Strategic Industrial Pricing," by Subhash C. Jain and Michael V. Laric, *Industrial Marketing Management,* 8[1979], pp. 75–80. Copyright © 1979 by Elsevier Science Publishing Co., Inc.

Measuring Buyer and Seller Strength

To determine the type of negotiating strategy to be employed, the strength of the seller's bargaining power relative to that of the buyer must be measured. It is possible to determine this power by a number of criteria. For instance, a buyer's bargaining power depends on such factors as the size of the organization, the amount of past purchases, future buying power, length of time in business, and the firm's need for the product. The strength of a seller can be measured by criteria such as company image, product quality and uniqueness, delivery capability, technical assistance, and postsale services. The strengths of both the buyer and the seller are a function of these various criteria and must be measured in relative terms (that is, the buyer's strength relative to the seller's). Therefore, once strengths have been evaluated for both the buyer and the seller, an overall measure of strength/weakness must be derived. This can be accomplished by rating the criteria on a scale of 1–10 (weak–strong) and then assigning weights to each criterion based on its importance in the negotiating situation. The score for each criterion can then be derived by multiplying the scale value by the weight, and total strength determined by summing the scores of all criteria. Table 17-8 illustrates this method.

TABLE 17-8 Measurement of Buyer's and Seller's Strengths

Measurement of Buyer's Strengths				*Measurement of Seller's Strengths*			
Strength Criteria	*Scale Value Range 1–10*	*Weights*	*Total Score*	*Strength Criteria*	*Scale Value Range 1–10*	*Weights*	*Score*
1. Organization size	9	3	27	1. Delivery service	4	3	12
2. Sales potential	7	2	14	2. Company image	6	3	18
3. Size of past pur- chases	3	4	12	3. Product quality	3	2	6
4. Desirability of maintaining as a customer [re- peat purchases]	8	5	40	4. After-sales services	5	2	10
				5. Trade-in policy	6	1	6
				6. Price	8	2	16
Total			93	Total			68

Total possible score = 140

Percentage score = $\dfrac{93}{140} \times 100 = 66.4$

Total possible score = 130

Percentage score = $\dfrac{68}{100} \times 130 = 52.3$

Source: Reprinted by permission of the publisher from "A Framework for Strategic Industrial Pricing," by Subhash C. Jain and Michael V. Laric, *Industrial Marketing Management,* 8 (1979), pp. 75–80. Copyright © 1979 by Elsevier Science Publishign Co., Inc.

As you can see, the buyer, in confronting the seller, is in a somewhat better bargaining position with a total strength score of 66.4 percent compared to the seller's 52.3 percent. The buying firm is quite large and represents desirable future business, even though their past purchases have been small. The seller's major strengths are company image, price, and trade-in policy. However, weaknesses exist in delivery capability and product quality. Unfortunately, trade-in policy is a minor issue, while delivery is important.

The two overall scores (66.4 percent and 52.3 percent) are used to determine where the seller is located relative to the buyer in the pricing strategy quadrangle, Figure 17-3. In this example, the combined buyer's and seller's scores fall in the northeast corner. Both parties are relatively strong, and a negotiated strategy would be most appropriate.

Evaluating Buyer and Seller Product Need

Once negotiation strategies are pinpointed, tactical maneuvers must be determined. While, in the illustrated case, the buyer and seller will attempt to negotiate price, the tactics to be employed in the negotiation process will depend on the buyer's need for the product with respect to the seller's need for the sale.

A buyer's product need can be classified as acute, moderate, or marginal. If the proposed purchase is an immediate replacement of a defective machine critical to the manufacturing process, the buyer is not likely to be price sensitive. In such a case, the buyer would be ready to pay a high price for the equipment, and the seller would classify the buyer's need as acute. (Any seller taking undue advantage of this situation through price gouging, however, would be open for retaliation in future negotiations.) A moderate need would exist if the buyer had some time, even though limited, to engage in a supplier search before finalizing the order. When a firm is searching for office supplies to replenish stocks three months later, the need would be classified as marginal, because the buyer has ample time to locate and obtain a satisfactory price from an acceptable supplier.

The seller's need to make the sale must also be compared to the buyer's need for the product. An acute product sale need could occur when a company is operating well below capacity, needs working capital, or desires to secure a prototype order that will probably lead to repeat business. On the other hand, if production is near full capacity, or a buyer is not likely to place repeat orders, the product sale would be classified as marginal. Table 17-9 illustrates the pricing tactics matrix. As you can see, when the buyer's need is greater than the seller's, the buyer is likely to yield to the seller (cells 4, 7, and 8). If the seller's need for the sale is greater than the buyer's need, then the buyer is likely to have the upper edge in negotiation (cells 2, 3, and 6). However, when the seller and the buyer have the same degree of need, neither can dictate price (1, 5, and 9).

Determining Key Negotiable Factors

It is essential for the seller to determine where the buyer stands with respect to all factors relevant to the negotiation. Some factors will be clearly irrelevant (for example, import tariffs when buyer and seller are in the same country). Other factors will fall into one of three categories: nonnegotiable factors, prime trade-off candidates, or nonvalue factors. For example, a buyer may require delivery of component parts

TABLE 17-9 Pricing Tactics Matrix

Seller	Buyer		
	Acute need	Moderate need	Marginal need
Acute need	1. Neutral ground	2. Buyer has leeway	3. Buyer in control
Moderate need	4. Seller has leeway	5. Neutral ground	6. Buyer has leeway
Marginal need	7. Seller in control	8. Seller has leeway	9. Neutral ground

Price elasticity of demand is inversely related to the acuteness of buyer need. When the need is marginal, price elasticity is high, and conversely, when the need is acute, price elasticity is low.

Source: Reprinted by permission of the publisher from "A Framework for Strategic Industrial Pricing," by Subhash C. Jain and Michael V. Laric, Industrial Marketing Management, 8 (1979), pp. 75–80. Copyright © 1979 by Elsevier Science Publishing Co., Inc.

in six weeks to support a planned production schedule that cannot be delayed, but the seller is unable to supply the component to complete specifications in that time span. In this example, the delivery date is definitely not a negotiable item. However, let us assume that a discussion with the buyer's engineers reveals that a product already in the seller's inventory and differing from the standard component in only noncritical details is acceptable, particularly when coupled with a price reduction. The coupling of specification revision and price reduction becomes a major trade-off item. Neither buyer nor seller care that the substitute component is painted green instead of blue.

This simple example illustrates that most industrial negotiations are clearly aimed at a win-win result, not a win-lose (or zero-sum) outcome. Experienced negotiators on both sides of the desk realize that any worthwhile transaction must yield something of value to both buyer and seller. The key lies in open-minded and flexible investigation of alternatives when the initial desires of either party cannot be satisfied without exception. Naturally, either party can exhibit the most creativity and initiative. Since this text is written from the seller's perspective, it is suggested that marketers develop such capability, if only from the standpoint of making their own jobs more productive and satisfying.

LEASING

Leasing in the industrial market is an alternative to selling capital equipment. In contemplating the purchase of capital goods, buyers examine the cost/benefit trade-offs of various financing alternatives, and when the benefits of leasing outweigh the benefits of owning, they will lease rather than purchase. Predominant among the benefits are those accrued under federal and state income tax laws and regulations.[14] Firms often find it more profitable to lease equipment and account for the charges as expenses rather than to purchase equipment and account for the charges as capital expenditures. In other words, leasing utilizes pretax dollars, whereas capital purchases use posttax dollars (retained earnings).

Leasing also provides other benefits such as minimizing equipment disposal problems, avoiding dilution of ownership or control through debt or equity financing, and protection against the risk of equipment obsolescence.[15] In a study of 191 American industrial firms, six factors were found that affected decisions to lease rather than buy: (1) leasing provides 100 percent deductibility of costs, (2) leasing does not dilute ownership or control, (3) leasing allows for piecemeal financing of large acquisitions, (4) the after-tax cost of leasing is less than the after-tax cost of equity, (5) leasing allows for the passthrough of the investment tax credit to compan-

[14]Paul F. Anderson, "Industrial Equipment Leasing Offers Economic and Competitive Edge," *Marketing News* (April 4, 1980), p. 20; and Monroe M. Bird, "Marketing to the Industrial Lease Buyer," *Industrial Marketing Management* 9 (April 1980), pp. 111–116.

[15]Anderson, "Industrial Equipment Leasing Offers Economic and Competitive Edge," p. 20.

ies with low or heavily sheltered earnings, and (6) lease payments provide a greater tax shield than depreciation or interest payments.[16]

Leasing has gained considerable momentum in the industrial market, and for the marketer of capital goods, it can be an alternative to selling those products to potential customers. Leasing has often proven beneficial for suppliers who could not otherwise make an initial sale to a company.

Leasing Arrangements.   There are three ways of leasing equipment to industrial customers.[17] First, the firm can lease directly to the customer by carrying the financing and working out the lease arrangements itself. Second, many large industrial firms such as International Harvester, John Deere, Allis-Chalmers, and General Electric are forming credit subsidiaries to provide leasing to their customers. This approach enables the company to tap an additional profit center and defer taxes through the use of installment sales treatment for tax reporting, while still recording a sale for financial records. Third, leasing may be arranged for customers through a bank that is involved in leasing industrial equipment or through one of the many companies specializing in industrial leasing such as CIT Financial, Commercial Credit, General Finance Corporation, U.S. Leasing, and U.S. Industrial Tools.

The two basic types of industrial leases are (1) financial, or full-payout, leases and (2) operating, or service, leases. Financial leases are noncancellable contracts, usually long term and fully amortized over the term. Lease payments over the contract term will normally exceed the original purchase price. The operating or service lease is usually short term, not fully amortized, and cancellable. The lessee is generally responsible for operating expenses, but the lessor provides maintenance, service, and sometimes, technical updating. Since the primary purpose is to provide customers with equipment that is only needed for a short time, contracts do not usually contain a purchase option.

Successful leasing strategy requires a careful assessment of its role in the overall marketing program, an understanding of the benefits and costs of leasing from the customer's perspective, and well-developed financial techniques that show potential customers the economic benefits of leasing. Evidence has suggested that many large customers employ financial analysis that fails to pinpoint the benefits of leasing.[18]

LOOKING BACK

The effect of price on subsequent sales volume and cost must be analyzed prior to the introduction of a new product, when initiating a price change, and when responding to competitive actions. This analysis is aided by the combined concepts of

[16]Robert W. Haas, *Industrial Marketing Management,* 3rd ed. (Boston: Kent Publishing Co., 1986), p. 369.
[17]Anderson, "Industrial Equipment Leasing Offers Economic and Competitive Edge"; and Bird, "Marketing to the Industrial Lease Buyer."
[18]Ibid.

marginal profits and learning curve cost reductions. Break-even analysis and return-on-investment pricing are excellent tools for interrelating market demand, production levels, and costs, which jointly impact company profits. Expected payoff analysis allows the price setter to quantify various market uncertainties and substitute these figures for pure intuition when making price decisions. However, certain qualitative factors must still be weighed.

Developing competitive bids is costly and time consuming. Attention must be given to the development of a bidding strategy that includes analysis of company objectives, screening of alternative bidding opportunities, and a method of assessing the probability of success for a particular bid.

Price negotiation, common in industrial marketing, is a bargaining process aimed at reaching agreement between two parties. The successful negotiation of a contract requires skill, experience, knowledge of the major factors relevant to the negotiation, and an objective appraisal of the seller's and buyer's relative strengths. Methods for measuring that strength and for determining tactical maneuvers during negotiation were discussed.

An alternative pricing strategy that is gaining great momentum in the industrial market is leasing. The three means of leasing equipment to industrial customers (direct, via credit subsidiaries, and bank leasing) were discussed along with the advantages for both buyers and sellers.

DISCUSSION QUESTIONS

1. Finding the optimal level for prices is a difficult task in industrial marketing. Outline specifically the approach that Prentice-Hall should take to find the optimal price for this textbook.
2. What factors make it difficult to use break-even analysis? Can they be overcome?
3. Why is return-on-investment pricing common in industrial markets that tend to be oligopolistic?
4. When should expected payoff analysis be used in establishing price?
5. Discuss how the learning curve affects price analysis.
6. To enhance the chances of winning contracts, a building contractor bids on every contract that comes up in his market area. Evaluate this method of developing bidding strategy.
7. Buyers and sellers spend a lot of time negotiating over price and other product factors during the exchange process. What steps can sellers take to improve their negotiating strategy?
8. Leasing is becoming increasingly important in the marketing of capital goods. What factors influence a buyer's decision to lease rather than buy capital goods?

EXERCISES

1. The Hot Ashes Laser Company (HAL) has developed a miniaturized plastic laser gun. Although the gun's beam is too weak to penetrate most substances, it appears to be an excellent etching tool for manufacturers of such products as personalized eyeglasses,

earrings, and hearing aids. In attempting to determine the optimal price for its new product, HAL has estimated market demand and variable costs over various price ranges. Given that HAL's fixed investment costs are $220,000, from the data given, estimate HAL's optimal price and production range for entering the market. If HAL decides to use a market penetration strategy, what should the entry price be? What would it be if HAL opted for a market skimming strategy?

Unit Price	Estimated Market Demand	Variable Cost per Unit
$4.10	90,000	$2.05
4.05	100,000	2.00
4.00	110,000	2.00
3.95	114,000	2.00
3.90	118,500	1.95
3.85	123,000	1.90
3.80	127,000	1.90
3.75	130,500	1.90
3.70	133,000	1.95
3.65	135,000	1.95
3.60	137,500	2.00
3.55	140,000	2.05

2. After Hot Ashes has produced 130,500 units, it obtains learning curve information for a similar but larger plastic laser gun, produced by Sianara, Inc. Sianara's gun production has an 85 percent learning curve. Using Sianara's curve, what does HAL predict its variable costs to be when production reaches 522,000 units? when it reaches 1,044,000 units?

3. HAL's standard costs for its guns are estimated to be $3.63 per unit. Given that HAL wants a 10 percent return on its investment of $220,000, what should price be if expected first-year sales are 127,000 units?

4. Consider that HAL entered the market at a price of $3.80, with fixed costs of $220,000 and variable costs of $1.90 per unit, and that by the end of the first year, market demand reached 127,000 units. To increase demand during the product's growth stage and protect its market share from competitors, HAL is considering a price reduction. Thus, several executives have gotten together and estimated the following possible reactions to (1) a 3 percent reduction in price from $3.80 to $3.68 and (2) a 5 percent reduction in price from $3.80 to $3.61. Using expected payoff analysis, which of the following options should HAL pursue?

    Option 1: Maintain price at $3.80.

    Option 2: Reduce price by 3 percent to $3.68.

    a. There is a 30 percent probability that competitors will not react. If this occurs, sales volume will increase by 15 percent, and variable cost will decrease by 5 cents.

    b. There is a 50 percent probability that competitors will exactly match the price reduction. If this occurs, sales volume will increase by 10 percent, and variable cost will decrease by 3 cents.

    c. There is a 20 percent probability that competitors will reduce price by 5 percent. If this occurs, sales volume will decrease by 5 percent, and variable costs will increase by 3 cents.

    Option 3: Reduce price by 5 percent to $3.61.

    a. There is a 20 percent probability that competitors will not react. If this occurs, sales volume will increase by 25 percent, and variable cost will decrease by 5 cents.

  b. There is a 40 percent probability that competitors will exactly match the price reduction. If this occurs, sales volume will increase by 15 percent, and variable cost will decrease by 3 cents.

  c. There is a 30 percent probability that competitors will reduce price by 8 percent. If this occurs, sales volume will decrease by 8 percent, and variable costs will increase by 2 cents.

5. HAL has learned that the Army base at Fort Still—which is in its market area—has let a closed bid for the development of plastic molded water canteens. Since HAL is anxious to get the contract, it has determined that a desirable bid opportunity exists and has developed the following information relative to its competitors' previous bids as they compared to HAL's direct costs on projects 1 through 20:

Project	HAL's Direct Cost	B's Bid	C's Bid	D's Bid
1	$32,000	$154,000	$51,000	$52,000
2	25,000	32,000	33,000	30,000
3	36,000	45,000	47,000	46,000
4	22,000	30,000	28,000	29,000
5	42,000	55,000	60,000	58,000
6	21,000	33,000	34,000	35,000
7	40,000	61,000	64,000	63,000
8	15,000	20,000	19,000	18,000
9	30,000	43,000	45,000	44,000
10	10,000	13,000	14,000	12,000
11	45,000	48,000	51,000	53,000
12	50,000	55,000	53,000	58,000
13	65,000	80,000	84,000	82,000
14	10,000	12,000	13,000	13,000
15	28,000	41,000	38,000	39,000
16	70,000	103,000	99,000	98,000
17	58,000	74,000	72,000	76,000
18	62,000	81,000	83,000	82,000
19	12,000	16,000	15,000	18,000
20	47,000	65,000	61,000	63,000

If HAL's direct cost for the upcoming bid has been estimated at $36,000, how much should it bid on this project? Hint: To figure HAL's optimal bid, you will have to determine by what percent each competitor's bid exceeded HAL's direct cost on projects 1 through 20. You will also have to assign probabilities of HAL's chances of underbidding its competitors.

SUGGESTED ADDITIONAL READINGS

BIRD, MONROE M., "Marketing to the Industrial Lease Buyer," *Industrial Marketing Management,* 9 (April 1980), pp. 111–116.

JAIN, SUBHASH C., and MICHAEL V. LARIC, "A Framework for Strategic Industrial Pricing," *Industrial Marketing Management* 8 (1979), pp. 75–80.

MORSE, WAYNE J., "Probabilistic Bidding Models: A Synthesis," *Business Horizons* (April 1975), pp. 67–74.

PARANKA, STEPHEN, "The Pay-off Concept in Competitive Bidding: A Way to Improve the Bidding Record," *Business Horizons* (August 1969), pp. 77–81.

PARANKA, STEPHEN, "Competitive Bidding Strategy: A Procedure for Pre-Bid Analysis," *Business Horizons* (June 1974), p. 39.

PART EIGHT

International Industrial Marketing

ATLAS COPCO SECURES THE MARKET

The Swedish-based multinational, Atlas Copco, had been serving South America with mining equipment for years when the Andean Pact was formed. Five major nations (Bolivia, Ecuador, Colombia, Peru, and Chile), comprising seventy million people, banded together to form the pact and told foreign suppliers they would face restrictive tariff barriers unless they were lucky enough to be chosen as exclusive producers within the Pact nations.

Atlas applied for the exclusive production rights and was selected as the sole producer of rock drills, large compressors, and pneumatic tools. It rented temporary quarters until a plant could be built in La Paz, Bolivia. Since local building know-how was not up to par, the new plant took longer to build than expected. But upon completion, it became apparent that it was almost impossible to find workers who had sufficient industrial experience to operate it. Under the pact, Bolivians had to be hired and trained as managers. Furthermore, seventy-five percent of the inputs for Atlas' products were to be of local content, which was impossible due to the lack of production facilities within the pact. Clearly, it was not an easy beginning.

The guaranteed and protected market then began to crumble as Chile withdrew from the pact, and an unpopular new Bolivian president threatened the continuance of that country's membership. Also, member nations were not able to agree on the nature of the restrictive, protective tariffs. Several of Atlas' competitors began selling their products within the pact, in part because Atlas' production problems in Bolivia hampered its competitiveness.

Even though all these problems have taken their toll on Atlas Copco, the company continues to operate, hoping eventually to make a profit in the pact, before ownership of the Bolivian plant, in accordance with Atlas' agreement, passes over to its Bolivian partners.

Source: See Dag Hovind, "Atlas Copco's Gamble in Bolivia," *International Management,* January 1981, p. 15.

International marketing is essentially a double-edged sword—to the marketer entering a foreign market for the first time, it is a challenge to the traditional way of doing business, and to the domestic marketer facing competition from a foreign competitor, it is a challenge from an "outsider" who neither knows nor cares how business is "conducted" in the country.

In this final part we discuss the formidable challenges international marketers face, the strategies they should consider, and the strategies that national firms might consider in response to the ever-growing presence of foreign competitors.

CHAPTER 18

Industrial Marketing in the International Environment

This, our final chapter, depicts the decision-making considerations of the industrial marketer operating in the international environment. It portrays, however, only the beginning chapter in the globalization of industry. Only now are we beginning to understand the totality of the impacts of international competition. While some industries in various nations have experienced phenomenal growth through multinational operations, others have been all but destroyed. We hope, then, that this chapter will leave you with

1. An appreciation of the inevitability and importance of international industrial marketing.
2. The numerous environmental differences between national and international marketing.
3. How strategic planning changes when a firm considers or enters the international arena.

Since the days of Adam Smith, we have been taught that specialization forms the theoretical basis of "comparative advantage"; that is, nations should specialize in producing and trading those products that they are most efficient at producing. Even if a particular nation cannot produce any product more efficiently than can another nation, both nations will still benefit from specialization and trade of those products they respectively produce most efficiently.

Since World War II, America has been the world's leading advocate of the theory of comparative advantage. We have done this by encouraging international

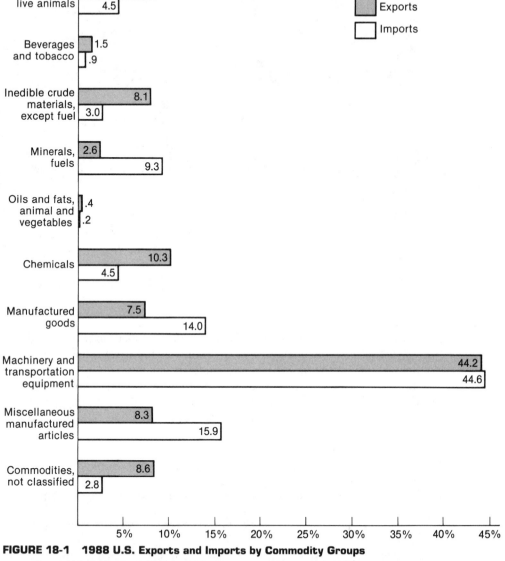

FIGURE 18-1   1988 U.S. Exports and Imports by Commodity Groups

Source: U.S. Foreign Trade Highlights, U.S. Department of Commerce (1988).

trade without government restrictions such as tariffs and quotas. Although this has been an uphill battle, much progress has been made toward achieving it. Nearly one-fourth of the goods produced in the world today cross national borders, nearly one-fifth of our industrial production is exported, and fully seventy percent of

American goods compete against products made abroad.[1] Thus whether a firm actually engages in international marketing or is simply challenged here at home by foreign competitors, it is essential that marketing decisions be made on the basis of international rationale. This is particularly so in industrial marketing because the majority of international trade is industrial trade, as Figure 18-1 highlights.

The critical issue facing industrial marketers is to remain competitive in what has become an increasingly competitive world. Today, all nations compete with one another for markets, capital, technology, supplies, and raw materials. Firms around the world have become more astute at assessing and overcoming political/legal risks, they have relocated to avoid barriers to trade, and they have become more knowledgeable about and effective in overcoming cultural differences among nations. Many international firms have become industrial giants, able to take advantage of learning curve effects on an international scale. National firms can no longer hide behind national borders but must now consider international competitors and adjust their strategies to meet them.

One study indicates that imports increased in relation to American production in thirty of forty-two industries, industries that account for 70 percent of American production.[2]

THE CASE FOR INTERNATIONAL MARKETING

While the United States had long been the number one exporter and importer, rapidly growing foreign competition began making dramatically increasing inroads since the early 1970s. United States merchandise imports exceeded exports in 1975 and continue to do so. Of course most other developed nations export a much greater portion of their output than does the U.S., which exports only 11.3 percent of its GNP. Table 18-1 indicates some long-term trends in this regard. You will note that West Germany's exports exceeded those of the United States in 1986. After a resurgence of United States exports in 1988 to $322 billion, the United States was virtually equal to West Germany with its figure of $323 billion; its exports far surpassed third-place Japan which exported $265 billion. However, the United States imported $441 billion, a large amount, eighty-one percent higher than those of West Germany and 168 percent higher than those of Japan.[3] Thus, international trade is both an opportunity and a threat. Domestic markets are often limited for some types of industrial goods. The increased volumes of going international can lead to lower marginal costs of distribution and help to pay for the heavy capital invest-

[1]John Young, "Global Competition: The New Reality," *California Management Review* 27:3 (Spring 1985), pp. 11–25.

[2]"Global Competition: The New Reality," *Report of the President's Commission on Industrial Competitiveness,* Vol. II (Washington, D.C.: U.S. Government Printing Office, January 11, 1985), p. 17.

[3]See *United States Trade Performance in 1988,* U.S. Department of Commerce, International Trade Administration, September 1989.

TABLE 18-1 Export Shares of Selected Countries

	1938	1948	1958	1968	1978	1986
World Exports	100.0%	100.0%	100.0%	100.0%	100.0%	100.0%
United States	13.5	21.8	16.3	14.3	10.9	10.2
Canada	3.8	5.4	4.6	5.3	3.6	4.1
France	3.9	3.7	5.0	5.3	5.9	5.6
Federal Republic of Germany	—	1.4	8.7	10.5	11.0	11.5
United Kingdom	12.1	11.5	8.8	6.4	5.6	5.1
Japan	4.7	1.2	2.6	5.4	6.1	9.9
U.S.S.R.	1.1	2.3	4.0	4.4	3.9	4.6
Other	60.9	52.7	50.0	48.4	53.0	49.0

Source: Calculated from United Nations, *Statistical Yearbook,* and United Nations, *Monthly Statistical Bulletins.*

ments that accompany many new technologies. Global marketing also allows a firm to take advantage of comparative advantages of supply sources, not only companies supplying inputs but labor and facilitating institutions such as financial organizations. Such firms can, given a certain finesse, take advantage of economic differences, such as exchange rates and inflationary considerations.[4] Because of such considerations, United States firms have invested $326.9 billion in other nations while foreign firms have invested $328.9 billion in the United States.[5] However, as long as United States imports continue to far surpass our exports, we can expect yearly foreign investment in the United States to be much larger than our investment abroad.

In this chapter, then, we discuss the economic, cultural, and political/legal environments of international marketing. Each of these environments must be analyzed although they become more involved, more difficult to understand, yet more interesting when a firm begins crossing international borders. It is also interesting to note that while the same marketing strategies used in domestic marketing are used in international marketing, they become more complicated to apply due to the differences in the international industrial environment. Thus, we shall also discuss those strategies to illustrate how differently they are employed when marketing across international borders.

THE INTERNATIONAL MARKETING ENVIRONMENT

Although marketing involves the same principles regardless of where it is performed, many differences exist between domestic and international marketing in the area of environmental influences. Not only do nations vary in their levels of eco-

[4]Martin Starr, "Global Production and Operations Strategy," *Columbia Journal of World Business* (Winter 1984), pp. 17–22.

[5]"Foreign Direct Investment: Effects on the United States," by the Subcommittee on Economic Stabilization of the House Committee on Banking, Finance and Urban Affairs (July 1989).

nomic development and the structure of their economic systems, but they have different monetary, legal, political, and cultural systems that place varying restrictions on the movement of goods and capital and marketing strategy. The differences encountered in the international marketing environment, as compared to the domestic marketing environment are shown in Figure 18-2.

While the demand for industrial goods is influenced more by technical factors than by cultural, the operating structures of many foreign industries are often considerably different. For example, in comparison to the United States and other developed nations, labor costs in underdeveloped countries are often so low that buyers may prefer to use labor rather than expensive capital equipment (see Table 18-2). Thus, marketing across nations requires the desire and ability to interpret an unfamiliar environment. Once these differences are recognized and understood, however, there is little fundamental difference in applying marketing knowledge in any part of the world.

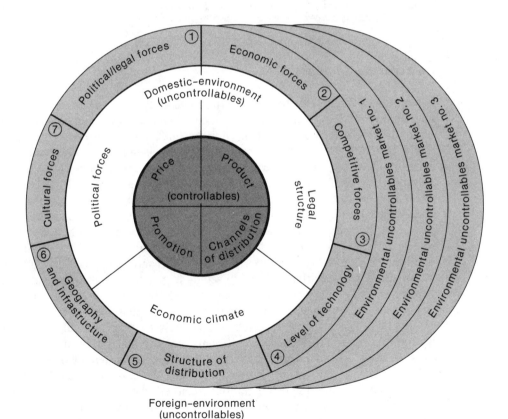

Foreign–environment
(uncontrollables)

FIGURE 18-2 The International Marketing Environment

Source: Philip R. Cateora and John M. Hess. *International Marketing,* 6th ed. [Homewood, Ill.: Richard D. Irwin, Inc., 1987], p.9. Reprinted with permission.

TABLE 18-2 Hourly Compensation for Production Workers in Manufacturing, 1972–1983

	1972		1980		1983	
	Rate	% of U.S.	Rate	% of U.S.	Rate	% of U.S.
United States	6.35	NA	9.89	NA	12.26	NA
West Germany	6.19	97	12.33	12	10.41	85
France	4.58	72	9.13	92	7.66	62
United Kingdom	3.26	51	7.28	74	6.48	53
Japan	3.05	48	5.61	57	6.20	51
Brazil	1.13	18	1.70	17	1.68	14
Mexico	1.92	30	2.95	30	1.45	12
South Korea	.36	.06	1.08	11	1.29	11

NA—Not available.

Source: U.S. Department of Labor, Bureau of Labor Statistics, Office of Productivity and Technology, October 1984, as found in Volume II, "Global Competition: The New Reality," *The Report of the President's Commission on Industrial Competitiveness* [Washington, D.C.: Superintendent of Documents, U.S. Government Printing Office, 1984].

The Economic Environment

Two economic factors that bear on international industrial marketing considerations are exchange rates and the balance of trade. Exchange rates depict how many monetary units (or portions of a monetary unit) of one nation's currency are required to obtain one monetary unit of another nation's currency. When exchange rates change, making one nation's currency more expensive and the other's less expensive, the effect is to change the price of products sold between nations.

The balance of trade is a monetary summary of the value of exports and imports between nations. For example, the United States balance of trade for 1987 was an all-time record, a negative $152 billion,[6] meaning that when the values of exports and imports were tallied, the United States had imported $123 billion more than it had exported. This is important to the international marketer as it indicates not only how well a nation is doing in selling its products, but it also indicates if a nation is selling enough products outside its own borders to have accumulated foreign currencies, currencies needed for purchasing foreign products.

Agricultural products, especially grains, have been traditionally a mainstay of our country's export trade. However, because of the dollar's overvaluation in recent years vis-à-vis other currencies, the short-term export potential of the principal grains (e.g., corn, wheat, rice, soybeans) has been bleak. In fact this abnormal situation stimulated former importing nations to either seek other sources or grow their own staple foods. Thailand is now an exporter of rice and is challenging the United States in markets long considered to be tied to this country. For example, Thailand

[6]*United States Trade Performance in 1988,* U.S. Department of Commerce.

is exporting rice to the Persian Gulf for approximately $200 per metric ton, c.i.f. (cost, insurance, and freight). That same grade of rice is available from California millers for $350 per metric ton, f.o.b. (free on board) Port of Oakland, California.[7]

Exchange Rates. Since the early 1970s, the values of all currencies in the free world have been allowed to "float" relatively freely; that is, their comparative values have been allowed to change in response to the supply and demand of money with little governmental interference. For example, in 1974 one U.S. dollar was equivalent to 2.58 German marks, by 1979 it was only 1.73 marks, but in 1985 it rose to equal 3.31 marks. Between 1974 and 1979, the purchasing power of the dollar, in terms of German goods, dropped thirty-three percent, and between 1979 and 1985, it increased ninety-one percent.

Firms involved in international marketing must monitor exchange rates closely if they are to take advantage of changing rates as well as to protect themselves. When a foreign currency is becoming more expensive compared, for instance, to the U.S. dollar (making U.S. products cheaper abroad), the U.S. marketer should consider such options as (1) expanding its overseas marketing efforts to increase world market share or (2) raising its price to increase profits. On the other hand, when a currency is becoming less expensive compared to the dollar (making U.S. products more expensive abroad), the U.S. marketer should consider (1) reducing price to increase quantities sold, with the hope that learning curve effects will make the price reduction profitable, (2) importing less expensive inputs from overseas, or (3) relocating its production facilities abroad.

To illustrate how some of these strategies are employed, during the early 1980s when U.S. firms were faced with a dramatic increase in the value of the dollar (as much as 100 percent against several currencies), Du Pont, Ingersoll-Rand, and Beckman Instruments, to name a few, transferred their export-producing plants abroad.[8,9] Not only did these companies follow the strategy of moving production facilities overseas, they also began purchasing more foreign inputs.[10]

When a firm relocates its production facilities abroad, it is exporting capital rather than products. The exportation of capital tends to threaten a nation's ability to compete in worldwide markets. It lowers the capital-labor ratio allowing labor productivity to fall, becoming less competitive, leading to a slower growth rate and possibly higher rates of inflation.[11] The estimated number of jobs lost to U.S. citizens due to American manufacturers moving abroad has been estimated to be between 1.5 to 2 million.[12] One authority estimates about 22,000 jobs are gained by

[7]John H. Gore, international marketing consultant (August 8, 1985), telephone interview.

[8]Gary Putka, "Moving Abroad," *The Wall Street Journal* (April 9, 1985) pp. 1, 12.

[9]"Drastic New Strategies to Keep U.S. Multinationals Competitive," *Business Week* (October 8, 1984), pp. 168-172.

[10]Gary Putka. "Moving Abroad," pp. 1, 12.

[11]The President's Commission on Industrial Competitiveness, quoted in John Young, "Global Competition: The New Reality," *California Management Review* 27: 3 (Spring 1985), pp. 11–25.

[12]Putka, "Moving Abroad," pp. 1, 12.

each one billion dollars of exports—in other words, if imports exceed exports by $100 billion, we could calculate a loss of 2.2 million potential jobs.[13] In 1987, before exports began to recover, imports exceeded exports by $152 billion. Such job losses could be a major cause of real hourly wages remaining relatively stagnant between 1973 and 1980, declining after 1980, and edging up with the beginning of 1988.

In the mid-1960s and early 1970s, when U.S. companies began the process of transferring some of their labor-intensive production lines abroad, the countries usually considered were Japan, Taiwan, South Korea, and Hong Kong. Today, companies headquartered in these countries are transferring their facilities to Malaysia and Sri Lanka. They, too, have been affected by the rising cost of labor.[14]

Balance of Trade.   Between nations, one of the major causes for changing exchange rates is the balance of trade. Trade balances are affected by the development of a nation's production facilities, the cost of its inputs (such as labor), and the quality of its products. Because of their effect on exchange rates, however, trade balances play an important role in international marketing. During the first seventy years of this century, for instance, the standard of living in the United States increased greatly as we experienced trade surpluses. Since 1970, the United States standard of living has leveled off and even decreased as trade deficits mounted.

Nations that experience long-term trade deficits, along with a decline in their currencies' exchange rates, have little foreign currency in reserve to purchase products from abroad. This dilemma does little to increase their standard of living. To counteract the effects of decreasing exchange rates, governments often take severe actions such as (1) devaluating their own currency, which has the effect of making their goods cheaper in world markets and foreign goods more expensive at home, and (2) directing the spending of scarce foreign currencies toward capital goods and away from consumer goods. In 1971, and again in 1973, the United States devaluated the dollar for this very purpose.

The Cultural Environment

Cultural considerations in international marketing are less concerned with perceptions of products and more with problems in personal selling. In part, this is because industrial products are more homogeneous worldwide than are consumer products. While the English, the Japanese, and the Americans have differing tastes and expectations in the purchase of cake mixes, such is not the case with industrial products. Steel, for instance, when purchased by an English, a Japanese, or an American original equipment manufacturer (OEM) is basically for the same purpose—to produce goods. Steel is steel no matter where it is sold, as long as it meets the buyer's standards.

Personal selling, on the other hand, presents the industrial marketer with special problems because of the differences in cultural attitudes among nations—differ-

[13]*United States Trade,* U.S. Department of Commerce.
[14]See Gore, personal communication.

AMERICAN CULTURE IS OFTEN A PUZZLE
FOR FOREIGN MANAGERS IN THE U.S.

A group of Arab oil workers sent to Texas for training found American teaching methods impersonal. Several Japanese workers at a U.S. manufacturing plant had to learn how to put courtesy aside and interrupt conversations when there was trouble. Executives of a Swiss-based multinational couldn't understand why its American managers demanded more autonomy than their European counterparts.

To all these people, America is a foreign country with a strange corporate culture. Just as Americans doing business abroad must grapple with unfamiliar social and commercial practices, so too must the European, Asian and Latin American managers of U.S. subsidiaries, a growing number of whom are coming to work here. The U.S. Department of Immigration and Naturalization says that last fiscal year 65,349 intercompany transferees, up from 21,495 in 1978, were brought here to work in an administrative or managerial capacity or to use some specialized knowledge.

In part, the transferees are following their employers' money. Direct foreign investment in the U.S. has increased from $30.6 billion in 1978 to $174.0 billion by the end of the third quarter of 1985, according to the U.S. Commerce Department. American companies too are bringing in more foreign managers for training that will enable them to replace high-cost American personnel in such places as Hong Kong, West Germany and Brazil.

To lessen the culture shock, many companies are relying on consultants to provide books, movies and special programs that educate foreign employees about corporate life in the U.S. Some have taken the language instruction, tax advice and orientation techniques used when Americans are sent abroad and modified them to accommodate foreigners transferred here. Others are trying a sort of buddy system, pairing foreign newcomers with American managers.

Culturally Determined

Most people think that culture is manners, food, dress, arts and crafts,'' says Clifford Clarke, president of IRI International, a Redwood City, Calif., consulting company. They don't realize that how you motivate a guy is culturally determined. Every managerial task is culturally determined.''

Occasionally, transferees find that behavior suitable at home may irritate co-workers here. "Living in the U.S.A.,'' a recent training film, portrays a Japanese employee angering an American colleague by repeatedly apologizing for a late report; the American expects explanations and solutions. "In America, if you talk around things people get frustrated with you,'' says Lennie Copeland, who helped produce the film.

Jose Carlos Villates, a business manager for animal health products at American Cyanamid Co., also had a problem with office protocol. Back in Puerto Rico and the Dominican Republic, where he was raised, business people would begin meetings with relaxed chitchat. At the company's headquarters in Wayne, N.J., though, he says he picks up "signals or body language'' that Americans find such sociability time wasting. But even after 15 months in the U.S., Mr. Villates feels uncomfortable plunging abruptly into business. "It strikes us as cold-blooded,'' he says.

Europeans, on the other hand, can be flummoxed by "a deceiving appearance of informality," says French-born Andre Rude. "They don't realize the urgency of the request and find themselves in trouble" when work isn't done on time. Mr. Rude counsels international transferees at Hewlett-Packard Co. in Palo Alto, Calif.

Classroom Difficulties

Many foreigners also have a hard time with American-style classroom training. Mr. Clarke of IRI says his firm teaches Japanese to be more outspoken in such situations and recommends that American teachers "count to 10" while waiting for a reply. He adds that Arab oil workers, for their part, learned more quickly when classroom time was supplemented with individual sessions and even home visits by teachers.

Managers don't need to be physically present in the U.S. to be confused about American ways. Foreign top executives are increasingly having to ponder how to manage and motivate the senior-level Americans who oversee their U.S. subsidiaries.

The problem is compounded by the fact that these subsidiaries are often larger than the parent companies' home headquarters. "The size and scope of responsibility is probably greater for those being managed than for the [executive foreign] managers," says Rodman Drake, a managing partner of Cresap, McCormick & Paget, an international consulting firm. "It creates natural jealousy."

Mr. Drake cites the case of a Swiss-based multinational whose U.S. unit made up thirty percent of the company's world-wide sales. The Swiss parent called in consultants to help eliminate the "ongoing friction" between managers here and at home over day-to-day pricing, planning and marketing decisions.

More Autonomy

The Swiss were persuaded to allow the American managers more autonomy. But they were uncomfortable doing so, says Mr. Drake, because they didn't run any of their seventy or eighty other international units that way.

"There's more of a macho, cowboy, I'm-in-charge style of operating here, in contrast to the collegial approach prevalent in Europe and Asia," he explains.

Some of the programs designed to speed acculturation are intensive and emotionally strenuous. One U.S. manufacturer has retained trainers to stage role-playing sessions for its Japanese managers, some of whom have had special difficulty with American bluntness. During one of these, in which a Japanese manager was told to criticize an American employee's performance, "it took five runs of the same situation until he was direct enough that the American could realize he was being criticized," says Gary Wederspahn, a director of the international division of Moran, Stahl & Boyer, the consulting firm that conducted the sessions.

Other programs provide help in a broader context. Dow Chemical Co. fears isolating transferees, says Donald Reed, manager of international personnel. So the company pairs them with American colleagues, who take charge of social and professional introductions and connections.

"There's a more rapid integration and buildup to total efficiency," he says. "You don't want them to come here and feel uncomfortable. You want them to feel good about the assignment."

Families of foreign managers can find the U.S. stressful too, and many companies try to accommodate them. Utaka Yamaguchi, a Hewlett-Packard engineer, was confident he would adapt to life here during a three-year California assignment. But he worried about his wife, who spoke no English. The company found them an apartment near many other Japanese families, who help Mrs. Yamaguchi with shopping and errands. Meanwhile, she's studying English.

On the whole, foreign managers seem pleased with the additional help they receive. "They made sure I had the best transition possible," says Mr. Villates of American Cyanamid. "They made us feel at home. I could sense the company was doing everything necessary to make us feel we were being accepted without pampering us."

Source: Amanda Bennett, "American Culture Is Often a Puzzle for Foreign Managers in the U.S." Reprinted by permission of *The Wall Street Journal.* Copyright © Dow Jones & Company, Inc., February 12, 1986, p. 12. All rights reserved.

ences that, if not recognized and adapted to, can critically affect marketing effectiveness. While many American firms are paying more attention to international communication, too frequently, due to ignorance of cultural differences, American marketers make embarrassing mistakes such as offering Japanese industrial buyers doormats as a token of friendship, not realizing that shoes are not worn inside Japanese homes.

Cultural attitudes, especially with respect to time, space, materialism, friendship, and contractual agreements, directly affect the climate for international business. Thus, sales people, as well as other company representatives, going abroad should be sensitive to these differences and how they influence the behavior of people within international organizations.[15]

Time Perceptions.   Perhaps, because of the synthesis of immigrants coming from different cultures or effects of the Protestant work ethic, Americans have developed an obsession for doing things in a timely fashion. Nowhere else in the world can such clock-worship be found. Although it is impossible to arrange countries on a continuum relative to "the concern for time," Germany, most likely, approaches the United States. When a German train is fifteen minutes overdue, there has been either an unexpected monumental event or a major holiday; otherwise, train arrivals and departures take place within two minutes of published schedules. On the other end of the scale are Latin nations, which are quite distant from the U.S. perspective of time, with Asian nations, perhaps, even farther; Ethiopians even go farther by holding an inverted view of time compared to ours.

The U.S. Embassy in Brazil, for example, warns that, "Many Brazilian executives do not react favorably to quick and infrequent visits by foreign sales representatives. They prefer a more continuous working relationship implying long-term

[15]Edward Hall, "The Silent Language in Overseas Business," *Harvard Business Review* (May-June 1960), pp. 87–96.

commitment in Brazil.[16] A more extreme view was given by one Japanese business-man who said, "You Americans have one terrible weakness. If we make you wait long enough, you will agree to anything.[17] In Ethiopia, on the other hand, the view is that the more important the decision, the more time should be devoted to making it, so that if a salesperson attempts to hurry things, the implication is that the "deal" is not too important. Some Ethiopians will even attempt to extend the time it takes to make a decision, simply to impress others with the importance of their decision making.[18]

The important implication of time-oriented differences in cultural perspectives is that time has different meanings around the world and the international industrial marketer must understand and adapt to these differences. While a thirty-minute wait to see an American buyer may indicate the buyer's lack of interest and inspire aggressive sales tactics, the same length of waiting and the same sales tactics overseas can cause the American salesperson to appear to be irrational, uninformed, and greedy.

The seasoned international businessperson knows from experience to set aside sufficient time for negotiations with parties for whom time is not measured in mone-tary terms. Often these officials will ask at the very outset how many days has the visitor set aside. Should he or she say seven, serious negotiations will usually be delayed for some unexpected reason until day 5. To prepare for this contingency,

---

WAITING MEANS DIFFERENT THINGS IN DIFFERENT COUNTRIES

In the United States, a corporation executive knows what is meant when a client lets a month go by before replying to a business proposal. On the other hand, he senses an eagerness to do business if he is immediately ushered into the client's office. In both instances, he is reacting to subtle cues in the timing of interaction, cues which he depends on to chart his course of action.

Abroad, however, all this changes. The American executive learns that the Latin Americans are casual about time and that if he waits an hour in the outer office before seeing the Deputy Minister of Finance, it does not necessarily mean he is not getting anywhere. There people are so important that nobody can bear to tear himself away; because of the resultant interruptions and conversational de-tours, everybody is constantly getting behind. What the American does not know is the point at which the waiting becomes significant.

Source: Reprinted by permission of the *Harvard Business Review.* Excerpt from "The Silent Language in Overseas Business," by Edward T. Hall, May–June 1960, pp. 87–96. Copyright © 1960 by the President and Fellows of Harvard College, all rights reserved.

---

[16]See *Marketing in Brazil,* found in International Marketing Series, OBR 81-23, prepared by Larry Garges and Stuart Barrowcliff. Office of Country Marketing and the U.S. Embassy in Brasilia and the American Consulate General in Rio de Janeiro (September, 1981), p. 17.

[17]Hall, "The Silent Language in Overseas Business," pp. 87- 96.

[18]Ibid.

the visitor should always be willing to extend his or her visit for several more days, and again for several days more if conditions warrant it.[19]

Spatial Perspectives. Proxemics is the science of the use of space in communications. South Americans, Greeks, and Japanese prefer to conduct business while standing or sitting close to their business associates.[20] Also, in many countries, business acquaintances tend to be more animated in their conversations, including touching, than their American counterparts. In our country this behavior could be considered improper. Even the degree of eye contact between business people varies considerably from nation to nation. Eastern Europeans and some Latin people, for instance, prefer eye-to-eye contact in business dealings. Such differences in spatial perceptions often lead to feelings of apprehension and uneasiness on the part of Americans, who fail to respond according to accepted norms, thus severely hindering successful business negotiations.

Materialism Perceptions. In the United States, materialism, and its rewards, have long been an important motivator in recruiting, keeping, and inspiring employees to be productive. Other people of the world, however, are much less materialistic. For example, Hindus and Buddhists avoid material things in their attempts to achieve nirvana.[21]

Also, what we consider to be wealth is not necessarily what other people think of as such. For example, some people value cattle over money, while others value camels, and still others gold.[22] Only in the United States are stocks and bonds so highly valued. American stock exchanges handle eighty-three percent of the world's stock transactions. Japan takes second place with approximately eleven percent.

The international firm that is establishing production facilities overseas or merely attempting to market products and services overseas needs to understand what people desire to attract and motivate them. United States business people who have traveled to nations such as Morocco have indicated they experienced cultural shock when seeing the "appalling" conditions of offices and other business facilities. In reality, the typical, successful Moroccan entrepreneur is more concerned with business friendships and achieves more from feelings of self-esteem and those friendships than from the size of a desk or expensive office decor.

Until the United States develops a professional corps of international businesspersons, it will lag behind other nations such as Japan. Just as we have raised the professional status of medical doctors and accountants, so, too, must we raise the status of international business people. Until business schools recognize the need for having a separate discipline in international business and companies come to

---

[19]See Gore, personal communication.

[20]David Ricks, *Big Business Blunders* (Homewood, Ill.: Dow Jones-Irwin, 1983), p. 16.

[21]Vern Terpstra, *The Cultural Environment of International Business* (Cincinnati, Ohio: Southwestern Publishing Co., 1978), p. 81.

[22]Ibid., p. 83.

appreciate the value of recruiting international business majors for their international operations, the problems will persist.[23]

Friendship Perceptions. In most of the world the marketing of industrial goods depends more on friendship, trust, and service than is the case in the more pragmatic, case-by-case basics-oriented United States. In Central and South America, for example, the industrial buyer prefers to buy from the foreign supplier who has expressed a long-term, genuine friendship and an interest in the buyer's country. Long-term business friendships are perceived as a kind of social insurance.[24]

Americans have separate social rules for business and personal relationships. This is not true elsewhere. In Saudi Arabia the same courtesies are provided a business caller as a personal friend. In Latin America a businessperson would never rush a counterpart. And, in Japan, should a business proposition become unsatisfactory, the Japanese businessperson will never flatly turn it down, but instead will suggest that "there are too many difficulties."[25]

Contractual Agreements. In America, we place a high value on carefully written contracts that have been negotiated under certain rules, regulations, and laws. However, the rules of contracts and contract negotiation vary from culture to culture. In fact, the vice president of international trade operations for AMF Corporation has warned, "Beware of contractual sales agreements. In some nations they're good for life."[26] In Latin America and Greece, the written contract is viewed only as an

---

THE LANGUAGE OF FRIENDSHIP

The American finds his friends next door and among those with whom he works. It has been noted that we take people up quickly and drop them just as quickly. Occasionally a friendship formed during schooldays will persist, but this is rare. For us there are few well-defined rules governing the obligations of friendship. It is difficult to say at which point our friendship gives way to business opportunism or pressure from above. In this we differ from many other people in the world. As a general rule in foreign countries, friendships are not formed as quickly as in the United States but go much deeper, last longer, and involve real obligations.

Source: Reprinted by permission of the *Harvard Business Review.* Excerpt from "The Silent Language in Overseas Business," by Edward T. Hall, May–June 1960, pp. 87–96. Copyright © 1960 by the President and Fellows of Harvard College; all rights reserved.

---

[23]See Gore, personal communication.

[24]Garges and Barrowcliff, *Marketing in Brazil,* p. 17; and Hall, "The Silent Language in Overseas Business," pp. 87–96.

[25]Edward Cundiff and Marye Hilger, *Marketing in the International Environment* (Englewood Cliffs, N.J.: Prentice-Hall, Inc., 1984), p. 119.

[26]Henry Rodkin, "Selling Abroad: 10 Rules to Live (and Sell) by Overseas," *Sales and Marketing Management,* April 2, 1984, pp. 63–64.

expression of intent at the time the contract is signed. Much importance is given to personal friendships after the signing. On the other hand, for many Moslems the written contract is offensive and is perceived as a reflection on their honor.[27]

In the United States, written contracts are usually upheld, while oral contracts are frequently broken. In Japan, however, oral contracts are considered to be as binding as written contracts. This is because relationships between two firms are "always assumed to be continuous." Thus, when problems occur between two companies, the firms' primary interests are to maintain a continuing relationship. And because both firms assume that the relationship will continue, they tend to be conciliatory. These continuing relationships are a type of insurance against the uncertainties of new contracts and allow firms to renegotiate without litigation. In fact, Japanese firms regard these continuing relationships as having a higher value than the economic benefits that might be achieved by changing relationships.[28]

Although no one can be familiar with the numerous contractual considerations worldwide, simply knowing the existence of a great number of divergencies among such considerations is extremely important to the international marketer.

The Political/Legal Environment

The practice of international marketing is significantly influenced by the politics and laws of host nations. What takes place in the political/legal environment affects (1) whether or not a firm will engage in international marketing in a particular country, (2) its form of international market entry, and (3) how it employs marketing strategies. Although many political actions and legal restrictions may seem to be unfair to exporting firms as well as firms locating abroad, we must remember that each nation must put the interest of its own people above others, and it is government and public officials who are charged with the responsibility of developing policies that will achieve that goal.

A nation's political and legal actions that normally affect the international marketer are (1) restricting imports, (2) establishing market and monetary controls, and (3) taking control of foreign owned assets.

Import Restrictions.   To restrict the inflow of foreign goods, as discussed in Chapter Three, nations use tariffs, quotas, artificial barriers, and voluntary agreements. Import restrictions help to protect the national economy. When foreign products are more expensive or inaccessible, jobs and capital remain at home. For example, during the 1970s and early 1980s when the world was experiencing high rates of inflation and unemployment, many governments imposed protective barriers to insulate their domestic economies.

While all nations control their foreign trade, they vary in degree and kind of control. Because of a long-term trade deficit, Brazil is attempting to direct scarce

[27]Hall, "The Silent Language in Overseas Business."

[28]Yoshi Tsurumi, "Managing Consumer and Industrial Marketing Systems in Japan," *Sloan Management Review* (Fall 1982), pp. 41–49.

foreign currency away from consumer goods and toward capital goods, while at the same time building essential industries. Brazil's tariffs, therefore, range from 0 to 205 percent, though most goods are in a 30 to 85 percent bracket. In its attempt to build a domestic minicomputer industry, Brazil is blocking the importation of a wide range of minicomputers, while allowing large mainframe computers to be imported.

Brazil also has numerous artificial barriers. At customs, importers must present copies of commercial invoices, bills of lading, and import permits. The American embassy has warned, "It cannot be overemphasized that the documentation must be completed and correct in all requirements in order to avoid heavy fines and penalties." These fines can be as high as the value of the imported goods.[29]

Because of such restrictions, some American firms have moved production facilities to Brazil. Companies from many other major free-world nations relocate in other countries for similar reasons. One estimate claims that sales of multinational corporations exceed twenty percent of the world gross domestic product.[30] At the end of 1988 the United Kingdom had $102 billion, Japan $53 billion, and the Netherlands $49 billion invested in the United States.[31]

Market and Monetary Control. To protect their home industries, governments worldwide also enact a number of forms of market and monetary control. These include (1) restricting the sale of particular foreign products, (2) levying various types of taxes on foreign-owned production facilities, (3) establishing price ceilings on products produced in foreign-owned plants, (4) requiring foreign-owned companies to employ a certain percentage of local workers, (5) requiring that products produced locally have a specified amount of locally produced components, (6) requiring that local foreign-owned companies be owned in part by local businesses or the local government, (7) limiting the amount of profits that can be remitted to the parent company, and (8) giving direct support of local businesses.

Although these various controls can hurt international firms, various strategies exist to overcome them. General Motors, for instance, was hurt in Argentina when the regime of General Videla placed price controls on assembled vehicles but not on what were mostly locally made component parts. Canadian Prime Minister Trudeau reduced foreign ownership (mostly U.S.) of petroleum reserves, to fulfill promises to his strong supporters in Canada's eastern provinces.[32] On the other hand, the H. J. Heinz plant in Zimbabwe is allowed to return profits to its overseas parents, though most other foreign-owned plants are not. Heinz owns fifty-one percent of the plant there, though most other foreign companies own less than half. The government in Zimbabwe even lifted controls on the price of cooking oil to benefit Heinz.

[29]Garges and Barrowcliff, *Marketing in Brazil.*

[30]John H. Dunning and John M. Stopford, *Multinationals: Company Performance and Global Trends,* May 1983, p. 53; in *International Direct Investment,* U.S. Department of Commerce, November 1988, p. 2.

[31]"Foreign Direct Investment," Subcommittee on Economic Stabilization.

[32]Thomas Shreeve, "Be Prepared for Political Changes Abroad," *Harvard Business Review* (July-August 1984), pp. 111-118.

Heinz employed two strategies that may account for its enviable position. First, four government representatives sit on the nine-man Heinz board of directors. They help "unjam things" and "they will also lobby for the industry," according to Heinz' operations manager in Zimbabwe. Many U.S. companies located abroad have found it advantageous to employ influential local citizens and government officials. Second, Heinz was careful and thorough in negotiating a contract with the government of Zimbabwe—a process that took nine months.

Taking Control of Assets.   There are five ways in which governments take control of foreign assets within their nations. These are expropriation, confiscation, nationalization, socialization, and domestication.[33]

Expropriation occurs when a government takes control of a foreign firm's assets and compensates the firm for the assets. *Confiscation* is expropriation without compensation. *Nationalization* occurs when a government takes control of a single or a few industries, including both foreign and local firms. *Socialization* involves a government taking control of all industries. And *domestication* is accomplished by various means, usually requiring a foreign-owned firm gradually to transfer control to local citizens.

Government take-overs are a source of extreme aggravation to companies with overseas production facilities. Perhaps the most notable example of companies retaliating against such actions is of ITT's efforts to thwart Allende from taking power in Chile in 1970. "A director of ITT and former head of the CIA, offered his successor a $1 million contribution" to finance a campaign to stop Allende from taking office. In spite of the efforts, Allende's government came to power and nationalized Anaconda's and Kennecott's copper mines. U.S. firms like Kennecott retaliated by suing in France, Sweden, Germany, and Italy, the buyers of Chile's nationalized copper. Other corporations were pressured to refuse to sell Chile spare parts for trucks and machinery, "even for cash."[34]

The international marketer should always be cognizant of political decisions, no matter how remote, that could ultimately affect business operations. Even today American farmers have still not rebounded from President Carter's decision to declare a grain embargo on the Soviet Union because of its invasion of Afghanistan in late 1979. Because the embargo virtually canceled our government's obligation under a long-term contract with the Soviet Union, Moscow reacted by buying grain from Argentina, Australia, Canada, and France. Never again would the Soviet Union depend on any single foreign source for its vital needs. Not only did the embargo destroy an approximately 10–20 million ton annual grain sale, but such ancillary services as milling, processing, and shipping as well. Although the latter were too numerous and extensive to estimate in value, their loss was also profound.[35]

[33]This discussion is based on Subhash Jain, *International Marketing Management* (Boston: Kent Publishing Co., 1984), pp. 224–226.

[34]Richard Barnet and Ronald Muller, *Global Reach* (New York: Simon & Schuster, Inc., 1974), pp. 81–85.

[35]See Gore, personal communication.

TABLE 18-3 Checklist for Analyzing the Political/Legal Environment

1. What is the country's political structure?
2. How do citizens, political parties, and special interest groups participate in political decision making?
3. What is the current government's political philosophy? How is it implemented?
4. What are the philosophies of opposing political forces?
5. What role does the current government see for foreign business?
6. Is foreign business treated differently from local firms in public policy? If so, how?
7. What is the country's history in dealing with different types of foreign businesses?
8. What is the process whereby changes in public policy are made?
9. What are the current and foreseeable trends in relationships between government in this country and in my home country?
10. What general role does government see for private business in this country's economic life?
11. What restrictions on international transfers of resources will affect my firm's operations in this country?
12. What are the major trends in the regulatory environment?
13. What incentives does the government give to private business and foreign investors?
14. What are the trigger points for increased nationalistic feelings in the host country?
15. How does the government assert its economic sovereignty?
16. What are the specific risks of loss of ownership or control of assets?
17. What are the chances of political harassment and what form is it likely to take?
18. What tools can we use to build a mutually beneficial relationship with this country's government? Will they survive a possible change of government?
19. What are the possibilities of a change in government or other expressions of political instability?
20. Are my firm, my industry, and/or my products likely to be politically vulnerable?
21. What is the basis of this country's legal system?
22. Will my firm's activities violate any of the home or host countries' extraterritorial laws?
23. What areas of my marketing strategy will be affected by the host country's legal environment?

Source: Edward W. Cundiff and Marye Tharp Hilger, *Marketing in the International Environment* [Englewood Cliffs, N.J.: Prentice-Hall, Inc., 1984], p. 167. Reprinted by permission.

Space here does not permit coverage of the many methods available for assessing the political/legal environment of foreign countries; nevertheless, Table 18-3 indicates the various forces that should be assessed by the industrial firm planning to expand into international operations.[36]

FORMS OF INTERNATIONAL MARKET ENTRY

Regardless of the problems and risks involved in international marketing, profit enhancement is a major stimulus for marketing in foreign countries. Increased profit potential rises from the opportunity to utilize unused plant capacity, to offset

[36]For further insights into such assessments, see Stephen Kobrin et al., "The Assessment and Evaluation of Noneconomic Environments by American Firms, A Preliminary Report," *Journal of International Business Studies* (Spring-Summer 1980), pp. 32–47; and Shreeve, "Be Prepared for Political Changes Abroad," pp. 111–118.

seasonal fluctuations in sales, to make wider applications of R&D findings, to recover manufacturing investments, to offset declining margins due to saturated markets at home, and to keep pace with competitors who have overseas plants. The impetus for international marketing can also originate from government activities, such as assistance in the financing of export sales, export expansion programs, or trade fairs, as well as through unsolicited orders from abroad.[37]

Whatever the impetus, once the decision has been made to expand into foreign operations and market choices have been made, it is essential that the strategy for market entry be well conceived for successful penetration. As Table 18-4 indicates, several alternative strategies are available for entering international marketing.

The terms "strategic" and "operational" reflect the degree of a firm's commitment to international marketing. Operational indicates the least company commitment and is reflective of tactical actions taken to implement strategies. For example, in the course of producing for a domestic market, a firm discovers that it has excess inventory and operationally decides to sell it overseas. Operational strategies include indirect and direct exporting and foreign licensing. Strategic, on the other hand, indicates that a firm is more committed to become involved internationally, and devises major strategies to allow it to do so, such as entering joint ventures or foreign production.

Indirect Exporting. The most common and least risky form of market entry is indirect exporting. Here the firm sells to intermediaries, who, in turn, sell to foreign markets. While indirect exporting is a good strategy when the firm has little knowledge of exporting to foreign markets, where markets are limited in size, or when the

TABLE 18-4 Forms of International Market Entry

Operational Strategies	*Strategic Strategies*
Indirect exporting	Joint ventures
Sells to domestic intermediaries; for example, export trading company or export management company.	Local and foreign firms share ownership. Foreign production
Direct exporting	Establishes solely owned production facilities in foreign country.
Sells directly to foreign buyer or foreign intermediaries—local company ships and handles financing and shipping documentation.	
Foreign licensing	
Exports "know-how" through management contract.	

[37]This discussion is based on Cundiff and Hilger, *Marketing in the International Environment,* pp. 29–38.

firm does not wish to commit its resources, it places constraints on other marketing strategies as well as on control.

Direct Exporting. The investment and risk in direct exporting are greater than in indirect exporting. Under direct exporting, the firm has to establish foreign distribution, increase production capacity, and adapt products for foreign markets. Direct exporting places the firm in an overseas market through either a sales branch or subsidiary, or an agent who represents the firm exclusively in the host country. The direct exporter, unlike the indirect entrepreneur, tends to have more control over the process and better feedback due to dealing directly with foreign buyers or foreign intermediaries.

Both indirect and direct exporters, however, receive less foreign market information than do firms using other methods (except licensing). This makes it more difficult for the industrial marketer to determine proper marketing mix strategies involving such areas as quality, packaging, and pricing. The advantages of direct over indirect exporting, however, are greater control, better marketing information, and the chance to develop expertise in international marketing.

Foreign Licensing. Foreign licensing involves an agreement between a firm in one country (the licensor) and a firm in another country (the licensee) whereby the former permits the latter the use of its manufacturing processes, patents, or trademarks in exchange for a royalty fee. Foreign licensing often occurs when overseas production facilities have been taken over by a foreign government. The experienced managers are asked to stay on and provide technical and managerial expertise.

"Turnkey" operations, a type of foreign licensing, involves a firm in providing experts to set up a foreign company, ultimately turning the operation over to the host entity (e.g., foreign firm or nation). Some form of royalties is also paid on turnkeys after the experts have left the scene. (Fiat was able to sell a factory in the Soviet Union through this method.)

The advantage of licensing is that the firm gains market entry at little risk. Foreign licensing, however, limits profit potential, and licensees often lack managerial and marketing expertise. Licensees may eventually even become competitors; however, if licensees do a poor job, they can hurt the parent company's image.

Joint Ventures. When two or more firms or investors share ownership and control over operations and investments, they have entered into a joint venture. Joint ventures provide better knowledge of local markets, a local identity, and a shared risk. Sometimes they may be necessary for political and/or economic reasons. The local government may require joint ownership as a condition for entry, or the firm may lack the essential financial or managerial resources to undertake market entry by itself. Joint ventures, however, sometimes result in conflicts in management and marketing philosophies, since foreign philosophies can be much different.

Foreign Production. Foreign production, often referred to as direct investment, involves the largest commitment and, thus, the greatest amount of risk due to the chances of blocked or devalued currencies or expropriation. It also allows the firm to establish a company image and gain knowledge of the foreign market, as well as to reduce costs of transportation and distribution—offering the greatest profit potential and market control. How successful a firm is in foreign production, however, depends on its ability to adjust its labor, organization, communication, and management requirements to the needs of local employees and operating conditions. Thus, direct investment is justifiable only when the market and potential for sales are substantial.

The form of market entry strategy depends on the firm's resources, its international marketing objectives, and the market potential and legal/political environment within the foreign market(s) under consideration. Each succeeding strategy involves the firm in more commitment, risk, and potential profits. Thus, before a market entry strategy is chosen, the would-be international industrial marketer should (1) estimate current market potential of chosen countries, (2) forecast future market potential and risk, (3) forecast sales potential, (4) forecast costs and expected profits, and (5) estimate the rate of return on investment.[38]

INTERNATIONAL ADAPTATION OF CONVENTIONAL MARKETING STRATEGIES

To illustrate how the use of conventional marketing strategies differs as a firm enters international marketing, we turn our attention to international market segmentation, target marketing, and marketing mix strategies.

Segmenting the International Market

In the international arena, market segmentation is usually referred to as "comparative analysis," that is, segmenting countries on the basis of their similarities and differences. When, a firm selects a number of countries as its target markets, on the basis of these comparative similarities and differences, it is said to be employing "comparative marketing" rather than target marketing.

Comparative Analysis and Marketing. Comparative analysis and marketing sounds simple enough and is no different conceptually from conventional market segmentation and target marketing. However, the term "comparative" emphasizes the international difficulties involved. Given the economic, cultural, and political/legal differences among nations, determining comparative similarities and differences can be a major undertaking not found in domestic markets.

While sources of information for assessing the differences may be obtained from such sources as the departments of Commerce and State, international organizations, major banks, foreign governments, and standard reference sources such as

---

[38]See David S. R. Leighton, "Deciding When to Enter International Markets," in Victor P. Buell, ed., *Handbook of Modern Marketing* (New York: McGraw-Hill Book Company, 1970), Sec. 20.

Business International, the information may prove to be inadequate or even deceptive. Egypt, for example, generates considerable secondary statistical data as does the United States; however, much of the Egyptian data are not useful for marketing decision making. The data may not always be timely and realistic, and they are published in Arabic.[39]

On line databases are beginning to supply a considerable amount of information, usually in the form of extracts from foreign publications.[40] Of course, such extracts cannot be expected to explain peculiarities due to subtle cultural differences. However, they offer the industrial marketer interested in technical facts much worthwhile information. For example, the Japanese do not rely heavily on written communications and contracts in their business operations; thus, their database abstracts do not provide the same range and depth as those on American databases.[41] However, foreign databases frequently provide technological information which the industrial marketer finds useful.

One way to perform comparative analysis is to limit the variables considered to those that have the greatest impact on a firm's decision making. For example, an exporting firm might find its purposes best served by performing comparative analysis on the basis of the level of industrial demand, exchange rates, and trade restrictions. There is, however, no universal model for comparative analysis and marketing, since the variables to be considered depend on whether a firm is planning to export, form a partnership, or establish production facilities within a foreign country.

If a firm is planning on exporting, however, it should consider such factors as the level of industrial demand, the nature and location of competition, exchange rates, amount of foreign currency available for purchasing foreign goods, the characteristics of distribution channels, and trade restrictions. In the case of direct investment, the firm should consider such factors as the level of wage rates, the level of employment skills, infrastructure conditions, import restriction on manufacturing inputs and facilitating equipment, market and monetary controls, the likelihood of a government takeover, and costs of shipping products to customers.

Performing comparative analysis is usually very difficult since there are many variables to consider and they vary considerably relative to their importance in decision making. The advantages of comparative analysis and marketing, however, are numerous. When properly performed, the firm can employ the same marketing strategies in several countries, thus avoiding costly adjustments to the marketing mix on a country-by-country basis. It can also take advantage of economies of scale and learning curve effects. Further, when nations are similar, comparisons make evaluating and controlling marketing performance much easier.

---

[39]Essam Mahmoud and Gillian Rice, "Marketing Problems in LDCs: The Case of Egypt," in G. S. Kindra, ed., *Marketing in Developing Countries* (New York: St. Martin's Press, 1984), pp. 76–94.

[40]For a partial list of international on-line services, see Tim Miller, "Around the World in Forty Keystrokes," *Online Access* (May/June 1987), pp. 42–57.

[41]Robert Chapman Wood, "Japan Online," *Online Access,* (September/October 1987), pp. 32–38.

When nations are determined to be similar but data regarding some variable exist for some but not for others, the missing data can be inferred with some degree of justification.

International Product Strategies

Although products in the international industrial market are more homogeneous than consumer products, there are more product variations internationally than domestically due to the greater number of international economic, cultural, and political/legal variables (see Table 18-5).[42]

Economic Considerations. Economically, infrastructures vary among nations. Infrastructure refers to the basic enabling facilities on which a country depends, such as transportation, finance, education, and power. Many nations, for instance, have more advanced railway systems and provide better passenger service than does the United States. Such differences in infrastructures require product adaptation to suit foreign market needs. For example, the U.S. Budd Company developed a prefabricated stainless steel rail car equipped for passenger service that can be assembled locally.[43]

Manufacturing equipment and inputs also differ throughout the world, even in many industries that produce similar products. For example, a lathe in a less developed country may be simplified and treadle powered, while in more advanced nations it is much more complicated and electrically powered.

Product adaptation for economic differences, then, involves simplifying for less developed countries and streamlining for more advanced countries. It also in-

---

2,000 IDLED TRUCKS

With the vast influx of oil dollars, many of the OPEC nations experienced major problems because of their lack of adequate infrastructures. Iranian officials, for instance, ordered thousands of trucks to handle that country's economic upsurge. The government, however, did not realize that the nation lacked trained drivers and mechanics. At Iran's main port 2,000 trucks sat idle for months while the government recruited South Koreans and other foreign drivers. And two years after the trucks had been ordered, one-third of them, due to a lack of mechanics, were idle— waiting for repairs.

Source: Ray Vicker, "Waste Is Draining Surplus Oil Money from Mideast Nations," *The Wall Street Journal,* October 14, 1977, pp 1, 35.

---

[42]This discussion is based on Cundiff and Hilger, *Marketing in the International Environment,* pp. 277–293.

[43]V. H. Kirpalani, *International Marketing* (New York: Random House, Inc., 1984), p. 365.

TABLE 18-5 Design Implications of Environmental Factors

Environmental Factors	Product Design Implications
Level of technical skill	Product simplification
Level of labor cost	Automation or manualization of the product
Level of literacy	Remaking and simplification of the product
Level of income	Quality and price change
Level of interest rates	Quality and price change (investment in quality might not be financially desirable)
Level of maintenance	Change in tolerances
Climatic differences	Product adaptation
Isolation (repair difficult and expensive)	Product simplification and reliability improvement
Differences in standards	Recalibration of product and resizing
Availability of other products	Greater or lesser product integration
Availability of materials	Change in product structure and fuel
Power availability	Resizing of product
Special conditions	Product redesign or invention

Source: Richard D. Robinson, "The Challenge of the Underdeveloped National Market," *Journal of Marketing,* 25 (October 1961), p. 22. Reprinted by permission of the American Marketing Association.

volves informing, educating, and training foreign product users, as well as providing services and repair parts in a timely fashion.

Cultural Considerations. Cultural considerations affect product strategy in many ways. For example, a Japanese manufacturer of calculators had to redesign its product to incorporate Arabic symbols.[44]

Cultural differences, however, affect services more than products because the sale of services involves continuous personal contact with host nationals. Thus, marketers of services should take steps to assure that their personnel are adequately trained in and knowledgeable of foreign cultural considerations. One American university, which provides educational services in various countries, devotes a good deal of money and time providing realistic job previews (informing prospective overseas candidates of the positive as well as negative points) and educating its employees in several aspects of international survival, including obtaining driver's licenses and living quarters, local customs, possible legal problems, map reading, exchange rates, and foreign language skills.

Political/Legal Considerations. Just as the various states within the United States have different political and legal systems that impact on the marketing of products (e.g., automobile emission standards), so do nations. Germany, for instance, has strict legal requirements regarding electrical wiring that carries 220-volt current as opposed to the U.S. 110-volt current. Products wired for 220 volts must meet more

[44]Ibid., p. 366.

PRICE NEGOTIATION CAN BE A TRICKY BUSINESS

Negotiating price can be a tricky business when negotiators are unaware of local customs. American executives, for instance, accustomed to making final decisions under pressure, are often anxious to complete a deal and tend to rush negotiations. On the other hand, Japanese executives, who tend to make group decisions, prefer to negotiate slowly, consulting group members before reaching final decisions. Thus, in the American's haste to end negotiations with the Japanese, he or she often commits blunders that can result in a higher price than necessary. In one instance, for example, an American "raised the price he was willing to pay three times after the Japanese were prepared to accept." In his haste to close the deal, the American failed to realize the effect of local custom on the negotiation process. In Japan, hesitation and discussion does not necessarily mean "no deal." It means that Japanese executives are politely listening to their colleagues' opinions.

Source: David A Ricks, *Big Business Blunders* (Homewood, Ill.: Dow Jones-Irwin, 1983), pp. 110–111.

---

stringent safety requirements than those using 110 volts. Most of the free world also uses metric measurements, thus requiring modifications in products made for United States markets.

International Pricing Strategies

Although pricing practices appear to be no different internationally than nationally, in some respects there is wide divergence. These differences occur in the areas of transfer pricing, dumping, and governmental influence over price.

Transfer Pricing. Transfer prices are the prices placed on products as they are transferred between units belonging to the same company. Transfer prices can be used to mitigate the effects of government regulation. Since tariffs are usually based on the value of imported goods, a producer can charge a low transfer price to a foreign subsidiary, thereby reducing the foreign tariff. It can also charge a high transfer price (making a large profit) as it exports from a country having a low tax rate, and then sell (making little profit) in a country having a high tax rate. Exporters to countries not allowing profit repatriation (the return of profits to overseas parent companies) can charge high transfer prices and make little profit in such countries. Price controls are often based on some markup on cost, so that by charging a high transfer price, the controls can be partially overcome.[45]

Adjusting transfer prices for the sole purpose of circumventing government

---

[45]Ruel Kahler, *International Marketing* (Cincinnati, Ohio: Southwestern Publishing Co., 1983), p. 264.

regulations is looked on with disfavor by governments and should be avoided. Our own IRS carefully watches transfer prices. In a two-year period, for example, the Internal Revenue Service examined 591 cases and decided in 174 of those cases that goods transferred from the United States had been underpriced. Its average settlement with the companies involved was $750,000.[46]

Dumping.   Dumping is disposing of goods in a foreign country at less than their full cost. Goods will sometimes be exported at prices that only cover direct costs to dispose of excess inventories. Companies sell their excess inventories overseas to avoid disturbing their own national markets (e.g., reducing prices or causing price wars at home). The purchasers of dumped goods may not mind the practice, but firms that produce the same products in nations where goods are dumped do mind. Such competitors call for protective legislation, as has the U.S. steel industry. Most nations have strong antidumping regulations. International marketers should take care to prevent the appearance that their firms may be dumping. Low transfer prices can, for example, lead to charges of dumping and investigation.

Government Influence.   Not only do governments influence prices through trade restrictions, they use other methods as well. Indirectly, subsidies in the form of grants and inexpensive loans enable a nation's manufacturers to sell at lower prices; currency devaluations make a nation's goods less expensive overseas, and imported products more expensive. Governments also place restrictions on foreign aid and challenge the efforts of international organizations, such as the International Monetary Fund, to impose restrictions, which affects prices.

Direct government controls over pricing are extensive. In this regard, for example, governments establish direct price controls. The United States, for instance, established price controls for all businesses in the early 1970s and has continued to use them in selected industries such as transportation, power, and utilities. The European countries that impose price controls on manufacturers are France, Ireland, The Netherlands, Spain, Sweden, and the United Kingdom.[47] Governments also exercise price controls through government-owned firms and stockpiles.

One of the most interesting series of governmental interventions occurred in Portugal where over ten years ago the government established a law preventing the firing of employees, but neglected to specify that workers must be paid. Today approximately 500 Portuguese companies owe back wages of $70 million to 150,000 employees, giving those firms a differential advantage in pricing, that is, a real advantage over firms in other nations that pay full wages.[48]

---

[46]"Business International," in Vern Terpstra, ed., *International Marketing* (Chicago, Ill.: The Dryden Press, 1983), p. 521.

[47]Ibid., p. 531.

[48]Barry Newman, "Sure, Keep Your Job, But Don't Expect to Get Wages, Too," *The Wall Street Journal,* December 12, 1984, pp. 1, 22.

International Promotional Strategy

In the international industrial market, the primary element of the promotional mix is personal selling, for only through personal selling can the coordination so essential to the industrial buyer–seller interface be effectively achieved.

Sales promotion in the form of trade fairs is playing an increasingly important role in international marketing because so many prospects can be contacted in one place and because they enable quick comparisons of products. Direct mail is also becoming popular, although mailing lists are usually difficult to obtain. The use of publicity, although growing in popularity, is limited due to language difficulties and media coverage. Advertising is given little attention in the international industrial market, perhaps because of the difficulties in determining media coverage and numerous, widely varying, governmental regulations. Here our discussion concerns personal selling.

Domestic versus Foreign Sales People. A firm's international sales force may be comprised of domestic, foreign personnel, or both. Domestic sales people tend to be more knowledgeable about the company and its products, which is an important industrial criterion. They tend to be better "connected" to obtain concessions, such as special product adaptations, from the parent company. However, they will likely be more expensive than a foreign sales force. Normally, the parent company pays not only their regular salaries, but also a bonus for overseas "hardships," as well as various travel and accommodation costs. The primary disadvantage of having domestic sales people working abroad is their lack of familiarity with cultural differences. In many cases, they will need extensive foreign language and other cultural training.

Because of these factors, many companies prefer to hire local nationals for their overseas sales forces. Such people offer a means of overcoming the shortcomings of using a domestic sales force and often are already familiar with foreign marketing procedures. American expatriates (U.S. citizens) living in a firm's foreign markets can also constitute an excellent source of sales force personnel. "The expatriates, or even third-country nationals, who can operate freely in the market's business environment, are immersed in its culture, knowledgeable of its history, fluent in its language(s), are politically neutral, and have retained their national identities, are worth their weights in gold to transnational organizations," says a veteran international business consultant.[49] Thus, the use of expatriates can provide a "best-of-both worlds" type of sales force.

International Distribution Strategies

The primary goal of international marketing is achieving wider distribution. But, just as in the United States, distribution involves more than physically moving a

---

[49]See Gore, personal communication.

product. It involves handling, storage, inventorying, sometimes assembling, protective packaging, paperwork, and forecasting. We have already discussed one aspect of distribution, and that is how to enter national markets (exporting, licensing, joint ventures, and foreign production). In this section we discuss three additional distribution considerations: (1) the international product life cycle, (2) international supply chain management, and (3) differential advantages achieved through international marketing distribution.

The International PLC. The international product life cycle (see Table 18-6) hypothesizes that most new products are developed by advanced nations and initially marketed in other advanced nations (the overseas innovation, or introduction, stage). Firms in other advanced nations, then, begin producing the product (the maturity, or growth/maturity, stage). As numerous advanced nations produce and sell to less developed countries, which also begin producing, the originating nation's sales fall dramatically (the worldwide imitation stage or decline stage). Ultimately the nation that originally developed the product becomes an importing nation (the reversal stage), because the now standardized product can be produced through simplified technologies and becomes labor-intensive rather than capital or technologically intensive.

For any product, nations are seldom at the same stage of the international product life cycle. A firm wishing to take advantage of this knowledge attempts to distribute to nations that are in the more profitable growth/maturity stage of the product life cycle.[50]

TABLE 18-6 International Product Life-Cycle Stages and Characteristics

Stage	Import/Export	Target Market	Competitors	Production Costs
Local innovation	None	United States	Few: local firms	Initially high
Overseas innovation	Increasing export	United States and advanced nations	Few: local firms	Decline due to economies of scale
Maturity	Stable export	Advanced nations and LDCs	Advanced nations	Stable
Worldwide imitation	Declining export	LDCs	Advanced nations	Increase due to lower economies of scale
Reversal	Increasing import	United States	Advanced nations and LDCs	Increase due to comparative disadvantage

LDCs = less developed countries.

Source: Sak Onkvisit and John J. Shaw, "An Examination of the International Product Life Cycle and Its Application Within Marketing," *Columbia Journal of World Business,* Fall 1983, pp. 73–79. Reprinted with permission.

[50]This discussion is based on Sak Onkvisit and John Shaw, "An Examination of the International Product Life Cycle and Its Application Within Marketing," *Columbia Journal of World Business* (Fall 1983), pp. 73–79.

Of course, any model that describes the evolution of worldwide distribution processes offers the industrial marketer an excellent starting point for developing strategies. For example, a firm can consider securing the most advantageous distribution networks when it is alone in the world market during the overseas innovation stage. This would relegate later imitators to inferior channels. The initial innovator firm can also consider linking with other firms in advanced nations during the worldwide imitation stage, as all four major American auto makers have done.

International Supply Chain Management

Wide fluctuations in industrial demand, caused by derived demand, are even more pronounced in longer and less communicative international supply chains.[51] Inventories and production are subject to wider swings the farther an organization is removed from ultimate buyers. The effects are similar to swinging a whip, the farther the point is from the handle, the wider the variability in its motion. This variability is accentuated in the international chain due to communication problems, accentuated by economic, cultural, and political/legal environments. For example, national governments are increasingly limiting information sharing between host and foreign companies.

Rather than continue conventional answers of drastically changing production schedules, inventory levels, and revamping control systems, supply chain management advocates an "integration" of channel efforts rather than the conventional "interface." This integration envisions supply as a shared objective of every channel firm and of functional units within firms.

Supply chain management involves a not easily attained, but essential, shared managerial philosophy among international channel firms. It envisions shared ownership of information regarding plans, allocations, and inventories; linking of different functions, such as purchasing and production; and the management of data gathering and its flow across international organizational and functional boundaries. In this context firms must be willing to share essential supply information, so that a small swing in demand does not turn into an unjustifiably larger swing farther up the supply channel. Also, firms and functional areas within them must be willing to negotiate on varying, often conflicting objectives. For example, it may be determined that a ninety-nine percent delivery reliability in four weeks is more acceptable than an eighty-five percent reliability on a two-week lead time.

Supply chain management requires developing trust and cooperation between and within firms separated by great distances and affected by different economic, cultural, and political/legal environments. Inspiring a multifirm philosophy that accomplishes such an integration represents a monumental challenge; however, the benefits would also be monumental.

Differential Advantages in International Distribution. It is only now becoming increasingly obvious that international distribution offers distinctive competencies to

---

[51]This discussion is based on John Houlihan, "International Supply Chain Management," *International Journal of Physical Distribution & Materials Management,* 15, 1, (1985), pp. 22–38.

international firms and thus differential advantages over their less worldly competitors. Whether such competencies have been derived intentionally is not fully known, but their existence continues to be documented. For example, Goodyear's tire market was challenged in the United States by the French manufacturer, Michelin. Michelin was able to use profits from its worldwide sales to challenge Goodyear's U.S. position while exposing only a portion of its own world market.[52]

During much of the last decade Japanese television manufacturers developed worldwide brand dominance. Achieving that dominance allowed Japanese manufacturers to move along the learning curve. Although American companies responded with improved technological processes, they were faced with ever lower competitive prices; that is, global distribution had effectively established real barriers to competition.[53]

Distribution strategies involving overseas production can be accompanied by purchases of nearby, low-cost foreign inputs (for example, in China labor costs are less than half a cent per minute, as compared to eight cents per minute in Japan and twenty-four cents per minute in the United States).[54]

International companies can also develop differential advantages by employing the principle of comparative advantage, that is, producing where production is least expensive and selling where the greatest profits are achievable. They can take advantage of lower wages, greater worker skills, reduced lead times, and readily available capital at production locations and concentrated, well-financed, high-producing markets at selling locations. For example, Massey-Ferguson, a Canadian-based global company, assembles French-made transmissions, Mexican-made axles, and British-made engines in a Detroit plant for the Canadian market.[55]

LOOKING BACK

International marketing is primarily industrial marketing and the United States has been the principal world advocate of encouraging international marketing through free trade. To perform well in the international arena, the firm must be aware of economic, cultural, and political/legal environments.

In the economic environment, major considerations are exchange rates and the balance of trade, both of which have been adverse for the United States in recent years. The world's very different cultural environments cause difficult interpersonal relationship problems in the important industrial interface environment. Political/legal constraints involve import restrictions, market and monetary controls, and foreign entities assuming control of foreign assets in their countries. International

---

[52]Gary Hamel and C. K. Prahalad, "Do You Really Have a Global Strategy?" *Harvard Business Review,* 85, 4 (July–August 1985), pp. 139–148.

[53]Ibid.

[54]"Capitalism in China," *Business Week,* January 14, 1985, pp. 53–58.

[55]Barnet and Muller, *Global Reach,* p. 28.

firms need to develop unique strategies to handle problems occurring in these international environment areas.

Firms engaging in international marketing do use, however, conventional marketing strategies. These strategies involve segmenting and target marketing that are referred to internationally as comparative analysis and comparative marketing. They also involve the marketing mix strategies of product, price, promotion, and distribution. Due to worldwide economic, cultural, and political/legal differences, these conventional marketing strategies, however, encounter many more contingencies and constraints internationally than nationally. The firm that carefully develops these international strategies can develop comparative advantages and even distinctive competencies.

QUESTIONS FOR DISCUSSION

1. Respond to Theodore Levitt's claim that multinational companies are in decline and must change themselves into global corporations that view the world as "one vast market rather than as slices of nations."

2. Foreign direct investment in the U.S. has now reached $329 billion dollars. It has surpassed U.S. investment abroad and is growing much more rapidly than U.S. investment. Should the U.S. place restrictions on such investments?

3. In efforts to strengthen a long-stagnant economy. Mexico has sharply devalued its currency (the peso) a number of times in recent years. Are these devaluations helping and what more might be done?

4. Discuss the cultural obstacles an American businessperson might have when making a rush trip to a Latin American nation to secure a large contract involving the purchase of a television station.

5. Although many Japanese firms have been eminently successful, U.S. firms have invested much more in Italy, The Netherlands, the United Kingdom, and other countries than Japan. Why is this so?

6. The single greatest loss in an initial international venture was that experienced by the billionaire Daniel Ludwig in Jari, Brazil. What economic, cultural, or political/legal problems did Ludwig encounter, and could they have been overcome?

SUGGESTED ADDITIONAL READINGS

ABEGGLEN, JAMES, and GEORGE STALK, "The Role of Foreign Companies in Japanese Acquisitions," *The Journal of Business Strategy* 5 (Spring 1984):3–10.

CALLAHAN, MADELYN R., "Preparing the New Global Manager," *Training & Development Journal* (March 1989):29–32.

"Global Competition: The New Reality," *Report of the President's Commission on Industrial Competitiveness,* Vol. I (Washington, D.C.: Superintendent of Documents, U.S. Government Printing Office, 1985).

HALL, EDWARD "The Silent Language in Overseas Business," *Harvard Business Review* (May-June 1960):87- 96.

KINKEAD, GWEN, "Trouble in D. K. Ludwig's Jungle," *Fortune* (April 20, 1981):102–117.

KOEPFLER, EDWARD R., "Strategic Options for Global Market Players," *The Journal of Business Strategy* (July/August 1989):46–50.

LEVITT, THEODORE, "Levitt: Global Companies to Replace Dying Multinationals," *Marketing News* (March 15, 1985):15.

ONKVISIT, SAK, and JOHN SHAW, "An Examination of the International Product Life Cycle and Its Application Within Marketing," *Columbia Journal of World Business* (Fall 1983):73–79.

SEASE, DOUGLAS, "Japanese Firms Set up More Factories in U.S., Alarm Some Americans," *The Wall Street Journal,* SW edition (March 29, 1985):1, 16.

SHREEVE, THOMAS, "Be Prepared for Political Changes Abroad," *Harvard Business Review* (July–August 1984):224–226.

TERPSTRA, VERN, *The Cultural Environment of International Business* (Cincinnati, Ohio: Southwestern Publishing Co., 1978).

TSURUMI, YOSHI, "Managing Consumer and Industrial Marketing Systems in Japan," *Sloan Management Review* (Fall 1982):41–49.

YOUNG, JOHN, "Global Competition: The New Reality," *California Management Review* 27: 3 (Spring 1985):11–25.

CN Information Services

David Orlinoff, the new director of marketing for Columbia National (CN) Information Services, was sitting at his desk, trying to list the various major tasks that he had to tackle in his new job. On the piece of paper before him, he had listed a number of major headings, each representing a major piece of the job of getting his new unit up, running, and producing revenue within a short period of time. One of the headings was staffing. David decided that this evening he was going to try to attack that piece of the job and that he would try to identify all of the various things that had to be done in order to build an effective staff.

BACKGROUND

Columbia National Bank (CN) is a major financial institution in a large city in the eastern United States. During the late 1970s, CN had been very concerned about the increasing costs of information processing and, in particular, the cost associated with the processing of information that had to do with retail banking, such as checks, credit card information, and so on. A major decision was made by the management of CN to invest resources in the development of the most advanced technology and systems for doing

This case appeared in David A. Nadler, Michael L. Tushman, and Nina G. Hatvany, *Managing Organizations: Readings and Cases.* Copyright © 1982 by David A. Nadler, Michael L. Tushman, and Nina G. Hatvany. Reprinted by permission of Little, Brown and Company.

this work. From 1975 on, the bank made considerable investments in the development of new computer systems for the support of retail banking operations. These systems were, by and large, successful. They enabled the bank to maintain service quality while expanding volume dramatically and in the process reducing the expenses of this "back office" operation.

Having accomplished the job of developing the state-of-the-art information technology, top management of the bank began to discuss other ways of gaining a return on the investment that had been made to develop the information systems. The executive vice president in charge of operations, whose responsibilities included the back office operations, developed a proposal that involved selling the bank's systems to other organizations facing similar information management problems. The executive vice president reported that he had received numerous inquiries about the information systems from other businesses and that many of these were willing and eager to purchase the expertise of the bank in this area. The executive committee of the bank reviewed the proposal and agreed to move ahead in this area.

The executive vice president appointed a senior vice president to head up the CN Information Services Group. This senior vice president, Matthew Diaz, in turn set up two major departments, operations and marketing. Operations would develop and implement the systems. Marketing would have responsibility for identifying customers, generating sales, and working with customers to pinpoint needs and thus determine the type of product that operations would be required to develop and install.

THE MARKETING DEPARTMENT

Diaz had recruited an old friend of his, David Orlinoff, to be the director of marketing. Diaz and Orlinoff had been in the same MBA program several years earlier and had kept in touch since then. Orlinoff had gone to a major computer firm in marketing after getting his MBA. After several years in a number of jobs in that firm, he had been recruited by a major consumer products organization. As a product manager, he had established a tremendous record of performance, but had been frustrated with the lack of opportunities for growth within that particular organization. Thus, when approached by Diaz, Orlinof decided to take the job at CN Information Services.

THE STAFFING PROBLEM

Orlinoff was given approximately six months to put together a marketing group. David knew that over the long run, his performance would be judged based on the performance of the entire Information Services Group (essentially Diaz, Orlinoff, and the operations director). More specifically, David knew that his responsibility would be to identify a marketing approach and generate sales volume. Obviously, he would have to work with the operations people closely.

It was now January, and Orlinoff had the goal of being "staffed up" and ready to start active marketing work by June at the latest. He knew that he had approximately $750,000 yearly in budget for direct expenses (salary) for staff for his department. As he began to plan for the next six months, a major concern was how he would go about assembling an effective staff for the department.

CASE 2

Crofton-Wagley, Inc.

Charles McDowell was worrying about a sales contract that he had counted on signing in a few days but that was now in danger of falling through. He thought, "If only those people in the accounting department and in navigation instrumentation would cooperate sometimes and get a team effort going."

This case is reprinted with permission of Macmillan Publishing Company from *Cases in Marketing,* 3rd ed., by Thomas V. Greer. Copyright 1983 by Thomas V. Greer.

McDowell was sales representative and contract negotiator in the sales department of Crofton-Wagley, Inc., a large company engaged in the manufacture of electronics, aerospace products, and sophisticated equipment. About 80 percent of its sales volume was to the military. Most of the military sales were to the U.S. armed forces, but there was significant business with the military procurement offices of Canada, Australia, and West Germany. Crofton-Wagley's plants were located in California, Texas, and the Middle West, and the company had just opened a small experimental facility in Appalachia following federal government pressure to "spread the jobs around."

Sales volume fluctuated somewhat more from year to year than in most other firms in this type of industry. Sales last year were $499 million, but the year before were $538 million. The ratio of net profit after taxes to sales was a disappointing 2.0 percent in the latest year. Long-term trends are given in Exhibit 1.

Experienced and age 35, Charles McDowell had been with Crofton-Wagley, Inc., about six years and was with an aerospace company for about seven years before that. He graduated from a well-known university with a BS in a combination engineering-business administration curriculum. In industry he had had experience in product design, product laboratory testing, liaison between various engineering departments and the marketing department and was currently in sales. He was on a straight salary. McDowell was considered a competent, personable, and loyal employee.

Recently McDowell had been negotiating a sale with Ronninger Corporation for $4 million worth of navigation equipment.

He and some others deemed it highly important not just for the large amount of money involved but for the possibility of follow-on orders from Ronninger and also because it would get Crofton-Wagley deeper into civilian markets. The president of the company wanted Crofton-Wagley to be less dependent on military orders.

Crofton-Wagley's pricing had been systematized. This meant that certain procedures adopted a little over a year before had to be followed in determining the asking price. The Crofton-Wagley approach was essentially cost-based pricing. Company practice was to figure the costs involved, then add a small contingency charge (sometimes hidden in slight overestimates of detailed items but sometimes spelled out separately) of about 2 percent of the costs, and then add a markup that averaged 14 percent. Special facilities needed for a specific contract, such as specialized testing equipment or new construction of testing rooms tailor-made for the contract, were charged to the contract and thus became part of the price quoted to the potential customer. The navigation equipment on which McDowell and Ronninger were negotiating required a special testing room that had to be constructed from the ground up. Estimates of cost to construct this room were $135,000, and the special testing equipment would add another $25,000. There seemed to be no significant error in these two estimates that anyone could discover. These two figures were part of the exactly $4 million total figure McDowell was asking the potential customer.

Ronninger had bought similar but technologically less advanced navigation equipment in the past from one of Crofton-Wagley's prime competitors, Kingston, Inc. McDowell had just learned that Kingston was trying to obtain the same contract and was quoting a total price of $3,930,000, or $70,000 less than Crofton-Wagley. Said Mc-

EXHIBIT 1 Sales and Profit Trends of Crofton-Wagley, Inc.

Number of Years Ago	Sales	Net Profit After Taxes
1	$499,000,000	$10,023,000
2	538,000,000	12,975,000
3	485,000,000	10,045,000
4	456,000,000	9,902,000
5	491,000,000	10,450,000
6	461,000,000	10,076,000
7	485,000,000	13,240,000
8	440,000,000	13,210,000
9	441,000,000	13,230,000

Dowell, "It not only is cheaper than our quotation by 1¾ percent but sounds a lot cheaper because it stays below $4 million."

At this point McDowell approached the senior cost accountant, Louise Bascomb and attempted to get a special exception to company costing procedures so as to delete from the estimate the $135,000 cost of the construction. Bascomb appeared to want to cooperate but replied in the negative. She pointed out that this costing policy was the result of the work of a pricing policy committee that included the marketing vice president, the sales manager, two other vice presidents, and the company president. In vain, McDowell argued that the testing room would still be in place and have some value after the order had been filled. An immediate appeal to the head of finance and accounting did not change matters.

Undaunted, McDowell next sought the exclusion of the $25,000 worth of special testing equipment, but to no avail. Next, McDowell began questioning the 2 percent contingency factor, but the reply to that

from everyone was a resounding "no." It was even added that the company's cost estimating was so imprecise that perhaps the figure of 2 percent should be raised in the future. Finally he questioned the 14 percent markup, but again without positive results.

At this point, these thoughts went through McDowell's mind: "Perhaps Ronninger would pay this price differential just to get what amounts to 'second sourcing,' because we all realize that Kingston can give Ronninger just as sophisticated technology as we can. On the other hand, they already know Kingston and Kingston's people quite well. And $70,000 is a lot of money." "Second sourcing" referred to an idea in which many industrial buyers believed strongly; that is, a company was likely to get into a poor position if over the long run it relied on only one source for an important product or category of products that no one else was making.

Advise Charles McDowell of Crofton-Wagley, Inc.

CASE 3

Edward F. Crow Company

The Edward F. Crow Company is an industrial distributor located in Memphis, Tennessee. Its principal product lines include materials handling equipment such as conveyors and transfer stations, electric motors and

This case was prepared by Ernest F. Cooke, Professor of Marketing, Layda College, Maryland. Reprinted by permission.

controls and power transmissions, and, finally, weighing scales, particularly those used as part of conveyor lines. The firm covers a territory consisting of parts of nine states: Tennessee, Kentucky, Alabama, Mississippi, Louisiana, Arkansas, Missouri, Illinois, and Indiana. Memphis is the hub of a trading area called the mid-South.

The firm was founded in 1937 by the late Edward F. Crow who had earned his mechanical engineering degree from Case School of Applied Science (now Case Western Reserve University) in the 1920s. Before starting his own firm, he had been a design engineer and then a sales engineer for a major manufacturer of conveyors. When he passed away about five years ago, operation of Crow was taken over by one of the lawyers who was handling the estate. There were no heirs interested in or capable of running the firm.

Over the last five years, annual sales have decreased from slightly less than $3 million to slightly more than $2 million (see Exhibit 1). Because of inflation, actual physical volume has decreased even more (about 40

EXHIBIT 1 Income Statement, 1978 versus 1982 ($000)

	1978		1982	
Sales				
Motors and so on	$669		$412	
Parts, repair and service for motors, and so on	642		516	
Materials handling/installations*	870		615	
Scales	361		224	
Parts, repair, and service for scales	374		298	
Total net sales		$2,916		$2,065
Cost of goods sold				
Motors and so on	458		288	
Parts for motors and so on	237		196	
Materials handling	556		406	
Scales	243		155	
Parts for scales	111		94	
Total cost of goods sold		1,605		1,139
Gross margin		$1,311		$ 926
Operating expenses				
Service and repair, labor and overhead**	501		412	
Warehouse and distribution expense	212		201	
General administrative and selling expense***	318		319	
Basically fixed costs				
Total operating expense		1,031		932
Operating income [loss]		$ 280		$ [6]
Interest expense less interest revenue		[13]		[4]
Net income [loss] before taxes		$ 293		$ [2]
Income tax [refund]		132		0
Net income		$ 161		$ [2]

*Actual materials handling sales are larger than indicated on the income statement because they usually include electric motors and controls, power transmissions, and sometimes scales. When these components are included as part of a materials handling installation, the sales dollars are shown under the category scales or motors and so on.

**About 10% of this is assembly labor and warranty labor associated with material handling sales.

***Basically fixed cost and includes the engineer's salary.

percent). Five years ago the corporation was very profitable, but last year Crow suffered a very small loss.

Five years ago there were five outside sales people. As conditions worsened, the sales force diminished in size. the last outside salesperson quit last week, and only two inside salespersons are left. They are both very competent but are overworked. As a result, the firm lost an opportunity to bid on seven large electric motors for the Tennessee Valley Authority when the closing date was missed.

At present (1983), volume is broken down as follows:

1. Electric motors and controls and power transmissions   20%
2. Parts, repairs and service for motors, and so on   25
3. Materials handling equipment, including parts and design services but not including motors, controls, transmissions, or scales   30
4. Scales   10
5. Parts, repairs, and service for scales   15

Over the last five years, dollar sales decreased in all five categories. The share of total sales held according to category has changed, with new motors and scales dropping from 35.3 percent to 30.8 percent, all parts and repair increasing from 34.8 percent to 39.4 percent, and material handling holding steady at 29.8 percent.

In addition to the two inside sales people, employees include a purchasing agent, a parts manager, a service manager, and seven service and repair people, an engineer who designs materials handling systems, some warehouse and delivery people, and clerks who handle bookkeeping, billing, and correspondence. There has been turnover among these employees; consequently, problems have arisen due to being short of help as well as having inexperienced help For example, there is a one-month backlog in billing for completed service work due to a shortage of help and inexperienced help.

The purchasing agent also acts as office manager. The engineer has increased the amount of his customer contact because of a decrease in outside sales people.

The firm is the exclusive distributor in the mid-South for Primax, a foreign manufacturer of electric motors whose East and Gulf Coast port-of-entry is New Orleans. Primax has a distribution center in Memphis that serves the entire country. Crow's annual Primax sales five years ago totaled 400 units, contrasted with sales last year of 200 units. Its sales quota last year was 200 units. So far this year, sales have been at an annual rate of 200 units averaging $1,000 per unit.

Crow also represents several divisions of Reliable Electric, a manufacturer of electric motors, control, transmissions, and so on. Sales of Reliable products this year are running at an annual rate of $300,000 including parts. Almost 10 percent is small power transmission components purchased from Reliable's Lodge Division for materials handling installations.

The firm is the distributor for several different manufacturers of materials handling equipment and scales. These manufacturers are competitors in some of their lines. In these cases, Crow sometimes uses more than one manufacturer for a given installation of materials handling equipment or scales. For most manufacturers, the firm is the exclusive distributor in the Memphis area even though they carry competitive lines.

In the almost 40 years that Mr. Crow ran the firm, he had built up an excellent reputation among suppliers and customers. Although this reputation has deteriorated somewhat in the last five years, the firm still enjoys a good reputation. If the situation continues to deteriorate much longer, it will reach a critical stage. It may even become an irreversible situation.

Recently the Fearhank-Moose Scale Company, which manufacturers a line of portable industrial scales, canceled its contract with Crow because it felt that Crow was not doing justice to its line of scales. Subsequently, Fearhank signed up with another Memphis industrial distributor who is in direct competition with Crow.

You have just purchased a controlling interest in the firm and have appointed yourself president, chief executive officer, and chief operating officer. The lawyer who was president is no longer with the firm. There is no doubt that he was ill-equipped to run the business. It requires someone, like you, with marketing and management know-how.

CASE 4

Cumberland Gasket Company, Inc.

"It's my problem and I've got to live with it," said Fred Barlow, vice president and general manager of the Maryland division of Cumberland Gasket Co., Inc. "There are 30 people out there in the plant working with asbestos, and even with all of the precautions we have taken, some of them may develop symptoms of asbestosis or lung cancer." Mr. Barlow went on to observe that the real moral issue for him was related to the fact that most of the scientific evidence of serious consequences from inhaling asbestos dust was based on asbestos miners and other workers around raw asbestos, while only a relatively modest amount of asbestos was used in the Maryland Division. "My trouble is," he said, "that I just cannot be sure how serious it is."

This case was made possible by the cooperation of a business firm which remains anonymous. Prepared by Professors Herman Gadon and Dwight R. Ladd of the University of New Hampshire. Copyrighted by the University of New Hampshire.

The Maryland Division of Cumberland Gasket Co., Inc., manufactured a wide range of gaskets, washers, and other nonmetallic fittings and parts which were primarily used in petroleum processing equipment such as pumps and valves. Some of these parts and fittings were made of asbestos because of the latter's exceptional resistance to wear and heat. The parts were relatively inexpensive, but were unusually critical components of the equipment in which they were used. Failure of one of these small parts could shut down an oil well or cause serious oil spillage, for example. Thus, Cumberland's products were of substantial importance. The parts in question were manufactured in two plants in Cumberland, Maryland. In 1977, the Maryland Division had sales of about $20 million. Cumberland, which in other plants in Michigan and California made parts for the automotive industry, had sales of about $60 million in 1977.

CUMBERLAND AND FRED BARLOW

Cumberland Gasket Co., Inc., had been formed in 1970 by the merger of three smaller companies. While the primary goal behind the merger was to enable the companies involved to serve better an increasingly dispersed nationwide market, the divisions, which were generally equivalent to the predecessor companies, retained a great deal of autonomy. The general managers of each division, who were vice presidents of Cumberland, were primarily responsible for the profitability of their divisions. Thus, Mr. Barlow had the authority to decide what was best for his division, although he would also be responsible for the consequences.

Fred Barlow had been vice president at the Maryland Division of Cumberland Gasket for three years. His career had been marked by determination to do well and to move on to more challenges when he felt he had come to grips with the ones he faced when he first took a job. Now 34, he had gone to work for a bearing manufacturer after he had finished high school. He worked there for a year to get enough money to get through college, went to college for a year, ran out of money, went back to the bearing manufacturer and finished his bachelor's degree at night. After completing college, he acquired an MBA in an evening program. When he was 22 he became works manager of the bearing company. At 24 he left that company and joined a larger one that made electromagnetic laminations and stampings. First employed as production control manager, he became manufacturing manager before he left at the age of 27 to manage a division of a company that sold to libraries. At the age of 30 he came to Cumberland Gasket Co., Inc., as manufacturing vice president. Two years later the company merged and he became a corporate officer and general manager of the Maryland Division.

Shortly after he joined Cumberland. Mr. Barlow read a book entitled *The Expendable American,* by Paul Brodeur. The book described the hazards of breathing asbestos dust and documented the long struggle to impose maximum exposure standards. The book convinced Fred Barlow that working with asbestos could be a major health hazard, and he concluded that dealing with that hazard should be one of his major responsibilities.

THE PRODUCTS

About 15 percent of the Maryland division's sales were of products containing asbestos. These products ranged from tiny washers and gaskets to relatively large vanes used in air compressors. All of these were parts which had to fit snugly with metal surfaces against which they moved, while also being resistant to heat and having a certain amount of give. The production process began with sheets of canvas and asbestos laminated with resin compounds which were purchased from another manufacturer. At the Maryland plants, the laminated sheets were sawed, cut, or drilled into the desired shapes and sanded as necessary. These operations created the exposure to dust which concerned Mr. Barlow.

ASBESTOS

Asbestos is a mineral which is impervious to heat and fire and which can be separated into fibers which, like wool, can be carded, spun, and woven or felted. It can also be crushed into powder and mixed with other substances such as paint or patching plaster. These qualities of asbestos mean that it has a multitude of applications in industry and consumer products. Some commonplace applications are brake linings, electrical insulation, washers, gaskets, and shingles.

Asbestos was known and used in classical times—for lamp wicks, for example—but widespread use began with the Industrial Revolution. For some applications—automotive brake linings, for example—there is no known substitute for asbestos. Unfortunately, it has been generally known since the beginning of this century that asbestos—or more specifically, inhaled asbestos fibers—is a principal cause of certain, almost invariably fatal, diseases. One of these is asbestosis, which is the scarring of the tissues of the lungs, which ultimately results in the victim being unable to breathe. Lung cancer is also a likely result of inhaling asbestos, as is mesothelioma (malignant tumors of the lining of the chest cavity). Asbestos-related diseases are of the sort which, in the absence of regular medical checkups, appear only 20 or 30 years after exposure, at which time they are generally untreatable. As yet, it is not known how much or how little exposure will cause one or another of these diseases, but it is believed that not a great deal of exposure is required and that build up of fibers in the body is cumulative and irreversible. Further, because asbestos fibers readily cling to other substances such as clothing or the skin, the dust can be widely dispersed. There is incontrovertible evidence that members of the families of asbestos workers have contracted these diseases in an abnormal degree even though they had never been near places where asbestos was handled.

REGULATION

Prior to 1972, the United States had no enforceable standard for maximum exposure to asbestos. In 1969, the American Conference of Governmental Hygienists recommended a minimum exposure standard of not more than 12 asbestos fibers longer than five microns in a cubic centimeter of air, over an eight-hour-period.[1] In spite of its name, this organization was a privately funded, nongovernmental agency, and thus adherence to the standard was entirely voluntary.

In 1970 Congress passed the Occupational Safety and Health Act, which, among other things, empowered the Secretary of Labor to set safety standards. The act also created the National Institute for Occupational Safety and Health (NIOSH), and during 1970 and 1971, NIOSH publicized a number of earlier studies showing the health hazards associated with asbestos. Trade union officials and independent investigators urged that a minimum exposure standard of two 5-micron fibers per cubic centimeter be instituted by the Secretary. This, incidentally, was the standard adopted by the British government in 1968. However, the Secretary chose, in early 1972, to impose a standard of five fibers. After continued controversy and public hearings, the two-fiber standard was promulgated in July 1975, and in 1977 OSHA proposed a new limit of one-half 5-micron fiber per cubic centimeter of air. NIOSH, at the same time, was urging adoption of a standard of one-tenth 5-micron fiber.

THE FABRICATION DIVISION

The Maryland Division's operations were carried on in two separate plants. One was housed in the original nineteenth-century

---

[1] A micron is equal to 1/5,000th of an inch. It is about the smallest fiber length that can be measured without an electron microscope. It is estimated that the presence of two 5-micron fibers in a cubic centimeter of air means the presence of up to 1,000 smaller particles.

The average person will breathe in about 8 million cubic centimeters of air in an eight-hour period.

factory where Cumberland began, but the other, in which most of the asbestos processing took place, had been constructed in 1976. In the old plant, only some machines were fitted with dust collectors, and therefore asbestos products could only be worked on those machines—thereby considerably limiting flexibility in scheduling. In the new, one-story, windowless plant, dust was collected from all machines and deposited through a central evacuating system into plastic sealable bags. This meant that products containing asbestos could be worked on any machinery in the plant. Though more costly, the application of dust collection to all equipment in the new plant provided a cleaner total environment as well as more scheduling flexibility. The sealed plastic bags were removed by a small independent contractor and buried within 24 hours in the city landfill dump.

Under OSHA regulations every employee working with asbestos was required to wear a mask. Mr. Barlow insisted on rigorous enforcement of the rules by decreeing that the supervisor of any employee working with asbestos without a mask would be immediately suspended for a week. Though Mr. Barlow made frequent inspections, no one had ever been found without a mask. In the early days of Mr. Barlow's tenure, Cumberland's insurance carrier had made annual surveys of dust conditions. In 1976, Mr. Barlow had his own testing equipment purchased so that the plant could conduct its own tests every month. In the three inspections by OSHA, particles of asbestos at every machine in the two factories had always been below the OSHA standard of two fibers. In accordance with OSHA regulations, any employee working with asbestos was required to have his pulmonary functions tested and chest X-rayed under the direction of a physician at least once each year. The company was required to keep records of these medical tests of each employee for 50 years.

ATTITUDES ABOUT THE HAZARD

In spite of various precautions being taken, Mr. Barlow was not sure that enough was being done, or whether any exposure to asbestos was acceptable. Though scientific evidence of the effects of small dosages was still inconclusive, Mr. Barlow observed, "If a 5-micron fiber is dangerous, why is a 4.9-micron fiber OK?"

Though his peers were aware of, and concerned about, the dangers of working with asbestos, there were differences of opinion among them about what more could or should be done. Some were resigned to the realization that hazards are all about us anyhow and in some minimum sense unavoidable. Others equated the risk with no more than occasional smoking and raised the question whether tests on animals of massive exposure to substances could really be used to evaluate effects of very small, albeit continuous, exposure of humans to those substances. By and large they had concluded from all the facts as they knew them that Cumberland's precautions provided workers with sufficient protection as well as early warning through regularly scheduled pulmonary inspections. This opinion was strengthened by the results of a study of the medical records of retired Cumberland employees who had died during the preceding 20 or so years. In no case was the cause of death apparently related to asbestos.

Mr. Barlow's greatest frustration was with the workers themselves, who, according to Mr. Barlow, "couldn't give a damn." Employees and others, Mr. Barlow felt, had seen so many ridiculous government regulations that they assumed that all government regulations were ridiculous.[2] Wiping the white asbestos dust off his finger after he had handled a small, in-process piece of asbestos-laminated sheet, a supervisor, showing the casewriters through the plant, shrugged his shoulders and said he had resigned himself to the exposure as an unavoidable part of his job, though he worried about the effect on his wife and children. He noted the thin layer of dust on all surfaces in the plant in spite of elaborate dust collection equipment and reflected about the consequences of asbestos particles carried home on his clothes and transferred to the clothes of other family members in the family wash.

Most customers were primarily concerned that asbestos and asbestos products were becoming more expensive and harder to get, but did not otherwise appear to be overly concerned about the health hazard since they only installed parts and did not machine, sand, or saw them.

THE MARKET

When Mr. Barlow took over management of the Maryland Division, Cumberland Gasket Co., Inc., had two competitors for its asbestos-based products. About the time that the two-fiber OSHA standard was introduced in 1975, one of the competitors left the market for reasons not known to Mr. Barlow. Thus, in 1978, only Cumberland and one other company were supplying the market. Mr. Barlow thought that the other company re-flected concern for the hazards of working with asbestos when they stopped selling trimmed asbestos sheets in 1977. (Trimming creates dust.) He had heard rumors from customers and other sources that the last competitor was planning to leave the market.

The market for the asbestos-based products made by Cumberland was dominated by a few large companies. In addition, there were 20 to 30 very much smaller customers. Mr. Barlow felt that the primary concern of these customers, especially in the replacement market, was with price and delivery. Early in 1977, the price of asbestos had increased by 16 percent following just six months after a 10 percent increase. Because there were now only two producers left, Cumberland and its one competitor, it was becoming increasingly difficult for customers to get timely delivery. Because of the general lack of concern about the hazards of asbestos, very little work had been done on developing a substitute. (There are hazards other than those related to workers. One estimate holds that 158,000 pounds of asbestos fiber is put into the air each year from the wearing down of automotive brake linings.) Nor could Cumberland, a relatively small company, afford to do much pure R&D on its own. Du Pont had developed a substitute, which tends to be four to five times more expensive than asbestos and was of inferior quality for some applications. The evidence of customer behavior was that they were unwilling to pay more for asbestos substitutes.

COMPANY POLICY AND ALTERNATIVES

In 1978, Cumberland's announced policy was to continue to manufacture asbestos as long as it could do so in compliance with OSHA or other standards, and as long as it

---

[2]Mr. Barlow believed that, contrary to much popular opinion, OSHA was good and effective. He observed that while OSHA had promulgated some silly and widely publicized regulations about the shape of toilet seats and the like, there was incontrovertible evidence that industrial injuries and accidents had declined since OSHA had come into existence. He was confident that these declines would not have occurred without OSHA.

could do so without further capital investment—unless the investment had a six-month or less payback. The investment limitation reflected management's view that standards very probably would be made more restrictive. Products using asbestos were always fully priced, including the costs of the air testing and special cleaning programs. Mr. Barlow would not discount products containing asbestos in order to promote other business. In his visits to and discussions with customers, he regularly tried to get them to try substitutes for asbestos, though with limited success. Mr. Barlow stressed the company's obligation to its customers and observed that Cumberland could not leave them without a source. Without Cumberland as a supplier, market demands could not be met. However, if the OSHA standard of one-half of a fiber were introduced, Mr. Barlow thought that Cumberland could not continue without major changes.

One possible change would be to move to a complete "white room," space-age environment. This would involve isolating equipment used in making asbestos from the rest of the plant. Employees using the equipment would have to make a complete change of clothing and to shower before leaving the room. Masks would still be required. In addition to the costs associated with clothing changes and the like, the white room would mean serious underutilization of equipment, since the machines would only by used with asbestos material about 30 percent to 40 percent of the time. A white room would require an investment of $750,000 and would raise operating costs by $100,000 a year. The fabrication division had $6 million in assets. Another alternative would be to process all asbestos under water or other liquid. However, since asbestos is absorbent, product

properties could change. Thus considerable research would have to go into developing the liquid used and testing the properties of the product after it had been processed in a liquid.

Processing in a liquid would eliminate dust but would substitute asbestos-bearing sludges. Interestingly, neither OSHA nor the state had any regulations preventing the company from dumping sludge containing asbestos into the river. (Eventually, asbestos in the water would be washed up on the banks, dry out, and enter the air.) The new Cumberland plant had a completely enclosed filtration system designed to prevent any discharge into the river. This system had not been required by law, but Mr. Barlow had included it when the plant was built, and even though it had added a substantial amount to the cost of the plant, top management had not questioned it.

The final option for Mr. Barlow and Cumberland was to leave the asbestos business entirely. As noted, this would do irreparable harm to customers and would raise the cost of many goods and services for society generally. Beyond this, there were serious financial consequences for the Cumberland Company and its employees. Unless substitutes developed for asbestos-involved materials and processes which were adaptable to Cumberland's capabilities, jobs in the plant would inevitably be lost. Furthermore, the fabrication division was only marginally profitable and the contribution of products containing asbestos was considerable. Loss of the asbestos business would place the division in a loss position—and would jeopardize the profitability of other divisions within the company.

Though Mr. Barlow had given considerable thought to the moral and business issues involved in Cumberland's processing of asbestos materials, he still faced unresolved questions and concerns about the extent of the hazards to which Cumberland's workers were exposed and of the ways in which he should respond to them.

CASE 5

Double L Company

Double L was founded in 1957 by Mary and Phil Lamount. It was born in the Lamounts' garage as a part-time business attempt to build a practical electric car. Though both Mary and Phil had considerable expertise in the electrical field, the reality of building the car seemed always beyond their reach, and the business remained hidden behind the closed garage door. It wasn't until Phil Jr. graduated from college and undertook operation of the business as a full-time job that Double L moved into more conventional "business" quarters.

Phil Jr. seemed to have his parents' expertise in technical competence. Initially he developed a number of inexpensive alloys—mixtures of two or more metals or of a metal and another material that adds some desirable quality to the original metal. These alloys allowed the company to produce inexpensive scissors, and, over time, a number of inexpensive small kitchen appliances. By 1981 Double L employed thirty-two people on its production lines and another five people who performed administrative duties, including a marketing manager, Ralph Egerton. Egerton primarily worked with industrial representatives and personally performed a small amount of direct marketing.

By 1984 Phil Jr. had begun tinkering with the use of alloys in the development of an engine that could be used to power a lawn mower. In 1986 he completed work on the engine and, given his innate inventive ability, he was able to make it fifty percent smaller and sixty percent lighter than conventional engines of equal power. The engine employed an entirely new and radically unconventional design. The improved alloys allowed the engine to withstand much higher temperatures than conventional lawn mower engines and thus permitted the improvement in the new design. The smaller and lighter engine promised to allow users to be able to lift the entire mower much more easily than conventional mowers.

Since Double L's limited capital would not allow the company to produce a line of lawn mowers in addition to its existent products, Ralph Egerton was asked to contact the second largest mower manufacturer, one of ten major lawn mower producers in the United States.

Breeze, Inc., the number two com-

Prepared by Robert Reeder

pany, was chosen because of the weakening reputation of its mower's engine reliability. Though it owned thirty-six percent of the company that supplied its engines, Breeze and its integrated supplier seemed to be unable to develop a competitive engine despite their best attempts. Phil Jr. might have asked Ralph to contact other companies in addition to Breeze, but he reasoned that in their oligopsonist market each producer would want to make the most of product differentiation.

In April of 1986 Ralph contacted Breeze. He spoke directly to Mary Mitchell, Breeze's purchasing agent. From the beginning, Mary seemed so taken with the possibilities of Double L's engine that she handled the entire matter herself, never allowing any other Breeze personnel to talk with Ralph. Ralph rationalized that Mary wanted all the credit once the Double L engine was finally purchased and proved to be successful. He didn't object to Mary's doing so.

As the weeks rolled by, Phil Jr. would occasionally become perplexed at the seemingly sluggish progress Ralph seemed to be making. Ralph had to constantly reassure the always impatient Phil Jr. Ralph was convinced of the progress. Since Mary never allowed him to talk to any other company personnel, or even see the factory operation, Ralph became more and more convinced of her sincerity and determination to adopt the

Double L engine. He knew she would buy.

Ralph reported the "big break" to Phil Jr. in March of 1990. He explained that Breeze was now so involved that Mary had asked that Double L ship one of its new motors to Breeze for testing. Within the week the motor was sent to Mary.

After receiving the motor, Mary was as quiet as she had been all along, never initiating calls to Ralph. He reasoned that she was becoming increasingly concerned about the importance of his new motor, and wanted to be even more sure of maintaining secrecy. In January 1991, when Mary did call, her voice was filled with concern and disappointment. She let Ralph know that Breeze's long-time supplier, N.R. Sud Co., would likely be continuing to furnish engines in the future. She said that Sud even reported that it was working on a unique engine of its own.

Suddenly Ralph felt drained, let down. He thought that Phil Jr. had probably set too high a tentative price on the Double L motor, so that the Breeze account might be permanently lost, though he further reasoned, "Why not try once again?" He jokingly asked Mary if Breeze had any openings for a good marketing manager. Mary laughed and said, "I just bet we have. I'll have our personnel people get right back to you! We can always use an excellent addition to our staff."

CASE 6

Grey Electronics, Inc.

Grey Electronics, Inc., a multidivisional producer of electronics equipment headquartered in Iowa, was founded in 1936 by John Forman, a graduate engineer with an interest in electronics. During its early years the company survived by assembling various types of radio equipment for midwestern manufacturers. Operations expanded substantially during World War II as the company obtained large amounts of subcontracting work, mainly of an assembly nature. During and immediately following the war, Forman changed the character of his firm in an attempt to develop a proprietary product. His first effort was an improved version of a high-frequency radio receiver which one of his associates had designed. The "new" product was immediately successful, and the profits generated enabled Forman to invest heavily in research and development. During the late 1940s and early 1950s the company successfully introduced a series of new products, and by 1960 sales had grown to almost $40 million a year. By 1965 the company consisted of three major producing divisions (consumer products, radio equipment, and solid state) as well as several staff departments (see Exhibit 1).

The Solid State Division's products were high-quality, technically sophisticated electronic subassemblies and integrated circuits designed for limited, specialized uses,

with about 75 percent of division sales going to the U.S. government. The products were constantly changing, and the division regularly worked near the "state of the art" in either its product development work or its production methods.

The division was organized with four major departments—all of which reported to a [division] manager. In 1964 a Solid State Oscillator Department was added to the division.[1] (See Exhibit 2.) This department was responsible for its own research and development, engineering, manufacturing, and marketing activities. Grey's market share for this product was estimated to be about 35 percent versus 40 percent for the industry's largest producer, Standard Parts.

Because such a large portion of its sales were to the government, the manager of the Oscillator Department, Ned Seymoure, was constantly troubled by the problem of bid pricing. Competition was severe and he was often forced to bid on a variable cost basis—or even below—to secure some business. In 1965, Seymoure asked Tom Moore, director of Corporate Operations Research, to investigate the feasibility of preparing a model which would help in determining the price to bid on contracts.

In his preliminary work, Moore found

---

[1]An oscillator is a source of power used in technically advanced laboratory and field tests sets. A test set might contain a series of oscillators, each capable of producing a signal over a given frequency range, making the set useful for checking the accuracy and receiving power of a piece of electronic equipment.

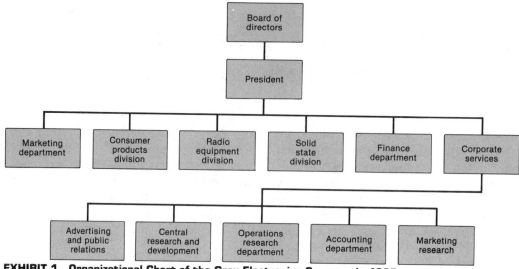

EXHIBIT 1   Organizational Chart of the Grey Electronics Company in 1965

that the oscillator subassembly group's cost on a job was often a function of the price bid. Thus, if a low bid was submitted and accepted the manufacturing group worked hard to keep its costs down. Conversely, if a "profitable" bid had been accepted, the manufacturing group did not strive as hard to hold down its costs. He also determined that substantial variations existed between contracts and bids in the gathering and utilizing of marketing information concerning the customer's needs and competitor's strengths, weaknesses, and probably bids.

At the end of three months, Moore and other members of the Operations Research Group had completed the job of constructing and programming the model. The actual construction consisted of two steps:

Determining the Objectives of the Model.

After careful deliberation it was decided that, since the manager of the Oscillator De-

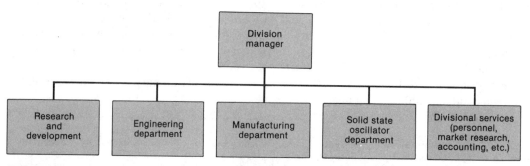

EXHIBIT 2   Organization Chart of the Solid State Division of the Grey Electronics Company in 1965

partment was the person who would ultimately accept or reject the model, it would be useless to try to sell him a model which did not meet his objectives. "Therefore," stated Moore, "I asked Seymoure what his own goals were relative to the operations of the division. It would have been possible for us to construct a model which best served the interests of the corporation, the product managers working for Seymoure, and/or of Seymoure himself. We knew, in advance, that the objectives of these three parties were not necessarily compatible. For example, the corporation tends to set year-to-year objectives on return on investment while product managers often become excessively concerned about winning or losing a particular contract. Seymoure, on the other hand, tends to look at the long run—the next five years. He worries about getting enough volume to hold his research group together, to hold his manufacturing schedule fairly constant throughout the year, and to attain a big share of the market. We finally decided we'd try to construct a model which would be predicated on the long run, but which would show what would happen in the short run also."

Determining the Bidding Process. The bidding procedure in the Oscillator Department involved the representatives of several functional areas. Chronologically, the steps appeared as follows:

1. A request to submit a bid was received by the department's marketing manager.
2. He referred the bid request to a product marketing specialist whose specialty was within the product line concerned.
3. The product marketing specialist requested a cost estimate from the Accounting Department.
4. A cost estimator from the Accounting Department obtained from the product line

manager estimates of the cost of manufacturing the product, that is, the cost data, both historical and estimated, that he could use to produce a bid. This bid was always based on full-cost-recovery pricing.

5. This analysis was returned to the product marketing specialist, who prepared an analysis of the market to supplement the financial analysis.
6. These analyses were presented to the product line manager. The product marketing specialist and the product line manager jointly prepared a bid which was submitted to the marketing manager for approval.
7. If the product line manager and the product marketing specialist could not agree on a bid, the marketing manager would resolve their differences.
8. If the contract to be bid was large or particularly significant for other reasons, the division manager approved the final bid. He also resolved any remaining disagreements or even changed the suggested bid to one which he felt was more appropriate.

FULL-COST-RECOVERY PRICING

A full-cost-recovery price, as prepared by the cost estimator, was designed to recover *all* variable costs plus all allocated costs of a contract. The procedure for preparing such a bid was

1. Direct labor for the contract was estimated. Direct labor included a 25 percent charge for employee fringe benefits.
2. An overhead charge was allocated based on 70 percent of direct labor. Overhead included depreciation on the division's equipment, the costs of the machine shop and service departments of the division (e.g., divisional R & D), and all fixed charges not included in the general and administrative allocation.
3. Material costs were estimated.
4. (1), (2), and (3) were totaled to get manufacturing costs.
5. General and administrative burden was

computed as a percentage of manufacturing cost. G&A included an allocation for the expenses of the corporate staff, corporate building, corporate service, the division manager's salary and his staff salaries, and costs of moving and rearranging equipment. G&A normally ranged from 35 to 65 percent of manufacturing cost.

6. An allocation for profit was computed as a percent of the total of (4) and (5). The percentage used depended on the type of contract being negotiated and also varied according to the federal government's pricing guidelines.

Description of the Model

The basic model represented an attempt to simulate the process by which an experienced manager prepared a bid. The probability of getting the contract if a given price were bid was of critical importance. By multiplying this probability with the expected payoff, the model showed the probable value of submitting a particular bid. Mr. Moore explained: "We repeat this process for many different bids until we find the optimal price, that is, the bid which was the highest expected value of those bids we are willing to submit. Naturally, we don't blindly accept what the model puts out. We know we can't describe all bidding situations in this one model, and even if we could, the cost would be exorbitant. We submit the model's output to the department manager for further action. If his intuition agrees with the model, we'll have done a pretty good job. If not, either some factor has been left out of the model or the manager is biased by some personal consideration. Once we determine what the problem is, the model's suggested bids can be accepted or rejected."

Inputs to the Model

In its completed form, the model made use of four inputs. The first input was an estimate of the most critical competitor's probable bids. Factors considered in preparing this estimate included the opposing firm's financial condition, the capacity at which the firm was estimated to be operating, its bidding history, and the bidding history of the person preparing that firm's bid, the firm's estimated cost structure, its capacity to develop or produce the product involved, the firm's policies relating to long-run versus short-run gains, any unique rivalry existing between Grey and that firm, the firm's position in (or out of) the market involved, the price structure of the market (e.g., firm or deteriorating), and any other information relevant to the opposing firm's probable bid.

One or several people might prepare this assessment. Usually those persons most familiar with the market would be the manager of the manufacturing group for that product and his counterpart in the marketing department. Their estimates were quantified in the model using a probability distribution. A normal-type distribution was assumed with the competitor's most likely bid equaling the mode.

(As an example, if a competitor's most probable bid was expected to be $50,000 and there was felt to be 1 chance out of 40 that he would bid below $35,000, a normal-type distribution was created with $50,000 equaling the mode while $35,000 and $65,000 equaled the plus and minus two standard deviation points.)

The second input involved an estimate of the amount of bias which the customer held for or against Grey or its products. To prepare this estimate it was necessary to determine the basis on which the contract would be let. A customer might be concerned about a number of factors including price, the ability of the supplier to meet delivery schedules, unusual technical characteristics of a product, and the backup service which a firm offered—or any of a number of other factors peculiar to a customer and a contract.

This estimate was quantified in terms of the probability of Grey's being awarded the contract if its bid [were] a certain percent above or below the competitor's bid. Such an estimate might appear as follows, for example,

Percent Grey's Bid Above [+] or Below [−] Competitor's Bid	Probability Grey Will Get Contract
+20%	.025
+5	.5
−10	.975

Once again, a normal-type distribution was assumed with the mean equaling the point at which there was a 50–50 chance Grey would get the bid. This estimate was prepared by the product sales manager and the manufacturing group manager.

The third input consisted of the production costs of the contract. An estimate of the labor and material costs was prepared by the manager of the manufacturing group. He considered historical performance, learning curve effects, start-up costs, equipment required and all other factors which influenced his production costs. Overhead rates were allocated by the division controller.

The fourth input was the long-run effects of the contract. Effects of the contract on catalog prices and prices which would have to be submitted on succeeding bids such as follow-on contracts, reduced overhead allowances on renegotiable contracts, gains and losses in market position and prestige, and any other factors not included in the costs of production were computed to determine the rewards and penalties of losing the contract. These payoffs or losses were present-valued at an annual rate of 10 percent to determine the "extra" benefits and costs of the contract. The manufacturing group manager and the marketing manager prepared this estimate.

Output of the Model

The model's output was a payoff table showing the expected value of a given bid. This table might appear as follows, for example:

Bid	Probability of Winning	Profits [Losses]	Probable Profits [Losses]
$70,000	.05	$40,000	$ 2,000
60,000	.3	30,000	9,000
50,000	.55	20,000	11,000
40,000	.70	10,000	7,000
30,000	1.0	0	0

Other Factors

Several additional factors were built into the model. The model could produce two suggested bids, one based on full cost and the other on variable cost. The model could also be used to compare the effect of several different estimates of cost and market inputs.

The SSI Job

An opportunity for the Oscillator Department to reach its goal of becoming the leader in the solid-state oscillator field arose in April 1966, when Systems Suppliers Incorporated (SSI) solicited bids for a large number of oscillators to be used in laboratory test sets designed for the military. SSI received the contract from Redstone Arsenal at a time when SSI was reportedly in financial trouble due to low sales volume.

The contract was for 57 sets. Each set contained two separate oscillator units, each of which required one oscillator subassembly for each of eight frequency bands, A, B, C,

D, E, F, G, and H. Bids were therefore being solicited on 912 subassemblies in total or 114 in each frequency band. In addition, bids were requested for a possible follow-on order should Systems Suppliers wish to raise the total procurement to either 1,200 or 1,600 units.

SSI did not restrict itself to one supplier for the entire contract. Bids were requested on several options so that SSI could split the contract if it wished. The options were

Option Number	Frequency Bands to Be Covered
1	A, B, C, D, E, F, G, & H
2	A, B, C, D, E, F, & G
3	H
4	A, B, & C
5	D, E, F, & G

Grey asked for and received permission to bid on one other option:

Option Number	Frequency Bands to Be Covered
6	A, B, C, D, & E

Grey requested this option because it closely matched Grey's present capabilities and its market expansion plans. Option 6, therefore, was the option the company was most interested in winning.

Grey believed it held a technical advantage in three frequency bands (A, B, and C) amounting to a virtual monopoly. Standard Parts, Grey's only significant competitor, was known to have started working on these oscillator subassemblies, but had not yet displayed any capacity to produce or deliver in quantity any oscillators in these frequency ranges. In the past year, Grey had successfully marketed an oscillator at H band, one which was expected to be extremely competitive in terms of the SSI contract. Grey did

not have, or plan to develop, an oscillator at G band, but at F band, an oscillator was in the final stages of development. At E band, the company was preparing a pilot production run, while both Grey and Standard Parts had successfully marketed D band subassemblies.

Grey believed it held a technical advantage on all oscillators from A through E band, and in H band, because its products were magnetically shielded. Magnetic shielding was important to SSI as Redstone's specifications required close physical storage of the oscillators, a layout which might cause equipment failure if their magnetic fields interacted. It was known that Standard Parts proposed to overcome this weakness by lining the storage containers with magnetic shielding material. It was not known with certainty if this technique would work.

The Customer

Determining the basis on which SSI would award the contract was relatively easy. SSI had the reputation of making decisions which maximized short-term profits. In other words, they were thought to be willing to take a high risk of a long-term loss in return for a high assurance of a short-term gain. Price, therefore, was thought to be the key to obtaining the contract.

This situation operated to Grey's disadvantage because, in issuing the contract, Redstone Arsenal had specified Standard Parts oscillators rather than "Standard Parts or equivalent." This oversight on Redstone's part had probably occurred because Redstone copied SSI's specifications when the contract was written. Grey was not successful in attempting to get Redstone to change this specification. Although Grey might legally have forced Redstone to change the specifications, this would have created ill will, which the company was reluctant to incur.

Redstone's oversight worked to both SSI and Standard Parts' advantage. SSI told Grey it would be willing to purchase Standard's oscillators in all frequency bands despite the risk of technical difficulties and failure to meet delivery schedules, knowing they could escape any repercussions by maintaining they had exactly followed the contract's specifications.

On the other hand, Grey was reasonably sure that SSI did not really wish to do this. Grey felt that SSI probably wanted to split the order, with Standard Parts getting options 3 and 5 and Grey getting option 4. It was also felt that Standard Parts would be determined to get as much of the contract as possible since their market share had dropped substantially over the past two years. This contract was quite large and the firm which got the contract would probably gain or hold a leadership position in the market for some time to come. The combination of these circumstances meant that the SSI job was a prize well worth seeking but one that would be difficult to attain.

		Bid Range	
Option	Frequency Band	Estimate A	Estimate B
1	A	$1,990–2,390	$1,530–1,630
	B	1,170–1,420	1,020–1,120
	C	765– 865	665– 720
	D	690– 740	665– 765
	E	665– 740	640– 690
	F	665– 740	640– 690
	G	690– 765	690– 740
	H	2,500–2,750	2,100–2,500
2		Same as option 1 except eliminate H band	
3	H	$2,500–2,750	$2,100–2,500
4	A	$2,040–3,040	$1,840–1,940
	B	1,220–1,720	1,220–1,320
	C	820– 920	870– 970
5	D	$ 720– 770	$ 720– 770
	E	690– 765	665– 720
	F	690– 740	665– 720
	G	720– 820	720– 770
6	A	$1,990–2,390	$1,530–1,630
	B	1,170–1,420	1,020–1,120
	C	765– 865	665– 715
	D	690– 740	665– 765
	E	665– 740	640– 690
7 Standards Parts' reaction to option 6	F	$ 690– 765	$ 714– 765
	G	700– 800	790– 840
	H	2,325–2,550	2,375–2,495

EXHIBIT 3 Grey Cost Data for Frequency Band H

Month	No. of Weeks	Labor Category			Total Labor	Material	Equivalent Effort*
		1	2	3			
1	4	$ 4,290	$ 5,110	$ 2,450	$ 11,850	$ 4,700	11.70
2	4	3,330	4,330	3,860	11,520	2,420	8.65
3	4	2,865	3,870	2,370	9,105	3,440	8.50
4	5	3,905	2,480	2,125	8,510	2,820	1.15
5	5	3,120	3,860	4,050	11,030	1,775	12.25
6	4	3,770	2,825	3,115	9,710	1,570	13.35
7	4	3,535	3,165	2,655	9,355	1,570	12.65
8	4	2,170	3,350	2,830	8,350	1,175	8.25
9	5	2,285	2,110	3,160	7,555	590	8.15
10	4	3,410	2,735	2,660	8,805	785	9.35
11	4	3,265	3,150	2,210	8,625	980	9.55
12	5	2,985	2,845	3,615	9,445	590	10.45
		$38,930	$39,830	$35,100	$113,860	$22,415	114.00

*"Equivalent effort" refers to the number of oscillator subassemblies produced during the period. With respect to the above, for example, output at the end of the first month might consist of the following:

No. of Oscillators	Percent Completed	Equivalent Effort
1	100	1
20	50	10
2	25	0.5
1	20	0.2
Equivalent effort at end of month 1		11.70

Estimates of Competitive Bids

Assuming the contract would be let on price alone, Grey prepared estimates of Standard Parts' probable bids.[2]

Estimates A and B were made by knowledgeable people who were intimately familiar with the market, historical bids made by Standard Parts, their general financial position, and other intangibles which might influence Standard's bid. They were

[2]While Grey was preparing bids on all seven options, only option 3 will be costed in this case; the cost per oscillator is given in Exhibit 3.

made independently, and there was no attempt to "correct" the estimates once each estimator knew what the other had estimated. They were therefore a reliable indicator of Grey's knowledge of Standard Parts' intentions.

Historical Costs

The company possessed a substantial amount of cost data on oscillator subassemblies in bands A, B, C, and D; several successful bids had been made for contracts involving these subassemblies, and the company was confident that this information could provide the basis for a successful bid on this occasion. The company had only been marketing band H subassemblies, on the other hand, for some four months. The technical breakthrough which had enabled Grey to manufacture band H oscillator subassemblies at relatively short notice had led to wide customer acceptance of the product. Nevertheless, Grey was a little uncertain of the value of the five months' cost data on band H components, in view of the relative experience of its competitors. In spite of this, Grey was very anxious that the company's bid on option 3 should be competitive, in view of the boost to development that would be provided by winning the band H contract. The five months' labor and material costs (Exhibit 3) are those actually incurred during the first production runs of band H components. The last seven months' costs (of the full year's contract) were estimated by the product line manager.[3]

[3]The company felt it had a good chance of being awarded the contract for option 4. At all events, Grey anticipated spreading the production of the subassemblies over a year's operations.

Although lacking marketing experience in bands E, F, and G, the company prepared bids using the following criteria:

1. Costs for the band E oscillator should equal band D. Equivalent effort should be the same.
2. Costs for band F should be the same as those for band D except that the costs for labor category 2 should be doubled. Equivalent effort should be the same.
3. Costs for the G band oscillator should be the same as for D band for labor category 1, the same as the F band for labor category 2, 1.25 times the cost of D band for labor category 3, and the same as D for material costs. Equivalent effort should be the same as the D band.

All labor costs included an overhead charge of 70 percent.

Additional Labor Costs

If Grey obtained an order, it was felt that additional people would be required. Estimates of these needs were as follows:

Labor	Salary [Not Including 25% Fringe Benefits]	Order Size*
Junior technician	$115/wk	Three or more bands
Assembler A	$2.75/hr	Three or more bands
Assember A	$2.75/hr	Six or more bands
Assembler B	$2.41/hr	Three or more bands
Experimental assember	$2.75/hr	Any order
Assembler B	$2.41/hr	Four or more bands
Technician	$136/wk	Six or more bands
Production engineer B	$180/wk	Four or more bands
Clerk [half time]	$88/wk	Four or more bands

*The necessity for these labor force additions varied with the number of types for which an order was received. If Grey received an order for any three oscillators, for example, it would have to hire four people: a senior technician, an assembler A, an assembler B, and an experimental assembler. If it obtained an order for all eight oscillators, it would have to hire all the people listed.

Equipment Required

In addition to labor force additions, an order from SSI would force Grey to purchase equipment. The table at the bottom of the page summarizes these requirements.

Other Costs

Several miscellaneous costs had to be considered. (See Exhibit 4.) Training cost historically equaled about six weeks' salary per person. There were also warranty provisions; about 5 percent of the oscillators in each of the top five bands would have to be replaced, while in the lower three bands, about 15 percent would have to be replaced. Royalties were also a factor; a royalty consisting of one-half of 1 percent of the selling price would have to be paid on the top six oscillators. Finally, there was the problem of deciding which, if any, of the bids would bear the departmental overhead of $480,000 a year. The management assumed that the contract, if awarded, would run for one year and that the overhead rate on all of the oscillator business was effectively the same. This did not mean, however, that a marginal cost bid could not be made.

In addition to these costs, increases would be necessary in some liquid assets. In general, a contract would increase cash requirements by about two or three weeks' total cost, receivables by between three and four weeks' total cost, and inventories by about seven to eight weeks' total cost.

Intangibles

No matter what the factory costs, Grey did not want to lose all of the SSI business. Recent technical developments in test sets indicated the feasibility of substituting integrated equipment for low-frequency oscillators. If Standard Parts got a contract for high-frequency units, they could develop a shielded oscillator subassembly and compete more favorably with Grey elsewhere. Grey, therefore, did not want Standard Parts to get the order for high-frequency oscillator subassemblies.

Output

The final output of the program, based on the information given in the case for band H subassemblies, is presented in Exhibit 5.

Equipment	Approximate Cost*	Order
Assembly station	$ 5,000	Three or more bands
Assembly station	5,000	Four or more bands
Processor	1,200/pair	Any order
Console	10,000	Any order
Console	10,000	Four or more bands
Microscope	600	Each added assembler
Spotwelder	1,000	Any order
Spotwelder	1,000	Three or more bands
Two spotwelders	1,000/ea.	Six or more bands
Test bench	500	Each added assembler
Furnace	7,500	Seven or more bands

*Installation costs included.

EXHIBIT 4 Evaluation of Cost of H Band Oscillator Subassembly: Options 1 and 3

Direct labor	$113,860	
Material	22,415	
Additional labor	11,690	
Training costs	660	
Additional equipment	1,590	
Manufacturing cost	$150,215	$150,215
Warranty provisions	22,530	
Royalties	—	
Other costs	485	
Miscellaneous costs	$ 23,015	23,015
Allocation of department overhead	42,860	42,860
Cash	10,660	
Receivables cost	15,275	
Inventory cost	30,545	
Total increase in liquid assets	$ 56,480	56,480
Total cost		$272,570
Units produced		114
Full cost per unit		$ 2,391
Marginal cost per unit		$ 2,015

Note: Costs are calculated on the basis of information given earlier and in Exhibit 3 of this case. General and administrative overhead of $42,860 (29 percent of manufacturing cost) was a result of (1) allcoating the total factory overhead "reasonably" between not only the expected SSI contracts, but also over the other work on which the department was engaged and (2) an assessment of the major long-term benefits to which success with the option 3 bid was expected to lead.

EXHIBIT 5 Grey Electronics, Inc.

Grey Full Cost Probability
Q = .95
A = $2,100.00
M = $2,500.00
B = $2,750.00
Alpha = 0.0 percent (competitive advantage)
First trial price = $2,000.00
Trial price interval = $10.00
Number of trial prices = 80.00
Product cost = $2,391.00
Number of units = 114.00
Extra profit = $.0
Extra penalty = $.0
PSTAR interpolation permissible error = .10 cents

Bid Price	Grey Full-Cost Probability of Winning	Expected Profit	Bid Price	Grey Full-Cost Probability of Winning	Expected Profit
$2,000.00	.991	$−44,182.81	$2,290.00	.813	$−9,364.50
2,010.00	.990	−42,997.70	2,300.00	.799	−8,286.62
2,020.00	.989	−41,808.76	2,310.00	.784	−7,235.26
2,030.00	.987	−40,615.91	2,320.00	.768	−6,212.89

[continued]

EXHIBIT 5 (Continued)

Bid Price	Grey Full-Cost Probability of Winning	Expected Profit	Bid Price	Grey Full-Cost Probability of Winning	Expected Profit
2,040.00	.985	−39,419.04	2,330.00	.751	−5,221.99
2,050.00	.983	−38,218.12	2,340.00	.734	−4,265.04
2,060.00	.981	−37,013.14	2,350.00	.716	−3,344.48
2,070.00	.978	−35,804.15	2,360.00	.697	−2,462.69
2,080.00	.976	−34,591.25	2,370.00	.678	−1,621.99
2,090.00	.973	−33,374.60	2,380.00	.658	−824.60
2,100.00	.969	−32,154.44	2,390.00	.637	−72.62
2,110.00	.966	−30,931.10	2,400.00	.616	631.98
2,120.00	.962	−29,704.97	2,410.00	.594	1,287.42
2,130.00	.957	−28,476.56	2,420.00	.572	1,892.06
2,140.00	.952	−27,246.46	2,430.00	.550	2,444.51
2,150.00	.947	−26,015.39	2,440.00	.527	2,943.54
2,160.00	.941	−24,784.16	2,450.00	.504	3,388.19
2,170.00	.935	−23,553.72	2,460.00	.480	3,777.74
2,180.00	.928	−22,325.13	2,470.00	.457	4,111.70
2,190.00	.921	−21,099.59	2,480.00	.433	4,389.86
2,200.00	.913	−19,878.41	2,490.00	.409	4,612.25
2,210.00	.904	−18,663.04	2,500.00	.385	4,779.23
2,220.00	.895	−17,455.07	2,510.00	.361	4,891.56
2,230.00	.886	−16,256.20	2,520.00	.337	4,951.25
2,240.00	.875	−15,068.27	2,530.00	.313	4,961.09
2,250.00	.864	−13,893.22	2,540.00	.290	4,924.44
2,260.00	.853	−12,733.11	2,550.00	.267	4,845.16
2,270.00	.840	−11,590.11	2,560.00	.245	4,727.52
2,280.00	.827	−10,466.46	2,570.00	.224	4,576.08
2,580.00	.204	4,395.64	2,690.00	.052	1,786.08
2,590.00	.185	4,191.08	2,700.00	.045	1,582.41
2,600.00	.167	3,967.30	2,710.00	.038	1,393.14
2,610.00	.149	3,729.	2,720.00	.032	1,218.82
2,620.00	.133	3,481.05	2,730.00	.027	1,059.66
2,630.00	.118	3,227.52	2,740.00	.023	915.55
2,640.00	.105	2,972.51	2,750.00	.019	786.13
2,650.00	.092	2,719.61	2,760.00	.016	670.82
2,660.00	.081	2,472.02	2,770.00	.013	568.89
2,670.00	.070	2,232.47	2,780.00	.011	479.47
2,680.00	.061	2,003.22	2,790.00	.009	401.62

Maximum profit = $4,963.18   Price = $2,527.10

EXHIBIT 5 (Continued)

Grey Marginal Probability
$Q^* = .95$
$A = \$2,100.00$
$M = \$2,500.00$
$B = \$2,750.00$
Alpha[†] = .0 percent (competitive advantage)
First trial price = \$2,000.00
Trial price interval = \$10.00
Number of trial prices = 80.00
Product cost = \$2,015.00
Number of units = 114.00
Extra profit[‡] = \$0.0
Extra penalty[‡] = \$0.0
PSTAR interpolation permissible error[§] = .10 cents

Bid Price	Grey Full-Cost Probability of Winning	Expected Profit	Bid Price	Grey Full-Cost Probability of Winning	Expected Profit
\$2,000.00	.991	\$−1,694.99	\$2,150.00	.947	\$14,572.93
2,010.00	.990	−564.27	2,160.00	.941	15,557.16
2,020.00	.989	563.46	2,170.00	.935	16,519.48
2,030.00	.987	1,687.64	2,180.00	.928	17,458.04
2,040.00	.985	2,807.62	2,190.00	.921	18,370.29
2,050.00	.983	3,922.68	2,200.00	.913	19,253.95
2,060.00	.981	5,032.00	2,210.00	.904	20,106.59
2,070.00	.978	6,134.66	2,220.00	.895	20,925.67
2,080.00	.976	7,229.68	2,230.00	.886	21,708.59
2,090.00	.973	8,315.93	2,240.00	.875	22,452.72
2,100.00	.969	9,392.19	2,250.00	.864	23,155.37
2,110.00	.966	10,457.13	2,260.00	.853	23,813.83
2,120.00	.962	11,509.30	2,270.00	.840	24,425.44
2,130.00	.957	12,547.14	2,280.00	.827	24,987.50
2,140.00	.952	13,568.95	2,290.00	.813	25,497.41
2,300.00	.799	25,952.61	2,550.00	.267	16,302.91
2,310.00	.784	26,350.65	2,560.00	.245	15,245.55
2,320.00	.768	26,689.19	2,570.00	.224	14,188.41
2,330.00	.751	26,966.04	2,580.00	.204	13,140.41
2,340.00	.734	27,179.20	2,590.00	.185	12,109.92
2,350.00	.716	27,326.81	2,600.00	.167	11,104.65
2,360.00	.697	27,407.32	2,610.00	.149	10,131.54
2,370.00	.678	27,419.31	2,620.00	.133	9,196.65
2,380.00	.658	27,361.74	2,630.00	.118	8,305.12
2,390.00	.637	27,233.72	2,640.00	.105	7,461.11
2,400.00	.616	27,034.78	2,650.00	.092	6,667.77
2,410.00	.594	26,764.75	2,660.00	.081	5,927.34
2,420.00	.572	26,423.66	2,670.00	.070	5,241.11
2,430.00	.550	26,012.09	2,680.00	.061	4,609.49
2,440.00	.527	25,530.72	2,690.00	.052	4,032.13
2,450.00	.504	24,980.73	2,700.00	.045	3,507.93

(*continued*)

EXHIBIT 5 (Continued)

Bid Price	Grey Full-Cost Probability of Winning	Expected Profit	Bid Price	Grey Full-Cost Probability of Winning	Expected Profit
2,460.00	.480	24,363.70	2,710.00	.038	3,035.21
2,470.00	.457	23,681.29	2,720.00	.032	2,611.76
2,480.00	.433	22,935.79	2,730.00	.027	2,234.97
2,490.00	.409	22,129.52	2,740.00	.023	1,901.93
2,500.00	.385	21,265.38	2,750.00	.019	1,609.48
2,510.00	.361	20,347.27	2,760.00	.016	1,354.37
2,520.00	.337	19,382.81	2,770.00	.013	1,133.28
2,530.00	.313	18,381,02	2,780.00	.011	942.92
2,540.00	.290	17,351.23	2,790.00	.009	780.09

Maximum profit = $27,422.98   Price = $2,366.70

*Q = the degree of certainty which Grey had for the estimates of its competitors' most probable bids. A = the minus 2 standard deviation point; B = the plus 2 SD point, and M = the mode.

†Alpha is an input measure of any (nonprice) competitive advantage that Grey was thought to have over the competitor. Alpha = .5, for example, would mean that Grey could bid 5 percent more than the competitor and still win the contract. If the contract was being let on price alone, then there could be no competitive advantage, and Alpha would equal zero.

‡Extra profit, extra penalty: These dollar inputs quantify the extra (particular longer-term) benefits (or penalties) that the company might expect as a result of winning (or losing) the contract. For example, success in this contract might lead to a reduction of costs in the production of another assembly.

§$P*$ is the allowed error in the estimate of the price (to produce the expected maximum profit)

Appendix A: Government Contracts

Among the problems faced by firms supplying sophisticated parts and equipment to the government or its suppliers is the contracts which the government negotiates.

As a first-order generalization, government contracts are very precise in terms of specifications, both technical and other. The custom of phoning or writing a customer to submit an order, common in some business and industries, is not common when doing business with the government. Technical specifications in government contracts are very specific and inclusive in describing the desired product. Other specific provisions of these contracts might include delivery dates, profits which the supplying firm is allowed to make, sharing of research and development costs, and privileges which the government reserves for itself with respect to the product, its development, and the knowledge which a firm gains from developing that product.

With respect to systems, the government reserves the right to accept or authorize the manufacture of a system until the pilot models have been demonstrated to be fully workable and the supplying firms have proved their capacity to supply the system and its components. Thus, if five firms are supplying components to a systems manufacturer and one of the components fails, neither the systems manufacturer nor the components manufacturers will receive authorization to commence production until the problem is solved. This can create many scheduling problems, as a firm might receive a contract for a component but not get authorization for production until some time later, with that time depending on another supplier.

Contracts which the government might negotiate with respect to profits can also create problems. In general, there are three types of contracts: a "fixed-price" contract, a "cost-plus-fix-fee" contract (CPFF), and a "target-incentive" contract.

A fixed-price contract means that a company agrees to supply a given quantity of a given product for a fixed amount of money. If the company loses money on the contract, it suffers the entire loss. If the company makes money on the contract, it enjoys the entire gain.

A cost-plus-fix-fee contract might cover a research and development project, with the government agreeing to pay for the cost of the project plus some amount of percentage of profit. Such contracts are renegotiable as differences of opinion may arise concerning exactly what the costs are or were. Disagreements can arise over whether machinery investments should be allocated fully to a given contract or should be partially supported by other aspects of a firm's operations. Overhead and administrative expenses are also common areas of disagreement, not only because of the difficulties involved in allocating these costs, but also because of the difficulties created by the fluctuating volume of business which a company might do. For example, an overhead allocation rate based on the level of business a firm is doing now might be unacceptable to the government six months from now if the firm's business increased significantly in the interim. The opposite would be true if the firm's business declined.

A target-incentive contract involves several negotiated figures—a target price, a target cost, a ceiling price, and a profit formula. Target cost represents the expected cost of the job. Target price is the price the government expects to pay and represents target cost plus an allowance for profit. Ceiling price is the highest amount which the government will pay for the job. The profit formula represents the division which will be made of the costs or profits if they differ from the targets. If target cost is less than actual cost, the government shares part of the cost and the company takes the rest. If actual cost is less than target cost, the government shares part of the savings and the company gets the remainder.

The government handles problems over CPFF and target-incentive contracts by reserving the right to audit a company's books whenever it chooses. For example, if a company is working on a CPFF contract and the company receives another large contract from the government or a significant amount of business from elsewhere, the government might audit the company's books to renegotiate the overhead and administrative allowances on the CPFF contract. As a consequence, when a company is bidding on contracts, it must consider the effect of those contracts on any government business it currently has, if that government business is renegotiable or requires cost breakdowns.

The government also audits a firm's books before it negotiates a fixed-price contract if there is insufficient competition for the contract.

Another aspect of government contracts deals with the ownership of products developed through government-sponsored research. If the government has financed the development of a product, it can require the firm which performed the work to supply blueprints to competing firms to allow the government to develop alternative sources of supply. It should be noted, however, that supplying blueprints does not imply that production know-how must also be supplied. In practice, the difficulties involved in manufacturing many technical items reduce substantially the usefulness of blueprints.

Appendix B: Some Competitive Characteristics of the SSO Market

SSOs are utilized as subassemblies of systems designed mainly for military use. It has been estimated that as much as 90 percent of the SSOs produced are ultimately delivered to the government. In this field, Grey is an "independent" producer. That is, Grey is not a systems designer but, instead, supplies SSOs to other firms which are systems designers and which often have their own SSO departments. Independent producers sometimes find that a systems designer will ask for bids from the independents, then offer the contract to [its] own division if it can produce the SSOs at a lower cost.

About 25 percent of Grey's SSO sales are the result of contracts for which bids are required. However, these bid contracts serve as the price leaders in the field. As the price structure of this and other electronics markets is historically deteriorating, it is necessary for a manager to consider not only the effect of a bid price on a given contract, but also the effect of that bid on his "catalog" prices and the profits resulting from these sales.

Producers compete in several ways in this market but not all firms elect to follow the same paths. As the products are often "state of the art" in terms of their advanced technical design, the capacity to develop and produce high-quality, technically advanced, and often highly specialized equipment is one area of competition. In general, too, allegedly competitive items produced by different manufacturers are not directly interchangeable. For example, if a system is designed to use company A's SSOs, it might be very difficult or expensive to alter that system in order to use company B's SSOs. This situation places a premium on being either the first producer of an item or getting a firm to design their system specifically to use your products.

Firms may compete by having an intelligence system which informs them of the probable need for a given new product or an adaptation of an existing product in order that they can develop the item. They may also compete through the use of highly skilled, technical field men whose job it is to sell the systems designer on the merits of their company's products and to suggest to the systems designer ways in which new uses or adaptations can be made of existing products. It is sometimes said that the field men must "live in the customer's pocket."

The importance of price in this market is very great. Systems designers must submit bids to the government which force the designer[s] to seek the lowest-cost suppliers [they] can. In addition, contracts with suppliers are usually negotiated by the business managers of a system design firm rather than by the technical men. Thus, even though the technical designers may be convinced of the merits of company A's products, it may be very difficult to convince the business managers of this fact. This problem is compounded by the fact that technical specifications of competing products are often the same while their performance characteristics may not be.

Several other factors also compound the price problem. The effect of volume on the costs of production is substantial. Learning curves play an important role in this industry, so that the variable costs of producing SSOs is significantly reduced with increased volume. In addition, the high costs of research and development represent a substantial fixed investment in a given product which often requires a large volume of production to recover. As government contracts are often followed by additional "follow-on" contracts for the same products, the necessity for volume production places another premium on securing the initial contract. Finally, as initial contracts sometimes include an allowance for R&D, yet another premium is placed on securing the first contract.

The characteristics described so far also apply to the systems manufacturers, so that price pressures are extremely strong throughout the industry. Systems designers and components manufacturers will sometimes deliberately take a loss on an initial contract in order to gain a competitive advantage. When a systems designer has done this, he will exert pressure on the components manufacturers for lower prices in order to recover part of the expected loss. Similarly, a components manufacturer may not do the same thing to its suppliers or to its own manufacturing groups in order to reduce costs.

One of the more interesting ways in which suppliers may be pressured is by means of a practice referred to as a "Chinese auction." A system manufacturer might solicit bids from components manufacturers with the understanding that the contract will be awarded to the low bidder. After bids have been submitted, the customer might call components manufacturer company X and hint that he would prefer X's products but that company Y submitted a lower bid. If X responds by submitting a lower bid, the process is then repeated with Y. Since X and Y do not know what the competing firm has bid or whether or not the customer is in fact telling the truth, the amount of uncertainty faced by a supplier is very great. X and Y cannot reveal their respective bids for com-

petitive reasons nor will they do so for fear the Justice Department might regard this as collusion. They cannot mutually agree to stop bidding since that would definitely be collusion. The only alternative is to elect unilaterally to stop bidding, inform the customer of this decision, and run the risk of losing the contract. Needless to say, the customer may not believe a company when it has made this decision and may find itself placed in an untenable position as a consequence. The Chinese auction is a practice followed by only part of the industry, so a supplier must know who might engage in this practice and be prepared to act accordingly.

Another practice consists of varying the technical specifications of a contract. A customer might specify loose or misleading technical specifications in a contract to be bid on. After the contract has been awarded, the customer will tighten and reinterpret the specifications, so that he gets an expensive part or component for the price of a cheap one.

It would be misleading to say that these practices prevail in the electronics industry. However, they are practiced enough, particularly on large contracts, that they must be taken into account by suppliers through strategic bidding. Some of the ways in which a supplier might combat these practices would include submitting an initially higher bid than the contract is expected to go for in order to be able to reduce the bid later. Alternatively, a supplier might demand technical concessions in exchange for a lower bid or even demand that his technical specifications be written into the customer's contract.

Another way in which a supplier might combat the Chinese auction problem or escape price pressures consists of reject bidding. If a components manufacturer is producing an SSO which must produce a certain amount of power, he may find that he is getting a significant number of rejects which do not meet the power requirements for the item he is selling. If he can find a customer for these rejects, he has the opportunity to make very large profits since, in effect, the cost of these items is virtually minimal to him.

Reject bidding, however, is also quite hazardous. It is based on the assumption that rejects will be available to be sold. If a production improvement eliminates the rejects or the market for higher-power products runs out, the supplier may find himself trapped with an unrealistic price. Alternatively, if the lower-power products are not acceptable, renegotiating the contract [will] be both difficult and embarrassing, if not impossible. The problem of renegotiation is further hampered by the responsibility a manufacturer assumes when he accepts a contract. If a system fails, even though it is the fault of the designer, the manufacturers whose components are involved suffer a very real loss of reputation and feel called upon to do what they can to correct the problem. If this involves supplying primary rather than reject products, they may be forced into this position to avoid the stigma attached to the failure of the system.

CASE 7

Huntington Electronics

NEW PRODUCT INTRODUCTION

Since the costs of electricity were expected to rise fourfold over the next few years for commercial and industrial users, the search was on for practical ways to cut costs and conserve energy resources. As a leading electrical equipment manufacturer, Huntington had been making a significant contribution to these efforts through the development of new energy-efficient products. The company

This case was prepared by Norman A. P. Govoni, Jean-Pierre Jeannet, and Henry N. Deneault, *Cases in Marketing,* 2nd ed. (New York: John Wiley & Sons, Inc. Publishers, 1983.) Copyright 1983 by Grid Publishing, Inc. Reprinted by permission of John Wiley & Sons, Inc.

was currently in the process of developing a new mercury vapor light which was designed to replace recessed incandescent down-lights found in lobbies, conference rooms, and similar public areas of hotels, motels, bank and office buildings, schools and universities, stores, airport terminals, and other facilities.

The problem lay in persuading, or rather, encouraging potential buyers to make the conversion from their existing lamps to Huntington's Superwatt and incurring the initial capital costs involved.

Huntington Electronics had been in existence for about 70 years and had always been active in the lighting business, producing such items as fittings and fixtures, searchlights, and signals for traffic control. The firm operated several factories in the United States and abroad and was traded on the New York Stock Exchange.

Huntington was considered one of the top outdoor lighting suppliers in the nation and carried one of the most complete product lines available. Huntington's products were used outdoors to light shopping centers, industrial parks and plants, apartment complexes, aircraft carrier flight decks, streets, malls, billboards, parking lots, and in numerous other situations. The firm had achieved a leading position in the field of aviation as well.

Superwatt was a simple kit that enabled recessed commercial incandescent lighting systems to be quickly converted to more efficient mercury vapor lighting at a relatively low cost and without the use of specialized labor. The advantages were as follows:

A. Energy costs were substantially reduced.
   By replacing an inefficient high-wattage incandescent lighting system with a highly efficient, lower-wattage mercury vapor system, power usage could be reduced by more than 40 percent without sacrificing light levels. The most common conversion would be from a 150W incandescent light to a 70W color-improved mercury vapor.

B. Installation was easy and inexpensive.
   The unit was simply screwed into the existing incandescent socket after the old lamp had been removed.
   1. No expensive rewiring was required.
   2. No specialized labor was required. Anybody could install it.
   3. No special tools were required for installation.
   4. Light levels remained the same.

C. Relamping labor costs were one-twentieth of those of the incandescent system.
   The mercury vapor source had a lamp life of approximately four years (16,000 hours total) as opposed to the incandescent source (rated at 750 hours).

D. Initial cost of Superwatt ($30.00 direct to a large user with lamp) could be recovered by energy and maintenance savings in less than three years (see Exhibit 1).

The unit consisted of two aluminum extrusions clamped together around a mercury ballast with top and bottom cover plates completing the basic external housing assembly. The compact mercury conversion kit construction and shallow lamp enabled the combination to fit easily into most existing fixture housings and permitted original fixtures hardware to be replaced in its original position so that the overall ceiling appearance remained the same as before.

The fixture housing had numerous fins to provide heat dissipation which insured that the kit would perform within safe operating temperature limits. A medium base plug body on top of the housing allowed the fixture to be screwed as a unit into the existing incandescent socket. A lanyard-type arrangement was provided with the fixture, which when attached to the existing housing, provided an additional securing device. The down-side of the unit consisted of the socket and reflector-type lamp which was provided as an integral part of the unit. Two locating clips insured proper positioning of the prong-base lamp.

The market for Superwatt consisted of any existing commercial or institutional building that presently utilized recessed incandescent lighting in any way for its indoor lighting system. Generally, this type of lighting fixture would be most commonly found in lobbies, hallways, executive offices, conference rooms, or where accent lighting of some kind would be required.

By drawing on several government and industry sources for background information, the market researchers refined this basic information in order to determine the actual numerical size of the potential market,

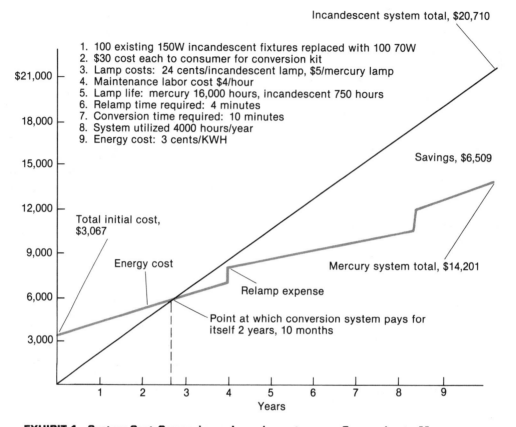

EXHIBIT 1   System Cost Comparison—Incandescent versus Conversion to Mercury

as shown in Exhibit 2. The study indicated that approximately 7,000,000 fixtures presently in use were mechanically capable of being converted to Superwatt.

The markets were further divided into segments according to their order of importance as perceived by the product marketing manager who was responsible for the introduction of Superwatt.

1. Office and bank buildings
2. Stores and other commercial buildings
3. Hotels and motels
4. Manufacturing facilities, offices and lobbies
5. Schools and universities

6. Hospitals and health treatment centers
7. Government buildings

Because the target areas were existing installations, the buying influences were expected to be considerably different from those encountered in new project situations.

The most important consideration was locating the individuals within each organization who were concerned with power and maintenance costs since the Superwatt product benefits were heavily weighted in that direction. The researchers estimated that approximately 25 percent of the potential conversion market was controlled by some corporate central organization.

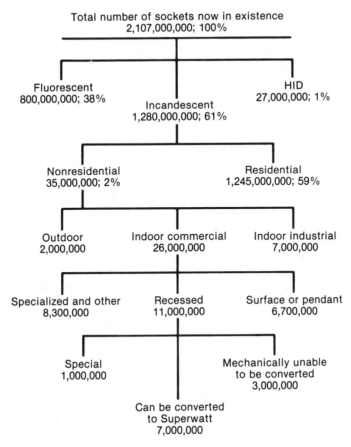

Total number of sockets now in existence
2,107,000,000; 100%

Fluorescent
800,000,000; 38%

Incandescent
1,280,000,000; 61%

HID
27,000,000; 1%

Nonresidential
35,000,000; 2%

Residential
1,245,000,000; 59%

Outdoor
2,000,000

Indoor commercial
26,000,000

Indoor industrial
7,000,000

Specialized and other
8,300,000

Recessed
11,000,000

Surface or pendant
6,700,000

Special
1,000,000

Mechanically unable
to be converted
3,000,000

Can be converted
to Superwatt
7,000,000

EXHIBIT 2   Market Potential—Mercury Connector Kit

Huntington's most significant competition in the area of interior lighting came from companies such as GTE Sylvania, Westinghouse, and General Electric. Although the industry had by nature been rather blatant in copying one another's product, there had not been any definite indication of competition within this new market thus far. It could be inferred by any means that other industrial firms had ignored the possibilities of manufacturing more energy-efficient incandescent lighting systems. Statistics provided by the U.S. Commerce Department revealed that incandescent lamps had enjoyed the most rapid growth rate of all available lighting sources.

Huntington's Lighting Division, which had been responsible for the Superwatt introduction, distributed its products through about 1,300 electrical distributors as well as approximately 1,000 equipment manufacturers who installed Huntington products in their own products and thus acted as OEMs (original equipment manufacturers).

Huntington's marketing organization was product oriented due to the technical nature of the products manufactured and the resulting differences in methods of use and purchase. The company believed that this organizational structure enabled all parties involved to participate in marketing a product or group of products (from marketing manager to field salesman) and to concentrate on one segment of technology involved with respect to that product and thus become highly expert in it. Huntington believed this resulted in better service to the customer and a more intelligent and effective presentation of the product's benefits on the part of the sales force.

Each division's marketing program was headed by a marketing manager who, based upon recommendations of the national sales manager and the product marketing manager, had complete authority in directing the manufacture and marketing of a product or group of products, subject to company policies and overall top management control.

The national sales manager directed six district salesmen and six specialists (usually engineers) who were assigned to the different districts according to their individual level of skill. In addition, there was an original equipment manager who was responsible for the manufacturing companies that Huntington serviced.

The product manager functioned as a source of information about his or her products. The product manager studied the markets, recommended courses of action, planned or assisted in planning the company's operations with respect to products, checked the efficiency of the firm's activities in manufacturing and marketing, suggested product modifications, and made other studies and suggestions designed to improve the performance of his or her assigned product. The managers of advertising and sales promotion, market research, and sales analysis lent support to the product marketing manager's decision (see organization chart, Exhibit 3).

Huntington planned to sell the Superwatt kit for $30.00 to its distributors who would in turn sell them at $37.50 to their customers. This price consisted of $24.75 for the fixture (where Huntington earned its profit) and a 70W vapor lamp for $5.25. Huntington's gross margin on the entire kit amounted to about 50 percent.

From the point of view of the assigned product manager, several favorable and unfavorable factors had to be considered before planning the introductory marketing program. Among the favorable factors were

1. Timing for this type of product appeared to be favorable. The shortage of energy which had been developing for several years had created a psychological climate where the conversion of energy was often in the minds of the consumers.

2. The savings that resulted from the lower power consumption realized by converting combined with savings that were realized from lower maintenance requirements, provided a strong sales story. Indications were that electricity rates would increase substantially, especially during peak operating levels, making this an especially important consideration.

3. With the recent improvement of the color rendition of high-intensity discharge light sources, mercury vapor lighting had been gaining acceptance for interior lighting in higher wattages. Superwatt could benefit from this trend by providing a method of utilizing more efficient mercury sources in low-wattage units as well.

There were, however, also some unfavorable considerations:

1. Several easy and inexpensive alternatives were available including
   a. "Power down" by replacing high-wattage incandescent bulbs with lower-wattage lamps.
   b. Remove some lamps completely.

2. There was substantial skepticism regarding the validity of the "energy crisis" and

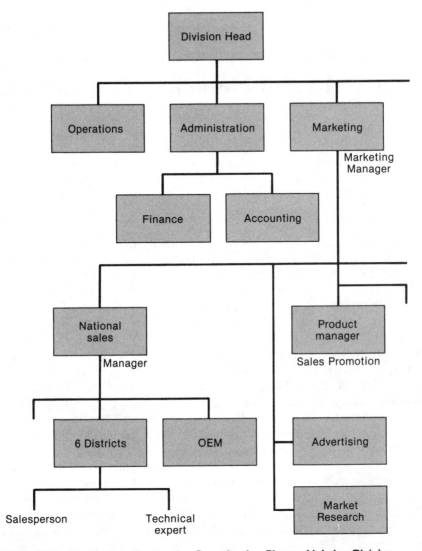

EXHIBIT 3 Huntington Electronics Organization Chart—Lighting Division

many were inclined to take a "wait and see" attitude.

3. Although acceptance might be good, financing might be difficult because the money to convert could be drawn from maintenance budgets which normally required management approval for an expenditure over a minimum amount. Consequently, even though a commitment to

convert existed, it would have to be done over a period of several months or years for financial reasons.

With these considerations in mind, it was now up to the product manager to recommend a complete plan to his marketing manager.

CASE 8

Kruger-Montini Manufacturing Company

The management of Kruger-Montini Manufacturing Company had just entered a new fiscal year and was rethinking its specific policies and general position on transfers of sales representatives. The decision was the responsibility of the sales manager.

Founded many years earlier, this well-established corporation was a medium-sized manufacturer of several related industrial products in rather wide use. The majority of customers were manufacturers. For quite a few years Kruger-Montini did not do its own personal selling. Starting about 20 years ago, it gradually phased out the various intermediaries and manufacturers' agents. After about 5 years of difficult transition, Kruger-Montini relied strictly on sales representatives who were on the company's payroll and who worked for no one else. Kruger-Montini was not truly national in coverage in its early years but became so 9 years ago when it added 5 sales representatives in 1 year and relocated 13.

The size of the sales force had increased as the company grew and prospered and had now reached 38. The sales manager had found it necessary to divide his organization into four geographical regions because of span-of-control difficulties as Kruger-Montini grew. Because the product line was fairly narrow, it was decided that geography, not type of products, would be the best basis

This case is reprinted with permission of Macmillan Publishing Company from *Cases in Marketing,* 3rd ed., by Thomas V. Greer. Copyright 1983 by Thomas V. Greer.

for the organization structure. Thus each sales representative sold all products. A contributing reason for deciding against product specialization as the basis for organizing selling efforts was that it would have resulted necessarily in a larger geographical territory for each employee to cover. That would have meant his being away from home overnight much more than under the policy adopted. The present sales manager, Henry Rosas, estimated that the average person on his sales force spent six nights a month away from home. This figure was a little lower, he knew, for people in the highly industrialized and densely populated areas of the Northeast; the Michigan, Ohio, Indiana, Illinois, Wisconsin region in the Middle West; and parts of California. The figure was a little higher for his people in all other areas. Rosas estimated that the difference was about five versus eight nights per month. During the past few years the company had noticed a sizable number of its customers relocate to the Sun Belt and many customers open branch factories in those milder climate areas of the nation. The demand for Kruger-Montini's products was slowly becoming more evenly spread across the country, and this trend was expected to continue.

Rosas had been with the organization about three years. He had been a successful salesman with one company and then assistant sales manager with another company before coming with Kruger-Montini. He had a good personality and was well liked by the sales representatives.

The company had always used a salary

plus commission pay plan. For the average representative the commission provided 25 percent of his compensation.

Kruger-Montini manufactured nine products, two of which had been introduced only in the past three years. Prior to that three-year period there had been no new product introductions for a great many years. It appeared highly probable that Kruger-Montini would introduce two more new products, closely related to the existing product line, and delete one during the next two years.

During the most recent fiscal year Kruger-Montini had transferred six sales representatives to different territories. In the four years previous to that, the company had transferred seven each year. Each was moved because of company need and/or the assigning of better territories to deserving sales representatives. See Exhibit 1 for earlier years and additional data on size of the sales force and average distances people were transferred. The mean distance of a relocation at Kruger-Montini had shown a downward trend for several years.

Every person on the sales force had moved at least once. The longest time in one

place anyone on the present sales force had experienced with Kruger-Montini was seven years. Rosas was tentatively thinking about moving from five to seven members of the sales force later this year.

The management did not know much about the geographical preferences of its sales representatives or their family life. Rosas could not legally inquire systematically about whether the spouses were also employed and whether that work was professional and managerial, which might make one less willing to move. Dual careers made it difficult for couples to handle relocations well, and some probably would not consider it at all. However, Rosas and his four regional sales managers had been trying recently to make observations and record facts and inferences about these matters for all the sales representatives. Three of the sales representatives were young, unmarried men who seemed to be mobile and flexible. Three middle-aged men were divorced, and 1 was a widower. The remaining 31 were all married. It appeared that 20 of them had working spouses and that 15 of these women had professional or managerial careers. Rosas also began to understand that most nonworking

EXHIBIT 1 Data on Sales Force of Kruger-Montini Manufacturing Company

	Size of Sales Force	Number Transferred	Mean Distance Transferred (miles)
Latest year	38	6	798
Two years ago	37	7	872
Three years ago	37	7	682
Four years ago	36	7	1122
Five years ago	35	7	1254
Six years ago	34	9	1360
Seven years ago	32	9	597
Eight years ago	32	12	1070
Nine years ago	31	13	793
Ten years ago	26	10	1035
Eleven years ago	25	10	640
Twelve years ago	24	11	510

married women had developed community ties and that moving for them could also be difficult and unsettling.

The unwritten understanding of personnel at Kruger-Montini had been that turning down a transfer would be suicidal. At the minimum, such a rejection would classify a person as unaggressive and unambitious. The U.S. culture for many years had perceived frequent transfers as evidence of fast-track career progress. Staying mobile was a "badge of honor," as business newspapers and magazines usually described it.

No one on the Kruger-Montini sales force had ever declined a transfer until two years ago, as far as Rosas could determine. The sales manager and other headquarters personnel had been surprised and perplexed when Charles Hopkins, a very satisfactory employee, had declined a move from a small, pleasant southeastern city to a much more lucrative territory in another part of the United States. Age 37 and a native of the upper Middle West, Hopkins explained that he like Kruger-Montini and wanted to continue working for the company but did not want to move. His wife was a business manager in another company, and they had a 13-year-old daughter in school.

The costs to relocate a sales representative had been rising quite rapidly. The most recently transferred person was Alex Kendall, a man with a wife and three children. It cost Kruger-Montini $30,880 to move the family approximately 2900 miles from one coast to the other, although the company was not any more generous than the typical American company. Of this amount, $11,475 was to ship household goods, $4,100 was for the premove housing search, and $3,680 was for one extra month of this man's average compensation in lieu of incidental expenses.

Final travel and temporary living expenses accounted for another $4,550. The remaining costs had to do with company subsidies on the sale of the couple's house and purchase of a replacement house. The management of Kruger-Montini was beginning to note the financial impact of moving costs of the company.

Kruger-Montini also recognized that a transferred sales representative required several months to get his work productivity back to normal. The recovery of productivity was much more difficult for people who worked with the public and who needed to understand the characteristics of a market than for other types of workers. A sales representative also needed time to establish rapport with the regular clients.

One managerial colleague whom Rosas respected was outspoken about the issue of moving. Bert Crane, who managed another department at Kruger-Montini and had been with the company about 12 years, believed that if employees were permitted to put down roots in a community they would lose their sense of corporate identity. Loyalties to the geographical community would overcome loyalties to the corporation. He stated that perhaps this had been an unconscious motivation of Kruger-Montini in past years.

Another colleague, Robert Mason, mentioned that a nice compromise might be to confine transfers to the region in which the sales representative was already living. For example, the ten sales representatives in 11 northeastern states would be transferred only within that region. Mason noted that each region had some life-style characteristics that set it apart from the others. He was an experienced manager and had been with the company for about nine years.

CASE 9

Lewiston-Copeland Company

"We would like to see your division come up with a statement of objectives and strategy which is consistent with that of the corporation as a whole," said Mr. Crawford. "In addition, you should lay out both the short-term and the longer-range plans for your division in as much detail as you can within the limited time available to you." Thus, Mr. Charles Crawford, president of Lewiston-Copeland Company, summarized his instructions to Mr. James Boyd, vice president in charge of the Copeland Paper Division.

Mr. Boyd, along with most of the other top executives of the company, had been attending a three-day long-range planning session held at a resort motel about 25 miles outside of Evergreen City, headquarters of the Lewiston-Copeland Company, and a community of about 100,000 population located in the Pacific Northwest. This three-day session, held in the spring of 1971, was the culmination of numerous meetings and discussions extending over a two-month period during which the company was trying to embark on a formal system of long-range planning. During the three-day planning session, overall corporate objectives had been agreed upon and general strategy guidelines had been set for the company, although none

This case is produced with the permission of its author, Dr. Stuart U. Rich, Professor of Marketing and Director, Forest Industries Management Center, College of Business Administration, University of Oregon, Eugene, Oregon. Copyright © 1978 by Dr. Stuart U. Rich. (ICCH CASE #9-373-669)

of the specifics of planning had been spelled out.

Toward the end of the planning session, the suggestion was made that rather than launching all of the company's ten divisions on any type of formal long-range planning, one division should be taken first as a "pilot division" and should go through a "complete planning performance." This division was to draw up a statement of divisional objectives and strategy, decide on the appropriate time frame for its plans, consider the roles of division planners versus corporate planners, and draw up some actual plans and programs.

After a relatively short discussion on the matter, the Copeland Paper Division was chosen to be the pilot division. The top corporate executives, whose experience had been mainly in timber, lumber, and plywood, felt that the Paper Division was a good one to start with because the complexity of its products and markets was not as great as in other divisions, and because Mr. Boyd had had long-range planning experience at another firm before joining Lewiston-Copeland several years earlier. He also had a reputation as a self-starter and displayed a zest for achievement in whatever job he undertook. Although some of his division executives were a little dubious about this honor bestowed upon their division, Mr. Boyd tackled the job with accustomed enthusiasm, determined to make his division a showcase of long-range planning during the three-month period allotted him.

COMPANY BACKGROUND

The Lewiston-Copeland Company was a large manufacturer of forest products with manufacturing, converting, and distribution facilities located throughout the United States as well as in Canada and abroad. Its sales of somewhat over $1 billion were divided up among lumber, plywood, particleboard and other panel products, logs and timber, paperboard, containers and cartons, pulp, paper, and real estate and housing. The company was organized along product divisional lines, with ten divisions coming under four different business groups. The Copeland Paper Division, along with the Pulp Division and the Paperboard and Container Division, came under the Fibre Products Group.

All of the divisions were separate profit centers, and some of the product divisions were the raw material sources for other product divisions. For instance, the Pulp Division furnished pulp to the Paperboard and the Paper Divisions as well as selling to outside customers. For its own raw material needs, the Pulp Division bought pulpwood from the Timber Division and wood chips from the Lumber and Plywood Divisions.

The company typically had millsite integration. For example, near one of its large tree farms there might be a manufacturing complex consisting of a lumber and plywood mill and a pulp mill. The latter used logs not suited for lumber and plywood manufacture as well as waste wood in the form of chips from the lumber and plywood mills. At the same site there might also be a paperboard mill and a paper mill using the output of the pulp mill.

The company also had two nonintegrated paper mills, that is, paper mills located by themselves, not near a pulp mill or a source of timber supply. Such paper mills, which were relatively old compared with the integrated mills, bought pulp from distant company-owned pulp mills as well as from outside sources.

COPELAND PAPER DIVISION

The manufacturing facilities of the Copeland Paper Division consisted of some 25 different paper machines, located in both integrated and nonintegrated mills in the Pacific Northwest, the South, and the Northeast. The company had both on-machine and off-machine coaters used in the manufacture of the higher-quality grades of printing papers as well as some types of technical papers. An on-machine coater was an inherent part of the paper machine and coated only the paper produced on that particular machine, whereas a more flexible off-machine coater stood by itself and could be used to coat paper produced by any paper machine, either at the mill where the coater was located or shipped in from another mill. On-machine coating was a less expensive method of manufacture than off-machine coating.

The average cost of a new paper machine of the type found in the Copeland mills was $30,000,000. A new coater cost $8,000,000. Plant capacity could sometimes be increased at less cost through rebuilding and speeding up old machines, with expenditures of up to $5,000,000. Typically, however, capacity increases in the paper industry came in sizable increments, and depreciation on machinery and equipment, along with other fixed expenses, represented about 30 percent of total product cost for the types of papers made by Lewiston-Copeland. Raw material costs accounted for 50 percent, and variable labor costs the remaining 20 percent.

The division's product line consisted of several hundred different types or "grades" of paper, ranging from standard uncoated offset printing paper to silicone-coated papers with water-repellent and nonadhesive characteristics designed for special industrial uses. As a first step toward simplifying the business of his division, Mr. Boyd had recently had the product line classified into 32 product groups, which were then combined into eight product families, based on their marketing and manufacturing affinity. Among these eight product families were premium printing papers, usually with fancy coatings; commodity printing papers, such as uncoated offset paper; converting papers, such as envelope and tablet stock; communications papers, including electrographic and other specialized office copy papers; and technical papers such as pressure-sensitive papers.

COMPANY OBJECTIVES AND STRATEGY

The basic corporate objective of the Lewiston-Copeland Company, which had been agreed upon during the recent planning meetings, was to "sustain an average growth rate in earnings per share of 15 percent per year over at least the next five years." Having set forth this objective, management then analyzed the major strengths of the company, and the nature of the businesses in which the company was engaged, in order to determine an appropriate strategy to achieve its objective.

The company's major strength was its several million acres of timberlands, much of which had been acquired at a cost far below current market value. The timber was a renewable asset, was readily accessible, and could be harvested and sold as logs or could be manufactured into forest products. The company also had extensive and well-integrated manufacturing facilities, a broad product line, and a sound financial condition with a debt-to-equity ratio lower than that of its major competitors.

Management felt that the company was basically in two major businesses: commodities and specialties. Commodities, such as dimension lumber ("two-by-fours" and the like), were manufactured to common specifications, with little or no product differentiation, and were sold on the basis of price and service. The commodity product line had a low rate of technological obsolescence, a low value added by manufacture, and a low profit margin on sales. Markets were large, worldwide, and well established. However, markets were also slow growing, very competitive, and prices might be highly unstable over short periods of time.

Specialties, such as particular types of overlaid paneling, had a high value added by manufacture and often carried a high profit margin, although market size was usually small. There was a real or perceived product differentiation; in fact, some specialties were manufactured to individual customer specifications. Product life was sometimes short due to rapidly changing technology, and the timing of market entry was often quite important. The successful management of a specialty business required a quite different set of skills than did the management of a commodity business. This was true whether the skills involved marketing, manufacturing, engineering, research and development, logistics, or resource allocation. The relative importance of these various functions also differed in the two types of businesses.

The basic strategy guidelines of the company which were developed at the recent corporate planning meetings were stated as follows:

1. Build a solid commodity business by improving and increasing the utilization of our raw material base and delivering products and required services to market at the lowest unit cost; and

2. Use this commodity business as a foundation for supporting investments in higher-risk, higher-return opportunities in present and new markets, by new technologies, and in new businesses.

DETERMINATION OF DIVISION STRATEGY

One of the major strategic issues facing Mr. Boyd was the roles to be played by the Copeland Division's nonintegrated mills and by its integrated mills. In the former were old, slow-running paper machines, suited to the manufacture of specialty papers, which included most of the communications and technical grades. These slow-running machines were also suited for the many trial runs required in the development of new types of specialties. In the integrated mills were large, modern machines designed for high-volume production of commodity papers, including most of the printing grades.

Complicating the nonintegrated versus integrated mill situation was the fact that the more successful specialty papers often developed into commodity papers. This was because their high profit margin and the expanding market demand attracted competitors, and new types of papers were very difficult to patent. As usage developed, their manufacture became more standardized. In order to keep costs down and keep prices competitive, the division then had to shift the manufacture of these paper grades from the old, slow-running machines in the nonintegrated mills to the modern, fast-running machine in its integrated mills. Technical difficulties sometimes had to be solved in making the shift. After such a shift, the nonintegrated mills often had the problem of filling the gaps in their machines utilization in order to keep the mills profitable.

Another problem that faced all nonintegrated mills, including those of the Copeland Division, was the fact that their raw material costs were about 15 to 20 percent higher than those of integrated mills. This was because in an integrated facility, pulp was fed in slush form from an adjacent pulp mill directly to the paper machines. To supply a nonintegrated mill, pulp had to be shipped in dry form from a distant pulp mill and then reconstituted into a slurry on the paper machines. Because of their location away from any pulpwood supply, it was not feasible to build a pulp mill adjacent to the Copeland Division's nonintegrated paper mills.

About three-fourths of the division's sales and four-fifths of its profits were from the commodity grades made in its integrated mills, with the remaining percentages coming from the specialty grades in the nonintegrated mills. Within these two categories, however, there was a wide variation in profit margins, particularly in the specialty papers. Certain grades of copy papers and release papers were the most profitable of the entire product line. Some of the older specialty papers had showed a loss for several years, but were kept as long as they covered their own direct costs and made some contribution to common fixed costs. The most profitable grades were often papers which had recently moved out of the specialty and into the commodity class, and enjoyed a strong market demand.

In working up a statement of strategy relating to the product lines and mills in his division, Mr. Boyd had decided that there were four major strategic alternatives from which to choose. The first was to operate the division's existing businesses without investing additional capital over and above that required for routine maintenance and replacement. If the company ceased being cost competitive in particular grades of specialty papers, it should withdraw from those particular products and the markets they served.

The second alternative was for the company to shut down and/or divest itself of all nonintegrated facilities. It should emphasize the commodity markets and should retain only those specialties which could be produced in the integrated mills.

The third was to provide adequate capital to modernize and speed up some of the machines in the nonintegrated mills in order to be more cost competitive in the fast-growing fields of copy and release papers. Expenditures would also be made to improve the capability of the integrated mills to produce specialties, including copy and release papers.

The fourth alternative was to close one of the company's nonintegrated mills, to drop all but most profitable specialties such as copy and release papers, and to increase the emphasis on commodity papers.

SHORT- AND LONG-RANGE PLANNING

In determining the appropriate time frame for his division's planning, Mr. Boyd reviewed the type of planning which had gone on in the past. In the Copeland Division, as in other company divisions, planning had been limited largely to an annual sales forecast, production forecast, and financial operating budget, which were drawn up during the fourth quarter of each year for the following year. At the corporate level, although no regular long-term planning had been carried on, special studies were sometimes made extending as far as 15 years ahead. For instance, if the company were considering the acquisition of timberlands, tied in with the construction of production facilities in a new region, a 15-year cash flow analysis was

made, and Copeland or other divisions affected might be called upon to contribute data.

Mr. Boyd knew that there were many activities in his division that could not be fitted into a 1-year planning cycle, but which did not require a 10- to 15-year look into the future. These included new product development, establishing positions in new markets, and adding new production capacity. As an example of the latter, the typical time required for a new paper machine to be constructed and brought to full production capacity, with operating problems all ironed out, was 3 years.

Regardless of which of the four strategy alternatives under consideration were to be adopted, Mr. Boyd knew that plans would have to be drawn up, built around an appropriate time period for their achievement. The division's annual operating budgets would also have to be made to mesh with any longer-term plans that were adopted.

DEVELOPING PLANS AND PROGRAMS

Before drawing up any long-range plans for his division, Mr. Boyd felt that it would be necessary to distinguish between those planning activities which had to be done at the corporate level and those which were more appropriately left to the division. Obviously the determination of overall company objectives, goals, and strategies was a corporate headquarters responsibility. Major capital investments in new regions or in new lines of business would continue to be planned at the corporate level, although Mr. Boyd felt that the divisions should play a larger role in such decisions than merely furnishing data inputs when requested.

The main planning areas in which corporate versus divisional responsibility had not yet been spelled out were as follows:

1. Identification and projection of economic, social, and competitive trends affecting the Lewiston-Copeland Company;
2. Identification and study of merger or acquisition candidates;
3. Anticipating and securing future resource requirements, and allocating resources to divisions;
4. Improving the utilization of raw materials, including raw materials not currently being converted at their highest potential economic return;
5. Identification and study of specific new product and market opportunities and of the application of new technology to products and processes;
6. Proposal of courses of action to be taken on obsolete, marginal, and unprofitable businesses, facilities, and products;
7. Setting of specific targets for such performance criteria as earnings and market share;
8. Determination of the particular economic and competitive assumptions upon which specific forecasts would be based;
9. Determination of the general format in which plans were to be drawn up, and the manner in which they were to be presented, approved, and implemented.

Mr. Boyd realized that this list was by no means complete, and he was trying to think of other areas which should be included. Some of the planning areas would apply equally to all Lewiston-Copeland divisions, whereas others would apply particularly or uniquely to divisions in the Fibre Products Group, or perhaps just to the Paper Division.

The role that the Copeland Division market managers should play in planning had yet to be decided. There were eight market managers, one for each of the eight product families. These people, who had all worked up through sales, now occupied these recently created staff positions. In the case of specialty products, several of the market managers still retained some of their old customer accounts. Mr. Boyd considered these managers as sales-oriented, but "not well trained in abstract thinking." Their main function was to help to develop the markets in their respective product areas. They studied demand trends and present and future customer needs and tried to determine how the division could better satisfy these needs. They helped the line personnel to balance customer demand with machine capabilities. They also provided "top-down" sales forecasts, which were combined with the "bottom-up" forecasts of the field salesmen and sales managers to arrive at a composite sales forecast which became part of the division's annual operating budget.

Some of the division executives, particularly those in manufacturing, felt that the creation of the new market manager positions had made the division too sales oriented. One of these executives, who had been with the company for many years, remarked, "It's nice to look at the market and see what it wants, but in a capital-heavy industry like ours it may be better to look at the paper machines first and see what they can make, and then ask ourselves how we can sell it. This is particularly true in our big new integrated facilities, where there are machine limitations, pulp mill limitations, and fibre species limitations."

CONCLUSION

As a start toward carrying out the directions given him at the recent planning meetings, Mr. Boyd decided to call his division management staff together and discuss with them what the requirements for success were in the commodity paper business and in the specialty paper business. From such a discussion he hoped there would emerge a consensus as to what division objectives were and what the appropriate strategy should be to accomplish those objectives. The main planning area noted earlier would have to be examined, priorities set, plans developed, and programs launched.

To enlist the full cooperation of his management staff in what seemed to them an awesome undertaking, Mr. Boyd knew he would have to show them how planning would help make their daily operating jobs easier. Some of the planning activities he would have to do himself and others he could delegate to his subordinates. One of his most important jobs, he felt, would be to provide everyone with a clear sense of direction as they worked their way through the planning process.

CASE 10

Modern Medical Products Company

Modern Medical Products Company (MMPC) had its inauspicious start twenty years ago when William Gardner decided to leave his position with Medical Supply Company and invest his life's savings in developing and producing a blood oxygenator. Gardner enlisted financial support and part-time assistance from two associates, Jim Cain and Bob Stacer. Development and production began in a small workshop in Gardner's garage.

A blood oxygenator is a life-sustaining unit used in conjunction with open-heart surgery. During open-heart surgery, the heart and lungs do not function; therefore, artificial means of adding oxygen and pumping blood through the patient must be employed. During the surgery the patient's blood is retrieved from the open chest cavity and moved through special surgical tubing by means of a pump to an oxygenator, which mixes the blood with oxygen gas, and then warms or cools the blood to the correct temperature for reentry into the patient. The development of a blood oxygenator permits the patient's blood to be utilized throughout the operation. Prior to development of the oxygenator, the patient's blood became contaminated and had to be discarded when extracted from the chest cavity. The blood oxygenator possesses two major advantages: first, the amount of blood transfusions is greatly reduced, and second, the probability of the patient's recovery is greatly increased when his or her own blood is reused.

The timing of Gardner's venture was fortuitous because open-heart surgery was just beginning to be accepted as a reliable technique for treating certain kinds of cardiovascular ailments by the medical profession. Additionally, MMPC's oxygenator could exceed the performance capabilities of any other brand on the market. When production was initiated, Gardner wore all hats: scheduler, orderer of materials, marketing manager, salesman, and financier. With the part-time assistance of Cain and Stacer, sales for the first year were $315,000 with a loss of $111,000. During the second year sales increased by 60 percent, and a profit of $65,000 was realized. At this point Cain joined the firm full-time, principally in the sales area. The firm's continued growth is illustrated in Table 1, along with balance sheets for selected years in Table 2.

Since Gardner owned 15,000 shares, and Cain and Stacer 5,000 each, Gardner was the controlling party. Three years after the firm's inception, the original founders elected to sell an additional 12,500 shares to friends. Four years later the firm elected to go public on the over-the-counter market.

An additional 16,250 shares were offered and quickly purchased.

After four years of operation, the original partners were growth oriented; however, a major problem existed. Because of the reliability and constant upgrading of their product, MMPC had acquired 80 percent of the market in oxygenators. To further compound the problem, the number of open-heart surgeries was leveling off.

Gardner described the situation in these words:

> Our immediate strategy was to broaden our product line, and to offer a full line of accessories for open-heart surgery. Over the next three years we developed and introduced a pump, a reservoir, tubing, and a bypass filter. But competition had already increased. There were six competing oxygenator models on the market, and all had comparable performance characteristics to

TABLE 1   Modern Medical Products Company Income Statement (000s)

	Last Year	Two Years Ago	Three Years Ago	Four Years Ago	Five Years Ago	Eight Years Ago	Eleven Years Ago
Revenues							
Net sales	$20,148	$17,109	$12,914	$9,574	$6,744	$1,463	$315
Interest	229	499	594	178	31	—	—
Other	101	199	—	—	—	—	—
Total	$20,478	$17,807	$13,508	$9,752	$6,775	$1,463	$315
Expenses							
Manufacturing costs	9,312	7,527	5,568	4,128	2,939	585	126
Selling costs	2,819	2,001	1,604	1,181	818	77	121
R&D	1,216	1,032	856	614	518	30	46
General and administrative	2,173	2,013	1,444	1,075	969	56	71
Interest	62	—	—	—	—	—	62
Total	$15,582	$12,573	$9,472	$6,998	$5,244	$748	$426
Income before taxes	4,896	5,234	4,036	2,754	1,531	715	(111)
Taxes	2,350	2,564	1,967	1,256	783	355	-0-
Net income	2,545	2,669	2,069	1,498	748	360	(111)
Dividends paid	162	162	162	143	143	17.5	-0-
Dividend per share	4.32	4.32	4.32	7.5	7.5	5	-0-

TABLE 2 Modern Medical Products Company Comparative Income Statement (in thousands of dollars)

	Last Year	Two Years Ago	Five Years Ago	Eight Years Ago
Assets				
Current				
Cash	$ 2,591	$ 4,286	$ 2,104	$1,073
Receivables	4,008	3,801	2,360	1,996
Other	38	129	3	6
Inventories	4,487	3,809	1,965	940
Prepaid expenses	231	193	72	51
Deferred income tax	267	286	46	23
Total current	$11,622	$12,504	$ 6,550	$4,089
Property				
Land	331	289	100	65
Building	4,779	3,247	2,200	902
Machinery and Equipment	5,017	3,720	1,932	870
Furniture and fixtures	414	370	132	35
Leasehold improvements	313	580	53	5
Construction in progress	816	183	213	0
Total	$11,670	$ 8,206	$ 4,630	$1,875
Less: accumulated depreciation and amortization	1,834	1,040	562	305
Property—net	9,836	7,166	4,068	1,570
Other assets	1,440	1,544	300	100
Total assets	$22,898	$21,214	$10,918	$5,759
Liabilities				
Current				
Notes payable	109	118	43	22
Current portion of long-term debt	7		31	50
Accounts payable	1,361	1,265	848	320
Accrued liabilities	433	754	232	120
Total current	$ 1,910	$ 2,137	$ 1,154	$ 512
Long-term debt	824		400	500
Original loan $830,000 @ 8% interest and annual payments of $60,000				
Deferred income tax	1,237	1,291	300	50
Stockholders' equity:				
Common stock	215	215	150	100
Paid-in capital	10,684	10,684	6,944	4,487
Retained earnings	8,028	6,887	1,670	110
Total stockholders' equity	$18,927	$17,786	$ 9,064	$4,697
Total	$22,898	$21,214	$10,918	$5,759

ours. Even broadening the product line wasn't going to help. We had to diversify if we were going to continue to grow. Our strategy was to acquire firms with new technological products without competitors in the medical field. In a two-year period we acquired four companies.

Of the acquired firms, one is performing satisfactorily; one has been sold because its product was not directly applicable to the medical market; the third is still in the development stage; and finally, there is Dee Jee, which has cost us dearly.

Dee Jee Co. was started by a dialysis technician turned inventor named Bob Hutchinson who decided to develop a new coil dialyzer. The product's design was complete; Hutchinson, with the aid of a consulting engineer, had designed the production machinery. However, at this stage, Hutchinson got cold feet because he lacked sufficient funds and marketing know-how and, as a result, began seeking support from larger, more established medical-supply firms.

We at MMPC felt attracted to Hutchinson and to Dee Jee Company because of the parallels in our origins, namely, having enough faith in your own idea to invest in it. Besides, we may have just stumbled onto another product that would sell like crazy. So we bought out Dee Jee Company and made Hutchinson the production manager of the dialysis operations.

Dee Jee's dialyzer had not been introduced to the market, but it had been well received by doctors when pilot production models were tested. In addition, Hutchinson had also built an inexpensive production machine that could be copied easily if sales demanded.

Before MMPC took over Dee Jee, it conducted marketing research to attempt to determine the potential dialysis market. The preliminary research is shown in Table 3. MMPC attempted to pursue Dee Jee's brand name, and at the same time merge the company into the present organization in such a manner that it was indistinguishable.

MMPC's organization chart is shown in Figure 1. Two years after taking over Dee Jee, MMPC began marketing the dialyzer. Sales did not come close to their forecasted level the first full year of operation, as shown in Figure 2. That did not alarm MMPC too much. MMPC experienced a "slight panic" when it looked at the income from dialysis sales, Gardner said. "It was pathetic, to say the least, when compared to market and profitability potential." This is shown in Table 4.

"But the best is yet to come," claimed Gardner. After four months of operation in this year, sales are still considerably below forecasted levels, and that is being kind. This is shown in Figure 2. Last year Dee Jee showed a 38 percent loss on sales. If that figure is projected for the five months from January to May of this year, Dee Jee would lose $345,040 on sales of $908,000.

As Figure 2 shows, sales have leveled off at about 2,000 dialyzers and blood-line sets per week. To compound MMPC's situation, a serious leaking problem in the blood lines has developed. Subsequently, MMPC dismissed the product manager. The firm has halted production of dialyzers and blood lines. Automatic blood-line assembly equipment was ordered that will double capacity and reduce costs by 21 percent, from $6.50 to $4.00 per set. However, MMPC has now learned that the equipment ordered will not assemble the blood lines to the configuration required by the large dialysis centers. Delivery of this equipment cannot be stopped. The high-production tooling on orders for piece parts can be modified to eliminate the leading problem for only a small charge, Gardner said:

> The question is, what do we do now? Our inventory of 40,000 dialyzers and blood-line sets should hold our present customers while we take action.

TABLE 3 Estimated Domestic Kidney Patient Population

	Four Years Ago	Three Years Ago	Two Years Ago	Last Year	Next Year	Two Years Hence	Three Years Hence	Four Years Hence
Ending population prior year	10,000	12,400	16,900	22,000	27,550	32,950	37,700	41,850
Mortality	[1,200]	[1,450]	[2,000]	[2,200]	[2,750]	[3,300]	[3,800]	[4,600]
New patients	6,000	8,500	9,500	10,500	11,000	11,000	11,000	11,000
Mortality	[900]	[1,250]	[1,400]	[1,550]	[1,650]	[1,650]	[1,650]	[1,650]
Returned from transplantation	500	700	1,000	1,000	1,000	1,000	1,000	1,000
Patients transplanted	[2,000]	[2,000]	[2,000]	[2,200]	[2,200]	[2,300]	[2,400]	[2,800]
Year-end patient population	12,400	16,900	22,000	27,550	32,950	37,700	41,850	44,800
Average patient population for year	11,200	14,650	19,450	23,775	30,250	35,325	39,775	43,325

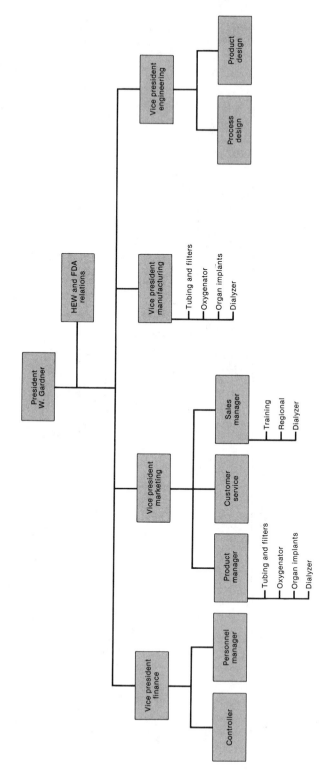

FIGURE 1 Modern Medical Products Company Organization Chart

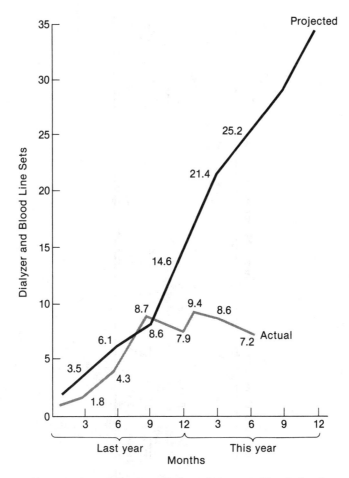

FIGURE 2 Forecasted and Actual Sales per Month (in thousands of units)

We've invested substantial money in an effort to enter the dialysis market, approximately $620,000 to produce a dialyzer that costs us $8.00 and sells for $16.20, and blood lines that cost $4.00 and sell for $5.50.

THE DIALYSIS PROCESS

Each kidney contains approximately 1 million nephrons, which are the functional units of the kidney. In addition to removing waste products from the body, the kidneys remove substances taken in, such as medications and poisons. They maintain the body's internal environment by regulating the water and electrolyte balance and by retention of substances necessary to normal body function, such as glucose, protein, and amino acids. They also play a role in regulating the blood pressure.

When the kidney function ceases, the items mentioned above are no longer removed, which results in the retention of

TABLE 4 Modern Medical Products Company—Dee Jee Division: Monthly Statement of Income, Last Year

	Jan.	Feb.	March	April	May	June	July	Aug.	Sept.	Oct.	Nov.	Dec.
Net sales	$16,200	$19,440	$29,160	$43,740	$59,940	$91,140	$123,690	$134,540	$188,790	$177,940	$184,450	$160,580
Cost of product sold	8,000	9,600	14,400	21,600	29,600	60,900	82,650	89,900	126,150	118,900	123,250	107,300
General and administrative	19,000	25,000	28,000	27,000	32,000	47,000	64,000	63,000	65,000	69,000	68,000	70,000
Selling	3,240	3,880	5,832	8,780	11,988	18,228	24,730	26,908	37,758	35,588	36,890	32,116
Total	$30,240	$38,480	$48,232	$57,380	$73,588	$126,128	$171,380	$179,808	$228,908	$223,488	$228,140	$209,416
Income before taxes	[14,040]	[19,040]	[19,072]	[13,640]	[13,648]	[34,988]	[47,960]	[45,268]	[40,118]	[45,548]	[43,690]	[48,836]

these products in the blood and body fluids. When this happens, it becomes necessary to use an artificial kidney to remove the wastes from the blood. The hemodialysis procedure cleanses small portions of the blood at a time until the blood is sufficiently cleansed to restore nearly normal conditions. Waste materials start building up in low concentrations shortly after the procedure, making it mandatory to come in two to three times a week to have the waste materials removed by the artificial kidney. The waste materials in the blood are filtered through a semipermeable membrane in the artificial kidney and eliminated. One type of artificial kidney resembles an automobile engine's oil filter in appearance except that, instead of threads to attach the filter to the engine, it has a place to attach two blood lines. The semipermeable membrane is a thin layer of material with microscopic openings. According to the size of these openings or pores, particles smaller than the pores pass through, while larger ones do not. The patient's blood passes through a compartment formed by the semipermeable membrane during the hemodialysis procedure. Surrounding this compartment is dialyzing fluid. Red and white blood cells and most plasma proteins are too large to pass through the pores of the membrane. Water and small particles, however, can pass freely across the membrane by diffusion in both directions until they are equal in concentration on both sides.

The function of the dialyzing fluid is to carry away waste materials and fluids removed from the patient's blood by the dialysis procedure. The dialysis fluid also prevents the removal of essential electrolytes and avoids excessive water loss during the procedure. These functions are achieved by making the chemical composition of the dialyzing fluid correspond as closely as possible to that of normal plasma.

THE DIALYSIS MARKET

Kidney dialysis has been available since 1965. It was not until 1973, however, that the U.S. government passed a law on catastrophic diseases (Public Law 92-603), which provides for 100 percent coverage of medical expenses for certain diseases. Kidney failure is one of the diseases covered. The Catastrophic Diseases Act made it possible for patients who previously had to pay $5,000 to $18,000 per year for the treatment to receive it absolutely free. The government is now paying for 95 percent of all dialyses in the United States. The typical patient requires three six- to eight-hour treatments per week. The dialyzer market is predicted to increase at the rate of 15–17 percent each year for the next five years (see Table 3). Dialyzer prices are also predicted to rise at a 7–10 percent rate per year, despite the expected entry of more dialyzer manufacturers into the market.

The dialysis treatment takes place at 710 dialysis centers throughout the country. The centers are run by nephrologists who are physicians under contract with the centers. They receive a fee for providing all materials and technicians for the centers. Occasionally the centers are also owned by the nephrologists.

Nephrologists are concerned with the performance predictability of the dialyzer on their patients, a low product failure rate, and, of course, price, since they are contracted on a fixed-rate basis by the center. Their technicians, on the other hand, are most concerned with the ease with which the dialyzer and its accompanying blood lines can be used. Often, both the nephrologist and the head technician must be sold on the product before a sale can be made.

There are four basic types of dialyzers. The equipment used by the dialysis center

TABLE 5 Estimated Share of Domestic Treatments by Dialyzer Family

	Six Years Ago	Five Years Ago	Four Years Ago	Three Years Ago	Two Years Ago	Last Year	Projected This Year
Coil	75.5%	79.4%	79.8%	73.1%	69.0%	66.5%	63.3%
Hollow fiber	—	1.2	7.0	13.0	19.0	19.6	19.3
Parallel flow	—	3.0	6.2	9.9	10.1	12.7	16.9
Reusable coil	24.5	16.3	7.1	4.0	1.9	1.2	0.5
Total	100.0%	100.0%	100.0%	100.0%	100.0%	100.0%	100.0%

determines the type of dialyzer to be used. The coil dialyzer is by far the most popular. The hollow fiber, however, is beginning to take a larger portion of the sales. The performance characteristics of the hollow fiber are superior to those of the coil and parallel-flow dialyzer, but it is priced approximately $5.00 higher. The use of the reusable coil dialyzer is diminishing because of the hazards of spreading disease from one patient to another by reusing the same dialyzer. The market share of each dialyzer type is shown in Table 5.

THE COMPETITION

The market shares of the various competitors are shown in Table 6. A brief description of each competitor follows.

Dexter

Dexter Co. has been in the medical supply field for 30 years. It offers an assortment of many types of medical supplies and equipment. Sales for the last year were over $300,000,000. They were the first to offer a coil dialyzer in 1955 and the design remains basically the same. Only minor modifications have been made. Dexter also builds dialysis equipment.

Diacoil

Diacoil Co. is approximately the same size as MMPC. Its principal products are two types of dialyzers (coil and hollow fiber) and blood infusion equipment. It is the parent company of a subsidiary that makes dialysis equipment for coil and hollow fiber dialyzers.

Nephrotek

Nephrotek is a division of Medical Supply Corp. a large company similar to Dexter. The company was founded three years ago as an institution to finance dialysis centers. It is expected that its centers will use its dialyzers exclusively, although no contractual agreement now exists.

Bentley

Bentley, Inc. is a small subsidiary of a medium-sized medical supply company. While it has been an innovator in the dialysis market, its management appears to be unclear about what the major thrust of its approach is—technological advances or mass production. Dee Jee views it as the most vulnerable to competition and the easiest to run out of the market in spite of its products' advantages.

TABLE 6 Estimated Corporate Share of Domestic Coil Market

	Six Years Ago	Five Years Ago	Four Years Ago	Three Years Ago	Two Years Ago	Last Year	Projected This Year
Dexter	71.5%	70.3%	69.1%	68.2%	66.7%	56.0%	51.7%
Diacoil	28.5	29.7	30.9	31.8	31.8	30.6	28.2
Nephrotek	—	—	—	—	—	2.0	8.5
Bentley	—	—	—	—	0.9	5.3	6.4
Dee Jee	—	—	—	—	0.6	4.1	5.1
Total	100.0%	100.0%	100.0%	100.0%	100.0%	100.0%	100.0%

MMPC's dialyzer does have a slight advantage in allowing the dialysis to take place at a higher flow rate. This allows for greater solute removal in a specific amount of time or, if desired, a shorter time for the dialysis process.

All the competitors are priced the same or higher than MMPC's products. Prices range from $15.00 to $24.00, depending on the dialyzer size, which is determined by the size of the patient. A 10 percent discount is normal, as well as a 15 percent discount on volume orders.

All four companies have established excellent reputations in the market. It is generally felt that the competing products are of equal quality. Therefore, it is difficult to persuade a dialysis center to switch brands of dialyzers. Price, service, and special features such as blood lines are used as competitive tools.

PRODUCTION

At the time of acquiring Dee Jee, the dialyzer component parts were made by vendors contracted by Dee Jee Company, and production was done on a newly completed production machine called a coil winder. The assembly process involved the winding of the plastic mesh and membrane around a plastic core on the core-winding machine and attaching the inlet (arterial) and outlet (venous) connecting lines. The assembly is then removed from the coil winder and placed in a rigid plastic housing which is sonic-welded to the cap. The unit is then bagged, boxed, and sterilized.

To ready the dialyzer for marketing, modifications were made to the coil winder to allow for closer control of wrapping tension, the housing was redesigned for appearance as well as functional reasons, and the packaging was changed to include MMPC's logo. All molds for the plastic components were machined by outside vendors, and parts were then produced by MMPC's own injection-molding shop. Three more coil winders were manufactured, making a total of four. A production facility containing 40,000 square feet was leased a few blocks away from MMPC, and production was started on a one-shift basis.

The coil winders each had a production capacity of 150 coils per eight hours. Production employed 8 people, plus a supervisor and production manager. This continued until the fall of 1975 when the blood lines were introduced. At that time three more coil winders were built, and production increased to two shifts, employing 27 people. Only 50 percent of the leased building was utilized. The remaining 50 percent was vacant.

When the design was finished on the blood lines, low-volume tooling for molding the piece parts was manufactured.[1] Since management was faced with high initial component prices and a line assembly time of approximately 11 minutes, it was decided to subcontract the assembly labor to a Bahamian firm until automatic assembly tooling could be manufactured. The labor rate of $3.09 per hour charged by the Bahamian firm included transporation of components and assemblies, plus all necessary facilities in the Bahamas. Burdened labor costs for Dee Jee is $6.37 per hour.

Production of blood lines began in June 1975 at the rate of 2,000 sets per week, and 14 people were employed. In October production was increased to 4,000 sets per week, and 20 people were employed by the Bahamian firm.

Automatic machinery was ordered in December 1975. The machinery would lower production time of the lines to approximately 5 minutes each.

At first the lines were sold as fast as they could be made. Since the component parts were still made on the low-volume tooling, much overtime was expended in supplying the Bahamas with parts. The overtime rate added to the already high cost of the parts. High-volume production tooling had just begun to arrive when operations were shut down until existing inventories had been sold.

Sales of dialyzers by the month for the last year and the first six months of the current year are shown in Figure 2.

---

[1]Low-volume tooling is made from aluminum and yields only one part per machine cycle, whereas high-volume tooling is made from hardened steel and produces as many as eight parts per machine cycle.

QUALITY CONTROL

Testing and refinements were made on the coil dialyzer, but because of the hurried situation of the blood lines, almost no quality analysis was performed. In addition, regular company inspectors were placed at the Dee Jee facility to carry out routine inspections and testing of the dialyzers. No inspectors were present in the Bahamas. Only one person from MMPC was assigned to the Bahamian facility, and this employee was responsible for both production as well as quality of the product. Full testing of the blood lines did occur in the Bahamas, however, and sample testing again was performed on finished assemblies at Dee Jee.

Problems occurred only after the product had aged for approximately one month. Therefore, at the time of manufacture, no leaks would be detected. It was only after the product had been sold and used by a customer that it was discovered that certain components would not remain properly bonded together and that a leak would occur.

In addition, the component that connected the dialyzer to the blood line would occasionally mismatch, and, again, a leak would occur. This connector was not made during the testing procedure because the lines and dialyzer were manufactured and tested at separate facilities.

MARKETING

After two years of developmental work, the dialyzer was placed on the market. The first sales were accomplished by four salespersons who had no experience in dialyzers and whose initial customers were the centers which had been given pilot production samples for evaluation. To increase sales, the company's staff of 30 salespersons started to call upon the various dialysis centers that used the coil dialyzer in their treatment. The salespersons attempted to sell the dialyzer principally to centers associated with hospitals, since they were calling on the hospital to represent MMPC's product line. The salespersons were paid a draw, plus commission on total sales, plus expenses. The average salary was about $60,000, plus 50 percent of that in expenses and fringe benefits.

When sales did not achieve their expected level, the product manager started to investigate. He found that the "free-standing" centers were largely being avoided. Sample calling on "free-standing" centers revealed that they were difficult to sell to because they were unfamiliar with MMPC's product line, and they were extremely reluctant to switch to an unproven brand, especially when no blood lines accompanied the dialyzer.

The product manager felt that MMPC should offer blood-tubing lines to accompany the dialyzer. The blood-tubing lines carry the blood from the patient to the dialyzer, and they are a convenience feature that eases the difficulties associated with using the dialyzer. Accordingly, the product manager asked engineering to design several sets of blood lines.

However, management, in order to make the blood lines available as quickly as possible to increase sales, imposed early deadlines on engineering and production. Consequently, the blood lines were soon available, although a minimum of design was utilized. When the centers attempted to install the lines, they were not to the configuration desired because each center uses slightly different equipment and methods requiring different features on the blood lines. The product manager then ordered the design and manufacture of 22 different configurations of blood lines. Sales then rose to 2,000 dialyzers and blood line sets per week.

The product manager also analyzed the sales pattern and found that the selling procedure went typically along the following pattern. A salesperson would first contact a dialysis center by phone and ask the physician or head nurse if the center would be interested in hearing about a new product on the market. Since the salespersons were paid on a salary-plus-commission basis, they would not call personally on a dialyzer prospect because this took a great deal of time and very few sales were made. The salespersons' time was more profitably spent selling the products they were familiar with to hospitals.

If the reply from the physician or head nurse was yes, a conference was arranged. If the reply was no, the salesperson would make a note to make a follow-up call on the center at a later date. When the salesperson would meet with the center's representative, he or she would first have to sell the center on MMPC since it was new in the field. This was not difficult with centers that were associated with hospitals, because the salesperson would call in person and the hospital personnel were already familiar with MMPC. For "free-standing" centers, performance charts and data were available for discussion with center personnel, which enabled the salesperson to point out the advantages of MMPC's dialyzer.

If the customer was still interested at this point, the salesperson then set up a demonstration. Following the demonstration, the salesperson would attempt to get the center to agree to use the dialyzer on a few sample patients for a month. It was felt that once the center used sample dialyzers, it would adopt MMPC's dialyzer and purchase them in large volume.

Following the sale, the maintenance of good relations is also important. Nurses and doctors appreciated it when the salesperson would occasionally drop by the center to ask about specific problems while helping the nurse set up for the first few patients. Any problems that might occur in the product's use could then be observed and reported by the salesperson. Most MMPC salespersons did not have any experience in dialysis and did not have a desire to spend a great deal of time assisting in the setup. As a result, the salespersons were unable to report the leaking problems promptly; this had delayed the taking of corrective action in the assembly methods and tooling of blood lines.

CASE 11

Parker Instruments Ltd.

George Parker locked the door of his car and walked across the parking lot toward the station entrance. Although it was a sunny spring morning and the daffodils and tulips provided welcome color after the grayness of winter, George hardly noticed. Within a few minutes the train from London would be arriving, and with it Bruce MacDonald, the export sales manager for Electro Industries—a Canadian firm that George's company represented in the United Kingdom. George would be spending the day with Bruce, and he wondered what the outcome of their discussions would be.

PARKER INSTRUMENTS LTD.

George Parker was managing director of Parker Instruments Ltd. (PI), part of a small family-owned U.K. group of companies.

This case was prepared by Professor Philip Rosson of Dalhousie University as a basis for class discussion rather than to illustrate the effective or ineffective handling of an administrative situation. The names of the companies and persons have been changed but in all other respects the case study is factual. Copyright © 1984 by Philip Rosson.

The company gained its first sales agency in 1923 (from a U.S. manufacturer), which made it one of the longest established international trading firms in electronics instruments. PI sales were the equivalent of about $1 million, with 75 percent coming from imported distributed items and 25 percent from sales of its own manufactured items. The company had a total of 15 employees.

PI was the U.K. distributor for 15 manufacturers located in the United States, Canada, Switzerland, and Japan. Like many firms it found the 80/20 rule held true; about 80 percent of the import sales of $750,000 were generated by 20 percent of the distributorships it held. With current sales of $165,000, the Electro Industries distributorship was an important one.

ELECTRO INDUSTRIES

Electro Industries (EI) was a younger and larger organization than its U.K. distributor. Located in southern Ontario, it was founded in the mid-1950s, had current sales of $2 million, and employed a work force of 90. EI had developed a strong reputation over the years for its high-precision instrumentation and testing equipment, and this led to considerable market expansion. As well as market expansion, the company had moved in a number of new product directions. The original products were very precise devices for use in standards laboratories. From this base it had more recently established a presence in the oceanographic and electric power fields.

As a result of this expansion, 80 percent of sales are now made outside Canada, split evenly between the United States and offshore markets. In the United States, the company had its own direct sales organization, whereas indirect methods were used elsewhere. In the "best" 15 offshore markets, EI had exclusive distributors; in 30 other markets it relied on commission grants.

WORKING TOGETHER

It was in New York City that EI and PI first made contact and the two companies agreed to work together. George Parker was on a business trip in the United States when he received a cable from his brother saying that a representative of EI wanted to contact him. George and his wife met the senior executive in their hotel room and after initial introductions settled down to exchange information. At some point, George—who had had a hectic day—fell asleep! He awoke to find that PI was now, more or less, EI's U.K. distributor, his wife having kept the discussion rolling while he slumbered.

The two firms soon began to enjoy good fortune together. For PI, the distributorship gave it a product line to complement those it already carried. Furthermore, the EI instruments were regarded as the Cadillacs of the industry. This ensured an entry to the customer's premises and an interest in the rest of the PI product line. As far as EI was

concerned, it could hardly have chosen a more suitable partner: PI's staff was technically competent, facilities existed for product servicing, and good customer contacts existed. Moreover, as time passed, George Parker's long experience and international connections proved invaluable to EI. He would often be asked for an opinion prior to some new move by the Canadian producer. George preferred to have a close working relationship with the firms he represented, so he was happy to provide advice. In this way, PI did an effective job of representing EI in the United Kingdom and helped with market expansion elsewhere.

As might be expected, the senior executives of the companies got on well together. The president and vice president of marketing—EI's "international ambassadors"—and George Parker, progressed from being business partners to becoming close personal friends. Then, after nine successful years, a tragedy occurred—the two senior EI executives were killed in an airplane crash on their way home from a sales trip.

The tragic accident created a management succession crisis within EI. During this period, international operations seemed to be left dangling while other priorities were attended to. Nobody was able to take charge effectively of the exporting activities that had generated such good sales for the company. Although there was an export sales manager—Bruce MacDonald—he was something of a newcomer, having been in training at the time of the accident. He was also a middle-level executive, whereas his international predecessors were the company's most senior personnel.

From George's point of view, things were still not right a year later. The void in EI's international operations had not been properly filled. Bruce had proven to be a competent manager, but lacked support since a new vice president of marketing had yet to be appointed. Also, although a new president headed up the company, as the previous vice president of engineering, he displayed a preference for dealing with technical rather than commercial issues. So, despite the fact that Bruce had a lot of ideas about what should be done internationally (most of which were similar to George Parker's), he lacked the position or support of a superior to bring about the necessary changes.

While the airplane accident precipitated the current problems in the two companies' relationship, George realized that things had been going sour for a couple of years. At the outset of the relationship, EI executives had welcomed the close association with PI. Over time, however, as the manufacturer grew in size, and as new personnel came along, it seemed to George that his input was more and more resented. This was unfortunate, because George felt that EI could become a more sophisticated international competitor if it considered advice given by informed distributors. In the past, EI had been open to advice and had benefited considerably from this. Yet there were still areas where EI could effect improvements. For example, its product literature was of poor quality and was often inaccurate or outdated. Prices were also worrisome—EI seemed unable to hold down its costs, and its competitors now offered better "value-for-money" alternatives. Other marketing practices needed attention also.

THE OCEANOGRAPHIC MARKET

One area where EI and PI were in disagreement was the move into the oceanographic field. George was pleased to see EI moving into new fields but wondered if EI truly appreciated how "new" the field was. In a

way, he felt that the company had been led by the technology into the new field rather than having considered the "fit" between its capabilities and success criteria for the new field. For example, the customer fit did not seem close. The traditional buyers of EI products for use in standards laboratories were scientists, some of whom were employed by government, some by industry, and some by universities. By and large, they were academic types, used to getting their equipment when the budget permitted. As a result, selling was "gentlemanly," and follow-up visits were required to maintain contacts. Patience was often required as purchasing cycles could be relatively long. Service needs were not large, for the instruments were used very carefully.

In contrast, the oceanographic products were used in the very demanding sea environment. Service needs were acute, not just because of the harsh operating environment, but also due to the cost associated with having inoperable equipment; for example, ocean research costs are already high but become even higher if faults in shipboard equipment prevent sea measurements from being taken. In such a situation, the customer demands service today or tomorrow, wherever the faulty equipment happens to be located. The oceanographic customer is also a completely different type—still technically trained, but concerned to get the job done as expeditiously as possible. Purchasing budgets are much less of a worry—if the equipment is good, reliable, and with proven backup, chances are that it can be sold. But selling requires more of a push than the laboratory equipment.

When EI entered the oceanographic field, a separate distributor was appointed in the United Kingdom. However, the arrangement did not work out. EI then asked George to carry the line, and with great reluctance he agreed. The lack of enthusiasm was due to George's perception that his company was not capable of functioning well in this new arena. Because PI was ill-equipped to service the oceanographic customer, there was the thought that there could even be repercussions in its more traditional field. George was loath to risk the company's established reputation in this way. However, while he would prefer not to represent EI in the oceanographic field, George worried that there was something of a "one-market, one-distributor" mentality at EI.

THE CURRENT VISIT

George Parker had strong personal and sentimental feelings for EI as a company. In his opinion, however, some concrete action was required if the business relationship was to survive, let alone prosper.

From his standpoint, George saw pretty good sales of EI products but shrinking profit margins over the last few years.

This resulted from the increased costs PI faced with the EI product line. Since EI was slow to respond to service and other problems, more and more frequently PI had been putting things right and absorbing the associated costs. However, these costs could not be absorbed forever. George had been willing to help tide EI over the last difficult year, but expected a more positive response in the future.

George Parker hoped that Bruce MacDonald would bring "good news" from Canada. Ideally he hoped to drop the oceanographic line and rebuild the "bridges" that used to exist between his firm and the manufacturer. A return to the close and helpful relationship that once existed would be welcomed. At the back of his mind, however, he wondered if EI's management wanted to operate in a more formal and distant "buy and sell" manner. If this were the case, George Parker would have to give more serious thought to the EI distributorship.

CASE 12

Power Tools, Inc.

Power Tools, Inc., was a large and diversified manufacturer of power tools and labor-saving devices for home and industry. Founded in the early 1900s, the firm's headquarters was in the Middle Atlantic states. It was included in the *Fortune* 500 list of large

This case is reprinted with permission of Macmillan Publishing Company from *Cases in Marketing: Orientation, Analysis, and Problems,* 3rd ed. by Thomas V. Greer. Copyright © 1983 by Thomas V. Greer.

U.S. corporations and produced and marketed its products on a worldwide basis.

During the early years of its existence, the company was primarily a manufacturer of a variety of machines and equipment. For example, at one time it manufactured industrial scales. As time passed, however, the firm expanded into the production of universal electric motors. This led to the placement of a chuck onto the spindle of an electric motor; this was the earliest electric drill. It was large and cumbersome but offered the user the ability to drill holes without being tied to the traditional fixed-in-place drill press.

During the 1930s and extending into the 1940s the firm grew to specialize in the manufacture of electrically driven portable power tools. The firm grew and prospered. It developed a variety of electrically driven tools, such as various sizes of drills, percussion hammers, and a variety of grinders. During the late 1940s and early 1950s, the firm entered the "do it yourself" market. It was able to develop the previously unexplored homeowner's market. This propelled the firm into a period of tremendous growth. In addition to the industrial markets, the firm increased in size by selling tools to the homeowner. This provided the firm with very large economies of scale. The price of the typical one-fourth-inch drill dropped from the $50 or $60 range to the $10 range. In the process, the firm doubled its sales about every ten years.

THE INDUSTRIAL/ CONSTRUCTION DIVISION

During its early years, the primary focus of Power Tools, Inc., was on the industrial user. As mentioned, the company provided grinders, drills, and a variety of other expensive engineered products. The company considered itself to be a pioneer in the growth of the industrial markets. It sold its products exclusively through the traditional "mill supply" houses. This emphasis on the industrial nature of the business was continued in the Industrial/Construction Division even as the phenomenal growth in the Consumer Products Division occurred.

During the 1950s, however, there was considerable growth in construction products offered by the Industrial/Construction Division. Circular saws, finishing sanders, routers, and a variety of other new products were developed in parallel with the Consumer Products Division. Thus, the Industrial/Construction Division was able to take advantage of the economies of scale being produced in the factories of the Consumer Products Division. Specifically, the construction type of product continued to be sold through a distribution channel intermediary now called "Industrial Distributors" that also included a new variety of business that served construction contractors directly. These new distributors were unlike the traditional mill supply houses in that they were considerably smaller and catered to a construction contractor rather than to the traditional plant engineer or plant maintenance manager.

The growth of the construction products portion of the Industrial/Construction Division propelled the division to impressive new heights. The company viewed its traditional industrial products as slow growth areas. The traditional products were now characterized by very cyclical and low growth rates. The construction products were viewed differently; their rate of sale growth was twice the rate of growth of similar industrial products.

THE DEVELOPMENT OF NEW PRODUCTS

The growth of the Consumer Products Division was visible to the public, which drove the price of the company's common stock to new highs. What was not as visible, although it was quite profitable, was the growth of new products in the Industrial/Construction Division. A variety of improvements upon existing products was made in addition to the introduction of completely new products. The division was well able to market these new products, often at a considerable profit. The circular saw was developed specifically for the Consumer Products Division, but it could be improved on and added to so as to make it a high-quality construction device.

In addition, the division prided itself on being a broad line manufacturer. It offered a variety of alternative tools in terms of size, quality, and performance. The division offered utility-duty products, heavy-duty products, and super-duty products. As an example, the division offered one-fourth-inch, three-eighths-inch, five-sixteenths-inch, half-inch, one-inch, and larger sizes of drills. It offered end-handle drills, pistol-grip drills, right-angle drills, all-insulated drills, and others.

The concept of driving a screw with a drill evolved as part of the development of the drill line. This led to the development of the electrically driven power screwdriver, which was essentially a drill with a chuck that was designed to hold a screw and then drive it into the material. This product development was quickly found to be popular, and soon the other major manufacturers of power tools were eager to enter the market. The product exhibited all the attributes of the life-cycle curve. Only recently had the annual rate of growth begun to taper, and, in fact, the sales of this product by Power Tools, Inc., recently started a rapid decline.

ELECTRIC SCREWDRIVERS TODAY

The total United States demand for electric screwdrivers was approaching $17 million per year. Because it viewed itself as the pioneer in the electric screwdriver business, Power Tools, Inc., was perplexed and annoyed by its present situation in that business. Several salient facts that had been gathered and are presented in Exhibit 1 seemed to portend danger to the company's valued and profitable line of electric screwdrivers. These products were manufactured in the company's oldest plant, which was located in the East.

THE INFLUX OF DOMESTIC COMPETITION

The concept of the electric screwdriver flowered in the late 1960s and was further developed throughout the 1970s. The fundamental economic strength of this product concept was the labor-saving aspect. Parallel to the labor-saving aspect were the many

EXHIBIT 1 Pertinent Data on Electric Screwdrivers

	Total U.S. Market Size	
	Dollars [millions]	Units [000s]
1970–71	$ 6.1	87.5
1974	10.4	146.7
Latest year	16.6	188.0

U.S. Power Tool Market as a Percentage of U.S. Total Tool Market [$]

1970–71	13%
1974	17
Latest year	20

Company Share of Electric Screwdrivers Market [$]

1970–71	32%
1974	24
Latest year	13

Makita Share of Electric Screwdrivers Market [$]

1970–71	NA
1974	NA
Latest year	8%

useful refinements and variations of the basic product. Depth-sensitive models, models with adjustable clutches, models with reversing features, and other variations were developed to serve specific market segments. However, no sooner had Power Tools, Inc., developed a new advance than a competitor would copy the idea and enter the market. This was possible because any manufacturer of a drill could convert it to a screwdriver by modifying the front end of the drill to accommodate the screwdriver attachments. Soon Power Tools, Inc., noticed that it had many competitors in the sale of electric screwdrivers.

This pattern of events led to a corresponding decline in the firm's market share. In the early years this organization had dominated the market, holding about a two-thirds share. As time had passed, its share had slipped gradually to 24 percent in 1974 and an estimated 13 percent currently. In a recent general sales slump, the electric screwdriver market declined as badly as, or worse than, other sectors of the power tool business. Sales of the product then increased but did not recover to quite the preslump level.

THE INFLUX OF FOREIGN COMPETITION

During the late 1970s the firm was intensely bothered by the aggressive new efforts of Japanese manufacturers in the screwdriver market. The introduction of the Makita brand of power tools was especially noteworthy. This line of power tools was offered for sale in the United States at prices that were well below the general price level. Power Tools, Inc., viewed the quality of Makita power tools as being commensurate with their price.

In recent years the Makita Company added insult to injury by announcing its intention to commence manufacturing at a West Coast facility that it proposed to finance in the United States. The total bond offering was made for $60 million and the plant was built. This new facility was soon to come on line. Power Tools, Inc., estimated that a majority of the new Makita plant's output would be electric screwdrivers that would compete directly with the company's own screwdrivers.

Advise Power Tools, Inc.

CASE 13

Precision Parts, Inc.

Mr. Vincent P. Sayles, vice president in charge of industrial marketing for Precision

This case was reprinted with permission of Stanford University Graduate School of Business, © 1968 by the Board of Trustees of the Leland Stanford Junior University. Written by James R. Miller of the Graduate School of Business.

Parts, Inc., viewed with some concern the tenfold increase in cost projected by Mr. Mark S. Timador, the company's senior market analyst, for preparing next year's annual sales forecast. Mr. Timador had indicated in a recent memorandum to Mr. Sayles (see Exhibit 1) that it would cost the com-

EXHIBIT 1 Mr. Timador's Memorandum to Mr. Sayles

TO: V. P. Sayles
FROM: M. S. Timador
SUBJECT: Preparation of Annual Sales Forecast
DATE: 8 April 1968

In thinking about preparing our annual sales forecast for 1969, I have made some rough cost estimates. I believe that we shall have to spend about $42,000 for next year. This compares with $4,552 in 1966 to prepare the 1967 forecast. I have not isolated the cost of preparing the 1968 forecast, but I believe it ran close to $4,500 on our 500 regular customers.

The cost increase is attributable to our recent acquisition of Nash in Chicago. They sell direct to some 1,500 customers, which means that we shall have to contact four times as many people as we have in the past. Moreover, I expect that it will cost us more to obtain information from Nash's customers than it will from our own, since we do not know whom to contact in these other organizations. You remember how long it took us to "train" our regular customers in the early 1960s to give us accurate information. I feel sure that we can "train" Nash's customers eventually, but for the next few years, it's going to be pretty rough.

Based on our early experience with our regular customers and adding a little for inflation and unforeseen contingencies, I think we shall have to spend about $25 apiece on the Nash group. This includes letters, follow-up phone calls, requests for documentation, and so forth. With diligence on our part and cooperation on theirs, I think we can get the accurate information we need for about $37,500. Assuming $9 apiece to canvass our regular customers, this will add $4,500 to the bill. I expect the whole job to cost about $42,000.

In addition, we should probably start earlier this year, particularly on the Nash group. We should also plan to spend more time preparing the forecast.

pany approximately $42,000 to prepare next year's forecast, whereas it had cost only $4,552 to prepare the same forecast for the year 1967. According to Mr. Timador, the principal reason for this cost increase lay in Precision's decision six months ago to acquire the Nash Grinding Equipment Company of Chicago, Illinois, as part of its ongoing diversification program. Nash sold grinding wheels and other standard equipment directly to some 1,500 industrial customers in the Midwest. Mr. Timador expected the cost of obtaining forecast information from these many new customers to fall at about $37,500.

Precision Parts, Inc., was founded in 1942 as part of the nationwide industrial mobilization effort to support World War II. Precision sold almost exclusively to the aircraft industry during the war years and en-

joyed a very handsome growth in both sales and profits. However, the outbreak of peace brought a significant decline in sales. Profits were reduced during this period to almost nothing. Imminent disaster was avoided by instituting a savage cost-cutting campaign, coupled with plantwide improvements in productive efficiency. By 1950, the company was eking out a modest profit on reduced sales, most of which were still to the aircraft industry.

The Korean War stimulated another significant increase in sales and particularly in profits, since Precision had managed to develop a highly skilled work force and efficient methods of production.

A second sales decline following the Korean War was treated as before—namely, by cost reductions and improvements in efficiency. This time, however, an effort was made to extend the efficiency concept beyond the production process to all phases of the company's operation. A new cost accounting system was installed, and detailed planning and control procedures were instituted to coordinate raw material purchases, production scheduling, sales and distribution activities, and even the recruiting of skilled labor. These efforts proved quite successful. Profits were restored to Korean War levels, even though sales remained somewhat depressed. In 1959, Precision achieved national recognition by being named one of the ten best managed and most efficiently operated small manufacturing concerns in the country.

Precision was threatened again throughout the early 1960s, but this time for a different reason. Many new companies entered the industry during 1961 in anticipation of supporting the recently announced space program. This produced a temporary condition of industry overcapacity, and a severe price war ensued. Consequently, Precision suffered a decline in dollar profits, despite a significant increase in production and a moderate increase in dollar sales volumes. It was not until 1965, after several of Precision's less efficient competitors had been forced to close down operations, that some semblance of price and profit stability was reinstated.

Precision's board of directors decided in early 1966 that diversification was the best long-run remedy for the "feast and famine" problem that had plagued the company since its inception. Efforts were made to add certain consumer goods to Precision's product line and to acquire another industrial manufacturing company that might benefit from the company's highly developed skill and technology, but whose sales would be unrelated to the aircraft industry, the space industry, or any other industry heavily dependent upon federal government expenditures.

The Nash Grinding Equipment Company was eventually selected and acquired in September 1967. This raised industrial sales from $4.76 million in 1966 to an annual rate of approximately $6.5 million by the end of 1967. Total company sales were close to $10 million during 1967, with after-tax profits falling just above $1.2 million.

The annual sales forecast, for which Mr. Sayles was responsible, became an important part of Precision's planning and control mechanism in 1958. Although rough sales forecasts had been made in prior years, the need for precise estimates did not arise until the detailed control procedures were implemented. It was decided in 1958 that a 5 percent forecasting error in either direction would be tolerable for planning purposes. By contacting all industrial customers six months prior to the beginning of each calendar year, Mr. Sayles had managed to generate forecasts that fell consistently within the 5 percent limit of error. In addition, the average cost of preparing these annual forecasts had been steadily reduced over the years with experience and the building up of continuing relationships with key people in each customer organization. Exhibit 2 shows Mr. Sayle's success in preparing forecasts for the years 1959 through 1967.

At this point, Mr. Sayles was not sure how to proceed. On the one hand, it was very important to obtain an accurate sales forecast. The entire planning and control process depended critically upon whatever estimate Mr. Sayles would develop over the next few months. And besides, Mr. Sayles was justifiably proud of his spectacular record of accurate forecasts. The company had come to place a great deal of faith in his method.

On the other hand, a tenfold increase in the cost of preparing next year's forecast seemed exorbitant. Acquisition of the Nash Company promised to increase industrial

EXHIBIT 2 Annual Sales Forecasts for the Industrial Division, 1959–1967

Year	1959	1960	1961	1962	1963	1964	1965	1966	1967
Total forecasted sales [$000]	$2,709	$3,043	$3,126	$3,295	$3,532	$3,610	$4,355	$4,785	$4,996
Total actual sales [$000]	$2,653	$3,009	$3,117	$3,328	$3,507	$3,632	$4,373	$4,775	$5,021
Error [$000]	+$55.7	+$33.1	+$9.4	−$33.3	+$24.6	−$21.8	−$17.5	+$9.6	−$25.1
Percentage error	+2.1%	+1.1%	+.3%	−1.0%	+.7%	−.6%	−.4%	+.2%	−.5%
Number of industrial customers	384	419	418	437	462	480	513	497	503
Average actual sales per customer [$000]	$6,909	$7,181	$7,457	$7,616	$7,591	$7,568	$8,525	$9,608	$9,982
Standard deviation [$000]	$1,688	$1,721	$1,703	$1,832	$1,844	$1,901	$1,956	$2,073	$2,002
Average forecasting cost per customer [in dollars]	$20.23	$15.52	$12.31	$10.37	$9.70	$9.33	$9.21	$9.09	$9.05

Note: All figures are exclusive of the acquisition of the Nash Grinding Equipment Company in 1967.

sales by only 30 percent. It did not seem reasonable to pay so much more to obtain the additional information.

Mr. Sayles decided to arrange a meeting with Mr. Timador the next day to discuss the problem.

CASE 14

Prentice Machine Tools

Prentice was a moderate-size, regional producer of consumer hand tools, such as planes, hammers, screwdrivers, saws, chisels, hand drills, and bits. Competition came from a number of large national competitors, such as Rockwell; Sears, Roebuck; and Black and Decker; and many small specialty producers. Low-cost imports were a growing influence in the American market and represented about 10 percent of total sales.

Prentice estimated its regional market share at 5 percent, with the top four competitors accounting for about 60 percent of the total. The largest competitor was substantially bigger than any of the others.

Prentice's strategy had always been to price 10–15 percent below the level of the top four. The company spent almost nothing on advertising, relying instead upon price to generate sales in major retail outlets. Point-of-sale material was above average in quantity and quality. Prentice also had an active private-label program, which accounted for a growing 30 percent of total sales. It was not unusual in some outlets to find one of

the majors, Prentice, and a Prentice-made house label.

Prentice realized a tight 3 percent profit on sales. This margin had been approximately the same over the past four years. Market share in the industry and in the region had not fluctuated much, although there seemed to be increasing price pressure from foreign competitors.

On January 15, 1979, one of the major competitors (the number three brand) announced a new national price program consisting of "permanent" price cuts of 10–25 percent at retail, a multimillion-dollar promotion program, and a redesigned product line. The firm's objective seemed to be to buy market share. This company had recently followed a similar strategy in the United Kingdom and had picked up about ten share points. Whether the gain was profitable or not was not totally clear, although it seemed evident that prices had been lowered permanently.

Prentice's alternative seemed to be:

1. Do nothing—which might put the firm at a price disadvantage if the other majors moved to match the new schedules.
2. Immediately drop to match the new price, which could cause severe retaliation by

some competitors and a major drop in profits.

3. Some combination of marketing effort which would provide the firm with some breathing time.

4. Try to reduce internal costs so as to be better able to handle any required price cuts. There were no obvious alternatives here, although some possibilities were to trim the

line, to increase the private-label business, to postpone some planned product redesigning, to cut point-of-sale efforts, or to switch from a direct salesman approach (the firm had six salesmen who worked with distributors and sold a few large private label accounts directly) to the exclusive use of reps who typically charged 5 percent on sales.

CASE 15

Starnes-Brenner Machine Tool Company

The Starnes-Brenner Machine Tool Company of Iowa City, Iowa, has a small one-man sales office headed by Frank Rothe in Latino, a major Latin American country. Frank has been in Latino for about 10 years and is retiring this year; his replacement is Bill Hunsaker, one of Starnes-Brenner's top salesmen. Both will be in Latino for about eight months, during which time Frank will show Bill the ropes, introduce him to their principal customers and, in general, prepare him to take over.

Frank has been very successful as a foreign representative in spite of his unique style and, at times, complete refusal to follow company policy when it doesn't suit him. The company hasn't really done much about his method of operation although from time to time he has angered some top company men. As President McCaughey,

Philip R. Cateora, *International Marketing*, 7th edition (Homewood, IL: Richard D. Irwin, Inc.), 1990, pp. 746–750.

who retired a couple of years ago, once remarked to a vice president who was complaining about Frank, "If he's making money—and he is (more than any of the other foreign offices)—then leave the guy alone." When McCaughey retired, the new chief immediately instituted organizational changes that gave more emphasis to the overseas operations, moving the company toward a truly worldwide operation into which a loner like Frank would probably not fit. In fact, one of the key reasons for selecting Bill as Frank's replacement, besides Bill's record as a top salesman, is Bill's capacity as an organization man. He understands the need for coordination among operations and will cooperate with the home office so the Latino office can be expanded and brought into the mainstream.

The company knows there is much to be learned from Frank, and Bill's job is to learn everything possible. The company certainly doesn't want to continue some of Frank's practices, but much of his knowledge is vital for continued, smooth operation. Today, Starnes-Brenner's foreign sales account for about 25 percent of the company's total profits, compared with about 5 percent only 10 years ago.

The company is actually changing character from being principally an exporter without any real concern for continuous foreign market representation to worldwide operations where the foreign divisions are part of the total effort rather than a stepchild operation. In fact, Latino is one of the last operational divisions to be assimilated into the new organization. Rather than try to change Frank, the company has been waiting for him to retire before making any significant adjustments in their Latino operations.

Bill Hunsaker is 36 years old with a wife and three children; he is a very good salesman and administrator although he has had no foreign experience. He has the reputation of being fair, honest, and a straight shooter. Some, back at the home office, see his assignment as part of a grooming job for a top position, perhaps eventually the presidency. The Hunsakers are now settled in their new home after having been in Latino for about two weeks. Today is Bill's first day on the job.

When Bill arrived at the office, Frank was on his way to a local factory to inspect some Starnes-Brenner machines that had to have some adjustments made before being acceptable to the Latino government agency buying them. Bill joined Frank for the plant visit. Later, after the visit, we join the two at lunch.

Bill, tasting some chili, remarks, "Boy! This certainly isn't like the chili we have in America."

"No, it isn't, and there's another difference, too . . . Latinos are Americans and nothing angers a Latino more than to have a 'Gringo' refer to the United States as America as if to say that Latino isn't part of America also. The Latinos rightly consider their country as part of America (take a look at the map) and people from the United States are North Americans at best. So, for future reference, refer to home either as the United States, States, or North America, but, for gosh sakes, not just America. Not to change the subject, Bill, but could you see that any change had been made in those S-27s from the standard model?"

"No, they looked like the standard. Was there something out of whack when they arrived?"

"No, I couldn't see any problem—I suspect this is the best piece of sophisticated bribe-taking I've come across yet. Most of the time the Latinos are more 'honest' about their *mordidas* than this." "What's a *mordida?*" Bill asks. "You know, *kumshaw, dash, bustarella, mordida;* they are all the same: a little grease to expedite the action. *Mordida* is the local word for a slight offering or, if you prefer, bribe," says Frank.

Bill quizzically responds, "Do we pay bribes to get sales?"

"Oh, it depends on the situation but it's certainly something you have to be prepared to deal with." Boy, what a greenhorn, Frank things to himself, as he continues, "Here's the story. When the S-27s arrived last January, we began uncrating them and right away the *Jefe* engineer (a government official)—*Jefe,* that's the head man in charge—began extra careful examination and declared there was a vital defect in the machines; he claimed the machinery would be dangerous and thus unacceptable if it wasn't corrected. I looked it over but couldn't see anything wrong so I agreed to have our staff engineer check all the machines and correct any flaws that might exist. Well, the *Jefe* said there wasn't enough time to wait for an engineer to come from the States, that the machines could be adjusted locally, and we could pay him and he would make all the necessary arrangements. So, what do you do? No adjustment his way and there would be an order cancelled; and, maybe there was something out of line, those things have been known to happen. But for the life of me, I can't see that anything had been done since the machines were supposedly fixed. So, let's face it, we just paid a bribe and a pretty darn big bribe at that—about $1,200 per machine—what makes it so aggravating is that that's the second one I've had to pay on this shipment."

"The second?" asks Bill.

"Yeah, at the border when we were transferring the machines to Latino trucks, it was hot and they were moving slow as molasses. It took them over an hour to transfer one machine to a Latino truck and we had 10 others to go. It seems that every time I spoke to the dock boss about speeding things up, they just got slower. Finally, out of desperation, I slipped him a fistful of pesos and, sure enough, in the next three hours they had the whole thing loaded. Just one of the local customs of doing business. Generally though, it comes at the lower level where wages don't cover living expenses too well."

There is a pause and Bill asks, "What does that do to our profits?"

"Runs them down, of course, but I look at it as just one of the many costs of doing business—I do my best not to pay but when I have to, I do."

Hesitantly Bill replies, "I don't like it, Frank, we've got good products, they're priced right, we give good service, and keep plenty of spare parts in the country, so why should we have to pay bribes to the buyer? It's just no way to do business. You've already had to pay two bribes on one shipment; if you keep it up, the word's going to get around and you'll be paying at every level. Then all the profit goes out the window—you know, once you start, where do you stop? Besides that, where do we stand legally? Perhaps you've missed all the news

back in the States about the Wedtech scandal, HUD (Housing & Urban Development) billion dollar rip off, procurement scandals at the Pentagon, and so on. Congress is mad, countries are mad; in fact, the Foreign Bribery Act makes paying bribes like you've just paid illegal. I'd say the best policy is to never start; you might lose a few sales but let it be known that there are no bribes; we sell the best, service the best at fair prices, and that's all."

"You mean the Foreign Corrupt Practices Act, don't you?" Frank asks and continues in a—I'm not really so out of touch—tone of voice, "Haven't some of the provisions of the Foreign Corrupt Practices Act been softened somewhat?"

"Yes, you're right, the provisions on paying a *mordida* or grease have been softened but paying the government official is still illegal, softening or not," replies Bill.

Oh boy! Frank thinks to himself as he replies, "First of all, I've heard about all the difficulty with bribing governments, but what I did was just peanuts compared to Japan and Lockheed. The people we pay off are small and, granted we give good service, but we've only been doing it for the last year or so. Before that I never knew when I was going to have equipment to sell. In fact, we only had products when there were surpluses stateside. I had to pay the right people to get sales and, besides you're not back in the States any longer. Things are just done different here. You follow that policy and I guarantee that you'll have fewer sales because our competitors from Germany, Italy, and Japan will pay. Look, Bill, everybody does it here; it's a way of life and the costs are generally reflected in the markup and overhead. There is even a code of behavior involved. We're not actually encouraging it to spread, just perpetuating an accepted way of doing business."

Patiently and slightly condescendingly,

Bill replies, "I know, Frank, but wrong is wrong and we want to operate differently now. We hope to set up an operation here on a continuous basis; we plan to operate in Latino just like we do in the United States. Really expand our operation and make a long-range market commitment, grow with the country! And, one of the first things we must avoid are unethical. . . .''

Frank interrupts, "But really, is it unethical? Everybody does it, the Latinos even pay *mordidas* to other Latinos; it's a fact of life—is it really unethical? I think that the circumstances that exist in a country justify and dictate the behavior. Remember man, 'When in Rome, do as the Romans do.'''

Almost shouting, Bill blurts out, "I can't buy that. We know that our management practices and techniques are our strongest point. Really all we have to differentiate us from the rest of our competition, Latino and others, is that we are better managed and, as far as I'm concerned, graft and other unethical behavior have got to be cut out to create a healthy industry. In the long run, it should strengthen our position. We can't build our futures on illegal and unethical practices."

Frank angrily replies, "Look it's done in the States all the time. What about the big dinners, drinks, and all the other hanky-panky that goes on? Not to mention House Speaker Wright, PACs (Political Action Committee) payments to congressmen, and all those high speaking fees certain congressmen get from special interests. How many congressmen have gone to jail or lost reelection on those kinds of things? What is that, if it isn't *mordida,* the North American way? The only difference is that instead of cash only, in the United States we pay in merchandise and cash."

"That's really not the same and you know it. Besides, we certainly get a lot of business transacted during those dinners even if we are paying the bill.''

"Bull, the only difference is that here bribes go on in the open; they don't hide it or dress it in foolish ritual that fools no one. It goes on in the United States and everyone denies the existence of it. That's all the difference—in the United States we're just more hypocritical about it all."

"Look," Frank continues, almost shouting, "we are getting off on the wrong foot and we've got eight months to work together. Just keep your eyes and mind open and let's talk about it again in a couple of months when you've seen how the whole country operates; perhaps then you won't be so quick to judge it absolutely wrong."

Frank, lowering his voice, says thoughtfully, "I know it's hard to take; probably the most disturbing aspect of dealing with business problems in underdeveloped countries is the matter of graft. And, frankly, we don't do much advance preparation so we can deal firmly with it. It bothered me at first; but, then I figured it makes its economic contribution, too, since the payoff is as much a part of the economic process as a payroll. What's our real economic role anyway, besides making a profit, of course? Are we developers of wealth, helping to push the country to greater economic growth, or are we missionaries? Or should we be both? I really don't know, but I don't think we can be both simultaneously, and my feeling is that as the company prospers, as higher salaries are paid, and better standards of living are reached, we'll see better ethics. Until then, we've got to operate or leave and, if you are going to win the opposition over, you'd better join them and change them from within, not fight them."

Before Bill could reply, a Latino friend of Frank's joined them and they changed the topic of conversation.

CASE 16

Frank Sud Furniture

Frank Sud Furniture is one of the many small companies that abound in the furniture industry. The plant's value is approximately $15 million, and it employs 186 people in management and production.

Established in 1893 by Frank Sud, the company has always dealt in high-priced, custom-made furniture. The market is relatively small, but profitability is high, especially since most furniture companies have now gone to mass-production techniques and products. Only a handful of the custom manufacturers now exist.

Remaining in Portland, Oregon, Frank Sud Furniture has expanded three times since its inception. In 1923, under Frank Sud, Jr., the capacity was doubled in response to the "roaring twenties" spending. In 1943, after the death of Frank Sud, Jr., his son, also named Frank Sud, foresaw the postwar boom in the furniture industry and expanded once again. Also under his direction, Tower Furniture, an across-the-street neighbor, was purchased in 1949 to almost double once again the productive capacity of Frank Sud Furniture.

Sales have traditionally been carried on by a very limited number of "high-class" furniture outlets and company salespeople-decorators. This allows Frank Sud Furniture almost complete control over both the marketing and the production processes. The stores work through a very small inventory,

Submitted by William VanManen, President, Mikioi Metalcraft, Honolulu

supplemented by company catalogs. The company sales force works mainly through these same catalogs, with the stores and with individual interior decorators. The company supplements these efforts with a large showroom in Seattle, Washington, and by participating in various expositions across the country throughout the year.

This type of sales structure is considered to be the most expensive by most furniture manufacturers. The forty national salespeople average $32,000 per year and the eight expositions cost $12,000 per show. This is equal to approximately nine percent of net sales. The extremely high selling expense is justified by Mr. Sud as necessary to maintain the image of the company's fine line of furniture.

Recently, however, Mr. Sud has been entertaining the possibility of changing his marketing structure. Offers from fine furniture stores and showrooms have been forthcoming regularly for years but have usually been rejected on the grounds that Mr. Sud himself would lose control. However, two large, established showrooms recently contacted him in reference to handling his product.

One, Sud Showrooms of New York, with five showrooms on the east coast, has been increasingly persistent. With approximately thirty excellent decorators per showroom, it is one of the highest caliber showrooms (and competitors) in the east.

The second one, Knife and Tubes, has showrooms in Chicago, Dallas, Los Angeles, and Denver. With approximately twenty-five decorators per showroom, it would give Frank Sud Furniture more coverage in large cities west of the Mississippi.

Both companies have offered to assimilate the present company sales personnel in their respective areas, and both have agreed to show substantial amounts of Frank Sud Furniture in all of the furniture expositions each attends.

Mr. Sud has spoken with Kristen Ludlow, marketing manager, and John Vandon-Brank, production manager, and has asked them to come to his office to discuss all possibilities.

CASE 17

Titan Controls Corporation

In the Titan Controls Corporation, the product manager for valves, Steve Stengel, was devoting careful thought to a new product in December 1975. This product had become his responsibility following its laboratory development and field-testing. The product was a plastic solenoid valve, which was to be introduced to the national market sometime in March 1976. Stengel was due to submit an annual marketing plan for the new valve to the corporation's general management on February 1, the time when all the products' plans would be considered for the 1976–77 fiscal year.

Before the date of our case, December 2, 1975, the product had actually been adopted by Titan's higher management, and the required investment had been approved. The marketing strategy for the valve had already been formulated also, but the task remained of writing the marketing plan for the coming fiscal year. In preparing to compose and write that plan, Stengel reviewed the following information.

BACKGROUND

Titan Controls Corporation had begun in 1928, on a small scale in a rented building. It survived the ensuing Great Depression, and after economic recovery, the firm enjoyed steady expansion and moved several times into larger facilities in its northeastern urban location. Plants in the South and West had been added during the 1960s. In 1975, Titan was producing and marketing a broad line of commercial control systems and components.

A major Titan line was a variety of valves, each with a number of applications. Titan was a major firm in this field, and its executives constantly looked ahead and studied trends that might seriously alter the market environment. Control valves had

Note: Names in this case are disguised, and data are fictitious.

This case is reprinted by permission of Prentice-Hall, Inc. from *Marketing Strategy and Plans* by David J. Luck and O. C. Ferrell. Copyright © 1979 by Prentice-Hall, Inc.

heretofore been made largely with brass or stainless-steel forgings, and management had been concerned about worsening problems regarding the costs of these metals, and tardy deliveries of them. Titan's research and development staff had therefore been directed to find substitute materials for the nonmagnetic components of the valves. Working with a chemical manufacturer and plastic parts manufacturers, they had found a tasteless and rigid plastic material that should be a satisfactory substitute for stainless steel in the general-purpose solenoid valve.

Small quantities of the plastic were tested in Tatan's laboratories and proved to have likely applications for coffee, tea, carbonated water, syrup, liquid sweetener, cream, and air service. This development was being coordinated by the company's New Products Committee, which was impressed with the new material yet wary of possible resistance to a plastic-bodied valve from buyers long and universally accustomed to brass and stainless steel as the exclusive materials. The committee recommended that its introduction be confined to some application market where (1) buyers would be unusually cost-conscious and receptive to lowering valve costs, and (2) Titan had such a small current market share that not much would be risked if the new valve failed.

Stengel, whose product line would include the new item, was asked to select a market meeting those criteria, and he selected vending machines. He next proceeded with tests of such plastic valves in vending equipment, in two phases:

1. Tests were made in-house, vending free coffee and soft drinks to Titan employees. In these machines, the valves were life-tested until they failed.
2. Arrangements were made with two leading vending-machine companies to place the valves for trial in some of their machines that dispensed both cold and hot drinks at retail, After several months, the valves were returned to Titan and then life-tested there.

Also, approval for the new valve was obtained from Underwriters Laboratories, the Federal Food and Drug Administration, and other necessary agencies.

After the valve passed its tests, the New Products Committee had an economic analysis made to determine the amount of investment needed and the expected return in profits and cash flow. The projections met the company's criteria, but at that stage they were not detailed as to the exact marketing strategies or costs. The development of this information was delegated to Stengel, to incorporate into a marketing plan for the introductory year of 1976. The plan was expected to meet the following established requirements:

Profit, as a percentage of sales, was to attain a rate of 15 percent annually within three years.

Annual sales growth was to be in excess of 15 percent.

Market share of total valve sales in the same field of application was to be over 20 percent within three years.

(There was also a return-on-investment criterion that our discussion will omit.)

THE PRODUCT

The product offering was to be in two models: (1) a normal-service model for vending of cold drinks and (2) a high-temperature model for hot tea, coffee, and soup. The valve would be two-way, normally closed, and a direct-acting, diaphragm type. Its connections would be of an "O-ring" type that could be rapidly and easily connected with existing machines.

Some notable aspects of the valves were these:

1. During life tests of this valve against the established valve of the largest competitor, using 100 of each, 68 of the competitor's valves failed before any of the new Titan valves did.
2. None of the valves field-tested by the two vending-machine manufacturers had failed. All were in workable condition when returned to Titan.
3. Neither in the field tests nor in those held on Titan's premises were any unusual tastes or odors reported by users.
4. Thanks to the O-rings, soldering or brazing by vending-machine makers was avoided, which reduced costs and labor and eliminated a fire and explosion hazard in assembly areas. Also, the use of snap rings provided with each valve and to be stocked by distributors made field conversion of existing machines a "snap."
5. The 35 percent reduction in valve weight achieved by using the new material would mean lower shipping costs and easier handling.
6. Valve orders could be filled more promptly. Stainless-steel valves were requiring order lead time of four months or longer, but the plastic valve would need only one month's lead time.

MARKETS AND FORECASTS

The markets would be in two categories, OEM and replacement, and Titan would market its valves to both of them.

> The original equipment manufacturers (OEM) would be the manufacturers of vending machines in which valves would be originally installed. There were known to be about 180 manufacturers in the United States, but some 30 of them made most of the output.

> Replacement markets would be largely vending-machine retail operators. Any sizable vending company was able to repair its own machines, and it would buy new valves to replace those worn out.

Stengel already had forecasts of the total vending-machine market, in terms of valve units. His figures were based on four valves being needed for each vending machine produced in the OEM market and annual replacement of each valve on existing machines. Machines in service were estimated to have an average life of four years. These markets were projected, along with the shares that he expected the Titan plastic valve to capture during the company's standard three-year payback period (1976, 1977, and 1978). The resultant figures are given in Table 1.

The OEM market would be reached largely through a direct channel, since all the larger manufacturers would be contacted and serviced by Titan personnel. The replacement market and the smallest manufacturers would be reached by an indirect channel, through industrial distributors.

PRICING AND COSTS

In view of the keen cost-consciousness that was known to exist among both the manufacturers of vending machines and the vending retailers, Stengel determined that price would be the most influential factor in the marketing mix for the plastic valves. The figures he had received from the cost-accounting people on the expected costs to make and distribute the valves would give them a strong price advantage over the stainless-steel valves currently used. He decided to offer them at as low a price as would yield the company's required profit levels within the three-year payback period. These prices are

TABLE 1 Forecasted Sales of Vending-Machine Valves (in number of units)

	Normal-Service Valves		High-Temperature Valves	
Year	Total United States	Titan Plastic-Valve Market Share	Total United States	Titan Plastic-Valve Market Share
OEM—New machines				
1976	1,050,000	8%	800,000	10%
1977	1,090,000	20	825,000	23
1978	1,150,000	25	860,000	30
Replacement				
1976	3,900,000	7%	3,000,000	8%
1977	4,050,000	15	3,050,000	17
1978	4,250,000	20	ʻ3,125,000	25

compared with the current ones of stainless-steel valves in the table at the bottom of the page.

These prices would be those received by Titan, and sales made by distributors would have their margins added onto these. It may be noted that the price spread below stainless steel would be greater for the high-temperature models, and that is why Stengel projected a larger share for that application. The profits projected at these prices (which were among the optional levels Stengel considered) will be given in Table 2.

Heavy weight was given to the estimated costs of these valves. The cost estimates that Stengel was using included all costs and taxes, with overheads, except those for promoting or selling the product. Stengel would determine the marketing program and add on its costs, as given in Table 2. Thus, subtraction of these costs from the foregoing prices would leave the contribution per unit toward both profits and promotion.

EXHIBIT 1

	Total Costs and Taxes per Unit	
	OEM Sales	Replacement Sales
Normal-service	$5.05	$5.95
High-temperature	5.60	6.50

EXHIBIT 2

	Minimum Plastic Valve Prices versus Stainless Steel			
	OEM Sales		Replacement Sales	
	Plastic Valves	Stainless-Steel Valves (average)	Plastic Valves	Stainless-Steel Valves (average)
Normal-service	$6.00	$8.30	$7.00	$10.00
High-temperature	6.75	9.30	7.90	11.20

TABLE 2 Projected Profits and Sales of Plastic Valves

	Sales		Costs [before marketing]	Contribution to Profits and Marketing
	Units	Dollars		
1976				
Normal usage OEM markets	84,000	$ 504,000	$ 424,200	$ 79,800
Replacement markets	273,000	1,911,000	1,624,350	286,650
High-temperature OEM markets	80,000	540,000	448,000	92,000
Replacement markets	240,000	1,896,000	1,560,000	336,000
Total		$4,851,000	$4,056,550	$ 794,450
Less: Promotional costs				−171,000
Contribution to profits				$ 623,450
Percentage of sales				12.8%
1977				
Normal usage OEM markets	218,000	$1,308,000	$1,100,900	$ 207,100
Replacement markets	607,500	4,252,500	3,614,625	637,875
High-temperature OEM markets	189,750	1,280,812	1,062,600	218,212
Replacement markets	518,500	4,096,150	3,370,250	725,900
Total		$10,937,462	$ 9,148,375	$1,789,087
Less: Promotional costs				−150,000
Contribution to profits				$1,639,087
Percentage of sales				15.0%
1978				
Normal usage OEM markets	287,500	$1,725,000	$1,451,875	$ 273,125
Replacement markets	850,000	5,950,000	5,057,500	892,500
High-temperature OEM markets	258,000	1,741,500	1,444,800	296,700
Replacement markets	781,250	6,171,875	5,078,125	1,093,750
Total		$15,588,375	$13,032,300	$2,556,075
Less: Promotional costs				−150,000
Contribution to profits				$2,406,075
Percentage of sales				15.5%

DISTRIBUTION

As stated earlier, Titan would deal with and distribute to substantial-sized OEM accounts directly. Some judgment of the magnitude of these accounts may be gained from the approximate proportions of vending-machine units produced by size groups of manufacturers:

EXHIBIT 3

	Percent of Output
Largest 5 manufacturers	40%
Next largest 25 manufacturers	45
Next largest 50 manufacturers	10
Smallest 100 manufacturers	5

Many of the small manufacturers produced only special types of vending machines or did a custom business. Some were machine shops that were mainly in the repair business. Many types of vending machines, of course, do not dispense liquids and would not have valves, but Titan did not have reliable information on the types made.

The indirect sales, whether for replacement or to very small manufacturers, would take place through industrial distributors who carry replacement valves and parts for them. Most of their sales would be for replacement on existing machines in service, largely to the retail vending-machine companies in the United States, estimated at approximately 10,000, of which a very large proportion (at least 80 percent) vended liquids suitable for the plastic valve.

Titan already had its established network of authorized distributors, which numbered about 115 and were located in 38 states. It was recognized that not all retail vending companies would be convenient to these (for instance, there was no authorized distributor in Alaska or Puerto Rico). The number carrying vending-machine valves might have to be increased by 25 to 30.

In Stengel's opinion, with those added distributors of the vending-machine valves, Titan would offer slightly wider distribution than any other control-valve manufacturer for that market. He also judged Titan's distributors to have capability equal to that of their most aggressive competitor. Strategically, there would probably be a slight differential in favor of Titan, but this would not be the critical factor.

PROMOTION

In Stengel's view, the two marketing variables in which Titan would have the greatest advantage would be, first, price, and second, product, with its outstanding test performance for durability, its great ease of field conversion (for replacement markets), and its obviation of soldering and brazing in vending-machine assembly. These advantages, especially in the product variable, could nevertheless be realized only if the message reached the prospective buyers clearly and convincingly. Hence, the promotion variable could be the third most influential, if well executed.

Personal selling would carry the main burden of promotion. The multiple buyers, especially among the OEM prospective customers; the technical nature and demonstrations needed of the product; and the need to get the story across of savings without sacrifice of quality—all these conditions would make the sales force most important among promotional means. The 15 sales representatives would be backed by three technical service people and guided by four district sales managers. Each representative dealt with about 120 direct customers for various Titan products and an average of seven authorized distributors, who handled virtually all contacts for replacement sales and were to keep inventories of all Titan products and parts.

The sales representatives would come to headquarters for training sessions of two intensive days on the new valve. Then they would call on every distributor and O.E.M. prospect in their territories, solely to sell the new valve. This work would entail about one month, typically, and after that the new valve would become one item in the product line, to be given normal promotional emphasis. Stengel recognized that even when the new valve obtained a mature hold in the market, presumably by 1978, it would make up only about 12 or 13 percent of the average representative's sales volume. However, both because it was an interesting and novel product to sell and because of the emphasis it would need, he expected that the sales reps would spend about one-sixth of their time on the valve, so he costed the product at that rate in his profit projections.

The plan required the sales force to call on their distributors in early February to get them to stock-in the product within a month. Some key OEM contacts would have begun in February also. The real kickoff, though, would follow the National Vendors Show, held in March. Titan would have an elaborate booth at that show, at which virtually all the leading OEM and replacement market customers would be present. Model valves would be in operation there, and catalogs, sales brochures, and souvenirs would be distributed to visitors. Such materials would also be carried by the sales reps, a normal and not unusual strategic feature.

Advertising would be heaviest at the time of the Vendors Show, when a double-page spread would appear in the four leading trade magazines and also in the show's program. A teaser single-page advertisement would appear earlier, in February, and three others during the remaining quarters of the year, in the same media. For 1977 and 1978, four insertions a year in the four trade magazines were planned. A direct mailing of brochures to some 10,000 vending-machine operators in March 1977 would be augmented with supplies given to distributors for placing with their replacement customers.

Stengel expected that the program just described would have the costs shown in the table at the bottom of the page.

Stengel looked forward to an effective promotion effort, both in print and, more important, in personal contacts. Until the themes and advertisements had been created, however, he was not considering it to be a strategic advantage.

PROJECTED FINANCIAL RESULTS

The reasoning and data that have been described formed the basis on which Stengel projected the financial expectations for the three-year payout period of the new valves. next two deciding what information would projections for the plastic-valve line are stated in Table 2. This utilizes the total market and share-of-market estimates that were given earlier, to arrive at the unit sales forecasts. Of course, in product managers' annual plans, usually only the projections for the coming year (the one under planning) are displayed. For new products, like the plastic solenoid valve, projections for three years are generally expected.

	1976	1977	1978
Advertising and sales promotion			
Media and preparation	$ 20,000	$ 16,000	$ 16,000
Direct mail	6,000	4,000	4,000
Trade show exhibit	10,000	5,000	5,000
Personal selling	135,000	125,000	125,000
Total promotion	$171,000	$150,000	$150,000

CASE 18

The Top Plastics Company

Prior to the energy crisis and the myriad raw material shortages which appeared in late 1973, the Top Plastic Company (TPC) expected 1974 to be its best year ever. Preliminary forecasts for 1974 indicated that production would have to be increased 6 to 8 percent over the 1973 volume of 8 million pounds in order to meet sales expectations. Initial projections called for rising demands in all five product categories and in all four sales regions. Only in TPC's Mid Region territory was the outlook perceived as somewhat uncertain and this derived mainly from a projected weakening in the market for automotive-related plastics products.

A sudden unavailability of liquid resin supplies (a critical ingredient input for plastics productions), however, coupled with sharp increases in resin prices caught Top Plastics' management unprepared. Within the span of just a few months, it became painfully apparent that the company's entire marketing strategy might have to be reappraised and perhaps drastically revamped to meet the realities of liquid resin availability. Moreover, the company's once-successful policies in dealing with liquid resin suppliers seemed to be in need of revision.

This case was prepared by Gary P. Shows of the University of Alabama under the supervision of Professors Morris Mayer, Arthur A. Thompson, and A. J. Strickland, all of the University of Alabama. Permission to use granted by the authors.

COMPANY HISTORY AND BACKGROUND

Top Plastics Company is a wholly owned subsidiary of Alpen Paper Corporation and was formed in 1960 as a result of Alpen management's decision to diversify its product line out of industrial paper products. In the late 1950s when plans for forming Top Plastics first were conceived, Alpen Paper operated three pulp mills, two paper mills, and ten paper products plants; Alpen's corporate headquarters was located in Meridian, Mississippi, the site of its biggest pulp mill. In addition to its Meridian facilities, Alpen had mills and plants scattered in several locations in Alabama, Georgia, Mississippi, and Tennessee.

As of the late 1950s, the parent corporation's principal products were linerboard, corrugating medium and cylinderboard which, in turn, were used in assembling corrugated cases and paperboard cartons. Alpen's annual sales totaled $50 million and had grown at a moderate pace during the firm's 80-year history.

In 1958, several developments prompted the management of Alpen Paper Corporation to consider diversifying its product line beyond the confines of the paper industry. Both company and industry profit rates were low, partly because the industry produced a "commodity" type product. Demand conditions and technology offered little or no opportunity for Alpen to manufacture a distinctively different product and thereby gain a profitable competitive edge over rival firms. Furthermore, market demand for Alpen's products had weakened over the past two years, leaving Alpen with excess production capacity and shrinking profit margins.

A number of alternative diversification strategies were considered and after much analysis and deliberation, Alpen opted for a cautious move into the plastics industry. Alpen executives, being leery of jumping too fast into what was for them a new industry, stipulated that Alpen's initial investments in plastics be kept small. Diversification into plastics was deemed attractive to Alpen for a number of reasons. First, Alpen had an opportunity to sign a contract with German Plastics Company for the American patent rights to a new plastics manufacturing process. This newly developed process was thought by Alpen officials to be superior to existing plastic processes and, at the same time, met Alpen's requirement for a small capital investment. Second, market research studies indicated that the plastics industry had an excellent growth potential in both volume and profit. Third, it appeared that many of Alpen's industrial paper products customers would also be potential users of plastics, thereby allowing the company to use its present distribution channels to serve both lines of products. Finally, a good possibility existed that technological interfaces between paper and plastic products might permit the development of several entirely new products.

Thus, in early 1960 the Alpen Paper Corporation established Top Plastics Company and $750,000 was allocated for the construction of a small multiproduct plant in Ellisville, Mississippi. The new management team at Top Plastics intended for the Ellisville plant to steer the company on a course which would (1) pinpoint the types of plastic products with the highest profit contribu-

tion, (2) test the effectiveness of the German process, and (3) build a base of technical and marketing expertise for further entry into profitable segments of the plastics industry. TPC's Ellisville plant began production in December 1961 and had as its initial products egg cartons, bakery trays, inner-carton partitions (such as were used in packaging cookies), and packaging containers for in-store use by supermarket chains.

The essential raw material required in the production of these products was a petroleum-based liquid resin produced by combining the petroleum substance with other polymeric materials in a series of petrochemical processes. Top Plastics selected Monsanto Company and Koppers, Inc., as its chief suppliers of liquid resin because of their ability to work closely with product development and assist where possible with technical expertise. Though other resin suppliers were available TPC chose not to do business initially with them because they also marketed finished plastic products which competed with TPC's product line.

During the early months of operation, the products manufactured at the Ellisville Plant were sold in Mississippi, Alabama, southern Tennessee, and western Georgia. TPC's marketing force was comprised of four salesmen, each assigned to a specific product classification. One salesman called on egg producers, another on wholesale bakeries, a third on supermarket chains, and one salesman sold to both wholesale paper jobbers and wholesale grocers. By early 1961 the demand for TPC's plastic products was sufficient to warrant the limited use of Alpen Paper's sales force who were also selling in the four-state area. Alpen's salesmen were mainly utilized whenever an Alpen customer was a potential user of TPC's products, but was not being visited by one of the plastics salesmen. In mid-1961, TPC further expanded its sales coverage by contracting with two independent distributors in Memphis and Birmingham for the handling of TPC's plastic products. Sales during the first year of operation alone were $1.5 million, and expansion possibilities quickly became a prime consideration.

GROWTH AND EXPANSION AT TPC

During the next ten years, TPC continued to grow and expand at a healthy rate. In 1965 TPC built a plant in Tawanda, Pennsylvania, the company's first plant outside of the Southeast. The Tawanda plant was designed to produce heavier plastic products than the Ellisville plant, but it still incorporated the patented and highly efficient German process. Another plant was built in Houston, Texas, in 1967 and still another in 1970 in Charlotte, North Carolina. These latter two plants were engineered to manufacture heavyweight plastic products while remaining versatile enough to produce lighter-weight items if and when demand conditions warranted. The Houston and Charlotte plants required significant capital investments, but the risks were deemed acceptable by TPC because of the projected long-term strength in demand. Throughout this phase of major expansion, TPC's management relied exclusively on internal growth rather than acquisition because TPC's patented German process was still felt to be superior to processes used by other companies in TPC's market area.

Between 1962 and 1972 TPC's annual sales rose from $1.5 million to $13.5 million. The initial 4-item product line was expanded into 25 different product groups and more than 250 separate items. As of 1973, TPC's product assortment consisted of five major classes:

Group A—Heavy-weight plastics (children's toys, cabinets, shelves)

Group B—Lightweight plastics (door and wall moldings, plastic notebooks, auto plastics)

Group C—Packaging materials (egg cartons, inner-carton partitions)

Group D—Disposable products (cups, eating utensils)

Group E—Miscellaneous (pocket calculators, plastic screws)

REORGANIZATION OF THE MARKETING FORCE

Within a few years of TPC's formation as a division of Alpen, Top Plastics' management realized the company's marketing effort was gradually becoming less effective. The parent firm had cut back its sales force to try to reduce costs. Alpen salesmen were consequently spending less time servicing the accounts of the TPC subsidiary. Additionally, disagreements between paper salesmen and plastics salesmen were arising over the servicing of a number of plastics accounts. In 1967 Alpen and TPC agreed to assign responsibility for the entire plastics marketing effort to an expanded TPC marketing department, timing the move to coincide with the start-up of TPC's Houston plant. The Houston plant doubled TPC's production capacity and of necessity prompted adjustments in the marketing of TPC's expanded product line.

As of 1973, TPC's marketing department consisted of a direct sales force plus affiliations with eight independent distributors. The distributors, located in Atlanta, Memphis, New Orleans, Dallas, Chicago, Detroit, Louisville, and Richmond, gave TPC a greatly expanded sales coverage as well as providing feedback on changing market conditions. Some of the distributors even suggested what prices and advertising allowances should be offered to various customers. Each of TPC's distributors seemed to have a well-trained sales force and TPC was generally well pleased with the sales performance of its eight distributor outlets.

TPC's marketing department was headed by a vice president, who reported to the senior vice president of Alpen Paper corporation responsible for the marketing of both Alpen Paper and Top Plastics products. Reporting to TPC's marketing vice president were the four regional sales managers. Sales regions were divided into five districts with one salesman assigned to each district. The geographical makeup of the four regions by district was as follows:

> South Region—Mississippi, Alabama, Georgia, Florida, and Tennessee
>
> West Region—North Texas, South Texas, Arkansas, Oklahoma, Louisiana
>
> East Region—South Carolina, North Carolina, Kentucky, Virginia, and Maryland, Delaware, West Virginia, Washington, D.C.
>
> Mid Region—Western Pennsylvania, Ohio, Indiana, Illinois, and Michigan

Regional sales offices were located in the same cities as TPC's production facilities.

RELATIONSHIPS WITH SUPPLIERS

From the outset of its plastics operations, TPC had encountered only minor problems concerning the availability and acquisition of raw material suppliers for its plants. The main raw material was still liquid resin and supplies were plentiful. As many as eight resin suppliers continued to solicit TPC's business. Resin prices were generally stable and both delivery time and service were considered good.

TPC's chief resin suppliers included Monsanto, Koppers, Eastman Kodak, Union Carbide, Foster Grant, Dow Chemical, and Diamond Alkali. It was company policy for each TPC plant to purchase its own supplies of raw materials based on economic order quantity calculations. Since most of the suppliers used were dependable, price was normally the determining factor in deciding which firm to purchase from. Typically, TPC "played" resin producers off against each other to obtain the best possible prices for resin. No long-term contracts were made with any supplier since the resin market was essentially a buyer's market. The average price TPC paid for liquid resin in the first quarter of 1973 at its Houston, Texas, plant was 25 cents per pound, with a range of 15 cents to 35 cents per pound.

THE FORECAST FOR 1973

As late as the third quarter of 1973, it still appeared that 1973 would be a record year for Top Plastics Company. Sales were ex-

TABLE 1 1973 Operations Forecast

Product Class	Expected Demand [in lb]	Production [in lb]	Cost per Pound	Selling Price [per lb]	Profit [per lb]
A	2,500,000	2,500,000	$1.40	$1.90	$.50
B	1,200,000	1,200,000	1.50	2.20	.70
C	1,500,000	1,500,000	1.80	2.10	.30
D	1,500,000	1,500,000	1.60	2.00	.40
E	1,300,000	1,300,000	1.00	1.10	.10

TABLE 2 Regional Sales Forecast for 1973 (in pounds)

Sales Regions	Product Categories				
	A	B	C	D	E
South	500,000	150,000	300,000	400,000	200,000
West	500,000	300,000	300,000	500,000	400,000
East	600,000	150,000	500,000	400,000	300,000
Mid	900,000	600,000	400,000	200,000	400,000

pected to top the $15 million mark and production volume was projected to reach 8,000,000 pounds. Table 1 shows the anticipated 1973 demand in pounds, scheduled production in pounds, per pound production costs, expected market sales price, and expected profit per pound for each of the company's five product classes. During 1973 Top Plastics Company had the plant capacity to produce 8,075,000 pounds of plastics without having to schedule overtime production.

Table 2 depicts the expected 1973 sales by region; the figures are in pounds and include both sales by the direct sales force and the eight independent distributors. In drawing up its 1973 sales forecast in pounds, TPC assumed that per pound costs and selling price in each region would be constant within each product category and also across all four regions.

Table 3 shows the estimated percent-

TABLE 3 Forecast of Distributor Sales During 1973

Sales Regions	Product Categories				
	A	B	C	D	E
South	30%	40%	60%	70%	20%
West	25	30	50	60	25
East	35	30	50	65	15
Mid	20	25	70	60	20

ages of total 1973 sales for TPC's eight independent distributors.

Top Plastics' 1973 budget allocation for advertising and sales promotion was $450,000—an amount 15 percent greater than 1972. The 1973 promotional effort was patterned after the 1972 campaign and called for $100,000 to be spent on trade journal advertising, $50,000 to be spent at trade shows, and $300,000 to be spent for direct mail advertising.

MOUNTING PROBLEMS AND UNCERTAINTIES

Although TPC management anticipated a record year in 1973, events ran counter to expectations. In the summer and fall, the rumors of a petroleum shortage became fact. In November the shortage grew sharply worse when the Arabs imposed their oil boycott. Almost immediately, the cutbacks in crude oil supplies affected TPC's supply of petroleum-based liquid resin. TPC's suppliers, chiefly Eastman Kodak and Monsanto, began allocating their reduced resin supplies, first to their own plastics plants and then to their contract customers. Buyers such as TPC who spread their purchases unevenly and irregularly among several resin producers according to who offered the best price found themselves last on their suppliers' priority lists. Resin prices climbed rapidly and by late November 1973 TPC was paying from 45 cents to 75 cents per pound of resin whenever and wherever it could be obtained.

As shortage conditions worsened, TPC's purchasing agents in December estimated that during 1974 the company could expect to obtain only 65 to 75 percent as much resin as was bought in 1973; this was enough to permit production of just 5.2 million to 6 million pounds of plastic products—a production level far below the once anticipated capacity output of 8,075 million pounds. Upon receipt of this estimate, TPC's man-

ufacturing executives called a meeting to consider whether and how to revise the 1974 production plan. TPC's marketing vice president also scheduled a meeting with his four regional sales managers to discuss whether adjustments should be made in the company's market strategy and 1974 sales plan; the marketing vice president was also wondering how the manufacturing people would react to whatever marketing change might be called for and the extent to which it might be necessary to compromise the marketing effort in order to meet the constraints of the manufacturing division.

CASE 19

Trans-Europa Business Credit

Trans-Europa Business Credit (TEBC), a commercial finance company, was acquired as a wholly owned subsidiary by a large conglomerate holding company . . . It is headquartered in New York and has 30 branches, most of them located in North America and Europe, and a few in the Middle East. The branches have always operated separately and autonomously.

This case first appeared in David A. Nadler, Michael L. Tushman, and Nina G. Hatvany, *Managing Organizations: Readings and Cases*. Copyright © 1982 by David A. Nadler, Michael L. Tushman, and Nina G. Hatvany. Reprinted by permission of Little, Brown and Company.

TEBC'S primary business is accounts receivable financing, but it also books loans secured by inventory or other collateral when a borrower needs more money than can be secured by accounts receivable alone. The minimum loan is $100,000 and the average is $250,000. The district manager, who usually has four or five branch managers reporting to him has authority to approve all loans.

When TEBC was acquired, the management of Trans-Europa Corporation decided it wanted more control over the subsidiary. There was an overall concentration of loans in a few business areas that could become dangerous should the world economy change and undermine one of those business areas. To reduce the risk, Paul Bergonzi, the president of the finance company, hired George Praeger, an experienced loan executive, as vice president of commercial finance lending. Praeger was to reorganize the branch system and diversify the loan portfolio. Bergonzi assigned Tom Baldwin as Praeger's assistant. Over the years, Baldwin had worked in several areas of TEBC and knew most of the branch managers personally.

One of Praeger's first decisions was to centralize the loan approval process by requiring that the head office be notified of all loans over $250,000 and that the head office made final approval on all loans over $350,000. This would include any increases in existing accommodations that would bring the loan line over $350,000.

Praeger discussed this idea with Bergonzi who presented it to the conglomerate management. They approved the plan.

Praeger then drafted the following letter to the branch managers:

Dear _____:

Paul Bergonzi and the directors of the Trans-Europa Corporation have authorized a change in our loan approval procedures. Hereafter, all Branch Managers will notify the Vice President of Commercial Finance Lending of any loans in excess of $250,000 before the preliminary approval and before TEBC's auditors conduct the survey. In addition, final approval of all loans for more than $350,000 will come from the New York office. This includes new accommodations and increases in the loan line which brings the limit up to $350,000 or more.

By centralizing loan approval, we can ensure that our monies are not concentrated in only a few areas and we can broaden our base of operation. I am sure you will understand that this step is necessary in such times of increasing economic uncertainty. By effect-

ing this change, the interests of each branch and the company as a whole will best be served.

Yours very truly,

George Praeger
Vice President of
Commercial Finance Lending

Praeger showed the letter to Tom Baldwin and asked for his opinion. Baldwin said he liked the letter but suggested that since Praeger was new to TEBC, he might visit the branches and meet the managers to talk to them in person about the new procedure. Praeger decided that there was so much to do at the head office that he could not take the time to go to each branch. He sent the letter instead.

In the next two weeks, most of the branches responded. Although some managers wrote more, the following is a characteristic reply:

Dear Mr. Praeger:

We have received your recent letter about notifying the head office about negotiations of loans of $250,000 and the change in the approval process for loans in excess of $350,000. This suggestion seems a most practical one, and we want to assure you that you can depend on our cooperation.

Sincerely yours,

Jack Foster
Branch Manager

For the next ten weeks, the head office received no information about negotiations of loan agreements from any of the branch offices.

Executives who made frequent trips to the field reported that the offices were busy making somewhat more loans than usual.

CASE 20

Universal Motors Parts Division

Six months ago, William Frank, general manager of the parts division of Universal Motors Corporation began to feel uneasy about certain trends that had been developing in the automotive parts aftermarket. Products in this market fall into two major categories, service parts and accessories. Service parts are those used in repair and replacement, including mechanical, body/frame, and chassis components. Accessories, either appearance or functional items used to improve performance or dress up the car, include fog lights, outside rearview mirrors, or interior floor mats.

Over the past ten years, total aftermarket parts sales in the United States had stabilized in the $70 billion to $80 billion range after growing steadily along with new car sales since World War II. In the last two years, the total number of outlets selling aftermarket parts had declined dramatically, and it was predicted by industry analysts that in five years there would be 20 percent fewer outlets than there are today. Last year the average U.S. car owner spent $405 per vehicle on tires, batteries, accessories, and service parts. In the last three years, service parts sales had increased from $19 billion to $23 billion nationwide.

Like many firms, Universal Motors had also seen its sales patterns shift to follow population trends. Sales in the South and

West were expanding at a faster rate than in the North and East.

The major types of outlets for aftermarket parts are service stations, garages, new vehicle dealers, specialized repair shops (for example, muffler shops), mass merchandisers, and jobbers. Exhibit 1 shows how market shares of these types of outlets have changed over the last five years.

Fifty-three years ago, the Parts Division of Universal Motors was established by consolidating the aftermarket service parts warehousing and distribution activities of three marketing divisions. Twelve years ago, the Parts Division of Universal Motors Corporation became a separate operating division with aftermarket parts responsibility for all six of the North American marketing divisions. This had been done to provide one centralized service parts organization which was devoted entirely to the nationwide distribution of replacement parts to UM dealers. Sales and marketing activities continued to be performed by the marketing divisions, whereas the Parts Division concentrated on improving service, warehousing, and distribution.

Then, six years ago, sales and marketing functions were also assigned to the Parts Division, thus giving it total responsibility for marketing and distribution of parts to UM dealers. This move was soon followed by incorporation of all truck division service parts into the Parts Division system, and finally, two years ago operations were expanded from North American to include all aftermarket parts marketing and distribution

EXHIBIT 1 Percentage Market Shares by Type of Retail Outlet

Number of Years Ago	Type of Outlet						
	Service Stations	Garages	New Car Dealers	Specialized Repair Shops	Mass Merchandisers	Jobbers	Total
5	25	12	30	18	10	5	100
4	24	11	31	17	11	6	100
3	23	10	30	20	14	5	100
2	18	11	29	24	13	5	100
1	21	9	27	22	17	4	100

activities to UM dealers worldwide. This remains its current status today.

Universal Motors Parts Division (UMPD) and Allied Division are UM's marketing and distribution arms that service the automotive aftermarket. UMPD distributes only to UM dealers, whereas Allied serves independent distributors. Each division maintains its own sales force and network of distribution centers. Many of the parts inventoried are identical; yet, for sales and merchandising reasons, the two divisions operate independently of each other. Also, many of the accessory items sold by both UMPD and Allied are contract manufactured for UM by independent manufacturers.

In an indirect way UMPD and Allied actually compete because independent jobbers are free to sell to UM dealers, as is shown in Figure 1.

William Frank realized that the sales trends he had observed, if continued, would call for adjustments in the distribution sys-

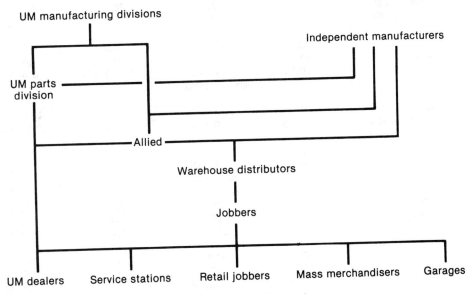

FIGURE 1 UM's Aftermarket Parts Distribution Channels

tem. He called in his director of operations, Dave Hert.

"Dave, I want to reevaluate our entire operational network. This division needs to operate even better and more efficiently than it has in the past. I know there is no fat to cut, but we have to trim someplace, and I'm depending on you to come up with some answers. Let's get together in 30 days and you show me what you've got."

Hert knew from past experience that such requests from the boss were not to be taken lightly and that completing an entire operational review in 30 days would be no easy task. He worked late that night and the next two deciding what information would be required. On the fourth day after his

meeting with Frank, he drafted a memo to each of his 23 regional distribution center managers, requesting a selected audit of the previous 12 months' operations.

Specifically, he wanted monthly average figures in each of the following categories.

1. Inbound freight volume in tons, broken down by shipment size. That is, what amount was received in less than truckload (LTL) shipments and what amount was received in full truckload (TL) quantities. For both the LTL and TL inbound freight he wanted to know average distance traveled and total freight charges billed. All of this information could be obtained directly from trucking company invoices and internal records.

EXHIBIT 2 Distribution Center Operating Review (for average 30-day period)

	Midwest		South	
	Toledo	Indianapolis	Atlanta	Memphis
Inbound Freight				
LTL				
Volume (tons)	125	260	152	171
Distance (miles)	77	86	380	275
Cost (thousands)	157.85	366.70	901.05	733.59
TL				
Volume	195	196	228	114
Distance	91	88	410	320
Cost	230.68	224.22	1,112.41	434.11
Inventory Carrying				
High turnover				
Amount (tons)	174	319	180	130
Cost (thousands)	22.45	37.64	19.44	11.96
Low turnover				
Amount	146	137	200	155
Cost	24.82	25.35	26.80	20.30
Outbound Freight				
LTL				
Volume	170	237	304	200
Distance	55	68	40	75
Cost	153.34	264.30	189.70	234.00
TL				
Volume	150	219	76	85
Distance	31	42	62	90
Cost	20.15	119.57	56.07	91.04

EXHIBIT 3 Inventory Carrying Cost Factors

	Midwest		South	
	Toledo	Indianapolis	Atlanta	Memphis
Number of Employees	20	26	17	14
Total Average Monthly Wage [thousands]	30.60	39.78	18.79	15.47
Cubic Feet of Storage Space [thousands]	200	275	220	140
Utilization [%]	78	84	87	88
Building Age [years]	12	19	14	6

2. Inventory handled in tons, again in two categories, high- versus low-turnover items. High-turnover items include routine service parts such as spark plugs, oil filters, and shock absorbers. Low-turnover parts include sheet metal and frame parts such as door panels and bumpers. Total inventory carrying costs for each category would also be needed.

3. Outbound freight volumes in tons, reported in the same manner as inbound freight.

Hert asked that the information be in his hands in two weeks. This was pressing things, but he wanted the remaining two weeks to absorb the information and do follow-up if needed.

After one week reports from the field began to come in. Soon 20 of the 23 distribution center managers' figures were in hand. Two had not been received because key people were on vacation, and in one location a newly installed minicomputer was experiencing start-up problems. Nevertheless, Hert was satisfied that he would be able to present an accurate picture of the current state of affairs when he met with Frank. Deciding to group the distribution center data by sales region, he displayed the highest- and lowest-cost operation in each region. The data for two of these regions appear in Exhibit 2.

Looking at these figures, it was obvious to Hert which operations were most and least costly; yet he still was unsure that the figures clearly pointed to any particular course of action. To get a clearer picture, Hert went back to the original reports and zeroed in on the sources of the inventory carrying costs. He believed these were the most directly controllable and therefore deserved the greatest attention. For each distribution center, he reviewed the figures on number of employees, total monthly wages, number of cubic feet of storage space in the building, percentage of space utilized, and building age. These figures for the Toledo, Indianapolis, Atlanta, and Memphis distribution centers are shown in Exhibit 3.

In the meeting, Frank mentioned that the sales figures continued to be unencouraging and that something would have to be done to reduce operational costs fairly quickly. Hert had been in the industry many years and he knew that it was highly cyclical. Sales often expanded dramatically during the early stages of a business cycle upturn, and he did not want to jeopardize the overall ability of the distribution network to respond. The ability to serve customers reliably and on time was still most important in the long run.

After an hour and a half of going over the figures in some detail, Frank turned to Hert and said, "What do you think we should do?"

Advise Universal Motors Parts Division.

Index